ELIZABETHAN LIFE:

WILLS OF ESSEX GENTRY & MERCHANTS

© ESSEX COUNTY COUNCIL, 1978

ISBN 0 900360 50 X

To
MISS ANNE E. BARKER
generous donor to the
Friends of Historic Essex

Essex Record Office Publication No. 71

ELIZABETHAN LIFE:

WILLS OF ESSEX GENTRY & MERCHANTS

Proved in the Prerogative Court of Canterbury

F. G. EMMISON

Author of *ELIZABETHAN LIFE: Disorder* (1970), *Morals & the Church Courts* (1973), and *Home, Work & Land* (1976)

Chelmsford : Essex County Council

1978

Printed by E. G. Ellis & Sons, Willow Street, Chingford, E4 7EQ

Contents

ACKNOWLEDGEMENTS

I am deeply obliged to the Library, Museum and Records Committee of the Essex County Council for sponsoring the book, which is additional to the three originally authorised. Once again a grant from the Friends of Historic Essex is gratefully acknowledged. Mr. K. C. Newton, the County Archivist, continues to help in various ways, and Miss Olwen Hall has again compiled the big Index of Personal Names. The *Index to Wills proved in the Prerogative Court of Canterbury* (British Record Society, Vols. 18, 25) was invaluable in the initial stages.

Ingatestone Hall, October 1977   F.G.E.

NOTE ON EDITORIAL METHOD

Dates between 1 January and 24 March are expressed in modern style. The present-day spelling of parishes has been adopted. The calendar preserves the original language. Preambles, routine phrases, lawyers' verbiage, clauses for children to have non-survivors' legacies, 'whichever happen first' (after 'at (the age of) 21 or marriage'), etc., and ordinary bed-linen, have been omitted. The word 'successive' has been inserted where several or many remainders are specified, sometimes in long but purely repetitive clauses. All personal, place or field names are given. Unless otherwise stated, all parishes are in Essex and all executors proved the wills. The Public Record Office reference for the Wills Registers is 'PROB 11', followed by the two numbers printed after the testator's name, but 'folio' should be read before the last number.

Introduction

For those unacquainted with the three earlier volumes of *Elizabethan Life* (their titles are given on the title-page of this book), it should be explained that they were the outcome of a scheme, approved by the Essex County Council in 1968, for preparing and publishing within the limits of about 1,100 pages a fairly full picture of social and economic conditions in the Elizabethan period: Volume I, drawn from the extremely rich Quarter Sessions rolls, supplemented by the Assize files; Volume II from the fine series of the Archdeacons' Courts books;[1] and Volume III mainly from the Wills proved in the latter courts and from the rolls of 74 Manor Courts. The Introduction to each volume described in detail how, by virtually ignoring the extremely common offences, routine legacies and legal verbiage, it has proved practicable to include within the restricted compass nearly all the material in these archives bearing on the other offences and aspects of Elizabethan life. Although presented in narrative form for the general reader, the Council intended that the volumes should be regarded primarily as source books, giving the maximum possible information from the original records in their custody, for scholars unable to visit the Essex Record Office. It was no part of the author's brief, therefore, to synthesise the evidence or to make extensive comment upon it.

The Introduction to Volume III envisaged the preparation of two further books beyond the original trilogy. The present volume comprises detailed abstracts of 339 Wills proved in the Prerogative Court of Canterbury, formerly at Somerset House and now in the Public Record Office (class 'PROB 11'). It was made possible by the purchase ten years ago at a cost of over £400 by the Friends of Historic Essex of negative photostats of all the registered Essex Wills. These number nearly 1,000 of which about one-third are upper class wills. The latter have such important and interesting contents that the Council's committee resolved in 1975 to publish a calendar as a fourth volume. The cost of printing the Wills *in extenso* would of course have proved quite prohibitive. However, the abstracts now printed do not omit a single personal or place name (except in two specified wills) nor do they leave out any clause apart from normal repetitive language, and legal phraseology, often very lengthy, has been condensed without excluding any material fact.

After careful consideration, the County Archivist and I decided not to print the Wills either in alphabetical or chronological order but to group them by status—Peers, Knights, Esquires, Gentlemen, and Merchants (and their wives or widows). While this brings together the wills of testators of much the same class, it has the slight disadvantage of separating those of a few of the same family, so cross-references, e.g. pp. 6, 111, have been made. The merchants prove to be a self-contained group. The authorised length of the book militated against including the Clergy. Most Essex clerical wills were in fact proved in the Bishop of London's Consistory Court (now in the Greater London Record Office), which had concurrent jurisdiction with the Archidiaconal Courts over the whole diocese of London except the peculiars. The same restriction prevented my dealing in the previous volume with the Wills of the gentry among those proved by the Archidiaconal Courts now preserved in the Essex Record Office, and indeed they called for similar treatment by way of full abstracts. Owing to current severe cuts in local authorities' expenditure, the Council has no funds for a fifth and final volume. It is therefore particularly gratifying that the Friends of Historic Essex have resolved to bear the whole cost of preparing and printing it. This has been welcomed by the Council's committee and publication is envisaged by 1980 of a similar calendar of about 150 esquires' and gentlemen's wills.

Definite provision for memorials in church was made by eight peers and knights (or their widows), nine esquires, twelve gentlemen and one wealthy clothier, Thomas Paycocke. Of these, thirteen were for 'tombs', fifteen for 'stones', and two 'in remembrance'. They included the fine monuments directed to be erected by the 3rd Earl of Sussex for himself and the 1st and 2nd Earls (Boreham), the 2nd Lord Darcy (St Osyth), the 2nd Lord Rich for himself and the 1st Lord (Felsted), Sir William Petre (Ingatestone), and Sir Thomas Smyth (Theydon Mount), also that 'prepared' in advance by Sir John Wentworth (Gosfield). Brasses as usual were not specified but included with incised floor-slabs in 'stones'. Testators whose brasses have survived are Thomas Collte (Waltham Abbey), Thomas Paycocke (Coggeshall), and Richard Twedy, who had asked for a 'tomb'. Rather high is the number of testators asking for 'stones' (some of marble) whose wishes were not acted upon or whose memorials are not preserved or were not identified in the Royal Commission on Historical Monuments *Inventory* for Essex (four volumes, 1916-23). Of the last, the brasses of Bartholomew Averel (Southminster), Robert Gaywood (All Saints', Maldon), and Thomas Whitney (Saffron Walden), all unnamed in the *Inventory*, now seem to be identifiable; and 'Thomas' may be filled in for the brass of 'Katherine wife of .... Reding' (West Thurrock). Instructions or requests for burial in church were also made by a few of the more substantial yeomen and others, whose wills are not abstracted; see Appendix B.

The Earl of Sussex and Sir William Petre provided for the addition of chapels to the parish churches. An independent chapel in Colchester for which we have little post-Reformation is mentioned : St Helen's with the chapelyard, stated by Morant to have been sold to George Gilberde in 1610,[2] was in his father's possession in 1583 (p. 201). Is 'Little Chapel' in Great Waltham an otherwise unrecorded name for Black Chapel, the picturesque surviving chapel-of-ease in that extensive parish (p. 178)?[3] St Albright's chapel in Little Stanway on the Chelmsford—Colchester road was likewise subordinate to the church at Great Stanway near the Hall, two miles away. In 1710 the former was used instead of the church, then 'utterly decayed'.[4] Hope for the restoration of the 'great church' was expressed many years earlier (p. 155).

Instructions for the expense of testators' obsequies range from a stern veto of 'pomp, pride and vain superstition' to at least £100 for 'black cloth and other things' (p. 106) and 'not above £1,500' for the Earl of Sussex. Very common was the provision of money for funeral and later

vii

sermons. Robert Camocke left 15 marks for ten godly sermons at quarterly intervals; had the rector—a witness to his will—used undue influence? Much less common were bequests for funeral 'drinkings' and other cheer.

A few cautiously-phrased bequests for providing burial tapers and obits are found in Elizabeth's first years, and several legacies of crucifixes and religious pictures by adherents to the Old Faith occur as late as 1599 (see Index of Subjects under 'Catholic'). But, as elsewhere, testators' minds shifted sharply towards secular endowments, though strong Puritan influence at Colchester and Dedham resulted in several bequests to the 'common (or town) preacher' or lecturer. The larger foundations embrace Brentwood, Chelmsford, Halstead and Elmdon grammar schools and almshouses at Colchester, Ingatestone, Stansted Mountfitchet and Stock. Sums left for the repair of roads and bridges include two for Hull Bridge over the Crouch (pp. 146, 226), then about to collapse or already down and never replaced;[5] also for the county house of correction for vagrants at Coggeshall (p. 181) and the market crosses (houses?) at Manningtree (p. 289) and Prittlewell (pp. 183, 226). The 'poor prisoners' in the London and Colchester gaols were sometimes remembered. But by far the commonest legacies were to the poor of the testator's own and neighbouring parishes, those in which he held land, or that of his birth; usually in cash, but occasionally for distributing winter fuel, an ox and bread at Christmas, twenty cows for twenty poor folks (p. 53), and so forth.

Among the larger mansions of which testators give important details, Sir Thomas Smith's Hill Hall, Theydon Mount, was to be remarkable for some of its advanced architectural features; but it was not finished, and Richard Kirkby, his 'chief architect', was left £20 to press on with its completion. For a few other houses we have the names of the main rooms and much about their furniture, e.g. New Hall, Boreham (pp. 2-4), Mark Hall, Latton (pp. 23-5), and Woolston Hall, Chigwell (pp. 126-7). Nearly all the Essex probate inventories were lost many years ago, but descriptions of furniture, furnishings and kitchen equipment in a number of wills are quasi-inventories. In some respects, indeed, as for plate and jewellery, wills yield far more details than some inventories in which only valuation totals of such items are given. The best description occurs in the will of the Earl of Sussex, which refers to the jewelled sword given him by King Philip as a reward for arranging the match with Queen Mary. Was Dean Colet (died 1519) the owner of 'Colettes Cup' (p. 108) and what lay behind the gift of a 'table[t] of gold with the Lord Cromwell's visage' to Sir Ralph Sadler, who had been one of Thomas Cromwell's henchmen in the 1530s (p. 51)? Deposit of plate and jewels for security with a City haberdasher (p. 157) may be contrasted with that of £2,000 in gold in a closet at Cressing Temple (p. 211).

The overriding concern of the landed testator was of course to pass his estate mostly intact where feasible to his eldest son. Four centuries ago the heavy risk of an heir apparent's death before reaching age or fatherhood might give rise to a series of remainders to all younger sons, then to daughters and even more distant relations, who would inherit in default of issue earlier in the succession. An extreme example is seen in the will of Sir Anthony Browne (p. 16), from which incidentally three folios of very long repetitive clauses have been abstracted in 18 lines without omitting a single fact.

Tudor parents' concepts of filial obedience are illustrated by legacies to daughters being occasionally made contingent on their submission in choice of husband to the wishes of mother, executor, supervisor or trusted friends (see Index of Subjects under 'Marriage'). The condition might also be applied to a son, a sister, and in one case to a cousin's daughter. A gentleman's son, 'Edward unthrift' (either thriftless or dissolute), got less than the other sons (p. 164), and several sons-in-law in disfavour are recorded. Only four testators refer to a bastard son; among them the first Lord Rich and John Barnabe, who persisted in claiming paternity in place of another deceased Barnabe.

In the previous volume the diverse means by which testators showed sternness or kindness, especially to their widows, was described. Those of affluent men received less consideration by way of houseroom, food or fuel; but generosity towards a faithful servant is a pleasant feature, as well as some long lists of menial servants' legacies.

Relatively few men, somewhat surprisingly, favoured university education for their sons. Petre earned the title of 'second founder' of his *alma mater*, Exeter College, Oxford, and both he and his widow made additional bequests, but he sent his son to the Middle Temple; and the Puritan foundation in 1585 of Emmanuel College, Cambridge, by Sir Walter Mildmay, brother of Thomas Mildmay of Chelmsford (p. 111), although favouring Northamptonshire and Essex scholars, seems to have influenced few Essex testators in the Queen's closing years. Sons at or intended for Cambridge are in fact referred to only in four wills (one with a view to obtaining a benefice), and a fifth had the choice of Oxford or Cambridge. Some caution, however, is needed with interpretation, as the contemporary meaning of 'school' may include university.[6] Girls' education received even less attention than in the wills of the lower classes;[7] an esquire's daughter who was to be 'placed in service' (p. 103) probably joined a household of like standing (Petre sent a daughter to enter the household of a great family).[8] Bequests of books yield some points of interest. Latin and Greek books were left by Sir Thomas Smith to Queens' College, Cambridge (as well as his globe—still treasured), and by Sir Anthony Cooke to his daughter, Burleigh's wife; and Sir Anthony's son passed on his 'whole library' at Gidea Hall (p. 69). Among law books we find mention of Fitzherbert's 'Great Abridgement', published in 1514 (p. 196). Of more significance is the reference by Sir Anthony Browne, justice of the Common Bench, to early Year Books (p. 14).

Various aspects of ownership and tenancy of houses and lands received attention in the previous volume (Part 1 : Wills, and Part 2 : Manors). The present book deals with much larger estates and is a chief source for the Elizabethan manors. Some of the wills should prove helpful in the compilation of the 'manorial descents' in the *Victoria County History of Essex,* which does not, however, give the names of the lessees (of non-resident lords) who lived in the manor-houses and farmed the demesnes.

The scope of this book excludes such yeomen's wills, but their leased manors are set out in Appendix A.[9]

An interesting facet of some wills is the plea for continued patronage by a royal court or local magnate to the testator's widow and children, sometimes accompanied by a request to accept the office of supervisor of the will and often encouraged by a generous *douceur* of money, plate, jewels or the best horse. Vincent Harrys of Maldon, for example, sought the influence of the Earl of Oxford and 'beseeched' the Earl of Sussex to be overseer (pp. 95-6). It was not uncommon for a substantial testator to ask the Master of the Rolls or another chief justice to act as supervisor; and a superior servant might beg his master to assume the office, e.g. Sir John Petre (p. 181). Among distinguished executors or legatees we note include the Earl of Leicester, Lord Burleigh, Sir Nicholas Bacon and others (p. 19); and Edmund Plowden, the jurist, was appointed overseer (p. 36); and among other notable names found in the wills are William Clowes the surgeon, George Gifford the Maldon divine, and William Gilberd the 'father' of electricity. Surnames prominent a generation or two later in early New England history are Alden, Pynchon and Winthrop, and other wills record the ancestors of Christopher Jones of the *Mayflower* (p. 324) and ancestors of General Sherman.

Although clerical wills have not been included, many incumbents and a few curates occur, chiefly as witnesses and writers. Witnesses who describe themselves as 'scr :', 'the scribe', or 'the writer' range from professional scriveners and 'writers of the court letter of London' (who were members of the Scriveners' Company) to the local attorney or literate neighbour. Nuncupative wills have their special interest and two preserve the actual deathbed words (pp. 71, 207). To us the courts' speed in action seems blissful : two days in one case (p. 251). For other aspects, the reader is referred to the full Index of Subjects, e.g. 'agriculture', 'wardships', 'weapons', 'war service', and 'trades and occupations'; in the last may be noted two moneyers.

[1] As foreshadowed in *Elizabethan Life: Home, Work & Land*, p. ix (n. 1), three chapters on Tithes, Perambulations, and Work and Play on Sundays, which had to be omitted from *E.L.: Morals & the Church Courts*, have now appeared in *Tribute to an Antiquary: Essays presented to Marc Fitch by some of his friends* (ed. F. G. Emmison and Roy Stephens, 1976), pp. 177-215 (enquiries to Essex Record Office).

[2] *History of Colchester* (1868), 153.　　[3] *E.L.: Morals*, plate 5.

[4] Newcourt, *Repertorium* (1710), ii, 553.

[5] Cf. *E.L.: Disorder*, 36.

[6] *E.L.: Home*, 122.　　[7] *Ibid.*, 123.　　[8] Emmison, *Tudor Secretary* (1961), 128.

[9] The corpus of Elizabethan Essex material now in print will probably be enlarged before long by a calendar of the Essex 'feet of fines', 1547-1603, thus bringing to the end of our period the existing series of four volumes of *Feet of Fines for Essex, 1182-1547*, published by Essex Archaeological Society between 1899 and 1964. (The continuation of the calendar, edited by Dr Marc Fitch, has already been typed for 1547-80 and enquiries may be addressed to the Essex Record Office.) These important property records, invaluable for ownership of manors and many smaller estates, if judiciously used and related to other evidence, will thus be complementary to Vols. III, IV and V of *Elizabethan Life*.

1
PEERS

THOMAS [RADCLIFFE, THIRD] EARL OF SUSSEX [of New Hall, Boreham], 1 April 1583. [29/52]

My body shall be by my executors decently and comely, without unnecessary pomp or charges but only having respect to my dignity and state, buried in the parish church of Boreham, where my funerals shall be performed, provided that they shall not dispend about my funeral obsequies above £1,500 and shall with all speed hasten my funerals. Therefore for the more speedy performance and of all other things in my will, they shall have all my plate which shall not be otherwise disposed, and I leave them a book signed by my hand of such plate. Whereas there is by me mortgaged to Thomas Newman, citizen and writer of court letter of London, by two indentures of bargain and sale of 31 January 1583 and 4 February 1583, 8,553 oz. of plate parcel gilt, gilt and white for £2,150 to be paid at certain days appointed, which number of ounces do far exceed in value the money to be paid for the redemption of the same, my desire is that my executors shall with such money as any ways shall come to their hands above the funeral charges redeem the plate at the days expressed and after shall make sale of it to the best advantage towards the performance of my will.

My executors with all convenient speed after my decease (if the same be not finished in my lifetime) shall see builded and finished on the south side of the chancel a chapel of brick already begun according to a plot and writing thereof made according to the order taken with the workmen or otherwise at their discretions, and shall also erect in the midst of the chapel where my body shall be buried a tomb of white alabaster, touch and other stones according to a plot or writing subscribed with my own hand. The corpses of my Lord my grandfather and my Lady my grandmother, my Lord my father and my Lady my mother shall be removed and brought thither and buried in the vault of the chapel and myself also when it shall please God to call me to be buried in the same place.

I freely give to the Lady Frances my wife (if she overlive me) the jewels, billiments, chains, buttons, aglets and other ornaments whatsoever dressed with precious stones or pearls or without which have been known to have been for the most part in her custody and use; with her apparel and other ornaments belonging to her person, saving one great table diamond, one great table ruby, one great pointed diamond, one other great table diamond and one great balas, all which five stones were given to me in a sword by Philip King of Spain when I was sent in commission into Spain for concluding of the marriages between Queen Mary and him and to bring him into England, saving also such other jewels and things as by this my will or any codicil I shall otherwise bestow, and saving all chains, collars, georges, buttons and other jewels which I did use to wear and remain in my custody whether they be garnished with stone or pearl or otherwise; which chains and other jewels used by me to be worn, except the five stones and such other as shall by my will be otherwise disposed, shall remain to my executors to be sold towards payment of my funeral charges and performance of my will. My brother, Sir Henry Ratcliff knight, shall have during his life the use and custody of the five stones; and after his decease they shall remain to my next heir male that shall be Earl of Sussex, and after his death to his next heir male that shall be Earl, and so from heir male to heir male being Earl, and for lack of such heir male to such of my heirs as shall be owners of my house of New Hall and their heirs for ever in like sort. And therefore I most earnestly charge my brother and the said heirs to see that the same may remain as an heirloom in my house for a remembrance of my service.

To my wife 4,000 oz. of gilt plate and 2,000 oz. of plate, parcel gilt or of plate with arms gilt or of white plate, such as herself like to make choice of. To her the coaches which she and her women used to ride in, the coach horses and other furniture to the coaches belonging, and the horses and geldings, saddles and other riding furniture which she or her women used when she rideth on horseback and 6 other geldings as she shall make choice of.

My linen and napery shall by my executors be equally divided into three parts; my wife shall have the first choice of one part, Sir Henry one other part, and the other to remain to my executors for performance of my will. For the better executing thereof she hath ever had the custody of my linen and napery, and now hath the books thereof, which I pray her to produce before my executors. To her my lease of Culvers in Boreham and of the field called the Wildes and other my leases of grounds in Bermondsey (Surrey).

To Sir Henry (if he happen to overlive me) 1,000 oz. of parcel gilt plate or of plate with gilt arms or of white plate, such as he choose after my wife; 10 pieces of hangings wrought with my arms and with the arms of my house, 3 pieces of the history of Polymenus and Oedipus, 8 pieces of forest work verders, 6 pieces of the Old Law and New Law, 7 pieces of forest work with fountains, 8 pieces of white lions, a standing bed of purple satin embroidered with lozenges of cloth of silver and gold with curtains and quilt, a standing bed of green velvet and cloth of silver with curtains and quilt, a standing bed of crimson bodkin and tawny velvet with stars and Stafford knots with curtains and quilt of red and yellow sarcenet, a standing bed of tinsel and crimson satin with letters T and E and curtains, a sparver of cloth of gold with murrey velvet with letters R and E and a quilt of red and yellow silk like birds' eyes, a sparver of crimson velvet and yellow damask and curtains and a quilt of red silk like to birds' eyes, all bedsteads, chairs, stools, cushions and other furniture commonly used with the beds and sparvers, 6 pairs of

2

fustians, 30 featherbeds (whereof 5 large beds fit for the standing beds and sparvers and the other ordinary beds), 6 pairs of pillows, 8 Irish rugs, 12 little Turkey carpets, and a long Turkey carpet of carnation.

For the true, faithful, kind and natural love which I have always found in my dearly beloved brother-in-law, Sir Thomas Mildmay knight, I bequeath him £500. To Sir Henry my armour, great horses and other horses, geldings, mares and colts, with the furniture to them belonging, not otherwise bestowed, and my apparel with buttons not being enriched with stone or pearl.

Whereas I, by my deed tripartite dated 20 November 1579, made between me on the one part and Sir Christopher Wraye knight, Chief Justice of the Queen's Majesty Bench, Sir William Cordall knight, Master of the Rolls, and Sir Gilbert Gerrard knight, her Majesty's Attorney General, and John Harrington esquire, have conveyed my manors of New Hall, Boreham and Wafer Hall [in Boreham], with their appurtenances, the manors of Woodham Walter, Ulting, Lexden, Burnham, Sheering, Wimbish, Fitzwalters [in Shenfield], Ashdon, Mangapp [in Burnham], and [West] Bergholt, with their appurtenances, and the manors of Attleborough, Hempnall, Diss and Watton (in Norfolk), to the use of my wife for life, and after to others of my heirs, with proviso so that it shall be in my wife's election to make choice whether she will have the manor of New Hall [etc.] or the manor of Attleborough [etc.]; I will that she shall possess the manors without trouble or let. Whereas I manifestly perceive by her speeches uttered privately to myself and divers times also in the presence of others that her direct meaning is to refuse New Hall cum membris and to make choice of Attleborough, and my meaning hath always been to have New Hall to remain honourably furnished as well for receiving of the Queen's Majesty when it shall please her to come thither as also for the honourable furniture of my heirs; I therefore bequeath to Sir Henry the suit of hangings which did hang in her Majesty's Bedchamber at New Hall at her Majesty's last being there and the suit of hangings which did hang in her Majesty's Inner Chamber Lodging, the hangings which I bought of Horatio Palavicino to hang the Withdrawing Chamber and the Privy Chamber for her Majesty, the hangings of gilt leather which did hang in the chambers where Mistress Frances Howard did lie, the hangings of the Dance of Death which did hang in the Presence Chamber, the suit of hangings which did hang in my Lord of Leicester's bedchamber, and the bed of lozenges of cloth of silver and cloth of gold embroidered on crimson satin which my Lord of Leicester lay in, with the bedsteads, cupboards, boards, chairs, stools, cushions, andirons and other furniture which at that time was used for the furniture of the bed and chambers of the Earl of Leicester, also the chairs of crimson velvet embroidered with cloth of gold and silver with the cushions, stools, chairs, tables and the other things belonging used in her Majesty's Presence Chamber, the table cloths, cupboard cloths, carpets, chairs, tables, cushions, stools, andirons and window cloths of crimson velvet embroidered with works of needlework or otherwise used in her Majesty's Privy Chamber, and the sparver of crimson velvet embroidered with hands and dragons and

3.

porpentines, with the quilts, chairs, stools, cushions, carpets, cupboard cloths, board cloths and window cloths belonging which was in her Majesty's Withdrawing Chamber.

Whereas I have heretofore conveyed to my loving friends Sir Christopher Wraye, Sir Gilbert Gerrard, Sir Thomas Mildmay, Sir John Peter, Sir John Higham, knights, John Harrington of Elmsthorpe (Leics.), esquire, Richard Wrothe, Thomas Wrothe, Robert Butler and Edward Anlaby, gentlemen, the site of the late dissolved monastery of Glaston alias Glastonbury (Somerset) and all other my lands in Glastonbury, to the intents declared in a pair of indentures made between me and them, dated 26 October 1582; now I for their better assurance to them bequeath the site and lands to the said intents, praying them according to the great trust in them reposed that, if the lands shall not fortune to be sold in my lifetime, they will with speed make sale of the lands in Glastonbury, and with the money pay such of my debts as I have by writing subscribed with my own hand, and the overplus shall be delivered to them.

I constitute executors my trusty and well beloved Sir Christopher Wraye, Sir Walter Mildmay knight, Chancellor of the Exchequer, Sir Gilbert Gerrard, Sir Thomas Mildmay, Sir John Peter, Richard Wrothe, Thomas Wrothe of the Inner Temple, and Edward Anlabye my auditor, praying them to call on my said feoffees for the sale of Glastonbury and to make earnest request to them to make speedy sale if not sold in my lifetime; and for their pains I bequeath to every of them 100 oz. of gilt plate. A book be kept by my executors of the receipts and payments and from time to time signed by them, each to have a copy, and Anlabye to see these books perfectly made. If it shall happen that the money from Glastonbury and of other my goods not given by my will exceed my debts, funeral charges and legacies, the remain shall be to the use of my heir male who at that time shall be Earl and shall be delivered presently to him if of full age and if not it shall remain in the custody of my executors to his use until he shall be of age. They shall have towards the performance of my will my corn, cattle and other goods not otherwise given away. Anlabye and one of my feoffees shall keep a book of the land sold and another book with the sums paid to anybody, to the end my feoffees and executors may be the more readily acquainted with their doings committed to their trusts; and for his pains he shall have an annuity of £20 over all such other charges as he shall be reasonably allowed for his riding charges, the annuity to be so long as my executors shall be thought good. I constitute the right honourable the Lord Burleigh, Lord High Treasurer of England, and the right honourable the Earl of Rutland to be the supervisors of my will, and do heartily require them to call earnestly upon my executors and my feoffees for the faithful performance of my will, and for their pains I bequeath to either of them 100 oz. of gilt plate.

In witness whereof I have subscribed my name and set my seal of arms in the presence of Humphrey Skinner H[enry] Maynard, Walter Cope, Herbert Crofte, Robert Boteler, Stephen Ridlesden, Ferdinando Stanton.   T : SUSSEX.

4

A codicil to be annexed to the last will of me Thomas Earl of Sussex.

Whereas I during the time of my sickness have sold to divers persons divers woods and timber trees on my manor and park of Attleborough and on my manors in Norfolk and Essex, if Sir Henry or the Lady Frances my wife or their heirs shall not permit all persons to whom I have sold such woods quietly to take the same, Sir Henry and the Lady Frances shall forfeit the benefit of my will.

Whereas Richard Wrothe my servant hath heretofore for many years had the receipt and payment of great sums of money and hath not yet given up his full account, he shall not in any wise intermeddle with the execution of my will or take on him to be my executor until he shall have so accounted to the residue of my executors. My executors shall have with such of my goods and debts as shall first come to their hands keep house and maintain hospitality in my house at Bermondsey for the Lady Frances and for such my menial servants as were ordinarily and daily attendant on me until my funerals be performed and also 20 days after, to the intent that my servants may have time to provide themselves some competent service. If my wife shall make her choice of New Hall, she shall have the use during her life of such hangings and other furniture of the chambers bequeathed to my brother, on condition that she shall first become bound to my executors with sufficient sureties that the hangings (reasonable waste and wearing allowed) after her decease shall remain to him.

Whereas I by my deed tripartite dated 20 November 1579 conveyed certain manors [as above] to my wife for life; to the intent that she may be the more assured to enjoy them, my brother shall become bound to my executors in £2,000 by a recognizance with condition that if she do quietly enjoy them the recognizance shall be void. Whereas by another conveyance since made I stand seized in fee simple to myself and my wife of the site of the monastery of Bermondsey; and whereas by my will I have bequeathed divers leases which I purchased of gardens and houses near the house of Bermondsey to my wife to dispose and give at her pleasure, at which time my hope and trust was that she would convey the house immediately after her decease likewise to remain to such uses and persons as in the indenture are expressed, and also the remain of the leases likewise to remain to such person as at the time of her decease shall fortune to be Earl of Sussex; therefore she shall become bound to my executors in £2,000 by recognizance with condition that if she shall within one year next convey the house and site to the use of herself for life and after to the only uses mentioned therein, and also convey the leases in such sort as they shall remain to such person being my heir as shall be Earl of Sussex, the recognizance shall be void; and if she do not become so bound then she shall not take any benefit of my legacy of £6,000 oz. of plate but such plate shall remain to my brother. I further bequeath to my wife a cup of gold remaining in her custody and all other plate of silver and silver with crystal set or garnished with precious stones or without and not being already expressed in a book subscribed with my own hand containing the parcels and number of ounces of all other my plate.

To William Dun my physician for his pains, travail and diligence taken about me in this my last sickness £50. To William Clowes my surgeon and servant £20. To Robert Perpoint my apothecary £20. To Robert Cannon steward of my house £20. To my servants Henry Cotten £20, Stephen Ridlesden £6 13s. 4d., William Monnynges £6 13s. 4d., Peers Conway £20, George Macabo £6 13s. 4d., Thomas Brewer £6 13s. 4d., Henry Heritage £20, Henry Oldfield £5, and George Gage £4. To John Gale my servant and one of the grooms of my chamber £10, Richard Carveth one of my footmen £4, and Glasney my footman £4. To my servants William Cooke £5, Richard Shawe 40s., Richard Sedell one of the grooms of my chamber £5, John Stannoppe another of my footmen £5, Scott of the scullery £5, and Henry Bacon and Richard Jones grooms of my stable, 40s. apiece. I forgive Garrett Alilmer my servant the £40 he oweth me. To William Preston my servant £20.

Witnesses, 21 May, 1583: William Dun, Joel Tynlye, Stephen Ridelsden, John Muschampte, Thomas Bedwell, Ferdinandus Stanton, Henry Cotton, Robert Nettleton, George Manwaringe.   T: SUSSEX.

Proved, 15 November 1585, before William Drury, doctor of laws, Commissary of the Prerogative Court of Canterbury, by the oath of Christopher Smith notary public, proctor of Walter Myldmay, Christopher Wray, Chief Justice of the Queen's Bench, Gilbert Gerrard, Master of the Rolls, Thomas Myldmay and John Peter, Thomas Wroth and Edward Anlabi, executors.

[Among the Petre family archives in the Essex Record Office (D/DP F240/1-12) is a volume and a number of papers relating to the executorship of the Earl's will. He died on 9 June 1583. The principal documents are the detailed accounts of his funeral charges at Boreham and the expenses of the Bermondsey household (he died there); inventories of his goods at New Hall (set out in full detail, room by room), of livestock and crops on the New Hall estate, and of goods at Woodham Walter and at Bermondsey; lists of jewels, plate, napery, clothes and household furniture bequeathed to his widow, and of napery at Bermondsey; a schedule of his debts; accounts of Sir Thomas Mildmay as executor; accounts of Richard Steephins alien, mason, for erecting the tomb at Boreham, 1588-89; and accounts of Anlaby and Gerrard as executors.]

[LADY] ELIZABETH DARCYE, widow [of Sir Robert Darcy, 1st Lord Darcy of Chich], — 1564. [For other Darcy wills, see pp. 77-79.] [8/35]

To be buried at St Osyth church by my honourable lord and husband, the Lord Darcye, with such ceremony as belongs to a Christian woman and to my calling. At the day of burial to the poor that is impotent and not able to work or aged £5 after 2d. dole or else as my executors shall think meet to give groats.

To my lord my son a gown and a coat and to my son [in-law] Edmund Pirton as much and two of his men to have coats, also to Thomasine Darcye such mourning apparel as belongeth to the daughter to wear for the death of her mother, to my daughter Pirton the same, and to my two gentlemen their gowns and coats and my gentlewomen a gown.

To my lord my son £10. To my daughter his wife a bracelet of gold flagon fashion. To Thomasine Darcie if she be unmarried 100 marks, a flower of diamonds, the best hedge of pearl, and my can of parcel gilt, a trussing bed sparver of tawny velvet and orange tawny damask with rotes of cloth of silver and curtain to the same, and a featherbed and a coverlet of coarse tapestry. To my daughter Pirton my other hedge of pearl, a ring with a diamond, a casting bottle all gilt, a trussing bedsteadle with gilt posts and a tester of cloth of baudekin and crimson satin with a word and curtains to the same, a gown of black velvet, my best kirtle, half a dozen of my best smocks, and kerchers as many.

To my son Robert a basin and an ewer with the Darcies' arms, a jug parcel gilt with the Darcies' arms, a dozen silver trenchers with the Darcies' arms, 2 wine pots all gilt, a trussing bedsteadle of walnut-tree with a tester of crimson satin paned with black velvet with my lord's arms and mine and curtains to the same, the featherbed that I lie on, a pair of fustians and a coverlet with leaves and conies and beasts, a long cushion of crimson velvet with mullets and another that is lesser with mullets, and a cupboard carpet. To my son Pirton a nest of goblets parcel gilt and 6 in the case, £10 to help towards payment of his livery, and £10 to keeping his son William to school. Also to Thomas Darcie my marriage ring and a crossbow of damascene work with the rack.

To my gentlewoman a gown, a kirtle of my own, 6 smocks, 6 kerchers and a bonnet. To Harper 20 nobles, a gelding, and half dozen of silver spoons. To Piren 20 nobles and a nag. To Roger my groom 40s. and a nag if he be my man, also to groom [sic] 4 beasts, i.e. milch kine, whereof 2 John Cooke hath to farm and 2 goeth with John Usherwode, a nag, and £4. To John Usherwode the rest of my kine that he hath in farm, i.e. 6, and a nag, and such money as he oweth me.

To my godson John Veer, my brother Geoffrey's only son, £10 in considering his bringing up in learning, which I do earnestly charge my executors to bestow to that use or else that way as may be benefit to the boy. To mistress Tey a little wretched ring if I die in her house, or else-where it is my chance to die to give it to her that is owner of the house.

If there remain any goods, they shall be evenly distributed between Robert Darcie and my son Pirton, whom I make my executors, as you [sic] will answer at the general day of judgement.

Memorandum, 26 December 1565, lying sick at the house of her son-in-law Edmund Pirton in the presence of Anthony Bisshoppe and George Peryn gentlemen, Edward Lloyde clerk, and others, she did acknowledge that she had made this will with her own hand and subscribed her name and that it did remain in a coffer of hers that was in her lodging at Mr [George] Tuke's house at Layer Marney, and she delivered the key of the coffer to her executors and willed for them to go for the same and to bring it unto her, at whose commandment they went and brought the will to Mr Pirton's house, but before they could come thither she was departed.

Proved 29 December 1565.

SIR JOHN DARCY knight, [SECOND] LORD DARCY OF CHICH,
3 February 1581. [24/1]

To be buried at Chich alias St Osyth by my father in such decent,
honourable, comely and convenient sort as is meet for my calling. My
executor shall erect at the place of my burial within two years after my
decease two decent and convenient tombs as well for Thomas Lord Darcy
my father and the Lady Elizabeth my mother deceased as also for myself
and the Lady Frances my late wife, meet for our estates and degrees.

Whereas my son and heir apparent Thomas Darcy esquire at my
special request hath entered into a recognizance in the nature of a statute
staple in £10,000 to my trusty and well-beloved friends Edmund Pirton
esquire, my brother-in-law, and Francis Harvye esquire, with a defeazance
thereof, on the date of these presents, for the true performance of my
will; in consideration thereof I give to my son as well the goods I have
as also all my lands and commodities [so] that he shall pay my debts
at the farthest within four years after my decease. To my daughter
Elizabeth Darcie for her preferment in marriage £2,000 at 23 or
marriage. My trust is in her that I have bequeathed an honourable
portion on her, so in the bestowing of herself in marriage she will be
advised and ruled by her brother Thomas and our good wife and discreet
friends. And until she shall have received her portion, for the better
maintenance of her meat, drink and apparel according to her degree, she
shall receive yearly £100. My youngest son Robert shall be brought up
in learning at Cambridge or elsewhere until 21 (if he do not before
marry) as it shall be thought most meet by the discretion of my executor,
and towards his bringing up in learning during his minority I bequeath
him yearly £30. To my two younger sons John and Robert £200 apiece
at 21 or marriage; to John my second son an annuity of £60 out of my
manor of Southminster, with remainder to such woman as he may marry,
for her life; to Robert my third and youngest son an annuity out of the
said manor, with like remainder. For the better advancement of John,
Thomas shall make to him a lease of my farm or wick in Southminster
called Mumsale for 21 years at the old accustomed rent now in being
granted to Brocke and Collins, further yielding yearly in the name of
provision to Thomas 20 wethers, 1 boar and 4 firkins of butter. To
Elizabeth Pyrton, my sister's daughter, £100 at marriage.

To every of my servants that shall be in wages or stipends with me
at the day of my death one year's wages above that shall be then due;
also to William Cooke my servant for his true and faithful service an
annuity of £3 out of the said manor.

I appoint Thomas my sole executor.

Whereas I have by way of communication agreed with Henry
Windham esquire for the demise of the site of my manor and demesne of
Elmswell (Suffolk) by indentures yet remaining unsealed, and have
granted to him the keeping of the Great Park in St Osyth in such sort as
John Barnes gentleman, my servant, had held it, and have also granted
to him in reversion a lease to be made of 53 acres in Norton (Suffolk);
and whereas I have agreed with John Brocke gentleman by indentures

8

not yet sealed for the grant of a lease in reversion to him of Walton Hall for £406 13s. 4d.; my will is that Thomas shall seal such leases.

Provided that, if Thomas shall have performed my will or else taken such order for performance thereof as shall be thought sufficient by Edmund Pyrton and Francis Harvye, to whom the said bond is acknowledged, and also by my trusty and well-beloved friends William Ayloff, one of her Majesty's Justices of the Queen's Bench, William Drurye and Robert Forth, two of the Masters of her Majesty's Court of Chancery, and Thomas Darcy of Tolleshunt D'Arcy esquire, or the more part of them, then the said recognizance to be cancelled.

Witnesses: Thomas Cannock, Nicholas Hilles, and others.

Proved 14 March 1581. [In margin: Darcy arms—three cinquefoils.]

SIR JOHN GREY knight, LORD GREY, in my house of Pyrgo [in Havering], —1564.   [8/2]

To be buried in the chapel of my house of Pyrgo. To my dearly-beloved lady and wife Mary, whom I make my sole executrix, my goods, farms and leases wheresoever they be, most heartily praying and requiring her of all loves to see my children virtuously brought up and well bestowed and to pay my debts. Witnesses: Caesar Adelmance and John Kerrol clerk.

Proved 29 January 1564 by John Kerrell clerk, proxy of Lady Mary.

SIR RICHARD RYCHE knight, [FIRST] LORD RYCHE, 20 May 1567.   [11/12]

To be buried in Felsted church, the order and manner of my burying and the charges I commit to the discretion of my executors. For my tithes negligently forgotten I bequeath to the vicar of Little Leighs 13s. 4d.

My executors principally shall cause my debts to be paid with as convenient speed as they may as well to our sovereign lady the Queen as to all other persons.

To Agnes Piggott, one of the daughters of my daughter [Margery wife of Henry] Pigott of Abington [Cambs.], 500 marks towards her marriage if she be not before married in my lifetime. To Lucy Barley, one of the daughters of my daughter [Dorothy widow of Francis] Barley [of Kimpton, Herts.], 200 marks likewise. To Dorothy Pigott, one of the daughters of my daughter [Anne wife of Thomas] Piggott of Stratton [in Biggleswade, Beds.], 500 marks likewise. To Anne Drury, one of the daughters of my daughter [Audrey widow of Robert] Drury [of Hawstead, Suffolk], 500 marks likewise. To Elizabeth Darcy, one of the daughters of my daughter [Frances wife of John Lord] Darcy, 500 marks likewise. Which legacies to be paid at marriage, to be levied of my goods and chattels and revenues of my lands. If any die before marriage, her portion to the next younger sister; if any shall marry without the consent of her father and mother, her portion to the next sister. To such of my executors as shall specially travail for the advancement in marriage of any of the same by his industry and travail £20.

9

To Sir Robert Ryche knight, my son and heir apparent, as much of my plate at his choice as shall be to the value of £200 and all my household stuff, being no silver or gold, at any houses of Leighs, Rochford and St Bartholomew, with my artilleries, guns, harness and munitions of war, and my great stoned horses.

To every of my gentlemen that be my servants at the time of my decease and not advanced to any farm or annuity £5, to every other menservants being my household servants not advanced 53s. 4d., and to every of my women and maidservants not advanced on their marriages 40s. To Anne wife of Thomas Shaa gentleman £10 and to my servant John Richardes £10.

My executors shall dispose in alms to the poor people coming to my burial 100 marks and shall be reasonably allowed for their expenses, pains and travail. To William Bourne my servant £10, and in consideration of his service heretofore done and to be done to me and to my son, taking like wages of my son, an annuity of £5 out of my manor and lordship of Rochford. Every person that stand bound for me and for my debt to the late kings Henry VIII or Edward VI or to any other person shall be discharged of their bonds by my executors [out] of the revenues of my lands.

To Sir Robert Catlyn knight, Chief Justice of the Queen's Bench, Sir William Cordell knight, Master of the Rolls, Mr Gilbert Gerrard, General Attorney, and to the said William Bourne, each £40, all of whom I ordain my executors. To them the manors of Great Waltham, Braintree and Newarks in Good Easter with the four prebends and parsonage there, lands called Watermans in Great Waltham, that parcel of Abchild Park called Waltham Quarter as is divided from the residue of the park, the manors of Broomfield Hall, Chatham Hall [in Great Waltham], Passelowe Hall [in High Ongar], Shelley, Brendish [in Moreton], Fyfield, Herons [in Fyfield], Upper Hall and Nether Hall in Moreton, Greensted Hall, the hundreds of Ongar and Harlow, the manors of Wanstead with the late park, Hatfield Broad Oak alias King's Hatfield with the mill and late park of Hatfield, Hutton Hall, Breames [in Great Leighs], Moulsham Hall [in Great Leighs], Warrakes [in Little Leighs], and Felsted with Grandcourts barn, the tithe corn of Fery Quarter in Felsted with the lands and pastures called Blakeley, the manors of Enviles [in Great Leighs], Glandviles and Whelpstones [both in Felsted], the messuages called Gales in Felsted and Frenches at Horne in Felsted, the Old Park near Pleshey, and the five pastures late parcel of the park, the manors of Leighs and Leighs Ryche with the farms or messuages called Camsex, Slampesey and Ravyns, the yearly rent of £5 out of the manor of Lyon Hall in Little Leighs, the manors of Westwicke Hall and Estwicke [both in Burnham], my part of the manor of Barlande [in Prittlewell] and Blakes in Prittlewell, and my lands in the same manors and parishes (except the site and capital messuage house of my manor of Leighs with Little Leighs Park and Lytley Park and the Forest of Hatfield, such lands, parsonages and tithes as I shall have in my own occupation towards the provision of my house at the time of my decease, and provision of corn, grain and cattle); and also my fair of Great St

Bartholomew with the profits; to hold the same for 6 years after my decease to the intent that they shall with the issues and profits perform my will.

To my son Sir Robert and his heirs male the site and capital mansion house of my manor of Leighs alias Leighs Ryche with all houses thereto belonging, the parks of Leighs and Lytley and the Forest of Hatfield, my lands, parsonages and tithes that I keep in my hands in Leighs and Felsted for the provision of my house, corn, grain and cattle, and the manors and lands bequeathed to my executors, after the expiration of the same years; and for default of such issue the remainder to my heirs male.

Whereas it hath pleased God besides divers sons to send me divers daughters, i.e. Margery Piggott my eldest daughter, wife of Henry Pygott of Abingdon esquire, Agnes Mordaunt my second daughter, wife of Edmund Mordaunt esquire, Dame Mary Wrothe my third daughter, wife of Sir Thomas Wrothe knight, Dorothy Barley my fourth daughter, late the wife of Francis Barley esquire, Anne Piggot my fifth daughter, late the wife of Thomas Pigott of Stratton esquire, Audrey Drury my sixth daughter, late the wife of Robert Drury esquire, Elizabeth Payton my seventh daughter, wife of Robert Payton esquire, Dame Winifred North my eighth daughter, wife of Sir Roger North knight, Lord North, and the Lady Frances Darcy my ninth daughter, wife of Lord John Darcy of Chiche; if I shall die without issue male, all the said manors shall remain to my several daughters and their heirs. [Mordaunt, of Thunderley in Wimbish; Wrothe, of Enfield, Middx.; Peyton, of Isleham, Cambs.; North, of Kirtling, Cambs.]

To Sir Robert the manors of Hockley, Hadleigh, Prittlewell and Pryors Marshes, Earls Hall alias Earls Field in Prittlewell, Eastwood, Sutton Temple, Southchurch, South Shoebury, and Milton Hall [in Prittlewell], my parts of the manors of Butlers in Shopland and the manors, lands, rents, reversions and services which were lately of Sir Henry Cary knight, now Lord Hunsdon, in possession or in reversion, in the hundred of Rochford (except such of the said manors late of Lord Hunsdon hereafter otherwise appointed); and for default of heirs male, the remainder to my daughters and their heirs. To Sir Robert the manors of Rochford and Combes and the farms of Myntons, Strowdwicke and Swaynes, the mill of Rochford and the tilekiln, and the rents of the same; and for default of such issue, the successive remainders to me and my heirs male and to Richard Ryche, my base son, and his heirs male; and for default, the remainder of the manors of Rochford and other the premises last before specified to Edward Ryche of Horndon [on-the-Hill] and his heirs male. Also to Richard, my base son, and his heirs male my manor of Patching Hall otherwise Woodhall Wall with those lands called Le Hyde in Broomfield and Chelmsford belonging.

My executors [out] of the issues aforesaid shall provide or buy one woman ward or some other woman having manors and lands of value of £200 yearly for a marriage to Richard, and shall pay him at marriage £500; and if he refuse to marry her or if no marriage shall be provided they shall pay him £1,000 and sell the ward or other woman if any such be provided to any other person to the uttermost advantage to the performance of my will. Anthony Browne shall have his government and bringing up in godly education and learning in the common laws or otherwise and shall receive the issues of the manors given to Richard towards his finding, apparelling and bringing up to the age of 21; and if he die before Richard is 21, Sir Robert Catlyn shall have his bringing up, and if Sir Robert die, Sir William Cordell shall have it.

The residue of all my manors and lands I leave to Sir Robert, provided that, if he willingly and advisedly shall practise in any court spiritual or temporal anything to molest, hinder, deny, vex or trouble my executors, then I bequeath to Richard, my base son, the manors of Brendishe, Shelley, Passelowe, Herons and Fyfield and to his heirs male, on condition that, if he or his heirs male shall at any time hereafter sell or give them, my heirs shall enter into them notwithstanding, and the gift to be void.

Witnesses : the Lady Elizabeth Ryche, John Boswell notary public, William Turner, M.A., and Thomas Mayew, with others.

Codicil, 10 June 1567.

To Edward Ellis, yeoman of my cellar, 53s. 4d. yearly for life out of my manor of Rochford on condition that he serve my son and heir in the same office justly, taking like wages as he now taketh of me. Whereas I have bequeathed the manors which lately were of Sir Henry Cary to Sir Robert, I bequeath out of them to the almshouse to be erected in Rochford 5 or 6 acres of wood, parcel of Strowdewicke, called Britchetley, other ground parcel thereof containing 3 or 4 acres, with Little Downes and Brickle Close, 5 acres in Rochford Park on the north side leading down where the vault shall go, a marsh called Wakeringes in Great Wakering in the occupation of Robert Edmondes, also as much ground within the clapgate leading to Rochford town as shall serve for the site, garden and orchard where the almshouse shall be builded as is now staked out. To John Planten my servant 40s. yearly out of my manor of Felsted for life. Witnesses : [as above].

Proved 3 June 1568, Sir Robert Catlyn renouncing executorship.

SIR ROBERT RICHE knight, [SECOND] LORD RICHE, 25 February 1581.   [24/21]

To be buried in Felsted church. The order and manner of my burial and the expenses I refer to the discretion of my executor being done according to my degree. He shall cause to be made for my father and me a comely and decent tomb, according to our degrees, to be erected in the choir or chancel of Felsted church or in some convenient chapel adjoined to the same, and the names of such as we have matched withal in marriage may be engraved in the stone, which my mind is shall be done within so short time as may be conveniently after my death.

My executor shall cause all debts to be paid with convenient speed as I owe to the Queen's Majesty as also to every other person.

To Robert Ryche, my son and heir apparent, my household stuff and utensils, jewels, plate, and all other my goods. To Edwin my son 200 marks at 21 towards the providing of some household stuff for him. To

Frances Ryche my daughter £1,500 at 21; provided that, if she shall not happen to marry to her advancement but otherwise without the consent of my son Robert and of Mr Robert Monsone, late Justice of the Queen's Majesty's Common Pleas, and of my cousin Robert Wrath, or of two of them, or if she fortune to die before age or marriage, the legacy to my sons equally to be divided; and she be placed by the appointment of Robert until age or marriage. To Edwin and Frances £50 apiece yearly payable, the former out of my manors called Burstead Grange, Whites, Gurnardes and Challwydden [in Great Burstead] and the manor of Hutton until he is 21, and the latter out of all my manors until she be paid the £1,500, for their educations [*sic*], maintaining and finding.

To all my menservants, other than such as have advancement by leases made by me, one year's wages. To my cousin Edward Mordante £5 yearly for life. To my brother Richard Ryche and Jane his wife £100. To William Bowrne my steward £20 and to Mr Wrighte £20.

To Edwin the manors of Great Burstead, Whites, Challwydden and Gurnardes and Hutton, with lands I have in Burstead and Hutton, at 21, and his heirs male; if he die without heirs, to Robert. To Robert the manors of Rochford and the tilekiln, and the rents of the same, and his heirs male; and for default of such issue the remainders successively to Edwin, to Richard my brother, and to Edward Ryche of Horndon, and the heirs male of each. Whereas there is conveyed by me to Lady Elizabeth my wife for life certain of my manors by reason of divers leases made by me, I declare that the intent should be for her jointure and that she should not have any part of the provision covenanted to be paid on them, but only the rent. The residue of my manors, lordships and lands to Robert. All lands and rents by my late father given to the erecting of an almshouse in Rochford shall remain and it shall be erected accordingly.

I make Robert my sole executor and I make Mr Monson, Mr Butler and Mr Morice my overseers and £10 apiece for their pains.

Witnesses: [none].

Proved 7 June 1581.

2
KNIGHTS

SIR ANTHONY BROUN of South Weald, one of the Justices of the Common Bench and one of the sons of Weston Broun of Abbess Roothing knight and of Elizabeth his wife, one of the daughters of William Mordaunte of Turvey (Beds.) esquire, deceased, 20 December 1565.

[10/20]

To be buried in the chancel of South Weald church with such funerals, alms, obsequies and ceremonies at my burial as becometh and in the Catholic Church is used by the discretion of my executors. To the reparation of the church 20s. and of the Cathedral church of St Paul 40s. To the church of Abbess Roothing where I was born 20s. To Serjeants' Inn whereof I am 40s.

Joan Reynolde be paid her annuity of 6s. 8d., according to a grant to her made by me at my mother's request, for her diligent service at the time of her sickness, and for charity for her relief 20s. yearly.

To my dear and well-beloved wife [Joan] my lease of the tithes of Clayton in Leyland (Lancs.).

I will that such person for ever as shall possess my manor of South Weald shall have the usage of all my books of all manner of sorts without having in them any property. The precedent book of my uncle William Mordaunt's and the Book of the Years containing ten the first years of King Edward III in parchment and an old book written of years of King Richard III and of other covered with boards and a great written book of precedents that I received of Robert Brooke to be delivered to my cousin Robert Mordaunte because the same I had by him and do belong to him as far as I do know. I will the precedent book of my old master John Jenour, much of it his own hand, be delivered to Andrew the son and heir of Richard Jenour, of which Richard I received it.

To my wife, of whose honesty, obedience, virtue and good life I have had good and long experience, thanks be to God, all my goods, plate, jewels and leases, not otherwise given, for her own use, desiring her to do such deeds of charity with part thereof as she shall think good, and I ordain her my sole executrix. I ordain my faithful friends Sir William Peter of Ingatestone knight, one of our sovereign Lady's Privy Council, and Sir Edward Saunders knight, Lord Chief Baron of the Exchequer, overseers, desiring them to assist my wife with their good advice concerning my will.

To the prisoners in the King's Bench, Marshalsey, Newgate and Ludgate prisons in London and Southwark 40s.; to every of the new founded houses at the Grey Friars and Bridewell 40s. To the poor brethren and sisters of St Dunstan's in London 13s. 4d.; to the poor folks in the Savoy £5.

To my sister Joan Bridges' lame son 26s. 8d. and her lame daughter 26s. 8d. and my sister Constance's boy 26s. 8d. yearly for life.

To my clerks Thomas Wallenger, Anthony Jebbe and Henry Hall each 5 marks, to John Fuller of my Chamber 40s., to every of my other servants a quarter's wages, men and women, and to the said Jebbe an annuity of 4 marks and in consideration thereof he should serve my wife one year after my decease.

To Sir William Peter for his pains a piece of plate for remembrance worth £5 and to Sir Edward Saunders a piece of plate of like value; to my executrix, to my Lord Ritche and to every of my overseers a ring of gold of 40s. and to their wives if they have any, and to my Lady Waldegrave, Sir Henry Tirrell, Sir Lawrence Taylarde, Robert Mordaunt, Edmund Tirrell, George White, Edmund Hudliston, Dorothy his wife, Wiston Browne, Richard Cutte, Alexander Scrogges and John Fowler each a ring of gold of 4 nobles, to be made like serjeants' rings and on the outside to be graven these words *Wee dye* and on the inside *Forgett nott.* To Robert Mordaunte in recompense for the board he gave me and my wife £20 and to Sir Lawrence Taylarde £5.

I will that there be given yearly for 20 years after my decease £20 by him or her that shall possess my manor house of South Weald, i.e. £5 to the poor inhabiting at Brentwood and other £5 to the poor in the Upland of South Weald, Brook Street and at the Churchgate, £3 in amending the highways and lanes in South Weald parish, and £7 towards the marriages of the poor children of such as have been my daily labourers in South Weald, of the poor inhabitants of South Weald, or of the poor tenants of the manor of South Weald, wheresoever they shall dwell, by the discretion of the owners of the chief mansion house of South Weald manor. And if the £20 be not paid I give a yearly rent of £30 to Robert Wrighte of Brook Street tanner, John Wright his son, John Wrighte of Kelvedon my servant, John Wrighte of Wealdside, John Lucas, George Monke my servant, John Tyler, John Haukyn, Roger Gittons and John Broman.

To my cousin Joan Mordaunte, daughter of William Mordaunte and of Agnes his wife, one of my wife's daughters, if she will during my wife's life be ruled in her marriage by my wife, 600 marks at 20 or at marriage; and if she live to 20 unmarried then to have the 600 marks and to marry at her free liberty. To Mary Charnawke, my wife's maid, £100, and to Joan Parker alias Loughton to her marriage £10. To my sister Eton 5 marks. To Anthony Cutte my godson £10 and Richard Cutte £20. To my sister Knighton £5. To the poor of Crofton (Lancs.) £21 and of Dagenham £5.

Whereas I have given by writings to the Schoolmaster of the Grammar School of Anthony Browne, serjeant-at-law, in Brentwood and to the Guardians of the lands of the school my late manor or grange called

Chigwell Grange with the lands belonging, and a messuage with a curtilage adjoining, a cottage with a garden, and an orchard in Brentwood, sometime of Richard Nytingale, for ever, the Master and Guardians shall have the same to such uses as in the same writings and by other ordinances made and to be made are declared. And because there is as yet no convenient place appointed to keep the School in nor apt place for the habitation of the Schoolmaster, I by virtue of sufficient licence granted under the Great Seal of England give to the Schoolmaster and the Guardians for ever the capital messuage called Redcrosse in South Weald and a close called the Conygre containing 4 acres adjoining on the north, which Redcrosse and Conygre I late purchased of Henry Becher, citizen and merchant of London, to hold for ever to such uses and ordinances as shall be declared.

To John Lyttell my servant my parsonage of Dagenham (except the patronage of the vicarage) for 20 years, paying yearly £24, the reversion thereof with the rent and five tenements in South Weald in the occupations of John Scotte, Thomas Barnes, widow Reynoldes, widow Fawvel and widow Margarett I give to the Schoolmaster and Guardians for ever to the intent that with the issues thereof they shall find five poor folks in South Weald to be named by such persons as shall possess my manor of South Weald.

Whereas my wife is joined with me for the term of her life in the manor and parsonage of South Weald, the manor of Coste[d] Hall, the fair and market of Brentwood, the manor of Calcot in South Weald, Shenfield and Doddinghurst, and the manor of Church Hall in Paglesham, and lands called Biggen in Great Stambridge, as by the writings of the purchase do appear; and whereas a messuage in Brook Street which of late was the free chapel there with 100 acres of land called Spyttell Lands or Chantry Lands in Brook Street, late in the occupation of Thomas Cappes deceased, except Style Field which is in my occupation, were conveyed to me and my wife; the writings and conveyances shall continue touching her for her lifetime, and she shall have the said manors and lands for life [the repeated names add the manor of Cockermouth [in Dagenham] before Church Hall]. And if I shall fortune to decease without heirs of my body, then all my manors and lands shall remain to Dorothy wife of Edmund Hudleston esquire for life; with further successive remainders to Weston the son and heir of my nephew George Broun, my brother's son, to Anthony Broun my godson, then to the son of Wiston Broun son and heir of George, and his heirs male, to the 2nd, 3rd, 4th, 5th, 6th, 7th and 8th sons of Wiston and their heirs male, to John Broun the brother of Wyston the son, for life; with successive remainders to Anthony Broun my godson; to the 1st, 2nd, 3rd, 4th, 5th, 6th, 7th and 8th sons of John and their heirs male; to Philip Broun, the eldest son of my nephew Henry Broun, son of John Broun my eldest brother deceased, for life, with successive remainders to the 1st to the 8th sons of Philip and their heirs male; to Connyngesby Broun the 2nd son of Henry Broun, for life, with the like successive remainders; to Sir Wiston Broun knight, my father, and his heirs male; to Richard Cutte esquire, my sister's son, and his heirs male; to Anthony

16

Cutte my godson, Richard's brother, and his heirs male; to Alexander Skeyef alias Scrogges, my sister Jane's son, and his heirs male; and to the heirs female of Sir Wyston Broun my father and of Dame Elizabeth his wife my mother.

The manors of Church Hall in Paglesham and Cockermouth in Dagenham shall remain to my nephew Wyston Broun and his heirs male, with remainders to my nephew John Broun and to Sir Wyston Broun and their heirs male; with further successive remainders of the manor of Paglesham to my nephew William Herberte of Colbroke [Colebrooke, Devon?], to sister Elizabeth's son, and his heirs male, and to the heirs female of Sir Wyston and Dame Elizabeth, and of the manor of Cockermouth to Alexander Scrogges and his heirs male, and to the heirs female of Sir Wyston and Dame Elizabeth.

I will to such person as after my wife's decease shall be my heir general a yearly rent of £20 out of all my leases (except Clayton tithes), provided that, if my heir general shall molest, vex or trouble my wife in any of the manors contrary to my will or shall meddle with any of my goods, then the yearly rent of £20 shall cease. To my wife the marsh ground that I purchased of Robert Tirrell and also the patronage of the vicarage of Dagenham for life; and to her for life and after her death to Dorothy Hudleston and her heirs the advowson of the vicarage of Crofton. To John Broun my nephew £4 yearly for life.

My wife's executors after her decease shall have the manor of South Weald for one year after her decease without any rent paying, and also Dorothy's executors if she overlive my wife shall have likewise.

Witnesses: Henry Hall, John Hasilwood, Mr Edmund Hudleston esquire, and others.

Proved 5 June 1567.

DAME JOYCE CARYE, late of Thremhall [in Stansted Mountfitchet], widow of Sir John Carye knight, 10 November 1560.   [4/3]

To be buried in Aldermanbury church in London beside my late husband Walsingham. To every of my sons, sons-in-law and daughters a gown of black cloth. To Agnes 6s. 8d. and Margery 10s. and my gentlewoman a gown of black cloth.

To Francis Walsingham my son a basin and a ewer of silver which was his father's, a bowl of silver gilt, a goblet of silver gilt, a ceiler, a tester of velvet with gold knots, a ceiler and a tester of yellow damask and black velvet with drops of gold, a quilt of blue sarcenet, a coverlet of arras work, 2 of my best featherbeds, a pair of fustian blankets, 2 pair of fine sheets, 2 pair of pillowberes, a long carpet of Turkeywork which was his father's, a tablecloth of diaper damask work, a towel of the same, 12 napkins of diaper damask work, a garnish of pewter vessel encrested, 3 of my best brass pots, and a great chaffer. To Wymond Carye my son the new basin and ewer of silver, a ceiler and tester of cloth of gold and crimson damask, another ceiler and tester of white satin and tawny damask with flower de luces and drops of velvet, a coverlet of arras work, 4 pieces of arras work which were made in my house, a bowl of silver and gilt, a goblet of silver and gilt, and all my silver spoons by estimation 18. To Edward Carye my son a bowl of silver gilt, a goblet of silver gilt, a ceiler and a tester of changeable sarcenet embroidered with yellow silk, another tester and ceiler of blue and black damask, a coverlet of red sarcenet with garters, and a coverlet of arras work. To my daughters Wentworth, Sydney and Tamworth each a bracelet of gold, to Wentworth my gown of satin, to Sydney my gown of damask, and to Tamworth my gown of velvet. To my daughter Myldmaye a salt of silver gilt which her father gave me. To Joyce Gates £6 13s. 4d. at 18 or marriage.

The value of my residue to my sons Francis, Wymond and Edward to be equally divided between them in money, saving that Edward shall have for his part £20 above the other parts, and the other parts shall remain in my executors' hands for four years after my death to be employed to their profit, and the goods before bequeathed to Wymond and Edward to be delivered at marriage or three years after my death. I appoint as my executors my sons Sir Walter Mildmaye knight and Francis Walsingham and my nephew Edmund Danyell, and to Danyell for his pains £5.

Witnesses : Margaret Willington widow, Elizabeth Andrew widow, Thomas Sydney.

Proved 30 January 1561, by Walsingham and Danyell only.

SIR ANTHONY COOKE of 'Guydyhall' [Gidea Hall] in [Romford in the parish of] Havering, knight, 22 May 1576. [For Richard Cooke, see p. 69.]   [20/10]

To be buried at Romford with convenient and not excessive charges.

To my son Richard my best basin and ewer of silver parcel gilt, my best gilt salt, a nest of bowls gilt the biggest, a pair of pots white of silver and a pair of parcel gilt, a nest of bowls white of silver, a dozen of spoons of the best. To my daughter [Mildred wife of William Cecil Lord] Burleigh another nest of bowls gilt and pinked. To my daughter [Anne wife of Sir Nicholas] Bacon another nest of gilt bowls plain. To my daughter [Elizabeth wife of John Lord] Russell my second gilt salt and 2 little salts gilt. To my daughter [Katherine wife of Henry] Killegrewe a nest of white bowls and 2 silver candlesticks. To my son William my second basin and ewer parcel gilt, 2 flagons of silver, and a dozen of spoons. To Richard my household stuff and harness which I have at Guydyhall and Bedfordes. Of my books my daughter Burleigh shall have two volumes in Latin and one in Greek such as she will choose of my gift, and after her choice my daughters Bacon, Russell and Killegrewe shall each successively have two other volumes in Latin and one in Greek; and the residue of my books to my son Richard and Anthony his son.

The lease of my farm in Minster in the isle of Thanet [Kent] with the stock of corn and cattle to my sons Richard and William jointly. To Richard £200 towards his charges at his entering in his lands after my decease. To William £500.

I appoint my executors the right honourable Sir Nicholas Bacon knight, Lord Keeper of the Great Seal of England, the right honourable the Lord Burleigh, Lord Treasurer of England, and Richard and William, and for their lordships' pains and travail £200 each.

The residue of my goods, ready money, plate and jewels to Richard. To William and his wife the manors of Magdalen Laver, Mascalls Bury and Haughams and Wythers [in White Roothing], with such remainders as is by covenant agreed between my Lady Graye and me in writing, on their marriage. To my daughter-in-law, Richard's wife, for her life, the manors of Chaldwell [in Chadwell St Mary] and Ryden Court in [Hornchurch in the parish of] Havering in full recompense of her jointure and dower with like remainders following. To Richard and his heirs male, the residue of my lands not before named, with successive remainders to William and his heirs male, to Richard's and William's heirs female, and to my daughters Burleigh, Bacon, Russell and Killegrewe and their heirs.

Witnesses, 9 June 1576 : W[illiam] Burleigh, Gabriel Goodman Dean of Westminster, W[illiam] Cooke, George Harrison notary, Richard Cooke's wife, Henry Killegrewe's wife, John Escott.

Schedule of [other] legacies. My Lady of Oxford £50, my Lord of Leicester the choice of two such stone horse as be in Havering Park, Robert Cicell £20, Elizabeth Cicell £20, my daughter Killegrewe £60, Anthony Bacon £20, Francis Bacon £20, Edward Hoby £10, Thomas Posthumus Hobie £10, Mary Cooke and Anne Cooke 3 portigues each, Anne Killegrewe 5 portigues, my cousin Skynner £10, my cousin Ogle £5. My servants John Escott £3 6s. 8d., Edward Davie £3, Richard Howell £3, my 3 other household servants at my death 40s. apiece, and every other hind woman servant and boy, in number 15, 20s. apiece, £15. Summa totalis £293 16s. 8d.

Proved 5 March 1577 by Richard Cooke, the other executors reserved.

LADY MARGARET CURSON widow, sometime the wife of Lord Curson and the late wife of Sir Edward Grene knight, deceased, of Halstead. 25 November 1568.   [20/42]

To be buried in St Peter's church, Ipswich, by the said Lord Curson and the Lady his first wife; and there to have a communion with the poor, and to every of the poor which shall receive communion 4d. and to the minister 12d.; to as many of the poor of Halstead 4d. and the vicar 6s. 8d. To the poor people of Sible Hedingham 10s., Earls Colne 3s. 4d. and Colne Engaine 2s. To William Goolde my messuage in Blaxhall (Suffolk) called Saxmadams, for life, with remainder to Robert his eldest son. To William Goolde, his wife and 6 children, each 20s., to every of Spicer's children 20s., Thomasine's children 20s., Arthur's children 20s., and Alice's children 20s., all at 18. To the poor people of St Peter, Ipswich, 40s., and the reparations of the church 40s., to every parish in Ipswich 5s., and to Halstead 40s., to be equally divided; to Blaxhall 20s., half to the poor and half to the reparations of the church. To goodwife Little £5, Alexander Brantwhat £5, James Richardson my

19

servant £5, William Goold the fool £5, and goodwife Little shall have the bestowing of it, Elizabeth Warde 20s., every of goodman Little's maids 6s. 8d., Mary Coote a black gown, and every of his menservants a black coat, Geoffrey Little 6s. 8d., William Little 20s., and every of my godchildren 3s. 4d. The residue to my executors, James Richardson my servant and goodwife Little. Witnesses: Robert Pierson gentleman, Henry Thomson, William Vigorus.

Proved 14 November 1577.

DAME MARY GATE widow, of High Easter, 28 January 1582. [26/28]

I revoke my will made 6 March 1580. To Wimond Brugges, son of my loving niece Prudence Brugges, £50, to remain in her hands for life. To my loving nephews John Carewe £100 and Henry Carewe £40. To my loving niece Mary Davye £60, Douglas Davye her brother, my godson, the same, at 21. To Christian daughter to my niece Wentworth £80 and Frances Wentworth, sister to Christian, £40. To the children of my nephew Jeffrey Gate £50 to be divided equally, to remain in his hands to their use. To Jeffrey the furniture in the chamber in my dwelling house called Garnettes [in High Easter] in which chamber he hath heretofore used most commonly to lodge and all hangings in the green chamber, which hangings have the Gate arms wrought in them. To Grace Shelton, daughter of my nephew Daniell deceased, £50. To my true and faithful menservants John Taverner and Thomas Heyward £10 apiece, my trusty and faithful womanservant Joan Birde £20, every of my other menservants 40s. apiece, my womenservants 20s. apiece, and my ploughboys 13s. 4d. apiece. To Francis son of John Taverner £10. To Robert Dacres my godson a silver cup parcel gilt. To Grace Joicelin my goddaughter a little silver salt.

Whereas my nephew Wimond Carye standeth bound to Sir Walter Mildmay for the payment of £300 to him, which bond was made on trust to my use, the benefit of the bond I appoint for the performance of my will, and for the same my executors to take of my nephew Roger Carewe so much money as he standeth bound to pay me for the purchase of Shenfield. Whereas there remaineth in my nephew Jeffery Gate's hands £100, residue of £400 with other £300 I have already disposed to the use of my nephew Anthony Gate his brother, which £100 remaining in Jeffery's hands and payable by a bond made to Sir Walter Mildmaye and Wimond Carewe, which was made to my use, I will to my executors for the performance of my will. The residue of my goods to John Carewe and my niece Katherine Mompesson.

I ordain my right trusty and dear friend and nephew Sir Walter Mildmaye knight, one of the Queen's most honourable Privy Council and Chancellor of her Highness's Court of Exchequer, and Matthew Carewe, doctor of law, one of the Masters of the High Court of Chancery, my trusty and loving nephew, and to him for his pains £20.

Witnesses: Lawrence Mompesson, John Taverner, Richard Nottige, John Smythe, William Motte.

Proved 16 May 1583.

DAME ELIZABETH HOBLETHORNE of Roydon widow, 4 July 1563. [6/28]

To be buried in the chancel of Roydon church by my good man Fuller deceased. I make my son John Fuller my sole executor. To John my leases of the lordship of Roydon Hall and of the Temple or Parsonage there, and all other goods, corn, hay or cattle. To my son Rice 20 nobles to make a ring, my daughter Barbara Rice £30, and my sister Jane Henry my black gown of cloth and 40s. yearly for life. To little Nan Boners £10 at marriage and she to be honestly kept and brought up at John's cost. To Mistress Morres my gown of unwat[ered?] chamblet. To Davie, John Gaunte, and Lawrence 20s. apiece, every one of my maids 5s. apiece. To Thomas Tuck 20s., William Colean 20s. and a ewe and a lamb, John Chester 10s., John Adams 5s., Joan Davie 40s. To Agnes Pye 5s. a year for life. To Mr Stichborne and his wife each a ring of 40s. To Margaret Rice 40s. Witnesses: Simon Adams, Thomas Tuck and William Curtis, yeomen dwelling in Roydon.

Proved 10 July 1563.

SIR FRANCIS JOBSON of West Donyland knight, 22 August 1572. [16/25]

To the poor people coming to my burial in the church of St Giles near Colchester £10 at the rate of 2d. apiece. To the poor of East Donyland 40s. and Halstead 40s.

To Edward my son £100. To either of my two younger sons Henry and Thomas each £100. To Mary Jobson my daughter towards her marriage 600 marks and two gowns of velvet which were my wife's. To Edward for life my office of mastership of the game and keepership of Wix alias Wix Park, and after his decease to Henry for life and after his decease to Thomas for life. To my nieces Frances Cole £10 and a gown cloth of black and Anne Cole a coat cloth of black.

To my servants Henry Howard 40s., Francis George an annuity of 53s. 4d. out of my manor of East Donyland, Robert Flint 26s. 8d., Margery Russell 40s., Martin Tegg my lackey 26s. 8d., Joan Barrowe widow that keepth my house of Moonkewicke 26s. 8d. and her daughter 26s. 8d., John Smarte 40s., John Keble 26s. 8d., John Sweie 26s. 8d., Thomas Atkin 40s., Robert Maydestone 40s., William Pigott £10, Cornelius Gelison 40s., [blank] my falconer 20s., and James my warrener 20s.; and to each a coat cloth of black. To John Smarte's wife and Margaret wife of Jeffrey Cole each a gown cloth of black. Further to Cornelius Gelison the bailiwick of the Friar[y] of St John's Green [in Colchester] with the profits for life as he now enjoyeth the same.

To my executors my mansion house and farm called Moonckwick and the lands in my occupation, my manor of West Donyland with appurtenances, Middlewick Wood and Reignoldes Grove, my manor of East Donyland with the woods, royalties and profits, the advowson of East Donyland, my farm and wick called Acres Fleet Marsh in Canewdon, my parsonage and tithe of corn and hay of the ground belonging to the Castle of Colchester and of the grounds in Lexden and elsewhere about the town and fields of Colchester, which tithe corn belonged to the Monastery of St John besides Colchester, for 12 years after my decease, towards the performance of my will. I give full power to them to sell or lease Acres Fleet, and they shall keep Monckwicke, wherein I dwell, for 6 weeks after my decease to carry away at their choice my goods there and on the demesne lands and park belonging. To Edward my manors, mansion house, lands, tithe and patronage, after my executors' interest shall be determined, and to his heirs male, with remainder successively to John, Henry and Thomas and their heirs male. To Edward, Henry and Thomas the manor of the Priory of Hatfield Peverel and the lands, parsonages and advowsons belonging, the fee simple or reversion whereof I obtained of John Allen gentleman, deceased, after the decease of John his father. To Edward an annuity of £20 which I ought to have of my lord Bishop of Worcester out of the manor of Hartlebury (Worcs.), and after Edward's decease to Thomas for life.

So many of my servants to whom I have given any legacy as my executors shall think convenient shall be resident at Moonckwick for 6 weeks after my decease and shall be ready to fulfil their reasonable commandments about the execution of my will.

The residue of my goods to my executors to pay my debts and perform my will, and afterwards to be equally divided among my three younger sons and Mary my daughter. I name my trusty and well-beloved friend Sir Thomas Lucas knight and Edward to be executors, and to each for their pains £10. Witnesses : John Beast, William Beriff, John Fludd.

Proved 15 July 1573.

DAME DOROTHY JOSSELYN of High Roothing, widow of Sir Henry Josselyn, knight, 10 June 1579. [For Henry Jocelin, see p. 100.]
[26/10]

To be buried in the church of Sawbridgeworth [Herts.], next to my husband. To the church towards reparations 6s. 8d. To High Roothing church towards reparations 40s. To the poor people of High Roothing 20s. at the day of my burial, and within one month after my decease 1 quarter of wheat to be baked and given in bread to the poor of High and Aythorpe Roothing. To the surveyors of the highways of High Roothing and their bridges 20s. To the poor of Hatfield Broad Oak 10s. To every of my sons a ring of gold price 20s. for a remembrance. To my daughter Jane Kelton [blank]. To Humphrey son of John Josselyn esquire £6 13s. 4d. at 21. To Richard Lucas my servant £6 and to all my household servants their full wages and to so many of them as remain with me at my decease 20s. apiece. To John Casse my servant a bullock of 2 years old. My executors shall pay Richard Lucas all debts due to him by an obligation long since and a bill of my hand of which some part is paid. I ordain my well-beloved brother Sir Henry Gate of Seamer (Yorks.) knight, in whom I put my whole trust that he will pay all my debts and legacies expressed in a schedule annexed to a deed made to him dated 17 July 1576. To Edward my son the moiety of all such my goods. To his daughter Mary Josselyn £20 at marriage or 18. I earnestly request Sir

William Cordell knight to be my supervisor, and for his pains a ring of gold price 40s. Witnesses: John Pickeringe, Hugh Glane [Glave?].
Proved 14 February 1583.

DAME MARY JUDD of Latton widow [(1) of Sir Andrew Judd, knight, and (2) of James Altham of Mark Hall in Latton, esquire], 20 February 1597. [For James Altham, see p. 51.]   [46/5]

To be buried in Latton church where my husband Mr Altham lieth, in such solemnity as my executors think meet for my calling.

To Emmanuel Wolley my son [in-law] the bedstead in my Lady Winter's Chamber, the bedstead in the next chamber being the Inner Chamber, the hangings of both chambers, and all other implements of household in them (except the linen in three chests), my quilt of purple taffeta, my best carpet of tapestry with water flowers, a window carpet with small flowers, a Turkey carpet lying on the ewry cupboard in the Great Parlour, my 6 best cushions of tapestry with roses, 2 long pillows for windows, one of printed velvet, the other of yellow satin embroidered, 2 square cushions of wrought crimson velvet, a pair of new woollen blankets, my white rug, my blue mantle, one chair of black velvet and 2 high stools covered with fugar satin in the Great Parlour, 3 low stools of scarlet cloth, and one great Spanish chair in the New Parlour, and the furniture in the Hall, a damask table cloth and a long towel to the same, 1 dozen damask napkins, a damask ewry towel, a cupboard cloth of damask, a diaper table cloth and a long towel, 1 dozen diaper napkins, a ewry towel of diaper, a cupboard cloth of diaper, a long fine table cloth and a long towel, 4 dozen plain fine napkins, 2 plain fine cupboard cloths, 3 plain fine ewry towels, 3 pair of fine sheets, 3 pair of new flaxen sheets, 6 pair of new canvas sheets, 6 fine pillowberes, and 2 pair of pillows. More to him, the furniture that doth belong to that chamber he usually lieth in, and these parcels of plate, i.e. the least basin and ewer I have of those 3 which are parcel gilt, my greatest nest of parcel gilt bowls, 3 jug pots of silver white with hanging covers, a gilt salt costed and a tun in the top of it, 1 dozen apostle spoons, and 3 silver trenchers. More to Emmanuel Wolley my son £400, and to my daughter Wolley his wife my ring of gold with an emerald in it, being a green stone.

To Mr John Barne, my son-in-law, and Jane his wife my daughter, the bedstead in the Chapel Chamber and its furniture, and the hangings of the chamber, with implements of household in the same; a covering for a bed paned with velvet and satin crimson, a long pillow of cloth of silver which hath Mr Altham's arms and mine, a pair of fustian blankets, a window cloth of small flowers, and belongeth to the Chapel Chamber, 2 high stools covered with tuftaffeta and stand in the Great Parlour, and [bed- and table-linen similar to that given to Emmanuel Wolley], my best basin and ewer parcel gilt, 2 gilt livery pots, a nest of new gilt bowls with a cover, and 6 silver plates. More to Jane, my chain of gold and my best ring of gold being a pointed diamond.

To Mr Robert Golding, my son-in-law, and Martha his wife my daughter the bedstead called the Queen's Chamber and its furniture

23

hangings and implements of household in the same. To them my best featherbed in the Green Chamber, the bolster in the press of the next chamber, my best coverlet of tapestry in the press next the Queen's Chamber, a Turkey carpet for a cupboard, a Turkey carpet on the table in the Great Parlour, a window cloth with flowers, a long pillow of crimson velvet wrought, a long pillow of yellow satin embroidered, 2 square cushions embroidered, 6 cushions in the Great Parlour with pomegranates and roses, a tawney Irish mantle, a red rug, 2 high stools of wrought velvet, a velvet chair in the Great Parlour, and [similar bed- and table-linen], my second basin and ewer parcel gilt, 2 livery pots parcel gilt, a nest of gilt goblets with a cover which were Sir Andrew Judd's, 2 gilt tankards, a dozen apostle spoons, 6 silver plates, and a costed salt. More to my daughter Golding, my ring of gold with the best ruby, a quilt of yellow and blue sarcenet, a silver pillow with my arms, and my coach with the stone horses and their furniture.

To Sir Edward Wynter my son 1 dozen silver plate trenchers, and to my lady his wife 1 long table cloth of damask, a long towel of damask to the same, a dozen damask napkins, a cupboard cloth of damask, an ewry towel of damask, and the same to be of the best I have. More to them a gilt French salt. To my daughter Morgan a gilt piece of plate of 30 oz. To my daughter Huntley my silver chafing dish and 2 gilt tankards. To Jane Huntley her daughter, my grandchild, £100 at marriage. To my daughter Welshe 3 gilt bowls chased and my arms in them. To my son William Wynter a standing cup gilt being the best I have and 3 white silver bowls with my arms and are somewhat shallow. To my cousin George Sare 1 of those gilt tankards which I bought of my son Derehaughe and £3 to make him a ring for a remembrance. To my cousin Thomas Sare and my cousin Richard Sare each £3 to make him a ring.

To Francis Roberts and Mary his wife, my grandchild, my bedstead in the chamber called the Iron Bar Chamber, with the furniture, hangings and implements, and [similar bed- and table-linen], a flat gilt bowl, a gilt tankard, a great jug of silver, 3 silver plates. More to Mary, a ring of gold being my second ruby. To Edward Alltham, my son-in-law, and his wife, the bedstead in my own chamber, with the furniture, and the silk curtains, the hangings and implements (except the little bed and the linen in any of the chests in that chamber and two little coffers in that chamber under the window with my wearing linen). To them a narrow carpet of Turkey work for the window in the Great Parlour and a long green carpet of broadcloth and 6 cushions with pomegranates and roses, and [similar bed- and table-linen], a gilt salt which I daily used at my table, a flat gilt bowl, a nest of silver bowls being deep and the last I bought, a bowl of silver to put spoons in, 3 silver trenchers, and my spice box of silver. More to Edward £100 and to Elizabeth his wife a ring of gold being a table diamond. More to Edward the tables and forms in the Hall, the cupboard in the Hall window, and the iron hearth that standeth in the Hall in the winter time. To William Derehaughe and Mary his wife, my grandchild, the bedstead in the Hall and chamber, and the bed in the little chamber next to that, a coverlet for a bed with roses, a long pillow of cloth of gold being old, a carpet of tapestry which serveth for the table in the Little Parlour, my little bedstead in the New Parlour within the Great Parlour, a cupboard, 3 little stools covered with scarlet, 2 Spanish chairs whereof 1 is high and the other low, a Turkey carpet for the cupboard in the New Parlour, and 3 cushions that be in the chairs in the parlour, and all that belongeth to the chimney in that room. More to them, [similar bed- and table-linen], my deep silver basin and ewer, 3 bowls to drink wine in parcel gilt, a French salt, a flat gilt bowl, a dozen spoons, 3 silver plates. More to them £100, and I forgive him the £100 he oweth me. To her a ring of gold with a turquoise.

To Mr Thomas Alltham, eldest son to my late husband Mr Alltham, a piece of plate gilt (weighing 20 oz.). To Mr James Alltham his brother a piece of plate gilt (20 oz.), and a black gown, and another to his wife. To Matthew Alltham their brother £10 and a black cloak. To Mary Gosnall my grandchild the hangings, bedstead and bed with all the furniture now in that chamber called my son Golding's chamber. To Mary Hawtrie my grandchild all such things of mine as be in my son Alltham's chamber and the bedstead in the Press Chamber. To Mary Derehaughe the younger my grandchild, the hangings and bed in the Green Chamber. To Barne Roberts my grandchild 1 of my parcel gilt tuns. To Edward Alltham my grandchild my cruet of parcel gilt which I daily used to fill wine in.

To Mistress Mary Barlee a casting bottle of silver and gilt and a black gown. To Mistress Jane Chaunce, my waiting woman, £20 and a black gown. To Mistress Edy Agar a black gown for a remembrance. To Dorothy Hodson, sometime my servant, a black gown, her husband a black cloak, and Anne Wrighte her sister a black gown.

To Mr Chatterton, Master of Emmanuel College in Cambridge, £5 for a remembrance and a black gown, and him I desire to preach at my funeral. To Mr Bland, minister of Buckland [Herts.], £20 and a black gown. To Joseph Birde, sometime minister of Latton, a black gown. To Mr Baines, minister of Hunsdon [Herts.], a black gown and 40s. to make him a ring for a remembrance. To Mr Linse, minister of Weeley, a black gown and 40s. to make him a ring. To Mr Denne, minister of Latton, a black gown and 40s. to make him a ring. To Mr John Napper a black gown and 40s. for a remembrance. To Henry Dondale a black cloak.

To Edward Mathewe my kinsman £50 and a black cloak. To Mary Allen of Colchester £5 and a black gown. To William Allen her brother £10. To Robert Allen his son £5, and to either of them a black coat. To Katherine Tilley £5 and a black gown. To Henry Stracie my tenant a black coat and to his wife a black gown. To Robert Welles my tenant a black coat and to his wife a black gown. To James Aydie my servant £5 and a black coat and to his wife a black gown. To Anne Brett a black gown. To every of my servants hereunder named, if they be in my service at the time of my death, a black coat. To Seth Haggar £5, Henry Gullyver £10, Thomas Ancepte [Aucepte?] my butler £6, Thomas Edward £5, Edward Rime £5, Andrew Plancke my footman 40s., Thomas Skingle 40s., Walter Godfrey my old servant 40s. To the rest of my servants in my service and not remembered by name, as well men servants as maid servants, 40s. apiece if they have served me for one year, to men black coats and women black gowns. To 40 poor women gowns of cloth at 6s. 8d. the yard to be worn at my funeral. My poor neighbours, specially those of Latton and Harlow, to have those gowns, and among the rest old Goddard's wife of Harlow and her husband a coat of the same cloth. To the poor of Great Parndon £3, Latton £4, Harlow £4, and Netteswell £3.

I ordain Emmanuel Wolley my son, John Barne and Robert Goldinge my sons-in-law my executors. The rest of my goods whatsoever I bequeath to my three executors to be equally divided amongst them.

Witnesses : Walter Thomas, John Bevis, Thomas Denne.

Proved 19 February 1602.

SIR THOMAS LODGE of West Ham knight, 14 December 1583.

[29/29]

To be buried by Dame Anne Lodge, my late wife, in the church of St Mary Aldermary in London in the vault or tomb appointed for the same.

Touching those goods which I promised to leave to my children begotten of Dame Anne lately deceased, contained in an inventory made between William my son and me by the appointment of Sir William Cordell knight, Master of the Rolls, late deceased, they be delivered or the value as appraised in the inventory by my executors to William, Benedict and Henry, my children. Whereas William hath in his hands £200 which he took for my lease of the manor of Sulton [co.?], I bequeath the said sum to my three children equally to be divided. My lease in the hands of Gamaliel Woodford, citizen and grocer of London, which I bought of goodman Gibson of Perryfield and other lands, shall be sold towards the performance of my will. To Sarah White, wife of Edward White, citizen and stationer of London, £10. To my cousin Jooet's wife £10. To Luke Williams, my apprentice, £10 and the remainder of his years. To every of my servants as well men as women and maidservants 40s. To Walter Walters innholder, now my servant, 40s. To my cousin Robert Pigott dwelling at Wood Green [Middx.] £5. To Margaret Stockmeyde widow a ring of gold worth 40s. and to my cousin Thomas Flammancke likewise. To my godson Thomas Pigott £5. To my sister Anne Edwardes £10.

To the poor people of West Ham £5. To 78 poor men each 2s. and a pair of new gloves, already bought, on the day of my burial, and they shall accompany my body to the earth. To every one of my neighbours and friends likewise a pair of new gloves. Mr Archepole, parson of St Peter, Cornhill, in London, shall make the sermon at my burial and 5 other sermons afterward, whereof 3 in the church of St Mary Aldermary and 3 in that of St Peter, and for his pains for every sermon 10s., and there shall be no other ceremonies. To George Samvell, citizen and writer of the court letter of London, 40s. to buy him a gown. All such duties as should be due to West Ham church, parson, clerk and sexton shall be paid to them as if my body should be buried there.

To my cousin Thomas Pigott, citizen and grocer of London, and to his wife, each a ring of gold of the value of 40s. To Gamaliel Woodford, my son-in-law, £3 to buy him a ring of gold. Whereas Richard Ledes, citizen and grocer of London, doth owe me money, such part as shall remain unpaid shall be yearly paid to my executors.

I constitute Gamaliel Woodford and Thomas Pigott the elder, citizen and grocer of London, executors, and to each 40s. above their legacies. I make my son William overseer and for his pains £3 to buy a ring of gold, also to him my seal ring of gold with my arms thereon.

To my godson Thomas, son of the said William, my basin and ewer of silver parcel gilt (weighing 82 oz.) at 21. To Anne Lodge, daughter of William, my acorn cup of silver all gilt (20 oz.) at marriage or 21. To my sons Nicholas my 6 hance pots of silver all gilt (67 oz.), Benedict my 2 silver salts gilt with one cover (46 oz. scant) at 21, and Henry my 3 silver gilt bowls (37¾ oz.) at 21. To my godson Thomas son of Gamaliel my standing cup of silver all gilt (27 oz.); to William, another of his sons, a silver trencher salt gilt (7½ oz.); and to Anne his daughter my maudlin cup of silver and gilt (6 oz.), my mazer with a band of silver and gilt, and my 4 stone pots tipped with silver, whereof 2 be gilt; both sons at 21 and Anne at 21 or marriage.

The reversion of my messuages and lands which I bought of Stephen Bull of West Ham yeoman shall be sold outright by my executors, who shall have the preferment in buying the same. If there remain [more] in their hands, my debts and legacies paid, they shall deliver to Nicholas, Benedict and Henry at 21 the residue of my goods equally to be divided. To Benedict a moiety of my manors, messuages and lands bought by me of Albon Lodge alias Broomley of Ashley (Staffs.) gentleman, and his heirs male, with remainder successively to Henry and to Nicholas. To Henry the other moiety and his heirs male, with remainder successively to Benedict and to Nicholas.

Witnesses : George Samwell notary public, Richard de la Rose, John Rose.

Proved 7 June 1585.

DAME JANE MEWTES of West Ham, late wife to Sir Peter Mewtes of West Ham, knight, 7 April 1577. [For Hercules Mewtas, see p. 109.]

[20/17]

To be buried in West Ham church.

To Hercules my son-in-law 6 silver pots, 6 silver spoons, my bedstead of walnuttree in the Great Chamber, a tester of red and white damask with a counterpoint of red and white sarcenet, 2 featherbeds, single valance of purple satin embroidered with silver, with curtains of yellow and blue sarcenet, a counterpoint of cut yellow satin lined with blue silver sarcenet, a tester of wood, a cupboard standing in the Great Chamber, 2 long cushions of crimson satin striped with gold and embroidered with silver, 6 pair of sheets, i.e. 2 of holland and 4 coarser, a damask table cloth, a dozen of damask napkins and a damask towel, a long plain table cloth and 2 short table cloths for a square board, 3 dozen of the best plain napkins with 2 plain towels of holland, a pair of latten andirons, my hangings in the Little Parlour with my table and cupboard in the same, with a carpet of needlework to the same cupboard. To my daughter-in-law Frances Howard my black velvet gown and my little silver cup. To Judith Elderton, my late servant, my great gilt bowl with a cover, a long damask table cloth with a towel, a dozen damask napkins, and my square carpet of needlework. To Mistress Margaret Johnson of Bedlem a pair of very fine holland sheets of two leaves apiece. To Robert Hodgeson of London, gentleman, my best gilt salt. To my cousin William Suppam my little gilt maudlin cup. To Joyce Johnson, my maiden, my 2 white bowls of silver, 6 silver spoons and my 2 feather-beds at Bethelem [sic]. To William Gibson of West Ham my white gelding and a year's wages. To John Turwell alias Butler my servant my little gilt bowl, £10, 2 kine, the stray nag, 2 platters, 6 dishes, 6 saucers, a dozen coarse diaper napkins, 2 pair of sheets, the featherbed in the Little Chamber, and the red covering on my own bed. To Margery my maid-servant 2 years' wages, to William Welborne a year's wages, and to every of my servants as much money as the black [sic] may come to, but no black cloth. To the poor people of West Ham £3 to be paid the day after my burial and not afore.

Whereas I have a basin and ewer of silver which lieth in pawn to Mr Hodgeson for £20, my son-in-law Hercules Mewtes shall have it, paying the £20. The residue of my goods to Hercules. I make my well-beloved son-in-law Hercules and my loving friend Robert Hodgeson my executors.

Witnesses: Rowland Yorke, Edward Saundershill, William Bate, William Gibson.

Proved 21 May 1577.

SIR WILLIAM PETRE of Ingatestone knight, 12 and 27 April 1571.
[16/1]

To be buried in the new aisle of Ingatestone church, and in the same aisle there be made and builded some honest monument with the names of me and my two wives, the ordering whereof I commit to the good discretion of my executors.

In alms to the poorest inhabitants of Ingatestone alias Ging Petre, Writtle, Ging Hospital [Fryerning], Buttsbury, Stock, Ging Mountney [Mountnessing], Gyng Margaret [Margaretting], East Horndon and Heron Green [in East Horndon] £40; and to the poorest inhabitants of Great Torrington (Devon) £5, Hawkhurst (Kent) 66s. 8d., Montacute and Tintinhull (Somerset) £6 13s. 4d., Kingsbridge and Churchstow (Devon) £4, my manor of Brent alias South Brent (Devon) £4, and St Botolph-without-Aldersgate in London £6 13s. 4d. To the poorest prisoners in the prisons in London and Southwark £20. To the relief of the poor in the hospitals of London and Southwark £20.

To Robert Gower my servant 20 nobles. Thomas Carmden £5, Arthur Ragland £4, William Bell 5 marks, and John Bell £4. To every other of my household servants at the time of my death his whole year's wages. Such of them as have long served me and done the parts of honest and true servants and have not been rewarded or otherwise advanced by my procurement in my lifetime or by my will shall further be considered by my executors as they shall think meet. To Richard Stoneley, John Clyff and Edward Bell, as well for service heretofore done as for their good advice and assistance to be continued to my wife and son and heir John, an annuity of 4 marks to every one for their lives out of my manor of Mashbury.

My will is that before all other things my debts be all paid; and if any have been wronged or extremely dealt with by me that it be largely and without delay paid and recompensed.

To Anne Baker, daughter of Katherine Baker my wife's late daughter, a jewel of the value of £20. To my good and loving wife Dame Anne Petre a basin and ewer of silver gilt and another basin and ewer of silver parcel gilt, 2 stock salts gilt, 3 goblets gilt, a dozen silver spoons, 3 bowls of silver white, a bowl gilt, 2 standing cups gilt, a dozen silver trenchers, a pair of quart silver pots, 2 beercups gilt and 2 parcel gilt, and 2 silver jugs gilt bearing my arms and my wife's graven on them. To my wife such apparel, jewels and chains of gold as she was wont to wear herself, one ring of gold with a diamond set therein given me by the Queen of good memory, Queen Mary, and a girdle of gold excepted, which ring and girdle I give to my son and heir John Petre for the use of his wife. To my wife 10 horses or geldings and such store of oxen, sheep and kine as shall be on my demesnes at Ingatestone or in my park at Ingatestone at the time of my death; and 10 featherbeds; willing nevertheless that my son have first the choice of 4 of my best beds. My wife shall have during her life my house in London freely to her own use without paying any rent. To her the half deal of my napery, sheets, pillowberes, table-cloths, napkins, towels and other linen, with the moiety of my pewter vessel, pots, pans and other kitchen stuff commonly used in my house at Ingatestone; also for life the use of all other my plate, household stuff, bedding, napery and household utensils at Ingatestone or London, if she remain sole and unmarried and will dwell and continue to keep house at Ingatestone or London. The residue of my plate, silver vessel, candle-sticks of silver, leases, debts, money, beds, bedding, hangings, napery, household stuff, horses, geldings, mares, colts, oxen, sheep and other goods, together with the household stuff, napery and utensils, the use whereof is given to my wife, I give to my son if he continue alive to 22, and if he die before leaving any heir male lawfully begotten the premises shall remain to such heir. And for want of such issue male my executors shall divide the said plate, [etc.] into four equal parts, whereof one to my wife, another to be equally divided amongst my daughters and their children, and the third and fourth parts to be distributed amongst the poor and for other good deeds of charity as to my executors shall seem best.

To my son-in-law Nicholas Wadham and to my daughter [Dorothy] his wife, £100 which he already hath by my order of my brother John Petre, Customer of Exeter now deceased. To Elizabeth Gostwicke my daughter £100 and to her son William 100 marks. To my son-in-law Lodowick Grevill esquire and to my daughter Thomasine his wife a basin and ewer of silver. To my son-in-law John Talbott esquire and my daughter Katherine his wife a basin and ewer of silver. To my god-daughter Gertrude Talbott £100, and to every other child of my said daughter Talbott 100 marks. My will is that the bequests to the children of Katherine and Elizabeth be delivered at marriage or full age. To my son John my lease of the manors of Montacute and Tintinhull, and if he die before the end of the lease then to my brother Robert Petre. To my son my leases of the farm of Imphy Hall [in Buttsbury], part of the possessions of the Bishop of Ely, and of certain marshes and fishings in South Benfleet, parcel of the lands of Westminster. To every child of any of my sisters £10.

Whereas I have of the Queen's Majesty's grant the wardship and marriage of Griselda daughter and heir of William Barnes late of Thoby [in Mountnessing] esquire, I give it and the profits to my wife to the use of the two younger sons of Thomasine named Edward and John Grevill and of Anne and Margaret Grevill her daughters, provided that Griselda maybe bestowed honestly without disparagement and according to her degree. To William Grevill, Thomasine's eldest son, a chain of gold worth £40.

Whereas I have by licence of mortmain of the late gracious lady Queen Mary erected a foundation of one priest and certain poor alms-folks at Ingatestone called the priest and poor of Ging Petre, and appointed lands, tithes and annuities for their sustentation according to my statutes, I require my son and heirs not only to continue the foundation as I have begun but also as occasion shall serve to increase it by any good means they may as they would God should prosper any doings of theirs in this transitory world. Whereas I have for part of the living of the priest and poor almsfolks granted them by deed an annuity of £16 out of my manors of Frern [in Dunton] and Bluntwalls [in Great Burstead] for divers years yet to come, if I do not in my lifetime grant other lands worth £18 by year in lieu of the said annuity for ever, I will give to my executors £400 to purchase after my death so much land as shall be worth yearly to the priest and almsfolks £18 yearly. To my wife £200 to be by her bestowed in alms and other charitable deeds in such sort as she is already instructed.

Whereas I have given to Robert Langthorne, late my servant, the farm [i.e. lease] of a tenement and lands in Sutton (Glos.), I grant the same to him for life. Whereas likewise I have given to John Taylor, my servant and cook, the farm of another tenement and lands in Sutton, I will that he shall have it for life with the farm of a half yard of land which his father held in the said manor. Whereas my son-in-law Richard Baker esquire granted by lease to Edward Walker, sometime my servant, a tenement and lands at Herongate, which lease I afterward redeemed, the years to come in the lease shall remain to my servant Barnard Geffrey. In consideration of the good service to me and to my wife and son hereafter by John Bell my servant, I give him my tenement and land in my manor of Toddenham (Glos.) for life.

To the 10 almsfolks of Ging Petre each 5s. and to the 10 other alms-folks each 3s. 4d., and to all 20 a black gown of coarse cloth.

To my brother Robert Petre, John Kyme and Edward Bell gentlemen each £10, requiring them to aid my wife, son and executors touching the execution of my will. Executors of my will I ordain my wife, my son and John Cliff of Ingatestone gentleman and give John Cliff for his pains £20. I pray Sir William Garrard knight, alderman of London, and Edmund Tyrell esquire to be overseers of my will and give them for their pains and for a remembrance of old friendship £10 apiece.

To Sir William Cecill knight, now Lord of Burleigh, Chief Secretary to the Queen's Majesty, £20. To the Rector and scholars of Exeter College in Oxford, to be laid in their treasure house for the use of the college £40. To Mary Percye widow [housekeeper at Ingatestone Hall] £4 a year for life out of my manor of Mashbury. To Mr John Woodward [rector of Ingatestone], my chaplain, £40.

Whereas upon extents there is delivered to me by process awarded out of the Court of Chancery all the messuages and lands of my son-in-law John Gostwike esquire in the counties of Bedford and Hertford, the revenues of which I have since bestowed on maintaining him and my daughter his wife and their children, on reparations of his houses and redeeming certain leases and grants by him unadvisedly made to other persons to the great disadvantage of him and his heirs, I will that my son shall have the said messuages and lands, and the revenues I require him to bestow about the reparations of the houses and the relief and comfort of my son-in-law, my daughter and their children (as I have done), which nevertheless I wholly refer to the discretion and conscience of my son; for if my son-in-law, my daughter or their children shall mislike this my meaning and shall attempt to vex or trouble my son in any court, then they shall be utterly excluded from any benefit thereof.

Towards the marriage of 8 poor maids 5 marks each, and my own maids in my house shall be specially remembered to be of this number. I give 100 marks on provision of firewood for the poor inhabitants of Ingatestone and Fryerning, viz. 20 marks a year for 5 years. Towards the reparation of Ingatestone church £10.

To my daughters Thomasine Grevill and Katherine Talbott each £100. Whereas my wife hath of long time had in her hands from me a stock of cattle and money worth £250 or thereabouts towards the finding of beeves, muttons and other provisions for my house, I give her the cattle, beasts and sheep of the said stock that shall be on my grounds at East Horndon and Horsefrith Park [in Writtle] at the time of my death, to be had freely to her own use.

Sealed and subscribed by me, 12 April 1571. Witnesses : John Clyff, Edward Bell, John Wodwarde, Robert Gower, John Bell.

As concerning all my manors and lands (one third part thereof as is holden by the Queen's Majesty *in capite* by me divided and set forth in writings only exвepted) I devise and give in form following. To my son John and his heirs male my manor of Brent alias South Brent (Devon) and the advowson of the vicarage, and for default of such issue the successive remainders to William son and heir of my brother John Petre senior of Torbryan (Devon) deceased and his heirs male, and to my son's heirs. To my son and his heirs male my manors of Downham Fravill (Devon) and Charmouth (Dorset), the successive remainders to John the younger son of my son-in-law John Talbott of Grafton (Worcs.) and his heirs male, to his next son by Katherine his wife and his heirs male, and to my son's heirs. To my son and his heirs male my manor of Comb Pyne (Devon) and my farm of East Membury (Devon), the successive remainders to Edward and to John the second and third sons of Lodowike Grevill, my son-in-law, by Thomasine his wife, and their heirs male, and to my son's heirs. To my son my manor of Chalenger and my farms in Branscombe, Sparkhayes and Hunthayes (Devon), the successive remainders to the said Edward Grevill and his heirs male and to my son's heirs. To my son and his heirs male my manors of Churchstow with the farm of Norton, Shute with the park of Shute, South Leigh, North Leigh, Wiscombe and Wiscombe Park, Dulshaies alias Dawlishehaies, Werrington, Uphay, Hitway, Humfravil, Axminster, Haccombfee and Borcombe, and my lands in Sidford, Sidbury and Harcombe with a mill and lands in East Allington, lands in Higher and Nether Stoford in Colyton, and a tenement called Kellenche in Torbryan (all Devon), with the advowsons of churches [unspecified], and for default of such issue to his heirs. To my son and his heirs male all my manors and lands in Essex, i.e. the manors of Ingatestone alias Ging Petre with the manor or farm of Hanley and the grange of Woodbarnes, East Horndon, and Crondon with the park of Crondon, the rectories of Ging Mountney and Buttsbury, the tourn and leet of Stock, and all other my lands in Stock, Buttsbury, Ramsden Bellhouse, Ramsden Crays, Downham and Runwell, my manor of Bacons in Ging Mountney with my lands there called Westlands, Adgores, Woolwards, Cuttells, Goughlands, Shemyngs, Sabrights, Nuttings and Wadlands, my lands in Little Burstead called Mynges, Tomlyns and Plummers, in Gyng Margaret called James land and late Gattons land, and in Ging Raffe alias Ingrave called Hopkyns, my manor of Bayhouse in West Thurrock, my lands in Chignall called Brettons; also my manors of Rokey and Water Andros (Herts.); my manor of Tatworthy (Somerset); and my capital messuage and other tenements in Aldersgate Street in London, with the advowsons of churches [unspecified]; and for default of issue to my son's heirs.

Sealed and subscribed by me, 27 April 1571. Witnesses: John Cliff, Edward Bell, John Woodward, Robert Gower, John Bell.

Proved 31 January 1572.

[Among the Petre archives in the Essex Record Office (D/DP F3) is a volume (*c.* 1575) containing copies of the indenture and schedule of the special livery of John Petre out of the Court of Wards, 1572, with a valuation of the estates in nine counties and London.]

[DAME] ANNE PETRE widow, late wife of Sir William Petre knight, deceased, 25 February 1582.   [25/15]

To be buried in Ingatestone church in the tomb where the body of my late dear husband, Sir William Petre, doth lie.

The distribution of such money, plate, goods and jewels as I shall have at the time of my decease shall be referred to my son, Sir John Petre, whom I make sole executor.

To the poorest inhabitants of Ingatestone £3, Writtle and Roxwell £6, Gynge Hospytall [Fryerning] 4 marks, Stock and Buttsbury £4, East Horndon and Heron Green 40s., and in Aldersgate Street [in London] £3, and to each of the four prisons in London, i.e. the two Counters, Newgate and Ludgate, £1. To 40 of the poorest householders in Ingatestone, Writtle, Mountnessing, Buttsbury and Stock £100, to be delivered within 5 years after my decease, viz. to each 10s. yearly at Michaelmas to buy wood or fuel.

Whereas my son doth owe me £400 by bond, I freely remit the debt. To my son such linen (not hereafter bequeathed) as I have by the gift of his father and is daily occupied in my house and in the custody of Mary Pytter, and the moiety of the pewter and brass remaining at Ingatestone Hall which I had of the gift of his father, and such bedding (not otherwise bequeathed) so remaining of the 10 beds which my husband gave me; and in consideration of his pains in executing my will £400.

To William son and heir of my son my best ring with a diamond and £40 to make him a chain at 21. To my daughter-in-law Lady Mary Petre a billiment of goldsmith's work with pearls and black enamel, viz. the pieces with pearls be 13 and every piece hath 9 pearls and the pieces without pearls be 14. To my daughter Griselda Grevill my tablet or book of gold with a rose of diamonds on one side and one ring with an emerald. To her husband [Lodwick] a basin and an ewer worth £20 or else £20 in money to buy him one. To my daughter [Katharine] Talbote a ring with a pointed diamond, the best, and my 65 black buttons of gold for a gown. To my son [John] Talbote her husband a basin and ewer worth £20 or else £20 to buy him one. To my daughter [Elizabeth] Gostwycke £6 13s. 4d. to make her a jewel. To my daughter [Dorothy] Waddam 4 marks to make her a jewel or a ring. To my nephew John Baker a nest of goblets gilt with his grandfather [John] Tyrrell's arms and mine on the cover (weighing 80½ oz.), 2 quart pots gilt whereon one hath my late husband's arms and the other mine (together 65½ oz.), 2 stocked salts gilt embossed (together 30¾ oz.), having a man with a hand-gun on the top, a dozen silver trencher plates ungilt, 2 pair of holland sheets of the best sort, 2 pair of fine holland pillowberes, a tablecloth of damask work, a dozen napkins, and a long towel of the same work. To his wife a piece of plate worth £7. To Thomas Baker his brother 3 white silver bowls having on it my husband's arms (together 62 oz.), 2 jugs gilt with my husband's arms and mine graven thereon (together 34½ oz.) and a standing cup gilt (24½ oz.) with a naked boy on the top of the cover, having a stase in one hand and a shield in the other. To Griselda wife of of Thomas Baker a border of gold enamelled black having to it 13 round pieces and 12 long (3¾ oz.), and a chain of gold (2½ oz.). To Anne Goodman, sister of John Baker, a tablet with a unicorn bone in the midst, a chain of gold worth £39 10s., a ring with a pointed diamond, a standing cup gilt (18 oz.), a dozen silver spoons (19 oz.), 2 pair of fine sheets of holland cloth, 2 pair of fine holland pillowberes, 2 long table-cloths of housewives' cloth, 2 long towels of the same, and 2 dozen napkins of like making of the finest sort. To John Goodman, Anne's husband, some pieces of plate worth £10 or £10 in money. To Anne Gostwicke my goddaughter £13 6s. 8d. at 20 or marriage, and if she die before then her sister Gertrude shall have it.

Whereas there doth rest in my hands in trust 200 marks of my husband's gift towards the preferment of Anne and Margaret, the two daughters of Lodwick Grevill by my daughter Thomasine, at 20 or marriage, the same shall be paid, and for their better preferment 50 marks apiece at 20 or marriage; and if either die before the survivor shall have the legacies. To Valentine, daughter of Lodwick by my daughter Thomasine, £100 at 20 or marriage. Whereas my sons-in-law Lodwick Grevill and John Talbote and my cousin John Goodwyn [sic] be severally indebted to me divers sums of money by bonds, I freely remit the debts. To my son-in-law Lodwick Grevill the use of all my lands which I hold by lease of John Edes of Acham alias Ashorn (Warws.) yeoman in Clifford (Glos.) until his son John Grevill is 21; and if he die before, then to Peter Grevill at 21, and if he die, then to Charles Grevill at 21; on condition that Lodwick yearly pay until their full ages to my son £30, which he shall yearly pay to my daughter Thomasine £5, to my daughter's son John £5, and if she decease before her three sons' full ages John shall have a yearly rent of £10. Out of the £30 a yearly annuity of £10 to 10 of the poorest people in Ingatestone, Writtle and Buttsbury, 20s. apiece. The other £10 remaining shall go to the perform-ance of my will. If Lodwick decease before his sons' full ages, the use of the lands shall remain to Thomasine until then.

To Gertrude, Anne and Mary Talbote, the three daughters of John Talbote by my daughter Catherine, 50 marks apiece at 20 or marriage. To my cousin Mary, late wife of John Paschall, and to her sister, my cousin Anne Clyffe, and to John her husband, 40s. apiece to make each a ring. To my godson Robert Paschall and John the eldest son of Mary Paschall each 40s. to make them a ring, and to his two sisters Thomasine and Bennet Paschall, Margaret Clyff daughter of Anne and John her brother, each 26s. 8d. to make them a ring. To my brother Sir Henry Tyrrell knight a ring worth 40s. and to my cousin Thomas Tyrrell of Heron [in East Horndon] a piece of plate worth £10. To my cousin Edward Browne, Charles Browne and Margaret Browne each a ring worth 4 nobles. To my brother [Robert] Petre of Westminster and to my sister his wife each a ring worth 40s. To my cousin Anne Hall a ring worth 26s. 8d. and to her sister Browne my goddaughter a ring worth 40s. To my cousin George White and to my godson Richard White each a ring worth 40s. To Mr [Richard] Stoneley £10. To the wife of my cousin Thomas Keible 26s. 8d. to make her a ring. To my brother-in-law Charles Tyrrell £10. To Thomas Fitch £20.

To such of my servants as shall be with me at the time of my decease, i.e. John Whyte 2 kine of his own choice, Mary Pytts and Robert Leyver each £4, Anne Haywodd my goddaughter 2 kine and 20s., John West 4 marks to make him a ring, John Beard 4 marks, Robert Rogers 4 marks and a cow, and William Sybberance and Valentine Wilkenson my cook each £6 13s. 4d. To every one of my household servants as well women as men (not otherwise in my will preferred) his or her half-year's wages after my death. I will that my house be kept for 6 weeks after my decease at my own cost so that my servants may there have meat, drink and lodging and also wages, by which time ended I hope every one elsewhere shall be the better provided.

My funerals, debts and legacies discharged, my son shall have the residue of my goods real and personal.

As to the disposition of my lands, my will is as followeth. To Peter Grevill my rectories of Cadbury and Nether Exe (Devon) which I lately purchased of the Earl of Lincoln and Christopher Gowgh, my messuages, glebe, tithes and offerings in Cadbury and Nether Exe, that portion of tithes which I also purchased of them, and the reversions thereof, to Peter and his heirs male; with successive remainders for default of issue to Charles and to John, Peter's brother.

Whereas by indenture, 20 May 1575, between me of the one part and John Baker, Thomas Grenewood, William Clederhow and John Royse of the other, I was contented to covenant that they should bring a writ of *entre sur disseisin* in the post against me and in the writ should demand the manors of Shepreth alias Shepreth Tyrrell and Meldreth alias Flamberds and divers land (all Cambs.) so that a recovery might be had to the uses in the indenture expressed, which recovery was had, in which indenture or by my will a proviso made it lawful for me to alter the use; whereas by another indenture, 17 June 1576, between me and them I did covenant that the recoverers should be seised to such uses as be declared in the second indenture; and whereas by another indenture, 8 June 1580, between me and John Baker, James Braybrooke and John Payne, I did repeal all such uses. And although I suppose and verily hope that by the last indenture, being made by good advice, the said uses by the first or second indentures are clearly dissolved so that the manors and lands are again in my free disposition. Nevertheless for the better avoiding of quarrels or doubts I now utterly repeal the uses, saving always the estate of any persons or of Baker, Grenewood, Clederhow or Robert Cawdwell; and my will is that the said recovery from henceforth shall remain and that Baker, Clederhow and Royse shall stand seised of the manors and lands to my use and that of my heirs for ever. Whereas by indenture, 27 May 1578, between me and Baker, Caldwell and Clederhow, I have assigned to them my estate and term of 19 years in a moiety of the manors of Forfield, Bromhill and Belbroughton and of the manor and capital messuage of Bovenhill alias Bonehill (all Worcs.) and my estate and term of 20 years in the other moiety on trust, hope and confidence that they shall faithfully employ the revenues to such uses as by my will I shall appoint; I will that they shall with the revenues faithfully pay such annuities or legacies as I shall appoint by my will, i.e. I give to Edward son and heir apparent of Lodwick Grevill £30 to make him a chain at 21; to George, my son's eldest son, £30 to make him a chain at 21; to Richard Norham a yearly annuity of 26s. 8d. if he be in my service at the time of my decease; to John Keygar my servant an annuity of 26s. 8d.; and to Baker, Clederhow and Caldwell an annuity of 40s. apiece in consideration of their pains taken during the several terms. I desire them to well manure and husband the woods in the premises so to them demised and that there be no woodsales thereof but the same be preserved to the best use of those to whom they are to remain. After such time as they shall have received so much of the profits as may fully pay the annuities, then from thenceforth of the residue I give to Katherine Baker, daughter of my nephew John Baker and Mary his wife, £40. To Richard son and heir apparent of my nephew Thomas Baker and to Griselda his wife £30 to make him a chain. To Elizabeth Goodwyn, daughter of my niece Goodwyn, £40.

Whereas on singular goodwill I have by a deed, 27 June 1578, given to my well-beloved cousin, Thomas Kebill gentleman, the office of keepership of my park at Writtle called Writtle Park and the custody of my houses and edifices thereon, with divers annuities and profits for his pains, for my life; if, after my decease, he do not (as I hope through my son's provision and goodness he shall) quietly hold for his life the keepership and custody with the annuities and profits, then from thenceforth for his life he shall have out of my manor of Shepreth an annuity of £10. To John Whyte my servant for life an annuity of 53s. 4d. out of the said manor if he shall be in my service at the time of my decease, and to John Hodge my servant an annuity of 40s. likewise. To my son and his heirs my manor of Shepreth and all messuages and lands belonging thereto.

Whereas I have conveyed one moiety of the manors of Forfield, Bromehill and Belbroughton and the manor of Bovenhill alias Bonehill, with the advowson of Belbroughton [Worcs.] after my death to the use of John Talbote junior, one of the sons of John Talbote of Grafton (Worcs.) esquire and Katherine his wife, and to his heirs male, with divers remainders, and the other moiety to the use of Charles, one of the sons of Lodwick Grevill of Milcote (Warws.) esquire and Thomasine his wife, and his heirs male, with divers remainders, by indenture quinquepartite, 20 May 1575, between me of the one part and Baker, Grenewood, Clederhow and Royse of the other, I devise for further security the same premises according to the true meaning of the indenture.

I constitute Edmund Plowden esquire assistant to my executor and overseer of my will, and my desire to him is with his counsel and good advice to aid my executor, and 20 marks for his pains.

Witnesses: Thomas Tyrell, Charles Browne, Thomas Kebill, Thomas Kemys, John Clyffe, Robert Leyver, Thomas Fitch.

Proved 26 April 1582.

[DAME] FRANCES POWLETT, widow [of Sir Edward Waldegrave, knight], 1 September 1599. [43/77]

To be buried in Borley church. For the making of a convenient tomb in the church over my body, I allow 100 marks, to be made within 3 years after my decease. My executors to distribute in alms among the poorest people of Borley, Sudbury [Suffolk], [Long] Melford [Suffolk], and other towns adjoining to Borley £40, whereof the poor of Borley 5s. apiece. My executors shall cause to be made against the day of my burial 24 gowns to be worn by 24 poor women of frieze or coarse cloth as the time of the year shall require.

To my son Charles my lease of the rectories and parsonages of Nave-stock and Borley; also for that I understand that he hath brought up my son Nicholas Waldgrave the reversion of the manor of Borley after my decease, the capital house whereof doth stand in part on the parsonage ground; all such money as he is indebted to me; a great gilt bowl embossed, with a cover parcel gilt, a dozen silver spoons, a chafing dish of silver; my household stuff in my house at Borley except such as I shall specially give away; my neats and bullocks, sheep, horses and other my cattle, saving such as shall be thought meet by my executor to be killed for the maintenance of my household at Borley for a month after my decease; and my provision of wheat, malt, barley and other grain, and hay and straw in the barns.

To my daughter [in-law] Jeronima Waldgrave my silver porringer with a cover, having a squirrel on it; 2 new-made silver candlesticks, my cross with the picture of Christ which my son [John] Sowthcott gave to me, a fair picture of Our Lady and St Elizabeth wrought with pearl and gold, my chain of pomander, my beads of coral with the Five Wounds which my Lady Jernegan her mother gave me, my claws of gold to wear about her neck, and half my physic and medicine books.

To Charles Waldegrave, second son of my son Charles, £50 at 21, and to Dorothy Waldgrave his sister £100 at marriage, and in the mean season both to remain in their father's custody. To the rest of my son Charles's children unmarried as a poor remembrance of their grand-mother 5 marks apiece. To my son Nicholas £140 and the money which my servant Jacob doth owe to me; one nest of goblets parcel gilt, a little bowl, all plain double gilt, and in the top a man with a bagpipe, 3 white bowls of silver with the arms of Sir John Peter on them, 3 jugs of silver, 2 salts of silver, a trencher salt of silver with a squirrel on the top, and a basin and ewer of silver parcel gilt; and after the decease of John Smith my servant and Margaret his wife my lands which I purchased in Twinstead of William Upchard and his brother. To my daughter Katherine Waldgrave, Nicholas's wife, a tankard of silver with a squirrel on the top, my cross of diamonds, an egg cup of silver all white, the other half of my physic and medicine books, and my still waters and medicines belonging to surgery and physic. To Philip Waldgrave, eldest son of Nicholas, £50 at 21, and Frances Waldgrave, daughter of Nicholas, £50 at marriage or 18, and in the mean season both to remain in their father's custody. To the rest of Nicholas's children, as above, 5 marks apiece.

To Thomas Powlett my son my manor of Fynges with the appurten-ances in Suffolk and Norfolk, and my lands purchased of Mr Francis Gawdie, one of the Queen's Majesty's Justices of the King's Bench, in Wingfield, Syleham, Isteed, Mendham, Stradbroke, Weybread (all Suffolk), and Pulham, Brockdish, Needham, and Metfield (all Norfolk),

37

and his heirs male, with successive remainders to Nicholas and to Charles; also £400; an ale jug all gilt made with the letters T and P, a nest of goblets parcel gilt, a broth cup of silver having the letters P and F, 2 little wine goblets parcel gilt with this verse *Soli deo honor et gloria,* a salt all gilt, a great goblet embossed and a man's head engraved in the bottom all gilt, a new jug of silver, a great salt bought of late of a minister, a crystal glass cracked all gilt, half a dozen silver spoons topped with gilt with the pictures of the apostles; 4 fair hangings of tapestry which I bought of William Powlett deceased, a fair feather-bed, a pair of woollen blankets with the name of Katherine Waldgrave on them, a counterpane of scarlet with tester and curtains of scarlet suitable to the same, my red bedstead, another convenient featherbed meet for his servant to lie on, and half a dozen pairs of my best hempen sheets.

To my son [in-law] Sir John Peter my cloak, and my daughter Mary his wife my cross of diamonds. To my Lady Katherine my best diamond, and William Peter her husband a portague. To John Peter a ring with an emerald, and Thomas Peter his brother a ring with a ruby. To my son [in-law] Mr Thomas Gawen and his wife [Katherine] £10, Frances Gawen their daughter £20, and the rest of his children, as before, 5 marks apiece. To my son [in-law] Mr John Sowthcott my pomander of gold, Elizabeth Sowthcott his daughter £20, and the rest of his children 5 marks apiece. To my sister Dingly a ring of gold with the words *Praye for me.* To my brother [in-law] Mr Robert Waldgrave £10. To Sir William Waldgrave my ring with a diamond, and my lady his wife a ring with the words *Praye for me.* To my three cousins Mistress Wigmore a stone of watchet colour, Mistress Willmott a ring with a death's head of the value of 33s. 4d., and Griselda Poole a cross of gold with five rubies on it. To Mr Henry Jernegan a ring with a stone called a jaffen, and my executor shall safely deliver to him after my decease the little cross of gold with wood in it which was his mother's. To Mistress Fytche my crystal cross. To Mr Francis Daniell my two cramp rings in one, and Margaret his wife a hoop ring with the words *Praye for me.* To old Mr Martin, Mr Richard Martin his son, Mistress Alice his wife, and Mr Robert Hare, each ring with a death's head of the value of 33s. 4d.; Mr John Downes the picture of my lady [Catherine wife of Henry 3rd Earl?] of Hunting-don, and his wife 4 angels; Mistress Littleton widow 6 angels; Mistress Mary Bentlie 20s.; Mr Oliver Stone £5; Father Needham £10 and one of my geldings; and Father Tilbie £3.

To my servant John Smith £30 and one of my best geldings, and Margaret his wife £30, my gown of grogram furred with squirrel, my blue cloth chair laid on with statute lace, my sapphire cross, a ring of black jet which I was wont to hang about my neck, and 2 of my milch kine; to Mary their daughter 40s. and the bed which she now lieth on; and little John Smith her brother 40s. To Audrey Mannocke £10 and one of my silk gowns which I use to wear, my grogram kirtle, and my worst scarlet petticoat. To Barbara Brest 40 marks, my gown of grogram furred with shag, one of my velvet kirtles, and my next best petticoat of scarlet. To John Boathe and Margaret his wife and the longest liver of the twain the house they now dwell in, with the lands belonging, paying only the rent yearly reserved; to John £10 and Margaret £3, and to both the land I purchased in Foxearth of John Clerke containing 3 acres for their lives, and after their decease to my son Nicholas.

To my servants John Butler £3 6s. 8d., William Cutler, John Storie, Roger, William Brome, each £5, Edmund Moule £3 6s. 8d., Tom Mewe £5, Hugh the husbandman £6 13s. 4d., Lawrence Cooper £5, Mark the brewer £6 13s. 4d., William the cook 40s., Edmund Clerke £3 6s. 8d., Westropp £3 6s. 8d,. Thomas Cranford 40s., Parnel Hacelinge £6 13s. 4d., William Maneringe £5, William Jacob £5, John Greene £4, Dobson and his wife 40s. and their dwelling at Jacob Wood for their lives, and Robert Keene £3 6s. 8d. To the rest of my servants, men and women, that have dwelt with me one year at the time of my decease their year's wages. To my servants a mourning garment to wear at my burial and their board and lodging within my house at Borley for one month after my decease, during which time my house be orderly kept as it was in my life with the provision which I shall leave behind me and the poor be daily relieved with meat, drink and money by the discretion of my executor.

The residue of my goods to Charles, whom I appoint my sole executor. And for that my intention is not further to charge and burden him with the execution of my will than he shall find sufficient money in my house or in due debts depending on Mr Derham's accounts for Western lands, if any such want of money shall happen I revoke all legacies in money either to my grandchildren or to any other foreign person, requiring my executor only to satisfy such legacies in money as are appointed to Nicholas Waldgrave and Thomas Powlett, the poor and my household servants, and with the rest of the money (if any shall remain) to pay those other legacies in part or in all as money shall come to his hands. Overseers of my will I make Sir John Peter knight, John Southcoate esquire, and John Derham gentleman, giving to each a mourning gown and coat. [No witnesses.]

Proved 19 October 1599.

SIR THOMAS SMYTH knight [of Theydon Mount], 2 April 1576.
[20/31]

To be buried at Theydon Monte with such ceremony as shall please my executors, having rather regard to the relief of the poor than to extreme manner of mourning not becoming Christians.

The ready money and debts owing me and my chains of gold and 1,000 oz. of my gilt plate and more if need be I will that they be bestowed on the finishing of my house at Hill Hall and of a tomb to be made for my wife and me according to the plat and design which I have made by Richard Kyrbie's advice, whose advice I would have followed in the finishing of my building and tomb, and all brick, timber, chalk, sand and all other stuff that I have prepared I would have employed to that use and none other, until that be perfected, which, if my executors do not see perfected with as convenient speed as they may, none of them take benefit by this my last will but he or they only which effectually do see that done and my house perfected and the ways after amended.

All kine, oxen, sheep, plough and cart horses and all such chattel as I have at Theydon at Monte at the time of my death called my stock at Hill Hall or Monte Hall which was at the last accounts £430 or thereabouts and is brought now to £300 by lavishing and expense this Christmas as shall appear by the bailiff's accounts, besides swine and the corn sown upon the ground and my wheat, malt and bargains of malt, hops and other such provisions, I give to my wife, the better to help her to keep house, and on condition she do maintain, until my buildings be fully furnished and the ways about the house amended, so many teams as be now occupied about carriages therefor effectually and on condition that what shall remain of my said stock at the time of her decease, and the corn sown by her on my grounds, do remain to my brother George or such as by my devise shall succeed her in Monte Hall. Likewise to my wife her apparel, jewels, chains of gold, such bedsteads and bedding, goblets, bowls and other plate which she brought with her from Hampden [Bucks.] to dispose at her pleasure and more to the furniture of her house. She shall choose out 700 oz. of such of my plate gilt or ungilt as she shall think will best serve her turn. The which 700 oz. I give to my brother George or to him who shall succeed him in my manor of Theydon at Monte, and also the bedsteads, which be now in my new building, and such other brass, pewter, iron and other implements as were bought or made at my charge, on condition nevertheless that he do suffer my wife during her life to have the occupation of them for her friends and mine in my house, but not to sell nor alienate them away, and my brother George do leave two third parts thereof to him that shall succeed him in Theydon at Monte, giving securities to my nephew John Wood and his heirs, and so each successor to do to his successor.

All household stuff, linen, beds, hangings, etc. that do belong to Ankerwicke [Bucks.] and so hath been appointed to my brother George to supply the taking away of such things as came from Hampden which my wife may dispose to the intent that the house of Monte Hall or Hill Hall be not disfurnished, and on condition that he leave two third parts thereof to him that shall succeed him in Theydon Monte and so each successor to leave to other. If any to whom any thing is left upon condition in this will be suspected that he will not perform this condition to his successor, it shall be lawful to him who should have it after the death of the suspected to require sureties for the performance of the condition, which if it be refused then the two third parts to the suspected left shall be immediately delivered to his possession who should succeed him as his own given from me, on this condition nevertheless aforesaid, leaving to his successor; and because the suspected would give no sureties I give to George 1,000 oz. of plate which I would should be sold and £100 or £200 of that to be lent to my cousin Twiford for a year or two upon good bonds and sureties but upon no interest in usury, that 1,000 oz. to be employed in the furnishing up of the stock which my wife may diminish in her life, on condition that my brother do leave three fourth

40

parts of that to him that shall succeed him in Theydon Monte and so that successor to his next and so each to other.

Mine apparel at home at the time of my death or else at the Court or at my house in Cannon Row or Fleet Lane [London] (except one gown of mine which my wife will choose and one piece of wrought velvet which two I give to my wife), and household stuff and implements there I will that it be sold and the money to be bestowed in paying the legacies made to my servants and the rest in reward to my ordinary and household servants and specially those whom my wife doth mind to keep, not equally but according to their longer more diligent and faithful service (besides those whom I shall especially name to be specially rewarded I refer to the discretion of my wife and my executors to reward the rest according as is before).

To my nephew John Wood the lease and the rest of my years which I have of the Clothworkers of the houses in Flete Lane by indenture. Out of my lease of the parson[age] of Theydon Monte the interest of the two parson's closes in the occupation of Walter Rawlins to him whom by my devise I assign Skynners and Bennettes unto, paying such rent yearly in discharging the parson's rent as is now paid, out of the which lease of the parsonage I give to my wife so many years as she shall live. The rest to him that shall succeed her in Monte Hall. Out of my two leases of the demesnes of Wyrardisbury [Bucks.] so many years to my wife as she shall live, and after her decease so many years as George or his successor shall enjoy Ankerwicke, and after his decease to him that shall enjoy Ankerwicke so many years of the said leases as he shall enjoy the same, and so after him as many to him as by my gift he shall enjoy Ankerwicke and no more than otherwise. To my sister Pettitt 300 oz. of plate to bestow on the marriage of her daughters which be to be married.

Whereas I have appointed Richard Kyrkebye to be the chief architect, overseer and master of my works for the perfecting of my house according to the plat, I give to him over and besides the wages for himself and his two apprentice carpenters for that work of carpentry for the overseeing of my works £20 to be paid so soon as my new house is tiled and all carpentry work for the setting of it up done there, and also to his marriage a silver salt, 12 silver spoons and 1 silver cup to drink wine in.

I will that Apollo Wyberd have for 3 years next following 5 marks every year to find him at Walden School and the fourth year 5 marks to find him at Cambridge or to be apprentice at his friends' will. To the two which be of my chamber now in my sickness 40s. to each and to Philip Taylor for taking pains in my still house 40s. and a new coat. Another cup or salt to Humphrey Mychell.

Executors of this my last will I do make my brother George Smyth and my nephew John Wood, and supervisor thereof Mr Henry Archer, to whom for his labour I do give £20 to see things done in good order.

The rest of my plate not appointed heretofore, my house builded, my legacies paid, and my funerals discharged, to be equally distributed amongst my three executors. If John Dighton will take pains to see the workmen do their work as they ought and see them paid weekly I give him for his pains £10, and for being steward of my house and keeping good accounts £10. To my cousin Nycholls for painstaking in my matters of law £10.

Because I see that none of those which shall succeed me of long time are learned I give my Latin and Greek books to the Queens' College in Cambridge, and my great globe of my own making, so the Master and Fellows, having warning so soon as I am dead or at the least so soon as I am buried or before, the which I would they should have with a true inventory carried to them of the said books, do send carts to fetch them away within 10 or 12 days, the which I give on condition that they chain them up in their library or distribute them amongst the Fellows such as will best occupy them, but so that they do it by indenture or condition that when they depart from the College they restore those books to the College, my Titus livius, Aristotle in Greek and Plato in Greek and Latin, and Tully's works, and 10 more of my books which Clement Smyth will choose I will that he have them, but yet on that condition that, when he doth go from the College, to restore them again to the College; my other little globes I give to Clement Smyth. If the Master and Fellows of the Queens' College will not fetch them away, sending some wise man to see them well trussed and packed, then I give them to Peterhouse on like condition as to the Queens' College. My standing massive cup all gilt which hath the seven planets in the cover I give to the Queen's Majesty as most worthy, having all the good gifts endowed of God which be ascribed to the seven planets, praying her Majesty to take that simple gift in good worth as coming from her faithful and loving servant.

My meaning is specially that he that should have Theydon at Monte should be able to keep house there to the relief of the poor and to set neighbours on work. If there be any ambiguity or doubts in this my will whereupon my executors cannot agree, they shall stand to the decision of my cousin Nycholls, Mr Archer and parson [Thurston] Shawe [rector of Theydon Mount] or the more part of them, whom I make the interpreters of this my will, because I would have no controversy in law.

Reviewed and corrected by me after the death of my nephew William Smyth of Walden and signed to every page, 18 February 1577.

Of my books I have given to parson Shawe Chrisostonii opera vol. v, Origines vol. 2, Lutheri opera, Bucerus, Galatinus, Felinus super Psalterium, Petrus Martir in libro Judicum. To my servant Thomas Crowe The Monuments of Martirs in two volumes which be now in the Parlour beneath, the new gilded books to remain in the Parlour instead of the old, Matheolus in French in folio and in Latin in quarto and octavo and folio, Galenus de composicione medicamentorum, Galenus de Antidarium facultatibus, Petrus pena de herbis, Methodus medendi, Galeni, Auditarium speciale, Turnor's Herball, Falliopii opera, Rondoletius, a Bible in Latin in quarto gilded. To Henry Butler the works of Chaucer.

I bequeath all my manors, lands and tenements as already I have given and disposed them by indenture made betwixt me on the one part and Francis Walsingham, Secretary to the Queen's Majesty, James Altham, Henry Archer, esquires, Humphrey Mychell and my nephew

John Wood on the other part, dated 4 February 1577. My executors to take care to set some good order betwixt my nephew William Smyth's widow and Skotte's children and the children be provided for to be well brought up in the fear of God. Reviewed and amended by me, 10 March 1577.

Proved 15 August 1577 by John Wood, reservation to George Smyth, and afterwards, 14 May 1580, by him.

LADY PHILIPPA SMITH of Hill Hall [in Theydon Mount], 21 May 1578. [22/30]

I make James Altham of Latton esquire my sole executor. To him and the Lady Judd his wife each a black gown of 20s. the yard, a chafing dish of silver and 12 yards of black raised velvet, and to two of his servants each a black coat of 10s. the yard. To my brother John Wilford and his wife each a black gown of 15s. the yard, and a bedstead of walnuttree carved in the Great Chamber, a mattress of linen cloth, a featherbed, a blanket of white woollen, a red Spanish blanket, a coverlet of tapestry, a testern of red velvet fringed with silk and copper silver, the curtains of red taffeta sarcenet likewise fringed, a bolster and 2 pillows, a long cushion of red velvet with copper silver fringed, the covering of buckram for the testern, a cupboard cloth of Spanish work, a damask table cloth and a towel, a dozen of damask napkins, 2 pair of fine sheets and 2 pillowberes, a long table cloth of holland, and a short table cloth; and £40.
[Nearly every legatee named below is to have either a black gown or a black cloak, value 15s. a yard for relations, 10s. a yard for others including servants, but servants of husbandry to have a black coat of 8s. and maidservants a black cassock of 8s. the yard. In addition, most relations are to receive bed- and table-linen, whether also given a bedstead or not, and some other legatees are to get a pair of sheets and a table cloth.]
To Agnes Nashe, my sister, in the Green Bedchamber a French bed of walnuttree, a testern of tissue to the same, a covering of tapestry, a quilt of green sarcenet, 5 curtains of green sarcenet, a chair and 2 stools, a cupboard of walnuttree, a table of wainscot, a long cushion of tissue; and £20. To my sister Copland and her husband, in the High Gallery a bedstead of walnuttree, 2 white rugs, a court cupboard, a chair and 2 stools, a square table of walnuttree; in the Great Chamber a quilt of red, green and yellow damask, a long cushion of red satin with copper silver fringe, a chair of yellow velvet with 2 stools to the same, the hangings of tapestry that was John Hamden's, 6 old needlework cushions; and £40; in my own chamber a great chest of fir board and another chest called a ship chest; and the lesser press in the Armoury. To my niece Barrett and her husband, in the chamber called Mr Altham's Chamber, a bedstead of walnuttree, a tester with curtains of green kersey with copper silver lace, a covering with Sir Thomas Smith's arms, a quilt of red, blue and green damask, a long cushion of tissue, a chair and 2 stools of green kersey with copper silver lace, a table and a chair of

walnuttree, a cupboard cloth of Spanish work, 2 creepers of iron; and £20. To my cousin John Nashe, son to my sister Nashe, and his wife, in the Compass Gallery a bedstead with a testern of blue damask and curtains, a table with a frame, a chair in the Green Bedchamber of red damask, a quilt of green sarcenet in the press in the Compass Gallery; and £20. To my goddaughter Mistress Philippa Fewilliams, daughter to Sir William Fewilliams, my best bracelets of gold for a remembrance. To my cousin Jane Lucas and her husband, in my chamber a home-made coverlet, a testern and curtains of blue say, a quilt of green sarcenet, a chair of red velvet and 2 stools suitable appertaining to the Great Chamber, a cupboard pane of damask edged with silver; and £20.

To John Wilford the eldest son of my brother £20; Jessam Wilford his other son £15; and William Wilford his youngest son £15. To Humphrey Nashe son of my sister Nashe £20. To Elizabeth Wilford my brother's eldest daughter £40, and the fir chest in my own chamber; Joan Wilford his second daughter £30; and Margaret Wilford his third daughter £20. To Elizabeth Lewcas daughter of Jane Lucas £13 6s. 8d. To my cousin Elizabeth Lyllingsley £13 6s. 8d. To Margaret Arthur wife of one Arthur a gilt silver pot which Sir Thomas Smith had of gift from the inhabitants of Walden, and one of my little French gilt salts.

To my brother George 10 quarters of wheat and 10 quarters of oats, so that he be no impediment to the quiet taking away of any the goods I have left to my friends, remaining at Hill Hall or on the ground there or elsewhere, which, if he be, then this my gift to be void. To John Smith his eldest son and Richard Kirby, each a black cloak. To my sister Petytt one of my tin [*sic*.] parcel gilt cups. To my cousin John Wood a cap of velvet with aglets and a brooch of gold. To Richard Lewter and his wife one of my little white silver bowls. To my cousin Kydson one of my little white silver bowls. To Margaret Wood [linen only]. To Thomas Crowe and his wife a bedstead of walnuttree in the Inner Chamber to the Greater Chamber, a testern of green and red sarcenet, and an old chest with iron bars in my own chamber. To Mr Cheveley and his wife a stone jug footed with silver. To my cousin William Heyward a gilt wine silver pot. To Katherine Bartley 2 partlets and a pair of sleeves of velvet. To my cousin George Nicholls of Walden a little chain of gold. To parson Shawe the bedstead in one of the chambers over the workhouse. To John Wybard 40s. To Walter Rawlyns £6 13s. 4d., the warrener's bedstead, and a barred chest in my own chamber. To my servants Robert Dawkes one of my parcel gilt cups, John Trapps 30s., and John Lightefoote 40s. and a cow. To Mr Archdeacon Mullens to preach at my burial a black gown, and if he should die then to some other good preacher. To Robert Westlowe a young heifer and 2 young shots. To John Wilson 20s. and I remit to his wife the 40s. she oweth me. To Philippa Wilson my god-daughter a heifer and 2 young shots. To the poor people of [Theydon] Mount 40s., Theydon Garnon 20s., and Stapleford Tawney 20s. To the poor people at the time of my burial £4. To the amendment of highways where most need is, to be bestowed at the discretion of my executor, £40 [*sic*]. To poor maids' marriages £6 13s. 4d. To Philip son of widow Taylor £3; Elizabeth Taylor £4, a bedstead of wainscot in one of the chambers over the workhouse; Philip Board 40s.; and John Andrewes and his wife my gilt silver cup.

To every of my servants half a year's wages from the quarter before my death; if they be then in my service, i.e. William Clarke, William Woodroff, John Buggs and Samuel Howell. To my other servants half a year's wages, i.e. Thomas Ayestropp, Thomas Reve, Thomas Rewle, John Drenter [Dreuter?], Philip More, John Sharpe, Francis Wybard and Edward Price. To my servants of husbandry half a year's wages, i.e. Thomas Browne and 2 ewes, 2 lambs and 2 shots, Philip Boerd and 1 weanling calf, and Harry Paltock, John Jackson, Thomas Dymsdalle, and Richard Asterleye. To John Clarke my old servant £20. To my maid-servants, a black cassock, i.e. Elizabeth Taylor, Amy, Agnes, Amy Dosset, Katherine Rawlyns and Philippa Bord, and more to Elizabeth Taylor a little fir chest and a wainscot chair in my own chamber. To Philip Rawlyns my godson 2 ewes and 2 lambs; the wife of Walter Rawlyns a smock, a kercher and a table cloth of my own spinning; good-wife Taylor a smock, 1 ewe, 1 lamb, a kercher, and a table cloth; goodwife Ededropp 1 ewe, 1 lamb, a smock and a kercher. To Mr Archer the lawyer one of my white silver wine pots. The charge and order of my funeral shall be at the discretion of my executor. The residue of my goods to be distributed at his discretion. I ordain my brother Richard Copland overseer.

Witnesses: Robert Marbeck *in medicino doctor*, William Hayward grocer.

Proved 13 July 1579.

SIR JOHN WENTWORTH of Gosfield, knight, 8 October 1566. [For John Wentworth, see p. 142.] [10/29]

To be buried within 48 hours after my departing out of this world, if my executors think it possible or conveniently as to be done, in the north aisle of Gosfield church in the tomb which I already have prepared. To the needy poor householders and inhabitants £100, viz. Wethersfield 40s., Gosfield 20s., Halstead 20s., Sible Hedingham 20s., Bocking 20s., Finchingfield 20s., Shalford 13s. 4d., Belchamp Walter 13s. 4d., Little Horkesley 13s. 4d. whereof 10s. to the almshouse there, Gestingthorpe 10s. and Otten Belchamp 10s., all yearly, to such honest men and persons as shall be thought meet by my executors' discretion. To the amending of the most needy places in the highway between St Anne's chapel [in Great Leighs] and Braintree 20s. every year, £10.

To my loving daughter Anne the Lady Mautarvers my best basin and ewer parcel gilt, a pair of livery pots silver and gilt, a nest of bowls of silver all gilt which I last bought at London, a pair of my best salts of silver all gilt, 2 silver spoons all gilt, 2 beer pots of silver all gilt being part of the 3 beer pots I bought at London, 6 of my best silver candle-sticks which I bought of the Master of the Rolls, 1 dozen silver spoons with the twelve apostles, a standing cup of silver and gilt, 1 dozen silver trenchers parcel gilt, and a chafing dish of silver; also 2 candlesticks and

2 cruets of silver parcel gilt which served for my chapel and a chalice of silver all gilt, and 2 little candlesticks which I lately bought of the Countess of Oxford [Margery, widow of John 16th Earl?], a casting bottle of silver all gilt serving for sweet waters; the whole hangings for the Parlour, the best tester and ceiler in the Chief Chamber, my best carpet of needlework I bought of William Wilford esquire and 2 cushions of cloth of gold.

Whereas William Walgrave of Smallbridge in Bures St Mary [Suffolk] esquire hath by his indenture, 9 September 1566, assured to me and my heirs the site of the manor of Bradfield Hall with the houses and lands in Bradfield Park as it is enclosed with pales, in Bradfield, Wix and Mistley; on condition that, if William Walgrave do not make payment of £500 to me at the site of the manor of Bellhouse alias Gosfield Hall at Michaelmas next, then the site of the manor of Bradfield Hall with the Park and premises shall remain to me; and for default of payment then Sir William Cordall knight, Master of the Rolls, shall have to him and his heirs for ever the site and premises, on condition that, if he pay to my executors £500 within 3 months after Michaelmas, they shall sell the premises and with £200 thereof shall buy 2 fair basins with 2 ewers of silver parcel gilt, 2 nests of silver bowls all gilt, a pair of silver salts all gilt, 1 dozen silver trenchers parcel gilt; and the residue of the £200 to be bestowed on silver plate by the discretion of my executors and taking the advice of my daughter, Lady Anne, to whom I give all the plate to the value of £200 besides such plate given her in my will; and the residue of the £500 shall go to the performance of my will; and in case my executors shall fortune to sell the premises for above £500 they shall have the same residue for their pains divided equally.

To Anne my well-beloved wife 2 basins with 2 ewers of silver parcel gilt, one of them which was my father's, a pair of my best livery pots of silver parcel gilt, a nest of silver bowls all gilt, a nest of silver bowls all white, a nest of silver goblets all gilt, a standing cup of silver all gilt, a pair of salts all silver, 2 goblets of silver parcel gilt, 6 candlesticks of silver all white which I caused to be made in London, 1 dozen trenchers of silver, a flat piece of silver parcel gilt which was my father's, a casting bottle of silver all gilt for sweet waters, and the residue of my silver spoons being all gilt or parcel gilt which are not before bequeathed to my daughter; also 500 marks; that whole hanging, bedding and stuff commonly used to the chamber called the Lord Wentworth's Chamber and the best tester and ceiler to the same, 2 of my long cushions of needlework, 2 square cushions of the same work, my best long carpets of needlework commonly used in the Parlour, 1 of my best cupboard cloths of needlework or carpetwork at her choice, 2 beer pots of silver all gilt with 2 covers whereof 1 was Sir Giles Alington's and the other is 1 of the 4 whereof 2 are given to my daughter, that whole hanging of the story of Moses, with those pieces of hanging which I bought at London to furnish the Dining Chamber there, and the tester and ceiling of needlework which hangeth in the Chief Chamber.

To my nephew John, son of my late brother Henry Wentworth, a pair of livery pots of silver parcel gilt being with leopards' heads, a basin with an ewer of silver parcel gilt being 1 of the 2 which I lately bought at London, at his choice, the standing bed with the ceiler and tester to the same paned with cloth of gold and crimson velvet, which is commonly used in the chamber over the Old Parlour, and the bedding and stuff in the Inner Chamber to the same; 1 demi-lance, 6 corselets and 20 almain rivets, 1 dozen pikes, 1 dozen livery bows, 6 sheaf of arrows, 6 halberds, 6 bills, and 6 javelins; also £100; all on condition that he be bound in £200 to my executors to suffer such leases as I have granted to any persons of any such manors as shall come to him after the deaths of me, my wife or my daughter.

To my nephew Henry Wentworth, brother to John, £40. To my nephew John Wentworthe of Bocking, son of my late brother Roger, a basin and ewer of silver parcel gilt, being 1 of the 2 which I last bought at London, a pair of livery pots of silver parcel gilt, 1 of my best geldings, and £20. To my nephew Henry Wentworth of [Steeple] Bumpstead, son of my late brother John, £100. To Elizabeth Barne, one of the daughters of my late nephew John Barne esquire deceased, £100. To Judith Bettenham, one of the daughters of my late brother-in-law Thomas Bettenham esquire deceased, £100. To such one of the daughters of my nephew Henry Wentworth of Bumpstead which first shall be 18, towards the preferment of her marriage, 100 marks at 18 or marriage.

To every one of my servants named in a schedule annexed such sum as is appointed, provided that, if any shall be departed out of my service when it shall please God to call me out of this world, they shall have no legacy.

To my nephew William Cardenall the younger my title of such manors, lands and goods in Essex as lately were delivered to me in execution of a recognizance of 1,000 marks in the nature of a statute staple acknowledged to me by William Cardenall of Great Bromley esquire, father of William, by an extent of record in the Chancery, to hold to him for such time as I now holdeth them, on condition that William Cardinall the elder and the younger during one year after my death observe the covenants in the assurances of the jointure of Mary Cardinall my niece, wife of William the younger, as in their marriage settlement between me and William the elder, and that William the elder and the younger discharge me and my executors against Thomas Sackforde esquire, one of the Masters of Requests, concerning an execution which I did lately take of the manors of Over Hall and Nether Hall in Dedham, parcel of the premises before bequeathed as parcel of the extent.

My executors shall sell my best chain of gold with all my aglets, buttons, brooches and jewels to the best value they can, and with the money shall buy plate of silver, all gilt, parcel gilt or white; half of the plate to John son of my late brother Henry and the other half to be equally and indifferently divided between John Wentworth of Bocking and Henry Wentworth of Bumpstead, provided that my executors shall not sell any jewels which my wife hath used or worn, all which I give to her. To my executors for the special trust and confidence that I have in them, each £10. The residue of my goods to my wife and my daughter to be equally divided. I ordain my executors my wife and my cousin Rooke Grene esquire.

Witnesses: Christopher Hill clerk, Thomas Leaper, Arthur Breame, Bartholomew Wayte, John Catterall.

Schedule of servants: John Barnishe gentleman 40s., Bennet Cornewall 40s., Arthur Breme £3, William Codwell £3, Robert Gosnolde 40s., John Catterall 40s., Thomas Woode 40s., John Spencer £4, Thomas Lawrence 53s. 4d., John Goldinge 40s., Thomas Wayte 40s., John Peace 40s., Robert Rowse —, George Gece 26s. 8d., William Osborne 40s., John James 40s., Robert Langden —, William Chapman 20s., Agnes Blithe £4, Alice Man 20s., Thomas Leaper 26s. 8d., Bartholomew Wayte 20s., John Kinge 20s., James Mare 20s., Robert Goldinge 20s., Roger Goldinge 20s., Cuthbert Toodd —, Henry Hunte 26s. 8d., William Clarke 26s. 8d., John Reve 20s., George Harde 20s., James Clarke 20s., Martin Neweman —, John Pasfield —, Thomas Bridge —, and John Shepparde 26s. 8d.

Proved 15 October 1567.

DAME ANNE WENTWORTH of Gosfield, widow of Sir John Wentworth, knight, of the same, 20 June 1575. [18/46]

To be buried in the chancel of Gosfield church next to the body of my husband in the tomb prepared for the same; there shall be bestowed on black and other charges of my burial 200 marks.

To my daughter the Lady Maltravers on the performing of certain conditions hereafter expressed £100, with one edge of great pearl to be valued at £13 6s. 8d. to be parcel of the £100; such my part of the brewing vessels and the tables and forms in the Hall and the table in the Great Chamber as were given to me by my husband's will, on condition she shall permit my executors peaceably to have the use of Gosfield Hall alias the Bellhouse, with the buildings, barns, stables, yards, gardens, orchards, dovehouses, lands, feedings, and the Park, and the demesne lands, with all profits belonging as I occupy in my lifetime, for 8 weeks after my decease to the intent that they pay my legacies and take away all my goods. To my nephew Arthur Breame of Gosfield £100 and the debt which my cousin Rooke Grene esquire doth owe me. Nevertheless, if she will within 30 days after my decease make to him a lease for 21 years of the houses and lands which my husband bought of Mr Roger Parker called Hancockes, Godholtes and Pere Field in the occupation of James Clerke and of myself, a tenement called Hodinges or Holdinges in that of John Grey, the dovehouses with the doves and barn called Hodinges, and 10 loads of round wood yearly to be assigned within a mile of the tenement, all in Gosfield, and my nephew to have all wood and timber growing thereon, then she shall have the £100. To my sister Dorothy Bettenham £13 6s. 8d.; my nephew Jerome Bettenham £30; and my nephews and niece Samuel, Peter and Hester Bettenham each £10. To Arthur Breme £100 and my customary tenement called Northes and Church Croft which I bought of Robert Walforde of Wethersfield deceased in Wethersfield and Shalford, Arthur to pay thereof towards finding his cousin Isaac Copwood 46s. 8d. yearly for life, and after his decease Arthur and his heirs shall pay 46s. 8d. for ever, if the tenement be let or otherwise, to the poor and most needy people of Gosfield.

To Rooke Grene a little tablet of gold which he gave me. To Mr Henry Drewrie of Lawshall (Suffolk) £10. To my niece Judith Breme my furniture that I have for myself or for my women, viz. pillows, saddles, pillion saddle cloths, bridles, peytrels, and a garnish of pewter vessel at her choice, a pair of sheets of my own spinning, a board cloth and a towel of plain diaper, a pair of beads of gold price 40s., a brooch of gold price £3, a tablet of gold price 20s., and another tablet of gold with an image.

To my servants Sir Robert Thompson 30s., Mistress Elizabeth Thursbee 30s., John Catteral 40s., John Peche —, Thomas Woodde 40s., Thomas Fytche 20s., Floode 20s., Richard Gomer 20s., George Cooe 40s., Thomas Lawrence 40s., Robin Smithe 20s., John Hames 20s., Andrew Mannock 40s., Agnes Wood 20s., Robert Gosnold 20s., William Clarivaunces 20s., Assheton 40s., Henry Hunte 10s., John Golding 10s., John Clarke 10s., William Osborne 10s., Spencer 10s., James Clarke 10s., Harde 10s., Reve 10s., William Clark 10s., and widow Howe 20s. The residue of my goods I give to the discretion of my executors, whom I ordain Henry Drewry and Arthur Breame.

Witnesses : William Hause, Robert Briant, John Curray.

Proved 19 November 1575.

3
ESQUIRES

JOHN ABELL of West Bergholt esquire, 26 June 1575. [18/46]

To be buried in the chancel of West Bergholt church. To Mary my wife all the bedding, implements and furniture in the chamber wherein we commonly lie and in the maids' chamber adjoining, the gallery and the new chamber, together with the custody of the residue of the bedding, implements and household stuff and furniture in my house until my eldest son is 21; 2 of my best geldings and one-half of my milch beasts, sheep and swine on my manor of Cookes alias Nether Hall [in West Bergholt] with half the corn growing there and in the barns and chambers, together with my plate not otherwise disposed.

Waldegrave my son, if he live to 21, and if he die in the meantime such other of my sons as shall inherit my lands at the like age, shall have my nest of goblets which were my grandfather Neave's, with my great silver salt and my chain of gold which containeth 207 links. I leave to descend to Waldegrave my heir apparent in full recompense of the third part of my freehold lands the yearly rent of £26 13s. 4d. out of my manor of Cookes, which rent is reserved on a lease with the reversion of the manor. To John my son for life an annuity of £10 out of my manor of Landymer Hall [in Thorpe] on condition that he make no claim to my copyhold land belonging to it. To William my son on like condition an annuity of £10, my tenement wherein Edmund Browne my servant dwelleth with the land for life, and an annuity of £5 which I bought of my brother-in-law John Waldegrave gentleman during John's life. To my two daughters Dorothy and Mary all my living cattle not otherwise disposed, with the other half of my corn equally divided, and £150 apiece at 21 or marriage; and the residue of the rents and profits of Landymere Hall over and above the two annuities and out of my customary lands being sokenhold until my eldest son is 21 shall be divided between them and the child my wife is withal at this present.

To Richard Darbie alias Page my servant my lands lying in the Soke, in the occupation of one Alleyn, for 40 years if he live so long at the yearly rent of 4d., and an annuity of 20s. out of my tenement called Merells in Fordham. To Edmund Browne my farm wherein he dwelleth for 40 years at the yearly rent of £5 as in his lease.

To the right worshipful and my dear friend William Waldegrave of Smallbridge [Suffolk] esquire my bay trotting nag which Sadler hath and all my hawks and spaniels (except 2 couple of my best spaniels and my lanner which I give to my nephew Charles Waldegrave). To my said nephew my bay gelding in the hundred. The residue of my goods to be equally divided between my two daughters and my child that my wife is with. I name my executors William Waldegrave and Charles Waldegrave and my loving wife.

Witnesses : John Waldegrave, Edward Lovell, Edmund Browne, John Fludd, Richard Darbie, James Game.

Proved 11 November 1575, the widow having died.

JAMES ALTHAM of Latton esquire, 17 December 1582. [See p. 51.]

[26/16]

I make my executors the Lady Judde my loving wife and my three sons Thomas, Edward and James. My goods, plate, household stuff and money I give to Thomas Altham, merchant of London, my brother, a basin and ewer of silver parcel gilt, the basin whereof hath a rose in the middest part; of that sort I have 2 basins and ewers, and my will is that he have the best of them. Whereas I have given in my lifetime to my son Edward £600 I now further bequeath to him 3 beer cups of silver parcel gilt called tonnel or else the value of them in some other of my plate at his own election, and have given to my son John £200 and a lease of a house in Cheapside in London that cost me other £200, I now further bequeath to him £200. To Margaret Goliver my maidservant £5 and Seth Hagar and Henry Turner, my two menservants, £3 apiece, the rest of my servants to be considered by my executors. The residue of my goods to be divided, one third to my wife and the other two thirds to my sons Thomas, James and Matthew equally betwixt them. Witnesses : Thomas Altham, James Altham, Seth Hagar, John Wilkinson.

Proved 19 March 1583.

THOMAS AVEREY of Berden esquire, 7 December 1576. [19/39]

To a boy called John Averey £6 13s. 4d.; Richard Jackson £6 13s. 4d.; Valentine Rufford, Thomas Simson, John Devell, Roger Warde, and Thomas Gregose, £5 each; George Holden £3 6s. 8d.; John Holden 40s.; and Joan Makrell £6 13s. 4d. To Sir Ralph Sadler knight, my table of gold with the Lord Cromwell's visage. I make my well-beloved wife Mary my sole executrix, and supervisors Sir Thomas Lodge and Mr John Harrington. My manor of Colne Engaine alias Gaines Colne with the gift of the benefice and the appurtenances to the manor, and my lands in Colne Engaine, with the reversion, to Mary for life, with remainder to John Everey and his heirs male. Witnesses : Thomas Lodge, John Harrington, Edward Elrington, Matthew Dale, Edward Atkinson, and John Cooper notary public.

Proved 20 December 1576.

WILLIAM AYLOFFE of Runwell, esquire, 19 January 1569. [12/5]

Margaret my beloved wife shall have my household stuff, plate, mixed corn in the barn and in the house or fields, stock of cattle as well kine, oxen, bullocks, sheep, hogs, and all other goods in my houses at Fleminges or Pencyes [in Runwell], also the household stuff at Braxted Lodge which was herebefore to her own only use, except certain plate which was brought from Brettens [in Runwell], i.e. 2 bowls and gilt salt, whereof she shall have the occupying for her life; and after her decease William my eldest son have it, except 4 oxen now going at Fleminges and my horses other than those which I shall hereafter bequeath her. Therefore to my wife the white nag which I commonly ride on, the grey double gelding which she useth to ride on, the sorrel nag called Owseleye, the black nag called Wrighte, the great bay trotting gelding at Braxted, the little bay mare, and the great bay trotting mare, the 2 cart mares, the great white curtal, the black ambling mare, and the white colt at Braxted; and towards the keeping of her house 4 fat bullocks in Braxted Park and my sheep there. For the consideration abovesaid she shall give to all my children one year's board after my decease in her house at Fleminges.

The residue of my goods, as leases, household stuff, plate, stock of cattle, and debts due to me to William, whom I ordain my only executor, paying £100 yearly towards my funeral expenses, debts and legacies until my will be performed; and to pay to my daughters Elizabeth Ayloffe 200 marks and Mary Ayloffe £100 at marriage, to my other children each £40 and to my sons Thomas, Giles and Ralph their sums of money as soon as it will arise of the £100. Whereas there is due to Mr Sullyard's daughters yet left unmarried 400 marks by their father's legacy to be paid at marriage, my executors do pay them at the day, if it will be so soon levied of the £100 a year.

Concerning the disposition of my lands, whereas I am bound to George Foster esquire and others, that if my wife overlive me I shall leave to her my lease of Wennington Hall, she hath promised that no advantage be taken hereof against my executors, she shall have in lieu my farm called Pencyes for life, with remainder to William. To Thomas, Giles and Ralph an annuity of £10 out of Brettens [in Runwell]; to Thomas the bay ambling gelding called Bay Jackson, to Giles the young ronded ambling nag new broken, and to Ralph the sorrel gelding with the cut off the leg. To Robert Bundocke, Martin Engledewe and John Jackson 20s. each, James my lackey 40s., Peter my cook 10s., and Raven my servant 20s. My cousin Darcye of Tolleshunt shall have Grey Jackson and my son-in-law Edward Sulliarde my bay stoned horse, desiring them both to be good to my children. To my wife's daughters a ring worth 40s.

I appoint my wife and my cousin Darcye overseers. [No witnesses.]
Proved 7 February 1569.

MARGARET AYLOFFE of Runwell, widow of William Ayloffe, esquire, 20 July 1579.   [32/21]

To be buried in Runwell church. To Jane Tirrell my sister for life my messuage and lands called Joyners in South Hanningfield, Runwell and Ramsden Bellhouse in the tenure of Thomas Harris which I purchased of Arthur Clarke gentleman; the remainders to Edward son of Thomas Tyrrell gentleman and Jane his wife for their lives and to Edward

Suliard my grandchild, son of Edward my son. To Edward Suliard my son my messuage and lands in South Hanningfield in the tenure of John Watson which I purchased of John Towle yeoman. To Edward my grandchild my messuage and lands called Markes in Rettendon with other lands I purchased of Sir Henry Tyrell knight and Thomas Tyrell esquire, his son and heir apparent, in the tenure of Robert Strete, and his heirs male; with remainder for want of issue to Thomas his brother and his heirs male; my son Edward to make a true account of the revenues and profits to my grandchild until he is 21; and if Edward my grandchild die before then, having one or more sons, Edward my son to do likewise, and if having one or more daughters to remain to Edward my son, on condition that he pay £200 to my grandchild's daughters at 18 to be divided between them; and if Edward my grandchild die without issue to Thomas my grandchild and his issue male or female likewise.

To 20 poor folks in Runwell, South Hanningfield, Ramsden Bellhouse and Downham 20 good and able milch kine, each 1 cow or else 40s. To John Vicarstaffe my gardener and servant £10; Thomas Decesse, Frenchman, my butler, £10; and my servants Margaret Clifte, Mary Withie alias Potter, and John Wade, each £6 13s. 4d.

To Anne daughter of Thomas Darcie of Tolleshunt D'Arcy £10 and his daughter Margaret £5. To Bridget daughter of William Forster of Crowhurst (Surrey), my brother, 40s. To Edward Siliard my grandchild my tablet of gold with a face made with a stone, and Margaret Darcie my daughter, wife of the said Thomas, the same until Edward is 22. To Anne Suliard my daughter-in-law, wife of Edward my son, my tablet wherein a unicorn horn with a ruby and a diamond are set and my ring with a turquoise engraven with a face. Edward my son and his wife and the survivor shall have 6 of my silver plates during their lives, and after their deceases to Edward my grandchild. To Dorothy Maxey my daughter my gilt bowl. To Edward Darcye my grandchild my gilt standing pot. To Anne Glascocke my daughter my gilt salt. To Jane Ayloffe my daughter 4 of my silver spoons gilt. To Bridget Wattes my daughter my gilt salt. To Edward my grandchild my gilt tankard, and his father shall have it until he is 21. To Jane Ayloffe my daughter my ring set with a sapphire. To Jane Tyrell my sister my little gilt salt, my silver salt with a cover, and my little pepperbox. To Henry Maxey my grandchild my silver tankard, and his father or mother shall have it until he is 21. To Edward Tyrell my sister's son an annuity of 40s. for 40 years if Jane his mother shall live so long. To Thomas Darcye my son-in-law and Margaret his wife my tester of a bed paned or guarded with purple velvet now in his keeping. To Edward my son my household stuff, on condition that he pay my executors £110 towards the performance of my will, £10 whereof for my funeral. To Katherine Breder my sister £5 which I lately lent her. To Henry Veniall my godson £5. To every of my grandchildren not before remembered a ring of gold worth 20s., and to every of my godchildren not being of my kin 6s. 8d.

My executors shall procure 20 sermons to be preached in Runwell church by some discreet and well learned preacher, to have 6s. 8d. for every sermon, and at every sermon 5s. to the poor of Runwell. To Agnes Foster daughter of Michael Foster my brother £3 6s. 8d. My son Edward shall take the revenues and profits of my messuage of Markes for finding of Edward my grandchild to school to the bringing of him up in learning until 21. Whereas Edward Suliard of Stanway esquire, my son, do owe me £200 by two bonds, which I have delivered in trust to my well-beloved and trusty friend Anthony Maxey of Bradwell [juxta-Coggeshall] esquire, my son-in-law, towards the performance of my will, my executors shall take of Edward my son within a year after my decease the £200 to buy lands to be conveyed to Edward my grandchild and his heirs, with remainder for want of issue to Edward my son.

To Martin Ingledewe my servant £4; Edward Bettes my servant and virginal player £10; Joan Whoode my cook 40s.; and Sarah Silvester my girl £10. I will that these legacies go out of the money that shall grow of the annuity of £10 which I did purchase for 55 years of Richard Cannon of Rettendon gentleman. After the legacies be paid my executors shall during the residue of the 55 years bestow yearly £6 13s. 4d. toward finding one scholar in the University of Cambridge, and shall pay the residue of the annuity being £2 6s. 8d. amongst the poor people of Runwell and other towns within two miles of Runwell.

To Edward my son a basin of silver with an ewer of silver (weighing 83 oz.), 2 quart pots of silver parcel gilt (62½ oz.), 3 silver bowls parcel gilt (in all 10½ oz.), 1 salt gilt (25¼ oz.), and an old casting bottle of silver parcel gilt, notwithstanding that he shall pay upon delivery of the plate in consideration thereof £70 towards the performance of my will.

I ordain Anthony Maxey of Bradwell juxta Coggeshall and John Glascocke of Roxwell, my sons-in-law, my executors, and for their pains £10.

Schedule, 24 December. I give to Edward my grandchild my messuage or farm lands in Downham, Ramsden, Wickford, South Hanningfield and Runwell called Sudburyes in the occupation of Robert Prentise which I purchased of William Nutbrowne the elder of Barking esquire, 2 November 1583, with remainder for want of issue to Thomas my grandchild.

Witnesses : Anthony Alderson, Michael Forster, 21 June 1586.
Proved 9 March 1587.

RICHARD BARLEE of Elsenham esquire, 7 June 1593.   [37/77]

To be buried in Elsenham church. Whereas heretofore I conveyed a tenement and lands in Kimpton (Herts.) and a yearly rentcharge of £6 13s. 4d. from my manor of Bybsworth [Herts.] for part of the jointure of my well-beloved wife for her life, and whereas she holdeth the manor of South House and its lands for life, all which she hath promised to resign unto her [sic] and my son Thomas, my will is that if she upon request by my executors assign her right in the same manor, lands and rent to my executors for their time and to Thomas after them, according to my will, then I devise to her for life in recompense thereof the lands in Elsenham which I have purchased at sundry times, also a yearly rent of £5 15s. 6d. from John Godfry's lands in Elsenham, which lands and rent are of much better value than the lands assured to her for part of her jointure. To my executors for payment of my debts and performance of my will my manor of Bybsworth with the lands belonging and Kimpton mill, and the reversion of my manors of Elsenham and South House in Essex, to hold to them during the minority of Thomas. If Thomas die without heir, the manor of Elsenham to my daughter Osborne, her child's part of the manor to remain to my three daughters Anne, Ellen and Mary. To my said three daughters for their advancement £300 apiece, to be paid out of the first money which shall come to my executors, and if I do not leave so much ready money they shall be paid £5 13s. 4d. apiece a year towards their maintenance; and I charge my daughters that they will be ruled in their choice of marriage as otherwise in all their affairs of credit or profit by my executors' loving advice and direction.

To my son and daughter Osborne as a remembrance of my love and goodwill 20 marks each, and their 5 children, viz. Anne, Peter, Christopher, Thomas and Richard, 20 marks apiece. To my sisters Wiseman and Hare 20s. in gold to make them a ring. To my well-beloved son my bedding in my chamber over the new kitchen with the furniture of the same chamber and one new featherbed which I made of late, price £8, and 4 pair of new sheets, and my books, and likewise the wainscots and glass of my houses, my brewing vessel, lead and copper for brewing, and a great cauldron or pan with 4 ears with a new trivet made for the same, 3 spits and 6 of the best coffers in the house, 1 carpet wrought of needlework that my mother made for a cupboard cloth, 6 of my best cushions, my armour and weapons and warlike instruments except so much thereof as my wife shall be charged to have by statute in readiness after the rate that she shall be assessed unto by subsidy, and my little clock that hanged in my hall.

The rest of my household stuff in my house of Elsenham, except my provision of victual in the house as fish, butter, cheese, hops and corn, and except my money, gold and silver plate, being gilt or not gilt, to my loving wife, together with £20. I carefully advise and heartily desire her as the last request I will give to her in this world that she will be heedful especially of ordering of herself and living to seek and follow the advice and direction of my faithful friends my son-in-law Mr John Osborne and my brother-in-law Mr John Hare, whom I make executors, and to whom I give for their pains £10 apiece.

Forasmuch as my son is of young and tender years and of weak nature and overmore inclined to much sickness and my great care is and hath been for his meet and convenient guiding according to the weakness and necessity of his state in such manner as experience hath taught me to be most profitable for his health and welfare, and I have not only of purpose heretofore acquainted my very loving brother and sister Hare with the same manner and secrets but also have noted such virtue and natural kindness in them as doth justly exclude all doubt of their kind and careful dealing towards my son, I therefore most heartily pray them immediately after my decease to take him into their custody and bring him up in virtue and godliness and by no means to suffer him to be in that of any other person. In case it shall happen my son to be a ward, I desire them by any means to procure or buy his wardship, without which I make account that the days of my poor child will not be long. I humbly desire of those to whom it shall appertain in this behalf that my brother may be preferred before any other person to the custody. To the intent that my brother may make less doubt to compound for his wardship in fear that the child might decease before his full age and composition for his marriage because he hath evermore been sickly even from his cradle unto this day, I devise that, if my brother shall buy his marriage and custody and also that the child shall decease before he hath agreed with my brother for the same and if he hath not assigned him his wardship to any other person than to my sister his now wife, my brother shall have £100 of my bequest towards his charges sustained in that behalf. To the poor of Elsenham 40s. and to Elsenham church 20s.

I appoint my brother Ralph Wiseman esquire with my son Thomas to be supervisors and to Ralph for his pains my best gelding. To my cousin Anne Goldwell £5. After my debts be paid the overplus shall be delivered to Thomas at 21 and to my other children if he die before age.

Witnesses: John Hare, John Tillinghast, John Turner, John Ive, Thomas Hodgkine, John Rice.

Proved 15 November 1599.

ELLEN BARLEE [of Elsenham], 22 February 1600. (Nuncupative.)
[44/17]

To my brother Osborne and my sister Osborne £20 which Mr Fitche hath of mine. To my two other sisters Anne Barlee and Mary Barlee £100 each of the money that my brother Osborne hath. To the poor of Elsenham £5 and £3 more at my burial. To the servants of the house £5 among them. To my uncle Mr John Hart and my aunt Mistress Hare to buy a ring 20s. each; my sister Anne my ring with the arms; my cousin Anne Osborne my saucer; my mother 20s., my brother 30s., and my sister Mary 20s., to buy them each a ring. To buy a stone to cover the grave I give £5. To my mother Bothe, goodwife Shelley and goodwife Godfrey 5s. apiece; my cousin Wiberde's wife, mother Mott, goodwife Pamflin and goodwife Godfrey [sic] 5s. apiece; Mr Barnarde and Mr Tillinghaste 20s. each. To Mr Gray to preach at my burial 20s. To little Frank Osborne my little ring of gold. To William Cockett for writing hereof 2s. 6d. My gowns and linen to my sisters Anne and Mary, and Anne to dispose of them. I desire my brother Osborne and my uncle Hare to see my will performed. Administration granted, 6 March 1600, to John Osborne esquire.

THOMAS BEDELL of Kelvedon esquire, 26 October 1591.   [35/88]

To be buried in Writtle church. To the reparations of the church 5 marks and to the poor of the same parish 40s. Whereas on good cause for divers debts and dangers that my kinsman William Bedell gentleman stood for me, for part whereof he was then in execution, I did in honest intent convey to him my goods by force whereof I remain dispossessed and disabled to dispose of any part, nevertheless for that some small portion of goods came since to my hand, which is by some order of law to be administered, I have by his licence and consent and by my earnest desire entreated him to be my executor, trusting he will discharge it. Witnesses : John Skerne alias Poule, Edmund Helmey, John Robertes the writer.

William Bedell having renounced executorship, 9 November 1591, administration granted 10 November to Robert Bond of Hythe [in Fawley] (Hants.), gentleman.

THOMAS BENDISHE of Steeple Bumpstead esquire, 28 March 1592.
[47/24]

To the poor of Bumpstead £5, and Haverhill [Suffolk and Essex], Leverington in the Isle of Ely and Wisbech [Cambs.] 40s. to each. To my eldest son Thomas my manors, lands and tenements in Bumpstead, Frating, Elmstead, Bentley, Great Oakley and Wix, and my parsonage and lands in Haverhill, and to his heirs male, with remainder successively to Richard my son and his heirs male and to the heirs male of John Bendishe esquire, my late father. To my son Richard my manors and lands in Leverington, Wisbech, Tydd St Giles and St Mary in the Isle of Ely (Cambs. and Lincs.), and his heirs male, with remainder to Thomas and his heirs male. To my three daughters Barbara, Elizabeth and Eleanor £20 each and their children £6 13s. 4d. apiece. To Richard my goods, implements of household, money, plate and jewels, at Leverington in my house there. To my mother Bendishe my gold ring which I now wear. To my brother John Bendishe gentleman a piece of plate worth £3 6s. 8d. To my two sisters Barbara and Margaret a piece of plate worth £3. Whereas I have in my hands £20 which was delivered to me by my mother to be paid amongst the children of my brother Robert as they shall come of years, I give in discharge thereof £10 each at 20. To Richard Stanfeilde, my clerk, £5; to my servants 13s. 4d. each. The residue of my goods, leases, money, plate and jewels unbequeathed to Thomas, whom I make my sole executor. Witnesses : Thomas Raynolde, Andrew Bendishe, William Bendishe, Thomas Bendishe.

Codicil, 12 February 1599. I bequeath the reversion of the manor of Chawreth alias Chace [Chawreth in Broxted] which I purchased and in evidences was assured to me by my uncle Thomas Crawley of Manuden esquire and the reversion of certain lands in Chrishall and Elmdon to Thomas Bendishe, my eldest son, and his heirs male, with remainder to Richard, my youngest son, and his heirs male.

The rest of my manors and lands not bequeathed to Thomas and his heirs male, with remainders successively to Richard and his heirs male and the heirs male of John Bendishe, my father deceased. Witnesses : Lawrence Faierclyffe, vicar of Haverhill, Thomas Bendishe senior, Lawrence Fairclffe.

Whereas I have given to Thomas the reversion of the manor of Thorney in Stowmarket (Staffs.), I revoke my will in that point only and give it to Richard and Margaret his wife and his heirs male, with remainder to Thomas and his heirs male. Witnesses, 3 September 1601 : Thomas Ady, William Bendishe, Anthony Gurney, Thomas Renoldes.

Proved 10 March 1603.

ROBERT BRADBURIE of Littlebury esquire, 7 January 1577. [For Henry Bradbury, see p. 162.]

To be buried in the chancel of Littlebury church besides my ancestors decently without pomp and a stone be laid over my grave and the grave of my father. To Littlebury church for tithes forgotten 5s. To the poorest people in Littlebury £5, i.e. 20s. a year; to the people at Meesden [Herts.] 10s., Langley 5s., Sampford 5s., and Walden 20s.

In consideration and upon special trust that my brother Henry will aid my wife with his best counsel and travail in the execution of my will and that of Edmund Terill, her father deceased, I bequeath him £20 and half my bedding, napery and household stuff, my wife to have the choice; my lease of the Bishop of Ely in Littlebury as appointed by the will of William my father. The reversion and remainder of my lands set forth before this time for my wife's jointure and the inheritance of all other manors after my decease shall remain to Henry.

To my brother Thomas Bradburie £10; my sister Mary Bradburie £10; every of my brothers and sisters 20s. to make them rings; and every godchild of my brothers and sisters 10s. To Samuel Donne 40s. To my cousins William Bradburie and Thomas Bradburye each 20s. To my uncle Mr Matthew Bradburie a corselet for a footman furnished. I acquit my cousin William of that which he doth owe me. To my said uncle, my brothers Henry and Thomas, my aunt Rutter, and my cousins William and Thomas, and Thomas Welbore, each a mourning gown. To Robert Fulnotby my godson an annuity of 26s. 8d. out of the manor of Giffordes [in Great Sampford]. To John Tremil, my sister's son, an annuity of 26s. 8d. out of my lands called Elizes. To Robert Holgate, my servant, in consideration of his faithful service to me, an annuity of £3 6s. 8d. out of my lands not bequeathed to my wife. To my wife Margaret for life my capital messuage with the appurtenances in Littlebury and Fulling Mill Lands and Bowsers Lands, in augmentation of her jointure and dower. Provided that, if Henry make her a sufficient estate for life of the manor of Langley Hall in Essex and Herts., the bequest to her of my capital messuage and other lands shall be void, and the lands to remain to him.

To Lady Anne Peter a ring of gold for a token. To my aunt Rutter 20s.; my cousin Katherine Keble 10s.; Thomas son of William Tyrrell 20s.; my sisters Platers and Susan each 20s. to make them a ring; my cousin Thomas Keble 5s.; and Robert Watson, Robert Leaver and Mr Withall, servants to Lady Anne Peter, 3s. 4d. apiece. To my cousin John Clyff a gold ring with an onycle, and I heartily desire him to be supervisor and to assist my wife with his friendly counsel. To Margaret wife of John Archer 20s. The residue of my goods to my wife, whom I ordain sole executrix.

Witnesses: Thomas Baker, John Cliff, Henry Bradburie, Robert Cranewise, William Cliderhowe.

Proved 4 May 1577.

JOHN BROCKE of Walton esquire, 6 September 1582.   [25/39]

To Mary my well-beloved wife £1,000. Witnesses: Andrew Paschall senior and junior, Richard Stone, Edward Bar, Lawrence Parker. Administration granted, 29 October 1582, to Mary Brocke widow.

THOMAS BROWNE of Flamberdes in Cold Norton esquire, 2 May 1567.   [10/15]

To be buried in Cold Norton church. To Jane my well-beloved wife my goods, household stuff, plate and jewels, except such as shall be bequeathed. To Thomas my son my manor called Porters in Prittlewell and my manor or messuage called Beake Hall in Rawreth, with all lands belonging. To William my son my messuages, lands and marshes called Sampsons, Hotes, Heddes and Campshedes in Tillingham and a tenement called Le Tyle Kyll in Thundersley. To Edward my son my messuages and lands called Freindes in Great Wakering and Waldens Marsh in Great Stambridge with all my free and copy lands in Wakering. To Anne and Ellen my two daughters and the child that my wife is now with child if she be with child my manor of Cottonton Court alias Cotmanton Court in Sheldon, Northbourne and Deal (Kent). My wife shall have the profits of the manors given to my children and shall therewith bring up my children with meat, drink, apparel and schooling to their age of 21 and without yielding account. To my sister Thomasine Harrison of London an annuity of £5 from two mansion houses in Lime Street in London. To Elizabeth Barnarde widow of St Mary Abchurch, London, £5. To William Gitto 40s. To John my son and heir 4 of my best featherbeds with bedsteads and 2 other beds for servants, my gilt bowl of silver, my standing cup of silver gilt, my 3 gilt salts of silver, 1 gilt bowl of silver, 3 bowls of silver, 3 silver pots, and 1½ dozen spoons, at 21. The residue of my household stuff to be equally divided after my wife's decease among Thomas, William and Edward.

To Robert Warde, William Maggott, Richard Smythley, Thomas Potter, William Baillye, John Blackmore, William Bullman, Thomas Ledes, John Wode and John Ellis, my servants, 20s. each, and each of my maidservants 20s.

The residue of my goods to my wife, my sole executrix. I appoint as overseers Mr Thomas Darcie of Tolleshunt D'Arcy esquire and Mr William Allington of Grays Inn esquire, and for their pains £10 each.

Witnesses: Philip Allington, William Anderkyn, Thomas Smith, John Locke the writer.

Proved 27 May 1567.

WISTAN BROWNE of South Weald esquire, son and heir of George Browne late of White Roothing esquire deceased, son and heir of John Browne late of Abbess Roothing esquire deceased, son and heir of Sir Wistan Browne late of Abbess Roothing knight deceased and cousin and next heir of Sir Anthony Browne late of South Weald knight and one of the Justices of the Common Pleas deceased, 16 January 1580. [24/15] [For Anthony Broun, see p. 14.]

To be buried in the chancel of South Weald church near the body of Mary my late dear and virtuous wife, one of the daughters of Sir Edward Capell knight, there buried, with such charges about my grave and funerals as shall be thought meet for a Christian man of my calling, by the discretion of my executors. At the day of my funerals dole be given to the poor people, viz. 6d. apiece to so many of them as will hold up their hands to take it, besides sufficient meat, bread and drink to every of them. To the poor people of White Roothing where I was born and christened 30s., Abbess Roothing 20s., South Weald 40s., Langenhoe where I am lord of the manor and patron of the parish church 10s., and Pagelsham where I have land and living 10s. To the reparations of the churches of White Roothing, Abbess Roothing, South Weald, Langenhoe and Paglesham 20s. apiece.

I bequeath the residue of my money, plate, jewels, goods, and leases in Abbess Roothing, South Weald, White Roothing, Langenhoe, Paglesham or Dagenham, as followeth. Firstly, the joined ceilings and joined work in my three mansion houses, viz. Weald Hall, Rookwood Hall [in Abbess Roothing] and Colvile Hall [in White Roothing], whether of oak, wainscot, chestnut, walnuttree or otherwise, being by any means made fast to the walls or freehold, shall remain to the owners for ever. Secondly, the bedsteads, presses, chests, coffers, tables, frames, benches, forms, stools, cupboards and chairs in the three houses shall likewise remain as heirlooms. Thirdly, brewing vessels and vessels for beer or ale as firkins, kilderkins, barrels and hogsheads, and stalls to lay beer, ale or wine upon, shall remain as heirlooms, and as they decay to be repaired or changed for so many other as good by the occupiers thereof. Fourthly, the copper pan and the great cistern of lead in the kitchen at South Weald Hall, the great cistern of lead in the pump house, the two great mustard querns in the kitchens at South Weald Hall and Rookwood Hall, and all dresser boards, tables, planks, shelves, troughs, tubs, cheese presses, coops, pastries, bakehouses, brewhouses, dairies, milkhouses or washhouses in the said houses shall remain as heirlooms. Fifthly, doors, gates, casements, glass of windows, locks, keys and iron work, gutters, spouts, pipes, conduits and cisterns of lead, lead work, horsemills with their stones, frames and utensils shall remain.

To Elizabeth my dearly beloved wife her apparel, linen, chains, bracelets, borders, billiments, rings and jewels which she is wont to wear, the gold rings with the three rubies which I had of her, and the money which she is wont to have in her custody without any account making. To my wife the gilt bowl which my lady Marquess Dowager Winchester sent us to our marriage, my second gilt salt-cellar having the manikin broken off, my little gilt salt, 6 of the second dozen of silver spoons with round knops, 6 of the silver spoons with maidenhead tops, my 2 silver tankards, and my great gilt bowl.

To Katherine my daughter 1 of my silver bowls parcel gilt, 3 silver spoons of the second dozen, 3 of my silver spoons with maidenhead tops, my white stoned pot covered with and trimmed with silver, and the little casket with white and black bone which was her own mother's. To Jane my daughter my silver goblet parcel gilt which my cousin John Cobden gave me by his will, 3 gilt silver spoons which were sent me by my lady Jane Browne, my aunt, at my daughter's christening, 3 of the silver spoons with maidenhead tops, and my brown stone pot covered and trimmed with silver. The residue of my plate in an inventory hereunto [not] annexed, to my son Anthony. To him his and my apparel and wearing linen, the flagon chain that he is wont to wear, the serjeant's ring of gold which my uncle Sir Anthony Browne gave me by his will with the agate, my border of gold buttons that are for a cap, and the little brooch with the agate in it. To Katherine my daughter her apparel, linen and the borders of goldsmith's work which she is wont to wear, her own mother's wedding ring, the little brooch with the agate that Mistress Fynche gave her, and the flagon chain of gold which she is wont to wear. To Jane my daughter her apparel and linen, the borders of goldsmith's work, and my round tablet of gold with the pearl hanging upon it. The residue of my goods to my wife, Anthony and my two daughters in four parts to be equally divided by my executors' discretion.

As concerning my manors, lands and leases. First, whereas Elizabeth my second wife standeth jointly seized with me for her life of the manor of Colvile Hall alias Knightes alias Brownes Manor with the appurtenances in White Roothing, Aythorpe Roothing, Abbess Roothing, Matching and Hatfield [Broad Oak], the manor of Church Hall in Paglesham, lands called Much Biggins and Little Biggins in Great Stambridge, the moiety of certain lands in Langenhoe called Haynes, Lexdens, Evelettes and Wades, with sundry remainders over as by sundry deeds and conveyances may appear (which manor of Colvile Hall as well by the office found after the death of John Browne esquire, my grandfather, as also by that found after the death of George Browne my father was valued at £11 a year, and which manor of Church Hall and Much and Little Biggins were after the death of the said Sir Anthony Browne, my great uncle, one of the Justices of the Common Pleas, then valued at £22 13s. 4d. a year, and which moiety of the lands in Langenhoe were purchased by me of the yearly value of £3 6s. 8d.); my will is for the further declaration of the assurance of the premises to my wife that she shall have the manors and lands by assurance in law conveyed to her, also during her life £10 a year which Richard Pease, farmer of the manor of Church Hall and Biggins, hath by his indenture dated the last day of January 1579 covenanted to pay me for certain years yet to come in consideration and stead of certain wethers, horse pasture, fowl and fish by his lease, on condition that my wife do not demand them.

John Wright of Markes in White Roothing, my servant and bailiff of that manor, shall have the occupation during my son's minority of my lease of the tithes of the demesnes of Colvile Hall and Markes in White Roothing from Harry Banckes, now parson [rector] there, for sundry years to come, to his own use, paying the parson yearly the rent of £6 reserved on the lease and to my wife yearly 10 quarters of malt during the nonage of my son; and after he is 21 I give the lease to Wright.

Whereas I have suffered a recovery of the manor of Markes and the advowson of the parish church of White Roothing to the use of myself for life, the remainder to my son and his heirs male, with other remainders as by the conveyance may appear, on which a question may grow whether the whole manor or but two parts thereof shall pass to him in tail, and the fee simple of the third part remaineth in me and my heirs; notwithstanding that conveyance, for that the manor being holden from the Prince by knight service in chief there was no licence of alienation sued on the conveyance, to avoid ambiguity after my death, I bequeath the said third part to my son and his heirs male with like remainders. The manor of Markes and the advowson to my son and his heirs male, which by office found after my father's death were valued at £10 a year. The exchange made with the farmer of Markes for the time being by my grandfather John Browne and continued by my father and by me of lands called Alderdownes, Spitle Croft, Hawkins Pytle and Hawkins Lane, parcel of the manor of Colvile Hall, for lands called Wilbrook Field, Wilbrook Mead and Wilbrook Lane, parcel of the manor of Markes, shall continue.

The churchwardens of White Roothing shall have my little pightle in Aythorpe Roothing in the occupation of [blank] Davye for so many years as they shall suffer my heirs to have a parcel of ground called Church Hope.

Whereas by assurance in law I have conveyed to me from Sir Edward Capell knight deceased and Thomas Leventhorpe esquire by lease for 80 years; if the Lady Dorothy Huddelstone, wife of Sir Edmund Huddelstone knight, shall so long live, two parts of the manor of South Weald and of the parsonage of South Weald, two parts of the manor of Costed Hall and of the market and fair in Brentwood, two parts of the manor of Calcottes alias Caldecotte, two parts of the free chapel or chantry in Brook Street, two parts of 100 acres of land, meadow, pasture and woods called the Spittell Lands in Brook Street and South Weald, and two parts of such manors and lands in South Weald, Brentwood, Brook Street, Shenfield and Doddinghurst, all in three parts to be divided, as lately were the inheritance of Sir Anthony, my great uncle, paying to Sir Edward and Thomas Leventhorpe the yearly rent of 1d., as by the deeds appeareth. And whereas I am seized of an estate of inheritance in fee simple of the third parts of the said manors, parsonage, market and fair, and lands that late were the inheritance of my great uncle and now that of me by descent as his next cousin and heir, at the yearly value of £21 10s. 0¼d., viz. the third part of the manor of South Weald and of the parsonage at £10 13s. 4d., of the manor of Costed Hall and the fair and market at £6 13⅓d., of the manor of Calcottes at £3 12¼d., of the chantry and the 100 acres of 35s. 6½d., I bequeath for the first 10 years after my death, if Lady Dorothy shall so long live, the rents and tithes from the said two thirds (the woods excepted) to my son and my two

62

daughters equally to be divided; and I bequeath for the first 10 years after my death the rents and tithes from the said two thirds of all such manors and lands as lately descended to me by the death of my great uncle to my two daughters; provided that they shall have of the revenues only £1,000, i.e. £500 each, and the residue of the revenues I will to be employed towards their bringing up and payment of my legacies and funerals, and the final residue to my son. My daughters shall be brought up by the oversight and direction of Sir John Peter knight. The right worshipful and my very good friend and neighbour Sir John Peter, my brother Henry Capell esquire, my cousin Richard Cutte esquire, and my loving friend Thomas Wallinger gentleman, whom I ordain executors, shall have the letting and selling of the said two parts and third parts and the receiving of the rents and profits; and they shall account once in the year amongst themselves. Sir John Peter be accountable in the first year, my cousin [Sir Richard] Cutte the second year, Thomas Wallinger the third year, and so to begin again with Sir John Peter in order. Item, on the account the money to be delivered to Sir John Peter and Mr Capell by even portions; and George Monke, my servant, to be bailiff, collector and gatherer of the rents, and for his pains 40s. yearly. The portions to my daughters of so many years as shall be then gathered shall be paid to them at marriage or at 21, and my son's portion at 21. Provided always that the executors shall not sell or fell any woods or timber on any of the two parts nor the third part but for necessary fuel to be spent in South Weald Hall or for necessary reparations of the Hall or of other the edifices and farm houses that appertain thereto, nor shall fell or give licence to any copyholder of my manors until my son is 21. If my son after he is 21 be desirous to have the mansion of South Weald Hall and the said two parts and the third part of the manors into his own hands and shall put in sufficient bonds to my executors to pay my daughters their yearly portions of money, he shall have all the said lands.

Whereas the patronage of the Grammar School of Anthony Browne, serjeant-at-law, in Brentwood and the gift and disposition of the school-mastership and of the gardens of the school and of the nomination of 5 almsfolks in South Weald, when any of their rooms is void, is descended to me and my heirs in fee simple as next cousin and heir to the said Sir Anthony, I bequeath them all to my son and his heirs male, and for want of such issue the remainders successively to the heirs male of myself, my brother John for life and his heirs male.

Touching my manor of Ruckewood Hall and other my lands in Abbess Roothing not before bequeathed, Beauchamp Roothing, Margaret Roothing and Little Laver, valued at £13 6s. 8d. a year in the office found at the decease of my father, I give as followeth. First, in consideration of the service of Edward Humberstone yeoman, heretofore and hereafter, to him the office of the keepership of my park of Ruckewood Hall Park for life, all fees and commodities as to the keeper of a park belongeth, and pasture, walk and feeding for 2 milch beasts, 1 mare and 1 hunting nag in the park; also for two parcels called Langelonds and Potters Croft; and there be yearly delivered to him 6 loads of sweet hay of the grass in Howe Mead and Carters Leaz and to be inned in the new hayhouse in the park at my executors' charges for the feeding of the deer in the park in winter; and he shall have sufficient browse for the deer to be lopped by himself, and the wood thereof remaining shall remain to the use of such person as shall dwell in my house of Ruckewood Hall to be spent for firewood and not elsewhere. My executors shall with part of the profits of the premises build a convenient house for a lodge for the keeper near the middle gate of the park within the compass of the old moat now dorved up near Watkyns Field; and he shall have his lodging in the chamber wherein he now lieth until the lodge be builded. My executors for the enlarging of the park shall take in certain crofts of land and woodground called Brickells, Watkyns Field, and one of the pastures called Costes Crofts, and the same shall enclose with post, rail and pale of the timber which I have felled for the purpose; and shall sever out from the park parcel of the lawn adjoining the Hall with three rails between every post.

To my executors my manor of Rookwood Hall with the appurtenances in Abbess Roothing and my lands not before bequeathed in Abbess, Beauchamp and Margaret Roothing and Little Laver for 10 years after my death to the use following. First, that they suffer my wife to dwell in the mansion house (except the study) for 10 years if she shall so long live sole and unmarried, and to hold the same by such rents as my executors and she can agree upon; and if she marry they shall let the house and lands by their discretion. My wife shall at her costs keep the house and buildings of the manor in reparations of tiling and daubing.

To my son my manor of Langenhoe to answer to the Queen's Majesty for the third part of all my manors and lands; and I most heartily pray that it might stand with her goodwill and pleasure to grant to my good friend Sir John Peter the custody, bringing up and marriage of my son. I likewise humbly beseech my honourable good lord, the Lord Burleigh, Lord High Treasurer, to give his consent thereunto and to be a mean for me to her Highness in that behalf.

I will that my wife and children and my family now in South Weald shall be and remain together and be maintained there with such goods and provisions as are on the demesnes of the manor for six weeks after my decease, and my servants shall each have one half quarter of a year's wages besides their due wages. My books as well of divinity as law books and other my books to my son, also my armour and weapons in Weald Hall and Rookewood Hall; all which I will shall remain in such studies, galleries and other rooms as they now be to the use of my son. To my executors for their pains £10 apiece.

Memorandum that, if my Lady Huddleston shall die within 10 years, whereby the two parts shall come to Mr Anthony Browne or to any other, then so much as shall be valued of £1,000 for the portions of my daughters shall be levied of the issues and profits of the third parts of the premises and of such woods as shall be to be felled in South Weald, Calcottes, Costed Hall or elsewhere in any of my manors and of the profits of Ruckwood Hall. [No witnesses.]

Proved 27 April 1581, Sir Richard Cuttes and Thomas Wallinger having renounced their executorship.

MARY BUTLER of Prittlewell, daughter of Henry Butler esquire, 21 October 1582. [27/6]

To my father my portion of money which was given by my late mother Dorothy deceased. To my brother Robert Butler a silver spoon, a silver and gilt whistle, and a gold ring with a toad stone, and my 2 sheep. To Elizabeth my sister a green silkcaul, a tinsel, a half shadow, a silver cowl, a coif of drawn work, 2 thread cauls, a square, a screen, 2 glasses, a little coffer, a face kercher, and a gorget. To my sister Susan Wylford a gorget of cambric, 2 forehead cloths, a caul of black work true stitch, and a gorget of loom work. To Joan my mother's maid a pair of new linen sleeves and a great coffer. To Mary and the other Joan each a pair of sleeves. To goodwife Marshe 2 kerchers and a pair of gloves. To my master Butler of Barrow Hall [in Little Wakering] a scarf, a pair of gloves and a band of cambric. To James Butler as much new cloth as will make him a band. To William Hodsoun as much as will make him 2 bands of new linen cloth. To my sister Prentice half an ell of new cambric. To Isabel Hodson my nurse my new taffeta hat; Mary Atkinson 2 coifs of cut work and a red petticoat; Robert Hodson my blue petticoat to make him a coat; John Frenchman a gown and a band; Sarah a petticoat; and goodwife Marshe more 2 old neckerchers, a pair of shoes and a square. To Margaret Sander my goddaughter a coif and 2 plain cross cloths. To my nurse Neale my blue gown and my nurse Hodson my new apron of blue. Witnesses: Richard Neale, John Mynyon, widow Marshe, William Hodson.

Administration granted, 15 October 1583, to Henry Butler, her father.

EDMUND BUTTS of [Wybridge in] Hornchurch esquire, 3 June 1577. [20/24]

To be buried in Hornchurch church before the place where the high altar sometimes did stand. To my very friend Mr Robert Mann, citizen and ironmonger, my ring of gold with a blue stone set in it. To Margery Bedell my sister-in-law all such goods as I have of hers, i.e. a featherbed, a bedstead, half a garnish of pewter vessel marked with a rose, a basin and a ewer of pewter, a brass pot and a brass pan. To Mary and Bridget her daughters £25 each at 18 or marriage. To Charles Butts £25 to be delivered to some honest man which will bring him up and also be bound to pay him the £25 at 21. To Margery 20 marks a year out of my manor of Wybridge in Hornchurch for life. To Audrey Butts my daughter my manor and the lands and tenements (except such as I appoint to be sold), with remainder in default of issue to my daughter Anne Butts. To Anne £200, i.e. £100 at marriage and £100 within a year after, if she marry with the consent of Thomas Butts of Biborough Magna (Norf.) esquire. To my cousin Thomas Butts my sealing ring of gold for a remembrance. Because my goods are not sufficient to discharge my debts, legacies and funerals, I command my executor to sell such lands as they shall think fit to discharge them. I appoint Thomas Butts my sole executor; if he refuse, Margery Bedell. I appoint Robert Mann and Basil Turberville my overseers. Witnesses: William Wager, rector of St Benedict Crechurch, London, Robert Mann, Steven Scarborough, Thomas Skipwithe, Basil Turberville, John Crafforde.

Proved 20 June 1577.

RICHARD CHAMPION of Hassenbrook [in Stanford-le-Hope] esquire, 25 February 1600. [44/17]

To be buried in Stanford-le-Hope church. To Richard Champion, citizen and draper of London, my nephew, my farm called Trappes wherein William Page dwelt, lands in East and West Tilbury in the occupation of Henry and William Pytman called Podwicke and other parts in that of John Parker and Robert Pake, lands in Burstead in that of [blank] Peche, and lands in Horndon-on-the-Hill in that of Henry Archer, William Kinge and Richard Woollwarde; and in default of issue male, the remainder to Humphrey son of my brother Arnold Champion deceased and to Richard Champion of the Isle of Wight, son of my brother Richard deceased, equally to be divided; and in further default to Philip and Thomas sons of Richard. To my nephew Humphrey, on condition that he convey to my nephew Richard of London all right which he may claim in any of my lands as my heir in my lands in Reading [Berks.] and the house in Horndon wherein John Slatirforde dwells, and the annuities in Weybread (Suffolk) to me due by conveyance from Edward Glemaunde gentleman deceased and due from Mr Stanley. Also to Humphrey £100 to be paid by my nephew Richard. Whereas I have heretofore conveyed by deed to my nephew Richard of London draper my manor of Hassenbrook and my farm of Shudden containing a clause of revocation, I signify that I have not revoked the same. To the poor of Godliman [Godalming, Surrey?] an annuity of 50s. out of Crayford (Kent), to Stanford 40s. and Horndon 40s. To the children of Richard of the Isle of Wight £10 apiece except Judith my servant to whom I give £20, and to Barbara daughter of my brother Arnold 20 marks. The residue of my goods to Richard of London, whom I make my sole executor. Witnesses: Francis Smaleman, Henry Archer, William Brookes, James Englishe, George Browne.

Proved 1 March 1600.

FRANCIS CLOVILE of West Hanningfield esquire, 2 April 1561. [5/16]

To be buried in West Hanningfield church. To Elizabeth my wife my manor of Barnes in the plain for life over and besides her jointure that I have made to her; also my sheep and lambs in Pampisford (Cambs.), paying for every sheep 3s. and every lamb 18d., my ploughs and plough beasts and the milch beasts, leaving them after her decease to remain to them that shall have the manor; 120 of my best udder beasts called milch kine, paying £240 for them; her own gelding, my grey geldings called Calton and Saddleback and my bay bald stoned colt that I bought of Foxe; all household stuff that I have in Norwich and Suffolk, 2 dozen silver spoons and 2 goblets of silver, £10, and 2 salts of silver. To Eustace my son and heir my household stuff in West Hanningfield, my plate there not given to my wife before, my cattle, i.e. my milch kine, steers, wennels, bulls and sheep, a bay horse, my sorrel bald gelding and my dun bay gelding that I ride on, my bay gelding that I bought of Foxe, my bay stoned colt of 2 years and the vantage, my roan stoned colt of 2 years, and my black stoned colt of 2 years which was of my fell mare. To Anne Clovile and Priscilla Clovile my daughters £400 apiece, and if the £800 cannot be levied then my manor of Wedsyde [recte, Widford?] shall remain with my executors until they receive so much money as shall make up £800 with my ready money, debts, goods, cheese and corn in the garner and fields. To my brother Thomas Clovile an annuity of £3 out of my leases of Crechurche of Norwich and of Garbelsham (Norf.), also for life my two tenements in Norwich; with remainder to Eustace, also my black stone horse and my grey ambling colt of 2 years. I make my wife and brother Thomas my executors. [No witnesses.]

Proved 19 June 1562. Administration granted, 24 October 1593 [sic], to Roger Osborne, one of the creditors of the deceased, Thomas Clovell not administering.

EUSTACE CLOVILL of West Hanningfield esquire, 5 November 1589. [34/9]

To be buried in West Hanningfield church. To the poor of West Hanningfield £5. To repairing West Hanningfield church 5 marks. To Percival my eldest son £200 at 21. To Frisewith my daughter £400 at 21. To my five younger sons, viz. Henry, George, Francis, Eustace and Edward, £700 to be equally divided among them, i.e. £140 each, at 21. [Elaborate clauses concerning the putting forth of these sums until they are 21]. To my sister Bramstone £5. To Francis Chewlyeye 5 marks. To Anthony Herington my man £6 13s. 4d. To Percival my plate and household stuff in my dwelling house in West Hanningfield, provided that he shall suffer my wife to occupy it for life, and if she marry her husband shall be bound in £300 not to alien or diminish the same otherwise than by reasonable use. The residue of my goods to my wife, and in consideration she shall bring up my seven children, and my overseers shall pay her yearly allowances towards their education. I make Jane my well-beloved wife my sole executrix, and I appoint as my overseers my loving and very good friends Edward Suliard of Runwell esquire, Thomas Bridges of West Hanningfield gentleman, and Roger Bramstone of Boreham gentleman, my brother-in-law, and to each £10; and to Thomas Bridges for his pains in making my will [blank]. To Thomas Burges of Runwell gentleman a ring worth 40s. [No witnesses.]

Proved 12 February 1590.

THOMAS COLSHILL of Chigwell esquire, 23 April 1593. [39/23]

To be buried in the high chancel of Chigwell church between the communion table and the wall of the south side of the chancel. To 70 of the poor people of Chigwell 4d. each. To Jasper Leeke my son-in-law a standing cup of silver and gilt which was my grandfather Weste's (containing 47 oz.). To my daughter Mary his wife a tankard of alabaster covered and bound about with silver and gilt. To my son-in-law Edward Stanhope a nest of pinked bowls of silver and gilt with a cover (66 oz.), requiring him to cause the Colshills' arms to be set on the cover. To my daughter Susan his wife a tankard of alabaster covered and bound about with silver and gilt. To my cousin Mary Manhood wife of John Manhood the featherbed in the little parlour wherein they both now lie.

Whereas by a deed dated 29 July 1588 I reserved a rentcharge of £66 13s. 4d. for 10 years to Sir Thomas Henage knight, Vice-Chamberlain to her Majesty and one of her Highness' most honourable Privy Council, Thomas Smithe of London, Thomas Harris of the Middle Temple, Thomas Barfoote of Lambourne, esquires, and Nicholas Crafford of Carshalton (Surrey), gentleman, the first payment to begin after the decease of the survivor of myself, Mary Colshill and Elizabeth Dacres, upon trust, I declare it to be bestowed as followeth, if Elizabeth Dacres die before 21; to my cousin Francis Smith, Thomas son of John Manwood, my godson, Anne daughter of Jasper Leeke, Katherine Leeke her sister, Anne daughter of Edward Stanhope, Jane Stanhope her sister, Susan Stanhope their sister, Winifred Crafford my goddaughter, Jasper son of John Manwood, and Kirkland my servant, each 100 marks.

To my son Stanhope and his wife each a mourning gown to be worn at my funeral, two of his men that shall wait on him at my funeral each a black coat, my son Leeke and my daughter his wife each a mourning gown, two of his servants a black coat, my brother Crafford and my sister his wife, my cousin Manwood and his wife and my cousin Francis Smithe, each a mourning gown. To Mr John Smithe, my deputy, a ring of 40s. and to his wife a ring of 30s., both with this posy *Quis fuerim nosti*. To nine of my menservants, John Hopkins, William Kirkland, John Parker, Hugh Mellens, Francis Smithe, John Stanhope, John Kellye, John Pett and Richard Cockrell, each a black coat. To my servants William Kirklande £5, John Parker 26s. 8d., Hugh Wellens and John Kellye, each 20s., Joan Lawe £5, Joyce Duckinton and Julian Turnage each 20s., all over and above their wages. To the wife of William Lumley a black gown and 5s. To Mr [Thomas] Atterbie vicar of Chigwell 20s. in gold to make him a ring. Towards the reparation of Chigwell church 20s. The residue of my goods to Mary my wife, whom I appoint my sole executrix, and overseers John Wood of the Middle Temple and John Manwood gentlemen, and to each for their pains a ring of gold of 20s. Witnesses: Arthur Crafford, Thomas Allen, John Sorrett, William Kirkland.

Memorandum, 28 February 1595. Thomas Colshill, lying in his bed in the inner parlour where he usually lay, being present his brother-in-law Arthur Crafford, John Manwood, gentlemen, and William Kirkland, Thomas Colshill's clerk, being in communication with the said Crafford of the death of John Smithe of London, Deputy Surveyor to Colshill of her Majesty's Custom House, said, 'Brother Arthur, John Smithe hath not remembered me nor my wife so much as with a mourning gown by his will, as William Warner his man hath told me, which he having been my man and Deputy afterwards so long as he was, he might well have done therefore I will have the legacies to him and his wife strucken out'. Witnesses: Arthur Crafford, John Manwood, William Kirkland. Proved 12 April 1595.

RICHARD COOKE of 'Guidie Hall' [in Romford] esquire, 31 July 1579. [For Sir Anthony Cooke, see p. 18.]   [22/74]

To my well-beloved wife Anne my best coach with 2 coach geldings, 6 other of my geldings which she shall choose, and £400; my manor house of Gidea Hall and divers other lands and tenements in the liberty of Havering for life, according to a former conveyance thereof to her use, by indenture made between me on the one part and George Noodes and Robert Badbye gentlemen on the other part; also my lands in Thetford (Lincs.) for ever. To my son Anthony my armour and weapons at Gidea Hall, with my whole library of books there; residue of my horses, mares, geldings and colts not before bequeathed, one-half of my beds, and household stuff, one-half of my plate, my stock of sheep in Dorset [Avon Dasset, Warws.] and such other cattle as I have going in my ground in Warwickshire, one-half of my milch kine, 100 of such wethers as are going in my grounds in the liberty of Havering, whereof 50 shall be of the fattest, and the residue as they shall fall out one with another, 10 steers or runts of the best, 2 yokes of oxen of my best draught oxen, 1 cart, one-half of my white meats, one-half of my brass, pewter and other furniture of my kitchen, one-half of my household stuff, and one-half of my swine, and also £500.

To my daughter Philippa Cooke towards the advancement of her marriage £1,333 6s. 8d., so that she be ordered and ruled by my executrix and overseers touching her marriage, to be by them employed for her maintenance until some convenient marriage may by their good means be had for her, according to my especial trust.

To the right honourable the Countess of Oxford a basin and ewer of silver to the value of £50. To my brother William Cooke esquire £100. To my sister [Katherine wife of Sir Henry] Killigrew a basin and ewer of silver of the value of £50. To my nephew Mr Robert Cicill £20 and to my niece Mistress Elizabeth Cicill £20. To my nephews Mr Anthony Bacon, Mr Francis Bacon, Mr Edward Hoby and Mr Thomas Posthumus Hobye, each £20. To Mr Thomas Foster my son-in-law two of my garments which he shall choose. To Mistress Mabel Brighte a mourning gown; Mr Francis Ramme £20 and a mourning gown; George Toone 20 marks; and Mr Robert Badbye a mourning gown and an annuity of £10 for life out of my manor of Chadwell.

To every of my menservants if they remain with me at the time of my death, viz. William Hobson £5, Thomas Conwey £10, Ralph Dickon 20 marks, Thomas Plompton 20 marks and the choice of such books as I have that were none of my father's, Richard Gresham £6 13s. 4d, Evans 40s., Stilman 5 marks, little Will Cooper £10 [and]

53s. 4d. yearly for life out of my manor of Rydden Court [in Horn-church] in the liberty of Havering, Thomas Browne 5 marks, John Turke £5, Horsnaile £5, Edward Savage £6 13s 4d., Stephen Brighte £6 13s. 4d., Robert Fulwood £5, John Estcott 5 marks, Humfrey Wrighte 5 marks, and every other of my menservants having served me one year or more 40s., and every womanservant not hereafter named having served me likewise 26s. 8d. To Mistress Ursula Norton 5 marks. To Mr Francis White, parson of Chadwell, £20 in consideration that he shall preach yearly at Romford yearly for 5 years after my decease as often as he shall think convenient for the goodly instruction of such as shall be there present.

I make my wife my sole executrix and appoint as my overseers the right honourable and my very good lords the Lord Treasurer of England [Willim Cecil, Lord Burleigh] and the Lord Russell, and to the Lord Treasurer a jewel of the price of £50 and to the Lord Russell £50 in consideration of their grave and faithful advice, counsel and pains, especially towards my daughter Philippa. The residue of my goods to my wife.

Witnesses: Francis Ramme, Robert Gadbye [recte, Badbye?], Thomas Plumpton. Memorandum, acknowledged to be his will, 2 August 1579.

Proved 17 November 1579.

WILLIAM COTTON of Panfield esquire, 13 August 1561. [For Thomas Cotton, see p. 186.]   [5/6]

To be buried in the chancel of Panfield. To Thomas my son with the legacy given by his grandfather Veisey £100 at 23. To Henry and John my sons each £100 at 23. To William my son my lease of the manor of Boyton Hall in Finchingfield at 23. To Giles and Robert my sons each £100 at 23. To Frances my daughter with the legacy given by her grandfather Veysie 300 marks at 21 or marriage. To Anne and Katherine my daughters each 300 marks at 21 or marriage. Provided that if William depart this world before 23 the lease shall remain successively to Giles and to Robert. My executrix shall have the profits of the yearly fall of my woods in Hempstead called Hempstead Woods until £100 be so raised towards the performance of my will. To George my son my best chain of gold, my best bed of down in the brewhouse chamber, and 3 of my best colts or geldings. The rest of my goods to Agnes my wife, whom I ordain my sole executrix. Witnesses: Henry Veysie, Adam Richardson clerk [rector of Panfield], William Vigerus the writer, John Glascocke.

Proved 23 February 1562.

GEORGE COTON of Panfield esquire, 6 September 1592.   [37/28]

To be buried in Panfield church or chancel in decent manner. Concerning my manors and lands holden of the Queen's Majesty for a third part of the same and for all other my manors whereof the Queen is after my death to have wardship, to my son and heir Thomas Cotton my manor of Panfield and the lands belonging in Panfield and the towns adjoining. To Beatrix Coton my well-beloved daughter £300; Mary Coton the elder my daughter £300; George my son £100; Mary Coton the younger £300; Frances Cotton my daughter £300; Abigail Cotton my daughter £300; Anthony Coton my son £100. To each of my said children successively my manor of Hempstead with the lands belonging until their legacies be paid out of the rents and profits thereof.

To Frances my well-beloved wife so that she shall have a motherly care for the godly education and well bringing up of my daughters until they come to be married or receive their legacies an annuity of £40 out of my manor of Panfield; her chain amounting to £50 or thereabouts, her borders, buttons, jewels, gowns, linen and apparel, my best coach and 2 coach horses, 2 livery featherbeds, one in the Larder Chamber and the other in the Pantry Chamber, with 2 other beds for her servants, 6 milch neats, 6 seam wheat and 6 seam barley or malt.

The residue of my goods to Thomas my son and heir. My plate and my principal and best household stuff shall remain to him as an heirloom. To every of my brothers and sisters for a remembrance a gold ring worth 20s. To my brother-in-law Anthony Felton esquire, Dr Barrowe, and my brother-in-law John Machine esquire each a gold ring of the like value for a remembrance.

To the poor people of Panfield 40s. at the day of my funerals. John Banges shall have my house and lands wherein widow Brett dwelleth for 20 years paying £18 a year.

I make my executors my well-beloved brother-in-law Richard Freston esquire, my brother William Coton gentleman, and Thomas Coton my son and heir, and to them a gold ring of £10 value apiece; and I appoint as my supervisor my loving brother-in-law John Machell [sic] esquire.

Witnesses: Thomas Dyke, John Banges, Edward Ascewe, Edward Banges, John Gooda.

Memorandum, my Lady Northe her words unto George Cotton esquire on Thursday in the morning about 7 o'clock being 15 March, on which he died about 3 o'clock in the afternoon, 'Cousin Coton, is it not your mind that your wife shall have £100 a year out of Langham and your two youngest sons £20 a year out of the same?' He answered, 'Yea'. Witnesses: Judith Northe, Robert Coton, John Banges, John Clemence, Edward Ascue. Also it was his will on his deathbed that his daughter Frances Coton should in like manner have £300 as the rest of her sisters and so was then set down in his will with a blank before being left for the same. These parties hereunder written do testify and are witnesses: Thomas Northe [sic]. Memorandum that my Lady Northe her words were 'Cousin Coton, I have seen your will, and there I find my cousin Frances have no portion. Is it your mind she shall have no portion?' He answered, 'No'. My Lady said, 'There is now a blank. Are you minded she shall have as the rest of your daughters have?' He answered, 'Yea'. My Lady said, 'They have £300 apiece, shall she have so?' He answered,

'Yea'. 'Is it your mind,' said my Lady, 'it shall be set in so?', and he said, 'Yea', and so it was written by his bedside. Judith Northe, Robert Coton.

Proved 20 April 1593.

THOMAS CRAWLEY, son of Robert Crawley deceased and cousin and next heir apparent of Thomas Crawley, of Wenden Lofts esquire, 5 February 1559.   [2/15]

To Mary my wife her apparel and the apparel that was of my late wife, and 800 marks which is parcel of 900 marks that Mr John Tamworth oweth me by bonds payable at certain days, and the other 100 marks I reserve to my executors to perform my will. To her my household stuff, linen, plate and jewels, except my chain of gold, my velvet cap with aiglets of gold, my hat of velvet with a brooch of gold, 4 rings of gold whereof 2 that I wear and 2 that were my late wife's, i.e. a wedding ring and a death's head, my apparel as damask, velvet, satin shirts, 1 featherbed, 1 stone pot garnished with silver all gilt, another pot of silver all gilt wrought in manner of scallop shells, which things excepted I reserve towards the performance of my will.

To my two daughters Anne and Jane Crawley my lands and tenements which my wife hath in jointure, as appeareth by record enrolled in Chancery, during the nonage of my daughters. To them the said 2 pots and 4 rings, 200 marks which the right worshipful Anne Cock, widow of John Cock esquire, and William Wrothe gentleman stand bounden to pay to my children at 17 and 18. To them also £100 which William Waters my servant oweth me and £40 which Michael Mede of Ware [Herts.] innholder oweth me. She of my daughters that shall be better learned at 20 shall have my books, which be worth 100 marks or better; and my friend Thomas Wilson, Master of Arts, shall have the use of them in the meanwhile. Provided that if both my daughters die before 18 their portions be bestowed by my executors according to their good discretions, provided that William Waters shall have the £100 and Sigismund Brooke shall have the £60 owing until my children are 18. To Thomas Wilson the featherbed above excepted and £40 and such of my apparel as he shall think meet and such things as be packed in his chest. To James Pers minister, William Allexander and Richard Hall, each £10. To my servant Thomas [blank] £10.

All such bonds and leases made between me and Thomas Meade my cousin shall be ordered by the discretion of my executors and overseers for the profit of my children. The residue of my goods to Thomas son of George Wilson of Kendal [Westmorland?], my cousin John Wentworth of the Middle Temple, son of Henry Wentworth of Mounteneys [in Elmdon] esquire, deceased, and my cousin Francis Walsingham, to employ the same to the profit of my children; which three I make my executors, and for their pains each £5. I make Sir Thomas Wrothe knight my overseer, and fo rhis pains £10.

Witnesses: William Wroth, Sigismund Brooke, James Tenant, William Layne, William Marshall.
Proved 18 May 1559.

THOMAS CRAWLEY of Wendon Lofts esquire, 22 May 1559. [2/47]

To be buried in Elmdon church in the chapel where my wife Mary lieth buried. To poor people at my burial and in other charges of my funerals £50 and at my month day other £50. Towards the reparation of Elmdon church 4 marks. To Frances my wife the household stuff which she brought me and one featherbed. To Katherine Cosyn my servant a cow and the household stuff that was her mother's. To Reynold Cosin, servant to my son-in-law [John] Bendisshe, 40s. and a cow. To John Cosyn, brother of the said [sic] Richard Reynold, 40s. and a cow. To Nicholas Webb, John Parker and Anthony Thorne, my servants, each 13s. 4d.; Thomas Awsten my servant 20s. To Thomas my son my household stuff not before bequeathed. The residue of my goods to be bestowed amongst poor folks and in other charitable deeds by my executors and supervisors.

I make my cousin Reynold Meade and Thomas Parker my servant my executors, and for their pains each £6 13s. 4d. I appoint as my supervisors Mathy Bradberi esquire, Thomas Meade, Robert Brickit and William Rutter gentlemen, and William Sheppard clerk, parson of Heydon, and for their pains each £5 except Sheppard £3 6s. 8d. My executors shall yield to my supervisors a true account. Whereas I have given to divers of my kinsfolk and friends divers obligations and bills of debt to the intent they shall receive such sums owing to me when they become due, my executors shall be aiding them to recover them, provided that, if they shall refuse so to do or disappoint any of my kinsfolk or friends or refuse to yield their account, Mathy Bradbury, Thomas Meade and William Rutter shall be my executors.

To Thomas Bull, Edmund Jaklyn junior, Edmund Pakman, John Stracie, Andrew Baker, John Pelham junior, Thomas Pelham junior, Thomas Goldsmith, John Bucke and Nicholas Thurgoode of Manuden an annuity of 13s. 4d. out of the manor of Manuden Hall, to the intent that they and their heirs shall yearly for ever distribute the 13s. 4d. among the poor of Manuden in the church by the discretion of the curate and churchwardens and the farmer or owner of the manor.

To Thomas my son and his heirs male the manor and other my lands in Manuden, Farnham, Ugley and Stansted Mountfitchet, and for default of such issue to remain to Thomas Meade of the Middle Temple gentleman, and successively to the heirs male of Thomas Meade my godson, son of Richard Meade, and of my daughters Joan Meade, Margery Bendishe, Philippa Pyne, and Joan Goldwell. To Thomas my son my manor of Chawreth Hall and my lands in Chawreth, Chickney, Broxted and Thaxted and to his heirs male, and for default to remain to the heirs male of my daughters. To Thomas my manor of Old Hall [in Corringham] and my lands in Corringham, Fobbing, Vange, and East and West Tilbury and to his heirs male with like remainder. To Thomas Peverells

Wood alias the Rose Wood, late part of the manor called the Rose, and a tenement called Brewsters and my other lands in Wimbish, Debden and Thunderley, and to his heirs male with like remainder; provided that, if Edmund Mordaunte of Thunderley esquire pay him £180 within 6 weeks after Thomas is 21, Edmund shall have them.

To William Shepparde clerk, parson of Heydon, Anthony Toppan clerk, vicar of Elmdon, Geoffrey Sewster, gentleman, Henry Trigge, Thomas Trigge, Thomas Newman, Thomas Kinge, William Perin, Robert Serle, John Fromonte, Thomas Fromonte, Walter Fromonte, and Thomas son of John Searle an annuity of £14 out of the parsonage of Elmdon, to the intent that they and their survivors and their heirs for ever shall bestow the £14 on an honest, convenient and meet school-master being a priest to be chosen by the patron of the vicarage of Elmdon, the vicar of Elmdon, the parson of Heydon, the vicar of Chrishall and the parson of [Wendon] Lofts, or three of them, to teach a grammar school within Elmdon, within which school I will there shall be taught freely without further reward such children and scholars as shall repair or be sent thither of the inhabitants of Elmdon, Chrishall, Strethall, Wendon Lofts, Heydon, Over [Great] Chishall, Nether [Little] Chishall, Arkesden, Barley, Barkway [both Herts.], Manuden, Langley and Clavering; and for the better order such orders as shall be prescribed by the said William Sheppard, Anthony Toppan, Matthew Bradberie, Thomas Meade, Robert Briket, William Rutter and Geoffrey Sewster, or four of them, shall be for ever observed by the schoolmaster and scholars.

To Thomas my son the said parsonage and other my lands in Elmdon, and to his heirs male with like remainder. The said Bradbury, Meade, Brickett and Rutter shall take the rents and profits of the said manors and lands, except the annuities, until Thomas my son is 21 and shall pay out of the same to every of the next heirs male of my daughters then living £40, and shall yield a true account to him at 21; but if he die without issue before 21 they shall bestow the rents and profits in alms and other charitable works for the health of my soul.

Witnesses: Thomas Meade, Robert Bryckett, William Rutter, gentle-men, Thomas Coldam, John Parker, William Parker, Nicholas Welles, Anthony Thoppan, and Richard Conwaye clerk.

Proved 17 October 1559.

EDMUND DANYELL of Messing esquire, 20 December 1568. [14/22]

To be buried without any pomp in the parish where I die. To the poor of the same in meat, drink or money 20s. if it be not at Messing, but if at Messing a further 20s. There shall be sent about the time of my burial to the parishes hereafter named, because I would not have them resort to my burial, to be distributed among the poor householders by the discretion of some honest men of the same, to Inworth 5s., Kelvedon 5s., Feering 3s. 4d., Coggeshall 10s., Easthorpe 3s. 4d., Marks Tey 2s., Cop-ford 2s., Great Birch 3s. 4d., and Layer Marney 4s., i.e. 2s. to the house-holders and 2s. to the bedemen there, and to the prisoners in Colchester Castle in meat, drink or money 3s. 4d. I give yearly during the nonage of my son John, or if he die before full age to the poor men's box of Messing for the discharging of the householders at my house at Messing, 10s.

As for the ceilings in my house at Messing with the glass, brewing and other vessels, the horsemill and such like, I will they shall remain as heirlooms with the house. As for the bedsteads and all other the furnitures in the Great Chamber, the New Chamber and the Old Parlour, I give them to John at 21. As for my household stuff (except such as is otherwise bequeathed), my wife Alice shall have it during the nonage of John and at 21 deliver to him the said heirlooms and half of the other household stuff, and she to have the other half for life and after her death to John. If she die before he is 21, my son-in-law Reynold Hiegate and my cousin Robert Hall gentlemen shall see to the safe custody of the same until he is 21. If he die before 21 without issue male and my wife then living, the third part of the household stuff to her and the other two parts (or all three parts if she be then dead) to the rest of my children to be equally divided. If John have a wife, one-third to her, another third to my wife, with the part assigned to her, and if she be then dead to the rest of my children and their children. As for the waste of the household stuff which shall be occupied by her or Hiegate or Hall, I remit the amendment and recompense thereof to my executors' discretion; and as long as she have the custody she shall be bound to Hiegate and Hall for the redelivery, and when they have the custody they shall be bound to my cousin John Tamworthe and my nephew Thomas Terye for the redelivery.

Concerning my plate (if need so require, otherwise not), the most part or almost all (except some portion meet for John to have for his house according to my executors' discretion and such parcels as I shall hereafter bequeath) should be sold by them. As for the portion of plate assigned by them to John, it shall be in the custody of my wife if she live, and after her death in that of Hiegate and Hall during his nonage, with like bond and the plate delivered to him at 21; and if he die as heretofore said for the household stuff. Concerning my jewels (except as before) my wife to have them for life and then to such of her children had by me and to her sister Jane Denham as my wife shall appoint. As concerning my apparel (except as before) it shall be distributed where and upon whom my executors shall think meet. Concerning my cattle, corn and necessaries for husbandry (except all the stock at Knipesho in Mayland which shall be made up and maintained to the number of 20 kine, 1 bull and 10 score ewes to remain there or to be delivered to John at 21), my wife shall have the occupying of as much as she will so long as she will keep house either at Messing Hall or at the house of my late brother John Danyell in Chapel alias Pontisbright called Brome House, and she to be bound as for household stuff to make it good again; and when she will not keep house the cattle, corn and necessaries shall be sold.

Touching my lands the Queen's Majesty shall have in full recompense of her third part due out of my lands holden of her for John's wardship during his nonage the rents (except the farm rents of the demesnes due to my two manors of Messing and Herdborough, my tenement called

Turnors alias Smythes in the tenure of John Haywarde, my tenement called Poignontes with Lukes land, the lands late Russells now in the occupation of John Mothe, and my tenement called Mulchaines in that of Edward Underwoode); and if these rents will not amount to her Grace's full third she shall have as much of the profits of lands called Cortelands in that of Thomas Coberton, of my tenement called Tyled House in that of Clement Furton, and of my house called the Vyne with the two houses under one roof and the smith's forge, all in Messing Street, and of my cottage called Lottes House, as will serve to make up the same.

My wife shall have during her life in recompense for her dower the demesnes out of my manor of Birch with the lands in the occupation of Thomas Russell with the rents of assize as well called Birch rents as Newardes rents due to the manor called Birch Hall with the Castle, my lands called Birch Heath (except the sale of Birch Wood) late in the occupation of Robert Wade, my garden plot in that of Nicholas Ingram, my tenement called Wades with the lands of Dolmesey late in that of William Barley, my lands called Goters Highfield Wood (except the sale of Eightacre Wood) late in that of William Burton and Hugh Stree, and my lands called Sleys in that of John Turner, also my lands in Stoke by Nayland [Suffolk] in that of John Bennett. As for the demesnes of my manors of Messing and Herdborough with the rest of my rents and lands not heretofore willed, my executors shall receive the profits (except wood sales) during John's nonage for the performance of my will and the woods (except Great Podde Wood and Conywere Wood), to be preserved until his full age so that he may have the profits at his entry, but those of the two woods now sold to Reynolde to go to the performance of my will. [A few further clauses concerning rents and profits, but no additional place or personal names.]

Whereas divers [persons] occupy my manors, lands and cattle for sundry rents, some having leases and some no leases, if they use themselves still as honest and good farmers they shall enjoy their occupation for the same rents until John is 23 and afterwards to have the preferment thereof, and the leases shall not be scanned so straitly against them to the uttermost advantage that may be taken because they put me in trust with the devising of their indentures, seeking no further counsel therein. My executors shall keep hospitality at my house at Messing for a quarter of a year after my death for as many of my household as will tarry and there to have meat, drink and wages and provide them masters in the meantime. To every of my servants one quarter's wages above wages, livery or other duties due to him or her; to Katherine Paine my servant 10s.

To Elizabeth my daughter towards the preferment of her marriage 100 marks and then towards her apparel 50 marks and all other charges 50 marks more, also yearly towards her finding during John's nonage if she continue unmarried 66s. 8d. To my daughter Grace Shelton a pair of sheets of three breadths marked with the letter G and £10. To my daughter Mary Hiegate one of my new bowls of silver white and £5. To my wife £20, all sums due to me at my death for my fee of the Clerkship of the Prince's Council Chamber at Westminster, a beer cup parcel gilt, having a rose at the top of the cover, a standing goblet plain silver gilt, a beer cruse gilt pounced with a trail of leaves having a knop like a standing cup on the top of the cover, 3 salts of silver white graven which were new made, a low standing goblet plain of silver gilt, 6 spoons of silver white plain of the greatest of them that are daily occupied, and 2 spoons of silver white with flat knops gilt having letters graven on them. Because I have no other house meet for her to dwell in, she shall occupy for life if she continue unmarried the whole row of chambers or other houses at the lower end of the court on both sides of the gate at my house of Messing Hall. To Elizabeth my daughter a salt of silver parcel gilt bought of John Gate in recompense for another little salt given to her by my uncle George Danyell, one of my new bowls of silver white, and £5.

To my godchildren Edmund Teye 10s., Rogers 5s., Edmund Bowyer 3s. 4d., Constance Bushe 2s., John Stoverd 2s., Daniel Hiegate 15s., and Daniel Shelton 15s. The residue of my goods shall be equally parted among my children.

I ordain my executors my wife, Reynold Hiegate and Robert Hall, and to Reynold and Robert for their pains £10, desiring my cousin John Tamworthe to be supervisor, and for his pains £10. [No witnesses.]

Proved 19 May 1571 by Alice, to whom administration granted, reservation to Reynold and Robert.

ROBERT DARCY of St Osyth esquire, 3 September 1568. [For Lady Darcy and Lord Darcy, see pp. 6-8.]   [12/21]

To my lord and brother a basin and ewer parcel gilt. To his two elder sons two standing gilt pots. To my sister [Constance] Pirton two beds, with my part of the hangings. To my brother [in-law Edmund] Pirton my brooch with a diamond. To my sister Thomasine a silver drinking pot with ribs. To my nephew Pirton a dozen silver trenchers. To Thomas Tey a black guarded cloak with velvet and with a cape lying in my lord's chest at London and my white leather hose lying in my press St Osyth. To my brother [in-law Edmund] Pirton a plain cloak with a cape lined throughout with unshorn velvet and a red pane of carnation rose trimmed fair with lace and never worn, being in my press at St Osyth, and a black Dutch cloak trimmed with lace. To my servant Valey all my cast apparel with my doublets and jerkins and 20s. I ordain my brother Edmund Pirton and Constance his wife, my sister, my executors and the Lord Darcy, my brother, supervisor. Witnesses : George Knightley, Robert Cotton.

Proved 22 November 1569.

THOMAS DARCYE of Tolleshunt D'Arcy esquire, 1 September 1586.
                                                                        [30/63]

To be buried in the chancel of Tolleshunt church in the usual place where my ancestors have been buried, with a convenient remembrance such as my executors shall think meet. To a learned preacher for a sermon at my funerals 10s. To the poor of Tolleshunt D'Arcy 40s.

To John my son my tenement called Brigges in Tolleshunt D'Arcy with the lands in the occupation of Nicholas Stanton gentleman, Pannelles Farm in Tolleshunt in that of Robert Pannell, my copyhold lands in Tollesbury in that of Sibley Stare widow holden of the Queen's Majesty's manor of Tollesbury and her Highness' rectory or parsonage of Tollesbury. To Esdras my son my lands in Tollesbury and Tolleshunt D'Arcy in that of Thomas Marche. My executrix during the minority of John and Esdras shall take the revenues and profits of the said lands for their maintenance and virtuous bringing up with the good advice of my supervisors, and the rest of the profits shall be paid to them at 21.

To Margaret my wife for life land called Gerandes containing 20 acres of my own tenure, abutting on my Hearnesewes Wood, part of my manor and farm called Skynners Wick, and the said wood, with the profits of the fowls breeding there, provided that she not do any wilful waste of the wood to the hindrance of breeding of any of the fowls of heronsews and shovelers that breed there; also my manor or farm called Skynners Wick in Tolleshunt D'Arcy for 4 years, paying Thomas and Camilla his wife £70 yearly. To Thomas the residue of my manors, lands and tenements. To Esdras my chain of gold at 21, but if Thomas will enter into bond to my executrix to pay him at 21 so much money for the chain as the goldsmith will value it then it shall be delivered to Thomas presently. To Margaret my daughter £500 at marriage or 25. To Anne, Bridget and Dorothy Darcy, my daughters, each £400 at marriage or 25, provided that, if any marry before 25 without the assent of my executrix or at the least with [sic] the assent of one of my supervisors, she shall lose £100 of her portion and the money forfeited shall be equally divided among the others. My wife shall pay each daughter yearly £13 6s. 8d. until marriage or 25. To my wife for life my plate, bedsteads, brass and pewter, my principal standings, cupboards, livery cupboards, tables, forms and trestles, which shall be put into inventory indented between her and Thomas; and after her decease to Thomas, on condition that she shall enter into bond to him not wilfully to pull down any of the wainscot, ceilings or glass in my manor house or dwelling called Tolleshunt D'Arcy Hall. To my servingmen of my daily household 20s. apiece, and my husbandmen, servants and maidservants 10s. apiece.

I ordain my wife my executrix, and I give her the residue of my goods. I ordain my supervisors my trusty and well-beloved brethren Edward Sulyard and Anthony Maxey esquires, desiring them to be assisting her with their counsel. Whereas John Fylde, my Lord Dacre's farmer, did mortgage to me lands in West Mersea for £168, which he did not pay at the time limited, whereby they are now mine, yet if he pay my wife £168 within half a year after my decease I will the same lands to him, but if not, to my wife to sell the same. To my wife my copyhold lands lying in the Hall grounds holden of the manor of Bowersers Hall [Bouchiers Hall in Tollesbury], for life.

Witnesses: Edward Sulyard, Anthony Maxey, Richard Wiseman, and William Tyterell.

Proved 17 November 1586.

THOMAS DARCYE of Tolleshunt D'Arcy esquire, 14 November 1593.
[38/75]

To be buried in the usual place of my ancestors in Tolleshunt D'Arcy church. To the poor of Tolleshunt 53s. 4d. To [Camilla] my well-beloved wife my household goods for life, with remainder to my daughters to be equally divided; if she die before they are 21, then Mr Thomas Bening-field, my brother-in-law, shall have their bringing up and the use of their portions aforegiven, and he to enter into bonds to Arthur Harris esquire for the payment of their portions at 21. To my wife my manor house called Tolleshunt D'Arcy Hall with the lands belonging and all other my lands, with remainder to be equally divided among my daughters. The residue to my wife, whom I ordain my sole executrix. Witnesses : C. Atkinson, doctor of physic, Henry Maxey, Eustace Darcie, Henry Eustace, John Bushe.
Proved 16 November 1594.

HENRY DENNY of Waltham Holy Cross esquire, 22 March 1574.
[19/18]

To be buried in Waltham church. My goods to be valued by such four persons as my executors shall think meet, and I give two parts thereof towards the payment of my debts and the use of my younger children, Edmund, Henry, Elizabeth, Katherine, Anne and Dorothy equally, and the third part to my beloved wife Elizabeth. Two parts of all my lands and tenements in the counties of Essex and Hertford to my executors for 14 years after the date of my will towards the payments of my debts and the advancement of my younger children in marriage; the remainder of the yearly profits shall be equally divided among them. I ordain the right honourable and my very good friends Arthur Lord Gray of Wilton, Francis Walsingham esquire, one of the Queen's Majesty's Secretaries and of her Highness' Privy Council, my well-beloved brother Edward Denny, my well-beloved brother-in-law William Cooke esquire, and my very loving wife to be executors. I desire the right honourable Sir Walter Mildmay knight, one of the Queen's Majesty's Privy Council, to be overseer. Witnesses : Francis Cooke, Douglas Dyve, Robert Hall, John Vavasor, Thomas Blenerhassett, Thomas Smithe, Richard Johns, John Cox.
Proved 5 July 1576.

EDWARD DEREHAWGHE of Markshall esquire, 20 May 1598. [42/48]

My son William to pay Margaret my wife an annuity of £40 according to indentures betwixt me and John Holmesteede, wherein I and William stand bound for saving Holmsteede harmless of the payment. She shall have for life the profit of my messuage called Hell House in Markshall and Feering with the lands, keeping the new house in good reparations, and so much of the lands in Gedgrave [co.?] called Highams, parcel of the manor of Gedgrave, as shall amount to the value of £6 13s. 4d.;

which two tenements I bequeath to her in satisfaction of my bond to Mr Lightfoote, my wife's brother, for the leaving her lands to the value of £20 a year for life or goods to that of £400; with remainder to William. To him also my stock of cattle at Gedgrave, Markshall or elsewhere, and all my plate, viz. a basin and ewer of silver parcel gilt, 4 silver tankards of silver all gilt, 4 silver bowls all gilt, 4 silver bowls ungilt, 4 silver hooped tuns ungilt, 1 silver chased bowl ungilt, 1 dozen silver spoons all gilt, 1 dozen silver spoons ungilt, my household stuff in Markshall or in my own lodging chamber at Gedgrave, and my corn and hay (my wife's expenses in corn and hay for one quarter after my decease excepted). My son William and no other shall take administration of my goods for his own use, and I ordain him my sole executor. Witnesses : Robert Plaile and John Grene.

Proved 29 May 1598.

EDWARD ELRINGTON of Theydon Bois esquire, 25 February 1578. [For Rowland Elrington, see p. 192.] [22/11]

To Dorothy my well-beloved wife the lease of my house and garden in St Katherine Coleman in London with the household stuff there and in my house at Theydon Bois, her jewels and apparel to her belonging, and my plate, for life, and my cattle at Theydon Bois.

Whereas the Queen's Majesty under the seal of her Duchy of Lancaster by indenture dated 22 March 1571 demised to me the manor of Barwicke in High Easter and other lands, to begin after the expiration of a former lease to Thomas Wiseman esquire, my executors during 20 years after the beginning of my lease shall pay to my four children £60 yearly for their good education and bringing up in learning, i.e. to Francis, William and Thomas and Jane £15 each, the residue of the yearly profits above the £60 to be paid to my loving brethren and sisters Christopher Elrington, Edward Elrington, Beatrice Whitebreade and Judith Elrington to be divided equally; and if they decease during the 20 years then his or her part shall be paid to my three younger sons, Francis, William and Thomas. To them the residue of my lease of the manor of Barwicke, and if every of them die then the residue to my eldest son Edward. The household stuff in Widdington Hall to be sold after my decease and the money equally divided and paid to my younger children (my daughter excepted) at 21. To every one of my brethren a ring of gold worth 40s. having these words graven on them, 'Dominus vidit', and to every one of my sisters a ring of gold worth 30s. with these words 'The Lord doth see'. To every one of my household servants to whom I give both livery and wages, 40s. besides such wages.

Whereas I am seised of my capital and mansion house called Widdington Hall and lands belonging and a meadow between the church and the house called Stockwell (containing 2 acres), a close of pasture called Layland (20 acres), an adjoining close called Godrales (3 acres), Widdington Park (80 acres), an adjoining meadow called Park Mead (6 acres), and the demesne lands of the manor in the tenure of John Cockett, viz. arable (173½ acres) and meadow and pasture (23 acres), and quitrents and services of the copyholders and freeholders, and Leylingioke Wood (20 acres), all in Widdington, and being a full third part in value and more of my lands, I give them to Edward, with successive remainders in default of issue to Francis, William, Thomas and Jane, to Rowland Elrington my brother, the said Christopher and my brother Edward, to Richard Cuttes esquire and Mary his wife being my sister, and their heirs male, and to the heirs of Edward Elrington esquire, my father, deceased.

Whereas I am seised of a farm called Vesis in Widdington in the tenure of Robert Howland and Dane Mead in that of [blank] at a yearly rent of £34 8s. 9d. and 5 quarters of wheat, a farm called Cambrigges in Widdington in that of Nicholas Lacie at £11, a mead in that of Mistress Howland lying beside Newport at 26s. 8d., Widdington windmill now in lease at 53s. 4d., a limekiln in Widdington in lease at 30s., a house and two pightles in that of widow Hawkins at 16s. 8d., and 6½ acres of arable in that of William Toller for which I have no rent, and the advowson of Widdington church, I give them for 14 years after my decease, viz. my executors shall for 4 years pay to Francis, William, Thomas and Jane the profits and revenues to the extent of £10 a year for their finding and good education and to Jane out of such profits £500 at marriage or 20, and the residue at the end of the 14 years shall be equally divided among all my children except Jane, and, if she decease before, to Rowland [etc. as before].

Whereas I conveyed to Thomas Averie and Richard Cuttes esquires my manor of Shortgrave Hall in Newport and my lands in Newport belonging, my parsonage or rectory of Theydon Bois with the lands belonging, my capital mansion house called Birch Hall in Theydon Bois, and other my lands in Theydon Bois or Loughton, to the use of myself and Dorothy my wife, with successive remainders in default of issue to Rowland and to Christopher, so that it shall be lawful to me by will to alter the estates, I declare that if my wife decease within 14 years after my decease the manor, rectory and lands shall be to the use of my executors for the performance of my will and thereafter to the uses declared in the conveyance. To John Davye, my old servant, my house and 5 acres which Robert Patche occupieth in Theydon Garnon for life without paying any rent.

I constitute my loving brother-in-law Thomas Sadler esquire and my very good brother Rowland my executors, desiring my wife and them to have especial care to the bringing up of my children in the fear of God and good learning, and to each £10. I make Sir Ralph Sadler knight my father-in-law overseer, and to him as a remembrance my crystal cup.

Witnesses : Henry Billengsley, William Cooche, Humfrey Broke notary, and Richard Rogers, servant to Humfrey Broke.

Proved 4 February 1579.

WILLIAM FITCHE of Little Canfield esquire, 13 October 1577. [22/2]

My body to be enclosed in a coffin and decently buried in the chancel of Little Canfield church next to the place where Elizabeth my wife was buried, and there be prepared by my executors a convenient and fair marble stone engraved with my arms and the pictures of myself, my wife and children and with such superscriptions as shall seem best to my executors, and the stone to be laid over my corpse for a perpetual remembrance as well of the day of my death as of the names of my wife and children. To everyone that shall bear me to church to be buried 2s. To everyone of my godchildren 2s. To the poor people coming to my burial £4 in meat, drink and money. To a good and learned preacher provided to make a sermon at the time of my funeral 10s. To the poor inhabitors of Thaxted 13s. 4d., Great Dunmow 13s. 4d., King's Hatfield [Broad Oak] 13s. 4d. and Lindsell 6s. 8d.

To Thomas Walker my old servant the reversion of the lease of the tenement called Tanners in the occupation of one Glascock belonging to the manor of Garnettes and Markes [in High Easter], which lease I have signed and delivered to him, paying the rent in the lease. To every of my servants besides their wages one quarter's wages. To Anne my well-beloved wife and to each of my children a featherbed, my wife to make the first choice and next to her Thomas my eldest son, next William my second son, and then [no name] my third son. To the parson of Little Canfield for the tithes negligently forgotten 3s. 4d.

Whereas I now hold the manor of Little Canfield Hall wherein I dwell for term of my life and 6 years after my decease, and whereas I hold for life and 1 year after a messuage and lands called Hodinges in Little Canfield, I bequeath the terms of 6 and 1 years to my executors to receive the commodities and rent of the manor towards performing my will, with remainder after the expiration to the heirs of Eleanor my daughter, late the wife of Rooke Grene esquire, according to the conveyance. To the heirs of Francis Mannocke esquire and of my daughter Mary his late wife my manor and lands in Toppesfield called Camoyes which I hold for life. To my wife my manor of Lindsell for life, with remainder to Thomas according to covenants made before marriage between me and my wife. To Thomas the reversions of my manors and lands called Garnettes and Markes. To my executors the yearly rents and profits of my two parsonages, viz. Lindsell Parsonage and Stebbing Parsonage alias Friers Hall in Stebbing, to go for the paying of my debts and the performance of my will, and then to Thomas. To William Great Canfield Park on condition that he pay yearly to Francis my younger son during my wife's life an annuity of £20 and such money as shall come of the park over £40 until my debts and legacies be paid, then the whole profits less the annuity, and after her decease to hold the park, and for default of issue to Francis. To my wife for life my manor of Abins [Albyns] and the lands, tenements, woods and free warrens belonging in Stapleford Abbots and Navestock, according to the assurance made by George Wiseman gentleman and Martha his wife to my wife and me, and after her decease to remain to Francis and for default of issue to William.

My wife shall have the education, nurturing and bringing up of William and Francis and shall take the yearly rents and profits of their lands and annuities until they are 21, and during their nonage she make a true account to them before my overseers, and to be allowed for her charges towards their apparel, meat, drink and schooling.

My muniments and evidences, after such time as my office shall be found before the Queen's Majesty's Escheator of the county of Essex, shall be delivered to the custody of my overseers. I appoint my uncle Thomas Wiseman and my brother George Wiseman overseers, and for their pains 40s. The residue to my wife, whom I make sole executrix, most earnestly charging her to be careful and diligent with an honest motherly care for the bringing up and well educating of our children, and to the intent that she should be so the better able to assist them I have dealt the more liberally towards herself in this my will. I ordain Thomas to be sole executor, and, if he refuse, William and Francis.

Witnesses : Thomas Walker the writer and John Howland.

Proved 12 January 1579.

KATHERINE FORDE of Great Horkesley, widow of John Forde esquire, 19 April 1570. [For John Foorde, see p. 195.] [13/14]

To be buried in the chancel of Great Horkesley church as near the sepulture of my late husband as may be. To the parson for my tithes and oblations not paid 3s. 4d. To the poor people of Stoke-near-Nayland [Suffolk] 13s. 4d., Polstead [Suffolk] 5s., and Frating 6s. 8d. The legacies of my late husband's will to be paid by my executor.

To John my son a piece of gold of the value of more than 20s., 4 silver spoons, a tablecloth of diaper, a corselet with a pike, a brass pot, a flat posnet, 4 platters, a little kettle, 4 dishes, 2 saucers, and 2 pottingers of pewter hanging in the parlour, with hangings in the hall, a table with leaves in the hall, a form in the parlour by the end of the press, a cushion of tapestry, a joined quiver and case for bows, a great bow with 3 arrows in the hall, a great spit of the biggest sort, and my halberd.

Whereas my son-in-law Thomas Bendysshe gentleman did owe me £20 by bond, I have delivered to him the bond on condition that he pay to Barbara Bendysshe his daughter £10 at marriage. To my daughter Eleanor the wife of Thomas Bendisshe my bracelet of gold, a goblet of silver parcel gilt to give to what child of hers she will, 6 silver spoons of the best sort, my French hood, a fine royal, a pair of pillows of fustian, my virginals with the joined table whereon they stand, a brass pot, a brass pan, a copper kettle, a little kettle of brass, and such pieces of pewter as I have already delivered to her.

To Margery my daughter, wife of Richard Smyth gentleman, my chain of gold, my silver salt, a joined chair with green cloth, a joined form, 3 curtains of green and red say, a great cauldron, a kettle being the least of the biggest sort, a skillet pan, a little kettle of brass, and pewter [as above], with a chamber vessel, a ship chest in the gallery, a cushion of tapestry, an almain rivet with a black bill, a little featherbed, a pillow of fustian, a flock bed, a long spit of the biggest sort, a joined cupboard in the hall, my greatest firefork, my biggest cobiron, a dripping pan of the lesser sort, a pair of pothooks, 2 candlesticks, a chafing dish, a wedge of iron, a half-hundredweight of lead with a ring of iron fixed in the same, and a pitch with a ladle of iron.

To William Lyster gentleman and Katherine his wife my lands and tenements in Polstead, Boxford and Assington (Suffolk), and in default of issue with successive remainders to Eleanor and to Margery, in consideration whereof William and Katherine shall within two years after my decease pay at the house wherein Nicholas Gryme dwelleth called Bakers in Polstead to Anne my daughter, wife of John Parker gentleman, £20 over and besides the £20 which William hath already paid to Anne. To Katherine my best coverlet, a mazer cup lipped with silver, a great brass pot, a little brass pot, a brass pan being the least of my two, my greatest wort kettle, my lead that hangeth in the backhouse, 2 less kettles of brass, a posnet, a skillet pan with a steal, my best chafing dish, a skummer, 3 candlesticks of the best sort, and pewter [as above], a chamber pot of pewter, a flat chest of fir, a bow with a sheaf of arrows, a counter table in the parlour with the almain rivet in the same, a table with leaves and a joined form in the parlour, a cupboard in the buttery, my hangings in the chamber wherein I lie, a pair of mustard querns of the biggest sort, a pair of malt querns, my best hand gown of the best sort, 2 cushions of tapestry, a little featherbed with the new tick, a flockbed, a pair of fustian pillows, a poleaxe, a brazen mortar with the pestle, a round table, my side saddle with the hounce, and my apparel. To Margery a yearly rent of £5 out of my lands in Great Horkesley, in consideration whereof Richard and Margery shall convey to John my son a messuage with lands called Wardes in Frating late in the occupation of Robert Hall and now of his wife. To Thomas and Eleanor Bendysshe my lands in Great Horkesley on condition that he shall pay to Margery £60 and to John £10. To my son-in-law Richard Smythe and Margery my white mare, my thill horse, and 3 milch kine. To William and Katherine Lyster my young dun gelding, my grey nag and my youngest colt now at Frating.

The residue of my goods to William and Katherine. I ordain Richard Smythe and William Lyster gentlemen my executors.

Witnesses : John Walforde clerk, William Foxe yeoman, John Fludde. Proved 2 May 1570.

HENRY FORTESCUE of Faulkbourne esquire, 30 September 1576.
[19/28]

To George my son my goods, corn and cattle in my house, and the manor and lands of Eyeworth (Beds.). To Francis my son and heir after the decease of Mary my wife all those goods which were my own before marriage and now in my mansion house or manor of Faulkbourne for life. To John Tyler my servant my new doublet, a shirt, and 20s.; Edward Bowzeye my doublet and hosen that I wear and 20s.; my servant William Browffe my best gown and 20s.; John Stockes my best cloak, a shirt, and 20s.; John Brooke 20s.; my cook John Wallyker 20s. and a shirt; Nicholas Barnarde a shirt and 10s.; Nicholas Rogers 40s.; Thomas Morfull my new canvas doublet, a shirt and 20s.; John Norres, Thomas Middleton my servant, and Edward Burles, each 20s.; John Sell my worst cloth gown and 40s.; George Wystock a shirt and 20s.; Mistress Frances, my wife's gentlewoman, my black coney skins to fur her a gown.

Forasmuch as my daughter Dorothy Nokes cannot enjoy quietly anything I should bequeath to her in certainty (being under covert baron and the yoke of matrimony, but that the same may be taken from her by her husband, of whom I have no good opinion), I request my wife to use her godly and good discretion to dispose her benevolence hereafter as well towards the relief and comfort of my daughter as to every of her children. The residue of my goods to my wife, whom I make my sole executrix. [No witnesses.]

Proved 27 October 1576.

THOMAS FRANCK of Hatfield Broad Oak esquire, 10 December 1573.
[25/5]

To be buried in the Jesus chapel in Hatfield church where my father lieth buried. To the poor inhabitants of Hatfield and Maldon £6 13s. 4d. on the day of my funerals or the morrow, to be thankful and give praise to God for the departing of my soul.

Whereas I made a lease, 1 February 1559, to Roger Warfilde, Henry Kinge and Edmund More of my manor or monastery of Beeleigh [in Maldon] and of other lands for the yearly rent of £13 6s. 8d. to commence immediately after my death until Thomas my son is 24 to the intent that the profits over and above the rent being of the value of £60 shall be employed to the performance of my will, the rent shall be paid to Mary my wife so that she shall bring my son up in learning or in some other trade of merchandise whereby another day he may be able the better to live, and the rents of the lands in Takeley which I late bought of Mr Wymond Carye shall in like manner be employed. Whereas I made a feoffment, 21 December 1557, of seven houses in St Martin-le-Orgar and St Clement in Candlewick Street in London to Sir Thomas Barrington knight of Hatfield and also to Edward Bugges and others enrolled in the Hustings [Court] in London to the use of myself and my wife for our lives and after to the performance of my will; the same shall be to the use of Richard my eldest son, with successive remainders in default of male issue to Arthur my third son and Robert my youngest son. Whereas I and my wife have executed an estate of all those houses in Bucklersbury in London for our lives and after to Robert, enrolled in the Guildhall of London, it shall so remain. Whereas of late I purchased of Robert Brockis and his wife a house in Hatfield called Hawettes, I bequeath it to Sir William Boreman, my chaplain, for life (if he survive me and my wife) if he keep himself without any other master and repair to the church and serve God; also the farmer of Robert a Braintrees and Howses for the time being shall of the ground of the farm crop and carry to the house of William yearly 3 loads of wood to his use; and he that shall dwell in the farm where William Polley dwelleth called Thomas by the Wood shall pay yearly to William 53s. 4d.

To my wife for life my manor or manors of Ryse and Morses in Hatfield and [Little] Hallingbury and the lands, rents and services belonging, the farm, messuages and lands called Ives in Hatfield, the messuages and farms called Robert a Braintrees which I had by deed from Thomas my late father and let to old Treasour by him, Ongers and Thomas by the Wood, Mashburyes and Seabrightes, all in Hatfield; also my manor of Ballingtons in Hatfield with its appurtenances; and after her death to Richard, with successive remainders to his wife, to his eldest issue male and to his wife for life, to the eldest son of the said eldest issue male of Richard and the heirs male of the said eldest son, to the second son of Richard for life and his wife for life, to the eldest issue male of the second son for life, to his wife, to the heirs male of the eldest son, to the heirs male of Richard, to Arthur for life, to his wife for life, to his eldest issue male [etc., as for Richard], and to Robert for life, to his wife for life, and to his eldest issue male [etc., as for Arthur].

To Richard my lease of part of lands called Hopkyns that I have of Robert Lucken. All the lands and tenements following shall descend to Richard according to common law, viz. those late purchased of one Dennise; a tenement wherein Jerome Browne dwelleth; a tenement wherein Poole's widow dwelleth purchased of Brockhurst; a tenement and lands wherein John Polle dwelleth; a tenement and a mill in the tenure of Thomas Kinge; a tenement wherein widow Phillipson dwelleth; a tenement wherein Brith dwelleth purchased of Robinson; a tenement called the Yealde Hall purchased of Lord Rich and Mr Borne; a tenement and lands purchased of John Fordes; a tenement wherein Adkyn dwelleth; lands purchased of William Twysers gentleman; a tenement wherein John Brockis dwelleth purchased of Robert Broke and his wife, widow of William Hewet, after the decease of William Boreman my chaplain; also the overplus of the rent of the lodge called Thornecrofte and Bolstmore.

My wife shall have the custody of four parcels of plate sometime that of Richard Hawle, my grandfather, viz. a salt of silver and double gilt and fashioned in proportion to a man, a standing cup of silver and double gilt made and commonly called after the fashion of a serpentine, a basin and ewer of silver parcel gilt, and a standing cup of silver and gilt with a cover of silver gilt polished with the cardinal's hat and the wheat sheaf. After her death I give the salt to Richard and the basin and ewer to Arthur.

My executors shall pay Arthur the money from the rents of the lands I bought of Mr Wimond Carye and shall pay Robert the money from lands in Bucklersbury, appointed to them at 24. I give the standing cup polished with the cardinal's hat to Robert. All which parcels shall be kept by my sons as a monument of their ancestors. The residue of my goods to my wife towards the bringing up of my children and maintaining of my house; after her death the goods or the value shall be equally divided among my four sons. I ordain my well-beloved friends Mr William Borne and Mr Roger Warfild my executors, and Sir Thomas Smith's honour, Chief Secretary to the Queen's Majesty, Sir William Cordell knight, Master of the Rolls, and Richard Franck my overseers, and to each for their pains £6 13s. 4d.

[No witnesses.]

Proved 25 January 1582.

HENRY GOLDING of Little Birch esquire, 20 March 1576. [20/8]

To be buried in such parish church as it shall happen me to depart this present life. To the poor of the said parish 20s., and of Great Birch, Little Birch and Easthorpe 60s. to be equally divided. To my well-beloved wife Alice my household stuff, plate, jewels and ready money in my dwelling house in Little Birch, and my corn, cattle and goods in my house and on my lands in Little Birch, except my own apparel, on condition that she suffer the heirs of John Frelove to possess quietly the moiety of the manor of Hawstead (Suffolk) which I sold to him and did covenant to discharge him of jointures. Whereas there is owing to Mary Waldegrave by Nicholas Mynne £400 and by myself £160, my executors shall pay the same to my wife and my cousin William Aloff to the use of Mary and until then she be allowed £10 of every 100 towards her living. Whereas Robert Waldegrave standeth bound in £700 to me for the performance of certain covenants concerning Mary, I charge my wife, cousin Aloff and my executor to further the matter. To my wife for her dower for life my manor of Little Birch and my lands and tenements in Little and Great Birch, Copford, Stanway, and Layer-de-la-Haye in my occupation and that of Swaffelde, John Baron, widow Budgman, Henry Clerke, Collett the miller, and Clover, with remainder to my brother Arthur for life, and successive remainders to my nephew Henry Goldinge and his heirs male and to my brothers George and William and their heirs male. To Elizabeth Waldegrave, daughter of Mary, £100. To my nephew Thomas Beeke £20. To every of my brothers a ring worth 40s. and sisters and sisters-in-law a ring worth 26s. 8d. To my servants Thomas Litle, Robert Beereman, Richard and Henry my horsekeepers 40s. apiece, and every other servant 20s. above his quarter wages.

I leave to descend to my brother Arthur the moiety of my manors of Easthorpe, Great Birch, and a tenement in Great Birch which I bought of one Waynewright and his wife. To my executor to pay my debts and legacies the profits of my lease of Campes which I hold of the right honourable the Earl of Oxford for 10 years; the residue of the term, after such payments, to my brother George, with the residue of my other goods not before bequeathed, whom I make my only executor and also for aiding my wife. My apparel (except my hoses which I give to my servants Robert Beereman, Thomas Litle and Richard) to be equally divided between Arthur and George.

Witnesses: Nicholas Mynne, Thomas Aglionby, John Myners.
Proved 12 February 1577.

ALICE GOLDING of Bradwell-near-Coggeshall, widow of Henry Golding of Little Birch esquire, 26 May 1585. [31/19]

To be buried in the parish church where it shall please God to call me, at which burial I bequeath 40s. to the poor and to a learned preacher for a sermon 10s. To the poor of Little Birch and Great Birch 20s., Easthorpe 10s. and Bradwell [juxta-Coggeshall] 10s. To Robert

87

Crispe of Little Birch gentleman and Mary my daughter my household stuff in Birch Hall except my great brewing copper and the long green table in the parlour which I bequeath to Thomas Peryn of Gray's Inn (Middx.) gentleman. Whereas £50 is due to me by Robert for my horse, bullocks, beasts, sheep and swine and other £20 of which I have received £10, and whereas he hath laid out certain money for me, the residue I give to Hatton Crispe his son except 1½ years' rent for my manor of Little Birch now demised by me to him and £4 for a black gelding which he bought of me.

To Mary Peryn, daughter of Jane Peryn wife of Henry Peryn, my daughter, £700 at marriage or 21, my black chest bound with iron with all the things therein, 4 of my best featherbeds with my best hangings in the chief chamber of Little Birch, my best table and 12 joined stools and my best carpet to the table, my press for apparel, 2 of my best chairs, one of needlework and the other of green cloth, my little woman's chair, 2 of my best livery cupboards, 2 brass pots, 1 brass kettle, 1 brass posnet, my pewter marked M and P, 2 of the best bedsteadles with 2 of the best testers belonging with silk curtains of red and yellow, 1 skillitory, 1 mortar with a pestle, 2 long window cushions of the best, 2 spits, the new tester which is now a-making and a new cover for a chair which were embroidered by Mary Peryn and Mistress Stutvell, and my wearing linen which is meet for her own wearing (the rest of my wearing linen to my maidservant); my jewels (except my signet of gold), my virginals and 2 chests in my chamber where I lie, a window carpet and 7 cushions of needlework, my coffers, and my best pair of cobirons with the tongs and firepan; all at marriage or 21.

To William son and heir of Robert Springe of Icklingham (Suffolk) esquire and the son of Jane my daughter his wife deceased £50 for life, to be paid out of the profits of the lands in Little and Great Birch that I bought of Robert, which profits Anthony Maxey of Bradwell shall have until he hath received the £50 to be paid to Robert within 5 years after my decease. To my cousin Eustace Cloveyle esquire a signet of gold of 40s. with a death's head therein engraved and to my cousin's wife my best damask gown. To my cousin Anne Stutvell, wife of William Stutvell gentleman, a gown and a kirtle and £8 which she borrowed of me. To Anne Huddleston my cousin one of my wearing gowns and £5. To my cousin Anne Robertes a wearing gown and £5. To the wife of my cousin Edward Sulyard esquire a signet of gold of 40s. with a death's head. To my cousin Dorothy Maxey a ring of gold of 40s. with a death's head and my best velvet kirtle. To Henry, William, Dorothy and Bridget, sons and daughters of Anthony and Dorothy Maxey, each a ring of gold of 20s. with a death's head. To Robert Beareman my servant £10 and a feather-bed; Richard Wilkinson my servant 20s.; my maidservant 20s.; the household servants of Anthony Maxey 20s. to be divided equally.

If Mary Peryn, sister of Thomas, shall contract herself in marriage without the consent of Anthony, £200 of my legacy shall be thenceforth to the use of Thomas. To my executor and Mary Peryn his sister all the rest of my featherbeds to be equally divided between them. The residue of my goods to Thomas, whom I ordain my sole executor, and I appoint my trusty and well-beloved cousin Anthony my supervisor, and for his pains a colt of the price of £6 13s. 4d. My executor shall decently by the advice of my supervisor bestow on my burial with a convenient remembrance in the place where I shall be buried £30 and in the charge of my funerals shall bestow among others on Jane Turrell, my sister-in-law, as much black cloth as shall make her a gown.

Witnesses : Anthony Maxey, Robert Beareman and Ralph Anneys.

Proved 4 April 1587.

WILLIAM GOLDING of Belchamp St Paul esquire, 8 February, 1588. (Nuncupative.)   [32/16]

Calling for Elizabeth his wife, he said to her, 'Besse, I have nothing to give thee in consideration of the long time that thou hast been with me, but I would you should have all that I have, and I pray you pay my debts and have consideration of my daughters'; and then she answered, 'Sir, I will pay your debts if I sell all that I have to my smock'. And after, about 3 o'clock in the night following, he died at his house in Belchamp St Paul. Witnesses : William Maslevile, James Armond.

Proved 17 February 1588. Administration granted, 22 June 1591, to Mary Golding, daughter of the deceased.

ELIZABETH GONSON [of Great Baddow?] 22 December 1582.
                                                                          [26/14]

To my brothers Benjamin Gonson £10 and Anthony Gonson £20 and to my sisters Ursula Peterson £5, Bennet Gonson £20, Thomasine Gonson £20, and Avis Gonson £20. To my niece Ursula Peterson £13 6s. 8d. To my sister Fleminge a ring of gold set with a diamond and 4 rubies. To Benjamin for his first wife in remembrance a purse and a pin pillow of crimson velvet embroidered with gold and pearl. To Ursula Humfrye my goddaughter £5. To Margery Savedge in remembrance to make her a ring 10s. To Joan Kinge widow and Joan Dawson each a ring of gold. To my cousin Mary Huse my gorgonet of gold. To by sister Bennet my chain of gold. To my sister Avis a jewel of the said chain. To William Note to make him a ring 20s. To Mary Porter, Amy Cornishe and Grace Bickner each 2s. 6d. To William Bushe, William Spillman, William Baker, Lawrence Couche, John Smyth and Thomas Turner each 2s. 6d. To the poor of the parish £3. The residue of my portion due to me by my grandfather I leave to my executrix towards my funeral charges and in consideration of my sickness and my portion of my father, whatsoever it be, I leave to my three sisters that be unmarried, to be equally divided. I ordain my dear and well-beloved mother to be my executrix. Witnesses : Christopher Amplefurth and William Note.

Proved 27 March 1583.

BENJAMIN GONSON of Great Baddow esquire, 1 September 1594.
[44/42]

Whereas indentures of covenants dated 4 June 1590 between me and Lawrence Hussy doctor of law, declaring the use of the recovery afterwards had in Trinity term 1590 of the manor of Great Warley and of all other my lands in Essex, I bequeath my lands in manner following. To my loving wife Mary for life my manor of Great Warley with its appurtenances, the right of patronage of Great Warley church, and all messuages, dovehouses, lands and commons, courts and other hereditaments in Great Warley, Shenfield and Stifford to the manor belonging; the Spittle Lands in St Peter, Maldon; the capital messuage called Sabrightes in Great Baddow and lands belongings; [and a few other closes]. To her for life also sufficient housebote, hedgebote, ploughbote, cartbote and firebote out of the woods. After her decease, to remain to my heirs, and for default of such issue the fourth part of the manor, advowson and lands of Great Warley to my sister Ursula wife of Robert Peeterson for life, with successive remainders to her first-begotten son and his heirs male, to Ursula the younger, the daughter of my sister for life, to her first-begotten son and his heirs male, to the heirs of my sister, and to my other three sisters Anne wife of Giles Flemynge, Bennet wife of Thomas Wallenger and Thomasine wife of Edward Fenton and their heirs. Another fourth part to Anne for life, with remainders to Benjamin her son and then likewise, and to Ursula, Bennet and Thomasine. Another fourth part to Bennet for life, with remainders to Thomas son of Thomas Wallenger and Bennet his wife and then likewise, and to Ursula, Anne and Thomasine. The other fourth part to Thomasine for life, with remainders likewise, and to Ursula, Anne and Bennet. To Anne for life, after the decease of my wife and for default of my heirs, in consideration both of the goodwill I bear to her and her husband and in discharge of such debts as I owe him, my messuage called Sabrites and my lands in Maldon, with successive remainders to Benjamin her son and his heirs, to the heirs of Anne, and to my three sisters.

My houses in the city of London shall be found by my executors and the rents and profits and such money as shall arise on any sale thereof shall be employed by them towards the payments of my debts, funerals and legacies. To my wife for life my household stuff at Sabrightes (except the stuff and furniture in the Great Chamber, the New Lodging and the Blue and Bell Chambers, and the wainscot, ceilings, bedsteads, tables, forms, stools and brewing vessels, but the said furniture so excepted shall remain to Anne); the stock of cattle on the grounds belonging to Sabrightes; my plate and her jewels, and £100; the occupation for life of my grounds called Grapnells [in Heybridge or in Wallasea island] which I have on lease; and after her decease to my sister Wallenger. To Benjamin the second son of my sister £30. To my cousins Katherine and Mary Wallenger, my sister's two daughters, each £20. To Ursula daughter of my sister Peeterson £30. To my godson Benjamin son of Benjamin Gonson £20. To my uncle Huse's three daughters, Mary Skepper,

Katherine Jordan and Margaret Rowe, each 40s. To my cousins Edward Moone £20 and Anne Natmaker 40s.

To my servants Thomasine Elkin £10, Marmaduke Hungate £3 6s. 8d., William Peare £5, William Note £13 6s. 8d., Nicholas Philip £10, William Bushe £5, and Robert Jordayne 53s. 4d., John Graing if I do not make him a lease of the house whereon Bricke dwelt £5, Peter Hogg £5, George Mault 53s. 4d., Thomas Snowe 26s. 8d., George Linstead 26s. 8d., and Ralph Bawkocke 20s., and among my maidservants to be distributed at my wife's discretion £10. I forgive Henry Bullington his debt of £5. To the churchwardens of Great Baddow to be distributed to the poor 53s. 4d. and of St Dunstan-in-the-East [in London] 40s.

To Sir John Hawkins knight for a remembrance of my goodwill towards him my piece of gold of 50 ducats, and I desire him to be one of my overseers, together with my brothers-in-law Thomas Wallenger, Edward Fenton and Robert Peeterson. I constitute my wife, my uncle Lawrence Huse and my brother-in-law Giles Flemynge my executors.

Witnesses: John Rose, Daniel Peeterson, Henry Bullington, William Note.

Codicil, 25 May 1600. To Edward Stoughton £50 and Harberd Butcher £10; to his servants John Evered, John Glascocke, Henry Thayer and John Milborne £10 to be distributed at his executors' discretion. Witnesses: John Nowall, William Clapham.

Proved 6 June 1600.

ROBERT HALL of Waltham Holy Cross esquire, 4 July 1580.   [27/11]

Whereas by a demise by Ralph Stafferton, one of the Queen's Majesty's gentlemen pensioners, to me, 23 September 1579, I hold among other things in reversion three parcels of land in Rippleside called Halfeld in Barking (containing 30 acres), also two parcels of marsh ground at Highehill in Barking (9 acres), my cousin William Hall, eldest son of my brother Godderd, shall have all the issues and profits for such term as I am to have if he so long live, and if he die before the residue shall revert to my executrix. To my cousin Richard Hall, second son of Goddard Hall, the issues and profits of several parcels of marsh ground (15 acres) in East Marsh in Barking and Dagenham now by me letten to Thomas Pierson of Dagenham for such said term, and if he die before the residue to revert to Edward and William, sons of Richard. I give and release to my cousin Richard Campe of Nazeing all debts he oweth me; and to his eldest son Robert 4 kine. To my brother-in-law Thomas Pawthorne an annuity of 40s. out of my 6 acres of meadow in Edmondsey in Waltham. To my cousin Robert Meade an annuity of 40s. To Joan my maidservant £3 6s. 8d., and my 4 servants John Allen 40s., William Breadstreete 20s., Richard Penne £5 out of my farm at Rainham, and Anne Gylbodye 20s. The residue of my goods to my cousin Robert Hall, third son of Goddarde, which Robert I constitute my sole executor, and I give him my freehold lands in Waltham and

Nazeing. I nominate my brother Thomas to be overseer. Witness : John Vavasor.

Proved 8 November 1583. Sentence, 27 February 1584, confirming Will in case between Robert Hall gentleman, executor, and Goddard, Thomas senior and Thomas junior, brothers of, and Anne Price alias Hall, sister of the deceased.

JOHN HARBOTTELL of Bradfield esquire, 24 September 1575. [21/6]

To the reparations of the church were my body shall be laid 20s. To the poor people £40 [*sic*]. To Joan my wife for life the lease of my manor of Crowfield [in Coddenham, Suffolk] and Bocking [in Crowfield], with household and profits of courts, timber and woods excepted, and it shall be lawful for her to take for her own and her farmer's use sufficient housebote, hedgebote, firebote, cartbote and ploughbote on the premises, to be spent there and at Ipswich; to her my moveable goods, gold, silver, plate, horse, neat, corn and debts, except my bedsteads, forms, tables, cupboards, chests and hangings in my house or chambers in Ipswich in St Margaret's parish; also to her for life my houses there which I bought of William Rene, Richard Burde and Edmund Leche. To Joan Resbye my daughter after my wife's death, the lease of my houses in St Margaret, Ipswich, which I bought of William Renne, Richard Burde and Edmund Leche. To Elizabeth wife of Henry Wynffielde gentleman and daughter to Thomas Resbye gentleman, after my wife's death, my manors of Crowfield and Bocking, and for default of issue to Joan wife of Edward Grimeston gentleman, on condition that Elizabeth and Joan pay yearly 100 marks out of the manors to their mother, my daughter, Joan wife of Thomas Resbie gentleman, for life. To Elizabeth Wynfeilde and Joan Grimeston, daughters of Thomas Resbie, my lands called Mansers and Waylandes in Shimpling[thorne], Cockfield and Lawfield [Lawshall] (all Suffolk). To Elizabeth also my houses in Layham which I bought of John Puntt and my meadows in [East] Bergholt (Suffolk), and in default of issue to Joan. To Elizabeth my part of Flatford Mill in [East] Bergholt which I hold by copy [of court roll] of the Earl of Oxford. To Joan, after my wife's death, and Joan Resbie her mother, my houses in St Margaret, Ipswich. To Josias Brande, James Brande, Margaret Dawson, and Thomas Punte, my sister's son, each £5, Richard Punte his son £10 at 21, and every child of Thomas Punte £5 at 21. To Naomi Lovett, daughter of William Clerke deceased, £5, and his children each 40s. at 21. To Mary Springe £5 at 21. To John Puntt of Layham for life 40s. a year. To my servants 10s. apiece. The residue of my goods to my wife, who shall have the government of Thomas Resbye, my son-in-law, if the laws will so permit. I institute my wife my executrix, and John Clenche of Crowfield shall be my supervisor, and for his pains to be a special comfort to her 5 marks.

Witnesses : Edward Grimston, Henry Wingfielde, Nicholas Couven, John Archer.

Proved 1 February 1578.

ROGER [sometimes called Robert] HARLAKINDEN of Earls Colne esquire, 2 January 1603. [47/38]

To be decently buried in the high chancel of Earls Colne, and a convenient tomb to be made for me there in the wall at the right hand of the door into the chancel, on which I would have mention made of all my 'wives' [Elizabeth and Anne] and children. To the poor people of the parish £5, 40s. at my burial and the other £3 to be kept in stock and employed to the use of the most honest and needy poor people at the discretion of the minister, churchwardens and overseers with the consent of 4 or 6 of the chief householders. To the poor people of Warehorne and Kenardington (Kent) 40s. each parish.

To Robert Cobb my servant for life the house in his tenure next to Hall Meadow in Earls Colne, and to his wife Edith, if she overlive him, for 1 year, and he shall be acquitted of money he oweth me for the house. To Anne Cobb his daughter a croft at Coleford Hill in the occupation of John Warde her grandfather until she is 21, paying yearly the rent of 2s. To Thomas Andersonne my servant two tenements called Crose House and the Tilekill in his occupation for 40 years for the yearly rent of £5. To Robert Pigott my servant, as an increase of his wages so long as he shall be the servant to either of my two sons, Richard and Thomas, the tenement in his occupation in Holl Street and another late in that of Stephen Champney in the lower part of Holl Street, paying only the rent of 2s. apiece, provided that, if he be unwilling to serve either or if both be unwilling to have him, he shall have the first tenement for 3 years only for the said rent, and his wife shall have the other for 5 years for herself and Thomas her son. To my other servants both male and female that have dwelt with me for 2 years 20s. apiece above their wages, and to my other servants 10s. apiece. To old William Mannors 20s. and Katherine wife of Randall Greene 40s. To my brother John Harlakinden's 5 daughters £10 apiece. To William Harlakinden my brother one of my best ambling nags and a ring of gold price £3 or £3 to make him a ring in remembrance of me. He shall have for life the use of the chamber and study that now he hath and his diet and lodging in my dwellinghouse freely as often as he shall take it for himself, his manservant and 2 geldings for life. To 5 godly preachers £10 to be distributed by my brother William within 2 years after my decease. To my son-in-law Mr Clement Stonard, Mabel his wife, and Francis their son £3 apiece to buy them a ring of gold; also to my said daughter my 3 bowls of silver which were mine before my last marriage.

Whereas I have heretofore promised to pay my son Stonard £50 after my decease in consideration of certain lands which he should have had of me, I declare that I have already paid him £20 thereof. To my nephew George Harlakinden of [Little?] Yeldham £3 to make him a ring of gold.

To Anne my loving wife such jewels as were hers before I married her and one other jewel which I gave her when I was a suitor to her and the new gold chain which she hath and I also gave her, with other pearls or jewels which then or since I have given her; 5 of my best kine

93

and my best coach with 2 of my coach horses at her election and the furniture belonging to them, and 5 quarters of wheat, 5 quarters of barley malt and 5 quarters of oats, all sweet and good, for her provision, for life; and 2 of my best featherbeds at her election. To her the lease of Hadham [Herts.] which I had with her; also a moiety of the lease of the house at Westminster which I had with her in marriage; the remainder thereof to my executors towards the performance of my will. To her a wainscot chest in the little chamber with the linen there, on condition that she ratify a lease heretofore made by me and her to William my brother and shall permit my executors quietly to have my other goods not before bequeathed to her. I heartily request her to be good to my children and to give my son's son reasonable time for the payment of money or goods by bond or otherwise. The residue of my goods to Richard and Thomas my sons towards the performance of my will. To my executors the lease of part of Earls Colne Park as is divided from the new way that leadeth from Colne towards Marshall Green on the east side of the way and lieth towards Coggeshall, and the lease of the manor of Earls Colne and the lands therewith leased after her decease towards the payment of debts and the performance of my will, with the reversion and remainder of the manor and lands and part of the park to Richard and his heirs male, and for default of such issue to Thomas and his heirs male. I constitute my two sons executors, and they shall enter into bond for £500 to William to perform my will, and if either shall not enter he shall not be my executor nor take any benefit by my will, and then my brother shall be executor with my other son and enter into like bond to his co-executor.

Witness: Robert Sandforde.

Proved 13 May 1603.

THOMAS HARLESTONE of South Ockendon esquire, 6 August 1572.
[15/30]

To Mary my wife in consideration of part of her dower the reversion of my messuage or farm called Mollandes in South Ockendon in the tenure of Robert Badbye, with the rents reserved on the lease to him. To her for life 40s. yearly out of my lands called Rowe Leaze in South Ockendon. If she overlive my mother-in-law £30 rent yearly for a further satisfaction of all her dower out of the lands which my mother-in-law holdeth for her jointure. After the death of my wife to my beloved father-in-law, Mr Rowland Lytton esquire, two parts of the lands which I have demised to her, a third part to descend to my heir, whereby the Queen's Majesty may be answered of the profits of the same for the wardship; after my mother-in-law's death two parts of the lands which she hath for her jointure; also two-thirds of all other my lands, a third part to descend to my heir, to hold to Rowland until my son is 22, for the payment of my debts; the residue to be equally divided between my son about the charges of his marriage and relief and my sisters for their preferment in marriage. The two parts and the reversion to my son John and his heirs male, with successive remainders in default of such issue to my brother William Harlestone and his heirs male and to my sisters.

The residue of my goods to Rowland, whom I make my executor, and I give him a ring of 40s. for a remembrance. Witnesses : Richard Smyth, doctor in physic, Robert Hodgekins clerk, Thomas Mitchell.

Proved 5th October 1572.

VINCENT HARRYS of Maldon esquire, 21 April 1574.   [17/44]

To Mary my well-beloved wife for life, for her jointure and dower, my messuages and lands called the Fryers and Branmeade in Maldon, Small Port and Temple alias Temple Marsh in Great and Little Wakering, Bettes and Bettes Wood in Hockley, Bakers and Colliers in Purleigh, [Cold] Norton and Stow [Maries], all which I purchased of William Waldeigne and John Higham esquires; and after her decease to remain according to a feoffment made to the right honourable my very good lord the Earl of Sussex, Arthur Harris, Edward Harris, esquires, and John Sammes gentleman. Whereas by the bequest of William Harris esquire, my father, I am possessed of a lease of the manor of Mundon with the rectory and tithes and other leases of quillets and lands in Mundon to myself and my heirs male, with divers remainders declared in his will; and forasmuch as by reason of divers charges and great expenses happened to me by suits in law and defence of the title of the leases and of the great charges sustained in the building of my mansion house in Maldon I am indebted in divers sums of money to divers persons, which debts though in equity and good conscience I find myself bounden and utterly desirous to pay, yet cannot perform the same presently without changing the condition of the lease of the manor of Mundon, whereunto having regard to my father's will and especial care to the performance thereof I am greatly unwilling so to do; I will all the leases to continue, i.e. first my executors shall receive so much of the yearly profits of the farm of Mundon and other the farms so to me given by my father as shall pay all my debts, and after such payment shall receive out of the yearly profits for my wife 400 marks and after that 500 marks for my daughter Mary at marriage or 18; and then I will that the leases shall remain to such uses as are declared in my father's will for payment of my debts and advancement of my wife and daughter; and for my legacies hereafter bequeathed I require my son Thomas to agree; and therefore I require that my leases shall be in the custody of my brother Arthur to be kept in the chest appointed by my father. The rest of my inheritance to descend to my heir and to remain in accordance with my father's will, and I most humbly desire the Earl of Oxford to be a patron and an especial protector, chiefly for payment of my debts and legacies and then for the preservation of my leases, to which my very good lord I give for his pains my best gelding or horse at his choice.

To my wife my household stuff, plate and jewels (except my chain of gold which I give to my heir), 6 geldings and her own colt called Fulgeam, my milch kine pasturing in Beanmead; and the rest of my cattle and goods to be employed to the payment of my debts. To Richard

Leversitche my servant £20, to Bridget my wife's maid £3 6s. 8d., and to every of my menservants in household 40s. and maidservants 20s., except Elizabeth Smyth to whom I give £3 6s. 8d. I ordain my brother Arthur Harris my sole executor, and I humbly beseech the Earl of Sussex to be overseer and to extend his lordship's favour and friendship for the stay of my wife and children and execution of my will.

Witnesses: John Sammes, John Locke, Thomas Kinge, Hugh Branham, William Bantofte, John Leedes, Thomas Chesse.

Administration granted; 28 November 1574, to John Leedes of Southminster, yeoman. [In margin: Harrys arms—on a chevron engrailed between 3 hares' heads erased, a lozenge between 2 roaches.]

ARTHUR HERRYS [Harris] of Creeksea esquire, 19 May 1597. (Nuncupative.) [41/50]

He gave to Dorothy Kempe his daughter an annuity of £20, Valentine Smith £100, Anne wife of Thomas Harrington £10, and Christopher Hanworth £10. To every one of his household servants one year's wages. To the poor inhabitants of those townships wherein he possessed land in Essex £20 to be proportionately distributed at his executor's discretion. The residue of his goods and plate to William Herrys his son, whom he appoint his sole executor. Witnesses: Edmund Freake, John Hildersham, John Lynsey.

Proved 30 June 1597.

EDWARD HUBARD of Stansted Mountfitchet esquire, 16 March 1601. [46/33]

[Preamble recites the Lord's Prayer.] To be buried in my chapel in Stansted church. I bestow on a tomb or monument for me and my late wife Jane £30 with the repairing of the chapel within two years after my decease if I shall not do it myself whilst I live; and if my executors refuse to do or do not perform in that time I do most humbly request the right reverend father in God my lord Archbishop of Canterbury and the Bishop of London to cause it to be done. To 12 poor folks of Stansted, Farnham, Manuden and Birchanger, whereof 9 of Stansted and 1 apiece for the others, 12 black frise coats at my burial, to George Dalton, Steven Skinner and Bartholomew Simons black cloaks, and to John Newman a black cloak, so they be all at my burial. To every manservant that I have black coats being at my burial and such mourning gowns as my executor shall think fit. I appoint £10 to be distributed to the poor people on the day of my burial, out of which 40 of the poor at Stansted to have 12d. apiece or more if it may be spared from the other poor to be distributed in quantity as my executor shall think fit, requesting him that shall preach for me that he would take some portion of this preamble in my will as to him shall be thought fit. To my household servants 10s. apiece, husbandmen 6s. 8d. apiece and my maidservants 10s. apiece. Whereas I have heretofore given for certain causes

96

to certain feoffees of Stansted a yearly rentcharge of 40s. for ever out of certain of my lands in the parish to be bestowed in the reparations of the church and to other good uses, I confirm the same.

Whereas Thomas Chapman deceased held of me 10 acres of copyhold land called the Gage Wood in Stansted, which he had forfeited by committing waste and so presented, yet because he was my bailiff and my servant, at his request (although I had made a seisure of the same) I was contented that he should enjoy it during his life and further gave my consent that 26s. 8d. should for ever go out of the land to such good use as I should appoint and also £5 given by him; now I declare that I have bestowed the £5 towards the buying of the fee simple of a house near Stansted chapel wherein one Fucas in his lifetime did dwell, yet I was contented because he was a poor man to give him for the house £10 and 20s. a year for life and his dwelling in a part of the house, towards which payment I have delivered the £5 in respect I appoint the house to go for ever to good uses, i.e. from the time I bought it I have freely suffered 10 poor people to dwell there, rent free. I appoint that old father Elliott and his son, who are in possession of part of the house, and his son's wife shall have the use during their lives and old mother Bennett to have that part she enjoyeth for life without paying any rent. For the ease of the parishioners I declare that old Elliott have for life 10s. yearly, 10s. yearly be paid to mother Bennett for life, and 6s. 8d. yearly to Elliott and his wife for their lives, and after their deceases the 26s. 8d. be bestowed on 3 poor folks that shall be assigned to dwell in the houses as an almshouse for ever.

Whereas I have an honest and dutiful wife Eleanor, whom if my ability would serve I would deal much more liberally with than now I can do, my estate considered, which I hope she will take in good part in respect she hath a very good jointure out of my small living; and touching her jointure I confirm to her for life all manors and lands specified in a writing. To her my 2 best coach horses and coach, she paying my executor for the same £50, to be at her choice whether she will have them or not. To her 2 fair chains, whereof one is gold and pearl and the other is gold, the bracelets that are mine, and her jewels, saving such rings of gold as I have left, which I desire her to see them delivered by my executor to every child that I have as well married as unmarried, to remember me and their own mother and in respect I have dealt so liberally with her. I earnestly request her as I have always found her to have a good conscience that she would not hide or keep anything of mine from my executor, and do take that which of right appertaineth to her and no more; and therefore I appoint her to have all such coin of gold as I now have, with such gilt plate as she brought to me. My executor shall let her have so much of my dwelling house as she shall think convenient for her to use, with 100 acres of land during such time as she shall keep herself a widow and no longer, she paying a yearly rent of £10 better cheap than the same is worth.

Whereas I receive certain rents in the right of Richard my youngest son of houses in London and Middlesex, bequeathed to him by his grandfather Sowthall deceased, my executor shall receive them during his minority to defray his maintenance at learning. Whereas I have purchased certain ground and lights of Mr Allforde very convenient for Richard standing over London Bridge, I freely give the inheritance to him on condition that he shall allow of the lease I have made of the house to Skinner.

To my son John my farm called Digbies in Birchanger and the grove that I bought of Robert Thorogood, for life, and to his heirs male, and for default of such issue to my son Francis and his heirs male, provided that no part of Stansted Park shall go to John and that my executor shall receive the profits until he is 21, bearing his charges; provided that, if John shall deny at Francis' request to seal and deliver a release of his rights in the lands of Luton (Beds.) which I know to be nothing worth in the law to Crawlie who purchased them from me, my farm given to John shall be void and remain to Francis. Because John may the better be persuaded to do the same I declare the cause, viz. that whereas I purchased the farm in Luton wherein one Bigge dwelt as farmer and after I sold it to John Sowthall, father to my then wife, for £400, whereof my wife paid privately £100 and Sowthall paid but £300, if Sowthall should have cause to sell it again I should have it at all times, paying his said money disbursed; if not, it should descend to me and to my then wife after the decease of him and his wife; at which time I was offered for it £700 of another man *bona fide,* which indenture of bargain and sale to Sowthall was never enrolled nor any feoffment with livery or fine levied to make good the same assurance, so as there passed nothing in law from me, whereby Sowthall's will for that farm is merely void.

To Jane wife of Edward Elliott, sometime wife of Edward Pulliver, an annuity of £20, Godfrey Frenche gentleman an annuity of £40, and John Skelton an annuity of £20. To my daughter Elizabeth £500 to be made up with such legacy as is given her by the will of John Sowthall and in the meantime my executor shall pay her £24 a year towards her maintenance in meat, drink and apparel; to my daughter Thomasine, if she live to be married, £300, to be made so much with the legacy given to her by Mr Sowthall and in meantime £16 for her maintenance; provided that, if any of my daughters die before they marry, to Francis.

Whereas my debts are great and speedy payment will be required, I appoint my executor to sell the reversion of the fee simple of the manor of Paken Hall in Manuden to any that will buy it with the most advantage that conveniently may be and to sell the copyhold tenement late Whelpstone's and John Smith's, whereof George Dalton and John Newman have the same and their heirs. All other my manors and lands on the conditions following to Francis, if he pay my debts mentioned in a book dated 14 January last, written with my own hand, at such days as they grow due or otherwise take order to pay them as he and my creditors can agree, whereby they shall have no cause to exclaim against me; if he fail in paying, my manors shall go to Edward eldest son of Francis at 21; provided that, if Francis enter into bond to my brother [in-law] John Wilshe for payment of my debts, Francis shall be my sole executor, and to have my plate and goods, corn, hay, and my quick cattle; but, if he refuse to deliver such a bond, John Wilshe shall be my

sole executor, and for his pains £10; and if there shall fall out any overplus, the same to be accounted to Francis. I request my right worshipful
good friends Mr Brograve, her Majesty's Attorney of her Duchy court,
Mr [blank] Golding of the Inner Temple, and my cousin Miles Huberd,
citizen and clothworker of London, to be my overseers, and to each a
ring of gold of the value of 20s. to have a death's head in it. [No
witnesses.]

Memorandum that I stand bound in sundry obligations for Francis'
debts with him which I have not put down in my book of debts because
they are his debts and not to be reckoned in the meaning of my will to
be my debts touching the speedy performance of the same.

Proved 14 May 1602.

JOHN IVE of Boxted esquire, 9 July 1600. [46/33]

To be buried in Boxted church near to the place where my wife lieth.
To my son Mark my manor of Rivers Hall with the meadows, pastures,
woods and feedings belonging and the live cattle thereupon, and my
woods bought of Shinglewood, Bogas and Fysher in Boxted. My house
called the King's Head in Colchester and my lands in Widford and
Writtle shall be sold by my executors towards the payment of my debts,
and if not sufficient Mark to pay out of my lands in Boxted £200. To
Mark my wood bought of Rose in Boxted. To my daughter Robinsonne
20 marks yearly towards her maintenance, and my son-in-law Mr Robinsonne her husband not to meddle with it. To every of her children £10
apiece. To my son William the lands which I have assured him already,
amounting to £80. The one-half of my goods and plate at Rivers Hall
in Boxted and at my house in Fleet Street shall be sold by my executors
towards the payment of my debts, if not sufficient before, and if sufficient
it shall remain to them. The residue of my goods to Mark and William,
whom I constitute my executors. To four of my men, John Graye, John
Gislingham, Thomas Twaightes, Thomas Bradstreate, £5 apiece. Witnesses: Brian Bradshawe, John Graye, John Gislingham, Thomas
Thwaites, Thomas Bradstreate.

Postscriptum. To Mistress Byshopp 40s., John Smithe my old servant
40s., and Elizabeth Cole my servant 20s. Witnesses: Brian Bradshawe,
John Graie, John Gyslingham, Thomas Thwaites.

Proved 18 May 1602.

JOHN JACKMAN of Hornchurch esquire, 7 November 1594. [38/84]

To Jane my well-beloved wife, whom I make my executrix, all my
goods. I desire my loving brothers Henry Jackman and Thomas Jackman
gentlemen to be my overseers. Witnesses: James Ley, Luke Lane, Hugh
Lee and Henry Shervile.

Proved 4 December 1594.

HENRY JOSCELIN of Torrels Hall [in Willingale Doe] esquire, 18 August 1587. [For Dame Dorothy Josselyn, see p. 22.] [32/5]

To Francis, Henry, Anthony and Christopher, my sons, each £300 at 21. To Grace, Winifred, Anne, Elizabeth and Katherine Joscelin, my daughters, each £300 at marriage or 21. To my servant Robert Cullin 20 marks. To Jeffrey Tanner my bailiff 40s. To Thomas Dennis my butler 20s. To Arthur Harris and Anne Harris, the children of my daughter Mary, each £40 at 21. Forasmuch as I cannot make perfect some things by my will which I desire earnestly to have performed, I therefore desire my well-beloved wife to grant to Robert Cullin, my servant, my windmill at Thurrockes [in Clavering?] for 21 years from my decease, paying yearly £3, he doing reparations, having timber delivered to him at Brentwood. My desire is that Gregory Smithe, my bailiff, have his dwelling in my manor house of Thurrockes where he now is and sufficient keeping on my ground belonging for 6 kine and 20 sheep for 21 years after my decease, and that a lease be made to my brother of my manor of Slade [in?] according to our agreement, and the rent to be bestowed on Thomas my son towards his maintenance. My especial request to my wife is that she will assure her lands from her decease to Thomas and his heirs male, with successive remainders for want of such issue to Francis, Henry, Anthony and Christopher and their heirs male. I make my wife sole executrix. [No witnesses.]

Proved 25 January 1587. Administration granted, 30 April, to Thomas, Anne not administering.

WILLIAM LARKE of Margaretting esquire, 13 August 1582. [25/24]

To Jane my beloved wife, whom I ordain my sole executrix, all my goods, and to her for life my lands, as already she hath no jointure thereof. I ordain John Nightingale gentleman and Paul Pope scrivener my overseers. To the poor of Margaretting 20 marks to be distributed at the discretion of Thomas Whitbred and [David] Wingate vicar of Margaretting and of St Bride in Fleet Street [London] £5. Witnesses : Paul Pope, John Nightingale. Postscript. To the poor of Mildenhall (Suffolk) 5 marks. To Paul Pope £6 13s. 4d. and to John Nytingale 40s.

Proved 29 August 1582.

THOMAS LATHUM of North Ockendon esquire, 31 July 1563. [2/42]

To be buried in North Ockendon church besides my mother. I will my executor to lay a monument or a stone over me. To the reparations of the church 20s. To the poor of the same parish 10s., Stifford 10s., Cranham 10s., and South Ockendon 10s. To my daughter Mary £40 at marriage or 20; if she die before, to be divided equally between my two sons William and Robert. She shall be brought up, kept and governed by my executor at his costs. To my two daughters being married each a black gown and 40s. The residue of my goods to Ralph Lathum my son,

100

whom I ordain my sole executor, so that he become bounden by deed to William Sheather and George Herde my sons-in-law, in £100 to perform my will, and I appoint them my overseers. To Ralph, my eldest son, my lands in North Ockendon, Cranham, Stifford, Aveley, Little Thurrock, Grays Thurrock and Chadwell, and to his heirs male, and for default of such issue the remainder according to the will of Robert my father. To William and Robert my sons my manor of Libere in Little Mundon (Herts.) and my other lands in Great and Little Munden. My overseers shall have the custody, government and bringing up of William and Robert and the rule of their lands until they are 21 and towards their bringing up in learning and virtue. There is in my house at Stifford a great chest and a brass pot which belong to William Herd of Bulphan and in my dwellinghouse a broad pan of Thomasine Hammon's which shall be restored. I forgive Richard Peacocke and Thomas Dauson the debts they owe me. To John Awoode my herd a cow. Witnesses: Peter Baylie, John Bawden, Roger Coies, William Sheather and John Sparrowe.

Proved 10 December 1563.

RALPH LATHAM of North Ockendon [esquire], 3 September 1565.
[11/20]

To be buried in the church or chancel of North Ockendon. To the poor people of the same parish 6s. 8d., Cranham 6s. 8d., and Stifford 6s. 8d. To my servants 6s. 8d. apiece. To John Awood, Richard Billinge, Thomas Wregeswood and Thomas Huntley each a cow. To George Herde's and William Shether's children 20s. apiece. The residue of my goods, my father's legacies and mine performed, to Audrey my wife, whom I make my sole executrix. To her my lands in North Ockendon, Cranham and Little Thurrock according to a feoffment to her made, and after her decease to remain to my heirs. To her my lands in Stifford and South Ockendon for life, and after her decease to my brother William Latham, with successive remainders failing issue to my brother Robert and to my sister Mary Latham. My executrix shall fell and sell all my wood at the Hyde and also in South Land for the performance of my will. Witnesses: Robert Badbye, Thomas Hammond of East Tilbury, Humfrey Barnes, John Awood, and others.

Proved 15 October 1568.

JOHN LUCAS of Ramsey esquire, 6 December 1596. [For Robert Lucas, see p. 228.] [43/50]

To be buried in St Michael's chancel in Ramsey church.

I confess that I owe William Bedingfeild of Bedfield [Suffolk] gentleman, my son-in-law, £116, and Reynold Marvine of Ramsey yeoman £10. Whereas I owe Edward Lucas, my loving cousin of London, gentleman, £20 by an obligation, yet calling to mind the account between us for loads of billet that he hath divers times received for me and £4 of her

101

Majesty's Cofferer in 1589, the debt remaining from me to himward is but £3 10s., with which I trust he will be satisfied. Whereas Sir Thomas Lucas of St John's besides Colchester, knight, hath a judgement for damages and costs on an action in her Majesty's Court of Queen's Bench for £100 and more, if he after my decease sue my heir and executor, my executor shall compound with him to his good contentment, but I trust Sir Thomas of his brotherly love will not proceed.

To the poor of Ramsey 40s. to be delivered to two substantial parishioners, charging them that they, with the vicar's consent, after divine service of the forenoon, call up 6 of the poorest persons and give them 4d. each and in like manner every Sunday 6 groats until 40s. be fully distributed; and to the poor of Wrabness 20s. likewise; and if any other poor of the adjoining parish do come to Ramsey church at my burial for my relief and charity my executor shall distribute among them 40s., willing the distributors to tell the poor of Ramsey and Wrabness that they be otherwise provided for. To Mr [Thomas] Bland, our vicar of Ramsey, or to some other learned minister in his absence, which shall preach the day of my funeral 6s. 8d. after the end of his sermon. To the bellringers that day 5s. To Audrey Mayas one of my maidservants for that she hath taken pains with me in this sickness, in satisfaction, £6; to William Freeninges, my servant, for the like pains, £4; John Levar my man 20s.; and Elizabeth my kitchen girl 40s. at marriage or 21.

Now among my loving friends and kindred. To Edward Grimestone of Bradfield esquire a ring of gold weighing 3 pounds on which his coat of arms shall be engraved. To my cousin, Mary wife of Thomas Lufkine, and William Bedingfeyld, my son-in-law, each a ring of gold price 40s., also to Mary Bedingfeyld my daughter, his wife, a ring of gold price 20s. I make him my only executor, giving him power to administer my goods now in Royden Hall [in Ramsey] and in the other houses and my lands in Ramsey and Wrabness, provided that he do not deal with the glass in the windows, doors nor ceilings. If my son John will buy my goods he shall have preferment before others, but if he refuse my executor shall sell them, paying him for their use by my executor for 6 months after my decease £5 10s.; and he then shall yearly resort to Royden Hall in the week of Pentecost and there before John and my cousin Clement Lucas my supervisor render his account of all sums to him paid; and the surplusage of the money and goods to Margaret my daughter. To Royden Lucas my second son an annuity of £20 out of my manor called West Hall alias Parkers and now Royden Hall and the demesnes belonging. To Edward my third son an annuity of £20 out of my purchased lands in Ramsey and Wrabness. To Edmund my fourth son an annuity of £20 out of my manor called Royden Hall. To Elizabeth my daughter an annuity of £15 out of my lands called Deuballs [Dunballs?] in Wrabness. To John my eldest son for life my manor of West Hall and my lands in Ramsey and Wrabness, and an annuity of 40s. called Free-stones rent out of a manor called Bondes Hall in Freestone (Suffolk); with successive remainders to his heir male, to the heirs male of the said heir, and to Edward and his heirs male. To John my great wainscot chest in the hall and all things therein and my best apparel and armour of proof. I ordain Clement Lucas of Bradfield gentleman my supervisor, giving him for his pains £5.

Witnesses : Jonas Goldingham, Robert Beddingfeilde, John Herde.
Proved 8 June 1599.

ANTHONY MAXEY of Bradwell-near-Coggeshall esquire, 18 October 1590. [35/91]

Whereas Sir Henry Gray of Pirgo [in Havering], knight, by a statute staple dated 30 September 1590, standeth bound to me in £1,500 for the payment of £500 to me at Michaelmas next, I bequeath the £500 to be at the disposition of Henry my son to pay Bridget my daughter and his sister £20 a year towards her maintenance until marriage; provided that she take such a husband as can make her a jointure of 100 marks of his own lands, and if not she to have but £250 and the other £250 so forfeited to be divided between Henry and William my sons, and if she die before marriage the £500 to be so equally divided. Henry to see his sister placed in service as a brother ought to do. To Bridget the best featherbed. To William £400 which lieth ready in my study, lately received of Sir Henry Graye, and for his maintenance during a year after my decease £20. Whereas there is in my hands £100 in trust committed to me with Henry for Mary Clarke, my wife's daughter and his sister, for his discharge I give another £100 which is ready in my study yet unbequeathed to Henry for her use. My executor shall permit William to have such corn as he hath in my barn here at Bradwell which did grow on his farm called Wildwood. To William his featherbed which he lieth on. My hops here and at Saling (except my wife's hops that grew in her garden called my wife's garden) shall be sold for the performance of my will. To my daughter and daughters-in-law and sons-in-law each a ring of gold of 40s. To my menservants and maidservants in household 20s. apiece. To the poor of Bradwell 40s., Great Coggeshall 40s., and Old [Great] Saling 36s. 4d. To the two daughters, children of Mary wife of Andrew Clarke, my daughter-in-law, £20 equally to be divided, at marriage or 21. To Dorothy my wife my plate with my household stuff. Whereas I delivered to Henry my chain of gold to be occupied by him and myself at my pleasure, I will it to him with my signet of gold which I wear daily. To Henry 3 of my best geldings with my stoned horse, excepting my wife's double gelding and coach horses. To William Maxey my brother a ring of gold of 40s. and a small piece of ground which is come to me by course of law by the decease of his own son in Beverley (Yorks.), according to promise. To John Maxey my servant and kinsman 53s. 4d.

Whereas I with Henry did assure him an annuity of £4 by our deed poll, and likewise to William my son a lease of the farm of Parkes for 50 years, both of which are in my custody, my executor shall deliver them. To Henry my furniture for the wars and my silk grogram gown with my velvet jerkin; the rest of my apparel to William meet for his wearing and the rest to be bestowed by my executors among my servants. To Henry my books of all sorts, except my new bible which I leave to my wife for the usual service in her household, which I desire her to continue that God may bless her and her household to live in his fear. The residue of my goods to my wife. I order her and Henry to be my executors.

My debts which I owe this 28 August 1590. To goodman Sorrell £20, the cause of this, I borrowed of him £60 for my son Jerome, of which Jerome paid to my cousin George Maxey £26 13s. 4d., of which George paid to my son Henry £20, and so there remaineth in his hands £6 13s. 4d. and the rest is still in Jerome's hands, which I will that ye procure of Jerome and deliver his bond and see it paid to goodman Sorrell with thanks. Jerome is likewise bound to you Henry and myself for £100 which we have to the use of your brother [in-law] Andrew Clerke and his children after his decease and which trust I advise you to see performed. My mind is that the £500 which Sir Henry Gray oweth me he should have it until my daughter is to be paid or they have cause to use it, Henry my son to have the profit thereof, paying his sister £20 a year until she is married. Whereas I used some barley of William's for want of my own malt to be converted into malt, my will is that he hath so much barley delivered to him.

Whereas there have been controversies betwixt the Friars of Clare (Suffolk) and me for certain land and rent out of land called Glansfields which [I] sold among other lands to William Sorrell of Saling the elder of 4 nobles a year rent, which rent hath been more negligently sought for than in default of me in withdrawing thereof, insomuch that it lieth in oblivion that it hath been unpaid since I have been owner of the same land, and finding in equity that it is due to them, as by a book of sundry remembrances set down to my wife and children of all causes of any title of any land or rent may appear, wherefore I bequeath such land in the tenure of widow Herde of Stebbing in Old Saling to Henry my eldest son on condition that he pay the arrerages of rent of 4 nobles from my first enjoying the land until my death, if the heir of the Friars do not wilfully refuse it. Whereas I with my wife did acknowledge a fine of the manor of Bradwell, at which time we did charge the manor with an annuity of £10 to Jerome Bonume, the second son of the wife of the said Anthony, my request is to my wife and Henry during their lives without any vexation [to pay the same]. [No witnesses.]
Proved 1 December 1591.

GEORGE MAXEY of South Ockendon esquire, 9 June 1598. [42/54]

To Edmund Hunt of Hawley (Kent) gentleman and William Mustchampe citizen and grocer of London, my executors, my goods, with the wardship of William Howe which I now have in trust and to the uses hereafter expressed, i.e. they pay such debts as in equity and conscience I owe and with the rest to divide it among my children Dorothy, Timothy, Edmund and Anne equally. I desire my executors to endeavour by all means they can to effect a marriage between Anne and William Howe, and in case it be brought to pass she shall have no part of my goods other than the wardship. To my executors my lands in the manor

104

of Huntspill de la Hay (Somerset) which I have in right of my wardship, to be sold to the best advantage of my children. Forasmuch as my desire is that my debts may be with convenient speed paid, I bequeath that Martha my well-beloved wife shall have the household stuff in my mansion house of South Ockendon, putting in sureties to my executors to pay them £50 to the use of Susan Maxey my daughter and Mary Howe her daughter equally between them, so that my wife deliver up a bond wherein I stand bound for payment of £10 yearly for the augmentation of their portions, otherwise the same to be wholly to Susan's use, the £50 to be paid by my wife at her decease or when Susan is 17. Such woods as are now cut down on the lands there and such other goods as are there and not bequeathed shall be sold by my executors towards the payment of my debts and the performance of my will; nevertheless my wife shall have the refusal of such goods, paying my executors according to their appraisement.

To George my tenements in Fleet Street in London called Brockhas Inn and my lands in Messing with the rectory and parsonage, on condition that he make choice of London or Messing; and after his choice he shall execute such deed for either by my executors' advice to these uses, i.e. to them for 17 years and then to Timothy and his heirs male, and for default thereof to George and his heirs male; and during the term the profits shall first be to my executors towards my debts, and after I will that 8 years' profits shall be to Dorothy and Anne equally and for the residue of the term to Edmund and Susan equally. My wife shall bring up Timothy and Susan according to her promise, to whose godly tuition and education I commit them. To Edmund for life the advowson of the parsonage or vicarage of Messing.

If any ambiguity arise on my will, it shall be determined by my well-beloved cousin Henry Maxey of Saling esquire and my loving brother Anthony Maxey of Repham (Norfolk) gentleman. I entreat Edmund Hunt and William Mustchampe to be executors, and I desire my well-beloved son-in-law William Holt to be overseer.

Witnesses: James Ireland notary public, Anne Mayow.

Proved 14 June 1598.

THOMAS MEADE, one of the Justices of the Common Pleas, [of Wendon Lofts?], 18 June 1584. [For Reynold Meade, see p. 230.]

[29/52]

To be buried in Elmdon church near the place where Joan Meade my mother doth lie buried or in some other place where it shall seem to my executors meet to bury my body.

To Joan my wife for life my manors of Pychardes, Banesbury and Foxleis in Guilden Morden (Cambs.) with all my lands (the woods and timber above the age of 21 years excepted) for her jointure and in lieu of her dower of my lands in the counties of Essex, Cambridge and Hertford, yet she make take sufficient timber for repairing the houses; and my manor of Sonninges in Ashwell and Hinxworth [Herts.] until my sons Robert and Matthew are 21 towards their bringing up in learning, and then to her for life. To my son Thomas my manor of Rockelles and the Lee and Lee Bury, my manor of Pigottes, and my lands in Elmdon (woods excepted) after due course of law, being a third part of my lands. During his minority my executors shall fell and sell my woods of Rockelles and Pigottes at convenient times towards the performance of my will. To my wife my messuages and lands in Wendon Lofts and Chrishall until Thomas is 24, she then paying £24 a year, with successive remainders to Thomas and his heirs male and for default of such issue to Robert and to Matthew and their heirs male. After my wife's death my manor of Morden with the lands in Morden, Ashwell and Hinxworth shall remain to Thomas and his heirs male and for default likewise. To Catherine Nightingale and Martha Clampe, my wife's daughters, my pasture in Huntingdon and such leases as I have of any houses in Huntingdon. Martha shall have the bond wherein Mr Roper standeth bound jointly with Philip Bassett in £300 for payment of £209 to her, besides £70 which she shall have, of which £100 was given to her by Mr John Clampe, her father. To John Wright my servant 40s. a year. To Robert and Matthew each a moiety of my lands which I bought of Sir John Cuttes.

There shall be bestowed at my burial and funeral £100 at the least to buy black cloth and other things, and everyone of my servingmen shall have a black coat; and a gown of black cloth to my brethren and their wives, my wife's daughters and their husbands, my sister Swanne and her husband, my brother Turpyn and his wife, my aunt Bendyshe, and Elizabeth wife of John Wrighte. To two discreet preachers and learned, to be chosen out of Cambridge by my executors, to preach at my burial and have 40s. To the poor of Elmdon, [Wendon] Lofts, Strethall, Littlebury, Ickleton [Cambs.], Chesterford, Newport, Wenden, Clavering, Langley, Chrishall, Heydon, Chishall, Arkesden, Morden, Ashwell, Stapleford [Herts.], and Huntingdon £20 a year for 6 years to be distributed by my executors' discretion. My wife shall keep such servingmen as I shall have at the time of my death one quarter of a year (if they will tarry with her) and at their departure 20s. apiece besides their wages, and to every other servant both man and maid 6s. 8d. apiece. To Robert and Matthew £100 apiece at 21. The residue to my wife and Thomas, whom I ordain my executors, and Mr Geoffrey Nightingale and Mr Reynold Meade my brother to be my supervisors, and for their pains £10.

Witnesses: Reynold Meade, Robert Symon, John Palmer, Geoffrey Palmer.

Proved 25 November 1585.

GEORGE MEDLEY of Tilty esquire, 20 May 1561.   [6/6]

To be buried without pomp, pride or vain superstition. Provision to be made by my executors for a sermon at my burial by a learned man of good conversation.

My daughter Elizabeth Medley be paid at her marriage £100 bequeathed by her granddame, Mistress Mary Danett widow, my mother-in-law, remaining in my custody. To Elizabeth £200 out of the yearly revenues of my leases above rehearsed [not described] and of other my goods for the preferment of her marriage at marriage; and towards her charges of apparel, meat, drink and finding until she be married £20 yearly. To my son Henry towards maintaining his learning and for his finding during his mother's life £30 yearly, and to my son William £30 yearly likewise. To my wife towards the performance of my will the profits of my leases and farms. To William after her death my leases of Bardon Park, Highborough Meadow and Shutermonhills (Leics.) and the lease of my house in London. To my wife for life my leases of Bedwelhaye in the Isle of Ely [Cambs.] and my lease of Tilty and Chawreth [in Broxted], with successive remainders to the issue male of my sons and daughters from eldest to youngest. To Henry at marriage 3 good featherbeds, bedlinen of the better sort, a garnish of pewter vessel, 6 candlesticks, and such harness and weapons as I have to serve in war. The residue of my goods to my wife, and at her decease she to leave two of three parts to Henry; the third part I clearly give to her to do as she shall seem best. My books (the English books excepted, which I give to her) to be divided between Henry and William. To the poor men's box or chest at Tilty 20s., Thaxted 40s., Dunmow 30s., Great Easton 20s., Little Easton 10s., and Broxted 13s. 4d.

I make Mary my well-beloved wife and Henry executors, and I most heartily require her that, of her portion given her in jointure for life which is that little of inheritance and purchase that I have, she will extend her motherly relief to my children so long as they shall humbly and reverently use themselves as obedient and loving children to her, and in this respect have I given to Henry by my will but £30 by the year during her life that both he by his deserving to her mought receive more at her hands and she by his humble duty doing as becometh a child in all points to his mother mought the rather be occasioned and provoked according to his need and her power to relieve and help him, not of constraint but of desert and good will. I make my singular good uncle Dr [Nicholas] Wotton, Dean of Canterbury and York, to whom I have from my 12 years age been always most especially bounden, supervisor, and for a poor token of remembrance a ring of fine gold of the value of 4 nobles besides the fashion, most entirely requiring him with his counsel to help my executors and that it may please him to receive this trust.

9 May 1562. To my wife such parcels of plate and other stuff which Mistress Mary Danett widow, her mother, did by her will or otherwise give me and my wife, to be used at her pleasure. To my wife for life 4 messuages in Tachbrook Mallory (Warws.) which I purchased of Edmund Downing and Bartholomew Brokes of London gentlemen. [No witnesses.] Proved 3 February 1563.

HENRY MEDLEY of Tilty esquire, 18 December 1577.   [29/22]

My body I commit to the earth without any vain pomp or ceremony, only with a sermon of some godly man.

To Frances my well-beloved wife £100, a silver tankard gilt, a square gilt salt, a gilt piece which Sir John Throckmorton gave her at her marriage, 2 great gilt spoons, a gilt casting bottle, and 6 of my best silver spoons; my English books, her wearing apparel and wearing linen and her jewels, 4 good featherbeds, whereof 2 to be of the best (my 2 great down beds in the two great chambers excepted) and the other 2 of a middle sort, and 10 pair of sheets, whereof 5 to be of the better sort (my 2 very best new pair of fine sheets excepted) and the other 5 to be of the meaner sort. My pantry linen and napery to be viewed by my executors and divided into four equal parts, and one part my wife shall choose. To her a good garnish of pewter vessel and 6 good brazen or latten candlesticks. My kitchen brass being equally divided, my executors shall deliver her one fourth part. To my wife such furniture for women to ride on as I have, 3 good nags or geldings, whereof her own ambling nag to be one. If my executors shall think meet that any house be maintained here at Tilty for bringing up my children, she shall have among my children meat, drink and lodging for herself, one maidservant and one manservant to attend on her for a year after my decease until she have received a year's rent of the profits of her jointure without paying therefor.

To Clement my second son the lease of Woodham Hall in Woodham Ferrers which I have by parole of my well-beloved cousin Mr Samuel Norton of Leigh (Somerset) for 27 years to come, and £200 at 21; and to Philip and Thomas, my two youngest sons, each £250 at 21; their portions in the meantime to be employed by my executors to some profit for their better education and bringing up and increase of their portions. To my three daughters Katherine, Mary and Margaret Medeley £250 each at marriage or 20, the sums in the meantime to be likewise employed. To my executors the profits of my farms and leases of the manor and grange of Tilty and of the farm of Bedwellhay in the Isle of Ely until my eldest son Henry is 21, the profits in the meantime to be employed for the performance of my will and his bringing up in virtue, godliness and learning, and to his heirs male.

To William Rawlinson, John Dennis and Alice Langeley, 3 of my servants that have a long time taken great pain with me as well in my health as in my sickness, each £5, Robert Browne 40s., and every other of my servingmen a quarter's wages besides in their purse towards providing them of other services.

I make executors my very good uncle Sir Henry Nevell knight, my very good cousin Mr Thomas Wootton of Kent esquire, my well-beloved brethren Mr William Medeley, Mr James Morrice and Mr John Throckmorton, and my dearly-beloved friend and kinsman Mr John Dannet of Croydon [Cambs. or Surrey?] and to each 40s. in gold to be made in rings, besides the fashion, humbly desiring them to accept my goodwill in good part, to see my will performed, and my children brought up in the fear of God in godliness, virtue and learning, especially in the study of the laws of the realm.

After my death my gilt cup known as Collettes Cup to be delivered to the right honourable my very good lord, my Lord Thomas Howard of

Walden, most humbly beseeching him not to regard the simpleness of the gift but the mind of the giver, which ever was ready to do him any service, and trusting that, according to his faithful promise made me of Mr Cuttes of Debden in the garden he will be good lord and master to my poor children, especially my eldest son. To my well-beloved uncle Kelham Thockmorton 40s. in gold to be made in a ring for him for a remembrance of good will. To my only and very good sister Mistress Morris £10 in gold in consideration of her release to be made to my son Henry of the right which she by outliving my brother William may seem to claim by my father's will for term of her life to my lease and farm of Bedwelhay, which release both she and my brother her husband promised me to make as strong as by law I could devise. To my niece Mary Morrice, my goddaughter, 40s. in gold. Of my horses, mares, colts and geldings, my Lord Thomas Howard to have first choice for one, my Lord William his brother second choice for one, and my brother William third and last choice for one. The residue of my goods to Henry. [No witnesses.]

Proved 8 May 1585.

HERCULES MEWTAS of West Ham esquire, 9 June 1587. [For Dame Jane Mewtas, see p. 27.]   [33/9]

To be buried in West Ham church where my mother, brother and kindred lie. To my loving wife Philippa for life my lease granted by my brother Henry, 1 April 1576; £1,000 now being in the hands of Sir William Fitz-Williams knight; £500 which I am to receive of my brother Mr Anthony Cooke which he is condemned in and have execution for; and my goods and household stuff in consideration that she carefully bring up my children and hers, as my only trust is in her. I ordain her my sole executrix and Sir Thomas Palmer knight and Edmund Yorke esquire my executors, and for their pains, to Sir Thomas my cast of falcons at Slattons and to Mr Yorke my bay gelding. To every of my servants a year's wages of 4 marks and to my now housekeeper 4 marks for his wages. To Sir Thomas Palmer, Mr Yorke and his wife, Mr Thomas Knowles and Mr Samuel Knowles and their wives, each a ring (weighing 1 oz. of angel gold) wherein my arms to be graven. Witnesses : Edmund Yorke, Samuel Knowles, Miles Leedes, Edward Moore and Philip Barton.

Proved 20 Nov. 1588.

MILDMAY : see MYLDMAY.

ROBERT MORDANTE of Hempstead esquire, 15 January 1570.
                                                                       [15/17]

To be buried in Hempstead chancel in the south side by the high altar that was, and a stone of marble to be bought price £4. To 22 poor households in Hempstead 22s. To the poor of every parish where I have any land, to every parish 6s. 8d. To every household servant men and women their quarter's wages above their duties. To John Coote £3 6s. 8d., willing John Mordante to be good to him. To Haymer and Bullocke each 20s., willing my heir to suffer them quietly to enjoy their leases, for they have deserved them. To Barbara Dixson £4, Elizabeth Harmer £3, Barbara Wilkins £20, and Barbara Crochworthe 20 marks.

To Barbara my wife, trusting she will be good to her daughters, my sheep on the Danie Ground and the West Ground in Little Massingham [Norfolk]. To her 5 horse with cart harness and 1 shod cart, the 5 horse are in Leder's stable, 12 of my best milch kine, and such bedding, linen brass and pewter as appeareth in a bill written by the hand of Mr Dericke clerk; and the keeping of my plate till John the elder come to 24 and then he to have it, except 1 salt, 1 goblet and 6 of the best silver spoons, and them I give to my wife, except she of her good will will give them to John. To John the elder my books, to remain as heirlooms. I will my sheep pasture named the East Pasture in Little Massingham and my lands in the said East Ground which extends from March Lane to Rainhamgate eastward and so to Great Massingham and Corner Wood, with my lease of Harpley [Norfolk] for 6 years after my decease, with the sheep on East Ground and Harpley Ground, to the performance of my will. I give my parsonage in Hempstead and my lands in Panfield for 6 years to the performance of my will, with my lease of the late Hospital lands for the said term; and after[wards] East Sheep Pasture, Harpley, the Parsonage, Hospital grounds and the part of the lordship of Old [Great] Sampford, with the sheep after the rate as they go now, with my lands in Panfield as Mayner occupieth them, to John Mordaunte, Philip's eldest son. To Robert Mordaunte of Westbury [Warws.] 40 marks. To Harry Mordaunte £40 and Edmund Mordaunte 20 marks. I will that my sheep at Congham [Norfolk] be sold to perform my will and my cattle in Hempstead except horse, mares and colts. The residue of my goods to John the elder, Philip's son. I make my executors my wife, Robert Mordante of Wesbury and Harry my son. The money that I must have of Unnion, if the land be not redeemed by John the elder, to him.

Witnesses: William Harrison, Official [of the Archdeacon of Colchester and rector of Radwinter], John Lodington clerk [vicar of Hempstead], John Mordante, John Leote, Robert Ratcliffe, Henry Williamson, John Frenche.

Proved 29 May 1572. Administration granted, 20 November 1639, to Sir Charles Mordant knight and baronet, next heir of Robert Mordante of Hempstead, according to the will, Barbara and Henry Mordant being dead, by Robert Mordant executor.

JOHN MORDANTE of Hempstead esquire, son and heir apparent of Philip Mordaunte late deceased, 29 June 1574.   [17/29]

To be buried in the parish church of Westbury (Warws.). To my brother James Mordant my goods and plate in my house of Hempstead, except one standing pot which is already with my brother John Mordant.

To him after the decease of my grandmother the moiety of the manor of Walton and Westbury (Warws.), my sorrel colt which is running in Hempstead, and my mares, colts and horses, except my bay nag which I give to my uncle Robert Mordant. To each of my servants 20s. and to every one in the house of my uncle Robert 5s. My servant Robert Leader shall enjoy his farm for his good and true service to me. To the poor of every town where I have land 10s. and of Westbury 5s. To Anne Cheswell my goddaughter towards her marriage £20; Barbary Wilkins 20 nobles; Robert Wilkin 20 nobles; and Christopher Snelloge my godson 20 nobles. I make my uncle Robert Mordant of Westbury sole executor, and he be paid his money which I owe him, and to his wife the ring which I wear on my finger. To my brother John Mordant my little turquoise ring which my uncle Harry Mordant laid to mortgage. I give to the performance of my will my part of my sheep course in Norfolk for 4 years, and after my uncle Robert to receive the profits of that ground in Little Massingham and Harpley with the stock that there should be left by my grandfather's will to me. Whereas there remain divers debts of my father Philip Mordaunt late deceased unpaid, my uncle Robert shall receive the residue of the profits which were received by deed of my father in Berners Roothing to my uncle's use. Witnesses : Emmanuel Chamond, William Bardesley clerk, John Wastley, Robert Sipwright.

Proved 2 July 1574. Sentence, 5 December 1580, confirming the sum of £420 in the accounts of Robert Mordant executor in case between Henry Mackwilliam esquire and him. Administration granted 20 November 1639, to Sir Charles Mordant knight and baronet, next heir of John Mordant late of Hempstead, according to his Will. [In margin : Mordaunt arms—a chevron between 3 estoiles.]

THOMAS MYLDMAY the elder of Moulsham in Chelmsford esquire, 24 January 1566. [For William Myldmay, see p. 232.] [10/3]

To be buried in Chelmsford church hard by or within the grave of Avice my late wife. To the church 40s. towards the reparations and to the church of St Thomas the Apostle in the city of London 13s. 4d. To the poor inhabitants of Moulsham £8 and to the poverty of Chelmsford 40s.

To Thomas my son my manors of Chelmsford and Moulsham and all other my purchased lands and tithes in Chelmsford and Moulsham, and to his heirs male; with successive remainders for default of such issue to Walter, Henry and Edward my second, third and fourth sons and their heirs male; then successively to the heirs of my four sons, to the heirs of myself, and to my brother Sir Walter Myldmay knight and his heirs male on condition that he distribute in alms to the poor prisoners of Colchester and Bury St Edmunds (Suffolk) 40s. yearly in each case and to the poverty of Moulsham £8, Chelmsford 40s. and Widford 40s.; and in default of such issue successively to my brothers William and John and their heirs male under the like condition. Howbeit, if I die, my heir then being within the age of the age of 31 years, then the manors and lands (except the chief mansion house of the manor of Moulsham and its demesnes now in my occupation) shall remain to my executors during 7 years after my decease to the intent that £4, parcel of the profits, shall be yearly bestowed among the poor people of Moulsham and the residue towards the performance of my will; and if I die, my heir being within 31 years, the chief mansion house and demesnes to Thomas for 7 years after my decease, paying my executors £60 a year. Nevertheless my manor of Moulsham to be always charged with the payment of three annuities by me given, viz. to Walter £20, Edward £20 and Henry £10 on the condition hereafter expressed, all for life.

To Thomas the profits of my capital messuage in the parish of St Thomas the Apostle in London with the great garden and stable and the small tenements adjoining until my next heir male be 31, paying yearly £10 to my executors, and thereafter to my heir male and his heirs male as long as there shall be any heir male; for my intent is that my heirs male shall keep the messuage to have continually a handsome house or lodging of their own ready at such times as they have occasion to resort to London, to the accomplishment of which my honest and friendly meaning I require them always to have a natural respect.

To my executors my manor and parsonage of Shouldham (Norfolk), my lands called Southwood in Chelmsford, my lands called Corpes with three parcels in Great Baddow, my lands called the Pype in Moulsham, my manors of Powers in Little Waltham, Little Waltham Hall, and Great Leighs with Bishop's Leighs [in Great Leighs], the reversion of the manor of Pisho [in Sawbridgeworth, Herts.] and the issues and profits, to the end of 7 years, to bestow yearly on Walter and Edward £10 each and on Henry £20 towards finding them exhibition for their good education and towards the increase of their learning and to employ the residue of the issues for the execution of my will; and after the 7 years to Thomas and his heirs the manor and parsonage of Shouldham, also to Walter and his heirs male my reversion of the manor of Pisho. [With further contingent remainders to the same persons.]

To the intent that the Free School of Chelmsford founded and erected by our late sovereign King Edward VI may be the better maintained and the youth and children may be the better attended and instructed in learning and virtue, I bequeath to the Masters, Governors and Rulers and to the Bishop of London a yearly rent of 20 marks to be taken of the tithe corn and hay of my parsonage of Terling for ever, on condition that they shall yearly employ 40s. thereof towards the finding of an usher to serve in the school, £6 among 6 aged, impotent and poorest people in Moulsham (3 men and 3 women) which shall be called the bede folks or poor almspeople of Moulsham, 40s. to buy an ox or bullock to be distributed amongst the poor people of Moulsham on Christmas Eve, and 66s. 8d. to buy 3 barrels of white herrings and 4 cades of red herrings likewise among the poor people of Moulsham and Chelmsford in the first and second week of Clean Lent; provided that the owner of the chief mansion house of Moulsham shall have for ever the nomination of the usher and almsfolk and the distribution of the salary and alms by the oversight of the Masters, Rulers and Governors and the Bishop.

112

The residue of my manors and lands above not willed, which amounteth above the yearly value of the third part of my manors and lands, i.e.
my manors and parsonages of West Bilney and Ayleswithorpe, my manors
of Wormegay, and my manor and parsonage of Ventney (all Norfolk)
to descend to my next heir to the intent that the Queen's Majesty may
take thereof the most profit by way of wardship, livery or primer seisin
as the case may require. My executors during the 7 years shall employ
the yearly profits of my leases of the manor of Fanton with the lands
called Bondviles [in North Benfleet] to Walter, Henry and Edward each
£10 yearly and for the performance of my will; and after the 7 years
the residue of such leases to Walter and Edward jointly, saving that I
give Henry £10 yearly.

To Thomas my lease of the late Priory of Wormegay, the manor of
Grantcourts in East Winch (Norfolk), and the parsonage of Wormegay
from his age of 31; and if he die before, then my next heir which shall
have my house of Ventney (Norfolk) at 26 shall have my lease of the
late Priory, etc. To Edward my annuity of £8 granted to me for term
of years out of certain lands in Coggeshall. To Thomas £300 in ready
money, plate to the value of £20, and my harness, weapons and munitions apt for service in the wars, my flagon chain of gold which I had of
the gift of his grandmother Mistress Gonstone; and if he die before me
then my legacies (saving my weapons) shall be equally divided between
all my sons at 21, and for want of my sons to my daughter Walldegrave
and her children. To Thomas my sealing ring that I wear on my forefinger; and if he die, successively to Walter, Henry and Edward at 21
and my daughter Waldegrave and her children. To Walter and Henry
each £200 and in plate £20, and to Edward £300 and in plate £10, all
at 25; and if any of my sons die before then, the money and plate to be
equally divided between my sons then living, and for lack of any son to
my daughter Waldegrave and Avice Waldegrave her daughter and other
of her children. To my daughter Elizabeth Waldegrave 500 marks and
in plate 20 marks.

All my children incontinent after my decease shall be in the order,
rule and governance of my executors, and they with the pensions
assigned for the education of my children shall provide that they be
honestly kept and brought up in virtue and learning, whereupon I
charge my executors to have great respect as they will answer before
God for the same.

Be it declared that, for the disposition of my stuff and implements of
household, as bedding, hangings, napery, brass, pewter, kitchen stuff, as
many of my children as shall overlive me and be of the age of discretion
and be willing to buy any part thereof as in part payment of their
legacies shall have the preferment of buying at such reasonable prices
as shall be specified in an inventory that shall be made. I bequeath such
jewels, brooches, rings and other things specified in a schedule [not in
registered copy] subscribed with my hand (except jewels and parcels
which Avice my late wife hath given to her children and friends by her
will) to my children equally to be divided by the discretion of my
executors. To my daughter Waldegrave a little salt of silver and gilt that

I gave her mother for her New Year's gift at Christmas 1557. The residue of my ready money, debts owing to me, plate, jewels and other goods, and also such money as shall come of the sale of lands and leases assigned to be sold, and the revenues and profits of my manors, parsonages, lands and annuities before willed to my executors for 7 years, shall remain in their hands concerning the execution of my will and shall be divided as following, i.e. of the overplus I give to the poor people in Moulsham £40 and the residue among my children equally, so the sum do not exceed 1,000 marks. Of the store of my corn and cattle at my manor of Moulsham there shall be reserved from my legacies 10 quarters of wheat, 20 quarters of malt, 5 oxen and 40 sheep towards the provision of my funerals and the maintenance of my house and servants by a convenient time after my decease.

To my cousin Margery Bell of London widow 26s. 8d. for life. In rewards among all my servants to be distributed at the discretion of my executors according to the worthiness of their service and time of the service 50 marks. To my sisters Payton and Thomas to buy each a pot each £4. To my brother William Myldmay one of my gowns, one of my jackets and one of my doublets, and a ring of gold price 30s. with the scripture on the same *Remember me.* To my brother John Mildmay one of my gowns, one jacket, one doublet, and a ring of gold price 30s. with the same scripture, and I forgive him £10 which he oweth me lent out of my purse. To William Waldegrave esquire, my right loving son-in-law, a ring of gold price 40s. with the said scripture, and two of my best geldings at his choice. To Avice Waldegrave his daughter £200 and a chain of gold price £10 at marriage or 21. To her brother William Waldegrave £100 and in plate £10 at 21.

My executors shall bestow upon a comely tomb or monument of hard stone, to be set up and builded by, near or within the church wall of Chelmsford adjoining to the place where Avice my late wife lieth buried, £40 within short time after my decease, in which shall be engraven my arms and the arms of my wife together with the pictures of us both and 15 children, the one half men children and the other half women children, as a remembrance of our being here together upon this earth and for a remembrance to our children and friends left behind us, without any pomp or glory or other respect.

To my brother Sir Walter Myldmay knight for a remembrance a ring of gold with the scripture *Remember me,* price 40s., and a like ring of gold of like price. To my brother Benjamin Gunstone esquire a like ring. To William Rede of Chelmsford 20s. yearly for life. To my cousin Rose Payton, now the wife of Lewger, £20. To Isabel my maid and nurse Sabian, if each remain in service with my children two years after my decease, each £10.

I have annexed [not annexed to registered copy] to my will for the better remembrance and instruction of my executors and to the world a codicil containing a declaration of my estimate concerning as well of what ready money, plate, corn, cattle, debts and other things I was possessed of the day above written, whereof the charges of the execution of my will shall arise, as also a near estimate to what sum my legacies, debts by me owing, and other charges will amount. I ordain my loving brother Sir Walter and my son Thomas to be my executors and my son-in-law William Waldegrave and Benjamin Gunstone to be supervisors, and for a poor remembrance of their friendly travail, diligence and pains, to Sir Walter 66s. 8d. and to my supervisors 40s. each. The moiety of my lease of Southminster shall be sold by my executors towards the execution of my will. To the said 6 poor people of Moulsham 6 loads of wood from my manor of Moulsham yearly for evermore and to be carried to their houses by my heir of Moulsham at his costs as he will answer before God.

Witnesses: Thomas Myldmay, William Waldegrave, Elizabeth Walldegrave, William Myldmay, Robert Dereham, Edward Anleby.

Codicil, 28 August 1566. To the intent that the 6 poor bedefolks of Moulsham should be assured, I bequeath to the Bishop of London a tenement and garden next the Friars gate, in the occupation of Richard Poulson, of the yearly rent of 16s.; a tenement and garden next the same in that of Richard Harrys, rent 13s. 4d.; a tenement with an orchard in that of Philip Walter, rent 13s. 4d.; a tenement adjoining the Greyhound in that of John Weaver, rent 6s.; and a tenement and garden in that of Thomas Haynes, rent 10s.; to hold to the bishop and his successors for ever to the use expressed in my will. To Henry my son, when the reversion of my manor of Pisho shall descend to Walter my son, an annuity of £20 out of it, provided that when the reversion shall fall chargeable with the £20 the annuity of £10 from my manor of Moulsham shall cease. If there remain after the execution of my will so much of my goods as shall discharge my debts and legacies, the moiety of my lease at Southminster need not be put to sale, and then Henry shall have out of it £20 a year for 20 years after the entry of the lease, and the residue to Thomas. Witness: Edward Baker.

Proved 29 January 1567.

HEWET OSBORNE of Parslowes [in Dagenham] esquire, 28 March 1599. [44/43]

Whereas I have two several stocks going or adventuring with Turkey, which if it shall please the Lord to bless them will advance unto £1,500, my will is that, the Lord sending them in safety into England, within two years after their arrival my executors shall with the money buy £100 by the year of good land of inheritance in my son Edward's name, of which notwithstanding he shall not have any profit before he is 21, but the use and profit thereof I give to my wife Joyce until then if she remain a widow; and if Edward die before the land be purchased it shall be in my son William's name and delivered at 21. If my stocks shall not be able to purchase £100 by the year, my wife shall pay so much out of my bequests to her as shall purchase the land; provided that, if any stocks shall happen to be cast away and not return to this realm, my executors shall not be bound to purchase the land nor my wife to make up the money wanting but shall employ or take bond for the rest of the money in the same sort as by my will I shall appoint the rest of my goods.

To my wife during her widowhood my two leases of Clacton and of Thorpe Parks with all the profits. My loving brother [in-law] Robert Offlie of London haberdasher and my brother Edward Osborne of the Inner Temple gentleman shall, with the help of two others whom they shall think good, take bond of my wife that, before her marriage or betrothing, she shall deliver my goods or the value as appraised by my brothers to them to be disposed of as I hereafter shall limit. If Edward die before 21, my brothers shall deliver my goods to William at 21; if he die before 21, to my daughter Alice at marriage; if she die before, my brothers shall have them to their own use. To my wife Cottam Closes (Notts.) for life. To my son Edward my manors or capital granges of Bilby and Randby (Notts.), being one third part of my lands. To my wife until Edward is 21, or if he die until William is 21, my manors of Harthill, Woodhall and Keeton (all Yorks.), my capital messuage of Wales Wood with the lands belonging, with the profits of my coal pits, my lands in Kinolmarsh (Derbys.), with my farm of Woodsetes (Yorks.), To my wife during her widowhood my rentcharge of £16 by the year out of Burton (Notts.) being sometime the inheritance of Hersy Neville esquire deceased, my manor of Parsloes, and my houses which are to descend to me after the death of my mother-in-law Lady Osborne, wife of Mr Baron Clerke, in the city of London, i.e. a tenement in Philpot Lane in the tenure of Robert Bringeborne, which (if by the laws it should have descended to me and not to have been sold with the great house adjoining by my father's will is commanded to be sold) I will she shall have as aforesaid, and four tenements in St Margaret Pattens, London, late the inheritance of Edward Osborne knight deceased. Provided that, if my wife marry or betroth herself, these lands shall remain to Robert Offly and Edward until my son Edward is 21, and if he die before 21 to William until 21; and the profits and rents to be received by my brethren to the best advantage of my two sons, reserving to themselves yearly £80 as long as they shall hold them for their pains and care of my children.

My cousin John Sadler shall be satisfied of his annuity of £24 granted him by my father, also my aunt Mellowes of her annuity of £10 likewise. To my sister Jane £200 at marriage, if she marry with the consent of her brother and sisters before the death of my mother-in-law, but if she shall not marry only £50 to buy her a chain to wear in remembrance of me, because after my mother-in-law's decease her portion will be very good. To Robert Offly and Edward Osborne £50 apiece, which I would entreat them to put in basins and ewers to keep for ever in remembrance of me, also to Edward Osborne £50 when he readeth in any of the Inns of Chancery towards his charges there. To my loving sisters, the Lady Alice Payton of Isleham [Cambs.] and Mistress Ann Offly, £10 apiece to buy them diamonds to wear for my sake. To my old servant Jeffrye Child for his good service done to me £40. All which last six legacies shall be paid out of my lands bequeathed to my wife during her widowhood and out of the profits of my coal pits. I make my executors my wife, Robert Offly and Edward Osborne.

Witnesses : Richard Cheswrighte, John Phippes.

Proved 20 June 1600.

116

JOHN PASCALL of Great Baddow esquire, 15 January 1581.   [24/9]
To be buried in the aisle of Great Baddow church where my friends
have been buried. To the poor people of Great Baddow £40, viz. every
year 20s. I leave to descend to my son John the third part of my manors
and lands to the end that the Queen's Majesty may be therewith satisfied.
To my son Robert my manor of Over Redstone and Nether Redstone
(Northants.) and the reversion or remainder (after the decease of Mary
my well-beloved wife) of my capital messuage or dwelling house in Great
Baddow with the lands belonging and of my lands called Brislandes in
the tenure of Jasper More and of 9 acres in Baddow Mead in that of
John Brooke; and my will is that he shall sell the said lands to him for
his profit. To my wife and to John my manors of Great Baddow and Sir
Hues in Great Baddow and my manor of Newbottle (Northants.), paying
my two daughters Thomasine and Bennet each 500 marks within two
years after their marriages. To my wife my marsh grounds called Hide
and Box Marsh, parcel of my lease of the manor of Dengie Hall; the
residue of my lease to my wife and John to discharge my debts and to
pay my daughters' marriage moneys if there be not sufficient on the sale
of my lands called Baddow Park and towards their maintenance until it
shall please God to send them convenient marriage; and the remaining
profits of the manor to my wife and John, equally during my wife's life,
with remainder to John. I ordain my wife and John executors and the
right worshipful and my very good friend, Sir William Cordell knight,
Master of the Rolls, my supervisor, and to him for a small remembrance
£20 towards the making of a death's head or some other gem of gold as
he shall most delight. Witnesses : John Lathum, Charles Tirell, John
Sammes, John Folderinge.
Proved 10 March 1581.

ANDREW PASCHALL of Springfield esquire, 10 August 1602.   [48/21]

To Philippa my well-beloved wife my household stuff in the little low
parlour where she doth usually lie, for as long as she doth remain in my
manor of Kewton Hall [in Springfield] with Andrew Paschall gentleman,
my son. To Isabel Paschall, my grandchild, his daughter, a chain of gold
at 18 or marriage. To my son my pied stone horse, my ronded mare and
her colt which I bought of Gilbert Damion of Sandon and my brown
young coach mare and her colt. To Thomas Hanchet esquire, my son-in-
law, my young sorrel gelding with a white rase on his face, which now
goeth at the park at Hatfield [Peverel]. To John Hayward my son-in-law,
doctor of the civil law, my grey gelding. To Zachy Farre my son-in-law,
gentleman, my young bay mare which was the colt of my young brown
coach mare. To Andrew my grandchild my young ginnet spayed mare
which now goeth at Bishop's Hall in Chelmsford. To William Paschall
my grandchild my customary tenement called Foxes alias Foxholes in
Great Baddow. To Philip Paschall my grandchild my little spayed mare
colt with a flaxen mane and a white face. Thomas Paschall shall have
Gray Lands conveyed to him by free deed of my manor of Kewton Hall,
paying to the lord thereof 12d. per annum. To Anne and Mary Paschall

my grandchildren each a ring of gold price 40s. To Edmund Paschall my grandchild my messuage called Bagleis wherein Thomas Miller doth dwell. To Andrew my grandchild my tenement called Snowrome Grove and Holdways Crofts adjoining. To Andrew my son my jewels, gold and ready money, together with my plate, my stock of cattle as well beasts as sheep in the occupation of Francis Smith yeoman and James Parker tailor, both of Springfield, with the residue of my goods, whom I make my sole executor, provided that my wife have the household stuff. Witnesses: Francis Smith yeoman, Robert Saye, Andrew Bruer of Springfield yeoman.

Proved 22 February 1604.

WILLIAM PAWN of Writtle esquire, 18 May 1569. [12/20]

To be buried in Writtle church in such place as shall seem good to Ellen my wife. To her for life my manor of Chevers Hall in High Ongar together with its appurtenances and manor of Packnell (Glos.), paying William my son £5 yearly. William Wyttam, Henry Wittam and Thomas Radleye shall occupy such lands as they hold of mine for 5 years after my decease at the same rents as they now pay. To my son my lease of Gold Crofts belonging to the Parsonage, on condition that he suffer his mother to occupy the same for 5 years, paying him yearly £5 6s. 8d. and to the Parsonage the farm rent due therefor. To Writtle church my two new tenements lately builded on the north side of the churchyard wherein William Jennynges dwelleth, my hampstall which I purchased of Thomas Beadell esquire near Deadman Lane, Lamp Croft near the highway from Writtle to Writtle Park and another croft and pightle adjoining near Lee Gate, which crofts are in the tenure of William Powle carpenter, so that the vicar and churchwardens shall place in the two new tenements two aged poor persons not being married, paying nothing therefor, and they shall have of the revenues 3 good loads of pole wood and receive the rest of the revenues quarterly. To William my chain of gold and my sealing ring of gold and £30. To Elizabeth Chappell the elder, one of the daughters of Thomas Chappell deceased, £4. To Alexander and to Mary, Elizabeth the younger and Margaret Chappell his daughters, each 30s. To William Cornelius my servant £4. Whereas Thomas Barker gentleman is indebted to me in £44 by obligation, if he pay £20 then I remit £24. To my loving friend John Rochester esquire £5. To William my lease of the windmill on Norton Heath [in Norton Mandeville] and my apparel and my household stuff in High Ongar. The residue to my wife, whom I make my sole executrix, and I make John Rochester overseer. Witnesses: Thomas Barrington, John Pynchion, William Pawne, Edward Cowper.

Proved 13 September 1569.

PIERCE PENNAUNT of Maylardes in the parish of Hornchurch esquire, 18 December 1589. [34/85]

To my brother William Pennaunt for life my manor or capital messuage called Mailardes alias Mailerdes Green and Naperse and my lands belonging, which within 12 years last past hath been letten as part thereof; my messuages viz. the sign of the Greyhound in the town of Romford and Culies Place alias Parkers, Harolds Wood and Broken Cross in the liberty of the lordship or manor of Havering at the Bower; with successive remainders to my nephew Pyers Pennaunt, to my godson and son of William and his heirs male, and to my brother John Pennaunt and his heirs male. To John my manor of Moyse Hall in Ardleigh and my lands there, and to the heirs male, and for want of issue to my nephew Piers Pennaunt and heirs male; and my houses in Hosier Lane by West Smithfield in the suburbs of London, and to his heirs male. To my nephew William Pennaunt, son of my eldest brother Thomas, and to my nephew Thomas Pennaunt, son of my brother Nicholas, each a coffer bed and a bedstead at Maylardes. To my brother William my bedsteads, linen, brass, pewter, and other household stuff at Mailardes, on condition that he grant to my brother John such bedsteads, linen, brass, pewter and other household stuff which he now hath at Mailardes. To my cousin Robert Gryffeth £6 13s. 4d. if he shall be in my service at my decease. To my cousin Richard Fulkes 53s. 4d. To my brother William my lease of the farm or grange called Fearnes in the liberty of Havering. To my nephew Thomas my lease of the parsonage of Denbigh (Denbighs.). To my nephew William, son of Thomas, the farm called Norton Priory (Yorks.); my niece Elizabeth Jacson £13 6s. 8d.; my nephew William, son of my brother Richard £26 13s. 4d.; my cousin Roger Jones a mourning cloak and 20s.; my cousin, his wife, as much cloth as will make her a mourning gown and 20s.; towards the bringing up of Roger's children £13 6s. 8d.

To the poor people of St Sepulchre-without-Newgate, London, 20s., Romford 20s., Marks Tey 40s., Ardleigh 40s., Hornchurch if I shall not fortune to be buried in that parish 40s., and if I be buried there £6 13s. 4d. and if not then of that parish wherein I shall be buried, and Whitford (Flints.) £5. To the poor prisoners in Newgate 20s. To my servants John Jesse, Elizabeth Thursbie and John Dickson each 40s.

To my well-beloved friend John Legate of Hornchurch gentleman a mourning gown of 16s. the yard at the least. The residue to my brothers William and John, whom I make my executors; and I charge them not to go to law or contend for anything that I have left but to stand to the order to be made by my dear friend Anthony Wingfeilde esquire, whom I make my overseer, and for his pains a black gown and 53s. 4d.

Witnesses : Gregory Kinge notary, George Boulton, Thomas Robartes. Proved 12 December 1590.

ROSE PINCHON of Writtle, widow of William Pinchon esquire, 20 March 1599. [43/28]

To be buried so near as conveniently may be to the place where my late husband lieth buried. To the poor of Writtle £5 at the discretion of my loving friends Mr Edwarde Hunte and Thomas Baker. To the poor of Pinner (Middx.) where I was born £5 at the discretion of my well-beloved brother Mr George Redinge.

To Elizabeth my daughter towards her advancement in marriage £1,000. To Jane my daughter £800 at 18 or marriage. To my sons Henry, William and Christopher each £800 at 21. My executor shall have the occupation and profits of my leases of the rectories and parsonages of Writtle and Roxwell, my leases of East Hall, Garmondes Marsh and Shell Marsh, and my leases of the watermill, windmill and pastures in Writtle and Roxwell granted to me by the Wardens and Scholars of St Mary College of Winchester in Oxford until Edward is 24, when he shall take the profits, provided that, if he die before 24, to Henry. To my executor my grant and lease from the Queen's Majesty and the Master of the Court of Wards of the custody of the body and lands of my son.

To my sister-in-law, wife of my brother-in-law Mr John Pinchon, 3 angels to make her a ring to wear in remembrance of me and a black gown. To my loving neighbours Mr Edward Hunt and his wife each 3 angels likewise and a mourning gown. To my loving friend Thomas Baker a black cloak. To every servant dwelling with me at the time of my decease 10s. To my cousin Mr Thomas Reydinge a black cloak. To John Whitebread my goddaughter 2 angels. To Susan Smewen my servant 40s. Alice Bennett my servant shall be sufficiently provided for in all things necessary for her maintenance at my executor's costs during her life. To every child of my brother-in-law John Pinchon 20s. To my uncle Edward Pinchon a black cloak and to his wife a black gown; and to my uncle Mr Henry Pinchon a black cloak. I forgive them such money as they owe me. To Arthur Machin £3 and a black mourning coat. To Joan Sawcer 10s. To Pleasaunte my late servant, now wife of William Bewtie, my bed in the maids' chamber on which the said Alice Bennett late did lie.

The residue of my goods to my very loving friend Jerome Weston of Roxwell esquire, whom I make my sole executor; nevertheless, if Edward my son after 24 take upon him to perform all things which my executor is to do, my son is to have my leases and goods and Jerome Weston to have only £20 paid to him by my son. Jerome to have the bringing up of my children during their minorities. If Jerome refuse as executor, I make my loving brother-in-law Mr John Leggat my sole executor likewise. I desire my loving brother-in-law Mr John Pinchon to be overseer and for his pains £3 and a mourning gown.

Witnesses: John Legatt, Edward Hunt, Edward Pinchon, John Willyams, Henry Glascocke.

Proved 19 April 1599.

JAMES QUARLES [of Romford] esquire, 21 September 1599. [44/57]

To my well-beloved wife my manors and lands in Hornchurch and Romford for life. To my son Francis an annuity of £50 out of my lands in Rawreth. To my son James an annuity of £50 out of my lands in Stanford Rivers. To my son Arthur my copyhold lands in Hadham (Herts.) according to the custom of the manor there, which is to descend to the youngest son. To my daughter Priscilla £1,500. To my daughter

Mary £1,000. I nominate my wife Joan executrix and my son [in-law] Cope Doylie supervisor. Witnesses: Francis Rame, Ralph Wilkinson, Cope Doylie.

Proved 9 September 1600.

EDWARD RICH the younger of Horndon-on-the-Hill esquire, 11 May 1598.   [42/62]

If the child my wife now goeth withal be a daughter, I will to my brother Robert Rich and his heirs my lands, on this condition that he and his heirs pay to her in the Hall of Lincoln's Inn £1,000 at 21 or marriage. To Robert £7,000 to discharge those sums of money in my hands as the marriage money of my cousin Henry Baker and the profit of the same and the rents of the leases put over by my sister Wiseman during her widowhood to me and Robert in trust for her younger children. To my sister Elizabeth wife of William Page £140 in satisfaction of all her money in my hands. To Judith my wife all the ready money in my trunk next to the press in my chamber and in my desk and all my plate, jewels, apparel, household stuff, nags and geldings. I ordain Robert my sole executor. Witnesses: Edward Rich senior, Thomas May, James Garetes. If it happen that my wife be delivered of a son and my goods will not suffice to pay all my debts and legacies, my executors to sell so much of my lands purchased since my marriage as may suffice, as shall be thought most meet by Sir Richard Saltonstall, Lord Mayor of London, or Edward Rich of Horndon-on-the-Hill esquire, my father, whom I make overseers. Witnesses: Edward Rich senior, Thomas May, Joan Aston.

Proved 4 July 1598.

ROBERT SAMPSON of South Ockendon esquire, 1 October 1589.
                                                                    [34/83]

To my executor my manors and tenement of Buckelers in Lindsey and Sampsons in Kersey (Suffolk), and lands [specified, in many other Suffolk parishes]; also my term of years which I have of the Queen's Majesty under the grant of Robert Wingefeild esquire deceased during the nonage of John Harlestone, her Majesty's ward, in the tenement called Rowles, late in the occupation of Richard Barton deceased, in South Ockendon, and the term of years in South Ockendon Hall; all for four years after my decease, for the performance of my will; and afterwards such manors to my son John. To the poor of South Ockendon 20s.

My executor shall make an inventory of my goods, whereof one part to remain with him and the other to be delivered to my supervisor. All the moveable legacies to John, other than corn and stock of cattle, shall be safely kept by my executor to his age of 21. To John a ring of gold set with a turquoise stone which was his mother's and my household goods at South Ockendon and Kersey to pay my debts, two of my best geldings at my decease, my books at 21 or before as he shall need, and part of my manor of Nether Hall in Harkstead (Suffolk) which I purchased of my nephew Thomas Blanerhassett gentleman and Frances his wife. To my daughter Elizabeth Sampson a gown of my late wife's of stitched taffeta with a satin or damask forepart, with her best petticoat, French hoods, and her wearing linen. To Mary Cave my eldest daughter a hoop ring of gold, which was the marrying ring of her own mother, a gown of satin with kirtle and bodice of fugar satin. To Jane Colthroppe my daughter a gold ring set with a diamond and a gown of my wife's of silk say with a satin forepart and bodice. Further to Elizabeth a plain hoop ring of gold. To my son Cave and his wife £3 apiece to make each a ring or jewel to wear in remembrance of my good will towards them. To my son [-in-law] Calthrop and his wife £3 apiece and to my son [-in-law] Audley 50s. likewise. To my brother [-in-law] Lathum 50s. and my sister Lathum his wife 50s. likewise. To my sister North £10 and a black cloth gown of my late wife's. To Margaret Lathum, daughter of my sister, £20 to be delivered by my loving servant Thomas Cotton, to the preferment of her marriage if she live to 16 or chance to marry before, and if she depart before to Susan Lathum her mother. To Mistress Anne Dinglie my daughter a hoop ring of gold which was the marriage ring of her own mother, late my wife, when she was married to Mr John Harleston esquire, her father, marked with H : M, otherwise to remain to my son John.

Whereas the right honourable the Lady Jane Wentworth in her widowhood did leave in my hands in trust to the use of Anne daughter of Clement Harlestone gentleman deceased £17, and there is £14 10s. 3¾d., the just portion of Mistress Mary Harlestone deceased, remaining in my hands and due to her, and £10 of a legacy given by her to one Mary, another of the daughters of Clement, and due to Anne, I appoint my executor to pay the same sums to her; to Anne, whom my loving wife did bring up, 40 marks. Whereas Faith Webb delivered to my wife 20 marks, which on her death came into my hands, I will my executor to pay the same. To my daughter Elizabeth the bedstead of wainscot with the green valance of say and the green curtains and the cupboard in the gallery chamber, with remainder to my son. To every of my household servants 6s. 8d. To Thomas Cotton my trusty servant 40s., and his wife 26s. 8d., to make each a ring.

My cattle, horses, mares, colts, sheep, udder beasts, hogs, poultry, carts, tumbrils, ploughs, harrows, cart horses and plough horses, yokes, oxbows, and iron work belonging to them; corn and hay in my barns and houses at South Ockendon and corn growing there and at Kersey; a frame of timber which lieth in South Ockendon barn, and other timber and wood ready felled at South Ockendon; I will to be sold by my executor for payment of my debts and legacies. He shall fell the wood and timber trees in Justice Wood in Polstead (Suffolk) within 4 years after my decease for such payments. To John my timber felled at the day of my death, framed, squared, wrought or lying in the pasture or pitle called the Grove between Sampsons Hall and the tenement called Mabiles; also my clamp of brick in Kersey containing beside the allowance for waste six score thousand of brick, as the brickstriker, marker and setter up did covenant with me to make and burn; which timber and brick I will to be safely kept to John's use. 1 require Thomas Cotton to take the care of selling my cattle, corn and other things devised; also to see to the letting of the manors and lands aboveremembered and the felling, stubbing and selling of my woods and trees devised, and to gather up the rents and money; and for his travail £5 a year during 4 years, besides his reasonable expenses. My executor shall yearly pay to Clement Colthropp and Jane his wife £5 towards their relief. The overplus to John, with remainder to my daughters Cave, Colthrop and Elizabeth and John Awdeley, son of my daughter Susan deceased, equally.

Whereas I have given the most part of my manors and goods to my beloved son, hoping that whereby he will bestow himself in some good virtuous house and to maintain the heirs, and for that it should be his quite overthrow to marry any daughters of Cecily Northe widow for divers reasons to me known and I fear my son may be thereto induced, I do hereby move him to take heed thereof. And if he shall not be hereby admonished I will for a further punishment that the manors and lands and the remain of my goods be distributed equally amongst my daughters until the issue of my son come to his lawful age of 21.

To Margaret wife of Thomas Cotton gentleman a black cloak of cloth and a safeguard of black cloth, both guarded with velvet. The rest of my goods, so as my son do not marry contrary to my mind, I give him, and I ordain him my sole executor. I appoint as supervisors my loving sons-in-law Mr Lysley Cave and Mr Clement Calthropp, and for their pains £5 each, and if my son refuse to be my executor I appoint Mr Cave and Mr Calthropp my executors, and they shall yearly make account to my supervisors, and for that purpose I appoint my well-beloved cousin Mr Thomas Beddingefeilde the [privy] councillor. I discharge my nephew Thomas Northe of his bond for repayment of £23 odd money he doth owe me.

Witnesses : William Lathum, Thomas Cooper.

Proved 2 December 1590.

LEONARD SANDELL of Hatfield Peverel esquire, 24 August 1570.

[13/33]

To the poor people of Hatfield where I now dwell 40s., Witham 20s., Terling 20s., Boreham 20s., Chelmsford and Moulsham 20s., Little Baddow 5s., Ulting 5s., Woodham Mortimer 5s., Woodham Walter 5s., Danbury 10s., Fairstead 5s., Wickham [Bishops] 5s., Springfield 5s., Rivenhall 5s., Great and Little Braxted 5s., Great Stambridge 10s., and Fairford (Glos.) where I was born 40s. To the poor prisoners of Newgate 20s., Ludgate 20s., the Fleet 20s., the King's Bench in Southwark 20s., and the Marshalsey 20s. To the poor people of the Spittle House of Moulsham 10s. To every of my household menservants 10s. and women-servants 5s. To Thomas Ivie and John Overed, my clerks, each a black gown and a coat, and my other menservants a black mourning coat.

To Besse Pilbarough, my [step-] son John Pilbarough's daughter, brought up in my household, 10s. To either of my wife's sons, John and Christopher Pilbarough, a ring of gold with a death's head worth 40s.

and a black gown and a coat. To Mr Tyte of London apothecary a like ring worth 40s. To Mary and Jane, my wife's daughters, each a ring of gold with a death's head worth 20s. and the like to my daughter Pilbaroughe of London and my cousin, wife to John Ivie of London, gentleman. To every of my wife's daughters, Elizabeth, Ellen, Mary and Jane [Pilbarough], a mourning cassock. To my daughter, wife of John Pilbaroughe, my ring with the pearl. To every of my godsons 10s.

To Richard Knighte of Rotherhithe [Surrey] my cousin my silver porringer which I had of the gift of his mother. To my cousin, wife of John Tyrrell of Warley esquire, my grey nag which I had of the gift of Mr Serjeant Knottisforde of Worcestershire. To my niece, my brother Robert Sandall's daughter, my ring with a pointed diamond in it and his wife my ring with a turquoise. To my brother Edmund Sandell my apparel at London and here in the country and my dun nag. To Ellen Pilbaroughe my wife's daughter £86 13s. 4d., so as her stock in my hands which is 20 marks shall make up with my legacy £100. To Elizabeth Cooke my wife's daughter, wife of Richard Cooke, my little signet ring with my signet engraved in it to wear for a remembrance. I give and forgive to my brother Robert Sandell all debts he oweth me on condition that he shall be good to his brother and mine Edmund Sandell. To Robert my great ring with my seal of arms and my seal of silver made likewise with my seal of arms and cognizance which I use to seal with, and one of my trotting geldings which he will choose, my two bedsteads at Stratford-at-Bow [Middx.] in my cousin Tyrrell's house there, the bedstead in my great chamber here at Hatfield, the andirons of copper in the same, my best carpet, a garnish of pewter vessel that I bought last, being of silver fashion, with the chargers and plates belonging, my great copper in the hall, my nest of gilt bowls with the cover, my dozen of gilt spoons, and my great salt gilt, all on condition that he shall not give or sell the same but whensoever God shall call him out of this world leave all to his daughter and other his children if he happen to have any more; if she die before him and he have no mo[re] children, I charge him to have them praised to the uttermost worth, and half the value to bestow on the poor and in other good deeds of charity where most need is and the other half to bestow on my brother Edmund and his children, if he have any, and if none I charge him to bestow likewise on the poor and in charity. To the wife of Christopher Pilbaroughe, my son-in-law, my serjeant's ring in my wife's custody.

To Robert my two leases of the manor of Great Stambridge, paying Edmund yearly £10; nevertheless he shall permit my wife to have the yearly use of the profits and rents for life; my lease of Rivers Hall in Boxted on condition that he shall not sell it to any other but to one of my executors or to my cousin William Dawtry esquire and his wife, of whom I had the same, so as any of them will give him £200, otherwise to be at his liberty.

The residue of my goods to Elizabeth my wife, whom with Robert, John Ivie secondary of my office, and Thomas Ivye my clerk, I ordain my executors, and for their pains to John Ivie a black gown and my ring which I have of the legacy of my son Anthony Pilbarough remaining yet in his wife's hands not delivered and to Thomas Ivie a ring with a death's head to be made for him worth 26s. 8d.

To my cousins John Tyrrell and his wife my lands in Little Warley called West House and the Crown tenement which I bought of my cousin John Tyrrell of Little Warley esquire; with remainder to their daughter Mary for life. If the marriage craftily and unhonestly had between William Porter and her happen to be dissolved and she marry with some other honest gentleman of honest parentage by consent of her parents and friends, I will West House and Crown tenement shall remain after her decease to her heirs; but, if the marriage be not dissolved but they join themselves together and so live together as man and wife, after her decease to remain to Stephen brother of John Tyrrell.

To my wife for life my lands at Langdon Hills called Goldsmiths in the tenure of Lawrence Pake and [blank] Hulke, which I had in mortgage of John Tyrrell, and the day of repayment being passed long ago so as by right of law the same is to me absolutely; the remainder thereof to my heirs; nevertheless if John Tyrrell or my cousin his wife do within two years after my decease pay her £200 he shall have the lands again for their lives, and after their deceases to remain to my cousin Mary their daughter for life, with remainders regarding her marriage as aforesaid.

Witnesses: John Tighte, Robert Turner, Richard Fissher, Jervis Malyn.

Proved 25 November 1570.

GEORGE SAYER of Colchester the elder, esquire, 16 March 1595. [For George Sayer gentleman, see p. 249.]   [40/73]

To Rose my wife for life the use of my 3 little white silver bowls, 4 white silver beakers, the second gilt salt, 2 silver ordinary salts, one dozen ordinary silver spoons, the best carpet, the silk quilt and yellow curtains and valance, the damask table cloth, napkins and towel, and so much armour as she shall be charged with. To my daughter Pretiman the second gilt salt. After my wife's decease the residue to George my son. To her the use of my furniture in the little chamber in my house, and after her decease to Thomas my son, and my coach and coach horses, provided that she become bound in £200 to my supervisors for the delivery to George and Thomas after her decease, as also to pay to William Greene my servant £100. Whereas certain lands are assured to her for her jointure for life, she shall yearly have 80 cartloads of cubit wood of the wood in Braswick, Kelpastures, Shrittes Woods and Chesterwell Woods and 10 cartloads of logs of the doted trees there for her necessary firing and shall permit George to dispose of the residue of my woods. I devise 8 loads of wood yearly to be taken in any of my lands to my poor almspeople which hereafter dwell in my four almshouses in Balkon Lane. To the poor of Colchester £5. My wife or my son George shall not take out of my house any furniture but after her decease it shall remain furnished to my son Thomas, to whom I give the furniture. To my wife my copyhold island in Colchester holden of the manor of

Lexden for life, with remainder to Thomas according to my father's will. I appoint George my sole executor and my loving brothers William Cardinall esquire and Charles Cardinall gentleman my supervisors and to each as a remembrance £5. To my good friends Dr Gilbert and Mr Robert Middleton junior to make each a ring as a token of my goodwill £3 6s. 8d. To my cousin Richard Sayer to make him a ring 40s. To my brother Pye 40s. to make him a ring and to Mr Samuell and his wife each 20s. To Rose Browne my grandchild a piece of plate worth £5 at marriage. To every of my servants 10s. Witnesses: John Pye, Robert Middleton, Richard Sideye, William Greene, John Carter, Richard Parker.

Proved 9 October 1596.

GEORGE SCOTT of Chigwell esquire, 22 May 1588. [For William Scott, see p. 250.]   [33/98]

To be buried in the chapel of Chigwell church between my two wives. To the churchwardens of Chigwell £3 to the reparations of the church. To the poor people of the parish £3. To Arthur Crafford gentleman and Thomas Allen of Chigwell yeoman £4 to be bestowed in the mending of the highways between Lambourne Bridge and Randolphs Mead 20s. and between Lambourne Cross and Billingborne Lane end next the Forest £3, where most need is. My executor shall pay such debts and legacies as of right I ought to pay as executor to the right worshipful Dame Julian Norwich deceased, i.e. to the poor of St Andrew Undershaft in London 40s. and to Christ's Hospital in London 40s., and as executor of Jane Spencer of London widow if any remain.

To George Scott my godson, son of William Scott my son, and to George's heirs my manor of Woolhampton Hall alias Wolston Hall with the appurtenances in Chigwell, which I hold for divers years by a lease made by Humphrey Browne serjeant-at-law, Richard Baron of Walden gentleman, Richard Gibson citizen and merchant tailor of London, John Lowen citizen and draper of London, Thomas Cheverell citizen and haberdasher of London, and Thomas Greene of Cottered [Herts.] yeoman, to Hugh Scott of South Weald, my father, dated 1534; and the use of the plate and household goods specified, i.e. my best standing cup of silver and gilt, my best square salt all gilt, a silver pot parcel gilt with my arms on the lid, 12 silver spoons of the Apostles, and a gilt spoon with letters engraved on the steal; the hangings of the Great Chamber, with table, frame, forms, stools, and the long carpet with my arms and my last wife's, the cupboard and carpet with the Browne arms and the window carpet to it; the hangings of the Green Chamber of leather, the walnuttree bedstead and the tester with my arms and my two wives', the curtains of red and green silk and the best covering, a chair embroidered with blue velvet, a tawny velvet cushion with a rose embroidered on it, the cupboard and carpet to it of tent work, a long cushion and 2 other cushions all like the carpet; the hanging of the Garden Chamber with the bedstead, the covering of imagery work lined with canvas, the sparver with the curtains of red silk, the cupboard and a carpet of carpet work, the ground black; the furniture of my chamber called the Gallery Chamber, i.e. the bedstead, the press in that chamber, and a covering of tapestry; a garnish of pewter vessel with the plate trenchers, all marked with my arms; and the great racks in the kitchen, 2 long round spits and a great square spit, 2 of the best brass pots, and the vats, leads and other implements belonging to the brewhouse. If he die without heir male, my lease of the manor and the use of the goods shall remain successively to Thomas, William, John, Edmund and Hugh, my second, third, fourth, fifth and sixth and youngest sons of William my son, and to each of their heirs male; provided that, if William shall at any time be minded to take the lease of the manor to his own use, on payment of £100 to such of the said grandsons as have it the bequest to them shall cease, and also the plate and household stuff shall remain in the possession of William for life and then be delivered to such grandson likewise.

To Robert my son a silver salt parcel gilt to be bought by my executor worth £3 6s. 8d. and a bowl parcel gilt worth £3 6s. 8d., and 6 silver spoons the ends gilt [? worth] 8s. apiece, Robert delivering to his brother William or George his son the 6 silver spoons which he hath now of mine; a good featherbed and tester in the Gallery Chamber with swans of gold and the curtains and a coverlet of tapestry. To Robert and Joan his wife a black gown each. To Prudence wife of my son William a book of gold and a ring of gold with a diamond in it which she hath of mine, and a black gown. To my daughter Anne Crafford my black nag and a black gown. To Elizabeth Scott, daughter of William, the use of a flagon chain and a pair of bracelets to the same of gold and a brooch of gold at 18, and a black gown; if she decease before that age or marriage, to remain to George my godson, her brother. To my nephew Hugh Base 2½ yards of black to make him a cloak to wear at my burial and 20s. to make a ring. To my niece Gouldes a ring worth 10s.

To John Mundes my man a black coat and 10s., and I charge William and George that they never put him out nor raise the rent of the field called Langlondes which he holdeth for the rent of 5 marks a year so long as he will serve them. To Peter Greene my woodward a black coat and 10s. To him that shall serve me waiting on me at the time of my death a black coat and 40s. To Richard and Robert Miles my nephews each 2½ yards of black cloth to make them a cloak. To my niece Holmes 20s. To Thomas, William, John, Edmund and Hugh £20 apiece at 21 and Elizabeth and Mary £20 apiece at 18 or marriage. To Mary Crafford, daughter of my son-in-law Arthur Crafford, a ring of gold with a ruby in it which my daughter, her mother, hath of mine at 18. To William Parris of Dagenham 1½ yards of black cloth to make him a coat. To Agnes a Lee, servant of my house, as much cloth as will make her a gown. The residue of my goods to William, whom I make my sole executor, and I make Robert and Arthur Crafford overseers; to Arthur a black gown and to Robert my ring with a death's head in it.

Witnesses: Arthur Crafford, Robert Scott gentleman, Thomas Allen, Nicholas Hill, John Mundes, and others.

Proved 15 December 1589.

GEORGE SCOTT (SKOTT) of Hatfield Broad Oak esquire, 3 February 1589.   [33/24]

To be buried at Stapleford Tawney without any pomp or great ado. To the child that my wife Dorothy, if she be conceived withal, if it be a son, my manor of Stapleford Tawney, and to his heirs male, after my wife's decease, paying my two daughters Elizabeth and Mary £500 piece at 21 or marriage; if the child be a daughter, to my three [*sic*] daughters jointly and to their heirs, with remainder to my brothers Roger, William, Richard and John, and their heirs male. To my wife my manor of Wolston Hall in Chigwell for life, with successive remainders to my son if it so happen and his heirs male, to all my daughters, and to my brothers. I will that the Queen's Majesty hath for a third part of my manors one third of my manor of Howsham Hall [in Matching]. To my wife the residue of the manor during my children's minorities towards bringing them up, with remainder to my son if it so happen or my daughters, with like remainders. After the decease of Elizabeth my mother, my wife shall have my manor of Lies Hall [in Hatfield] to pay the legacies of £400 to my two sisters bequeathed them by my father Roger Skott esquire deceased, which my manor of Stapleford Hall is charged withal and to pay such sums as my wife shall be charged and for repairing my manor house of Stapleford Hall; and after such charges the manor of Lies Hall to my son and his heirs male, with successive remainders to my daughters jointly and to my brothers, paying my brothers £6 13s. 4d. yearly. The residue of my lands to my wife for life, with like remainders; also the residue of my goods to my wife, whom I ordain my sole executrix. I appoint my father-in-law John Francke esquire and my uncle John Skott of the Inner Temple esquire overseers, and for their pains £5 each. Witnesses: Robert Franck, John Bridges, Nicholas Michell notary public.

Proved 13 February 1589.

THOMAS SHAA of Terling esquire, 27 March 1600.   [44/58]

To be buried in Terling church. To Thomas my eldest son my best gilt salt and my best gilt bowl. To my daughter Mary Deresley my second best gilt bowl. To my son Robert my signet ring with my arms graven therein and my book of Acts and Monuments. To my reputed son Edmund, one of the sons of Philippa Shaa alias Rochester, daughter of one John Rochester of Terling esquire deceased and now my wife or reputed wife, £100. To John, Thomas and Richard, three other of the sons of Philippa, £100 apiece at 21. Philippa shall convey to her son John a messuage in Terling wherein one Smith dwelleth or else £25. To Mary, Faith, Eleanor and Judith, daughters of Philippa, £100 apiece at 18 or marriage, and if any marry before that age the legacy to be void; and Faith, Eleanor and Judith shall be maintained by my executor until the time appointed. The residue of my goods to Philippa. I ordain her and Edmund executors. Witnesses: Edward Rochester, Anthony Lowe.

Proved 22 October 1600. Sentence, 23 November 1601, confirming

Will in case between (1) Philippa Shaa *alias* Rochester, executrix, and Thomas Shaa, eldest son, Mary Deresley *alias* Shaa and Robert Shaa, children of the deceased.

CHRISTOPHER SIBTHORP of Writtle esquire, 14 January 1601.
[45/2]

To be buried in Writtle church as near as possible to my father; if I cannot my desire is to be buried in the chancel. To the poor of Writtle £5. To my wife her apparel, jewels, household stuff and plate. My other goods as well corn as cattle shall go to the payment of my debts. The messuage called Branwoodes with the lands belonging should be sold to the payment of my debts, and Mr John Pinchin should have the offer of it, giving within £10 as another will give. In like manner the Stoke House shall so be disposed of. Out of these sales my mother shall have £40. To Samuel Perry and Christopher Perry my nephews £6 13s. 4d. apiece, Anne Sibthorpe my niece £6 13s. 4d., Christopher son of George Haughton £10, Christopher son of my brother Elmer £6 13s. 4d., and Christopher son of John Sibthorpe my brother £6 13s. 4d., all at 21 or marriage. I ordain my beloved wife and my brother William executors and my overseers my father-in-law Mr Bynnyan, George Haughton, Robert Sibthorpe my brother, and my cousin William Bedwell of Sheering. Witnesses : John Monke, Richard Benyan, Thomas Ascham, John Woolmer.
Proved 26 January 1601.

JOHN STONARDE of Luxborough in Chigwell esquire, 1 October 1579.
[23/50]

My body which is but dust and ashes shall be comely covered with earth by the discretion of my executor. To Anne my well-beloved wife for life my manor and mansion of Luxborough and the lands belonging, and my farm in Chigwell in the tenure of Robert Spakeman. An inventory indented be made by my wife and my executors of my household stuff and plate in Luxborough, one part of which to be delivered to Susan my daughter, wife of Robert Wrothe esquire, and the other to remain with my wife; and she shall have the use of it for life, being first bound with two sureties by recognizance in the Chancery to my executor in £200 that it shall remain after her decease to Susan and Robert. My wife shall have the profits and use of 24 kine and 1 bull on my manor of Luxborough and Chigwell Hall, serving for the provision of my house, 6 draught oxen and 4 cart horse which I cart withal and use in husbandry, and my carts and ploughs, carting ware and plough ware, provided that she be bound in £100 that they or the like in number and goodness by the judgement of two honest persons shall after her decease remain to Susan and Robert. To my wife my manor of Steeple Grange with the lands belonging heretofore (as I trust) sufficiently assured to her for life. Whereas I sold for £1,100 to Robert both leases of my manor of Loughton, i.e. my lease in reversion as in possession of the manor of Loughton alias Lucton Hall, parcel of the possessions of the Duchy of Lancaster, with an agreement that I take the profits for the yearly rent reserved, and after my decease my wife likewise for life, for the love I bear to Richard Stonerd my brother I give him an annuity of £10 out of the manor during her life. To Robert and Susan another annuity of £40. My wife shall have for life the residue of the profit of the manor, heartily praying Robert to see the same truly paid to her. To my wife £100 and 5 of my best geldings. She shall after my decease renounce to them her title in my marsh grounds called Barking Marshes in Barking and [West] Ham. To Francis Stonarde my brother £20. To my sisters Fuller, Barefoote and Hunte £10 apiece. To my brother Tyrell and my cousin Stacy a ring of gold price 40s. in token of my goodwill. To Philip Grenly a ring of price 40s. To my menservants and maid-servants ordinarily attendant in my house 20s. apiece. To Matthew Losell 20s. for the pains taken in this my last sickness. To Thomas Bettes 40s. The residue of my goods and my leases, stocks of cattle and corn, plate, jewels and money to my son-in-law Robert Wrothe esquire, whom I make my sole executor. Witnesses : Thomas Wrothe, Richard Dawes, Matthew Lanhill, William Palmer.

Codicil. To my niece Anne Mayes and to William Ingleton 40s. apiece. Proved 12 December 1580.

WILLIAM STRANGMAN of Hadleigh esquire, 4 December 1573.
[17/28]

To be buried in Hadleigh church. Bartholomew my eldest son shall have my leases in Hadleigh with the stock of cattle there and the profits for 7 years after my death, on condition that he grant my son James an annuity of £20 out of my lands in Purleigh, Rawreth and Rayleigh. Whereas I have made my wife a jointure of certain of my lands, I will that in no wise she be molested or troubled thereof during her life. To Bartholomew my lands in Essex, and for default of issue to James. To James £200 at 21. To my daughter Thomasine 500 marks at 21. To my serving men 20s. and the residue of my servants 6s. 8d. apiece. To my brother John Barmston 40s. yearly for 6 years after my death. To Ursula Rochester £6. The residue of my goods to my executor to per-form my will. I nominate Bartholomew my eldest son my sole executor. Witnesses : Richard Burrowes, Edward Erington and John Sturdye.

Proved 19 June 1574. Administration granted, 3 November 1604, to Bartholomew and Mary Strangman.

JOAN SYMPSON of Chigwell, widow and sole executrix of Nicholas Simpson esquire, one of the Privy Chamber of King Edward VI, 6 November 1560. [5/13]

To be buried nigh the place where my late husband lieth. My execu-trix shall expend £80 about the reparations of the highway between London and Chigwell. To the Hospital of Christ in London £20 on con-dition that my idiot Julian Herne shall be first admitted to the Hospital, there to continue and be found at the costs of the Hospital during her life, otherwise the legacy to be void, she to be sufficiently apparelled at the time of her delivery into the Hospital at the costs of my executrix.

To Michael Pott my late servant and Agnes his wife 2 kine, a featherbed, 2 brass pots, one of 2 gallons and another of 4 gallons, 2 of my middle pans, a long plain tablecloth, and a dozen plain napkins. To Richard Cutwarde my late servant 2 kine and a featherbed. To 4 poor women of Chigwell 4 gowns of London russet. To Audrey wife of Hamnet Brasie, citizen and haberdasher of London, my smaller ring of gold with a sapphire set in it.

Whereas Nicholas did bequeath besides other things to Robert his son, Thomas Northropp, citizen and clothworker of London, and Nicholas son of William Sympson, citizen and barber surgeon of London deceased, my husband's son, the moiety of divers parcels of silver plate to be delivered to them at my marriage or decease, which should first happen, which Robert is now deceased, whereof his part remaineth to me, I bequeath it to Joan Sympson, sister to Nicholas, and to Thomas, Nicholas and Joan the other moiety, equally among them. To Joan a garnish of vessel, 2 fair brass pots, 2 pans of 4 gallons apiece, a tablecloth, a dozen napkins and a towel, all of damask. To Susan Simpson, sister to Joan, a tablecloth, a towel and a dozen napkins, all of diaper, and a hoop ring of gold with the Five Wounds in it.

To Roger my servant 5 marks. To Margaret my maidservant 5 marks, a wool mattress, a featherbed, a plain tablecloth, and half a garnish of vessel. To my servants Joan Gowlde 5 marks and Ellen Stewarde 40s. My said servants shall have after my decease one month's meat and drink at the charges of my executrix at my house wherein I dwell. To every of my godchildren a silver spoon with an apostle.

I make Audrey Bracie my sole executrix and for her pains £10, and I make overseer Hamnet Bracie, and for his pains a great ring of gold with a sapphire in it. To Nicholas son of William Sympson my mansion house called Stiche Marsh with the messuages and lands belonging in Chigwell, with a lease of Brache Close and 3 acres in Stame Mead granted to me by John Stoner gentleman and others for 99 years, and my household stuff at Stiche Marsh; and for lack of issue the house and the lease to be sold and the money distributed among the poor where most need shall be; provided that Audrey shall occupy the premises in Chigwell until Nicholas is 23, paying him yearly £4. To him my great messuage called the Crucifix with shops, cellars, sollers, stables, yards and gardens in St Olave in Southwark (Surrey); and for default of issue it be sold and the money distributed likewise, Audrey paying £4 to Nicholas for occupying it until he is 23. [No witnesses.]

Proved 9 May 1562 by Audrey or Ethelreda Braci executrix.

CLEMENT SYSLEY of Eastbury Hall in Barking esquire, 1 September 1578. [21/36]

To be buried in the chancel of Barking church near the place where my late wife lieth. To Anne my wife for life my house called Eastbury

Hall, with the barns, stables, dovehouses, orchards and gardens, reserving the greatest barn and garden to my heir; my lands in my own occupation adjoining the said manor as it is fenced with pale and ditch; 12 load of wood out of the Forest called my livery wood belonging to the farm; the marsh grounds and meadows in the occupation of one Somner; the Mill Field alias the Conigree or warren of coneys in my occupation; and 50 acres of ground in that of one Collen for the yearly rent of £7; and after her decease to my son Thomas. To him my tithes of corn sheaf and hay in my occupation in Ripple and Chadwell wards in Barking; the meadows and house in that of Collen called Upney Place; the lands in that of Jeffrey Snagges the younger; ground called Woulfennes Piece in that of William Nutbrowne gentleman; certain grounds in that of George Mayle yeoman; ground called Fishponds in that of one Devell; and my manor called Bayers Hall [Barows in Chadwell St Mary] with the appurtenances in that of Jeffrey Snagges the younger; and for default of heirs male to remain successively to Edward my son and his heirs male, to Cordell my son and his heirs male, to Elizabeth my daughter and her heirs male or female, to Anne Sysley my daughter and her heirs male or female, to the heirs male of Thomas, to Mary Harman my daughter and her heirs, and to Clement Elliott my sister and her heirs. To Edward a farm or grange called Maybelles in the tenure of Jeffrey Snagges the elder and a parcel of ground called Foremans alias Lurchendown. To my wife her jewels and apparel, my sorrel gelding, my grey curtal, and half my household stuff to be equally divided between her and Thomas. To Elizabeth my lease of East Ham Hall with the appurtenances, which is 28 years yet to come, paying yearly to Arthur Breme esquire the rent reserved. To Anne and Cordall my lease of the manor of East Ham Burnelles and West Ham Burnelles, the manor of East West Ham and the manor of Place, to be divided equally between them. My leases shall remain in my iron chest wherein my evidences lieth, my Lady Allington, Peter Osburne and my executrix each to have a key and the chest not to be opened without the consent of all three. To Anne and Cordall my lease of Plometree Marsh, which is 77 years to come, equally to be divided. Provided that my wife shall have my leases for 10 years after my decease.

To my Lady Allington my mother, Peter Osburne and Edward Osburne, aldermen of London, each 5 marks to make a ring or some other jewel for a remembrance. To my brothers Richard Argall and Lawrence Argall esquires 40s. apiece to make a ring. To Thomas Elliott my servant 20s. a year for life. To all my menservants and womenservants 20s. apiece.

To Thomas my armour and furniture of armour, my guns, dags, pikes, bills, targets and crossbows, and they are to remain as standards and implements of household to him and his heirs for ever at Eastbury. To my brother Michael Flemming esquire 5 marks. To my sister 2 kine, she to take her choice. I make my well-beloved wife my sole executrix. I ordain my very loving mother, my Lady Allington, Peter Osburne and Edward Osburne my overseers, trusting that they will be good to my wife and my children, hoping that Peter will get the wardship of Thomas to the use of my wife for her money.

Witnesses: Thomas Lynn, Hugh Launder, Thomas Elliott, Katherine Kysse, Elizabeth Hall.

Renunciation of executorship, 4 October 1578, by Anne widow of the deceased.

CONSTANCE TEY of Layer-de-la-Haye gentlewoman, 15 January 1575. widow of John Tey of Layer esquire. [18/40]

To be buried in the earth near the place where my late husband lieth, and for the decency of my burying I give £4 to the engraving and working of a stone to be laid on my husband and me. To the poor of Layer-de-la-Haye 20s., Copford 20s., Marks Tey 20s., and Aldham 20s. To my eldest son Thomas Tey esquire one book of gold and £20. To Eleanor his wife a chain of gold. To William my son £20 and a pot with a cover and foot of silver and gilt. To Parnel his wife my best gown and a kirtle of worsted. To Edmund my son £60. To Henry my son £60 at 24, until which time Thomas to have the use of it for the finding of Edmund, but if he die before it be divided among the residue of my other children. To Elizabeth my daughter the bed which she lieth in, £10 at 32 [sic] or marriage, and my lease of the vicarage of Layer, Thomas to dispose of it for her most commodity, and if she die before the lease be expired then the profits to Harry my son towards his finding and augmentation of his living. To Jane my daughter the bed in which I lie and £80, and if she die before marriage £40 to the poor of Layer, £10 to Elizabeth, £20 to the poor of Layer for a continual stock as by Thomas and two of the chief inhabitants shall be best devised, £20 to William's eldest child, and the residue equally divided among my other children. My stuff named and not appraised in an inventory made between me and Thomas shall remain in the manor house of Layer-de-la-Haye as perpetual looms, implements and necessaries. I ordain Thomas only executor, who shall enter into sufficient bonds with Edmund Pirton esquire, Dr Pennye and William for the performance of my will. The residue of my goods shall be equally divided among my children. Witness: Thomas Teyrum.

Proved 4 November 1575.

EDWARD THURSBYE of Bocking esquire, 9 October 1602. [47/17]

To be buried in decent manner in Bocking church near the place where my late wife was buried. To the poor people of Bocking £4, Braintree 40s., Stisted 20s., Panfield 13s. 4d., and Gosfield 13s. 4d.

To Elizabeth wife of John Westhrop gentleman £40. To the children of John Smith my son-in-law which he had by Katherine my daughter £100, to be equally divided, at marriage or 18. To Edward Thursby the eldest son of my son Edward £40 at 21, and the rest of Edward's children £20 at 21 or marriage. To William Thursby my grandchild and his heirs male my messuage called the Cardinal's Hat in Bocking in the tenure of Richard Baker and Edward Jegoe. To Henry (whom I have brought up) £20, and to Thomas, John and Edward Thursby, all four sons of my son Christopher, each £20 at 21. To William Dennys my kinsman £30 at 21. To my cousin Anne Jenney £10. To Henry my messuage in Bocking in the tenure of William Barnard glover, an annuity of £10 out of my lands called Dorewardes Park in Bocking. To Thomas my messuage in Bocking in that of Naboth Hodge. To John my messuage in Bocking late in that of Jeremy Hodge deceased. To Edward my curtilage and ground where a dwelling house is appointed to be built adjoining said tenement in that of Jeremy Hodge.

To my servant William Hull my gravel pit, parcel of Dorewardes, to be fenced at his costs, and for erecting a dwelling house on the same, also £5 towards its building. To my servant Robert son of Robert Cooke another parcel of ground, parcel of my Bickmans Piece, lying between the two ponds in Bocking, to be likewise fenced for erecting a dwelling house, and £5 likewise; also a bullock of 2 years old. To Anne Hodge my servant £3 and a bullock of 2 years old. To Christopher Smarte my servant £5. To my farmers and tenants, i.e. Jeffrey Lingwood, Martin Skynner, Gilbert Joslyn, Erasmus Sparhawke, [blank] Barnerd yeoman, Anthony Hide, Henry Robertes, Naboth Hodge, Barnaby Fenner, William Wryghte, Richard Tebalde, old Ounsted, Richard Woodwarde, Thomas Gilbert, John Davy, John Turner, William Barnerd glover, and Richard Belsted, each 13s. 4d. to buy so much black cloth as shall make each a mourning coat, to accompany my corpse. Naboth Hodge and Philippa his wife shall enjoy my messuage from the end of my lease which they now have for the life of the longer liver at the existing rent.

My executors for a year after my decease shall maintain my household and family at my mansion house of Dorewardes Hall where I dwell or so many of them as will remain with my executors as servants with them and with such hospitality and housekeeping as I have maintained. The residue of my goods to John and Edward, whom I make my executors, and supervisors I nominate and entreat to be my worshipful good friends Mr Francis Gawdy, one of her Majesty's Judges of the Court of King's Bench, and William Towse esquire, counsellor at the law, entreating them to help my executors with their advice. [No witnesses.]

Proved 12 February 1603.

TIRRELL : see TYRELL.

GEORGE TUKE of Layer Marney esquire, 1 September 1572. [17/23]

To be buried in hallowed ground where God shall dispose and with costs of funerals at my burial as best shall seem to the discretion of my executors.

To my loving wife Margaret sufficient household stuff meet for the furniture of one chamber, her own apparel and jewels, and my plate. My other goods I leave to my executors to employ them towards the payment of my debts and legacies; and if any of my household stuff be sold by my executors, my wife shall have the preferment in the buying. To them the custody of my lease of the manor of Brook Hall [in Tolleshunt Knights] to see it occupied to the most advantage until George my son, son of Amy Easton otherwise called Amy Carter, commonly called George Tuke, is 21, and the yearly profit employed towards his education and bringing up and the residue delivered to him then; if he die before, to Peter my son, and if he die before 21, to Brian my son. To every of my household servants 13s. 4d.

Whereas I and my wife hold to us and our heirs male the manor of Abbots Hall [in Great Wigborough], a messuage called Morrells, lands called Ulkins and Wimpledon, lands called Sawmans in the occupation of Richard Saverie, lands called Mathens with parcel of land called Purches Lands in that of Edward Mutton, 3 parcels of land called Widdowes Lands, and lands and a tenement called New Park in that of Edward Crefeld; to the yearly value of £60 8s. 7d.; all which shall continue as by the conveyances is assured. Whereas I hold to myself and my heirs male the manors of Thorpe and Thorpe Hall [in Southchurch] and East Lee [in Basildon]; and whereas I hold to my heirs in fee simple lands and a tenement belonging called Vyners in Messing, How Field Meadow and Taylors Crofts and divers other lands, parcel of the demesne of my manor of Layer Marney in the tenure of Robert Camock, a tenement and lands belonging called Rockinghams and Argents in his occupation, Clerkes Lands in that of Richard Saverie, a tenement and lands in that of Thomas Gage called Haines Purches and Brises Broome, Great and Little Ackendons, two tenements and lands called Bettes and Bettes Meadow and Makins or Smithehouse, a croft of 2½ acres sometime Richard Camock's, Pipers Croft in that of Henry Makin, a tenement and lands called Browninges and Cock Croft in that of Thomas Tunbridge, a cottage called Thedoms in that of one Pope; which manors and lands are of the yearly value of £88 11s. 8d; I leave the manors and lands to descend as a full third part of all my lands to Peter according to the statutes I have in the same.

Whereas I hold to myself and my heirs in fee simple the mansion house of the manor of Layer Marney, with the greens, gardens, orchards, waters, ponds, moats, and 27 acres of meadow and pasture, parcel of the demesne of my manor of Layer Marney, called Hall Meadow and Shortland, the park of Layer Marney, Layer Marney Wood, the glebe lands, and a messuage with divers lands called the Dairy or Wick of Layer Marney, part in my own tenure and part in that of John Wayde, I bequeath and dispose the mansion house and the premises for 14 years after my decease, so that my executors shall out of the rents and profits bring up Mary, Elizabeth, Margaret and Katherine my daughters and also Hester and Dorothy daughters of Amy Easton alias Carter commonly called Hester Tuke and Dorothy Tuke my daughters, until 21 or marriage, as well in convenient apparel, commons and other necessary finding and education as in such learning or bringing up as shall be thought most meet for them according to their wits, ages and capacity, and that by the discretion, oversight and appointment of my executors; and also that they shall with the profits repair and maintain the mansion house of my manor of Layer Marney now in my occupation, during the 14 years, so that at the time Peter, or such other as by God's provision shall be my heir, is 21 the mansion house and premises to my executors demised shall be of like sort, plight, good estate and condition as I shall leave it. My executors shall not fell, sell or suffer to be wasted any manner of timber wood growing in the Park or elsewhere of any other wood other than necessary hedgebote and stakeboate to be spent only on the premises; and therefore I will and desire them to maintain and cherish the standing and safekeeping of the timber and wood, provided that they may fell timber for the maintaining and repairing of the mansion house and other buildings. My executors shall not plough any parcel of the Park. My wife, if she will, shall have the manor place and house of Layer Marney, the Park and the 27 acres which lie directly against my orchard called the Vineyard for the yearly rent of £40, so that she keep it in her own hands and keep her abode there, and so that she be bound for the preserving of the woods and for not tilling the lands; and Layer Wood shall be of the growth meet to fell, when she thenceforth shall have out of it yearly 40 loads of the underwoods for her firewood to be expended in the manor place and not elsewhere, and the same wood to be assigned to her by my executors. My executors shall pay to Mary, Elizabeth, Margaret and Katherine and to Hester and Dorothy out of the revenues and profits of the premises devised to them £1,066 13s. 4d., i.e. to Mary, Elizabeth and Margaret £200 each and Hester and Dorothy 200 marks each at marriage or 21 at their election, if my executors shall have sufficient in their hands, and thenceforth none of the six [Katherine omitted above in the original] shall have any further keeping, charge and provision. After the 14 years be expired, the residue and overplus of the revenues shall be paid to Peter. Also to Peter the mansion house of my manor of Layer Marney, the 27 acres, the Park, Layer Wood, the glebe, and the Dairy or Wick.

George son of Amy Easton shall remain in the custody of Mr Peter Osborn during his minority, if it shall so please Mr Osborn, and my six daughters to remain in that of my wife, if it shall so please her, my executors making to her allowance for the keeping of them as they can agree, and I desire her for my sake to be good to them and to see them brought up virtuously. To my child with which my wife is now enceinte 200 marks as to my other children. My executors, or such of them as conveniently may, shall once in every year for 3 years after my decease, and after as often as best shall seem good to their discretions, during the minority of Peter or such other as shall be my heir, assemble at the mansion house and oversee the state and usage of the house and timber and premises; and my executors shall have in keeping to the use of my heir my charters and evidences until he or she is 21. I make my executors my very loving friend Peter Osborne esquire and my wife's brother James Morrice, and for their pains each £10 and a gelding of the best I have. [No witnesses.]

Proved by James Morris executor, to whom administration granted, 25 May 1574.

ELIZABETH TUKE of Layer Marney, 31 July 1593. (Nuncupative).
[37/63]

To every one of her brother Mr Peter Tuke's sons, being four, 5 marks
apiece. To her sister Katherine Tuke her taffeta gown. To her brother
Mr Brian Tuke 40s., Thomas Tuke £20, and Maurice Tuke £20 on
condition that he shall go either to Oxford or Cambridge and there
apply himself to learning, if he may have convenient maintenance to
follow his study. The residue to Mr Peter Tuke, whom she ordained her
sole executor. Witnesses: Thomas Tuke, Maurice Tuke, Thomas
Maurice, Bartholomew Balden, with others.

Proved 9 August 1593.

JOHN TURNOR of Crepping Hall in Wakes Colne esquire 6 October
1578. [22/34]

To be buried in the church of that parish where it shall please God
to take me from this life. To the poor men's boxes of Wakes Colne 40s.,
Chapel 10s., Great Tey 13s. 4d., Fordham 10s., Aldham 10s., Mount
Bures 10s., White Colne 6s. 8d., and Earls Colne 20s. To the poor
strangers, the French congregation in London, £6 13s. 4d. My executrix
shall give yearly to some godly preacher to preach the Gospel of Jesus
Christ truly £5, if it shall please God to suffer the same in England so
long, and if not the payments to cease.

To Christian my loving wife for life my manor of Bacons and
Flories [in Chapel and Great Tey] with appurtenances, the land in the
occupation of John Craymer, the lands which John Finche holdeth of
me, my tenements and lands called Mathons, Bottislie, Bakers and
Trasshes, Cobbes Fen, Cobbes Field, Green Grasses and Trendle Fen,
and my tenements and lands called Fisshers and Pages, in Great Tey,
Feering, Earls Colne, Pontisbright [now called Chapel], Mount Bures
and Fordham; and after her decease to remain to Margaret Smythe my
daughter for life, paying Charles her son £20 yearly; and after her
decease to Charles, with successive remainders to the eldest, second and
other sons of Charles, on condition that he or his issue male pay Thomas,
John and Arthur his brother £6 13s. 4d. yearly. To my wife my lease of
the manor of Crepping Hall in Wakes Colne, Great Tey, Fordham,
Mount Bures, Wormingford and White Colne, which I hold of the
right honourable the Earl of Oxford; if she die before the lease be
expired, with like remainders.

To Thomas Smyth of Blackmore gentleman and Margaret his wife, my
daughter, my lease of the Castle of Camps (Cambs.) and the demesnes
and late parks belonging, late holden of the Earl of Oxford, in Castle
Camps, Shudy Camps (Cambs.), Bartlow and Ashdon, on condition that
they shall discharge my executors as well against the Queen's Majesty as
against the Earl of all covenants and payments to which I stand bound
by the lease and shall also yearly expend on the education and bringing
up in learning of Charles and Thomas, son of Thomas and Margaret,

40 marks for 12 years after my decease, and after the decease of Thomas and Margaret it shall be bestowed at the discretion of my wife, my brother-in-law William Fissher, and my cousin Richard Lambert of Colchester merchant.

To my wife my lease of the manor of Lamarsh Hall with the rents, profits and appurtenances for 12 years after my decease for the payment of my debts and the performance of my will, and after to Charles, Thomas, John and Arthur his brothers, on condition that they pay my wife yearly 20 marks during the remainder of the lease. To Margaret Smyth, my daughter's daughter, 300 marks at marriage or 21. To Abigail Smyth, another daughter of Margaret, 200 marks at marriage or 21. To Thomas, John and Arthur, each £40 at 21. To the Earl of Oxford in that he shall be good to my wife and such poor friends as I leave behind me £40, and, if he die before, the £40 to my Lady his wife. To my son-in-law Mr Thomas Smyth 6 milch kine. To my daughter Smyth 12 of my silver spoons and 1 of my bowls of silver, 1 of my beer pots of silver, and 1 of my tankards of silver, also 1 of my featherbeds. To Thomas son of Thomas Smyth my tenement at Wakes Colne church wherein Robert Swaine dwelleth. To my servants Robert Loveney £6 13s. 4d. and Thomas Turnor 40s.; Rachel Lyvinge £3 6s. 8d., at 21 or marriage; my servants Christian Turnor £6 13s. 4d. and John Keble 40s.; and every other of my servants in covenant with me 26s. 8d.

I desire my wife to give Charles such portion of other stuff for the furnishing of his house as she shall think best. To my sisters Baker and Symond each 20s. To William Turnor my brother £3 6s. 8d. To every of my brothers' and sisters' children to whom no legacy is heretofore bequeathed 20s. To John Fissher 40s., my riding cloak and one of my doublets. To my sister Byrd 40s. To my wife's other sisters Joyce Lambert and Elizabeth Tottie 20s. each. To George Goldinge esquire £3 6s. 8d., desiring him to aid and befriend my wife as he hath heretofore to me. To Rose Byrd, my sister's daughter, £3 6s. 8d. at marriage or 21, so that she do attend and serve my wife. To William Fissher's wife 20s. To every of her children and the children of John Fissher 20s. at marriage or 21. To my cousin Richard Byrd 40s. To William Byrd 20s. To Alice wife of Richard Barrett a half seam of wheat and 2 ewe sheep. To my sister Elizabeth Addams a seam of wheat. To the reparations of Wakes Colne church £4, if the churchwardens go about to repair it. To Philip Bloyse, Martha Knappe and John Berye my godson each 10s.

The residue of my goods to my wife, whom I make sole executrix. I make overseers Thomas Smyth, Thomas Waldegrave, gentlemen, William Fissher my brother-in-law, my cousin Richard Lambert, and my friend John Cockell, and to every of them £5. If my wife marry again my legacies to her shall be utterly void and shall remain to Thomas my son-in-law and Margaret, paying yearly to my wife 100 marks. If any doubt shall arise with my will it shall be determined by my right worshipful good friend Sir William Cordell knight, Master of the Rolls, to whom I give in token of his great friendship to me showed always £6 13s. 4d., or by Mr Justice Ayliffe, to whom I give for his pains 40s. To Margaret my daughter's daughter 100 marks besides the legacy to her given.

Witnesses : Alexander Mathew, John Langbroke, Bartholomew Chirch.

Proved 1 August 1579. Sentence, 11 June 1589, confirming Will in case between (1) Mary Pellett and Thomas Turner minor and (2) Robert Browne and Richard Browne.

RICHARD TWEDY of Boreham esquire, 23 January 1575.   [18/41]

To be buried in Stock church in the chapel where my grandfather is buried, with a tomb to be made by the discretion of my executors. To the reparations of Boreham and Stock churches each £3 6s. 8d. To 10 poor men of Boreham and 10 of Stock 20 gowns.

Whereas I am fully minded by God's permission to purchase a piece of ground in Stock as near the church as I can and on the same to build four almshouses for four poor men to dwell in, to be chosen of the poor inhabitants of Stock and Boreham, i.e. two from each, and every one of the houses shall be assigned to one poor man for life and every man to receive 12s. a week towards his finding and 8s. every year for a livery, with such a portion of fuel as may conveniently be had by the discretion of my executors, and so to remain for ever; I require them, as they will answer before God, that whatsoever shall be left undone by me in my lifetime touching the building and finishing of the almshouses and the endowment of such lands and tenements as in my will shall be appointed, they perform and finish the same of such lands and goods as I leave to them. I devise all my lands and tenements in Stow Maries called Prentises, with my lease of the same, to Peter Osborne, Thomas Wilmott and John Latham to convey the same to the endowment of the four almshouses.

To my brother Robert Twedy for 7 years after my death the profits of my copyhold lands in Boreham, except my mansion house there with the outhouses, barns, stables, orchards and gardens, also the profits of my little lease called Marshes for 7 years only, being altogether worth £20; my apparel and household stuff in my house in London and my apparel for my own body now remaining at Boreham, except my best gown of damask and such other things as I give away in my will; also my debts, specialties and other writings; provided that he do not release his title in a tenement and land in Stock in the tenure of widow Dale. To my very good friend Mistress Julian Penne widow my mansion house in Boreham so excepted from Robert, and my free lands in Boreham and Stock, with the use of my household stuff in the same, for life; and after her death the household stuff to Richard, son of my brother William, and the reversions of my mansion house and my lands in Boreham and Stock. My lease of Marshes shall remain to Richard and his heirs male, and for default of such issue with successive remainders to William and to Robert and their heirs male.

To my brother Thomas Wilmott my lease of Boreham Hall, on condition that he pay Mistress Penne an annuity of £30 at her dwelling house in London; and after his death to my sister, his wife, and to Edward her son. To Richard my lease of Old Hall with the appurtenances in Boreham which I have in reversion from the Queen's Majesty.

To Baptist Hickes my lease of the tithes of Stamerden [Stamfordham?] (Northumberland), paying out of the profits to Rowland Hackthrop, sometime my servant, £6 13s. 4d. yearly during the term. To Mistress Penne £200. To William, son of my brother Edmund Twedy deceased, towards his exhibition an annuity of £8 6s. 8d., parcel of my annuity of 20 marks which I have out of the Court of Wards during the minority of Mr Averell's heir. To Mistress Penne my great nest of silver bowls with a cover parcel gilt (weighing about 100 oz.). To my worshipful good friend Peter Osborne esquire my basin and ewer of silver and to Mistress Osborne his wife my chafing dish of silver. To Mr John Latham £10. To my brother Mr Thomas Wilmott my jerkin of black leather with 20 buttons of gold. To Cresner and Richard, my men, 40s. apiece, and to Broke, Carder and Say, my men, 10s. apiece, and to all a black coat. To Hatcheman a black coat. My friend Mistress Penne shall have delivered at her house in London so much fuel and wood from my lands in Stow called Prentises as will serve to find her house for life. To Geoffrey Skott my best night gown furred with coney, and I forgive him all money he oweth me. To my Lady Darell my signet of gold. To Mistress Latham and Mistress King a ring of gold of 3 angels apiece. To Gilbert Hanham, vicar of Boreham, a black gown and a black coat. To the poor of Baddow, Danbury, Sandon, Little Waltham, Hatfield Peverel and Springfield 20s. to each town.

To Dorothy my sister Wilmott's daughter £20 at marriage, and if she die the £20 to the rest of her children. To my friend Mr William Clarke my trotting gelding. To Baptist Hickes my bay trotting gelding. To Mistress Penne my own grey gelding. To my worshipful friend Mr Pole of the Chancery my black footcloth nag and my footcloth. To Dr [John?] Walker [Archdeacon of Essex?] my best velvet coat and to Anthony Higgons my short gown of taffeta guarded with guards of velvet. To my brother William my damask gown furred with wolverenes. More to Mistress Penne my black tablet. To my sister Ferne my nest of white bowls (weighing about 63 oz.). To my brother William's wife my 2 little white bowls of silver and 2 stone jugs garnished with silver. To Thomasine Barker, goodwife Farmer and goodwife Hixson each a black gown.

Whereas Sir Thomas Kempe of Ollantigh (Kent), knight, and Anthony Kempe of the same, esquire, stand bound to me in 500 marks by a statute staple dated 20 May 1569, I give the same statute staple and 500 marks to Michael Hickes, whom I ordain my sole executor as touching only the statute staple and 500 marks. I ordain Mr Peter Osborne, Thomas Wilmott and John Latham my executors touching my legacies and the building and endowment of the four almshouses and the placing of the four poor men; and to my executors the residue of my goods.

Witnesses: Thomas Powle, Edward Atslowe, George Walker, Anthony Higgons, notary, William Sansbury.

Proved 9 November 1575.

EDMUND TYRELL of Ramsden Barringtons [Bellhouse] esquire, 6 November 1576. [19/33]

Being visited with sickness and calling to my remembrance that I have made my will written with my own hand, the contents whereof being now troubled with sickness I do not well remember, I do affirm the same. Whereas I did appoint Sir William Petre, my dear friend deceased, to be the receiver of such profits and revenues as be given and willed by me to Thomas Tyrrell, my daughter's son, I appoint Mr John Clyff and Robert Bradberie gentlemen to receive the revenues and profits to Thomas.

Because I left divers other lands in Essex to dispose at my pleasure, John Archer shall have for his life the house and lands in his occupying, paying no rent. Annuities to my servants—to William Taylor 26s. 8d., William Madyson 20s., Piers Powell 13s. 4d., and Robert Staunton £3 6s. 8d. To Mistress Anne Browne, wife of Mr Philip Browne, for her life, for the gentleness and goodwill that I have found in them and in consideration of their troubles, an annuity of £3. To Dame Anne Crispe widow £20. To William Randall and John Haselherst gentlemen each 10s., and to Isaac Spracklinge, Lactance [*sic*] Cole, Stephen Mylles and Robert horsekeeper, my Lady Crispe's men, each 10s., and to Mr Browne's men each 10s.

Whereas, since the making of my former will, I have purchased the manor of Ramsden Barrington with the lands, rents and services in divers parishes, I give to Susan Tirell my daughter £40, parcel of the manor. To Robert Bradburie and Margaret his wife, my daughter, for their lives, £40, parcel of the manor, with remainder after their deaths to Thomas son of William Tyrrell and Thomasine my daughter and his heirs male. The residue of the manor to the said Thomas and his heirs male; the profits shall be taken for the reparations thereof. I make Robert Bradberie and John Clyff my executors and George White gentleman my overseer. Witnesses: Ciricius Petit, William Darrell, John Haselherst, William Randolf, Thomas Lake.

Proved 29 November 1576. Sentence, 13 July 1579, confirming Will in case between Susan Tirrell *alias* Cutler and John Cliffe surviving executor, which refers to the testator's death at Whitstable (Kent).

HENRY WENTWORTH of Steeple Bumpstead esquire, 27 April 1590. [34/34]

To be buried in the chancel of Bumpstead church. To Elizabeth my eldest daughter £100 in discharge of 100 marks given her by Sir John Wentworth knight deceased and which I have received to her use. To Mary my daughter £100 in discharge of 100 marks which I received for her and was given by William Bendlowes, serjeant-at-law, my late father-in-law. To Alice my daughter £25 in discharge of £20 which I owe her. To John my son £10 at 21. To Thomasine my daughter £10. To Peregrine Goddard my godson my messuage in Wisbech in the Isle of Ely (Cambs.); if he die before 21, remainder to Margaret widow of Thomas Goddard, his mother for 6 years, then to John my son. To Anne my youngest daughter £20. Whereas one Thomas Goddard became indebted to me in divers sums of money I acquit him. To Margaret his widow my grey nag and a featherbed whereon I lie and the counter table with all other furniture in the great chamber over the buttery wherein I lie. To Peregrine a featherbed. My lease of the rectory or parsonage of Bumpstead and the tithes and glebe shall be sold by my executors, and the residue of the money remaining shall be equally divided among all my children. I ordain Thomas Bendishe esquire my executor and I give him the lease of the rectory to the use of my will and 20s. in remembrance. To the poor of Bumpstead 40s. To Margaret my wife £10. Witnesses: E. Eyre, William Constable, John Edlyn.

Proved 29 May 1590.

JOHN WENTWORTH of Gosfield esquire, 27 January 1588. [For Sir John Wentworth, see p. 45.] [33/21]

Whereas by a deed indented, 2 April 1565, between my uncle Sir John Wentworth deceased of the one part and Sir William Cordall deceased, then Master of the Rolls, Sir Giles Alington, Sir Christopher Heidon, knights, Richard Tyrrell, then Warden of the Fleet, Rooke Grene and Henry Mackwilliams, esquires, of the other part; and also by a feoffment, 10 April 1565, divers manors and lands be conveyed to me for life after certain estates ended with divers remainders over; and whereas in the first deed there is a proviso giving me authority by my will to devise one-third part of the revenues of certain such manors whereof I shall die seized for 5 years or less after my decease, to be received by my executors for the advancement of my daughter or daughters, the payment of my debts or the performance of my will; I now devise for 5 years one-third of the revenues to bestow at the discretion of Dorothy my wife, hoping that she will be a natural mother and take some order for the help and advancement of her children as she hath by me. To her all my goods, whom I ordain my sole executrix. Witnesses: Robert Awdley, Peter Caige, John Tyler.

Proved 29 January 1589.

GEORGE WILMER of West Ham esquire, 28 January 1594. [38/16]

To be buried in West Ham church, and towards the charge of mourning attire, liveries and other occasions of necessary expenses of my funerals, I allow £100. To the churches of West Ham £5 and Barking £4.

Whereas I have by purchase of Richard Stonley of London esquire a lease for 8 years and another lease in reversion for 31 years of certain lands in West Ham, the reversion of which leases are in her Majesty, on which are reserved to her the yearly rent of £13 5s. 2d.; my will is that Anne my wife shall have the profits for life; and after her decease the residue of the leases to my son Thomas; and if he die without issue then to my son George; provided that she shall not claim any dower in any other of my lands in the city or suburbs of London. Whereas I have in mortgage by purchase from [blank] Cade a mansion house and two tenements adjoining in Aldersgate Street, I will the same to my wife and

142

her heirs, and for default of issue the remainder to Thomas, the mortgage being redeemable by Cade on payment of £360. To her £500 and such goods as are set down in a schedule annexed. Whereas I purchased of Mistress Mary Smythe widow certain lands or burgages in Southwark (Surrey) I appoint that after my wife's death without issue George shall have the reversion or remainder. To the second child of myself and my wife my lands freehold and copyhold in Goodman Street in Barking; and for default of issue or second child to George. To him my lands in Green Street which I purchased from James Plott, my lease of my lands in East Ham Marshes lately taken in lease by fine from John Hungerford esquire for 60 years, and my lease for 200 years by purchase from Richard Stonlye dated 20 January 1589, and the reversion also of which lease is since purchased and is in the hands of my son Andrew.

Whereas I have by purchase from Mr Anthony Hungerford lands in East Ham Marshes to myself, my wife and George, my executors shall receive the profits as also of all other lands given him by my will until he is 21. Whereas I have by deed of bargain and sale from Anthony Hungerford other lands in East Ham Marshes in the tenure of Edward Kyscuppe, my executor shall receive the rent and profit until he is 21, and then to Thomas; and for default of issue to George. Until Thomas is 21 my executor shall take the profit of the lands given to Thomas, rendering the yearly rent of 26s. for every acre to my brother Bullocke for the benefit, education and bringing up of Thomas and my other son and daughter, my brother accounting to them at their full age. To Andrew after the death of my wife without issue the remainder of the houses and lands I purchased from one Tirrowe and his wife in Angel Alley and Horne Alley in St Botolph-without-Aldersgate; the lease of my house in West Ham I bought of Mr Fanshawe; and £400. To my daughters Alice Wilmer Great Tun Marshes in East Ham, the profits according to the order prescribed, and £300, and to Eleanor Wilmer £500; and until they are 16, my executor, giving good security by statute staple to my overseers for re-answering the same, shall retain the money, yielding yearly for every £100 £6 13s. 4d. to be paid to my brother Bullock towards their bringing up and increase of their portions. Within 8 years after my decease my executor shall pay to my overseers and brother Bullocke £900 above the sums already mentioned, to be distributed as followeth, i.e. if Alice die before marriage or refuse to be ruled in her marriage by my overseers or by my wife and Bullock, £400 thereof shall be bestowed on George, Thomas and my other daughter, but if she consent and be so directed the £400 shall go to her and to such husband as by the same direction she shall fortune to marry; and likewise £500 to Eleanor. I will and entreat my wife to undertake the care and the charge of the bringing up and education of my two daughters in humility, good nurture and the fear of God until 21 or marriage; and towards the cost my executor and Bullocke shall allow her for each daughter £16 yearly and more if it shall so seem fit to my overseers. To my daughter Smythe of Plumstead (Kent) £100. To my brother Richard Wilmer's children each £4, and to the rest of the children of my brethren and sisters not named each £3 6s. 8d., at marriage or 21.

Whereas there is controversy between me and Philip Greenley, servant to Mr Wrothe, about some reckoning of 40s., because he shall not hold himself wronged, being a poor man, my executor shall pay him £5. To the rest of my servants each 40s. To Mistress Brampton and Thomas Nodin each 20s. more than their fellows. Whereas by deed of bargain and sale and by fine I have purchased from Mr Francis Bacon of Gray's Inn certain marsh grounds in Woolwich (Kent), my executor shall take the profits for 10 years after my decease towards the levying of my legacies, and afterwards George shall have the grounds. Nevertheless, whereas it is provided that, if Mr Bacon, Francis Windham, Edward Bacon, or Henry Gouldinge esquires, pay me or my assigns £940 on 24 March 1595, the deed shall be void, if the condition be performed my executor shall have the £940 towards the performance of my legacies. Whereas I have a lease from Mr Alderman Rowe lately deceased of certain lands in Kent yielding the yearly rent of £186 13s. 4d., Andrew and my executor shall occupy them and render account for and employ the residue of the annual profit that shall arise (besides the rent to Alderman Rowe's heir) towards the bringing up and increase of the portions of George, Thomas, Alice and Eleanor, wherein they be liberally allowed a competent yearly reward for their pains. The residue of my goods to be employed for my will.

I ordain my faithful and loving brother John Wilmer of Shrewley (Warwicks.) to be my executor on condition that he enter into bond of £4,000 to my overseers to discharge my will. I nominate and heartily entreat Thomas Fanshawe, Edward Doyle and John Strode of London, esquires, Henry Fanshawe of the Inner Temple gentleman, and Hugh Bullocke, citizen of London, to be overseers, and for their pains as token of my remembrance and goodwill each £5.

Witnesses: Edward Doylie, John Strode, Thomas Colffe, Clement Wilmer, and William Albert the writer.

Schedule of such goods bequeathed to his wife, all or most part the goods of Anne before their marriage. A basin and ewer of silver parcel gilt; a pair of gilt silver pots; a double cup embowled all gilt; a cup or bowl of silver gilt all; a nest of silver tuns with a cover; a double bell salt of silver; 3 silver bowls; 2 silver trencher plates; a little silver cup; a silver porringer; 8 spoons of silver; the basin and ewer of silver which my wife gave to me double gilt I give to her again; the silver chafing dish and the silver sugar box; a chain of pomander and gold; a short rope of small pearls; 3 chains of pomander pearl and coral; a table[t] with a cross of diamond in it; a little cross with right diamond; a ring with a table diamond; a hoop ring of gold; a ring with a deck diamond; and a chain of gold given to her by me. Six pieces of verdure hangings new; 2 pieces of verdure hangings of busky work; a suite of coarse verdure hangings of 4 pieces; 8 pieces of gilt leather hangings; a suite of white network hangings lined. A tester of a bed of crimson velvet laced and fringed with gold and silver, and 5 curtains of crimson taffeta to the same; a field bed tester of black velvet and damask embroidered with castles, and 5 curtains to the same of chequer work or stuff; a cupboard cloth of the same stuff; a tester of a bed of blue and red silk capha fringed, and 5 curtains to the same of blue and red chequer stuff; a new field bed of walnuttree covered with green say gilt buttons and curtains; 2 down beds, one of fustian and the other of tick; 7 featherbeds; 3 Spanish blankets white; 10 other blankets; 2 green rugs; a rug striped blue and red; 4 ordinary coverlets; an Irish rug; a quilt of taffeta. A long carpet of Turkey work for a table; a square little carpet of Turkey work; a long tablecloth, a square tablecloth, and a cupboardcloth of green cloth. Six stools covered with needlework new and a little chair of the same; 2 chairs and 2 stools covered with leather gilt; a chair and 2 low stools of crimson velvet with silver and gold lace; a chair of crimson satin; a low chair covered with scarlet; a chair and 2 stools of silk capha blue and red; a large cushion of crimson and velvet; 5 carpet cushions; 4 other old carpet cushions. A fair cupboard; 2 field bedsteads with posts. Such pewter, brass, spits and other furniture commonly used in my kitchen at London. Such coffers, chests, cupboards, stools and other such furniture of household as my wife had before I married her. Her coach and coach horses with the furniture. Such other horses or geldings as were my wife's before marriage. Such household stuff as was mine before marriage remaining in my house at London my wife shall have at such rate as they shall be appraised reasonably after my death.

Proved 27 February 1594.

JOHN WISEMAN of Felsted esquire, 4 January 1559. [For Thomas Wiseman, see p. 264.]   [3/8]

To be buried in such parish as I shall inhabit the time of my death, after the usual fashion, without great charge only it be to the poor people as shall be thought most expedient by my executrix. To the curates of my habitations in Essex for tithes withheld, each 10s. To the poor parishioners of Felsted 40s. yearly and Bermondsey (Surrey) 40s. yearly for 10 years to be taken out of my farm of Bermondsey, and 20s. yearly for an obit to be kept for the same term for my father's and mother's soul, my soul, and my mother [in-law] Anne Lethey's soul, and all Christian souls, taken likewise. To London highways £20.

To John my youngest son £6 13s. 4d. yearly; and the order thereof to be in my wife's hands until he is of full age, and then to his use during the term of the lease; the residue of the profits to be in my wife's disposing during her life to the use of herself and my children which she shall think have most need; and if she die before the end of the lease my eldest son shall receive the rents and profits and give to every of his brethren £5 yearly above the £6 13s. 4d. given to John. To Anne my daughter £20 to be levied out of my manor of Mucking Hall [in Barling and Shopland]. To all my servants both men and women with me in household half a year's wages besides their wages. To Thomas my eldest son all manors and lands as are not hereafter given to Joan my wife and my other sons except the manor of Mucking Hall, out of which to 40 poor maidens each 40s., to be given at their marriages by my executrix, inhabiting in Felsted, Little Dunmow, Great Dunmow, Great Waltham,

Thaxted, Debden, Wimbish and Braintree. Towards the new making of Hull Bridge [in Hockley] £20. To a priest to sing for my soul and all Christian souls for 2 years after my decease £24. I bequeath to be levied out of the said manor £10 yearly for 20 years after my decease, i.e. £6 13s. 4d. for shirts and smocks for poor people at the discretion of my executrix and £3 6s. 8d. towards the finding of a priest at Black Chapel [in Great Waltham] to sing for my soul and all Christian souls if the chapel so long continue. The residue of the profits of the manor to Thomas and his heirs.

After my wife's decease Thomas shall have the reversions of my lands in Essex and of such lands as I have presently given to him and Jane his wife for their lives, lands hereafter given to my other sons only excepted and except my lands in Kent, which shall be parted among my sons as well the reversions after my wife's death and the deaths of Thomas and his wife; and Thomas to have his part therein according to the custom there used, which is much more than is limited by the statute, considering that my wife is joint purchaser with me of a great part of my lands in consideration of her jointure. To my wife my manor or tenement of Seborowe Hall [in Mucking].

To Ralph my son my tenement called Moyndes in the tenure of William Hawes, my manor of Yerdley Hall with appurtenances in Thaxted, the reversions of my manors of Goshallayes with appurtenances in East Tilbury and of Seborowe Hall; and for lack of heirs my said manors to remain successively to my son George and his heirs, to Richard my son the eldest of that name, to Richard my son the younger, and to William my son. To Ralph my copyhold land in Braintree. To George Beeleigh Mills and the lands late in the tenure of Robert Gayewoode bought of William March; and for default of heirs to remain successively to Ralph, Philip my son, Richard the elder and younger and William. To Philip my grange and manor called Takeley Grange. To Richard the elder my lands in Langdon Hills late in the tenure of Gayneforde; and for default of issue to William. To Richard the younger my grange called Venors Grange in Thaxted and [Great] Easton with lands belonging; and for default of heirs to John. To William my tenements in London in Gunpowder Alley lately bought by me of the King's Grace; and for default of issue to John. To John my lands called the White House in Thaxted letten to divers persons; and for lack of issue to Philip. If Thomas do not suffer my executrix quietly to receive all such money out of the manor of Mucking Hall, then she shall have power to sell my manor called Welbernes in Debden and with the money to perform my legacies. My wife to have the liberty of three chambers in Broadoaks [in Wimbish], i.e. those which were last builded, if she be disposed to lie there, and pasture for 3 horses and 2 beasts and liberty to dress her meat there as long as she is unmarried. To George Boote my servant £6 13s. 4d.

The residue of my goods to my wife. I make her my sole executrix and Thomas my son and Thomas Wyseman my brother my supervisors. To my son my best horse, my best gown, my best coat and my best doublet, and to my brother another horse the next best, besides my wife's horse, and the next best gown.

Witnesses: William Rust vicar of Felsted, Thomas Rogerson clerk, William Fytche, Thomas Wiseman gentleman, John Courtman, George Boote the writer hereof, and others.

Proved 23 January 1560. Administration granted, 23 July 1576, to Thomas Wiseman esquire, son of the deceased, to administer the goods of Joan Wiseman alias Strangman, widow of the deceased.

ANNE WISEMAN, wife of John Wiseman of Great Canfield esquire, 1 August 1597. [46/10]

To John my husband my ring with a turquoise, which I commonly wear, for a perpetual remembrance. To Anthony Wever, my kinsman, a tablecloth, 12 table napkins and a towel, all of damask work, a tablecloth, 12 table napkins and a towel, all of diaper work, and a tablecloth, 12 table napkins and a towel, all flaxen, all of the best, a pair of my best flaxen sheets, and a sealing ring of gold which I daily wear which was sometime my late husband Symons' ring with his cognizance on it. To Peter Slutter, Richard Weaver, Edward Lewis and George Pumfrett, each a gold ring price 20s. To Anne Pumfrett a gold ring with a diamond which was my wedding ring, two pictures, one made for myself and the other for my late husband Symons, and the pewter she hath of mine, to the intent that if God send her any issue this my gift shall be bestowed on them or else on some of her kinsfolks at her discretion. To Margery Fytch, my waiting gentlewoman, and to Edward Smyth, each a gold ring price 20s. To Elizabeth Hawkins, my servant, 40s. and a red petticoat. To my daughters-in-law, Dorothy Glascock my damask gown, Jane Meade my grogram gown with 3 welts, and Anne Lygatt my taffeta petticoat. To Alice Weaver and Susan Lewis, my kinswomen, the rest of my apparel and wearing linen which was mine before I was married to the worshipful John Wiseman esquire, equally to be divided. The residue of my goods to Anne Pumfrett, Anne Slutter daughter of Peter Slutter, Susan Lewis for her eldest son Scott, Alice Wever and Anne Bostock, at marriage or 21, so that whosoever shall receive their portions shall stand bound to my executor for the safe custody and delivery of their portions; also such things of mine as are in the hands of George Pumfrett, except before excepted, shall be equally divided between them by my executor. I make Richard Weaver my kinsman my only executor, and my overseers Thomas Clarcke of London, sometime my servant, and John Bickner of Great Canfield the elder, and for their pains each a gold ring price 20s. Witnesses: William Edwardes, Margery Fitch, Robert Brewer, Edward Smyth, John Bickner, cum aliis.

Proved 9 March 1602.

EDWARD WYOTT of Tillingham esquire, 14 August 1571. [For Edward Wyott gentleman, see p. 267.] [14/42]

To my well-beloved wife Mary for life the use and profit of my lease of the manor of Bradwell-juxta-Mare and the wicks, marshes and lands belonging, which I have of the grant of the Queen's Majesty, saving a

147

piece of marsh lately inned by me in the occupation of William Paine; and after her decease to my son Edward Wiott. To Edward my leases of the manor and the parsonage of Tillingham and of lands called South Wick and Sheldwick Hoke. If I shall have another child before my decease or leave my wife with child, to the child £300 at 21 or marriage. To my wife one half of my household stuff and plate, the other half and my goods to Edward, my executors to have the use of the leases and goods until he is 21, making a just account during his minority. I earnestly require them to see him well and virtuously brought up in the fear of God and good learning, and the like request for any other child. To my wife my stock and store of cattle in the manor of Bradwell; and if she die during the term of my lease, my child or children being deceased, to my nephew Edward Wyott, youngest son of my brother Francis deceased; and if he die to William his brother. If my son or children die without issue, the other leases to my nephews Isaac, William and Edward and the longest liver. To my wife one half of my household stuff and plate, and if Edward die before 21 or there be no issue of my body living to my nephew Edward. If my son Edward die before 21 without issue and my other child (if any such shall happen) die before 21 without issue, I bequeath to Isaac Ashely my cousin, Edward Ashely my godson, Edward son of my nephew James Morris, William my brother Harris's son, Edward, Bridget and Margery children of my uncle Edward Waldegrave, brother of these eight last named, £10, for the payment whereof and my legacies I will my executors to have the said farms and stocks (the legacies to my wife excepted and to her only reserved), and after the same be paid I give the stock and store on the farm of Tillingham to my nephews Isaac, William and Edward; and if my son Edward or any other child live to 21 to each £40. To my cousin George Heigham in consideration of his pains for me divers ways £10. To each of my menservants being in covenant with me 40s. and to each of my maidservants their year's wages doubled.

If my son Edward and other issue decease before 21, I give the profits of my leases to the younger children of my brother William Waldegrave esquire, the children of my nephew James Morris esquire, of my niece Christian Spere, and of my nephew John Roos, and to my nephew Thomas Morris, to be equally divided among them. I ordain my wife, my loving friends Edward Waldegrave esquire my uncle, and Arthur Harris esquire my brother-in-law, my executors, and for their pains each £20, and I require my loving brother-in-law William Waldegrave esquire and my nephew James Morris to be supervisors, and to each for their pains a gold ring of price 10s. and a gelding.

Witnesses : Thomas Peninge, William Emerye, George Heigham.

23 August 1571. The debts which I owe without specialty to pay and yet not as legacies and so to be twice challenged, i.e. as a legacy over and above the same debt but to be paid once only as the debt and in conscience I am to pay. To my niece Mary Wyott, daughter of my brother Francis deceased as in his will, £100 at marriage. To William Thimble £40, Richard Payne £40, Thomas Bavet £30, and Gregory Kene £20.

Proved 3 November 1571.

4
GENTLEMEN

WILLIAM ADDAMS *alias* TASKER of Walthamstow gentleman, 12 January 1581. [25/36]

To Joan Vicars a petticoat and 2 kerchers. To Elizabeth wife of Thomas Addams alias Tasker, one of my sons, 10s., Thomas, Roger the younger, and Blanche Tasker, sons and daughter of Roger my son, 10s., 6s. 8d. and 5s. 8d. [*sic*, respectively]. To my wife the rest of the apparel and linen which belonged to Agnes my late wife. To William Tasker my son 2 shirts. To Thomas Peate, servant to my son Thomas, a doublet and a pair of hose which I use to wear myself. To Geoffrey and Richard Tasker my sons 12d. each. To Matthew Fawkes of Packington (Warws.) 12d. in recompense for certain cloits for a scythe which he saith I borrowed of him. To my sons Thomas Addames £3 and Roger Tasker 10s. and to Humphrey Brownsword 13s., which I owe them. The residue of my goods, leases, plate and ready money shall be indifferently valued and divided into three equal parts to Thomas, Roger and William my sons. I make Thomas my executor. Witnesses: John Wynge, Anthony Gall the writer.

Renunciation of executorship by Thomas, 24 September 1582.

THOMAS ARMYGER of Layer Marney gentleman, 25 October 1583. [27/28]

To be buried in the chancel of Layer Marney church. To my well-beloved wife Jane and our heirs the manor of Canewdon Hall in Canewdon with the lands belonging, which by law is due to my wife; and the lease of the parsonage impropriate of Wickham [St Paul?] which I hold by indenture of the Earl of Oxford. To my son Thomas £20 yearly out of my manor of Canewdon towards his learning and bringing up. To Susan my eldest daughter and Elizabeth my daughter each £100 at 20 or marriage. To the poor of Layer Marney 20s. To Thomas a high salt and a goblet, both of silver double gilt, which goblet was my father's, at 21 or marriage. The rest of my plate, jewels, goods and household stuff to my wife, my children and Mary wife of Robert Cammock to be equally divided and my wife to take her first choice. To my sister-in-law Mary wife of Thomas Badby esquire 2 angels of gold for a remembrance of me. I ordain my wife my sole executrix. To the menservants of my cousin Robert Cammock 10s. apiece. Witnesses: Robert Cannock [*sic*], Henry Cannocke.

Proved 10 February 1584.

GEORGE ASINALL of Audley End in [Saffron] Walden gentleman, 1 August 1594.   [38/71]

To my loving wife Dorothy the lease of my house and lands in Audley End which I had of the gift of the right honourable Lord Thomas Howard my singular good lord and master; my corn, cattle and household stuff to her only use; my lease of ground which I bought of John Greenwood gentleman in the manor of my lord and master called Brinkworth (Wilts.) until such time it please God she marry and on condition it may be let to the uttermost value for the payment of my debts and legacies; and if she marry my son shall have it, provided that she have the lease for the bringing up of my son in godly and virtuous learning until he is 18. To my brother Lewis Asinall an old lease which I have of escheated lands in Lancaster in hope he will be careful of my wife and son. The residue of my goods to my wife, whom I ordain my sole executrix, and my brother Lewis overseer. To the poor in Audley End 10s.

Debts due by me : to Lewis £15 10s.; to my cousin Alexander Prescott goldsmith £7; to William Browne of Audley End tailor £28 12s. Legacies given by me : to my lord's six children each a gold ring of the price of 6s. 8d. to be made with some pretty posies at the discretion of Mr Greenewood, to whom a pair of taffeta hose and 50s. to make him a satin doublet; to my brother Peter Asinall £3 6s. 8d.; to my cousin George Donne who now serveth me 40s., his mother 10s., and his brother Richard 10s.

Witnesses : Thomas Dove, Lewis Asinall.
Proved 19 October 1594.

BARTHOLOMEW AVEREL of Southminster gentleman, 1 May 1562.
                                                                    [5/18]

To be buried in Southminster church before my pew between it and the chancel, and a marble stone to be laid on me with the pictures and names of my wife and children on the same. To the poor walking people that resort to my burial £6 13s. 4d. and at my month's day £6 13s. 4d. To every poor householder in Southminster and Althorne that have neither lands nor chattels 6s. 8d. To the reparations of Southminster church 40s. To my household servants except Barnaby and Elizabeth 20s. apiece and to them each 40s. To Henry Hall my coats of cloth of what colour soever and my hosen and doublets of fustian. To my brother William Averell my other apparel. To every of my covenant servants a black coat of 6s. the yard.

To Mary my brother Bennett's daughter, my good [god?] daughter, £3 6s. 8d. at marriage or 21, and if she die before, then to be equally divided among my sister Eleanor Tredgold's children; to them £20 to be divided equally at full age or marriage. To Felice my wife my napery, household stuff, fuel and poultry; £200; my stock of cattle on my manor of Herons [in Althorne] and Bridge Marsh; 17 silver spoons called slips, a salt parcel gilt of silver, a great square salt of silver parcel gilt, 2 bowls parcel gilt, a silver goblet parcel gilt, a white silver pot with a hance and a lid, 3 white pots of silver with hances, a casting bowl all gilt with a chain, and a maudlin cup all gilt. To my daughters Grace and Elizabeth each £100 at marriage or 21. My wife shall have the profits of the manor of Southminster called the Moor with the windmill and of a marsh in Althorne called Bishops Hook during my term of years to come; and my stock and store of cattle and my corn there growing. My executor shall have the profits of my marshes called Mumpsdell [Montsale], Middle Wick, South Wick and Althorne Barns and my stock and store of cattle there during my term, paying the rents due to the lord of the manor of Southminster and charges due to our sovereign lady the Queen, and paying yearly to my three daughters Mary, Grace and Elizabeth £120. To my daughters my lease of an inn in Smithfield, i.e. the Rose at the Bars [in London]. At Michaelmas after my decease an account shall be made by my executor to my loving friends, my cousin Robert Gynes of the Temple, my brother-in-law Vincent Harris, William Averell my brother, and John Sammes my son-in-law of the profits of my farms and lands for that year, which shall remain to my three daughters. I ordain my cousin Gynes, Vincent Harris, William Averell and John Sammes my overseers, to whom I give 40s. apiece after the account made, also to each a black gown of 10s. the yard and a ring of 40s.

Whereas the Queen's Majesty is entitled to the third part of my manors and lands whereof I am seized in fee simple after my decease, by reason of the wardship of any that shall fortune to be my heir, I ordain my part of the manor of Franks in [Great] Warley and Rainham, my marsh called South Marsh in North Fambridge, a tenement called Chamberlains in Althorne, my manor of Burses in Thundersley, and my marsh called Raye Marsh, all which amounteth to the third part, humbly beseeching the Queen's highness to accept the same in recompense of her third.

To my wife, with whom I have lived quietly and have found her my loving and gentle wife, in token of my goodwill I bear her and for the augmentation of her living and the better maintenance of herself and my children in their young ages, my manor of Herons and Bridge Marsh in Althorne, and my messuage at St Swithin's Lane end in London, for life; and after her decease my executor shall have the profit as hereafter declared until my heir is 21 or married, and then he shall pay my daughter's portions. To my wife my copyhold lands called Rumbolds in Southminster and in [Great] Hallingbury holden of the manor of Walbury, for life; and after her decease to my heir; and my messuage and lands called Warners in Southminster, and after her decease to my three children. Concerning my manor of Barton alias Bretton Hall in Great Stambridge, my manor of Pudsith Hall in Canewdon, South Marsh in Fambridge, and my free chapel of Whempstead [in Watton-at-Stone] (Herts.), I will the same as followeth, i.e. my executor shall make the most advantage for my daughter's benefit and take the profits until they are of full age or married, and then pay them their parts of the profits. To my brother Henry Averell an annuity of £4 out of my manor of Barton Hall. The residue of my goods to my three daughters. I ordain my executor Arthur Harris.

Witnesses: John Levet, William Levet, James Sheapard, Henry Guynes.

To my wife 6 of my best horses after my heriots be paid, and my grain and corn and my woods felled to her own use. To Henry Guynes of Southminster 20s. To Agnes Fyne 20s. To Elizabeth my daughter my manors of Barton Hall and Pudsey and my free chapel called Weinforde chapel in Watton; and for lack of heirs successively to Grace and Mary and to my brethren William, Henry and Bennet Averell. To Grace after my wife's decease my manor called Herns and Countisbridge in Althorne; and for lack of heirs successively to Elizabeth, to Mary and to my brethren; and my copyhold lands in Southminster. To Mary South Marsh, and my house in London; and for lack of heirs successively to Elizabeth, to Grace and to my brethren. To Thomas Averell my servant 40s. To Thomas Averell of Domney 40s. I forgive Langaris' wife all the debts she doth owe me. The residue of my plate to my three daughters to be indifferently divided among them; in which Grace and Elizabeth shall have 2 great gilt salts, 2 dozen silver spoons, the one with maiden-heads and the other with round knops, towards their portions, and Mary shall have her portion within 14 days after my decease, and the other two parts shall be put in a sure chest to remain in my executor's custody locked with two locks whereof my wife to have one key and Robert Guynes and John Sammes to have the other. Whereas I have sold to John Steven of Mayland divers lands in Southminster and Mayland; and whereas I have a recognizance acknowledged to me by my Lord Darcie for the performance of the covenants in a bargain and sale of the same lands with others; when John Steven shall acquit and discharge my heir and executor against my Lord Darsie of the covenants, my executor shall deliver the recognizance to him. Whereas I stand indebted by the will of my uncle Henry Averell in £7 to be bestowed in marriage with 7 poor maidens, my executor shall bestow the same. He shall have to his own use during my lease of the manor of Southminster the quitrents and other profits payable to me out of North Wick, Land Wick, Broadward and the Park towards the payment of the lord's rent and my daughter's annuity. To my sister Eleanor Tredgolde a gown cloth as other hath. To my brother Tredgolde an old bay gelding that I was wont to ride on. Spoken and declared in the presence of John Levet, William Levet, Henry Ellice and James Sharparow.

Proved 29 June 1562.

JOHN AWDELEY of Berechurch gentleman, 21 July 1588.   [35/52]

To my cousin Thomas Awdeley of Berechurch my lands and tenements called Butlers in Peldon and Abberton, on condition that he pay to the children of my brother Thomas Awdeley of Gosbeckes [in Stanway] deceased, i.e. to Richard, George, Frances, John, Elizabeth wife of Richard Blenerchasset, and Mary wife of Robert Cooke £40 apiece to be taken out of the profits and paid orderly from the youngest to the eldest; my cousin to make my farmer Reynold Wakering a lease of Butlers

152

with the stock and store for 15 years at an annual rent of £36, leaving the stock at the end, i.e. 20 milch beasts and 60 mother ewes, in as good case as he shall now receive them; and to my cousin my bay ambling nag. To my cousins Francis Awdeley and John Awdeley, two of the sons of my late brother Thomas of Gosbeckes, my farm called Trumpingtons and Fithelers in Great Tey to hold part and part like, desiring them to be content with my bequest without any vexation one with another. To the poor's box of Berechurch £10, and £5 more to be distributed to poor people at my burial.

To every one of my sister Awdlie's children of Berechurch a piece of gold of 10s. or a mark. To Mistress Mary Southwell 2 pieces of gold called ducats; to Margery Pigge 40s.; to Mistress Elizabeth Gynes a piece of gold of 10s. To every one of my sister Awdlie's servants in household with her at Berechurch 6s. 8d. To Oliver Pigge the elder 20s. To Robert Cooke of Colchester 10s. To my cousins Mary Cooke my joined cupboard and my pewter, Elizabeth Blenerchasset my featherbed I now lie on, and Richard Awdley my best buff hose and a canvas doublet; and the rest of my apparel to my cousins Francis and John Awdeley, saving that Margery Pigge shall have 2 shirts. To my cousins Richard Blenerchassett my 2 longbows and my arrows, Robert Cooke and his wife my 2 coffers, Robert Awdley my nets and other engines to take partridges and hawks, and Thomas Awdeley of Gosbecks £5. To the children of Richard Blenerchassett the £10 that is owing to me, i.e. by Richard Underwood £6, mother Lambert 40s., and Richard 40s.

I ordain my very good sister Mistress Katherine Awdley my executrix. To my sister Beatrix Awdeley the debt she oweth me and £10 besides, and to my godchildren, i.e. my cousin John Nutbrowne, Stanstede's son and Clerke's son, 10s. each.

Witnesses: Anne Ashe, Jane Gilberde, Ambrose Gilbarde.
Proved 20 August 1588.

JOHN AWDELEY of Berechurch gentleman, 10 December 1597.
[43/17]

To my brother Francis Awdley £30; to my sister Hassett £30; to my mother Mistress Beatrix Awdley £5; to my brother and sister Hassett's children equally to be divided among them £30 at 21 or marriage. To my nephew Thomas, son of my brother Richard Awdeley deceased, an annuity of £10 granted by deed to me out of a messuage and lands in Layer Breton, Layer Mawlden [recte Marney] and Layer-de-la-Haye called Neverdes by Henry Addames of Abberton Hall yeoman, provided that if he pay to my executor £100 within one year after my decease then the deed to be void and the annuity to cease. To my little niece, sister of my said nephew and natural daughter of Richard, £10. Towards a stone to be laid over my father's and uncle's grave who lie both in one grave £5. To poor people in bread and money at my funeral 40s. and to poor and aged people where my executor shall think needful 40s. Thus entreating my very good cousin Mr Thomas Awdley as a charitable deed to take the executorship. [No witnesses.]

Proved 6 February 1599.

THOMAS BARKER of Chignal St James gentleman, 25 July 1577.
[32/13]

Because I have made a conveyance of my lease of the manor of Chignal Hall late to me granted from Sir John Peter and Dame Mary his wife to Thomas Catcher of London on trust to divers purposes, my desire is that Catcher shall assign my lease to Dorothy my loving wife and to Henry my son by her. The residue of my goods to my wife.

I appoint as my overseers my good friends Mr Baron Clerke and Mr Edward Eliott, and to each 40s. to wear in rings, and as my executors my wife and my son. Widow Stiles shall enjoy the small tenement and lands she dwelleth in for my term in Chignal lease at the same rent. To Jane Clerke daughter of Mr Baron Clerke my white cow. To every one of my servants 10s. To my brother [in-law] Massey 40s. to make him a ring. Witnesses: John Hassoll, John Pargrave, Thomas Gooche, John Taverner, Bedell Hole, John Stebbinge.

Proved 13 February 1588.

JOHN BARKLEY of Shenfield gentleman, serjeant of the Queen's Cellar, 1 May 1586.
[31/13]

To John my eldest son my house and land called Pages in Collier Row [in Romford] adjoining to the Forest of Waltham; and for default of heirs with successive remainders to Edward my son, to my daughters Elizabeth and Mary and the longer liver, and to the next heir male of my name. To John my copyhold lands in Chigwell and [the] Forest called Barnes in the occupation of John Campe; and for default of heirs likewise. To Edward my house in Enfield (Middx.), and for default of heirs to Elizabeth and Mary; and an annuity of £5 out of Pages until he is 21. My featherbeds and household stuff shall be equally divided among my children, i.e. John, Edward, Elizabeth and Mary; my apparel between John and Edward, and my wife's apparel between Elizabeth and Mary. My own chain and my wife's chain shall be sold by my executors to the use of my daughter's marriage money. My executors shall increase the said money, i.e. to Elizabeth and Mary £100 each if they find my substance to be sufficient or at least 100 marks at marriage, so that they shall be ruled therein by the discretion and order of my executors. The lease of my house at Shenfield shall be sold by them towards the performance of my will. To John my ring with the turquoise stone. To my servant John Ouer 40s., and to Garrett my servant for the great pains and travail he hath taken in my sickness and otherwise 4 marks. The residue of my goods to my executors towards the performance of my will. I constitute my executors my well-beloved friends Richard Wroth esquire and Mr

Richard Breame, one of the officers of her Majesty's Cellar, and to each for their pains 5 marks to make them a ring in remembrance.

Witnesses: Roger Jonnes, [blank] Carter.

Proved 22 March 1587.

JOHN BARNABE of Inworth gentleman, 15 April 1563.   [7/23]

To be buried without pomp in the parish church, chancel or chapel where it shall fortune me to decease out of this miserable world. To the reparations and other needful causes of Inworth church 20s., the church where I be buried 20s., Stanway the great church £5 conditionally so it may be well bestowed with other help so that the church may be for ever used as the chief parish church there with divine service where Mr Knevet Mistress Bonham is buried [*sic* : see Will of Katherine wife of John Barnabe gentleman, formerly wife of Edward Knevett esquire, of Stanway, 1535 (Essex R.O., D/ABW 3/44)]. To the curate, being a lawful priest, the day of my burial and at the 12th day or month or so after my death 12d., and he do say such divine service as then shall be used, and 7 poor folks or more every of the days to receive the holy communion each 8d., and to all other poor folks 4d. who shall be at my burial at the church to take the common dole, if they be 40 score or more, which I trow will not be, and to have bread, cheese or other victual and good drink sufficient and plenty in the church or some other meet place there. All priests that cannot say the holy communion for lack of tables to have but 6d., which I trow will not be 12 priests, and such priests and clerks with the most rich and substantial persons of the parish where I shall be buried and other substantial men that then be there, they taking no money at the dole, to have a dinner together with meat and drink and victuals in some convenient house or mine own, and the poor specially well refreshed with some things as bread, drink and cheese, and to every poor 4d. The sexton for his attendance and for ringing and making of my grave to have largely, and I a gravestone at Inworth to lie on me and a scripture thereupon to be set. I will be bought very thick frize of russet colour so much as will make 12 large gowns for 12 poor folks against my burial and to be given them ready made at my charge to such as dwell where I be buried. To every poor householder in Inworth, Tolleshunt D'Arcy, Tiptree, All Hallon parish and the late Crouch Friars Street and Maldon Lane in Colchester, Kelvedon and Stanway, to every such 8d., not being at the common dole. I will be distributed yearly during 7 years after my death £4 quarterly 20s. to most needy poor folks every 4d., this in anywise where and near the town I shall be buried. To such as will keep an almshouse for lodging of poor people in some great town or where is a great thoroughfare town 2 mattresses with bolsters, 2 pair of blankets, 2 coverlets, and 4 pair of strong sheets of canvas of my best and strongest meet for that purpose, to be bought of new cloth. Towards the acquittal and payment of fees and apparel of poor prisoners after they be acquit in Colchester Castle yearly during 7 years every year 40s., and the poor prisoners in the Castle every year 16s. 8d. for victuals in Lent time or any other time most needful. Towards the finding of poor fatherless and motherless children and other poor needful children within young age to be relieved and after they come to meet age of 6 or 7 years to serve then to be apparelled and put to service or made prentice, in all £21 evenly to be distributed during 7 years; but I having no sons and having a son or Thomas the bastard then but for 4 years, and having no son nor the said Thomas alive then more money for 10 years; out of the profits of my farms if need so be or else of specialties with Harbottell and debts specially of Mr William Tusser.

To Thomas Barnabe, by some people called bastard son of the late Peter Barnabe but is my bastard son, living to his full age of 23 or shall be out of his apprenticehood or be married, towards a stock after he become out of apprenticehood £60 besides Peter Barnabe's gift of £40 in my hands, conditionally as followeth; nevertheless Thomas is my bastard otherwise called because I [was] then a suitor in a marriage therefore so named at my desire to Peter Barnabe. To the said Thomas called the bastard of Peter such bargain and lease which I have of Robert Bonham deceased of sundry parcels of Kelvedon Hall to begin immediately after my Lady Hasset's death, freely to him and he live to 26 years or be married or have children; and if he die before and without children I give my lease to him that shall enjoy of my gift my lands; and I give thereof after the first 7 years £40, then to the youngest children of Robert Bonham deceased; provided that Thomas nor none other take profits of the parcels of master Tusser till after 7 years.

Towards the amendment of highways in London highway where great need is between Rivenhall smithy and Cross-in-the-hand £20 or else in any other place as to Colchester ward, trusting the country will help; and I will a footpath be made with a footbridge and a cartway at the watering place by my oodhouse [sic] at Easterford [Kelvedon] great bridge and so to my house there, or at Rivenhall broken bridge at Rivenhall smithy watering, with other charitable help of near dwellers and country. Towards the amendment of highways between Hecford bridge and Stanway Hall and so forth to Colchester where most need is, by oversight of Mr Bocking and specially of Mr Bonham £10, for my soul, my wife's and specially for Mr Edward Knyvit's soul.

To every my servants 40s. and their livery besides their wages; to other of lesser time as one year 20s. and by lesser time 13s. 4d. To Agnes my woman living unmarried a livery featherbed and a flockbed of such that was in the time of first making hereof which was July anno 2 Elizabeth at the parsonage of Inworth, 2 bolsters, 1 pillow, 2 pair of blankets, 2 coverlets, 3 pair of sheets, bedsteadle with posts, ceilure and tester, and 3 curtains of buckram, and the boarded bedsteadle, and £6, she being with me and continue true and diligent, part of the kitchen stuff as pewter, brass and latten and of other houses of office at the parsonage, and other linen that was there July anno 2, on condition being unmarried to keep my house and my stuff and gardens at Colchester or elsewhere, also under the same condition 40s. yearly for life out of my lands. In like condition to Alice Spiltimber some small part of the stuff but no featherbed nor stuff of household but money only 10s. or a dwelling near together. To every other such dwelling under me as servants 20s. My best apparel to Thomas Barnabe my boy, the rest to my kinsman in Lincolnshire and part of the rest to other poor neighbours. To every my godchildren 5s.

To Thomas eldest son of William Bonham deceased £3 and to the second son 40s. To the daughter of Robert Bonham late of Bradwell deceased, my goddaughter, £3 at 21 or marriage, to use it well or else his other eldest daughter.

Whereas I have plate, jewels, specialties and money with master Christopher Harbottle haberdasher of Ludgate in London, I will my executors to put it in safety with the gains that may be had thereby to the use as followeth. They shall not take any advantage of the light covenants in indentures against any of my farmers but only for the yearly rents stocks and farm rent, and I forgive all poor debtors their debts not able to pay. To Thomas Barnabe of Kirton in Holland (Lincs.) £3 for his children. To the son of Thomas Staleworthe, my brother-in-law, of Frampton by Kirton. To the poor bedemen of the Lord Marney in Layer Marney 10s. My copyhold lands holden of Pete Hall in Peldon are in feoffment of Henry Wykes and Thomas Hythe of Peldon by lawful surrender in court to the use of me and my heirs by my will, of which the copy is in a box in the counter table. My copyhold lands holden of Tillingham Hall of the Church of St Paul's in London are in feoffment of Mr Robert Gynnes of the Temple and Thomas Barnabe younger the bastard by surrender to the use of me and my heirs.

If I shall have issue male lawfully begotten, I give to such my issue my lands free and copyhold, patronages, leases and their appurtenances and to their lawful heirs male, also my stuff and plate in my house in All Hallon parish in Colchester or elsewhere and my plate etc. with Mr Harbottell; and for lack of such issue successively to (except what I have appointed to Thomas the bastard) the said Thomas and his lawful heirs, to the next heir male of me and of my surname Barnabe which is Thomas Barnabe of Kirton, and to the lawful issue male of Thomas the bastard and their lawful heirs male; and for further default of such issue the lands and goods to be sold by my executors and the money to be bestowed in charity.

If any doubts about the meaning of my will shall grow, the same to be determined by my supervisors and specially by Mr Carell and by Mr Stapleton of the Temple and by Mr Robert Gynnes, Mr Mariant or by 3 or 4 of them that shall be near my burial, and masters and governors of my children if need be. Provided that if Thomas the bastard be advanced to my lands and other the premises then he lose the £100. To the sister of the late Peter Barnabe my nephew buried in Inworth church to the use of her children £4. Nevertheless I will Mr Beste and Mr Daniell of Messing to have the rule, keeping and governance of my children within age if any such shall be, and also of Thomas the bastard, with all bequests given them or him; and I pray Mr Robert Gynnes whose aid I pray to [my] children and Thomas the bastard to see them have their right, [especially] of Thomas, who is my son which I so confess and will have him so to be taken and preferred as he ought to be. I

157

ordain Mr John Beste (£6) alderman and Mr Edmund Daniell (£4) esquire of Messing my executors, and supervisors and counsellors I make Edmund Daniell esquire, Robert Gynnes (£3) gentleman, and Mr Beest (£6) alderman of Colchester, and Mr Anthony Stapleton (40s.).

Witnesses : Guy Douse, Robert Middleton, William Mowlde, Thomas Barnabe, George Durbar.

Proved 28 July 1564.

GEORGE BIRD of [Saffron] Walden gentleman, 8 June 1600.   [44/63]

To Eleanor my wife for life my messuage called Bruettes, and my lands free and copy in Walden; and after her death to remain to the heirs of myself and my wife. To the child wherewith she is now big £100 at 21 or marriage, and if it die before to be equally divided between the children of my sisters Hammond, King and More at 21 or marriage. The residue of my goods to my well-beloved wife, hoping she will be careful to bring up my child in the fear of God. I make my wife my sole executor. Witnesses : William Bird, Edward Bird, Christopher Bird, Mary Mead.

Proved 3 July 1600.

JOHN BLACKSTON of Brightlingsea gentleman, 30 March 1593.
[37/91, 38/57]

To be buried in Kirby church. To Joan my wife my moveable goods. To my cousin John Cotton my tenement called Carvers in Kirby with 21 acres of land, after our decease. To my wife £10 a year during the original lease of How Wick and East Wick, with one gelding's pasture. To John Cotton £10 a year out of the lease. Provided that my executor shall divide the rents to the use of the poor of Kirby and St Osyth, and two or three other persons whose names he shall specify to John Tredgolde and father Bonner. I ordain John Cotton the elder my only executor. To Margaret Chandeler 5s., Parnel Chaundeler 20s., Matthew Glascocke 20s. Witnesses : Robert Ores, Robert Allen, William Jackson.

Memorandum that John Blackston, after he had perused the will, said that his meaning was that John Cotton should have the said land to him and his heirs in fee simple after the death of his wife. [Same witnesses.]

Proved 17 January 1594.

THOMAS BLAKE of Little Baddow gentleman, going into her Majesty's service in the Low Countries, 4 June 1599.   [47/108]

I bequeath my temporal goods, money, plate or jewels to my dear and well-beloved brother Christopher Blake, whom I make my sole executor. On the day of the making of my will I delivered to Christopher a certain note of a bill of debt made to me by my brother Giles Blake. Witnesses : William Wentworthe and John Hobson the writer.

Proved 12 December 1603.

158

WILLIAM BONFIELD of Pattiswick gentleman, 10 June 1599.
[45/13]

I will that 2s. worth of bread in penny loaves shall be yearly delivered by John Bonfylde, my cousin and next heir, to 24 poor folks in Corfe Castle in the Isle of Purbeck (Dorset) every Sunday, Good Friday and the Eve of the Annunciation of our Blessed Lady the Virgin for evermore for their relief, to be given at the tomb of my father in Corfe Castle churchyard; and in consideration thereof to John £100, being in the hands of one Ket's widow, for payment whereof she standeth bound to Morgan Hayne, my brother-in-law.

To my sisters Mary Domine £25 and Elizabeth Snooke widow £10. To William eldest son of William Bonfeild of Woston in Corfe Castle £20. To Sir Edmund Huddylston knight, my very good master, my gelding, and to my very good lady and mistress the Lady Huddylston £12 10s. which she oweth me and 40s. of the £7 which is owing me of the beerbrewer. To Mistress Fortescue £6 10s. and a little hope ring of gold. To my sister Mary a little seal ring which I have in my coffer. To my godsons Thomas Stonard of Pattiswick and Titterell's son 20s. each. To William Stonard my old cloak and a blue coat in my coffer. To old Woodward of Pattiswick a blue coat. To the poor folks in Pattiswick 40s. and Sawston (Cambs.) 20s. To my fellow Odell of Sawston 20s. To my son [in-law] John Byatt of Sawston 5s.; my fellow Wratham 5s.; Anne Swett of Sawston 10s.; and Duttesbury of Chelmsford at the sign of the Blue Bell there 10s. To William Bonfeild my cousin that serveth in my Lord of Sussex' house £5, my buff hosen, my best hat, my best cloak, my chest and desk at Pattiswick, and such things as I have in my press at Pattiswick, and Mistress Fortyskue to have the press itself and my desk at the Spittle. To the said John Bonfyld my chest standing at the Spittle. To Thomas Reynoldes of the Middle Temple, London, gentleman, my rapier and dagger. To Mistress Katherine, Mr Fortescue's gentlewoman, 5s., Alice Greenwood 5s., George Lee 5s., and Charles 2s. 6d. To my fellow-servants Ralph Rigbye and John Rigbie 2s. 6d. each. To master John Fortescue 2s. 6d. I ordain Mistress Isabel Fortescue widow and Thomas Reynoldes my executors, desiring them to perform the same.

Codicil, 16 August 1600. I owe Mr Myldemaye £10 as Mr Raynoldes do know, towards payment whereof there is in my chest at London £6; the rest my white gelding will discharge. My cousin John Tucker doth owe me £10 to be paid at Michaelmas term, which I bequeath to my sister Jane his mother. There is in my chest at London a bond of £60 forfeit, for which no interest is yet paid. To my cousin Thomas Hayne my Turkey gold ring in my chest. To my Lady Huddilston my crucifix, and I forgive 17s. interest which I paid for her ring. I forgive the wages my master oweth me. To Mistress Fortescue my watch, desiring her to be good to my sister Mary. To Mary my chest at Pattiswick and all things in it. To William Bonfeild my chest and desk at London and all things in them except before bequeathed. To Alice my Lady's maid 10s. To Skippe 10s. Witnesses : Thomas Wells and Robert Coote.
Proved 17 February 1601.

WILLIAM BOURNE of Bobbingworth gentleman, 29 April 1581.

To my very good and loving wife Margaret for life my tenement in Bobbingworth wherein John Garrolde dwelleth and now holdeth, my copyhold lands called Ryves land holden of Bobbingworth Hall [manor], and my copyhold lands called Bushy Lez in Shelley near Awkingeforthe Bridge holden of the manor of the Parsonage of High Ongar. To her my leases of my farms called the moiety or half part of South Hall in Paglesham, Strowde Wick in Rochford, and the watermill called the New Mill in Rochford, on condition that she shall for 5 years after my decease pay my son Robert an annuity of £5 and my son John another of £5. To my wife my household stuff, viz. bedding, linen, napery, brass, pewter, latten, iron, and all other things appertaining to household; my silver, plate, rings, or other jewels, together with her own apparel; her own saddles with the furniture thereunto belonging, her pillion and pillion cloth; my corn growing at Gippes alias Billesdons and my corn and grain as well there as at Blake Hall and Upper Hall [all in Bobbingworth], threshed and unthreshed in the barns, garners or chambers; 20 kine and a bull, 7 knowe bullocks and 1 bulchin at her choice, and 6 of the small steers which I bought at last Cold Fair [at Newport], my hogs, 50 sheep, 6 draught oxen, 2 cart horses, 2 of my best rode geldings with the furniture for the same, old [mar?]bette gelding, and a little grey ambling colt in Shelford in Foulness, and 1 grey young ambling mare in Shelford, my hay and store at Gippes alias Billesdons, and 4 horse colts whereof 1 remaineth now in Shelford and the other 3 at Moreton; my oats growing at Weald late Park and my wool and cheese at Billesdons; and £300. To my wife my leases of the manor of Blake Hall with the appurtenances in Bobbingworth, the stock and store of 20 milch kine and a bull, 50 sheep, 6 cart horses or geldings, my ploughs, carts, harrows, cart harness and plough harness there, and my wheat growing on the grounds of the same manor (if my wife shall live so long). To her my lease of the site and demesnes of the manor of Upper Hall in Moreton with the appurtenances, with the stock and store of 14 milch kine and a bull, 80 hoggerel sheep, 8 cart horses or geldings, my ploughs, carts, harness, cart harness and plough harness there, and my wheat and other grain, on condition that she pay to William and Mary his wife an annuity of £66 13s. 4d. ending at Michaelmas 1582, an annuity of £40 which I have granted to them by deeds out of Upper Hall, and to Robert and John for 5 years after my decease an annuity of £5. If my wife die or depart out of this transitory world and vale of misery before the expiration of the lease of Blake Hall, to Robert, and that of Upper Hall, to John. To Robert and John my lease in reversion of the farm and wick called East Wick in Foulness, jointly betwixt them, on condition that they pay William an annuity of £20. To Robert and John each a trotting horse colt and a mare colt being at Shelford, whereof Robert have his choice. To Richard and James my sons equally to be divided betwixt them £400 at 24, which shall be used to the best and uttermost commodity by my loving friend Roger Abdye, citizen and merchant tailor of London, he entering into sufficient bonds to my executors for answering as well the said stock as the increase of the same. To Margaret Bourne my daughter £100 at marriage, if she shall be advised and ruled therein by my wife, if then living, and if dead she shall be advised by her brethren or the most part of them. To Eleanor Milborne and Margaret Milborne, daughters of my daughter Milborne, each £10 at marriage, if they shall marry with the assent of their father and mother. To William my greatest grey ambling gelding in Shelford and to my daughter-in-law his wife a dark grey ambling colt bred in the said ground.

To Edward Rise my servant £5 which William Rise his father oweth me; to John Wapulles, Richard Tunbridge, Henry Litborne and Richard Casse 40s. apiece; to William Ellys and Robert Browne 10s. apiece; and every other of my servants as well men, women and boys 3s. 4d. apiece. To the reparations of Bobbingworth church 20s. To the poor people in Moreton 20s. and Bobbingworth 13s. 4d.

I ordain William my son and Richard Glascock my son-in-law my executors, and for their pains £20 apiece. I ordain James Morrice esquire my supervisor, desiring him to vouchsafe to take upon him the same, and for his pains 100s. To my sons William, Robert and James my apparel to be divided equally betwixt them (except my Dutch cloak lined with bays which I give to my son Milborne). To the same Milborne my old black ambling nag in Temple Marsh. The residue of my goods shall be equally divided betwixt Robert and John.

Witnesses: Thomas Glascocke, parson of Bobbingworth, John Glascocke, John Poole, George Milborne.

Further to my wife a tester of a bed of crimson and gold and black velvet, with the tables, forms, chairs, stools, cupboards and bedsteads in my house at Billesdons alias Gippes, the chests in the house and all things there (except £400 and my apparel). Whereas I have given to Robert immediately after the decease of my wife the rest of the years to come in Blake Hall, with the stock and store, he shall not sell the same before he be married, and dying before he be married the lease to come to William and John. Whereas I have given to John likewise the rest of the years to come of the site and demesnes of Upper Hall with the stock, he shall not sell it before he be married, and if he die before he be married the lease shall remain to William and Robert equally to be divided betwixt them. If it fortune that both die being unmarried, the rest of the years to come in Blake Hall and Upper Hall to be equally divided between William, Richard and James. Whereas I have given to Robert and John the reversion of a farm in Foulness called East Wick, if either die unmarried before the other the survivor to have the other's part; and if both die unmarried the rest of the years to come to William, Richard and James equally. To William £100. This codicil, 17 May 1581, I desire shall be annexed to my will. Witnesses: Glascocke clerk, Thomas Warner.

Proved 25 September 1581 by William, Richard Glascocke having renounced.

MARGARET BOURNE of Bobbingworth, widow of William Bourne, 7 December 1594.   [39/4]

To my son Richard £400, on condition that he shall not demand any interest or allowance for the use of £200 which my late husband did bequeath him. To my son James £400 on like condition. To my son Richard a featherbed and a coverlet of dornix. To Richard and James equally to be divided between them an old cypress chest of linen standing between the windows in my chamber. To my son-in-law Richard Glascocke £100. To my son-in-law Robert Mason £100. To John Whalpoole of Brentwood £10. To Agnes wife of Thomas Fanne of Parndon £10. To Henry Lilborne, Richard Tunbridge and Richard Casse, my servants, each £6 13s. 4d.; to Edward Whalepole my servant £5 and his sister 50s. and John their brother 50s. To Elizabeth Bourne, daughter of my son William, a diaper tablecloth with a towel, a dozen of napkins of diaper, and my best cypress chest. To Mary Bourne, daughter of William, my stone jug with a tip and lid of silver. To William son of William my stone jug with a gilt tip and cover. To George Milborne, my son-in-law, £100 which he doth owe me without any specialty. To William such sums of money as he doth owe me by bill or annuity, and 10 pair of sheets, 5 of them of the better sort and 5 of the worst sort. To my daughter Milborne my cloth gown faced with wolverene and guarded with velvet, my velvet hat, and a kirtle of grograine. To my daughter Mason my black cloth gown guarded with two guards of velvet. I ordain Robert my executor and William my supervisor and for his pains a silver and gilt goblet. The residue of my goods to Robert. Witnesses: Hugh Inse [rector of Chipping Ongar], George Milborne.
Proved 31 January 1595.

HENRY BRADBURY of Littlebury gentleman, 26 February 1597. [For Robert Bradburie see p. 58.]   [41/23]

To be buried in the chancel of Littlebury church as near as conveniently may be to Jane my late wife, and there shall be some convenient gravestone laid on me by the provision and discretion of my executors. To the churchwardens towards the repair of the church or churchyard 6s. 8d. To the poor people in Littlebury 40s., Meesden (Herts.) 6s. 8d., Sampford 5s., and Langley 5s.

My dear and well-beloved wife Marian shall have for life in recompense for her jointure or dower my manor of Langley alias Langley Hall in Langley and Meesden alias Missenden, my manor of Giffordes alias Stanleys in [Great] Sampford, and my messuages and lands in Langley, Great and Little Sampford, Hempstead and Finchingfield, according to a conveyance to my father [in-law] Mr George Niccolls and my brother [in-law] Mr John Michell to the use of my wife for life. To her for 12 years my house in Littlebury wherein I dwell, with the orchard and garden, the house wherein Mr Woodley dwelleth, and an orchard between Mr Woodley's yard and Mr Hely's house. After her decease, the manor of Langley shall remain to William my son and his heirs male; and for default of issue successively to Henry, Robert and George, my second, third and fourth sons, and the heirs male of each.

Whereas my sister-in-law Mistress Margaret Daniell, sometime the wife of my eldest brother Robert Bradbury, doth hold for life the manor of Meesden (the patronage and advowson of the church excepted) and certain messuages and lands in Meesden, Clavering, Brent Pelham, Anstey and Stortford (Herts.), the reversion or remainder of which is in me and my heirs; after her decease the premises and the advowson shall remain to William and his heirs male, and for default of issue as above. To William and his heirs male my manors, messuages and lands in possession and reversion except my mansion house and lands bequeathed to my wife, and for default of issue likewise. After my wife's decease, to Henry my manor of Giffords alias Stanley and his heirs male, and for default of such issue successively to Robert, George and William and their heirs male.

To my wife her wearing apparel and jewels and my great gilt salt; and she shall have my best featherbeds such as she will choose, with the chairs and stools in my great chamber; and all tables as well dormant as other, forms, chairs and stools other than such as are in the great chamber, great chests, cupboards, presses, brewing vessels and cisterns of lead, the great pair of andirons, and the great iron firefork in the kitchen, and wainscots, portals and glass shall remain in my house and be used by her during the 12 years; and after her decease they shall remain to my heir male. To William my armour, books and muniments (such bonds or bills which shall belong to my executors excepted); and the residue of my plate, jewels, linen and household stuff shall be equally divided between my wife and William.

If John Muffett, husband of my daughter Mary, put in such security as shall be liked of by Thomas Pagytt of the Middle Temple esquire for the leaving of Mary at the time of his death in money or goods, or if she die to leave to their issue £300 equally to be divided between them, William shall pay John £100. William shall pay my daughter Anne Bradbury £250 at Michaelmas 1598 and in the meantime allow her sufficient maintenance. To my daughters Barbara and Ellen each £250 at 21 or marriage. If the three sums of £100 and £250 be not paid after the time limited all bequests of my lands in Littlebury shall be void, and Mr George Niccolles, my father-in-law, Ferdinando Pulton and George Pulton gentlemen shall sell them and the money taken to employ to the said portions.

To Henry towards his education an annuity of £20 for life, provided that if my wife die it shall cease. To Robert and George each an annuity of £20; if she die, to Robert and George an annuity of £5 above the £20. She shall have the custody, education and bringing up of Barbara, Ellen, Henry, Robert and George and receive their annuities until 21 or my daughters are married. After my death there shall be an equal division of my corn in my barn, sollers and chambers, my growing corn, horses, bullocks, swine, sheep, milch kine and calves between my wife and

William. To her my coach. To George Niccolles my bay nag on which I use to ride. To my cousin Mr Robert Fulnetby £10. To Henry Baldwyn 20s. and Giles Keffer 26s. 8d., whom I have brought up from children. The residue of my goods to William, whom I make my sole executor.

Witnesses: Bennet Burton, Thomas Woodly, Robert Raymond.
Proved 19 April 1597.

HUMPHREY BRIDGES of Rayleigh gentleman, 28 August 1591.

[36/55]

My will is that as little charge as conveniently may be shall be at my funeral, only to the poor thereat 20s. in small money and 10s. to a preacher for a sermon, and £3 6s. 8d. to be bestowed on some drinking on such friends or neighbours as shall be at my burial.

To Dorothy my wife 100 marks and my best salt at her choice, with the little trencher salt, one of my goblets, the silver cup which my aunt Tirrell gave me, the 2 purled wine cups, the little silver cup to warm meat with the covered stone pot, 6 silver spoons, my household [stuff], and the stock of cattle on my grounds except such as shall be hereafter excepted.

To Edward unthrift my son my white silver salt and £10. To Richard my son my ring of gold with the death's head, 1 of my 3 silver wine bowls, and £20. To Thomas my son my ring with my seal of arms, 1 of my gilt salts, and £20. To Humphrey my son 1 of my wine drinking bowls and £20. To Anthony my son 1 of my silver beer pots and £20. To George my son the third drinking wine cup, £20, and 2 white silver spoons. To John my son my other goblet and £20. To Samuel my son my other white silver beer pot and £20. To Elizabeth my daughter my brooch of gold and 100 marks in satisfaction of any other legacy due to her. To Anne my daughter my third gilt salt and 100 marks. To Dorothy my daughter my little chain of gold in my desk, 2 white silver spoons, and 100 marks. My wife shall only have 4 of my kine, whereof the 2 bullocks to be 2 if she will, and of the horse only my nag and the northern white gelding, and the rest shall be sold towards some performance of my legacies and debts. To Thomas my law books at Lincoln's Inn or here at Rayleigh, with my bedding and stuff at Lincoln's Inn except my apparel. To Anthony and George my other books equally between them, except such as I hereafter dispose. To Richard my armour, except the musket which I give to Thomas with my best crossbow, but my wife shall have the use of such armour as she shall be charged with. To her only the use of my table, cupboards, stools, hangings or wainscot in my parlour, with pictures there, the table and forms in the hall, the press and bedstead in the great chamber and hangings there, the brewing vessels and other vessels in my brewhouse, cellar, larder, milkhouse and boulting house; and she shall leave them with my house without spoil.

To every manservant 6s. 8d. and every maidservant 5s. My apparel not otherwise bequeathed shall be given among my children by my wife's discretion. To her for life my principal house in Rayleigh, my lands I purchased of Mr Willis, Chapel Mead, Bennetts Croft, and the lands I purchased of Thomas Philipson, on condition that she shall claim no other jointure or dower of any other my lands, and after her decease to Richard and Thomas and their heirs male; and the common use of the pump, yard, waters and outhouses, hoping that they will agree like brethren.

To Edward Maldon Field, parcel of Seelie House land, in the tenure of Peter Jervis rented at £6 13s. 4d. yearly. To Humphrey Cocks Croft, parcel of the said lands in Maldon in the tenure of Nicholas Collin, who shall pay yearly to Humphrey during the lease £4. To Anthony my meadow, parcel of Seelie House land, in that of Oliver Skinner. To George my lands and wood in that of Edward Legate except the first crop of wood. To John my tenement and lands I purchased of Nicholas Broadwater in that of Thomas Buntinge. To Samuel my woods in Thundersley called Magis, Severall and the Grove, and my wood and land in Hadleigh and Leigh. My loving friends Richard Carr and Edmund Reade shall enter into Seelie house and the marsh grounds adjoining in the tenure of Nicholas Collin and sell the same to Arthur Harris esquire, or Collin, or any other that will buy them, and the money to be divided towards the payment of my children's legacies. Such of my children as be of full age or able to be placed by themselves or any other in any service or trade of life shall have their portions with as much speed as can be made, and the others by means of my said friends and executrix to have their stocks and legacies employed to some good use towards their maintenance until they shall be fit to receive them. To my wife the first crop or fell of my woods for the maintenance of her expenses, she sufficiently enclosing and preserving the springs and fencing the wood. To Richard and Thomas out of my lands given to her for life each 26s. 8d. yearly payable by her.

I ordain her my only executrix and Richard Carr and Edmund Reade my overseers, and to Carr my gown at London whereof I have taken out the face, my Calvin upon Job, and a ring of gold price 20s., and to Reade my cloak which I had of Mr Cooke, my lute, and a ring of gold price 20s. [No witnesses.]

Proved 2 June 1592.

JOHN BRIDGES of Chelmsford gentleman. [Undated.]   [20/26]

To Anne, my well-beloved wife, my lands and tenements as well copy as free, except one tenement in Moulsham in the occupation of John Bridges my brother, for life, provided that if she marry she have only a third part according to the laws of this realm.

To Thomas my eldest son, my parcels of land called Pond Land, Pit Croft and Band Croft, and the residue of the lands I purchased of Ralph Nalinghurste gentleman; my lands called Warrens, Great Broche Croft Field, Little Broche Croft Field and Bridge Croft, with the buildings on the same, which I purchased of John Tamworthe esquire; my houses in Dartford (Kent) with a wood wharf belonging which I purchased of Edward Dytchefielde, my son-in-law; my tenement in Moulsham called the Tabor, wherein John Worthlye dwelleth, a tenement next the same in the tenure of Thomas Pechye, and two tenements in Moulsham in that of Christopher Sex; to hold to Thomas and his heirs after my wife's decease or after she marry, with successive remainders to my sons John, Matthew and William and their heirs. To John my house wherein I dwell called Toppyes which I purchased of John Lyvinge; the tenement which I have now joined to my house lying next to Colchester Lane which I purchased of Henry Tyrrell knight; and 3 acres of meadow in Baddow Mead; to hold likewise, with successive remainders to Thomas, Matthew and William; a garden with a milking yard sometime belonging to the Boar's Head in my own occupation, to hold for 21 years; and so many unexpired years of my lease of my mead called Tunman Mead. To Matthew a parcel of meadow called Keye Mead in Broomfield and a tenement called Diers I purchased of William Raynolde and two crofts of land called Great Oxney and Little Oxney letten with the inn called the Cross Keys; to hold likewise with successive remainders to Thomas, John and William. To William my inn called the Boar's Head with the barn and garden letten with the same and Boar's Head Mead, and the reversion or remainder of the yard and garden devised to John for 21 years; to hold likewise with successive remainders to Thomas, John and Matthew. To my brother John for life the tenement before excepted wherein he dwelleth, the remainder to Matthew; provided that, if my brother or his wife behave towards my wife to her vexation, the term shall be void.

To Thomas my best salt gilt, 6 of my best silver spoons, 1 spoon of silver and gilt, and 1 white bowl of silver (weighing 8 oz.); my best ring with the death's head; my best bed standing in the New Chamber, the frame table with 6 stools, 1 settle, 1 less table with a cupboard in it, 1 chair covered with needlework, 1 pair of creepers, my best carpet for the great table, and another of my carpets for the little table, with the hangings in the said chamber, with the curtains about the bed and the windows, 2 little joined stools covered with silk wrought with gold in the said chamber; and £500. To John a salt of silver and gilt which I bought of Ralph Nallinghurst (16 oz.), 3 of my best silver spoons, a little goblet of silver (6 oz.); the bed in the Parlour where I lie, a coverlet of tapestry lined, a cupboard and a settle of wainscot, a frame table, a side table, 6 joined stools with 2 small joined stools, 1 chair, a pair of Flanders cobirons, 7 flower pots, 8 cushions of Turkey work in the Hall, with the hangings or painted cloths there; and £100 to be paid within 2 years after my decease. To Matthew my little silver gilt salt (8 oz.), with 3 of my best silver spoons, my best goblet parcel gilt (18 oz.); the bed that standeth in the Long Chamber nearest the window next the street; and £100 to be paid within 3 years, also £100 after my wife's decease. To William a salt of silver and gilt (15 oz.) which I bought of Mr Anderkynne, with 1 pot of silver and gilt (14 oz.), 6 of my silver spoons of the second sort; a bed in the Long Chamber nearest the window towards the yard; and £100 to be paid within 4 years. To my daughter Ditchfielde 2 of my silver spoons of the third sort. As for my other legacy to her I refer it to my wife's discretion. To my daughter Ellys 2 of my silver spoons of the third sort; and £100 to be paid in as convenient time as my executors can get in my debts. To my daughter Mary 2 of my silver spoons of the third sort; and £100 at marriage so that she do not marry contrary to my wife's consent. To my brother John £5; my old gown, 1 of my doublets, a pair of my hose, 1 of my jerkins, and my best hat. To Agnes Bridges, his daughter, 40s. at marriage or 21. To John his son 40s. at 21. To Roger Stokes 40s., a pair of my hose, a cloth jerkin, a hat, and my blue cloak which I made for my horseman. To my sister Tabor and her children 10s. apiece. To Joan Worthley, my wife's sister, and her children 6s. 8d. apiece. To Agnes Rotchell, my maid, £5, and Joan Anderkyne, my maid, £3, at marriage or 28. To Thomas Knotte the elder 5s., Mr Ruste 6s. 8d., Mr Fermery 6s. 8d., and Thomas Ruste my godson 5s.

I bequeath £4 a year to be bestowed among my wife and children, so that they meet together twice a year at such place as she shall think meet at Christmas and Whitsuntide. To my daughter Ellis's children £5 apiece, the men children at 21 and the daughters at marriage or 24. To John Dytchfielde, my godson, my daughter Dytchfielde's son, £5 at 21. To John Lyvinge's wife, my wife's sister, and to every of her children 6s. 8d. Towards the reparations of Chelmsford church 10s. To Mr [Thomas] Howlett, parson of Chelmsford, 6s. 8d. To Giggins the sexton 3s. 4d. To the poor of the parish 40s. I make my wife and Thomas my executors and John Ellys, my son-in-law, overseer. [No witnesses.]
Proved 27 June 1577.

RICHARD BROCKE (or BROKE) of Radwinter gentleman, 14 December 1563. [7/10]

To the right honourable William Brooke knight, Lord Cobham, my especial good lord, one dozen of silver spoons with acorn heads, parcel gilt. To William Broke, my only son, my signet of gold of the value of 40s. To Elizabeth my wife a bedstead standing in my parlour at Radwinter with my best bed and the 16 rings of gold which she hath in her custody. To William Stevens my cloak. To Hugh Dorrell esquire my curtail nag. To John Wilkins gentleman 40s. The residue of my goods to be sold by Hugh Darrell and John Wilkins, whom I make my executors, and the money to be equally divided into three parts, one to my wife and the other two to Lord Cobham and he to have the use of the money until William Brock my son is 21 towards his keeping and bringing up, and the money to be repaid to him at 21; if he die before, my executors shall each have £10 and the overplus to Lord Cobham, whom I make overseer if it please his honour to take the pain. [Signs 'Broke'.] Witnesses: William Page gentleman, John Harper, John Bugby.
Proved 3 March 1564.

WILLIAM BROCK of Boxted gentleman, 7 July 1598.   [43/48]

To the poor people of Boxted 20s., Holy Trinity in Colchester 20s., and Little Leighs 20s. To Elizabeth my wife my brass, pewter, bedding, 4 milch beasts, half my corn on the ground, half my hay, the household stuff in the house I dwell in at Boxted, the poultry, half the swine, and the little bay mare. To her an annuity of £30 in recompense of her dower, i.e. £15 a year out of my lands in Willingale Doe and Spain and £15 to be assured by my son Bartholomew as hereafter; which annuities I appoint on condition that she shall release to him and my son William, Robert Mott and the heirs of Mr Buckingham deceased, to whom I have conveyed any lands, as by the advice of William Brock of Upton (Cheshire) esquire and Robert Mydleton of Colchester gentleman shall be thought meet. To Bartholomew my chief messuage with the gardens and grounds belonging in Colchester on condition that he shall convey to my wife an annuity of £15 out of the lands purchased of Mr John Abell at Mile End. To William Brock my son my lands and tenements in Little Leighs, Great Waltham, Willingale Doe and Spain, and Black Notley, and my copyhold lands in Boxted and Great Horkesley; and my title in the lands in Little Leighs, Felsted and Great Waltham made to me by a lease by Lord Riche deceased. To John Reeve my son-in-law and his wife, my daughter, £10. To either of my brothers an angel for a remembrance. To Francis Moones my late servant 20s. The residue of my goods to Bartholomew and William, whom I make executors, and I ordain William Brocke esquire and Robert Myddleton supervisors, and for their pains 20s. apiece. Witnesses : Thomas Thurston, John Thedrun, John Youngs.

Proved 13 June 1599.

EDMUND BROUGHTON [of Orsett] gentleman, 14 October 1576.
                                                              [19/36]

To be buried in the side chancel by my father. To the poor of Orsett 20s. To my sister Gressham 6s 8d. for 10 years out of the rent of the manor of Orsett. To my wife out of my rent in Orsett Hall for 10 years £20 a year, and if she die before to my children equally. To Edmund my eldest son, Christopher my second son, and William my youngest son each £10 a year out of the same rent. To them equally to be divided my part of Lese; and if they die without heir then to my brother John. To Andrew Broughton my kinsman my best cloak, a pair of mockado breeches, and 10s. To my brother John my sealing ring and my best hose. The residue of my goods to my wife, whom with her father I ordain my executors to see my children godly brought up in learning. I make overseers Christopher Chibburne gentleman, Giles Buskell clerk, and John Broughton gentleman. Witnesses : Edmund Hurte, William Cherie, John Charvile, with others.

Proved 14 November 1576 by Audrey widow of the testator and William Holstock executors.

168

HUMPHREY BROWNE of Porters in Prittlewell gentleman, 30 August 1592. [36/78]

I make my will after the custom of London where I was of late a citizen. My freehold lands in Essex to my well-beloved wife Gertrude for life, and in default of issue with successive remainders to Humphrey my eldest son, Charles my second son, John, Thomas and William my sons, and to my three daughters Alice, Anne and Elizabeth. My goods to be divided into three equal portions according to the laudable custom of London, the first to my wife, the second to my five sons and three daughters equally, sons at 21 and daughters at 21 or marriage, and the third to my wife for life and after to be equally divided among my children. To Joan Kerkett 20 marks. To St Thomas's Hospital £5, and to St Bartholomew and Christ Church 50s. apiece, and £5 more to the poor of Prittlewell to be divided by my wife at my funeral. To Alderman Offeley £3 to buy him a ring. The residue of my goods to my wife, whom I make my sole executrix, and I appoint as my overseers Mr Charles Browne of Wood Street in London, my brother-in-law Mr John Haull of Lombard Street and my son-in-law Mr Thomas Francklynge, and for their pains £5 apiece. Witnesses: Robert Rowland parson of Sutton, Edward Turner, Anne Masoun.

Proved 5 October 1592.

WILLIAM BROWNE of Colchester senior, gentleman, 18 January 1573. [16/6]

To Edmund Pirton of Little Bentley esquire, Anthony Bisshoppe gentleman, Robert Browne my son, and George Martin, and to the survivors, the occupation of the farm called the Gerdner in Wormingford now in my occupation, demised to me by John Wentworthe knight lately deceased, and my stock and store of oxen, kine, carthorses or mares, sheep, corn and implements of household, for 7 years after my death, so that they with the profits pay the rent and keep the premises in good reparations and also provide my sons William, Richard and Edward and my daughters Susan and Margaret with sufficient meat, drink, cloth, fostering, teaching, schooling and setting forth according to their behaviour and intelligence, and the residue of the profits they shall at the end of 7 years pay to Susan if she shall then be bestowed in marriage but if not then they shall safely keep the residue to her use until marriage. To the same three persons the use of the farm for 6 years after the end of the 7 years in the same manner, and the residue of the profits to Margaret as above. The same persons to maintain the stock during the 7 and 6 years; and after both terms to my sons. To John Scotte my servant 20s. My son Robert to give to the poor people of St Peter in Colchester in which I dwell 20s. in each of the first, second and third years after my death. To Margaret my wife the occupation of half my household stuff for life, then her half to Robert and the other half

169

to be equally divided among my other children. The residue of my goods to Robert, whom I make executor. Witnesses : George Sayer, Thomas Turner, Richard Cabell, John Fludd.

Proved 19 February 1573.

ROBERT BROWNE of Colchester gentleman, 10 April 1595. [39/69]

To Mary my wife for her full jointure, for life, my lands in Wormingford, Little Horkesley, West Bergholt and Fordham called Cookes, in the occupation of Gilbert Freeman, and my lands called Huningtons in St Giles in the Old Hythe in Colchester; with remainder to William my son, and his heirs male, and for want of such issue to Robert my son and his heirs male. To my wife 100 marks, half my household [stuff], except my plate, also my mansion and dwelling house in my occupation so long as she remain my widow. To William for his maintenance until 18 £10 yearly, and after £20 yearly if my wife is still living. If she be with child, to the child £100 at 21 if male and 18 or marriage if female, and for its maintenance £6 13s. 4d. yearly till 10 and after 10 till 21 £10 yearly. To my daughter Rose Browne £400 at 19, and to Frances Browne my daughter 400 marks at 21, and for their maintenance £13 6s. 8d. to Rose and £10 to Frances yearly. To Robert my son my lands and tenements in the town of Colchester and elsewhere in Essex, my lease of Peldon Hall and the lands belonging and my goods and stock of cattle there, the lease of my farm called the Gardiner in Wormingford, and my other goods, household stuff, plate, jewels and money unbequeathed, at 24, with remainder in default of issue to William at 24, and in default to the rest of my children part and part like. Provided that my legacies to my wife, William and the unborn child are given on condition as in a bond by which I stand bound to Robert Suckling, citizen and alderman of Norwich deceased, and Joan his widow in 1,000 marks for conveying by me lands of the yearly value of £40 to my wife for her jointure in satisfaction of her dower, and after her death to my heirs male. To the poor people of St Peter, Colchester, 40s. at my burial, and the yearly rent for ever on New Year's Day of my two butcher's stalls with the chamber over them in the tenure of William Dow butcher, provided that no part of the rent shall be given to the maintenance of any bastard child or parent of any bastard child. Peldon Hall and lands shall be used and let with the stocks to the best profit to him or them to whom the same by my will is appointed, and for the better discharge of my legacies my executors shall have the government of all my lands until my children are capable and to have their ordering by the good advice of my supervisors to be brought up in learning and other virtuous behaviour. For the good opinion I have of the love of my brother-in-law Mr William Burgcher and my cousin Richard Symnell towards me, my wife and children, I make them executors, and I appoint my uncle Mr Richard Browne and my father-in-law Mr George Sayer supervisors. Witnesses : Richard Putto, Richard Sawyer, William Greene.

Memorandum 1 May 1595. I give my wife my ordinary silver salt parcel gilt, one of my silver beakers, my silver tun, one of my white silver bowls, and a dozen silver spoons.
Proved 22 November 1595.

THOMAS BURGEANT of Walden gentleman, 7 December 1569.
[13/13]

To be buried in Walden church. To Agnes Rabbet my servant my shop in the Bocherye Row in Walden, for life, with remainder to George Nicholles esquire, Anthony Calton, William Strachye the elder, William his son, and John Strachye of Walden, willing that they, their heirs and assigns for ever shall bestow the yearly rents and profits on the poor folks in the almshouse in Walden, also for the same purpose a meadow called Hooke Meade in Wimbish in the occupation of Richard Sexten; also to Agnes for life 1 acre held of the manor of Walden which I purchased of Nicholas Ersewelle of Walden, with remainder to Thomas son of William Byrde, my brother. To Elizabeth Bridgman, late my servant, a close containing 4 acres in Walden by the farm called Powncys about Mell Hill which I purchased of Margaret Smyth of Walden and Michael Smyth, for life, with remainder to my brother Christopher Byrde. To Nicholles [and the other parties] and Christopher Byrde Bryden Mead in Walden containing 2½ acres in the occupation of James Woddall of Walden, late of John Lawes of Walden deceased, which I purchased of Alexander Raye gentleman and Elizabeth his wife, [blank] Lawe widow, and George Lawe, willing that the feoffees for ever bestow the rents and profits on the poor folks in the almshouse, also for the same purpose my lands, late Thomas Myddelton's.

My other lands in Essex and Suffolk [no details] to my executors to sell for legacies as follows. They shall take the rents from my farm called Powncys for 10 years after my decease as follows. To my mother [in-law] Beatrix Byrd £100; my brother [in-law] Christopher Byrd £100; my sister Anne Calton £50; Anthony Calton her son £20 and Mary and Susan Calton her daughters £15 each, at 21, to be paid to my brother-in-law Anthony Calton, their father, for their use; my brothers Josias and Samuel Byrde each £100; my sister Elizabeth Byrde 100 marks; my cousin Elizabeth Rymson £40; my cousin Margaret Cowldam £20; my cousin Thomas Stutevyll £6 13s. 4d.; Andrew Byrde my brother the 100 marks he oweth me; my cousins Edward Stutevyll, Henry Stutevyll and Charles Stutevyll £3 6s. 8d. each; the children of my cousin Margaret Archer deceased 5 marks; and my cousin William Worrlyche £6 13s. 4d. To John Cowell, sometime my servant, now with Mr Thomas Parker of Walden cordwainer, 40s. To William, one of the sons of my brother William Byrde deceased, 100 marks at 21. To Thomas Byrde my godson and George Byrde, two others of his sons, each 100 marks at 21. To Mary Byrde, daughter of my brother William, £40 at 21. To Philip Byrde, son of my brother John Byrde, £30 at 21. To Anne Byrde, daughter of John, £20 at 21.

Whereas John Boyton of Icklingham (Suffolk) doth owe me £5, he shall pay it to Joan Boyton his daughter. Whereas William Runnam my servant and Andrew Bridgman of Walden each owe me £10, they shall have the use till Susan Boyton my servant is 24, to be paid to her then. To my brother John Byrde 30 quarters of barley and the term of years I have in the farm called Butlars; Thomas Clarke of Walden 10 quarters of barley; the said Elizabeth Bridgman, in consideration of the crops which I had of 1 acre of barley which was hers at the last harvest, 5 quarters; Anne Free and Mary Rabbet my servants each 5 quarters of barley; George Mydson my servant 2 acres of wheat; and to William Runnam my servant the crop of wheat in 2¾ acres in the lease I have of Mattins Mead.

To George, son and heir apparent of George Nicolles of Walden esquire, my best carpet. To Christopher Byrde my lease of the manor of Powncys Hall after the 10 years bequeathed to my executors, paying my mother Beatrix Byrde yearly £20 if she so long live. The residue of my goods to Beatrix and Christopher, whom I make my executors.

Witnesses : George Nicolles, William Strachie senior, Nicholas Ereswell, John Strachie, Anthony Calton.

Proved 20 April 1570.

Administration granted, 8 November 1603, to Gregio Byrd of the city of London gentleman.

EDMUND BURIE of Moulsham in Chelmsford gentleman, 30 April 1600. [40/42]

To the poor people of Moulsham and Chelmsford 20s. on the day of my burial. To my brother Benjamin Burie 40s., my riding cloak, a new fustian doublet and a pair of new cloth hose, on condition that he make a release and deliver it to Thomas Rawlins esquire. To my sister Middleditche 40s. To my brother Bradford Burye my pictures on condition that he deliver a bill obligatory of £8 which he hath of mine for payment of the 40s. To my daughter Dorothy wife of Thomas Addams 20s. to make her a ring. Whereas Bradford and I stand bound to one Richard Carre of Hockley clerk [vicar] in the penal sum of £200 for payment of £100, being a gift by my daughter Rebecca, £50 the moiety thereof, which is my part, shall be disbursed out of the money which Thomas Rawlyns is to pay me in November next. The residue of my goods to Elizabeth my wife, whom I make my sole executrix. Witnesses : Anthony Averill, John Cooke, Robert Cradocke.

Proved 29 May 1600.

THOMAS BUTLER of Loughton gentleman, 23 February 1577. [20/25]

To be buried without any pomp. To Mary my well-beloved wife, for life, £60 yearly out of my manor of Castle Thorpe (Bucks.) which I hold by two leases, one in possession and the other in reversion, for divers years yet to come. To my sons Richard and George each £20 yearly out of the manor. To my wife the manor or farm of Loughton Hall, which is to be made to me by Mr John Stonarde of Luxborough [in Chigwell] and for which I have paid him, on condition that she and sufficient sureties become bound to my loving friends George Carleton and Peter Wentworthe esquires as well for the good and virtuous education of Nathaniel, Mary and Sarah Butler, our children, during their minorities as also for the payment of 200 marks each to my daughters at marriage or lawful age and to Nathaniel 200 marks at lawful age, also for payment of £18 yearly out of the manor to my brother-in-law George Maxey for 18 years in consideration of the surrender of a lease which he had of part of the manor. To my wife £50 in goods and household stuff as it shall be valued by four indifferent persons whereof two be chosen by her and two by my overseers. To Nicholas Standon, Thomas Wilcockes, Thomas Edmundes, John Fielde, Nicholas Crane and Giles Seintclere each 40s. The residue of my goods to my son Ambrose, whom I make my executor, and I appoint as overseers Mr George Carleton and Peter Wentworthe, and they shall have the custody, tuition and government of my three children and of their legacies to see them brought up in learning and the fear of God as my special trust is in them. To Ralph Walker, Ambrose's schoolmaster, £4. To Alexander Morgan my manservant £4 and Ellen my maidservant £3 6s. 8d. To my wife's sister Susan Maxey £10. I remit to my servant Robert Walbye the £10 he oweth me. Witnesses: William Fuller, William Butler, Arthur Wake, Robert Preston.

Codicil, 5 March 1577, concerning the remainders for the legacies of 600 marks. Witnesses: Nicholas Crane, William Butler, Giles Seyntclere.

Administration granted, 19 June 1577, to the supervisors during Ambrose's minority.

JOHN CAMBER of East Tilbury gentleman, 6 March 1602.   [47/23]

To Anne my well-beloved wife 200 marks and my household stuff, except my plate which during the minority of my son John shall be in my executors' custody, the joined bedstead and court cupboard in the chamber over the parlour, and the wainscot, glass and glass windows in my mansion house, which she shall have for life; to remain to such person to whom the inheritance of my house shall descend by my will; on condition that she enter into a bond in £200 to my executors not to stub or fell the two elm springs on the back-side of my house, one end abutting on my woodyard on the west and the other on land belonging to South Hall on the north. To my cousin Isabel Harris £10. To Margaret Eglesfylde £5 and to every of the rest of the children of my cousin William Eglesfylde and his late wife Margaret 40s. at 21 or marriage. To my godson Thomas Phippes £10 at 21 and every one of my godchildren 10s. To the poor inhabitants of East Tilbury 50s. and South Benfleet 50s. To poor and needy people at the day of my burial 5 marks.

The residue of my goods to John. I appoint him as my sole executor at 21 and during his minority my well-beloved friends Robert Rich of Lincoln's Inn and Richard Gislinge of Stow [Maries] gentlemen. They shall have his education and bringing up, finding him meat, drink, apparel and all things meet for his degree and putting him to school wherein I desire he may be trained as soon as he shall be capable; towards which they shall allow an annuity of £34 due to me out of the lands of Roger Appleton esquire, until he be 10 £15 a year and from 10 to 16 40 marks a year, and shall make a true account to him at 21, for which they be allowed for their pains 200 marks, to be equally divided. To Robert Camber my nephew, son of my brother Thomas, my lease of the marsh grounds called Court Weekes [Wicks] and the stock of cattle therewith letten. The rest of my goods which besides the lease should have been due to my son on this account I give to Robert, Isabel Harrys and my cousin Thomas Phippes, to be equally divided. I appoint as overseer my assured good friend Ralph Wiseman esquire, and for his pains £10. To my executors during my son's minority, with one part of the profits of my lands to repair them and with the other part to defend causes of law if any be. To him my lands at 21, with remainder in default of issue of my lands in East Tilbury and Little Burstead to Robert, to whom an annuity of £5 out of my lands in Little Burstead. Witnesses : John Duninge, George Geslinge, Edward Charnocke scrivener, and Owen Bett his servant.

Codicil, 25 February 1603. Touching lands I purchased since my will, the evidences shall be in my executors' custody until my son is of full age. To Anne my wife 200 marks. Witnesses : John Drywood, Edward Charnocke, William Holmes and Owen Bett.

Proved 19 March 1603. Sentence, 4 June 1603, confirming Will in case between (1) Richard Ritche and Richard Geslinge executors and (2) Anne Camber widow, Thomas Camber brother, Isaac Geslinge nephew and Edward Phippes next of kin of the deceased.

ROBERT CAMOCKE of Layer Marney gentleman, 29 January 1582.
[30/14]

To be buried honestly in Layer Marney church. To Mary my wife, in consideration that she claim no dower or third in my lands, my lease of How Field and Rockinghams from George Tuke esquire deceased and my lease of the manor and lands called Abbottes in Wigborough and Layer Marney as specified in the lease taken of the Abbot of St Osyth or St Tosies to me; which leases I have delivered to my faithful friend and brother-in-law George Everton gentleman to the use of his sister Mary, my wife. To her my house in Layer Marney called Dukes with the grounds belonging, for life, and 40 loads of good wood (except timber and other woods not usually lopped) delivered for her necessary fuel yearly from Crammers or Dickes; and she may lop and shred so much wood meetest of such trees as heretofore have been lopped or shred. If she do not inhabit my house but put the same over clean out of her hands to be occupied with a farmer, such farmer to have yearly for his fuel but 20 loads. To my wife for life the four fields called Stampes with a little pightle next to Couper's house, Hockley abutting on Layer Breton

Heath, and two other fields called Hockley; two fields called Syons between the lands of Stampes and Dukes; land called the Harp (containing 9 acres) parcel of the messuage of Crammers between the causy leading to Colchester and lands of Dukes; a messuage called Moones and Belldammes in Langenhoe with the lands belonging; and lands called Beldammes now in three pieces, and my fields called Waddes (7 acres) in Langenhoe in the occupation of Ralph Baker. To my wife a gown of mine furred with white, and all the hay and straw in the rooms and barns about Dukes; my new bible of the greatest volume for life and after to Mary daughter of my son Thomas Camocke; and my household stuff, except my furniture of armour which I give to my son Thomas, except also my horsemill, the brass called the lead in the brewing house with the yeald vat, the cowl vat, the mash vat and troughs, and a press in my chamber, which are to remain in my house to my heirs. In consideration that I have given my household stuff to my wife, she shall pay Mary £10 at marriage. Thomas to have the pasturing of his cattle in Howe Field, Nightingales Queache, Howe Field Meadow, Barunden Hill and all Layer Fields in my own occupation. To my wife 6 seam of wheat; 5 silver pots parcel gilt, a tun pot double gilt which my son bought last at London for me, 12 silver spoons marked with her name and mine, my goblet of silver, a silver bowl, my silver salt parcel gilt, one of my stone pots with silver and gilt, and one pot of silver and gilt which her uncle Eyre gave her; my best and next best geldings; her own apparel and jewels; and 20 of my best milch neat at her choice. To her for life my lands and the lease of them which John Baron holdeth in lease of me in Layer Breton, i.e. 6 crofts called Moones, 3 crofts called Thorn Crofts, 2 called Smith Crofts abutting against the lands of Henry Bretton gentleman called Green Field on the south and against Layer Breton Heath [and] the highway from Garland towards Salcot on the north; a croft with a meadow called Manes lying before the parsonage gate of Layer Breton; and a meadow with a grove called Nor Meadow between the lands called Shoters on the north and those of John Makin on the south. To her also £40.

To my daughter Dorothy wife of Richard Whitlocke £6 13s. 4d. To my very friend Mistress Margaret Tuke widow 3 angels for a ring in remembrance of me. To my sister Mistress Spilman widow, my cousin Thomas Armiger and his wife, my brother-in-law George Everton and my sister, his wife, each a royal of gold for a ring. To my cousin Sammes' wife of Aldham Hall an old angel for a ring. To my daughter-in-law Ursula Camocke 2 old angels for a ring. To Elizabeth Westbrowne the eldest an angel for a ring. To Richard Whitlocke my son-in-law 2 old angels to make him a ring to wear for my sake, and my daughter, his wife, 2 old rials of gold of 20s. apiece likewise; to him 5 of my best cart horse and a shod cart. To Robert Camoke, my son's child and my godson, and George, Mary, Elizabeth and Ursula his brother and sisters, and Jane and Francis, each £10 at 21. To Mary Whitlocke my goddaughter £8, Dorothy her sister £6 13s. 4d., and John Whitlocke, their brother and my godson, £5. To Robert Cammocke, my brother's son, £5, and Elizabeth his sister £6 13s. 4d. To Jane wife of John Barington £4.

To Robert Tye my late servant 20s.; Alice wife of Lewis Barnard 10s.; my late servant Anne Holmes now wife of William Tompson 20s.; Rose Westwood my late servant 20s.; and to every of my other servants 20s. To Robert Bridgman 40s. I bequeath 5 marks for 10 godly sermons to be preached in Layer Marney church for 2½ years after my decease, every quarter a sermon, for every sermon 6s. 8d. To the poor people of Layer Marney 40s., Layer Breton 20s., Langenhoe 20s., Messing 10s., Great Birch 10s., and Copford 10s. To the poor prisoners in the Gaol or Castle of Colchester 20s. To the repairing of Colyton Haven (Devon) 3s. 4d., and the erecting of the town of Chard (Somerset) 3s. 4d. To John Wilton, parson of Aldham, 40s. to preach my funeral sermon and 4 more sermons within a quarter after my decease in Layer Marney church. To the churchwardens of Layer Marney 40s. to the mending of the church.

I ordain Thomas my sole executor. If he do not execute my will, he shall not have any goods of mine but my son-in-law Richard Whitlocke shall be my executor. I appoint George Everton supervisor, and £3 6s. 8d. for his pains. The residue of my goods to Thomas.

Witnesses: Thomas Moris clerk [rector of Layer Marney], George Tuke, John Morris.

Proved 5 March 1586.

THOMAS CAROWE of Berners Roothing gentleman, 22 October 1591.
[35/81]

To Joan my wife my lands free and copy in Berners Roothing and Hornchurch for life in recompense of her right of dower, with remainder to Thomas my son; and for want of issue those in Berners Roothing to my two daughters Susan and Lucy and in Hornchurch to George Carowe my boy, son of Jeffrey Carowe. To my brother William Sorrell my lands in Bishops Stortford (Herts.) and my lease of North Weald Park for 4 years after my death, so that of the profits he allow towards the keeping and bringing up at school of Thomas the first 2 years £40, and to be brought up and schooled with John Leeche of Hornchurch schoolmaster, and the residue of the profits to be bestowed on him during the last 2 years towards his maintenance at the Inns of Court and Chancery; provided that, if he refuse and obstinately deny to be brought up during the 4 years by the advice of William Sorrell his uncle and of his uncle Crane, to whose government I commit him, William Sorrell keep the profits and lease to his own use, and from the end of the 4 years I bequeath the lands in Stortford and my lease to Thomas, and for want of issue to Susan and Lucy. To my wife the remnant of years I have in the manor of Berners Roothing, my corn, my horses (2 nags and 2 mares which came lately from Navestock excepted), the sheep and lambs, hay and hogs, ploughs and carts, the household stuff at Barnish Hall which were her late husband's Dyer's, the household stuff by her renewed since our marriage, also 3 kine on Berners Hall grounds and 7 of the best kine at Loft Hall [in Navestock].

To Susan £210. To Lucy the occupation of my farm of Loft Hall for 10 years after my decease, the stock of corn, hay and cattle, and household stuff there (the 7 kine excepted), also the household [stuff] at Barnish Hall not before given to my wife, out of which Susan shall have 2 featherbeds whereof 1 be of the best. To Thomas Goodday, my sister's son, £13 6s. 8d., and his sisters Grace and Anne £13 6s. 8d. each. To my brother Crane £60. To my sister Stane £60 and her two daughters £10 apiece. To three daughters of my sister Cheny now living £10 apiece. To Mr Edward Josselin's wife, Mr Thomas Josselin's wife, Mr Robert Leigh's wife, Mistress Grace Josselyn, and Mistress Winifred Josselyn, 2 angels apiece to make them rings.

To John Greene and William Grave my men 40s. apiece and Bartholomew my man 30s. To Bessie Speller 30s. To George Carowe my boy £10 at 24. To Thomas my son the remnant of my years in Loft Hall after the expiration of Lucy's interest, and £300 at 21 if he shall observe to be brought up and if not my executrix to detain one half to her own use and the other to Susan and Lucy. To the poor people of Navestock 40s., Stortford 40s., Berners Roothing 20s., Shellow 20s. (of which the children of Mr Platt shall have 10s.), both Willingales 30s., Beauchamp Roothing 10s., and Margaret Roothing 20s. (of which Oliver shall have 10s.). The residue of my goods to my wife, whom I make my sole executrix, and my brothers William Sorrell and Crane my overseers, whom of all friendship I require to be aiding her.

Witnesses: William Dune, Edward Crane, William Sorrell, James Wilie.

Proved 12 November 1591.

PHILIP CAWSTON of Weeley gentleman, 28 September 1584. [29/9]

To the poor of Weeley 20s. To Cecily my wife £200 a year during my lease of Great Clacton Hall. To Thomas my youngest son my interest in land called Pylcrofts, parcel of the lease, in the occupation of Thomas Wolmer, on condition that he make to Robert my eldest son an assurance by surrender of such right as he have in the copyhold lands in Great Clacton in the occupation of one Barton. To Agnes Cawston my daughter £66 13s. 4d. to be paid out of my goods at marriage on condition that she marry with the consent of my two sons; Robert shall provide for her a convenient place and find apparel until marriage for the benefit of that money. To Agnes Boggas my kinswoman a silver tun. To Catherine Daniell my kinswoman £20. To John Dobye my kinsman £3 6s. 8d. at 21, and if he die then to Agnes Godfrye alias Dobye his mother. To Susan Godfrye alias Ballard my kinswoman £3 6s. 8d. My wife shall have all her wearing apparel and linen, a gelt mare colt, a featherbed, one of the new chairs, and a piece of plate which is in the goldsmith's hands at Colchester. To Edward Boggas a suckerel of the mare that was John Frenchman's which is in Weeley Park and its keeping at Clacton Hall for a year. To my kinsman Daniell £3 6s. 8d. to buy him a gown. To the right worshipful Mr Edmund Pirton £5 requiring him to take it in good part as a token of my poor goodwill towards him. If my goods will not pay all my debts and legacies, the profit of Clacton Hall and Geyuoyck

[Jaywick] be employed to them, my daughter's legacies to be last paid, and towards them my executor shall receive such money as is due from the right honourable my Lord Darcye deceased for the keeping of Nicholas Steward's son, viz. for 4 years' board £20 and for his apparel £10 and of old debt which I paid for his wardship £3 6s. 8d. I appoint Robert my sole executor.

Witnesses : Thomas Pirton esquire, Robert Bogas gentleman, John Danyell, Samuel Danyell clerk [vicar of Thorpe-le-Soken].

Memorandum that whereas I with Robert Bogas have entered into several bonds to Edmund Cotton and Robert Cotton for £160, whereof parcel is paid, which bonds are now set over to the latter, my executor shall pay the bonds and discharge Robert Bogas.

Proved 3 February 1585.

ROGER CHADWICKE of Great Waltham gentleman, 1 April 1585.
[30/21]

To Gilbert my son Little Chapel in Great Waltham, with the lands and tithes belonging, if he shall come to the Chapel and claim the same in proper person within a year after my decease, but if he shall not come to Rachel Hadland my cousin, wife of Henry Hadland of Braintree clothier, but if Gilbert come and claim notwithstanding Rachel shall have such rent and profit as be due therefor from the time of my death until my son's coming over. To Margaret wife of John Marrett of London the lease of my land in Norfolk. To Margaret my bay nag and an obligation wherein Francis Lovett of Buckinghamshire gentleman standeth bound to me for payment of 50 marks. To John Marrett my gold ring. To Margerty Selye my servant 40s. To the poor people of Great Waltham 40s. yearly for 20 years to be paid out of the Chapel lands and tithes by them who shall have the fee simple. The residue of my goods to Margaret and Rachel to be equally divided. I ordain that John Marrett and Henry Hedland my executors and my loving friend Charles Dabbes of Chelmsford shall have the custody of my will until the Court shall come that my executors shall prove the same.

Witnesses : Richard Ponde, Gregory Cavell, George Turner, Charles Dabbes notary public.

Proved 27 April 1586.

PETER CHARD of Great Warley gentleman, 17 April 1597.   [41/67]

To my cousin John Settle £5 to be paid him by his aunt, my loving wife Joan. To my cousin Matthew Settle 40s. to be paid by my wife at 21. My wife to have the use of my goods for life, and after they have been appraised she shall have and give the third part (excepting the lease of the farm of Bayles which I have) to whom she will, and the other two parts and the lease of Boyles [sic] to my daughter Margaret Browne, willing and requesting my wife and my son George Browne and his wife

Margaret during my wife's life to keep the house and ground and stock as now it is in Great Warley, with the ground at Boyles now in our occupation. To my wife for life my two tenements in the tenure of [blank] Robynson butcher and Martin de Custer coachmaker in St Botolph's-without-Aldgate in London; also my dwelling house in Great Warley, with barns, stables, outhouses, orchards, gardens, meadows and pastures, and with the barn, stable and orchard in the tenure of Thomas Wright oatmealmaker in Great Warley. After her death the two tenements to remain to John Muschampe, son and heir of Edmund Muschampe and my late daughter Elizabeth his wife deceased, with successive remainders to Margaret Browne, Francis Browne her son, and Mary Browne her sister. After my wife's decease my dwellinghouse to remain to Margaret and George, my son-in-law, with like successive remainders. If any of these frustrate my will touching the entailing of the messuage and lands in Great Warley, the churchwardens and constables have authority to enter into them and make 6 or 8 feoffees inhabiting there, so that they and their heirs may be seized in fee to the relief of poor decayed householders and poor and old lame men and women. To my wife for life the yearly rent of £6 out of a pasture in the county of Leicester by a lease to me by Sir Henry Grey, if the lease so long endure. To my old man, Miles Dawson, every Hollontide 6s. yearly for life for his winter coat, to be paid by them who enjoy my house. I make my wife sole executrix and the overseers my loving and good friends and neighbours Thomas Veare and Walter Gwye the younger of Great Warley, and for their pains 6s. 8d. each. Witnesses: Rowland Hodges, Edward Badbye.
Proved 30 July 1597.

ROBERT CHEEKE late of Dovers in Hornchurch gentleman, 21 September 1590. [34/68]

To my daughter Anne, wife of Robert Gardner gentleman, £50 to be paid out of the annuity which Richard Crafford of Grove Place (Bucks.) esquire, and Richard my son stand bound to pay me yearly for 10 years. To my son Robert £20 to be paid likewise. To my daughter Frances Southerton in remembrance and token of goodwill £5, Mary her daughter 40s. at 14, and Frances her daughter 20s. at 16. To my godson Robert Baccus £3 when he can read the Testament of our Saviour Christ and can declare his catechism, and if he die in the meantime to my daughter Emme Baccus. To Mary daughter of my daughter Mary Smalepece 20s. at 17. To Anne wife of Robert Gardner my goods in the chamber wherein I lodge in the house of Alice Colley widow in St Michael Bassishaw in London. The residue of my goods to my two sons-in-law Thomas Southerton and Robert Gardner gentlemen equally, whom I make my executors. Witnesses: John Mayle and Edward Bullocke scriveners of the court letter of the city of London, Edward Preston, Alice Colley widow.
Proved 1 October 1590.

CLEMENT CLARKE of Stisted gentleman, — 1583.   [5/9]

To the poor people of Stisted 40s. to be bestowed by the discretion of my kinsman and loving neighbour William Maye of Stisted. To the vicar 6s. 8d. and the sexton or parish clerk 3s. 4d. To some learned preacher 8s. to make a sermon at my burial.

To Elizabeth my wife for life such lands and tenements as I have heretofore assured her by conveyance before and since marriage for her dower, with remainder to John my son; provided that, if she be with child of a son, to such son my lands in Bocking and Sible Hedingham. If both die without issue, my messuage called Jowers and lands belonging to my brother William, and for default of his issue to my brother Andrew Clarke; provided that if William alienate any of the lands he shall pay to Robert Cole my brother and Jane and Anne my sisters 40 marks each, and if Andrew do so he shall pay £40. If John and my second son, if my wife be with child, die without issue, my messuage and lands in Bocking and a meadow in the tenure of John Wentworth esquire to Anthony Clarke, Andrew's eldest son, my messuage with shops, cellars, sollers and warehouses in St Mary Wolchurch Howe in London to John Clarke, Andrew's second son, and my freehold tenement and lands in Sible Hedingham called Curpis in the occupation of John Brytayne and the reversion of my copyhold lands of the manor of Graves Hall [in Sible Hedingham] to [blank] Clarke, Andrew's third son. To my wife my goods for life, with remainder to John. Such corn and quick cattle as I have at the time of my decease shall be sold and the money paid to my trusty friend Mr Robert Deraughe of Gray's Inn to be put in stock by him for the better advancement and bringing up of my child or children; to him a ring of gold with a death's head of the value of 30s. To every of my manservants and maidservants 5s. To John my prower and his wife 40s., and to every of my godchildren 5s. The residue of my goods to my wife and John, whom I make my executors. I appoint as my supervisor my trusty and well-beloved friend Mr Thomas Hunt of Witham.
Witnesses : Thomas Wysman, William Maye, Thomas Hunt.
Proved 26 June 1584.

JOHN CLIFF of Ingatestone gentleman, 9 September 1587.   [33/35]

To Sir John Petre a ring of gold worth 20s. and to the Lady Mary Petre his wife the like, and I desire them most heartily to continue their goodwill towards my poor children as they have done to me heretofore. To my loving daughters Anne Amery and Mary Lawe one of my gilt goblets each. To my daughter Margaret Cave my standing gilt cup for wine, 12 silver spoons, 1 of my silver jugs for beer, and £40; and I require my son John Cliff the younger of the Middle Temple, to whom I have devised my lands, to suffer her if she stands in need of a dwelling house of her own to have a convenient part of my mansion house for herself, her children (if she have any) and servants.

To the poor of Ingatestone, Fryerning, Buttsbury, Stock and Margaretting £10, and of Writtle 40s., requiring my executor to have the chiefest

180

consideration of the poor of the parish where I dwell and in no wise to give any to vagabonds. Towards the reparation of Ingatestone church 20s. and to Fryerning church 20s., and further to Ingatestone church for some special causes me moving £4; and if I die within 10 miles of Ingatestone to be buried in the chancel of Ingatestone church with some stone or other monument having my name and the names of my two wives graven in it, but not be buried with any solemnity but only in honest and sober sort.

I ordain my son, student of the Middle Temple, my sole executor, to whom I give my leases and goods. I desire the right worshipful Sir John Petre to take pains to be overseer, for which I give him 40s. To every servant his or her half-year's wages. To my father-in-law George Kebill esquire, my sister Joan Maddick widow, my sons-in-law Ralph Amery, Anthony Lawe and Brian Cave, and my daughters Anne, Mary and Margaret their wives, and my cousin Thomas Kebill, each a ring of gold worth 20s. Towards the maintaining of the house of correction for vagabonds erected at Coggeshall £6. To every child of Anne Amery and Mary Lawe 40s.

To my son my house where I dwell in Ingatestone called Bedells, with the croft called the Ridden (containing in all 15 acres), my tenement called Haldens (80 acres), and my land called Burres (13 acres), my tenements called Algores sometimes Fosters (18 acres), Morecocks where Robert Chamberleyn dwelleth, Besses Bigges in the occupation of Nicholas Lake, and that wherein John Payne dwelleth, and my land called Streets Bridge in his tenure, all in Ingatestone; my land called Myches and Haywards Crofts in Fryerning; and other my lands in Ingatestone, Fryerning, Buttsbury, Stock, Great Burstead, Hutton, Ingrave, Margaretting and Witham; with remainder to my three daughters.

Witnesses, specially required, 10 September 1587: Anthony Brasier [rector of Ingatestone], Anthony Lawe, Nicholas Lake.

Memorandum, 18 October 1588, I perused this will again and did alter the legacy to my daughter Margaret Cave to only £40.

Memorandum, 5 March 1589, between the hours of 9 and 11 in the forenoon, the testator lying sick in his bed in his own house, did acknowledge this his testament, all in his own handwriting. Witnesses: Anthony Lawe, Brian Cave, Thomas Kebill, John Price.

Proved 14 March 1589.

JOHN COCKE of Little Stambridge gentleman, 12 December 1574.

[18/1]

Visited with great sickness and in peril of death. To be buried in Little Stambridge church. To the poor people of Prittlewell 40s. yearly for 5 years.

To Elizabeth for life my well-beloved wife in recompense of her courtesy showed to me and of her dower my lease of my farm called Reynoldes in Shopland and Creekes Croft in Southchurch which I demised to Robert Collin for 17 years at Michaelmas last at the yearly rent of £38, and my lands called Jesus Hamstalls, Frises, Chaundlers, Diddons, Tickfields, with my house wherein Thomas Blake dwelleth, a wood lying by Goldesfields Hamstall and Brymynge in Prittlewell; with remainder to Richard my son, and for default of issue to John my son. The residue of my lands copy and free in Leigh, Eastwood, Prittlewell, Milton [in Prittlewell], Southchurch and Hockley, and two crofts in Ashingdon, whereof one is called Rombaldon, parcel of my manor of Little Stambridge Hall, to Richard from the end of 9 years after my decease; and for default of issue to John.

To my wife £200, her dwelling in Little Stambridge Hall and pasturing in the fields of the manor nearest my house, 12 kine, 40 ewes, 3 geldings, her swine and poultry, and sufficient firewood, with necessary stover for her cattle and commodities necessary for her degree, from the day of my death till Michaelmas come twelvemonths without any rent; an annuity of £26 13s. 4d. out of my lease lands called Shelford and Bradworth in the island of Foulness; also my nest of great silver bowls with the cover parcel gilt and all my silver plate marked with an E and C, my silver spoons, a stone jug covered with silver parcel gilt, a small silver bowl, and my least silver salt, and my rings and jewels of gold and silver which she useth commonly to wear, my brass, pewter, linen and napery, my household implements, half my featherbeds, 12 kine, 40 ewes, my swine and poultry, and so much wheat, barley and oats as shall serve for the reasonable expenses of her house and family until harvest next cometh twelvemonths; also my obligation wherein one Clerke and one Galtie standeth bound to me for £5 yearly during certain years to come; provided that before she receive the legacies she become bound to my executors and my overseer in £2,000 not to claim any dower.

I leave to descend to John so much of the residue of my manor of Little Stambridge Hall as doth amount to one third part of my manors and lands in Little Stambridge, Canewdon, Prittlewell, Leigh, Eastwood, Southchurch, Ashingdon, Hockley, Great Stambridge, Rochford and Hawkwell; the other two parts to my very loving friend William Borne gentleman for 9 years, on condition that with the profits he pay my legacies, educate and bring up my two sons in virtuous exercises and good learning, and of the overplus yield a true account yearly to my loving friends Henry Butler and John Cooke gentlemen, Thomas Bewleye, Robert Lawson and John Harrison of Thorpe [in Southchurch] and yield the overplus to my sons at the end of the term. To Borne an annuity of £10 from my lands in Foulness and to the others a yearly fee of 40s. for their pains, and Borne shall provide a strong chest with 6 locks and keys in my house in the safest place and my evidences and leases be speedily put into it in their presence or so many of them as upon warning given will be present, and each shall have a key. John, being 12 on 16 November last, from the end of the term shall have those two parts, residue of my manors, and in default of issue to Richard. To John my lease lands in Foulness and in the parish of Little Wakering, with the stock on the same, with remainder to Richard. The residue of my farms and leaselands called Stanesgate [in Steeple] and Tiled Barn [in Wallasea island?], with the stock and store on Stansgate, to Richard; and Borne shall take

182

the profits and pay my wife the said annuity of £26 13s. 4d. and Lawrence Hollingsworth, late of Little Stambridge gentleman, and Amy his wife the yearly rent of £140 for 6 years. My executors shall during the lease of Shelford Marsh [in Foulness island] distribute at Christmas an ox and half a quarter of wheat baked among the poor people of Prittlewell according to the gift of my uncle Thomas Cooke. To Alice Cole widow a cow and pasture for it in my ground in Ashingdon. To the reparations and new building of the marked [market?] cross of Prittlewell 100s. and to the reparations of Prittlewell church 10s.

Richard Browne shall have the two crofts, parcel of my manor, in the occupation of Peter Walker, for life, paying the yearly rent of 12s. To my servants their wages due at Christmas. To Anne Creke 100s., to Mabel Seborowe 20s., Thomas Dotterell £4, Edward Dampson 40s., Timothy Bourdman 40s., Thomas Cooke 20s., and William Crabbe the elder and the younger, Alice Rowell, Elizabeth Rawlins and Elizabeth Lawrence 5s. each. The residue of my goods to my executors, saving to Richard £100 and a silver tankard which was my father's. To Edward Camber my lands called Catawaie lands, parcel of my manor, in the occupation of William Stele, in Ashingdon for 9 years, paying the yearly rent of £5 6s. 8d.

Witnesses: John Cooke, Thomas Bewleye, Giles Alington, William Taynter, John Bastwick, Edward Camber, Thomas Heynes, Thomas Blake, Edward Cooe.

Codicil [undated]. To Sir Thomas Wentworth Lord Wentworth, my wife's brother, a portegue of gold, praying him to be good to my wife and two sons. To Mr William Wentworth, my lord's eldest son, a piece of gold of 20s. To Mr Henry Wentworth, my lord's brother, a piece of gold of 20s. To Mr Henry Wentworth, William's brother, an old angel. To Elizabeth Cocke his wife, besides the legacies he gave her, £20 towards her housekeeping, 2 horses and a gelding. To John Cocke gentleman, besides the 20 horses which I did sell him, another of my colts. To Mistress Margaret Wentworth, my wife's sister, my nag called Button. To Thomas Bewleye of Great Stambridge Gilbert my gelding and to Thomas Blake a ronded wort carthorse in recompense of his pains. Witnesses: Thomas Bewley, John Cooke, Elizabeth Cocke, Thomas Dottrell, Edward Cooe, Thomas Blake.

Proved 27 January 1575.

JOHN COLE of Markshall gentleman, 25 September 1567. [11/11]

To be buried in Markshall church. To Margaret my wife my lands in Essex for life, and after her decease to William my son, with remainder in default of heirs to Robert my son. To William £50 to be employed towards his education in virtue and learning during the life of my wife. The residue of my goods to my wife, whom I make my sole executrix. Witnesses: William Cardynall, Robert Veysey, John Betune.

Proved 25 May 1568.

ROBERT COLFORD late of Navestock gentleman, 20 December 1601.
[46/34]

To Emme Colforde my mother £40, already in her hands, to dispose thereof to my brother John Colforde, Richard Colforde and my loving sister Finche as she shall think most meet. To her my apparel which shall be ungiven at my death. To my brother George Colford £15 which he oweth me. To George and my well-beloved friend John Wright of Kelvedon Hall the elder, gentleman, my annuity of £10 payable to me at the dwelling house of Thomas Albery in Chancery Lane (Middx.) gentleman by the grant of Gabriel Leventhorpe of Sawbridgeworth (Herts.) gentleman on consideration of £100 to him by me paid by a deed of feoffment dated 1 December 1601. To my uncle Gabriel Leventhorpe in consideration of my diet £5 which he is to pay me for the half year rent of an annuity at the Feast of the Annunciation of Our Lady next. To Edward Gadburie, son of Richard Gadburie of London gentleman, 50s. which he oweth me. To John Coo of Grub Street, London, chandler, 40s. I will that 50s. be given in pious uses. I appoint my mother and John Wright executors. Witnesses: Edward Leventhorpe, Thomas Leventhorpe, Richard Meadowe, William Adams.
Proved 7 May 1602.

THOMAS COLLTE of Waltham Holy Cross gentleman, 26 May 1559.
[2/38]

To the poor people of Roydon £3, Waltham Holy Cross £5, and Nazeing 40s., and as much money to the poor people of Twickenham [Surrey] as Mary Hygham, my late mother, did by her will appoint.

To Magdalene my wife my house and lands in Halesfield [Holyfield in Waltham], the lease grounds for life, except the household stuff, and my cattle. To my cousin Edmund Lysle a cloak of black cloth guarded with velvet and embroidered, to be assistant to my wife and children. To Mr Harry Denye my grey hobby. To Mr Tamworthe my crossbow with 2 racks, 2 longbows, and my shafts, to be good to my wife and children. To my nephew Henry Coultte my arming sword, my target and my two-handed sword to my nephew John Coullte. To Mr William Fenstbye my sword, buckler and dagger and my damask cloak furred with black coney. To Sir George Somersett ½ oz. of angel gold to be made in a ring to his device, trusting that he will wear it for my sake and accept so poor a remembrance in good part. To Edith Thorpe my sister in token of charity 40s. a year for 10 years, provided that if she claim anything of duty it shall be void. To my brother George Collt ½ oz. of angel gold to be made a ring according to his device, desiring him to be an aid and help to my wife and children and to be good to them according to right, equity and conscience. To Thomas my boy 26s. 8d. a year for life on condition that he shall serve my wife and children. Goodman George that dwelleth by Nether Hall to have every year a new cap for term of life for a remembrance. My old apparel to be distributed among my servants, especially to Dyer and Waystaf.

If a close called Couldhams in Nazeing be recovered by Richard Banaster, then according to his bond to me he deliver estate thereof to my wife and daughters. Within or at the end of 10 years such sums of money as are due to me be employed on some good land to be purchased to the use of my daughters Katherine and Jane by my loving nephews Robert Kemp of Finchingfield esquire, John Kemp the elder of London draper, and Arthur Kemp of Lincoln's Inn gentleman, and my cousin Edmond of Battersea [Surrey] gentleman. If Katherine and Jane die without issue, my land in Hallyfield shall go to the erection and setting up of a free school for ever for the teaching of poor men's children, and none others in that school, by the appointment of the four Kemps. To my wife my lands in Edmonton [Middx.] for life, with remainder to Katherine and Jane, and in default of issue to Edith Thorpe. If Katherine and Jane marry against the goodwill of my wife, Robert Kemp and John Kemp or two of them without their consents or go about to break any part of my will, they shall take no benefit of my will. My wife shall have the lease of Parndon Hall which I should have of my brother George Coullt, and to her 100 marks. Whereas there be divers sums of money owing to me by specialties in my custody, they shall be paid to John Kemp, out of which he shall yearly pay my wife £50 towards the education and bringing up of my two daughters during their minority. To my brother Myddleton my rapier and dagger.

I make my wife and my nephew John Kemp the elder my executors and my trusty friend Mr William Fensby my overseer. My executors shall bestow at my burial as they shall think meet and shall cause 10 sermons to be preached, 1 every month after my decease on Sunday, 5 each in Waltham Holy Cross and Roydon, and to the preacher for every sermon 10s. To my brother Myddleton my best doublet, 2 of the best pair of hosen, and my best hat. To my nephews Robert and Arthur Kemp each ½ oz. of fine gold to be made in a ring for a remembrance.

Witnesses : John Kemp draper, William Fenclyf, Edmund Lysle.

Proved 17 August 1559.

WILLIAM COLMAN of Thorrington gentleman, 29 July 1586.

[30/63]

To the poor of Thorrington 20s. and to every poor widow there 3s. 4d. To my beloved wife Anne an annuity of £10 out of my farm of Thorrington Hall from Michaelmas next for 12 years; also £100 accounting the £20 I lent her in widowhood. If she be with child of a male child she shall have his bringing up and £10 a year till he is 20 and if a female child £6 13s. 4d. till she is 18. My brother-in-law Richard Symnell shall have the custody and bringing up of my daughters Jane, Elizabeth, Martha and Joan in good and virtuous education and £8 a year till 18. Whereas I have 20 years to come in my lease of Thorrington Hall, the residue of the profits thereof to my four daughters and the child wherewith my wife is (if she be with child), viz. each four years. To Jane her mother's marrying ring. Richard Symnell to have the possession, letting

185

and government of my lease of Thorrington Hall grounds. To my brother Edward Colman £20, my sorrel mare, the colt of the young white mare, and my apparel. To my sister-in-law Jane Simnell my black gelding. To Richard Symnell my biggest black colt. The residue of my goods to my children, part and part like. To Elizabeth my brass cobirons in the hall. My cousin John Colman shall within 2 years be put to prentice by my executors with double and decent apparel and in the meantime to be kept by him, he being allowed therefor from the profits of my farm. To John £20 at 21. To my brother-in-law Thomas Symnell my sorrel colt with flaxen mane and flaxen tail. To my servants Anne Lane 40s. besides the 18s. I owe her, Henry Cooke 26s. 8d., and Rand 13s. 4d., Helen 2s. 6d., and nurse Lawrence 20s. To my sister-in-law Martha Saffolde 13s. 4d. and my sister Taylecote 13s. 4d., each to make her a ring, and to Taylecote's daughter Jane Lambert a French crown. To my sister Rachel, my wife's sister, 10s. To Mr Forbere 10s. To Sluithe the sheepmilker three loads of brush. To my brother-in-law Lawrence Symnell my best black hat lined with velvet. To John Cole 4 loads of brush. To William Daye 26s. 8d. at 20. To Greaneleafe 2 loads of brush. To the Master and Fellows of St John's College, Cambridge, £3 6s. 8d. to buy a piece of plate, praying them to be good to my children and to grant licence to my executor to let my farm to the most profit for my children. I make my brother-in-law Mr Richard Symnell my sole executor. Witnesses: John Meridale, William Walle, John Hubbord, John Coll.

Proved 18 November 1586.

WILLIAM COOKE of Great Chishall gentleman, 7 April 1597.

[41/61]

To be buried in Great Chishall church. So much of my free land as I purchased shall be sold by my executrix for the payment of my debts. To Joan Cooke, Bridget Cooke and Alice Cooke, my daughters, £200 apiece, to be paid at 21 out of such lands as shall be thought meet by my executrix to be sold. To William my son £500 at 21 to be paid by Thomas my eldest son, provided that if Thomas default in payment then it shall be lawful for William to occupy my manor of Chishall Hall and Nigles until the £500 be paid. To Alice my wife my goods, and I make her my sole executrix. Witnesses: Thomas Mead, John Bownest, William Fordham, John Sulman, Reynold Eves, Henry Hithcok, Hugh Seaman.

Proved 11 June 1597.

THOMAS COTTON of South Ockendon gentleman, 15 February 1591. [For William and George Cotton, see p. 70.] [35/12]

To be buried in South Ockendon church. To the poor people of South Ockendon 13s. 4d., North Ockendon 6s. 8d., Aveley 10s., Stifford 6s. 8d., Orsett 13s. 4d., Horndon [on-the-Hill] 13s. 4d., Hadleigh 13s. 4d., Prittlewell 13s. 4d., and Stypington (Northants.) [recte Stibbington, Hunts.] 20s. To my loving brother William Cotton gentleman £20. To his wife 20s. to make her a ring. To my sister Alice Platt £5, and I acquit her husband £5 which he doth owe me. To my cousins Mr John Bewell and his wife and Mr William Taylor and his wife 20s. each to make them a ring. To John Hopkins of Norwich, my wife's sister's son, £5. To Mary Dennis, my wife's sister's daughter, £10 at marriage or 21, and if she die before the £10 to be divided between her brother William Dennys and her sister Prudence. To Nicholas Dennys and his wife, Stephen Wilkinson and his wife, William Gefferys and his wife, 10s. each. To my sister Jane Cotton 40s. To Alice my servant 6s. 8d. To my loving wife Margaret my goods, and I make her my sole executrix. Witnesses : Clement Calthorpe, Thomas Taylor, John Breattyn.

Proved 26 February 1591.

HENRY DANIELL *alias* PILBROUGHE, late of Blackmore, gentleman, lying sick in the parish of All Hallows, Thames Street, London, 2 March 1592. [36/20]

To Agnes wife of Thomas Eysam all his goods whatsoever. [London witnesses.]

Proved 9 March 1592. Administration granted, 5 September 1593, to Agnes.

JOHN DARNELL of Manningtree gentleman, 13 February 1563.
[6/20]

My mind is to have all my lands and houses sold, both by lease as in fee simple, and the money thereof and of my woods and other goods to be taken as follows. To William my eldest son £100 of my goods, being content with the sale of my lands and goods, to be delivered to his master with whom he shall dwell, putting in good bond to pay William at the coming out of his years. To my eldest daughter Josian £66 13s. 4d. at marriage. To my sons Anthony £66 13s. 4d., Roger £40, Richard £40, and Humfrey £40, all at 21. Goodwife Cowe shall have the parts of Richard and Humfrey in her custody till they come from nursing, putting in assurance. To my sister Agnes Woodward 40s. and my wife's wearing apparel, linen and woollen, and to her husband Robert Woodward my best cloak. If after the sale it be more, to be equally divided among my six children; if it will not come to so much, to be abated among them part and part like, as thus, if £60 be lacking, to abate £10 apiece. Also I have another daughter [unnamed] to whom I will £6 13s. 4d. out of my goods; if there be not so much, the rest of her brethren and sistern to give it her out of their portions. I ordain Robert Dickley and Richard Norden, both of Mistley, as my executors, and for their pains 40s. apiece. I require Robert Rand of Manningtree my neighbour to be my overseer. Witnesses : John Darnell citizen and haberdasher of London, Thomas Sheppard, William Arrowsmyth, Thomas Coo.

Proved 15 May 1563.

ROBERT DICKLEY of Manningtree gentleman, 15 February 1571.
[16/13]

Towards the reparations of Mistley church 20s. To my son Robert £60 at 25. To my son George both my houses called Roothy and Larrys on Mistley Heath at 21, with successive remainders in default of issue to Robert, my eldest son John, and my daughter Anne Dickley. To Anne £200 at 21 but before if my wife die, and if Anne die before 21 £20 of her portion to the poor people of Manningtree and the residue to be equally divided between the rest of my children. To George my stock of cattle being 5 milch beasts priced all at £6 13s. 4d., with the said farm at Mistley Heath. To my servant William Deryffall a heifer of 3 years old. To [Anne] my wife my dwelling house in Manningtree and the yards and gardens, for life, with remainder to George, the profits of the two tenements at the Heath during George's minority towards his bringing up, and an annuity of £20 to be paid by John out of the manor of Dickley Hall in Mistley and Little Bromley in the name of dower. To my wife for life 300 of good and able cubit from the woods belonging to the manor. The residue to my wife, whom I make my sole executrix, and I ordain my son and heir John my supervisor. Witnesses: Robert Glascock, George Wood, Thomas Warner, Henry Johnson parson there.

Proved 24 April 1573. Administration granted, 20 June 1578, to George Dowett, now Anne's husband.

JOHN DODD of Little Ilford gentleman, 15 January 1560. [3/12]

My goods shall be divided by my executors, one half to Mary Milles, daughter of John Milles, citizen and brewer of London, and the other divided among Isabel Dodd my mother, George Dodd my brother, Alice and Margaret Dodd my sisters, John Long, Thomas Brea, Robert Frenche, John Bilbroughe, Robert Trippitt, servants to the right honourable the Earl of Shrewsbury, William Ekin, Elizabeth Pole, John Branton, my servants, and goodwife Goddred, my keeper, at the discretion of my executors. I ordain William Newell, grocer, and George Henry, butcher, citizen of London, my executors. Witnesses: Henry Francke, William Acharte, John Benet, servant with Anthony Bond scrivener.

Proved 6 February 1560.

JOHN DRAWATER of Stambourne gentleman, 3 November 1597.
[4/112]

My manor of Ingesthorpe alias Inglesthorpe in White Colne with the profits and appurtenances shall be sold to the best advantage, and I entreat my loving friends Robert Plumbe the elder of Nether [Little] Yeldham, William Harrington of Maplestead, John Choett of Stambourne and Richard Choett of Bumpstead, all yeomen, to sell, and for their pains £5 each; yet in consideration of much kindness to me shown by Mr Stephen Soame, citizen and alderman of London, they shall sell to him before any other at such price as shall be agreed and he shall buy it £20 cheaper than any other will give if he shall accept; and the money shall be divided thus. To my sister Joan Dison widow £20, to be paid 40s. a year and in the meantime she shall have her diet and lodging with my wife in my dwelling farm in Stambourne. To her children and her children's children £20 to be equally divided among them. To my sister Margaret Lucas widow £10, her son John £10, Mary and Eve Lucas her daughters £5 apiece, and the rest of her children £10 to be equally divided. To my brother Denis Drawater £10, his son John £10, and the rest of his children 20 marks. I discharge Denis of debts he oweth me. To Seth Drawater my eldest brother's son £10, and Jonas and Susan, his brother and sister, £6 13s. 4d. each. To my brother Anthony Drawater £5, his son Oliver £50, his daughter Anne £6 13s. 4d., and the rest of his children (except John) £20; to Oliver my books, black apparel, and a ship chest to put them in. To Richard Choett my wife's father £10 and a russet cloak. To my wife's brother John the rest of my apparel not black and £6 13s. 4d., and the rest of my wife's brethren 40s. apiece.

To the poor people of Stambourne £4 by 20s. a year and of Islip (Northants.) where I was born £5. To Zachary Jackson scrivener, the writer hereof, for his pains about my affairs 40s.

To Joan my wife my leases of my farm and lands in Stambourne and Finchingfield with my stock of cattle, corn and household implements, conditionally that, if it shall please God to marry again, she shall marry with the consent and to the good liking of her father, otherwise she shall be utterly debarred from this bequest and from all right to my lands and goods and shall rest contented with £100 to be paid her by Oliver, who shall have her portion; to him also the overplus of such money from the sale of my farm after my legacies are paid. I ordain executors Richard Choett, Oliver, and Thomas Paynell [rector] of Stambourne clerk, and 40s. apiece for a remembrance.

Witnesses : Zachary Jackson, Richard Balthorppe, John Wilson, William Lapidge.

Proved 13 December 1597. Renunciation of executorship, 19 June 1604, by Thomas.

JOHN DRYWOOD of Dunton gentleman, 1 February 1579.   [21/15]

To be buried on the south side of the chancel of Dunton church, and upon my grave there shall be laid a marble stone whereupon to be graved a picture of my remembrance and the day of my death with such farther style as shall appertain.

To Frances my well-beloved wife my messuage in Dunton and lands belonging which I bought of John Edgiot and my lands bought of [blank] Gylman of Little Burstead for 60 years if she so long live unmarried, on condition that she release all right of dower and shall well maintain the orchard that I have newly made belonging to my house and the trees therein; also to her all manner of firewood felled at the day of my decease for the only use in my house. To her 2 of my best geldings and 1 bay mare colt that was sometimes a colt of my mare which she called her mare; also £200; my bedsteads, brass, pewter, linen, 1 of my best carts and 1 of my best ploughs, and my household stuff (except my silver plate, jewels, wainscot, and ready money), 12 silver spoons of 2 oz. apiece, 12 of such my best kine as I usually keep to be milked at my dwelling house at Dunton Wallett, and 60 ewes; and 20 quarters of malt which I bought of [blank] Harrys and 20 quarters of wheat with the wheat that is in the granary to keep her house withal. To my wife during my lease of the manor and farm of Dunton Wallett a yearly payment of 10 quarters of wheat and 10 quarters of oats; and such parcels of land of the manor of Frierne alias Friren [in Dunton] as are in my occupation and not demised to William King for such term of years as I have in the same manor by lease to be made, if she pay my son John 40s. yearly and shall permit him to fell the woods.

To John my son my lease from Sir Henry Tirrell knight of lands called Thirty Acres and Prenver Lands, and my lease from Sir John Peter knight of a parcel of land called Stryland. To Thomasine Drywood my daughter 500 marks at 20; if she die before, to the rest of my children [unnamed] to be divided equally; if none be then living, to Robert, George and William Drywood my brethren, equally amongst them; and if they be then all dead, to three persons being next of my kin. To Frances Drywood my other daughter 400 marks at 20; if she die, likewise; if all my brethren be dead, to the relief of the poor in Dunton, Horndon [-on-the-Hill], Laindon, South Benfleet, Childerditch, Brentwood, [South] Weald, and Orsett, and to the mending of the highways in Dunton. Thomasine and Frances during their minorities shall be nurtured and brought up in virtuous education by my wife, and John shall pay her yearly £5; if she die, John to bring them up.

To Thomas my son £300 at 21, my lands called Blankettes and Males Meads in Childerditch which I bought of Thomas Legate gentleman, and my inn called the White Hart in Brentwood, and in default of heirs male to John; an annuity of £19 which Legate by indenture, 12 June 1568, did grant me; an annuity of £6 13s. 4d. which John Lentall of Spexshall (Suffolk) gentleman, by his deed, 8 December 1572, did grant to me; my lease of Corne Mead [no details]; my lease from the City of Norwich of the same [sic].

John immediately after my decease shall take the profits of my three manors and farms of Dunton Wallett, Fryerne, and Pitsea and the lands belonging, which I hold by three leases. To John my annuity of £10 which Thomas Legate did grant me by indenture, 18 December 1571, and an annuity of £5 which William Bretton husbandman did grant me by deed, 12 June 1572. Copies of my leases and other deeds shall be kept in a strong chest with four locks and keys, whereof each of my executors and overseers shall have one. John shall pay for the keeping of Thomas at school and learning in one of the universities 20 marks yearly.

Whereas I was charged by the will of my brother Nicholas Drywood, to whom I am an executor, to bestow for repairing the highways £6 13s. 4d., John shall bestow it on the common roadway from Rayleigh to Horndon-on-the-Hill between Bowers Cross and Vange church without delay. To the poor people of Dunton 40s., Little Burstead 20s., Great Burstead 40s., Laindon 20s., Laindon Hills 13s. 4d., Hutton 10s., Shenfield 13s. 4d., Ingrave 20s., Fobbing 20s., Horndon 26s. 8d., Stanford [-le-Hope] 13s. 4d., Bulphan 20s., North Benfleet 13s. 4d., South Benfleet 20s., Mucking 20s., Orsett 20s., Grays Thurrock 20s., South Weald 20s., and the town of Brentwood 20s., to be paid to the churchwardens at or before the day of my burial, giving my executor a receipt.

To Mistress Legate my mother-in-law 40s., my Lady Petre wife of Sir John Peter 20s., Thomas Tyrrell esquire 20s. and his wife 20s., Edward Rich esquire 20s. and his wife 10s., my brother-in-law Thomas Legate £3 13s. 4d. and my sister Legate his wife 20s. To every of my godchildren 10s. To every of my maidservants 13s. 4d. To Thomas Browne, bachelor in divinity, parson of Dunton, £3 6s. 8d. To my cousin George Drywood £3 6s. 8d. To Thomas Meredith £3 6s. 8d. £50 shall be bestowed by John in black cloth to divers of my friends, whereof certain coats to my tenants, viz. Henry Edgiot, William King, George Mounes, Humphrey Drywood, Thomas Norrys, Thomas Witham, Andrew Daffil, Henry Ponde, Thomas Veare, and Edward Harvie, and the same tenants to bear my body to the church. The residue of my goods to John. I ordain my wife and John my executors, and John shall yearly give up accounts to my wife and overseers. I ordain Sir John Petre knight, John Lentall gentleman, and my brothers Robert and George my overseers, and for their pains £6 13s. 4d.

Proved 12 April 1578.

RALPH DUCKETT late of Roydon gentleman, 18 February 1587.
[31/17]

To my most dear and loving mother Mistress Coult a gilt goblet, my ring with the stone which she gave me, my great chest, and £6 13s. 4d. to bestow on something in remembrance of me. To my very loving brother Mr Swifte and my assured loving sister Mistress [Frances] Swifte each a gilt goblet and 40s. to bestow on a ring. More to my sister my gown violet and black, fine clothes and some of my best bands, and my great bible. To Francis Swifte, James Swifte, Jane, Dorothy, Margaret and Elizabeth their children in all among them £60, each £6 13s. 4d., to the men children at 21 and the others at marriage or 24. More to Jane my trunk and 3 of my cambric bands to make her ruffs, a little ring of gold, my small bible, and my linen unbequeathed. To my sister Joan Lovell £6 13s. 4d. to have the yearly profit, and a ring of gold which is about my scarf. To Thomas Swifte, my brother's third son, my lands in Pope Street in Eltham (Kent) and those tenements in lease to Thomas Hasellwoode, alebrewer of London, in Knightsbridge by St James' House [Middx.], and for lack of issue to James his elder brother; also my books unbequeathed. To my uncle and aunt Bladwell 10s.

To the Compter [prison] in the Poultry [in London] 10s. To the poor of Roydon 20s. To Besse Davye, my keeper, 20s. and my broad hat. To G. Gildersonne my old black doublet and frize jerkin, a shirt, a holland band, and a pair of stockings. To R. Palmer my brother's servant my riding cloak, black hat, rapier and dagger, black doublet, shirt, 2 good holland bands, and a pair of stockings. To Miles my buff hose according to a former promise. To Mistress Anne my mother's waiting maid my silver tooth picker. To Margaret her maid 3s. 4d., Jeanne 3s. 4d., Ralph and Slater 10s., and to each a holland band, Margery 6s. 8d., Joan my sister's maid 5s. and my old black cloak, Julian 3s. 4d., and the rest of my brother's servants unnamed 20s. To Mr [John] Fale the minister [vicar of Roydon] 20s. and my Latin bible. To my cousin Cowper 10s. To one John Scoller, a tailor in Barbery, £6 and my bill of £6 to be taken in, wherein I promise to pay him £5 at such times as they were certainly known who robbed me there, the certainty whereof will never be known, yet I would have him paid the £6 at one Laxfield's, a tailor in Bow Lane he will be heard of, the payment whereof I would have to be made of wood at Eltham or of the rents of both. To R. Bickerton a French crown to make him a little ring and his wife my ring with the blue stone.

28 February 1587. Memorandum, the testator after the will delivered to his mother Mistress Margaret Coulte widow, in the presence of Frances Swyft his sister and Margaret wife of William Butler of Roydon, being put in mind by his mother of disposing of such things as God had sent him, and being demanded by her if his meaning were not that his brother Swifte's children should have the most of that which he had, answered 'Yes' and that he had in writing already set down how he would have everything done and likewise that he would have his land go to Thomas son of his brother Swifte according to his writing. Moreover, 13 March following, the testator took the writing out of his gown pocket and read it over to his mother and sister, and next day delivered it to his mother, his sister standing by and others, and desired his mother to deliver it to his brother, who said he knew well what was to be done therein. Witnesses : Margaret Colte, Frances Swifte, Mary Bickerton.

Proved 14 April 1587.

CHRISTOPHER DUNSCOMBE of Orsett gentleman, August 1600 'or thereabouts'. (Nuncupative.)   [44/57]

To Grace his well-beloved wife all his goods, saying that it was all too little for her, whom he made his sole executrix. 'Divers and sundry witnesses'.

Proved 23 September 1600.

ROWLAND ELRINGTON of Woodford gentleman, 20 July 1593. [For Edward Elrington, see p. 80.]   [39/62]

To be buried in comely manner. To the discharge of my funerals £120, whereof £15 shall be bestowed in some monument in the church for a remembrance. To the making of a fair foot causey from Woodford Row to Woodford church £10, so as the inhabitants on the Row as it decay will yearly repair the same.

To Agnes my well-beloved wife £2,000 in satisfaction of such as she may in any wise claim by the custom of the city of London or otherwise. Whereas I am possessed of a house and warehouse in St Benet Fink in

London for divers years to come in the tenure of James Wilcockes, I give my lease to my wife, and my household stuff, quick cattle and utensils in my house at Woodford and in London (wainscot, painted cloths, glass and lead only excepted), also £130 in consideration that she hath disbursed money for the purchase of the tenement wherein I dwell in Woodford. Also to my wife a chain of fine angel gold of the value of £50, a pair of bracelets of like fine gold worth £14, and £60 towards her maintenance until she receive the said sums.

To William Elrington my brother £300, so as he enter into a bond to my wife to deliver yearly during her widowhood 5 quarters of wheat, 5 quarters of malt, 1 quarter of pease and 2 quarters of oats, also between Christmas and Candlemas 2 tierces of good Gascony wine of the best, being the third part of a tun. To Edward Elrington my brother my two messuages called Carters and Fennars in Matching and High Laver, with lands belonging, purchased by me of Nicholas Thoroughgood of Rowney [in Southill] (Beds.) gentleman, and £400. To William Elrington my brother my parcel of marshground called Sheep Lease (containing 9 acres) and 3 acres of marsh at Pond Lease next to a marsh called Phillippes Lease in Barking, and £600. To Richard Whitebread my sister Whitbread's son my annuity of £12 13s. 4d. payable to me by an indenture dated 29 May 1590 by Edmund Lewkenor of Kingston Bowsey (Sussex) esquire, and £20. To my sisters Mary Cuttes and Judith Catlyne each 100 oz. of gilt plate, every oz. worth 6s. 8d. To my niece Elizabeth Elrington, my brother Edward's daughter, £100 at marriage or 20, to remain in the hands of Edward Cage my brother-in-law till then, allowing her yearly £5 towards her poor maintenance, and if she decease before to be equally divided among her brothers; and I discharge my brother Edward of all money I lent him by his bonds, which are cancelled. To my brother William's children, i.e. his daughters £50 apiece at marriage or 20 and his sons £40 apiece at 21, to be delivered to their father to be employed for their commodity. To my brother Edward's children (his daughter Elizabeth excepted) £40 apiece at 21 or marriage to be likewise employed. To my sister Cuttes' children a ring of gold worth 40s. each. To my sister Catlyn's children £50 to be equally divided among them. To Mr Alderman Billingsley a ring of gold worth £3, my brother Lawrence a ring of gold worth £3, Mr Henry Beecher, Richard Hull's wife, my brother William's wife, and my brother-in-law Edward Cage's, each a ring of gold worth 40s.

To the poor children of Christ's Hospital in London £10. To the poor of Theydon Bois £5 and Woodford £5. To my household servants 40s. apiece. I constitute my loving brother-in-law Edward Cage and my very good brother William my executors, and to Edward £20 and William £5. I make my good friend Richard Hull of London draper my overseer, to whom I give 60 oz. of gilt plate of the value of 7s. the oz. The residue of my goods to the children of my brothers Edward and William Elrington equally to be divided among them.

Witnesses: Edmund Wynche, Robert Clarke, Thomas Taylor, Samuel Mason.

Proved 16 October 1595.

ROBERT ETON of Springfield gentleman, 20 October 1571.   [35/29]

To be buried in Springfield church. To my son Thomas my lease of the parsonage of Broomfield. To my loving wife Joan £20 a year for life out of my lease of the mansion house of the manor of Springfield called Springfield Hall and the demesne lands belonging, on condition that she claim no dower in my lands and shall after her decease and that of Anne Salmon, widow of John Salmon of Chelmsford, woollendraper, leave the inheritance of the tenement in Chelmsford called the Robin Hood to Thomas; and on that condition I give her my copyhold land called Kingstones for life, with remainder to Thomas. My household stuff and plate shall be brought into an inventory and remain in my house till Thomas is 21 under my wife's government to his use, and when 21 be divided by my executor, one half to my wife so long as she remain unmarried and dwell there and the other to Thomas, and if she marry her half be left to his use. She shall have the parlour at the upper end of the hall of Springfield Hall and the other parlour or under-chamber at the nether end of the hall, also the use of the hall, buttery and gardens and the stable within the pales as long as she keep herself unmarried. Thomas to have to his own private use all the other rooms and the use of the hall, buttery, gardens and stable together with my wife, according to my plain meaning that I would have them live quietly and charitably together. Whereas I purchased of Thomas Wallinger gentleman a lease in reversion of a tenement and lands in Springfield called Gardens, my loving friend and brother-in-law Harry Bridge shall have the lease for £40, whereof he has paid £30, and £10 shall be paid when William son of Thomas Mundes is 21. Whereas I am possessed of a lease of a messuage in Springfield with lands called Dukes in the occupation of Thomas Mundes, to whose father I was executor, he shall enjoy one half of the farm and his brother William the other.

My executor shall have the government of Thomas and his lands until he is 21, and I earnestly desire him that Thomas shall be well brought up in learning and that he be ordered by my executor. To the poor of Chelmsford yearly for ever out of Mill Field in Springfield 13s. 4d., so that the parishioners shall not charge the same lands for any other yearly rent heretofore supposed to be given thereof by Simon Swaffeld. To the poor people of Springfield 20s. and of Chelmsford 20s. To every of my servants over and above their wages 3s. 4d. To Jerome Motteley of his father's legacy £6 13s. 4d., and the third part of £6 13s. 4d. which was the third part of the legacy of his sister Mary. To Mistress Salmon my mother-in-law 6s. 8d.. the wife of Thomas Wellenger gentleman 6s. 8d., and Katherine Cordall wife of William Heditche, John Wallenger, Edmund Shether, and Katherine daughter of Andrew Paschall gentleman, 6s. 8d. each. To every of my godchildren other than Katherine Paschall 12d. To Harry Devenishe 3s. 4d., Lawrence Salmon otherwise Smythe 10s., mother Pamplin 6s. 8d., the wife of Thomas Mundes 20s., Harry Bridge 20s., and Jerome Mottelie £3 6s. 8d. To John Hones yearly for life 10s. out of the rent of the tenement he dwelleth in and to his wife 10s. in money.

To the solemnising of my burial my wife shall have a black gown and

Thomas a black gown and coat. I make my trusty friend Thomas Wallenger my sole executor, and for his pains 40s. The residue to Thomas, and to my wife her own apparel and jewels. I make overseers my very loving friends George White esquire and Thomas Tirrell gentleman, son and heir of Sir Henry Tyrrell knight, and for their pains 20s. each. Witnesses: Thomas Wallenger, John Brewer, Lawrence Smyth alias Salmon, Henry Bridge.

Proved 20 December 1571.

WALTER FARR of Great Burstead gentleman, 8 February 1588.

[34/25]

To be buried in Great Burstead church. To the reparations of the church 20s. To some learned preacher to make a sermon at my burial 10s. To the poor of Burstead 40s. To Henry my son £100. To Walter my son my lease I have of him of the farm of Buckwyns in Buttsbury, so that he release to me all actions of account. To Benjamin my son 100 marks. To Richard my son 20 kine, 1 bull, 80 ewes and 2 rams which Thomas Clemente hath in stock with the dairy at Bromehill, such corn as I have growing on the grounds of Westhouse and the hay housed and stacked there, my light horses with all the furniture to them and my other armour, corselets and calvyers, also my plate, provided that he permit Thomas Clemente to have the hardwick of Bromehill until Michaelmas after my decease. The residue of my goods to Richard, whom I make my sole executor. Witnesses: Humphrey Blake, Robert Blake, Timothy Ockley, John Brathwaite.

Codicil, 20 September 1588. If Richard do not within two months after my decease prove my will, Harry to be my sole executor and he to have all bequeathed to Richard.

Proved 5 May 1590 by Richard.

JOHN FOORDE of Thorpe gentleman, 31 May 1576. [For Katherine Forde, see p. 83.]   [20/4]

To be buried, if I die within the liberties of the Soken, in the chancel of Kirby church.

To Audrey my wife £11, 5 silver spoons, and a brewing lead remaining with my farmer of Dengewell Hall [in Great Oakley], my youngest gelding, my household stuff except hereafter excepted, and one coat of plate and one harquebus with a murrion, flask and touchbox, on condition that she shall not presume after my decease to open any of my chests or my desk before my executor hath perused the same, for if she do her legacy to be void. To Thomas Bendishe gentleman, my brother-in-law, my grograine gown furred throughout with lamb faced with coney and laid with lace and buttons, and my grograine coat guarded with velvet. To the children of my sister Eleanor Bendish deceased, each 20s. at 18, her eldest son excepted to whom I give my ring of gold with my seal of arms on it. To Richard Smythe gentleman, my brother-in-law, my grograine cassock furred throughout with lamb and laid with lace. To my sister his wife 2 old angels. To her children 20s. apiece at 18, her eldest son excepted to whom I give a ring of gold with a seal fixed therein. To my cousin Catherine wife of Edmund Mannocke gentleman 20s. To my nephew James Stuarte my copyhold lands in Great Oakley called Cuttes at 18, on condition that he pay his sisters Elizabeth and Anne £3 6s. 8d. each when he is 21. My executor shall pay him such revenues of his lands as I have received as his guardian. To Mr Rochester clerk, parson of Great Oakley, a Book of the Abridgement of Statutes and a Book of Kings. To my chirurgeon John Amott of Stock £5, one wyned trendle bedstead. To the children of Thomas Sayer of Frating 15s. each.

To the servants in the house wherein I die 2s. each. To Richard Deye my servant 53s. 4d., my shirts and handkerchiefs, and the residue of my apparel, a posted bedstead, and a great chest with a hollow lid wherein my apparel lieth; sufficient meat, drink and lodging for a year after my decease or else £5; two liveries, one of frize and the other of azure, and 4 does' skins; also £10. To Amy Wardle, late of Stratford [St Mary, Suff.] 40s. To Richard Webb sometime my servant 10s. To the poor people of Great Oakley 30s., Wix 13s. 4d., Frating 30s., Great Bentley 26s. 8d., Little Bentley 6s. 8d., and Elmstead 13s. 4d. To the poor that shall resort to my burial and the poor of the parish where I die £18 [sic]. To the poor prisoners in the Gaol and Castle of Colchester yearly at Lent for 21 years 4 bushels of peasen, 4 bushels of rye and 1 cade of red herrings. To Richard Wrighte and William Morse, both of Stratford, 10s. each. To Thomas Bendishe gentleman for 21 years the yearly rents and profits of Dengewell Hall and Blountes Hall in Wix and Great Oakley to perform the legacies in my will. The residue of my goods to be at the free disposition of my executor, whom I ordain Thomas Bendishe.

Witnesses: Robert Hasteler and Thomas Freman writer hereof.
Proved 6 February 1577.

HENRY FREEMAN of Woodham Mortimer gentleman, 19 November 1592.   [36/90]

To the poor people of Woodham Mortimer 20s. on the day of my burial and 20s. within a year following.

To Elizabeth my wife the lease of my farm of Woodham Mortimer Hall wherein I dwell, with the stock of 30 of my best kine and 1 bull, and if she shall happen to mislike of any 6 or 8 of the 30 kine she shall have for every of the kine misliked 50s.; 10 wennels of this year's weaning and 100 of my best ewes with 4 of my rams to be chosen by her out of my sheep on my grounds belonging to the Hall in the keeping of my brother [in-law] William Gage; 5 carthorses, with the carts and ploughs, my black crop-eared gelding, my grey mare with her colt, the stoned colt which is her own; my hay and corn, hogs, boars, shoats and pigs; my plate, jewels and household stuff at the Hall (the young timber which I bought of Mr Twedy only excepted), with the pasturing of a mare in

Barn Marsh all the years to come; also £110, whereof £10 presently after my decease and £100 within a year. To Bartholomew Freeman my brother's son £20, and Thomas and Mary his other children £10 apiece at 21 and the daughter at 18 or marriage. To my sister Furnes £3 6s. 8d. To William and John, my brother Thomas Furnes' sons of Maldon, £10 apiece at 21. To my sister Barbara wife of John Dannbrooke £6 13s. 4d. To John son of Ralph Freeman £3 6s. 8d. at 21, and Cecily, Margaret and Elizabeth daughters of Ralph £3 6s. 8d. apiece at 18 or marriage. To Elizabeth Wattes my sister 40s. To Cecily daughter of William Gage and Alice daughter of Thomas Harrys of Northampton, each 40s. at 18 or marriage. To William Claryvaunce 40s. and William Barker of Northampton 40s. To my servant Matthias Metheringham £3 6s. 8d. To the boy John Sharpe £3 6s. 8d. at 21 if he so long continue in service with my wife or where she shall place him and not depart without licence of her or such other as she place him with. The residue of my goods to Bartholomew my brother, whom I make my sole executor.

Witnesses : Thomas Furnes, John Mannynge, John Rothman, Thomas Chese.

Proved 12 December 1592.

ROBERT FREMLINGE of Romford gentleman, 19 November 1596.
[41/16]

To Elizabeth my wife £40, with remainder to my daughter Elizabeth Barker and Elizabeth her daughter to be equally divided between them, Robert Barker my son-in-law to procure sureties in bond for the same. To Thomas and John at 23 and Joan at 20 or marriage, my three children, £20 apiece. To Elizabeth, my daughter's daughter, £15 presently after my goods shall be sold, and the money to remain in Robert's hand to her best use until 16 or marriage. To the poor of Farningham (Kent) 10s. and Aynesford (Kent) 10s. The residue of my goods to my children equally to be divided. I make Thomas Fremlinge my brother and Robert Coleman my cousin, gentlemen, my executors. I ordain Richard Darbie, Henry Titheburne and Lawrence Atwill, my very good friends, my overseers, and for their pains 5s. apiece. Witnesses : William Titheburne, Richard Darbie, Henry Titheburne, Lawrence Atwill.

Proved 17 February 1597.

THOMAS FRENCHE the elder of Wethersfield gentleman, 23 June 1599. [43/73]

To the poor people of Halstead 40s., West Wratting (Cambs.) 20s., Snettisham (Norfolk) £3, Great Bardfield 40s., Little Bardfield 20s., Wethersfield 40s., and Arkesden 20s. To Mary my daughter, wife of John Collin, £20, and John, William, Mary and Elizabeth, her children, each £20, to be paid at the south porch of Great Bardfield church. To Elizabeth, my daughter, wife of John Meade, £20, and Edward,

Elizabeth, John and Agnes, her children, each £20 likewise. To every of the children of my son Thomas £10 at 21. To Thomas Girton, one of my son's servants, 10s. To John, one of Elizabeth Meade's sons, one of my silver bowls, and William, one of Mary Collin's sons, the other. To John, son of my son Thomas, another silver bowl parcel gilt. To Bridget my wife £5, her wearing apparel, and such goods as I had with her at marriage. The residue of my goods to Thomas, whom I ordain my sole executor. Witnesses: Thomas Reynoldes, William Younge, William Purcas.

Proved 31 October 1599.

PETER FYGE of Writtle gentleman, 12 June 1573.   [18/23]

To be buried in the chancel of Writtle church before my stool where I use to sit. At the day of my burial a sermon to be made and 6s. 8d. for the preacher's pains. To the poor people at my burial 20s. To every servant dwelling with me 12d. To Cliffe's wife of Moulsham in Chelmsford 20d. To Thomas my son my best bed in the great chamber and my coverlet of arras, whereon my arms are appensed and set, my best apparel, and my greatest brass pot. To Jane my well-beloved wife my houses and lands called Mumpillers alias Willingales in Writtle and Chelmsford for life. After her decease such in Writtle to Thomas; and for default of issue to Thomas Emery, my son-in-law, and Thomasine his wife, my daughter; and for default to be sold by my supervisors, and of the money one half to be given to the most poorest people of Writtle and Chelmsford by £10 yearly so long as any shall remain and the other half towards the exhibition of poor scholars in the University of Cambridge, poor maidens' marriages, and the repairing of highways and other deeds of charity in the said parishes by £10 a year at my overseer's discretion; and such in Chelmsford to Thomas and to his heirs male, and for default of such issue to his heirs female, so that there be paid to Thomas Emery £30 at his dwelling in Danbury. To Thomas my son my houses and lands called Pycottes alias Amys in Prittlewell, Eastwood and Hadleigh. The residue of my goods to my wife and Thomasine equally to be divided, whom I ordain my executors. I ordain my loving friend and kinsman Thomas Whitebreade the younger my overseer, to whom I give 10s. [No witnesses.]

Proved 3 June 1575.

EUGENE GATTON of Mucking gentleman, 10 November 1590.
                                                           [35/77]

To be buried in the aisle by the chancel of Mucking church. To the poor of Mucking 40s. To my godchildren 20s. apiece. To the children of Edward Webbe deceased 40s. apiece. To William Whetnall 5 marks. To Mary and Anne Brookman, my cousin Brookman's daughters, 5 marks apiece. To Rebecca wife of John Stonard of Horndon [on-the-Hill] and Agnes wife of Richard Cooke of Gravesend [Kent] each an old sovereign

of 30s. To every one of my servants over their wages 5s. All such legacies to those under age to be paid at their lawful age. To Elizabeth my wife my manor of Jenkyns [in Hazeleigh?] with lands belonging, my copyhold lands holden of the Dean and Chapter of Paul's [London] as of their manor of Mucking, and my other lands in Stanford-le-Hope. I ordain my wife my sole executrix and Edward Sulyarde esquire and Thomas Burges, my wife's father, supervisors, and to Edward for his pains 5 marks. Witnesses : John Stonerd, John Pease, Anne Cooke, William Howe, John Stampbredg, Joseph Page.
Proved 29 October 1591.

ROBERT GAYWOOD of Maldon gentleman, 11 November 1559.
[3/2]

To be buried in All Saints' church in Maldon, if it may be, next to my father, with a stone representing in Latin myself, my wife and my two sons, with a note of the day and year of my burial. To the vicar in recompense of my tithes negligently forgotten 10s. There be provided at my burial 5 tapers of wax of ¼lb. apiece and 10 of 1d. apiece during the time of the administration and other observances and to be borne by five honest freemen and they to have 4d. apiece; to 10 poor people of the borough town of Maldon about my hearse at the time of my body carried to the church and burial and to every of them for their labour 2d. There be provided at my burial such honest help and service as the law will suffer, with clerks to minister, and every of the priests to have 8d. and their dinner and every clerk to have 4d. and their dinner, and to 4 poor men which shall bear me to church 4d. apiece. There be provided at my burial ½ seam of wheat to be baked into bread, 2 barrels of beer, and ½ wey of cheese, and 40s. in money to be distributed to the poor people. To the two bailiffs and every alderman and head burgess of the town at my burial 4d. At my month's day 15 tapers to be occupied about my hearse, every of the said poor people to have for their labour 2d., and every of the bailiffs, aldermen and head burgesses at service in the parish church at my month's day shall have their dinners. To the poor people of All Saints 6s. 8d., St Peter 3s. 4d. and St Mary 10s., and Layer Marney 5s., in the month after my decease.

To Joan Gaywood my sister for life the yearly rent and profit of my messuage in St Mary between the tenement sometime of John Gate, late of John Thomeson tailor, and that late of John Gaywood, afterwards of Sir Thomas Darcie knight and now of Nicholas Harker, one head abutting on the highway against the north and the other on Mel Field against the south; and after her decease to remain to John my son.

To Marian my wife 4 featherbeds and bedsteads, so she take neither the bedstead in the new chamber nor the great chamber over the parlour, John to have the first choice of one and she the next, so dividing by turn for 8 of the best. To her and John in like manner 12 of my best pillows, 12 pair of sheets, 8 broad cloths, 8 towels, 3 dozen of napkins, and 4 cupboard cloths, and all other kind of linen and napery to John (except her linen which she weareth), brass, pewter, copper, spits, cobirons,

199

candlesticks and suchlike to be otherwise divided. To John my 12 best silver spoons, with a measure which my mother-in-law gave him. To my wife the occupying of all tables, stools, forms, trestles, cupboards, hangings, carpets, 8 cushions of arras work, my cushions of cloth of gold, velvet and silk in my house, for life, with remainder wholly to John; and if she chance to marry, she to have 2 tables joined, 2 forms and 6 stools at my son's appointment. To my wife her apparel and jewels, so much good corn and grain as wheat, malt and oats as shall be for her necessary occupation a year after my decease; 6 kine at Little Maldon at her own choice, there to be kept, wintered and summered during the term of my lease of the farm, 2 geldings, 1 trotting and another ambling, each worth £4 or to have £8, and pasture for 1 gelding on the same farm; and £10 a year for life out of my farms of Little Maldon and Layer Wick in Layer Marney but to cease if she marry again; my house that I dwell in, which she is possessed of, and the houses annexed and joined together, i.e. the tenement which mother Parke sometime dwelled in and my garden on the backside late of Sir Thomas Darcie; lands called Stickhers Redens sunderly in North Totham and Little Totham; my tenement called Bawdes in All Saints in which Robert Cowke dwelleth, my tenement, forge and garden called [blank] in All Saints wherein William Payne smith dwelleth, for her life; and my lease of a tenement and garden in All Saints which I had from John Huddlestone esquire. To my son John my two farms and leases of Little Maldon and Layer Wick with the stock of cattle, implements and corn. To every godchild 12d. apiece. To my sister Joan Crowe 3s. 4d. quarterly for life, and John Tedham 6s. 8d. for life and the dwelling in the house wherein she dwelleth, without payment. To John the profits of all other my farms and leases to the performance of my will. To Mr Bowswell of Maldon 10s. in gold and Joan Boswell his daughter 10s. To Mr Crestener one pistolet. To Mr Tucke one old ryal of gold.

If John may obtain to marry one of the daughters of Edmund Tirrell esquire and will not do so, he shall pay Thomasine Tirrell, one of Edmund's daughters, £10 at marriage, and if she shall happen to decease before, the £10 to her sister that shall marry next after. To Kelham Throgmorton esquire my black mare with the white star in the forehead. To Gregory Crow my second gown, my second coat, with a doublet and a shirt. To my sister Joan Hayward's children and of John Crow's children 6s. 8d. apiece at marriage or 20. To Edward Reade my skene which I had last of Leadge the butcher and a bullock of 3 years. To Joan wife of John Bright a bullock of this year's weaning. To Agnes Rumpton my servant 6s. 8d. at marriage. Wyseman shall not be removed out of Little Maldon during my lease without it be by his own folly and shall have the going there of 1 bullock and 2 lambs above his covenants. To Barbara Tedham 20s. at 18. To Alice Momperd a bullock of this year's weaning, and it shall be kept while she dwell with my wife, and my son shall deliver to Barbara Momperd her father's legacy and see her honestly brought up at his costs or pay my wife for doing so. The residue of my goods to John, whom I constitute my sole executor. I ordain Edmund Tirrell esquire, David Sympson, Thomas Sandes and

John Gaywood of Tillingham my overseers, and to the first two 40s. and the last 20s.

Witnesses : William Hale, William Jarves, John Newe, Edward Logge, John Locke, with others.

Proved 11 December 1559.

GIFFORD : see GYFFORD.

JEROME GYLBARD [Gilberd] of Colchester gentleman, 1 May 1583.
[26/38]

To be buried in Saint Trinity church in Colchester. Towards the repairing and glazing of the church 3s. 4d.

To my eldest son William Gylbard alias Dr Gilbard my capital messuage and head house in Trinity parish with the rentaries, gardens and orchards belonging, and my lands called Celers in Elmstead in the tenure of Humfrey Lane; but if he die before marriage or without issue all the premises shall remain to Jane my wife, and after her decease [successively?] to my two sons Ambrose and William Gylbard the younger and their heirs male. To my wife my lands called Ryddelles in Wivenhoe and Ricardownes in Elmstead with my pasture called Brockfield, for life and towards the good education and bringing up of the children had between her and me, and after her decease to remain as my lands called Kelers. To her my messuages, rentaries and lands in St Botolph's Street, sometime Lytelle's and after William Wyseman's, and my copyhold lands in Donyland in the tenure of Egell, for life, and after her decease with successive remainders to Ambrose and William the younger and their heirs male, to George my younger son and Thomas Gylbard my nephew and their heirs male, and to my four youngest daughters. To my wife for life and towards the bringing up of her three sons and four daughters my tenements and lands called Goldinges in Greenstead and Freemans and Freemans Fen in Greenstead and Ardleigh, and after her decease [successively?] to Ambrose, William the younger and Thomas.

To my son Jerome two messuages next to North Bridge and my tene-ments called Little Goodyeares at Mile End, and for default of issue to the use of my wife and her four daughters during my wife's life to remain and be divided among Ambrose, William and George. To Thomas, son of Thomas Gilbard my son deceased, my tenements and gardens, chapel and chapelyard called Saint Ellen's, and for default of issue to remain to Ambrose and William, provided that my wife shall have the bringing up of Thomas till he is 21. To George Gylbard my son my tenement in the parish of St Peter in North Street sometime William Wyseman's, with the shop and house adjoining to the broad gates there, with the moiety of the barn and yard behind it, with free ingress, egress and regress to the river.

To my wife my customary lands and pastures called Ten Acres with the grove called Pope's Head in Lexden for life for the maintenance of her houses in Botolph's Street. To my son Dr Gylberd my pasture named

Partridge Fen to go and continue with the head house in Trinity parish. To my wife my meadow called the Moor against Middle Mill for life, and after her decease to be divided between Dr Gilberd, Ambrose and William; and my lands called New Hammans and Old Hammans in Elmstead and my pastures and woods called Sumpters Heaths. To Dr Gylberd my part of grounds in Shotley [Suffolk] with the advowson and part of the patronage of Shotley, and to his heirs. To every of my four youngest daughters £20 at marriage or 21 and one featherbed and bedstead. My tenement and lands in Bradfield shall be sold by my executors, and the money to be divided among the children of my daughter Margaret, part and part like.

The half of my brass and pewter shall be divided among my wife's children that I had between her and me, and she to have it until they come of age or marry; and Ambrose shall have his part also given him by his grandmother there at Clare [Suffolk]. To Dr Gylbard half of the pewter that was his mother's and is in my chest, my best standing salt which was his mother's and 6 spoons with maidenheads, on condition that he redeliver the other salt parcel gilt that he hath of mine to my wife. To Jerome my son a gilt goblet when he shall have issue, then the custody thereof, putting in surety to render it to William the younger. To my wife the custody of the residue of the plate and spoons for life, except that bequeathed hereafter, and after her decease to Ambrose, William and George or two of them that will best intend to keep them in remembrance of me. To William the younger the standing cup or bowl gilt at marriage, and if he die before to my daughters Agnes and Elizabeth at marriage.

The woods (except the timber trees at Sumpters Heaths) and both the Hammans shall be felled and sold by the agreement of my executors and supervisor, and the money to pay my debts and towards the reparations of my houses in Botolph's Street and both the Hammans houses and the rest to be divided among the children that I had by my wife at 21. The residue of my woods at Keelers and Ryddelles to Dr Gilberd to the maintenance of his houses in Colchester To my son-in-law Harryes and his wife yearly 2 load of good wood to be delivered at his house in Colchester for 7 years. To my eldest son half the linen in the chest in the closet and the best featherbed and coverlet of silk, the best tester, curtains and hangings, and the residue to be divided between my wife and her children. My lands and tenements in Somersham and Nettlestead (Suffolk) shall be sold and the money parted among my three youngest sons at their lawful ages and be put in a stock during their minority that some profit may arise, and the part of such as shall die shall be divided among my said four youngest daughters. Provided that if Dr Gilbard shall infringe any of the bequests to my wife, all gifts to him shall be void.

I make my well-beloved wife and my especial friend Dr Drurye my executors. To Mistress Drury one pot and to Mistress Audley the other pot both bound about with silver. To my special friends Mr Thomas Tey, Mr Robert Audley and Mistress Elizabeth Audlye each an angel in gold, and to Mr Thomas Audlye the second son of Mistress Audlye my book of the Great Abridgement of Fytzharbett with the table belonging, and the residue of my books to Ambrose and William the younger.

Witnesses : William Langleye, Geoffrey Lovell, John Patche.

Proved 17 July 1582.

JANE GILBERDE of Colchester, widow of Jerome Gilberde gentleman, 1 August 1589. [33/83]

To Ambrose my eldest son a featherbed, 2 stools covered with silk, a livery cupboard, my great press, the long table and frame and an old long form in the Dutchman's house, 2 of my best chairs, a pair of andirons in the parlour, a firefork and a pair of tongs. To William my son a table with a frame, 2 little forms, with the bedstead that stood in the great parlour, and a pair of andirons. To George my son a bedstead, a feather-bed, a table with feet, 4 joined stools, my marrying ring of gold, and a chair, at 21 or marriage. To Thomas Gilberd my nephew a green chair, a table with a frame, a bedstead, 2 carpet cushions, and a coarse table-cloth, at 21 or marriage. I have appointed to my daughter Anne for her bedding stuff bequeathed to her by my late husband a bedstead with a canopy and curtains, a featherbed, a flat chest in the closet, 2 joined stools, a trundle bedstead, a trammel, a pair of great andirons, a firepan and a pair of tongs; to my daughter Agnes likewise a bedstead and a featherbed; to my daughter Elizabeth likewise a bedstead, a featherbed, a trammel, a pair of andirons, a pair of tongs, a table with leaves in the great chamber, and 2 frames with carved sides; and to my daughter Prudence likewise a bedstead, a featherbed, the cupboard table in the hall, with the cupboard where my glasses be kept, a trundle bedstead, and a chest wherein my household linen lieth. My brass and pewter and my half part bequeathed to me by my late husband's will, also that part bequeathed to my said children by his will, shall be equally divided between them over and besides any one's part given him by his grandfather.

To my sister Edith Wingfeilde 20s. and her daughter Elizabeth 20s. at 15, and to each a cornered handkerchief. To my goddaughter and niece Jane Wingfeilde and my nephew Thomas Wingfeilde each 10s. To my godsons Humfrey Huggens 5s. and John Piggot 5s. To Margery Piggott a holland sheet and a pair of holland pillowbeers marked with the letter M, and to Elizabeth Piggott a one-yard kerchief. To my sisters Mistress Drury and Mistress Hunstone and my nieces Ruggle and Wingfeilde each a ring of gold. To Dr Gilberd and Jerome Gilberd, my sons-in-law, each a spur royal of gold. To my brothers John and Anthony Wingfeilde and my nephew Humfrey Wingfeilde each an almain rivet. To my especial good friend Mistress Katherine Awdley a spur royal of gold. To the right worshipful my singular good friend Dr Drury a piece of gold of 20s., whom I ordain and humbly desire to be supervisor of my will.

If either George or Thomas my sons die before marriage or 21, their gifts shall be equally divided among my daughters. The iron stocks, my sawn boards, square and rough timber in and about my house shall remain to Ambrose and William. To my seven children to each a chest or coffer in my house and all such stuff in them, whereof there is an inventory with the names of my children therein written. To the poor of St Botolph in Colchester 13s. 4d. The residue of my goods to be equally divided among all my children. I ordain Ambrose my sole executor. To Ambrose and William my customary lands holden of the manor of Lexden called Popes Head and Ten Acres.

Witnesses: Here Osborne, William Stere, Jane Gilberd.

I will that £30 of £40 due to me by bond from my brother John Wingfeilde be paid to my daughter Elizabeth in payment of £20 bequeathed to her by my late husband's will. Witnesses: Katherine Awdley, John Wingfeilde. Thomas son of Robert Gilberd, my late son-in-law, shall be bound apprentice or otherwise appointed to be brought up by the advice and consent of his uncle Dr Gilberd.

Proved 20 October 1589.

JEROME GILBERD of Dovercourt gentleman, 2 February 1594.
[38/78]

To be buried in the church where it shall please God my life to depart, and towards its reparation for the breaking of the ground 13s. 4d., and to some godly preacher for a sermon at my burial to edify God's people 10s. To the poor people of Dovercourt, Ramsey, Harwich, Shotley [Suffolk], Holy Trinity and St James Colchester, to each parish 40s.

To my sister Margaret for life 40s. every half year during the lease I took jointly with Jonas Goldingham gentleman of the Queen of the manor of Michaelstow in Ramsey; and £3 6s. 8d. to buy her a gown, and to her children 40s. apiece at 21 or marriage. To William Harris her eldest son £20, to be paid by my brother Dr Gilberd at 21 out of my houses in St Martin [in Colchester], and Dr Gilberd to pay him yearly 40s. towards his maintenance to learning till 21. To Elizabeth Barwicke my goddaughter £20 at 21 or marriage. To William Gilberd my godson, son of Ambrose my brother, £20 at 21 out of my houses in St Martin which I purchased of the children of John Robards, on condition that he pay the gift to William Harris, William Gilberd and Elizabeth Barwicke. To John Marvyn her son 20s. To William, Abraham and Margaret Segges, children of my wife's son deceased, 40s. each at 20, and Adam Barwicke, Philip Barwicke and Josan Sacke's children 10s. each. To Thomas son of Adam Barwicke 20s. To my cousin Hubard one of my stone pots covered with silver, and to William, George and Margaret Hubard 10s. each. To Joan Manners my wife's sister 20s. To my servants 3s. 4d. each and to John Letton, servant with Mr Goldingham, my buff doublet and hose and my worst riding cloak. To my brother Weston's children 20s. apiece, and such brass and pewter which I have which was my brother's shall be equally divided between Dorothy Weston and Elizabeth Weston the younger; and the 6 silver spoons which were my brother's equally divided between the 6 youngest children of my brother Weston deceased. To my brother William Gilbert the younger all my books and the goblet of silver and gilt which my father gave me in his will. To my brother George Gilbert 40s., my brother Ambrose 20s., and my sisters Anne, Agnes, Elizabeth and Prudence each 20s.

To my wife Margaret £20 a year during the term of the lease which I took jointly with Jonas Goldingham gentleman of our sovereign Lady the Queen. To Dr Gilberd my part in the lease in possession and that in reversion which I hold together with Jonas of the Queen of the manor of Michaelstow [in Ramsey], on condition that Dr Gilbert pay my wife the £20 yearly as also the £4 yearly given by me to my sister Margaret, and on like condition that he suffer my wife to enjoy the house and land wherein I dwell, for life, paying him yearly £5, and that he pay his part of such money as Jonas and I stand bound to pay to Thomas Richmond, Thomas Spencer and Cecily Spencer. To my brother doctor a piece of copyhold land which I purchased of Thomas Harvy in Dovercourt. He shall receive my debts and shall pay my legacies. My wife shall quietly suffer Jonas to have his way through the ground belonging to my house. If Dr Gilberd be minded to sell his part of the leases given to him, he shall make offer to my partner Mr Jonas Goldingham and let him have it £20 better cheap than any other. The residue of my goods to my wife, whom I nominate with my brother Dr Gilberd my executors, and I heartily desire my loving partner Jonas to be my supervisor, and for his pains my ring with my seal of arms, the arms to be defaced, and 20s. to engrave his own arms thereon.

Witnesses : Adam Barwicke, Thomas Clarke, Thomas Hale.
Proved 19 November 1594.

RICHARD GLASCOCKE of Roxwell gentleman, 7 July 1598. [42/88]

My wife shall sell two parts of my lands for the payment of my debts and the preferment of herself and her daughter. To my two daughters Anne and Elizabeth £100 apiece at 18. I make my well-beloved wife executrix. Witnesses : Henry Glascocke, Edward Barber.
Proved 21 November 1598.

RICHARD GOLDINGE of Great Henny gentleman, 29 December 1584. [29/46]

To be buried in All Saints' church in Sudbury (Suffolk) or else in the churchyard near my father Roger Goldinge and before him my grandfather William Goldinge. To the vicar of All Saints 3s. 4d. and the parson of Great Henny for tithes forgotten. To All Saints' church 20s. when any great reparations be made. To the reparations of the stone bridge in Sudbury called Ballingdon Bridge 20s. with the good advice of the Mayor and Brethren of the town when need shall be and masons and workmen shall be working thereon. To the repairing of the highways from Ballingdon End to Great Henny 20s. in such parts as shall be thought most needful by my executors and the chief inhabitants of Henny. [The remainder of this abnormally long Will comprising 10 folios of small handwriting relates chiefly to a capital messuage and other properties in Sudbury, together with small properties in Ballingdon (now in Suffolk), Great Henny, Bulmer, Twinstead and Middleton, bequeathed mostly to his wife Margaret and his son George, who are appointed executors. His friends William Goldinge esquire and William Tyffyn gentlemen are appointed overseers.] Witnesses : Richard Goldinge, John Skynner, Michael Newman.

Proved 27 October 1585.

THOMAS GOOCHE of Roxwell gentleman, 20 January 1589. [33/85]

To Thomas my son my lease of the manors or prebends of Fawkners and Barrowes alias Bowers with the appurtenances in Good Easter and Norton Mandeville, which I hold among other things by indenture dated 1 July 1567 for 5 years from the Annunciation of Our Lady next; and thereafter to William my son, provided that he pay yearly to the Lady Elizabeth Riche, wife of Sir Robert Riche knight, Lord Riche, deceased, such provision reserved by the lease, i.e. 8 quarters of barley malt, 5 quarters of oats, 10 wether sheep, 2 suckling calves, 2 barrow hogs and 1 boar, with the yearly rent of £21. To Thomas my messuage called Bedfords and my lands in Good Easter, High Easter and Mashbury; and for default of heirs male with successive remainders to William and Richard, paying to the issue female of Thomas at marriage or 21 £100 at the church porch of Good Easter. To Richard my lease of the manor or prebend called Imber with the appurtenances in Good Easter and Norton Mandeville which I purchased of my well-beloved cousin William Lewen, doctor of civil law.

My executors shall have the disposing of my two leases of the messuage or farm called Boyton Hall in Roxwell with the lands letten which I hold of Sir John Peter knight and of the site of the manor or farm called Dale Hall with the appurtenances and all the demesne lands with the stock of cattle or other things (except household stuff) and of the stock of cattle, utensils for the husbandry and corn on Imber or Bedfords, and after to dispose of the residue among Thomas, William and Richard and my two daughters Katherine and Margery. To Katherine and Margery each 200 marks, on condition that they do not claim any part of a legacy of £40 given by Thomas Wiseman their grandfather among seven of my children which I then had by Clemence his daughter. To my godson Richard Glascock 40s. to make him a ring. To my daughters Eve and Taverner each £5. To the children of my daughter Jane £5 equally to be divided. To my three sons and two daughters my household stuff. To the poor in Roxwell £3, Good Easter 20s. and Lawford 20s. To William Kendall, curate of Roxwell, 20s. To William Quilter, Richard Taylor, David Garrolde and Martha Sadler my servants, 20s. each, and to the rest of my menservants and maidservants 6s. 8d. each. To every of my seven children a gold ring. To my cousin Luther's man, John Ockolde, 20s. The residue to my executors to dispose at their discretions. I constitute my well-beloved nephews Richard and Anthony Luther my executors and well-beloved nephew [*sic*] William Lewen, doctor of the civil law, my overseer, and for their pains £6 13s. 4d.

Witnesses: William Luckin, John Taverner, William Durden, Hugh Keelinge, John Ockolde notary public.

Proved 26 November 1589.

RICHARD GOOCHE of Good Easter gentleman, on or about 2 November 1599. (Nuncupative.) [44/23]

Lying sick at the Cross Keys in Moulsham in Chelmsford, Richard Rollffe his tenant came to him and asked him whether he should hold out the whole term of years of his lease or no, and Richard Gooche replied, 'Aye, paying your rent'; and when he was gone Mary Pennyfather, being then in the chamber where Richard Gooche lay, asked him who should have the rent of the said farm and the rest of his goods if he died, and he said, 'One not far off', and Mary asked who that was and said, 'Is it my mistress?' (meaning Anne Gough alias Gooche widow). 'Aye', said Richard Gooche, 'who should have it else?' 'I had thought', said Mary, 'your younger brother William should have had it'. 'No', he said, 'he shall have nothing to do there nor with anything that I have being mine', and with that, as soon as he had spoken these words, he took Mary's keys until her said mistress came. In the presence of Mary Pennyfather, Joan Squire, Elizabeth Pennyfather, and others.

Proved 22 April 1600. Sentence, 22 April 1600, confirming Will in case between Agnes Gooche executrix and William Gooch brother of the deceased.

JEROME GRENE of Tolleshunt D'Arcy gentleman, 16 June 1572. [15/28]

To be buried in Tolleshunt D'Arcy church. To William my eldest son, Jerome my second, Richard my third, and Bryant my fourth son, £25 each at 22; to Margaret my eldest daughter, Mary, Anne and Jane my daughters, £20 each at 20 or marriage; and to the child my wife goeth withal if it be a boy £25 and if a daughter £20. The residue of my goods to Jane my wife, and I constitute her my sole executrix, provided that if she marry again before the performance of my legacies to my children she shall put in sufficient bond to Mr Thomas Darcy and Richard Barnarde of Braxted, whom I appoint overseers, and for their pains 20s. in gold to Mr Darcy and 20s. in 2 old angels to Richard Barnarde. To the poor of Tolleshunt D'Arcy 3s. 4d., whereof the poor wench that hath the child in the parish have 20d. To Margaret Osborne my maid 6s. 8d., George Dandye my man 3s. 4d., Thomasine Gage my maid 2s. 6d., and Benjamin my man 2s. 6d. I desire that William Jeyner, William Malden, William Hodge and John Weles shall carry me to church and have 12d. apiece. Witnesses: John Welles fletcher, Hugh Walden, William Hodge, Hugh Allen writer hereof.

Proved 18 September 1572.

RICHARD GRENEACRES of Walthamstow gentleman, 16 August 1593. [37/69]

To be buried in Walthamstow church. I remit and forgive Mr Canon of such debts as he oweth me, £13, on condition that he pay the rest without further suit and trouble according to his bond to me; my cousin Richard Grenacres of Worster [*recte* Worston?] (Lancs.) and such debts as are owing to me by the executors of Brian Parker, my sister Katherine Hammerton widow, and my brother Arthur Greneacres. All my creditors whosoever be forgiven on condition that they pay without suit of law the principal according to their bonds or otherwise. To my godson John Reignolds 20s. To Mr [John] Reignolds vicar of Walthamstow 40s. To the poor people of this parish £5. I make my well-beloved wife Frances and my trusty and well-beloved friend Mr William Rowe gentleman executors, and for his pains £10 and my white nag. To his son John a brooch with a stone in the same. To Jane Rogers sometime my servant 40s. and such of my servants as my executors shall think good 40s. apiece. The residue of my goods to my wife.

Witnesses : William Rowe, Roger Tasker, John Reignolds, Richard Harrett.

Proved 10 October 1593. Sentence, 3 December 1594, confirming Will in case between Arthur Greenacres and Katherine Hammerton *alias* Greenacres, brother and sister of the deceased, and Frances Greenacres widow, executrix.

EDMUND GREYE of Moulsham [in Chelmsford] gentleman, 16 October 1571. [14/46]

To Anne Downes my sister's daughter £5. To the household servants of Mr Arthur Harris to be distributed 10s. To Nicholas my master's horsekeeper a pair of sky-coloured hose with the leather moulds; John Hartlie a new lockram shirt; Browne baker a lockram shirt and my felt hat; John Hartley my black cloth hose; Cobbes my old grey cloak; John Strange a holland shirt; my fellow Rookwood a holland shirt; and Shyres my brother Springe's man my red stammel hose. To my brother Thomas Graye my black velvet hose and black satin doublet. To Brian my sword and my dagger and a holland shirt, and Thomas my boy my old blue coat and old pair of boots. To my keeper 3s. 4d. To my brother Anthony Graye my canvas doublet with the hose which my master now lately [Will unfinished.]

Administration granted, 18 November 1571, to Elizabeth Springe, sister of the deceased.

THOMAS GREYE of Great Chishall gentleman, 16 May 1566. [9/16]

To be buried in Great Chishall church. To Alice my wife for life all my lands in Layston, Aynswick, Westmill and Buntingford [Herts.] called Answick or Down Hall, on condition that, on request by my cousins Andrew Grey and Andrew Mallerie, she convey the lands and tenements called Owls Barn in Hormead [Herts.] to the use of herself and after her decease to Elizabeth Grey my second daughter. To my daughters Katherine, Elizabeth and Alice Grey at marriage or 19 each £50. The residue of my goods to my wife for half a year after my decease, whom I make my sole executrix, and if on request to her by my cousin Andrew Grey and Ion Grey she assure to the uses hereafter expressed her moiety of such lands being freehold as are descended to her from John Serle her father deceased, i.e. to herself for life and after to Alice Grey my third daughter, then I give the said residue to her; but, if she refuse, the residue to Alice, whom I make my executrix. Witnesses : William Barley, Ion Grey, Matthew Grey, William Barlee, Grace Brockett, William Fordam, Elizabeth Barley, Margaret Newman, and others.

Proved 15 June 1566.

JOHN GRIFFETHE of St Botolph, Colchester, gentleman, 23 May 1590. [34/45]

To my loving brother Richard Griffithe of London gentleman my books that are here at Colchester and London, and my best cloak faced with velvet. To my mother a ring of 20s. and my aunt Canocke who dwelleth at Croft (Herefs.) a ring of 10s., both which I require my executrix to have made and sent with all speed after my decease. To my loving friend William Ramme of Colchester 40s. To John Jenipe my servant my riding cloak and such other apparel of mine as my executrix shall think good. To Andrew Stephens my servant my hose last made for me and the white stockings which are not yet dyed. To my servant Dorothy Trevor 40s. at marriage, and if she deserve well towards my wife and children after my decease she shall pay her more. To my good neighbour Agnes Halesworthe widow my gown guarded with velvet and faced with coney which is at London. The residue of my goods to Mary my most loving and good wife, requiring her to advance our two children and as they shall deserve, and I name her my sole executrix, being heartily sorry that I am not able to leave her in better estate, considering her good deserts and behaviour towards me as well in times of my health as sickness. Witnesses : William Ram notary public, Andrew Stephens.

Proved 12 June 1590.

ROGER GYFFORDE [of Tollesbury, gentleman?], 27 January 1597. [41/77]

To the right honourable Sir Thomas Egerton knight, Lord Keeper of the Great Seal of England, my honourable and very good lord, the jewel wherein the Queen's Majesty's picture is which I used to wear about my neck, in remembrance of my duty and unfeigned affection towards his lordship. I will that £500 of my money which remaineth in the hands of my friend Mr Humfrey Wemes and Thomas Sallm of Durham, whereof Mr Wemes hath £400 and Mr Sallm £150, shall be bestowed by my loving wife on my daughter Mary Giffarde to prefer her in marriage, if she marry by the advice and direction of my wife and my son-in-law Thomas Harries. The lease which I have already assigned to my son-in-law and to my friend Mr William Gall of my lands in the county of Durham shall be employed to such uses as by my deed to them dated yesterday are appointed. My farm of Tollesbury must go between my wife and my eldest son Thomas according to the lease which they and I have. My executors shall deliver to Merton College in Oxford, whereof I was sometime a Fellow, such of my books as Mr Henry Savill shall choose, to be placed in the library for the use of the Fellows and Scholars; nevertheless my executors shall deliver to my friend Henry Cuffe such of my French, Italian and Flemish books as he shall choose. My executors shall bestow before [*sic*] my death on my servants Randal, Robert, John, Eyton and Walter, 4 marks apiece and to Drury £4. The residue of my goods to my wife Frances. I make her and my son-in-law executors.

Witnesses : Henry Atkins, Henry Cuffs, W. Gall.

Proved 1 August 1597.

RICHARD HARBOROUGHE of Weald Hall in North Weald Bassett gentleman, 14 March 1597. [41/31]

To be buried in North Weald Bassett church. To Martha my wife my lease of Weald Hall and the stock of corn, cattle and household stuff, with my two leases of Weald Park and the stock of cattle there, other cattle of mine in Sheepcote Field and Gallow Mead, and 10 oxen at Richard Hopper's house in [Theydon] Mount; and a lease in reversion in Staffordshire granted to me by the Earl of Essex with £80 which my brother Miles Harboroughe oweth me, £80 which my brother Burton oweth me, and £100 which Springe of Canes [in North Weald] oweth me. To Elizabeth Burton my sister £40. To Anne Smith my sister £20. To my brother Miles £10. To the poor of North Weald £5, to be distributed at Easter next in corn at the direction of Mr Linse and the chief inhabitants. The residue to my wife, whom I make my sole executrix, and I desire Mr Edward Altham of Latton to be my overseer. Witnesses : Simon Linche [vicar of North Weald], Richard Spranger.

Proved 19 April 1597.

FRANCIS HARVYE of Cressing Temple, one of her Majesty's gentlemen pensioners, 11 February 1602. [46/40]

To be buried in the chancel of Witham church and in the same vault and under the same monument that I there made for my late wife Mary, and such obsequies and orderly observances be used at my burial as shall be meet for my calling in every condition. I will that 10 of my kinsmen or such of my good friends, gentlemen, with other that do serve me or will be present at my burial, shall have black mourning gowns or cloaks and all my other servants mourning liveries of black cloth. To such poor people as be there present in alms, men, women and children, 4d. apiece so that it amounteth not above £20. My executrix shall cause a fair white marble or touchstone tablewise 2 yards long and 3 feet broad to be set with pillars 3 foot high over the grave or vault where I shall lie with my former wife in Witham chancel, and I appoint £20 for the charges and more as it shall be thought needful. To the poor people in Witham 40s., Cressing 40s., Hatfield Peverel 10s., Ulting 5s., Terling 10s., Fairstead 5s., White Notley 13s. 4d., Black Notley 10s., Faulkbourne 5s., Rivenhall 10s., Bradwell 5s., Little Braxted 5s., Great Braxted 6s. 8d., Kelvedon 13s. 4d., the hamlet of [Little] Coggeshall 6s. 8d., and the hamlet of Chatley [in Great Leighs] 5s.

To Camilla my dear and well-beloved wife such goods as I had by her which Mr Thomas Darcy her former husband gave her; the wardship and tuition of her husband Darcy's children, Margaret Darcye, Mary Darcye, Elizabeth Darcye, Bridget Darcye and Francis Darcye, as I have them by her Majesty's grant; the lease I have by her Majesty's grant of the demesne lands in Tolleshunt D'Arcy during the minority of her children and wards; my manors of Drayton and Bringhurst and the sheep's close (Lincs.), for life, according to a deed which I made to her before our marriage; and after her decease to my only daughter and heir Elizabeth Harvie, and if my wife depart this life before my daughter is 21 my overseers shall have the manors and profits to her use till she is of age or married; and if she depart without issue to my nephew John Harvie's eldest son William and his heirs male. To Elizabeth my plate, household stuff and silver vessel, except such as I have before bequeathed to my wife, being her late husband's, provided that her mother shall have the use for life, putting in good security to my daughter (if my wife shall fortune to marry again) to deliver it to my daughter by inventory which shall be made; and if she die before her mother (not being married or 21), to my wife one half to her use and the other to my first wife's children equally to be divided. To my servingmen one whole year's wages. To my nephew and servant Robert Vasie my apparel; the annuity of £20 which I purchased of Mr Francis Newberie by deed dated 1 August 1598, which annuity is charged on the parsonage of Waltham Lawrence (Berks.); and the statute of £200 and all bonds concerning the same, which I bought purposely for him.

To Elizabeth towards her godly, virtuous and good education and bringing up and her better advancement £2,000 which I have in gold lying in my closet in Cressing Temple ready to be paid to her use, and I desire it be employed in good and lawful sort as shall be meet and fitting for a gentlewoman until she be of full age or married; and for the employment thereof I repose great trust and confidence in my wife and overseers, desiring them to have a tender and special care over her herein and also for her preferment in marriage, and I enjoin her to be directed and governed by them accordingly; provided nevertheless that £300 of the £2,000 shall be employed in stock for the help, sustentation and maintenance of my sister Ursula Vasie during her life or £30 a year. To Robert Vasie my lease of the houses which I hold of the demise of Sir Francis Flemynge knight deceased, sometime Master of the Hospital of St Katherine near the Tower of London, by indenture dated 20 February 1551; also £100. To my worshipful good friend Sir John Scudamore knight my best horse at his choice. The residue to my wife, whom I constitute my sole executrix, and I desire Sir John Scudamore and Sir William Harvie, to which Sir William I bequeath another of my best horses, to be overseers, desiring them of all loves to have due care of the bestowing of my daughter to a fit gentleman.

Witnesses : J. Scudamore, Richard Wotton scrivener, J. Giuceiardin. Signed with seal of arms. Proved 22 June 1602.

JOHN HAYES of Rettendon gentleman, 8 October 1566.   [10/15]

To be buried in Rettendon church, with a marble stone and super-scription thereupon, with my image, my wife's and my children, to be laid on my grave.

To John my son my messuage called Goodwyns in Rettendon with lands belonging in the tenure of Thomas Rawlyns, but if he die before 21 to Thomas my son. To John immediately after my decease, as soon as this crop of corn is taken, my moiety of Sowterdown, parcel of the manor of Rettendon Hall, for 60 years if he so long live, with remainder to such uses as the residue of my leaselands hereafter is by me limited. Dorothy my wife shall receive the yearly rents and profits of the residue of my messuages and lands, and my mansion house of Rettendon Hall, with my moiety of the leases of the residue of my lands belonging specified in a deed of partition thereof made between my brother George Hayes and me dated 26 September 1559 for 16 years after my decease, and with the profits educate and bring up my son Thomas in virtue and learning and my daughters Elizabeth and Hester in good nurture and pay my debts and perform my legacies; and after the expiration of the 16 years the lands and the mansion house to Thomas, yielding to my wife in recompense of her jointure 40 marks yearly; and if Thomas die without issue, to John, and for default of issue to Edward Hayes my cousin, paying to Elizabeth and Hester £100 to be equally divided; with remainder to my wife for the 60 years, paying John £10 yearly, and after decease to John and his heirs male, with remainder to my brother George's son. John Astley, John Athaye and William Fuller shall enjoy their several farms. To Elizabeth and Hester each 100 marks at 18 or marriage; if both die before, £10 each to Thomas and John at 21 and the residue to my wife. To my father-in-law Byer and his wife, my brother Henry Byre and his wife, my brother Nicholas Biere and his wife, my brother Pyncheon, my cousin Steward and his wife, my brother George, my cousins Judith and Horton, and Richard Canon, each a ring of gold with a death's head, the price of each ring 13s. 4d. Further to Henry Bire my coat of plate trimmed with red silk and silver, Nicholas Byre a colt, George my grey nag, and my cousin Henry Baker, my godson, my crossbow and rack and skene. To the rest of my godchildren each 12d.

To every servant in my house 10s., old Peter 13s. 4d. and Durrant's wife a bullock. To 10 poor housemaids in Rettendon yearly for 10 years 10s., and 5s. yearly during so many years to a preacher yearly on the day of my burial. My wife shall freely give to John competent meat and drink for 5 years after my decease. To Thomas Hastler, John Athayes and William Prentice each a felt hat price 4s. The ceilings of wainscot and all glass of my mansion house, with the furniture of the hall, viz. tables, trestles, forms, cupboards and hangings, also the copper and brewing vessels in the brewhouse, shall always remain as implements incident and annexed to the house. The residue of my goods, household stuff, napery, hangings of cloths, brass, pewter, jewels, plate, ready money, and my cattle as well horses, mares, kine, oxen, sheep, corn, and other implements of husbandry to my wife, whom I ordain my sole executrix.

Witnesses : H[enry] Bire, George Hayes, Thomas Steward, Nicholas Byre.

Proved 10 May 1567.

EDMUND HODILOWE of Kelvedon gentleman, 16 December 1586.
[31/36]

To be comely and decently buried in Kelvedon church. To my dearly beloved father in consideration of £200 which I lately had of him £10 a year for life out of the rents of my lands. To my son John my house at Witham, and my lands called Cantlings and Segmyers alias Sedmarsh in Latchingdon, Lawling and Mayland. To my daughters Anne Hodilowe £100, Katherine £40 and Mary 100 marks, and my daughter, the child newborn and yet unchristened, 100 marks, each at marriage or 20. My wife Barbara shall have the use of my lands during the minority of my two sons to the bringing up of my children and payment of my legacies, and to her my goods. To my brother Thomas a ring of gold price 40s. and to every one of my sisters a ring of gold price 15s. To Edward Tillingham my man 40s. To the repairing of Kelvedon church 4 seam of barley. I ordain my loving wife my sole executrix and my brother Thomas my overseer. Witnesses : Thomas Simson, John Upcher, William Aberford.

To Mr [Thomas] Simpson, vicar of Kelvedon, 40s. to preach five sermons within a year after my decease and for writing my will 10s. To goodwife Upcher and goodwife Waters for their pains 10s. apiece. To my father for a remembrance to make him a ring for his finger of what fashion he liketh best 40s. Provided that, if my wife shall marry again, he that shall marry her shall before marriage stand bound to Thomas my brother or my father (if he be living) in £1,000 that he shall bring up my children in the fear of God and good learning and perform my legacies. To Mr Cawston's wife 40s. Confirmed — witnesses : Matthew Causton, Thomas Simson, John Upcher.

Proved 27 June 1587. Sentence, 20 June 1587, confirming Will in case between Thomas Hodilowe and Barbara executrix.

RICHARD HOVENDEN of West Ham gentleman, 11 September 1602.
[44/65]

To be buried next to my mother at the discretion of Elizabeth my wife, whom I ordain sole executrix. I appoint my wife to be sole guardian to my two youngest daughters, Jane and Elizabeth, for their portion of my

213

lands in Norton Falgate [Middx.]. To Mary Hovenden my daughter, whereas my mother granted her £20, it shall be made £40, and to Jane and Elizabeth their portion given by my mother to be doubled, viz. £40 apiece. To Bret's wife 40s. to buy her a ring in remembrance of me. To John Jacson £5 and his wife 40s. to buy her a ring. To be delivered to the poor in bread 20s. The residue of my goods to my wife. I appoint Henry Sacheverell and John Jacson my overseers, and for their pains 20s. apiece. To John Harrison my best cloak and Richard Roberts my other cloak. Witness: Nicholas Boorman the writer.

To Robert Picking my fustian hose and doublet. To Henry Sacheverell, my father-in-law, my best nag. Witnesses: John Harrison, Pernell Sacheverell, Henry Sacheverell, John Jacson.

Proved 27 October 1602.

JOHN HOWE of South Ockendon gentleman, 17 April 1591.   [35/74]

Whereas I have by deed conveyed to Martha my well-beloved wife my lease of a messuage or inn called the Rose in Smithfield in London and divers messuages in St John Zacharias and St Thomas the Apostles for her jointure, she shall have them for life; and in augmentation of her jointure and for her better maintenance and good bringing up of our children I give her my capital messuage where I dwell in South Ockendon and my lands there which I purchased of [blank] Cotton of London gentleman, also my messuages in St Giles-without-Cripplegate in London for life; the remainder to my heirs, provided that, if she shall die before any my heir male is 21, to her executors and assigns until he is 21, the profits to be faithfully employed on my two daughters Martha and Mary equally for their better preferments in marriage or otherwise; if either die before, to Thomas my son or any other my heir male, and for default of such issue to my sister's children equally. If my son William shall disturb my wife in the quiet holding of any of the messuages conveyed for her jointure, she shall have my messuages in St Giles. My possession for many years to come of sundry messuages in Christchurch in London after the death of my wife shall remain to Thomas. The residue of my goods to my wife, whom I make my sole executrix. Witnesses: George Drywood smith, Gabriel Sparrowe, Davy Hancock.

Proved 16 October 1591.

WILLIAM HUMAYNE *alias* Rutter of Clavering gentleman, 6 August 1566.   [9/24]

To be buried in Clavering church.

To my son-in-law William Barlee my tablet which I bought of my cousin Wodham. To my sister Rutter 20s. To the poor people of Clavering 40s. of that which I am charged to pay in charitable deeds for Mr Crowley. To the curate of Clavering for my tithes negligently forgotten 3s. 4d.

To Barbara Bradburie which serveth me 10s. To my brother Stringer 10s. of that which I am charged to pay for Mr Crowley's charity. To my daughter-in-law Grace Serle 40s. and her husband 20s. of that which he oweth me. To William Taylour my servant 40s., John Herde 10s., and my cousin Lawrence Wodham £5, of that which I am charged to pay of Mr Crowley's alms. To Lawrence also the best gown I have at London. To my sons-in-law Thomas Wilbore my damask cassock and the sleeves of taffeta which belong to it and Philip Wilbore my Norwich worsted gown. To my brothers John of Anstey [Herts.] and Richard my two other gowns. To Thomas Dellowe my best coat saving one and to my servant William Taylor my old cloak. The residue of my goods, crop, corn, stock and household stuff to my executrix towards the performance of my will.

Touching such money as I am bound to distribute in alms for Mr Crowley deceased and in my hands, my executrix in satisfaction shall distribute £100 in charitable deeds at the assignment of master parson of Heydon and my sons-in-law Mr Bell of Writtle and William Barlee. I constitute Philippa my well-beloved wife my sole executrix, and Mr [William] Sheperd, parson of Heydon, supervisor, and for his pains 20s. My wife shall distribute 40s. to the poor people of Chrishall, Elmdon 26s. 8d., Newport 40s., and Langley 20s., all for Mr Crowley's alms which shall be accounted for as part of the £100.

Witnesses: William Barley, William Sheperd, Thomas Cloughe, Andrew Glascock.

Proved: 24 September 1566.

WILLIAM HUNWICKE of Halstead gentleman, 15 November 1569.
[12/24]

To be buried with such funerals and exequies as shall be thought meet by my executors respecting my ability.

To Joan my well-beloved wife and John my son, my executors, my goods and jewels, the lease of the parsonage of Halstead and the leases of the lands in Lincolnshire and of the parsonage of Stebbing only excepted; with this condition that, if she shall not, after being required by my son William or by my well-beloved kinsman John Hunwicke of Colchester, my kinsman Andrew Byat of Sudbury [Suffolk] or Allen Hamme my servant and kinsman, enter into bonds to prove my will, John my son, and the others, shall be my executors. To every of my sisters £3 6s. 8d. and to every of their children 20s. at marriage or 21.

To the poor people of Halstead and other parishes adjoining at the day of my burial £6 13s. 4d. to be distributed in my house among them that shall take pains in my sickness and funerals. To every poor householder in Halstead that liveth upon alms 3s. 4d., and if they be of my kin to have four loads of wood also of my pollinger wood. The farmer of my manor of Boyes [in Halstead] shall during seven years after my decease on New Year's and Midsummer Days bestow 20s. at a time of the rent on a dinner for relieving so many of the poor folk as conveniently it will suffice by the discretion of my executors and my supervisor.

To the said John Hunwicke of Colchester merchant, Andrew Byat gentleman, John Hunwicke of Halstead yeoman, and Allen Hamme my manor and lands to the use following that, if my plate, debts and other goods to my wife and John my son do not discharge my will, my said devisees shall be seised of one part of my said manor of Boyes alias Dynes and of my lands called Prynters, Long Croft, Water Croft and Snowdon Croft, my house in London, my marsh called Russhenes and my lands in Stebbing, and my lands in Lincolnshire, to the use of my executors until they shall receive so much of the revenues as may perform the residue of my will; and then to the use of my wife and John until William is 21; and then my feoffees shall stand seised of my manors to the use of William and his heirs male on condition that, if he decease without such issue, to John my son and his heirs male, and for default of such issue successively to the child which my wife is now withal if a male and his heirs male, and to all my daughters, i.e. Margaret, Parnell, Philippa and the child that my wife is withal if a female and their heirs male, and to the heirs of William.

Whereas I am possessed of the lease of the parsonage of Halstead and a lease of certain lands in Quadring and Gosberton (Lincs.) and of the lease of the parsonage of Stebbing and the manor of Friars Hall there, I give them to my devisees to the use of John and his heirs male, and in default of such issue successively to his heirs female, to my child that my wife is withal if a male, and if a female to my said daughters and their issue male, and to the next issue of William.

I require my children, as they will avoid the plague of God that happeneth to disobedient children, to be ruled in their bringing up and in their marriage by my wife; and if she die before they are married then by John Hammond of Colchester, John Hammond of Halstead the elder, Andrew Byate and Allen Hamme. To every of my daughters £66 13s. 4d. at marriage if they marry not before 18 and marry afterward by the said consent. To Ede Hunwicke late my servant £10. To every of my other servants that have dwelt with me for a whole year 20s. and to them that have not 10s. To every godchild 2s. 6d.

To Allen Ham for 7 years after my decease out of my lands in Halstead £6 13s. 4d. if he be some lawyer's clerk or shall live in the Inns of the Chancery or court at his book, whereof 20 nobles at his entering thereunto and £3 6s. 8d. half-yearly after, and in the meantime he be kept at school in Halstead. To Thomas Turnor my houses and land in Lincolnshire for 6 years after the teste [date] of my will.

If my wife shall not willingly bind herself in £200 to my devisees to prove my will, my cousin John Hunwicke of Colchester, my cousin Byate, Allen Ham and my son John shall be my executors, and if every of them do refuse my cousin Thomas Hunwicke that was my servant shall be my executor with my son John, for since that neither of them, if they mean truly and honestly to do for me cannot be my cousins by being my executors, for my debts that I owe be not above £100, whereof £40 I owe to Mr Alstone, £10 to John Prentice, £10 to my brother Bell and £50 to my cousin Hunwicke of Colchester, and towards that I have £40 in ready money and £125 owing me for 200 marks by Mr Bull. Thomas Hunwycke shall have the sale of my 46 steers in the park so long as there shall be no untrustiness showed of his part, and to have for his labour 40s., and every of my executors £3 6s. 8d. I make my brother Bell my supervisor. To my wife my lease of the parsonage of Stebbing and the park till John is 21.

The residue of my goods to my wife and all my children equally to be **divided.**

[No witnesses.]

Codicil [undated]. To Hardinge 5 marks and Chote 40s., Bragge a bullock the price 24s. and pasture for a year, Westwood a bullock price 24s. and keeping for a year, and Stevyns 10s. To Mr Cornewell £5 on condition that he shall do me no hurt as touching Stebbing and deliver me the counterpane [counterpart deed] of Tiffin's bargain, Jane Cornewell his daughter 20s., Susanna 20s., Westwood's wife 6s. 8d., Thomas Barker's wife 6s. 8d., Langleye 26s. 8d. and his dwelling till Our Lady Day, other debts discharged. To my wife my best gelding and the next, that only excepted which is at Knightes. To my cousin Thomas Hunwick which is at Knightes. To mother Paige 6s. 8d. and her dwelling till Our Lady Day. To John Hunwick £4 on condition he release his right in the house that Tokeley dwelleth in. To my wife's brother and sister each one genewe of gold price 3s. 4d. To all my kinsfolk that can prove themselves to be of my kin each 5s. To John Stenors 6s. 8d., Katherine the joiner's wife 3s. 4d., William Vigorous a porkling, and Edward Nottingham 10s. Sansom shall have a lease of his house for 11 years, paying 6s. a year. To Lyngwood a ring price 3s. 4d. and William Vegres 5s.

Proved 7 December 1569.

NICHOLAS HUNTE of Loughton gentleman, 22 May 1569.   [13/3]

I devise the two parts of my manors and lands in three equal parts to be divided whereof I am seised of any estate of inheritance to Jane my wife for life towards the maintenance of herself and of our children, with successive remainders to Edmund and Richard my sons for life, then to Paul my son and his heirs male, and for default of such issue successively to Edmund and his heirs male and to Richard. To my wife for life my goods and leases such as I have in Loughton, except a lease called Cockthorpe Hall in Norfolk which I devise to Jeffrey Hunte my brother. The profits of my leases lying out of Loughton other than Cockthorpe Hall to my executors towards the payment of my debts and legacies. I make my wife and my brother and my three sons my executors. To every of my wife's daughters £16 13s. 4d., besides their father's legacies, at marriage. To my daughter Jane £200 at marriage. Witness : Edward Baber.

Proved 1 February 1570.

WILLIAM HUNTE of Great Totham gentleman, 15 May 1598.
[42/45]

Whereas I have made an assurance of a tenements and lands in both Tothams in the occupations of John Felsteed and Richard Wythers, also of certain lands and tenements called Borowe Marsh and Borowe Hills with all fishings, weirs and other profits belonging, to Katherine my loving wife for life, the reversion and remainder of Borowe Marsh after her decease to William my son and the residue thereof to Richard my son. To her my lands called Sowriers containing 10 acres in both the Tothams for life. Although my eldest son Thomas is joint purchaser with me of my capital messuage and lands called Fryerne in Great and Little Totham, he shall permit her to use the messuage, orchard and garden until he is 26 without paying anything therefor. To her and her heirs my house and orchard called Newemans and 8 acres belonging in Little Totham, in consideration whereof she hath faithfully promised to see my youngest daughter Agnes brought up and provided for, by reason whereof I do not give anything of value to Agnes. Whereas I am tenant and farmer to the Queen's Majesty of certain lands and tenements in [Great] Tey, Wakes Colne, [Mount] Bures and Springfield, the same shall be immediately sold and the money to be towards the portions of my three daughters. To my wife my plate and jewels, the chairs and stools which I had from my Lady Petre, the best featherbed, the best linen, her own apparel and furniture for horses, a featherbed for her servant, 10 of my best kine and 20 of my best ewes such as she shall choose, the Upper Field sowed with wheat and half the barley field, and my bay gelding and my best grey mare.

To every of my daughters a featherbed. To Ellen Hunt and Margaret Hunt, my two eldest daughters, each 100 marks, and to Mary my daughter £20, if after my debts and legacies to my wife are satisfied the residue of my goods will amount to so much; and if not then to those three daughters so much proportionably abating of their portions. I require Thomas to give allowance to my two younger sons until they shall be bound as apprentices if they will be so bound, and to see them bound to such trades in London as are fit for them at his charges, which I lay upon him in regard that I have to my extraordinary charge brought him up in learning at the university and elsewhere and that he is joint purchaser of my house and part of my lands and thereby I am the more disabled to provide for my younger sons. I ordain my wife sole executrix, and I most humbly beseech the right worshipful Sir John Peter knight that it will please him to be the protector and overseer of my will.

Witnesses: John Wright and Reginald Bretland.

Proved 20 May 1598.

JOHN INCENT of East Ham gentleman, 10 November 1588. [33/13]

Towards the reparations of East Ham church 20s., whereof one half of the 20s. to the poor of the parish. To Elizabeth my wife my goods and leases, she performing my will; and she shall pay Andrew Norborne in satisfaction of my debts £12 10s. To her 3 acres of marsh being freehold at Wall End in East Ham for life, and after to William Hollidaye of London merchant, Thomas Redman of London notary public, and Zachary Jones of West Ham gentleman, to the use following, viz. to the heirs of Matthew Incent the younger, my son, in discharge of legacies bequeathed to him by Thomas Blackmore of London. Whereas Arthur Bell standeth bound with me to Edward Elliott of East Ham yeoman for payment of £3 6s. 8d. on 20 December next, my wife shall discharge Bell. She shall pay Thomas Ward, late of East Ham weaver, 15s. and Basil Dighton of London skinner, 56s. 6d., which Bell standeth charged withal, and her brother Ambrose Barker £6 which I owe him. The wainscot and ceilings of my dwelling house at East Ham shall remain continually to the use of such persons as I have by surrender appointed to enjoy the house. To Bell my servant for his wages past £3. I make my wife sole executrix and for overseers Ambrose Barker of East Ham gentleman, my son-in-law, and Zachary Jones. Witnesses : John Payton curate there, Zachary Jones, Ambrose Barker, Andrew Norborne, Arthur Bell the writer, Maud Walker.

Proved 7 December 1588. Administration granted, 28 January 1601, to Dorothy Jones *alias* Incent, daughter of the deceased.

EDWARD JERHAM of Maldon gentleman, 24 March 1582.   [25/26]

To the poor of the three parishes in Maldon £4 to be equally divided. To Mary my wife my lands called Bishops Castle Field alias Castle Croft in Maldon and those called Maschalls and Smyths alias Ivotts in Woodham Mortimer and Hazeleigh, for life; those called Bacons in Woodham Mortimer and Hazeleigh after the death of Joan Coker widow, my grandmother, for life; also the yearly profits of my lease of Bacons during my grandmother's life, and after my wife's decease to Edward my son, and if he decease before her the lease shall remain to such other my son as shall be then living. To Edward my lands, freehold and copyhold, in Essex other than such as I have before conveyed or in my will have given to my wife, together with the reversion and remainder; and for default of issue of Edward before 21 and of myself, after the decease of my wife, the remainder of my lands in Bradwell and Steeple to my cousin Mary wife of Abel Clark; that of my lands in St Lawrence to John the elder son of John Sammes of Langford gentleman; that of Bacons and Smyths alias Ivotts to John the younger son of John Sammes of Langford; that of my lands in Woodham Ferrers and Maldon to Edward Anderkin my kinsman; that of Mascalls to William Lovedaye; and that of my lands in Latchingdon and Lawling to my aunt Stammer's children. Nevertheless if my wife be now with child with a man child, after my grandmother's decease he shall have yearly £10 out of the profits of my lands which shall descend to Edward presently during the life of Peter Jerham my father and Jane his wife, and after the decease of the longer liver to such man child now in my wife's womb £20 yearly for life; and if it be a daughter £100 after my grandmother's decease and £5 yearly until marriage or 21. To Edward £40 at 21. To Henry Spacye my servant £5 and to every other of my servants 6s. 8d. The residue of my goods to my wife, whom I ordain my sole executrix, and John Sammes my father-in-law my overseer. Witnesses : George Gyfford, John Locke, Richard Williams, Theophilus Lancashere, Thomas Chesse.

Proved 27 June 1582.

JOHN KENT of Little Bardfield gentleman, 16 May 1585.   [29/51]

To my wife my lands in Little Bardfield, Great Bardfield and Shalford for life, and after to Andrew my son, as well that in lease as the other lands. To my son John my houses and lands in Bocking. To Mary, Frances and Anne my daughters each 100 marks at 21 or at my wife's appointment. The residue of my goods to my wife, whom I make my sole executrix, and she shall have the profits and rents of my lands towards the payment of my debts and legacies and the education of my children and until Andrew is 30. Witnesses: Charles Cardinall, Henry Colte, Robert Allyn.

Proved 20 October 1585.

RICHARD KIRBYE of Henham gentleman, 14 April 1590.   [34/59]

Being very aged, I give all my goods to Mary my well-beloved wife, hoping that she will have a motherly consideration of my children, and I ordain her sole executrix. Witnesses: Thomas Newce, John Clarcke.

Proved 30 September 1590. Administration granted, 18 February 1595, to Thomas son of the deceased.

BRIAN KYNNISTONE of St Osyth gentleman, 5 October 1602.
[47/34]

To be buried in St Osyth's church. To Thomas Kinystonne a brown pot tipped and footed with silver, £15, my greatest joined chest, and my trotting roan colt being two years old and the vantage. To my son Edward a pot tipped with silver which I promised to give him, £15, a joined chest next in bigness to the biggest, and my black roan gelding. The residue of my goods to Cassandra my wife, whom I ordain my sole executrix. Witnesses: J. Wakline, Thomas Jefferie. [Signs 'Kinaston'.]

Proved 4 May 1603.

RICHARD KYNWELMARSHE the elder of Great Dunmow gentleman, 1 October 1574.   [18/18]

To be buried in Great Dunmow church or churchyard.

To my executors my lands leased to William Longe, Nicholas Moyne, Thomas Bowde, George Deane, Thomas Edwick and William Barker, all of Great Dunmow, being parcels of my ground pertaining to the site and manor of Newton Hall [in Great Dunmow], until payment be made of my legacies. To Thomas Kynwelmarshe my son £3, Richard my son £3, Katherine Gosnoll my daughter 40s., and Jane Kynwelmarshe my daughter 40s., all yearly for life. To Philippa my wife out of the said lands £10 for life in recompense of her third or dower and of my lands in Derbyshire. My son Andrew shall receive to his own use my annuity or fee farm rent due to me out of my manor of Long Eaton [Derbys.] for the maintenance of his study in the University of Cambridge and not otherwise, and he shall enjoy the same until he be preferred and advanced to a benefice of the value of £20 a year by my son Robert or any other person, immediately after which the annuity shall remain to Robert and his heirs male, and in default of such issue successively to Andrew, Katherine, Jane, and to Richard Kynwelmarshe my brother's son of St Osyth, and their heirs male, and in default to the next heir male of that name. So long as she keepeth herself a widow, my wife shall have her dwelling at Newton Hall, i.e. two chambers and one cellar at the east part of the manor house and a closet in the hall for her thirds of the manor house, and the use of the kitchen with her necessary firewood. To Robert my son my manor of Newton Hall with the demesne, rents and services belonging except before bequeathed, also a tenement called Bartlemewe Tylers with the lands belonging in my occupation in Dunmow, and to his heirs male, and for default of such issue successively to Thomas, Richard, Andrew, Katherine and Jane. The tables and forms in the hall shall remain with the manor of Newton Hall for ever. I give to the manor for the service of the Prince, whensoever the same shall be charged, my armour, i.e. 1 corselet, 2 almain rivets, 1 jack, 1 caliver, 1 hagbut with flasks and touch boxes, 1 sword, 1 dagger, 1 black bill, 1 bow and a sheaf of arrows. Robert or any of my other sons to whom it shall please God my manor shall remain shall not fell any timber other than for reparations or their firebote, gatebote, cartbote and ploughbote. To my wife, in consideration she claim no dower of any of the lands that I have sold, one half of my goods and household stuff that are unbequeathed, she paying Jane £20, but not until £20 be paid to William Glascoke of Dunmow gentleman which I owe him by obligation, and my wife shall put in good surety to my brother Christopher Scotte of Barnston for the payment, and he shall have the use of the £20 until Jane is 21 or at marriage. To Robert the other half of my goods, he paying Jane £20 [as above]. To Richard my lease of Park Land of the demise of the Queen's Majesty.

Of such overplus of rent as cometh into my executors' hands yearly from my lands which is 40s., one half to the poor people of Great Dunmow for 20 years to be distributed by the vicar and churchwardens and the other 20s. to be bestowed on reparations of my manor house yearly.

To my brother Humfrey Kynwelmarshe 13s. 4d. yearly for life. I ordain him and Thomas and Robert, two of my sons, executors, and I appoint John Holland gentleman and William Longe overseers.

Witnesses : John Holland, Christopher Scotte, William Longe, Ralph Smith.

Proved 6 May 1575.

MILES LAKIN of Ardleigh gentleman, 14 November 1598.   [43/1]

To be buried in decent sepulture according to my calling. To 6 honest householders to carry my body to the church 12d. apiece. To the parishioners 40s. towards the maintenance of the stock for deeds of charity.

To Mary my daughter the fourth part of my goods (my leases excepted) at 21 or marriage, and if she die before to remain to all the children of my daughter Griselda Overed, part and part like, at 21 or marriage. To Mary my leases of my houses and gardens in St Martin-in-the-Fields (Middx.), with the glass, casements, wainscots, ceilings and other screens which were set up by me at my costs and which she may take away lawfully at the end of the terms or before; and if she die before to Margaret my well-beloved wife, but she shall have the occupation and profits of my chief house where I lately dwelt in St Martin so long as she shall keep herself widow, paying Ronninges' children yearly 40s. and the Earl of Bedford 14s. for my part of the garden plot. My wife shall have the letting of all my houses until Mary is 21 or marry. The other three quarters of my goods to my wife, whom I make my sole executrix. She shall have Mary's portion until 21 or marriage, bringing her up at her own charge without impairing her stock and putting in good bonds to my supervisor to pay her portion when due. To my wife my chief mansion house in Ardleigh as it is furnished with lead, fixed glass, irons, locks, keys, doors, windows, boards nailed, vessels of lead, fixed couching dressers, wainscot, ceilings, portals, and screens, as also my other copyhold and freehold lands in Ardleigh, Dedham and Langham, for life; to remain to Mary and her heirs, and for default of issue to Griselda for life, with successive remainders to Thomasine Overed, to Mary Ferris daughter of my nephew Mr Henry Ferris, and to Dorothy Ferris her sister.

To my godchildren 6s. 8d. apiece (they be not many). To John Whettle, my late servant, certain law books whereof I have double and in the beginning of every which book I have written with my own hand 'To John Whettle'.

I ordain my worshipful good friends John Ive of Rivers Hall [in Boxted] esquire and Mr Edmund Churche of Ardleigh gentleman and my good friend John Stevens the elder of Ardleigh yeoman to be my supervisors, and to each for their labour 20s. to make a ring of gold, requesting them to have my name engraven in the inside and to be good friends to my wife that she be not spoiled by her evil children. To Mr Ive my regals and Mr Edmund Churche my little lute for one of his children. To Mr John Stephens the elder my musket. If my wife die before Mary is 21 and unmarried, my supervisors shall have the custody of Mary and her lands to bring her up in virtue, yielding to her a reasonable account. Yet if my wife by sinister counsel shall refuse to prove my will, my legacies to her shall be void and she shall have only her dower of my freehold lands and half of my goods (except my leases), the residue to Mary, and I then discharge my wife of her executorship and ordain Mary my sole executrix.

Witnesses : Lawrence Lide the younger, the writer hereof, Lawrence Lyde the elder, vicar of Ardleigh, Thomas Ferres, John Stephen.

Proved 19 January 1599. Sentence, 13 November 1601, confirming Will in case between (1) Mary Lakin *alias* Whetle, daughter and legatee, and (2) Margaret Lakin executrix, and Philip Lakin, Griselda Lakin *alias* Overed and Margaret Lakin *alias* Hedges, children of the deceased.

THOMAS LANCASTER of Finchingfield gentleman, 30 March 1581.
[24/31]

To Mary my wife the lease of the farm that I now dwell in and the copyhold land which I purchased of Henry Hearington in Finchingfield, for life, and after to John my son. To my sons Matthew my lands in Ousden (Suffolk), John £73 13s. 4d., Matthew £53 6s. 8d., and Thomas £60, and my daughter Anne £20 and my daughter Marcus [sic] £20, all at 21. The residue of my goods to my wife, whom I constitute executrix, and Matthew Lancaster my brother supervisor. Witnesses : Thomas Smythe, Matthew Lancaster, Agnes Smythe.
Proved 16 November 1581.

THOMAS LARDGE of Borley gentleman, 5 December 1574.   [21/20]

To be buried in the next church or churchyard where I shall happen to end this my mortal life. To the help of the church there 6s. 8d. To the poor there £5. To William Lardge my brother 20 marks and one of my cloth gowns, and if he be dead all shall be bestowed in deeds of charity as my executrix shall see most need. To every of my menservants their year's wages and to every womanservant 13s. 4d. To Mistress Katherine Waldegrave and Mistress Waldegrave [sic] a gilt spoon for a poor remembrance and to Nicholas Waldegrave 2 of my best silver spoons parcel gilt. The residue of my goods to Elizabeth my wife, whom I make my sole executrix, and I desire Mr Roger Martyn to be supervisor, and for his pains 40s. and my quilted doublet of black satin. Witness : Francis Powlett.
Proved 10 May 1578.

ELIZABETH LARGE of Borley, widow of Thomas, 28 August 1589.
[35/55]

To be buried in Borley churchyard as near to my husband as conveniently it may be. To the poor people of Borley £6. To my trusty and loving friend William Bragg of Smeton Hall in Bulmer yeoman my copyhold house in Borley and the lands free and copy belonging, on condition that he pay me in my lifetime £100 and Thomas Powlett esquire £40, and shall permit John Gouldinge, my servant and tenant, to hold the same (the lower parlour and the chamber within only excepted) for 3 years after my decease if the custom of the manor will permit, without paying anything for it but the out rents due for the premises only, and shall keep the house and barns in good reparations. To Thomas Powlett a post bedstead and a painted picture of Our Lady. To my brother Lancelot Baker 40s. To my sister Thomasine Hill 40s. and my best gown. To Peter Baker's children 40s. to be divided part and part like. To my goddaughter Mary wife of Michael Ford 20s. To my late servant Margaret Haveringe 20s. To that maidservant of mine who dwelleth with me at the time of my death £6 13s. 4d. To Thomas Tynker, servant to Roger Marten esquire, 6s. 8d. The residue of my goods shall be sold towards the payment of my funerals and legacies and the overplus to be given in deeds of charity. I ordain William Bragge sole executor and Thomas Powlet, John Clerke and William Greene overseers, and to Clerke and Greene 2 old angels apiece. Witnesses : Edmund Clerke, John Clerke, William Greene, John Goldinge.

Proved 31 July 1591.

JOHN LATIMER of St Nicholas, Colchester, gentleman, 30 March 1575. (Nuncupative.)   [18/20]

To be buried in St Giles's church, Colchester, by his late wife.

Whereas Mr Price of Tendring did owe him £26 15s., viz. on a bill £10 15s., an obligation £8, and two letters and a piece of plate £8, he willed that his cousin Latimer, who then as he said kept with Mr Cockinge, should have £18 of the debt. To his sister Wainwright of London a black gown. To his kinswoman, Thumblethorp's wife of Manningtree, a velvet hat which was his late wife's. To John Vale sometime servant 10s. To the wife of Thomas Buxton of Colchester 40s. and a gold ring and a red stone, and Thomas Buxton a cloak cloth of fine black and a sapphire stone. To William brother of Thomas and to Mary Buxton his sister 20s. between them and his apparel. To Nicholas Wildbore a sealing ring of gold. To the poor of Colchester 40s., to be given to those whom Thomas Buxton shall think good. He confessed to be greatly in debt to Thomas and willed him first to satisfy himself. The residue of his goods and his own debts owing, which as he said did not amount above 10s. 8d., to Thomas, and he thereof to give at his own discretion and pleasure to his sister's daughter what he thought good, and made him his executor. Witnesses : Nicholas Wildbore, Thomas Palyfoote, William Buxton, Rachel Buxton, with others.

Proved 13 May 1575.

ROBERT LAWSON *alias* Edmondes of Prittlewell gentleman, 6 October 1577.   [32/18]

To be buried in the chancel of Prittlewell church as nigh to the place where my late wife lieth buried as conveniently as may be. During 40 years after my decease there shall be yearly paid out of the rents from my copyhold lands in Prittlewell £4 to the churchwardens and collectors for the poor and by them distributed among the poor.

To John Lawson alias Edmondes alias Celye my son an annuity of £3 6s. 8d. out of my freehold lands in Great Wakering. To Margery Celye, daughter of Nicholas Celye gentleman deceased, my wife, my messuages and lands freehold and copyhold (except my freehold lands in South Shoebury) for life; if she fortune to marry again, for 11 years only after my decease, on condition that she shall keep and bring up at her own charges my son Henry Lawson alias Edmondes alias Cely until 21 and shall by deed release her right of dower. To my said son my freehold lands in South Shoebury. To John and Henry each £500 at 21, if the same may be raised out of my goods and my farms.

224

To my wife my stock of cattle on my farm in Great Wakering, and my farm called Rugworth in the isle of Foulness, she paying to Richard Ceyle my brother-in-law for 6 years after my decease £10. To my wife and Robert Lawson alias Edmondes alias Celye my son my silver plate equally between them. To her my household stuff in and about my dwelling house in Prittlewell and the wick house there, except corn and implements of husbandry and a featherbed which I give to Robert, and an annuity of £4 if she continue a widow. My executor shall yearly for the term of my lease of the manor of Prittlewell deliver to her for the provision of her household and family out of the profits of the manor 12 quarters of wheat white or red and 15 quarters of barley, every quarter to contain 8 bushels at the least, 5 quarters of oats and 5 quarters of hens' meat or offcorn of the said measure, and 20 crone ewes, the ewes to be delivered yearly within 14 days before or after Michaelmas; if she marry again, this gift shall cease. She shall peaceably have her dwelling with sufficient corn, malt and other provision necessary for her and such family as she shall keep within my mansion house of Prittlewell from the day of my decease until Michaelmas following. To her 7 milch kine good and profitable, 40 ewe sheep and 2 geldings, one for herself and the other for her man. To William Tilford my son-in-law my interest in those parcels of ground called Graunce belonging to the manor of Prittlewell, by virtue of my lease of the manor; also the lease of the tenement called Pottmans in Prittlewell, paying yearly £3 and discharging the quitrents and tithes and not to fell any timber trees on the tenement nor cut any bushes in Cloddes Mead. I freely forgive him all debts due to me on condition that he leave the house which he holdeth and lately did dwell in at Milton [in Prittlewell] in good reparations. He may have my lease of Prittlewell Priory at a reasonable rent (except it shall please my brother John Celye to have and dwell upon it himself), reserving out of the demise the bushes for repairing marsh walls. To Robert son of William Tylford 100 marks at 21; if he die before, the 100 marks with £33 6s. 8d. amounting to £100 shall be paid to Anne Tylford my daughter, wife of William; and if Robert die before 12, the £100 be paid to Anne within 4 years after he should have been 12.

To William £10, Edward £30, Nicholas £10, and Elizabeth Drywood £20, the children of William Drywood and Elizabeth his late wife, my daughter, at 24; and if Elizabeth marry before, at 21. £160 which I am to have of my brother John Celye for my interest in the farm of Little Haye, with £40 more, be given to Mary Lawson alias Edmondes, daughter of my late son William Lawson alias Edmondes, at the Feast of the Annunciation of the Blessed Virgin Mary in 1590, on condition that Edward Bode gentleman and Frances his wife shall not claim any legacy. To Joan, Alice and Margaret Sansom, children of John Sansom deceased, £20 among them. To Margaret Sansom my sister an annuity of £5 for 10 years after my decease. To James Sawmon £10. To my servants, men and women, 20s. apiece. To one Leper's wife, my sister's daughter, £5. To the right honourable and my singular good lady, the Lady Penelope Riche, 20 angels in gold. To the Lady Elizabeth Riche,

225

my very good lady and mistress, £20 out of such debts as her honour oweth me. To Richard Celye my wife's brother £100.

To the relief of the poor people in Great Wakering £20 and Southminster £20, i.e. 40s. for 10 years. To the reparations of Prittlewell church £40 as need shall require. My executor shall pay the £5 which was committed into my hands by the gift of John Cocke late deceased for the setting up of a cross in the town of Prittlewell. If it shall happen that Hull Bridge [in Hockley] be set up and made again in good order with stone and lime, as heretofore it was, I give £100 to be paid £20 yearly for 5 years.

William Hodson shall keep the bailiwick which he hath during my lease of the manor of Prittlewell; also £6 yearly until my son Robert is 21 in consideration of his writing of accounts about the stocks and doings for my children and for his other pains. The residue of my goods and leases, cattle, corn and other things unbequeathed to Robert, whom I ordain my sole executor. My trusty and well-beloved brother-in-law John Celye to have the custody, bringing up and rule of Robert until 21, making a just account, and to John £10 yearly for his great pains. I make my trusty and loving friends John Catcher, now sheriff of London, Robert Cotton of the Queen's Majesty's Wardrobe, John Cooke of Rochford and Edward Bode of Canewdon gentlemen my overseers, to whom I allow 40s. apiece yearly.

Witnesses: John Bonner, Barnabas Barker, William Johnes.

Proved 8 March 1588.

Administration granted, 6 February 1589, to Margery widow of the deceased during the minority of Robert. Proved 28 January 1600 by Robert being of age.

PETER LEGAT of Aveley gentleman, being sick. (Nuncupative.)
[46/15]

Memorandum that about three weeks before Easter 1599 he gave all that he had to Magdalen Sadler and made her his sole executrix. Witnesses: Thomas Dawes, Mary Seamer and Magdalen Sadler.

Proved 5 February 1602. Sentence, 5 February 1602, confirming Will in case between John Legat and Margaret Legat *alias* Sadler, widow of the deceased.

THOMAS LEIGH of Loughton gentleman, 31 January 1571. [17/28]

To my eldest daughter Mary the lease of a tenement in Augustine Friars in the city of London wherein I dwell after the decease of her mother, my wife; if Mary die without issue the lease to be divided between her two sisters Margaret and Lucy. To Mary £100 at marriage. To Margaret the lease of half of Hatfeldes in Loughton held of the Queen's Majesty, with the stock of cattle, corn and implements of household at 20 or marriage, which my wife shall possess until then; if Margaret decease before without issue, to Lucy; and if likewise, to Mary. To Margaret 100 marks at marriage. To Lucy my youngest daughter my lease of St John's Mill in Horsey Down (Surrey) at marriage, with the rents between my death and her marriage except £10 yearly to be allowed to her mother for finding her in meat, drink and apparel. To Lucy £100 at marriage. Provided that my wife shall have the leases if she keep herself unmarried. £30 to be bestowed on my burial, whereof my brothers Partridge and Mariot and their wives and my brother Hamonde's wife to have a mourning gown. To Dorothy wife of my brother Hamonde 12d. a week for life. To Hugh Chadsey my tailor my gown faced with wolves' skins. To Sir William Poullet a complete harness, desiring him to be good to my wife and children, and to my Lady his wife a gold ring with a Turkey stone wound about with snakes. The residue of my goods to Anne my wife, whom I make my executrix. Witnesses : Hugh Chadsey, Henry Evans the writer, Margaret Chadsey.

Proved 19 June 1574. Administration granted, 14 May 1575, to Thomas Mariott of the Inner Temple, London, esquire, and Dorothy his wife, and Anne, Margaret and Lucy Ligh, daughters of the deceased, during the minority. [In margin : Leigh arms—2 bars.]

ABRAHAM LENS [LEUS?] of Ulting gentleman, 12 April 1596.

[41/95]

To Julian my well-beloved wife my lands free and copy in the city of London and Essex for life, and after her decease to John my son and his heirs male, and for want of such issue successively to Isaac and to Francis my sons and their heirs male. To John my leases in Berkshire likewise. To Isaac, Francis, Elizabeth, Susan and Mary my daughters such gifts as I have set down in writing remaining with my wife, whom I make my sole executrix. The residue of my goods to my wife. Forasmuch as I am called upon into her Majesty's service very suddenly, and I have no further consideration to surrender my copyhold lands according to the customs, I humbly desire the lords of the manors to admit my wife. Witnesses : Thomas Ive, John Whitacres, Thomas Sollers, John Lens [Leus?], Thomas Yonge.

Memorandum, 30 May 1597, whereas I wrote that, being called in her Majesty's service so as I could not surrender the copyhold lands at Easter last a year past, but afore my going this last voyage I had surrendered them, and whereas I mention in my will that I give my children certain portions that I have set down in writing, I give Elizabeth, Susan and Mary each £100 at marriage, also I leave the portions to Isaac and Francis to the discretion of my wife, who I do not doubt but will bestow on them to her power. If it should happen (which God forbid) that any of my daughters should marry without their mother's consent, they shall be void of this gift.

Proved 25 November 1597.

JOHN LOCKE of Langford gentleman, 21 May 1597.   [41/47]

To my two sons Lawrence and Thomas my messuage and lands called Steedes, with the orchards, gardens, lands, meadows, pastures, woods and moors belonging in Langford and Great Totham; nevertheless I give out of the yearly rents to John Wade my servant £10. I earnestly require Thomas Chese of Maldon scrivener, according to the trust I have reposed in him, that when he shall be required he shall convey to Lawrence and Thomas the lands in Stock and Buttsbury which he holdeth by copy of court roll of the manor of Blunts in Stock. I order Lawrence and Thomas to pay my funeral charges and debts, and in consideration thereof I give them my goods and household stuff to be equally divided, and I make them executors. Whereas I have at my great costs and travail planted an orchard at Steedes whereby the lands are become of the greater price and value to [be] sold, I require my sons, with the advice and consent of my good friend John Sammes of Witham Hall esquire and Thomas Chese, to put to sale to the most advantage of my sons my lands in Langford and Great Totham, and the money raised I require them to lay out in the purchase to my sons of two annuities of equal value for 21 years. Witnesses: John Nashe, Thomas Wells, John Clerke, Thomas Chese, John Wade.

To my brother-in-law William Soan £20. To Allen Paine and Sarah Parishe, servants with him, each 10s. To widow Cullen 6s. 8d. Witnesses: John Nashe, Thomas Chese, John Wade.

Proved 3 June 1597.

ROBERT LUCAS gentleman, lying in the house of St John's, Colchester, 2 July 1576. [For John Lucas, see p. 101.]   [19/20]

To be buried in the church of the parish where I die. To my elder brother Sir Thomas Lucas knight my lands holden by copy of court roll of the manors of Rivers Hall in Boxted, Stoke (Suffolk), and Great Horkesley; which lands in Great Horkesley and Boxted were my late mother's by the will of my grandfather Abel. To my brother John in hope of friendship which I trust shall ever continue between them £20 which he doth owe me, also £20 in consideration of debts that he may demand and on condition that he shall not sue Sir Thomas. To my servant John Bostock £3 and his wife 20s. in consideration of his dutiful service. To my keeper, the wife of Thomas Cawson, 10s. To my sisters Penny, Elizabeth and Mary each 20s. The residue of my goods to Sir Thomas, whom I ordain my only executor. Witnesses: Robert Bogas, Robert Smith, William Markant, William Hills, Robert Waylande, John Smith.

Proved 17 July 1576.

WILLIAM MARLER the elder of Kelvedon *alias* Easterford gentleman, 11 December 1596.   [42/20]

To be buried in Kelvedon church where many of my ancestors lie buried. To the poor people of Kelvedon 20s. To William my son my manor or capital messuage called Palmers with my lands in Halstead, Tey, Coggeshall and Feering; my copyhold lands which I hold of the manor of Feering Bury; and my messuages and lands free and copy in

228

Kelvedon, Rivenhall and Great Braxted; and to his heirs male, and in default of such issue to Arthur my son. To William my lands called Royses, Blackbards and Gunters in Burnham which I hold of the manor of Burnham. To Arthur my capital messuage in Witham called the Swan and my lands in Newland in Witham; and to his heirs male, and in default to William; provided that Arthur shall not enter on the premises until he is 22, but in the mean season William shall receive the yearly rents, and if they amount to £40 he shall pay the same to Arthur at 22 and if not he shall make up the £40. To George my son an annuity of £13 6s. 8d. out of the freehold lands which I have bequeathed to William. To Anne Marler and Alice Marler my daughters each £66 13s. 4d. To Jane my daughter, wife of John Lyngwood, £66 13s. 4d., whereof 40 marks to be paid to them when he shall have made to her use for life a surrender of his copyhold lands of the manor of Church Hall in Kelvedon and £40 within 6 months after his decease if she survive him. To John Knight, son of my daughter-in-law, 20s., Arthur Knight his brother 40s., and Edmund Knight his brother 46s. 8d., each at 21; William Knight my godson £5 at 21; and Stephen Knight, another of my daughter-in-law's sons, £3 at 21. To Anne Marler, my son William's daughter, my greatest ring of gold which was her grand-mother's, at 18; and Anne Marler, my son William's wife, my other ring of gold. The residue of my goods to William, whom I make sole executor. Witnesses: George Archer scribe, William Sache, Nicholas Ringeley, John Guy.

Proved 6 February 1598.

JOHN MARTIN of Maldon gentleman, being very weak and sick, 8 February 1599. [43/24]

To Alice my well-beloved wife my messuages and lands freehold and copyhold in Bildeston (Suffolk) for life, with remainder to Samuel my son. To Samuel my goods in my capital messuage in Chelsworth (Suffolk) in which heretofore I dwelt, on condition that he become bounden by his deed in £200 to her to assure the copyhold lands in Bildeston to her for life. To her my leases of the farms or wicks and marshes called Iltney in Maldon and Shrill in Dengie, and my stocks of cattle and the cheese, butter and other profits on them. To Samuel my messuages and lands freehold and copyhold in Chelsworth; and for default of issue to Anne, Mary, Susan, Alice and Elizabeth, daughters of Alice my daughter, wife of John Harrison, by equal parts to be divided. Samuel shall have the use, occupation and rents of my lands in Wattisham (Suffolk) and during my lease employ the income on the better maintenance of my daughter Alice and her children, and at the end of 12 years give the lands to my daughter's children to be equally divided. To my daughter's children £10 apiece at 21 or marriage. To Mr George Gifforde preacher of Maldon £10; Mr Ralph Hawden of Langford [rector?; vicar of All Saints, Maldon, 1600] £5; and Mr Thomas Carewe parson of Bildeston £5. To the poor of All Saints, St Peter and St Mary, Maldon, Bildeston and Chelsworth, to each parish 40s. The residue of my goods to my wife, whom I make sole executrix. Witnesses : Thomas Carewe, William Lowthe, Thomas Cheese.

Proved 20 March 1599.

EDMUND MAWDET of Great Braxted gentleman, 28 October 1587. [32/6]

To the poor of Rettendon 10s., Woodham Ferrers 10s., and Great Braxted 10s. To some godly preacher for two sermons, one at my burial and the other at some convenient time after, and for his painstaking 13s. 4d. To Margaret my wife freehold land called the Corpes in Old Newton (Suffolk) for life, with remainder to Edmund my son; my tenement called Boodes in Old Newton for 14 years after my decease for the bringing up of my children to 18 or marriage, and thereafter to my son Humphrey. To my four daughters Elizabeth, Frances, Anne and Prudence each £100 out of my lease of the manor of Dagworth Hall [in Elmdon] at 18 or marriage. To my brother Andrew £10, my sword and buckler, my best cloak but one, 2 of my wearing doublets, a pair of hosen that I use to wear, and my new buff hosen, or 15s. in lieu of them. To Agnes my maidservant 33s. 4d. To Elizabeth Stelloman, Lettice Stelloman and Judith Stelloman, 10s. each, and Judith Wheler 10s. To my sister Phillipps' two sons John and William each 20s. at 21. To Edmund Francis my godson 20s. The residue of my goods to my wife, whom I make sole executrix, and she shall bring up Humphrey in honest studies and learning, provided that she enter into bond of £500 to John Stelloman of Woodham Ferrers, Thomas Vicars of Rettendon and Elie Saunder of Woodham Ferrers for the performance of my will, whom I ordain overseers, and to each for their pains 20s. Witnesses : Robert Bryan, William Fountaine, Robert Archer, George Archer.

Proved 27 January 1588.

REYNOLD MEADE of Elmdon gentleman, 2 December 1589. [For Thomas Meade, see p. 105.] (Nuncupative.) [34/32]

By word in the presence of Barbara his wife, Thomas Cloughe clerk, vicar of Elmdon, Thomas Meade, Richard Meade, John Meade, and Mary wife of Thomas Meade. To be buried in Elmdon church.

To his wife his household stuff in his house in Elmdon, half his sheep at Chrishall, 4 of his horses, and the profits of Crowlbury Farm [in Chrishall] and of the sheepwalk, for 3 years ensuing his decease, to the intent that she keep and bring up Edward his fourth son and pay the annuity of £20 to John his third son; and after the 3 years the profits of his lease of Crawlebury Farm and sheepwalk to Edward for the life of his wife; and after her decease to John. To his wife an annuity of £7 out of the quitrents of the manors of Mounteneys and Dagworths in Elmdon. To her for life the messuage in Elmdon he dwelt in, the lands to it called Coxes and the lands that were Streats and Cosyns; the rest of his free lands in the corn fields of Elmdon, being no part of the

manors; Pill Croft; the profits of the pigeon house at the Bury; ½ acre of wood yearly to be taken out of his usual fellable wood for her fuel; his free land in Chrishall Fields; and 3 acres copy land called Taylors adjoining the messuage. He expressed that he dealt the more liberally with her because she should be good to her children and should not trouble them. After her death, Coxes and the land in Chrishall Fields to John; and Cosyns, Streats and the other lands in the corn fields (Bury Lands excepted) to Edward. The legacies to John for his maintenance and preferment in study and learning at the Inns of Court. The profits of the woodlands in Chrishall, Great and Little Chishall, which he held of the lease of Mr Penruddock, to Thomas his son and Richard his second son to the intent that they should pay Martha, Agnes and Mary Meade his daughters £100 each at marriage or sooner if his sons could levy it of the wood sales, not hindering themselves. To Frances his daughter and wife of Edward Wise £40 to be paid out of the profits of the woods and grounds. To Thomas the profits and fellings of the woods of the manors of Dagworths and Mounteneys to the intent by his discretion he give one part to Frances and the rest he satisfy to Barbara daughter of Thomas towards her better preferment in marriage. To his wife for life his lease of the moiety of the said two manors held of Mr Cuttes. To Richard 4 of his plough horses and sufficient corn to sow his lands. To Thomas the other moiety that he had purchased in fee simple and the manor place, site and other edifices and the pastures adjoining and the Bury garden. The residue of his goods to Thomas and Richard, whom he constituted his executors. [No witnesses.]
Proved 26 May 1590.

LAWRENCE MIDLETON of Stratford Langthorne [in West Ham] gentleman, 27 April 1589.   [33/44]

To my loving mother [Dorothy] £400 in the hands of John Chambers her brother. She shall be paid such money as is limited to her by indenture between Sir Henry Cuningsbye and me. All legacies given by my late father to my kinsmen by his will to be well paid by my executor. To the poor of St. Gregory in Paul's Churchyard in London 26s. 8d. and so much to St. Faith. To either of my men £4 apiece and to Comber my black cloak. I ordain my mother and my uncle John Chambers my executors and my overseers William Shatswell and Richard Bennete, and for their pains each a mourning cloak and their wives a mourning gown. To Margaret Devenishe £50 at marriage or 20. To Sir Henry Cuningsbye and his wife each a mourning gown, their menservants a mourning cloak, and his daughters a mourning gown. A cloak or two and some other of my meaner sort of apparel to my two men. To my four uncles, Arthur, Richard, Stephen and William Midleton, and my cousins, John, Alexander and Arthur Midleton, each a mourning cloak. Witnesses: William Statswell, John Hughes, Richard Bennett draper, John Comber, Robert Androwes scribe.
Renunciation, 6 May 1589, by John Chambers; proved by Dorothy Midleton, mother of the deceased.

FRANCIS MYCHELL of Theydon Garnon gentleman, 4 April 1582.
[25/16]

To Jane my well-beloved wife for life the new house and lands belonging, late parcel of the demesnes of the manor of Theydon Garnon and in the occupation of Francis Michell my son, also my new house and 3 crofts adjoining, and Taylors Croft in Theydon Garnon in that of John Richardes or else of him and John Harte; after her death the house to my son and the rest to Richard Hatleye, my son-in-law, and Jane his wife, my daughter. To my wife my close called Little Woodwards in Theydon Garnon in the occupation of George Chapman of Epping. To my wife for life my two copyhold houses in Epping Street in that of George Chapman and James Carr, and after her death to Francis. To the children of John Newman deceased £8 equally to be divided. I make my wife my sole executrix. Witnesses : Henry Beche, Henry Bett, Thomas Beeche, William Richardes, Grace Bartridge.
Proved 8 May 1582.

WILLIAM MYLDMAY of Springfield gentleman, 13 February 1571.
[For Thomas Myldmay the elder, see p. 111.]   [14/10]

To be buried in Springfield church. To the poor people of Chelmsford 20s. and Springfield 12s. To the widow Jenkenson a house of 6s. 8d. a year for life. To the poor folks in Moulsham 20s. To Thomas Free 2s. To William Myldmay, my son's eldest son, Sampford Barns and Barnes Mill [in Springfield] after 20 years be expired. To Sarah Myldmay, my son's daughter, my 2 crofts of land at Springfield Hill after 20 years be expired. To George, my son's second son, my copyhold houses in Moulsham and my copyhold at the Marsh stile. To Mary Celey £10. To Susan Wyntroppe £10 at marriage. To Alice, Margaret and Margery my maids 5s. apiece. To Thomas Byckner my man the house that he now dwelleth in for life and 40s. a year out of my manor of Barnes. To Robert Robynson my man 20s. The residue of my goods to Thomas my son to pay my debts, whom I make my executor, and I make Hugh Baker my overseer, and for his painstaking 40s. To Mr Robert Twyttey a doublet of velvet and a jacket of damask. Witnesses : Hugh Baker, Thomas Byckner.
Proved 24 February 1571.

THOMAS NOKE (or NOCKE) of Hatfield Broad Oak gentleman, 1 May 1559.   [3/16]

To be buried in Hatfield church, and for breaking the earth for my grave 10s. To the poor people of Hatfield £4. To the church in recompense of my tithes negligently forgotten 3s. 4d.
To Mary my well-beloved wife £12 yearly to be taken out of my manor called the Priory for life, on condition that she shall not claim dower in my other lands; 5 quarters of good wheat and 8 quarters of good barley malt during such time as she shall keep herself widow, out

of my lease of the parsonage; my house and garden wherein I dwell for such time as she keep herself unmarried, and after to Elizabeth my daughter and her heirs male; 2 beasts or kine feeding on the lands of the Priory, but not until the lease of George Raye be expired. To my wife one of my beds. To Cecily my wife's sister 20s. To Christopher Hilsdon sometime my servant my best pair of hose. Elizabeth Harwood to have her dwelling rent free for life, and Hugh Webbe the house, whereof Richard Gogyn hath the manurance and occupying, for 60 years paying yearly 8d.

To Robert my son at 21, if my debts and legacies be then paid, and to his heirs male my manor and lands called the Priory. To Edmund my son at 21 likewise my tenement and land called the Brewhouse; my tenement and garden called Buttes, my parcel of mead and the reed in the Common Marsh of Hatfield in the tenure of William Clarke; my lease of the house called the Brick Wall and the Stone Mead in Hatfield; the lease of the house and garden that sometime was Bedwettes and the lease of the stable and garden that sometime was mother Suttons; and a croft of land called Paynes, Yonges Croft and Wakelles Croft. To Elizabeth my daughter, with her grandfather's bequest, £100 at 20 or marriage, and a cow. To Margery my daughter, with her grandfather's bequest, 100 marks at 21 and a cow. To my cousin John Paschall the elder of Great Baddow my best gelding. To Elizabeth such household stuff and plate as her grandfather hath given her, as doth appear in a bill of parcels thereof made by Sir Robert Noke my father. The residue of my household stuff shall be equally divided among my wife, Robert, Edmund, John, Elizabeth and Margery, my children, saving that Robert shall have 2 beds, my best carpet, the 3 best cushions, and his part of the residue. If Robert decease without heirs male, the manor called the Priory shall remain to Edmund and his heirs male on condition that he assure to John the tenement called Waters; and if Edmund decease without heirs male, the Priory to John and his heirs male.

I give my executors authority to sell my lands, meadows and pastures called Estlondes, Wyche Field, Grenstedes, Tene Mead, Priors Moor in Sabesforde's tenure, and ground called the Little Stane, parcel of the manor, towards the performance of my will; and they shall have the profit of my lands and leases of the parsonage of Hatfield until they have sufficient to pay my debts and legacies and to see my children virtuously brought up. My lease of the parsonage shall remain to Robert my eldest son on condition that he do not marry without the consent of John Pascall and William Pascall the elder, my kinsmen, and of Thomas Shaxforde, but in the choice of his marriage he be ruled by them, or else not. Henry Rowland shall have his dwelling in the house he dwelleth in, paying 12d. yearly and keeping it in reparations for life.

I ordain John Paschall and Thomas Samforde of Willingale my executors, and for their pains 5 marks apiece, and I humbly desire and most heartily pray the right honourable and my especial good lord Robert Catlyn, Lord Chief Justice of England, to be overseer, and for his pains £3 6s. 8d. My wife shall have towards the bringing up of my children, so long as they may well and quietly agree together, to keep them to school and virtuously to bring them up till they be able to receive their bequests, and after that it shall remain to my eldest son, the rents of assize, the sum of £9 13s. 9¾d., and 2 quarters of malt more besides that I have given her and 5 quarters of wheat.

Witnesses: George Raye, John Bridges, William Clarke, John Burle, Thomas Huet, Christopher Hilsdon.

Proved 9 February 1560.

JOHN OLDAM of East Tilbury gentleman, 23 August 1599.　　[44/8]

To be buried decently in East Tilbury church. To Frances my wife such lands and reversions of lands as I have, for life, and after her decease to Mary my daughter. If Mary live to 21 or marriage, she shall have a lease of a messuage or farm called Griges in Coggeshall; if my wife be with child of a man child at my decease, he shall have the lease at 21 and the rest of my lands, so that he pay Mary £500 at 21 or marriage. To Grace Oldham my sister £200. To Reynold Oldam my uncle an annuity of 46s. 8d. To John Saunders of Coggeshall my cousin a messuage called Peaseland with the land belonging, provided that he pay my wife £60. To William Saunders my cousin £5. I confirm that William Haywarde of Coggeshall butcher shall have a lease of Griges, wherein he dwelleth. To William Haywarde the elder of Coggeshall £5. To Anna daughter of John Saunders late deceased £5. To William Hutt the younger £5. To my sisters Butler and Bucknam £5 each. My wife shall have authority to sell a messuage in Sandwich [Kent] which I bought of Thomas Crammer of London deceased on condition that she pay my debts. To the poor of East Tilbury £3 and Coggeshall £3. To Richard Browne of Chelmsford 40s. Witnesses: Robert Watson, Thomas Fuller, William Hayward, Richard Brown.

Proved 8 February 1600.

EDWARD ORMESBY late of Wood Grange [in East Ham] gentleman, 21 March, 1563. (Nuncupative.)　　[6/29]

My goods to Elizabeth my wife to bring up our six children, whom I make my only executrix, and my dear friend Thomas Wood, my brother John Ormesbie and Rice Edwardes to be my overseers. Witnesses: R. Edwardes, Joan Ormesby.

Proved 3 August 1563.

ROGER PARKER of Aldham gentleman, 5 November 1575.　　[19/19]

To Anne my wife my leases of the Howe with the lands belonging, and after her death the residue of the term, if any, three parts to Wentworth and one fourth part to Peregrine my sons. To Anne my daughter and Cecily Cowper my daughter each a gold ring price 20s. To William Cowper, my son-in-law, a gold ring price 10s. To Roger and Anne Cowper, my daughter's children, a lamb each at May Day next. To Richard Childersley and Margaret Botley my servants each 20s. To

Wentworth my eldest son my signet of my finger and Peregrine a gold ring price 20s. To Joan Martyn my servant a lamb at May Day. The residue of my wife, whom I ordain my sole executrix. Witnesses: John Wiltonne, William Sammes.

Proved 25 July 1576.

JOHN PEERS of Mountnessing gentleman, 19 January 1583.   [27/23]

The funeral of my body be only such as may beseem a Christian at the discretion of my executor and overseers. To my son [in-law] Brewster my ring which I usually wear on my forefinger; to Thomasine his wife, my daughter, two rings of gold which I commonly wear on my little finger, one a wreath of gold, the other a torquoise; and to my son [in-law] Browne a gold ring with my mark in it; which they should wear as pledges of my goodwill.

A true inventory of the rest of my goods be made and twice written indented, to the end that my well-beloved wife may keep one part and my executor the other, and that out of the goods she may take £100, as they be appraised, at her election; and for the rest she shall have them for life.

To the poor of Mountnessing where I now dwell 40s. To the wardens of the Fishmongers, of which Company I have been, towards a dinner for them £3 6s. 8d. To certain of the poorest of the ward in Bread Street £3 6s. 8d.

To my daughter [Anne] Collston after my wife's decease, first, in the great parlour at Arnoldes my great instrument, my great chest, six viols the high joined stools in my house, a long table and a short with 2 frames, and 2 chairs of needlework; in the hall, a long table and a square table with 2 frames, a long table with the trestles and 3 forms; in the little parlour an iron hook to hold a basin, a pair of virginals and the frame they stand on, a long table and a square table with frames, 2 forms, 2 joined chairs, a leathered chair and a little cupboard; in the chamber over the great parlour, a bedstead, a truckle bedstead, 2 settles, a court cupboard and a chest; in the great chamber, a bedstead with a settle, a square table and a court cupboard; in the counting house, an old counter table, a settle of wainscot, and an old chest; in the chamber over the pantry, a bedstead, a settle, and 5 chests; in the chamber over the kitchen, a great bedstead, a little bedstead, a little cupboard, 4 chests, and a settle; in the chamber over the little parlour, a bedstead, 2 settles, a court cupboard, and 3 chests; in the maids' chamber, the bedsteads there; in the long gallery, the bedsteads; in my great millhouse, my mills with the stones and things belonging; the firewood about my house that shall be left unburned after my wife's decease, and my hop poles likewise left; my carts, ploughs, plough chains, harrows and yokes; and the lumber in my brewhouse and dairyhouse; to the end she may have them ready standing in the house, if God grant her life to enjoy the same after her mother's decease.

To Thomas Reade and Anne Brewster, my daughter Brewster's children, £30 apiece; Alice the child of my daughter Anne Collstone

£30; William and Thomas, sons of my brother Richard Peers, and my cousin Hull 40s. apiece; all after my wife's decease. To my good friend Edward Colthurst, William Lincolne, Mr [Anthony] Brasier [rector of Ingatestone], and goodwife Allen, 20s. apiece. To my loving friends Charles Troughton 40s. and to Mr Edward Fage, Mr Robert Folkes and Mr Thomas Folkes, for the old friendship that hath been between them and me, to each £6 13s. 4d.; all after my wife's decease. To John Hester, Thomas Hester, William Hester, Richard Hester and Joan Hester, my kinsfolk, 40s. apiece. To my sister Parnell £5. To my son £20 at Michaelmas next and £6 13s. 4d. after my wife's decease.

To John Butcher my servant in consideration of his faithful service and that he shall do to my wife, if she survive me, £6 13s. 4d. To Mary Barries my servant £3, Anne Whittfeilde, Elizabeth Blatche, Richard Powlter and John Wratton, each 40s. after my wife's decease if they shall remain in my service at the time of my decease, and the rest of my servants likewise 20s. apiece.

To my loving wife my best featherbed of down with the usual furniture and such fine linen as doth usually lie in a curtain barred chest with iron remaining in my usual lying chamber; provided that she put such stock and goods as I have given to her during her life into the keeping of such honest men who may yearly pay some competent sum to her for her livelihood, so as the principal not given to her may at all times be forthcoming to perform my will, in which dealings I desire her to have a special regard. The residue of my goods to Richard and Henry my sons and Thomasine my daughter equally between them to be divided after their mother's decease. I ordain executor John Brewster, my loving son-in-law, and appoint Edward Fage, Robert Folkes and Thomas Folkes overseers. To my daughter Cowlstone my greatest portraiture made for my counterfeit hanging in my great parlour.

Witnesses: Thomas Folkes, Anne Colston, John Wratton, Richard Powlter, Elizabeth Blatche.

Proved 24 January 1584.

FRANCIS PELLS of Stanford-le-Hope gentleman, 10 December 1600. (Nuncupative.) [46/47]

To Joan Simpsonne his servant 20s. The residue to Joan his wife, and he also willed that her daughter Anne Dawson should have some part thereof. He made his wife executrix. Witnesses: Rep[ent] Savage [rector of Corringham], John Atkinson, Richard Meredith.

Administration granted, 23 June 1602, to Joan.

FRANCIS PETT of Nazeing gentleman, 6 May 1569. [12/15]

To be buried in Nazeing church by my wife. Towards the reparations of the church 3s. 4d. To the poor of Nazeing 10s. To Ralph my eldest son my farms and tenements in the city of London and suburbs, the city and county of Oxford, and the shire of Buckingham, with an annuity of £5 granted to George Gyfforde esquire for 41 years out of the late Minories by Tower Hill who gave his years by will to Ralph Gifforde his brother, who gave it to his son Roger, now doctor of physic, who sold to me the years to come (except two tenements in St Botolph-without-Aldersgate late belonging to the Priory of Hounslow [Middx.] which I purchased in the time of King Henry VIII); on condition that Ralph perform my will, first, that he make a sure estate in the law to George my second son for life of my lands in the county of Oxford and to Henry my youngest son for life of my farm in the county of Buckingham [details given]. To George one tenement in St Botolph before excepted, paying yearly to Ralph 13s. 4d.; and to Henry the other, paying yearly to Ralph a red rose if demanded. Ralph shall keep Henry at school and find him sufficient meat, drink, books and clothing until he live by his own industry. To George £20 and Henry £40. To Bridget my daughter £20. To Mary £3 which I owe her husband for part of her wedding money and £10 beside in reward. To Ursula and Elizabeth my daughters £20 each. To Elizabeth a black gown guarded with velvet, which was her mother's, a kirtle of black satin, 4 indifferent good smocks lacking a little sleeving, 4 good whole and fine neckerchiefs, and a pair of white sleeves worked. To my godsons Francis Dowset, Francis Awger and Francis Campe 2s. apiece, and Francis Browne 10s. To Bridget her mother's great ring of gold and Elizabeth her mother's ring which was a serjeant's ring of gold. To Florence Lawe my servant £5, Thomas and John my men 3s. 4d. apiece, and Mary and Ellen my maids 2s. apiece. Ralph shall lay a stone on me and his mother. To Mr vicar [Edward Hopkinson] one of my books and to Mr Randawle another book, such as they or my executor shall think meet. The residue of my goods to Ralph, whom I ordain my executor, and I pray my Lord Chief Justice of England, Sir Robert Catline knight, to be overseer, to whom I give for his gentleness to look to it 40s. [No witnesses.]

Proved 25 June 1569.

EDWARD PIGOTTE of Luxborough [in Chigwell] gentleman, 21 November 1580. (Nuncupative.) [23/47]

To Anne his well-beloved wife all his goods. Witnesses: Anne Stoner, Ellen Mercer, William Palmer.

Administration granted, 22 November 1580, to Anne.

RICHARD POULTER of Leigh, one of the principal Masters of her Majesty's Royal Navy, 14 November 1599. [44/17]

To Mr [William] Negus our minister of Leigh 40s. To the poor of the parish 40s. To my son-in-law Thomas Harrison 20s. and my sisters Margaret Oughan and Margaret Smithe of Leigh each 10s. To my cousins Richard Murcock 10s. and Thomas Oughan 20s. at 21.

To my well-beloved wife for life the occupation of my house wherein I dwell at Leigh, on condition that she surrender her right to Thomas

Harrison and my daughter Elizabeth in the houses [called] Richardes, Bagmans and Cobbes at the Corner in St Mary, Maldon as also in the houses [called] Piper Hatche and Arketelles in Brightlingsea; the use of my household stuff and the wainscotting and hangings fixed and belonging to the house for so long as she shall keep herself unmarried; and during the lease she shall receive the rents and profits of my lands copy and lease towards the education and bringing up of my children virtuously and in the fear of God until 21 or of my daughter's marriage and for her own better maintenance; and my ready money to the intents herein expressed. To Edward my son the lease of my house, provided that she have the occupation; my lease of Coggeshall Hay which I bought of John Archer; my lease from her Majesty which I have under the Duchy seal of Lancaster in Coggeshall Hay in reversion for 31 years.

There shall be sold by my wife and my executor and overseer my apparel both linen and woollen, with all my sea and land instruments, books, charts, maps, seabed and furniture, as also the lease of my house at Upner (Kent) with my household stuff therein; and the money thereof coming, with my ready money, shall be employed to profit by my wife and overseer for the benefit of my wife and children. To Edward at 21 my gold ring and £20. To my sons William and Benjamin each £13 6s. 8d. at 21. To my daughter Elizabeth wife of Thomas Harrison, besides that which I have already bestowed on her, £20 at 21. To my daughters Margaret and Mary Powlter each £50 at 21 or marriage if they do marry to the liking of my wife and overseer. After my children are 21 or married my wife shall at those times confer with my overseer that he may know how things hath passed and how her state standeth for the good of my children, that on the said conference he may according to his wisdom counsel her for the furtherance of her estate and my children's, which counsel I hereby admonish her to observe. Immediately after my death she shall take unto her my overseer and so many honest, able and sufficient men of Leigh as my overseer shall think fit and before them shall expose to view my goods and household stuff in my house at Leigh and shall cause them to be inventoried and truly valued, for which or the like value she shall be answerable to my executor; and she shall enter into bond of £200 to my executor and overseer for the performance of my will according to her faithful promise to me, which being forgotten and broken then she lose the benefit of my will. My overseer at the end of the minority of my executor shall render an account to him for such receipts and disbursements as hath happened during the time of his intromission in the execution of my will; and my executor shall then presently enter into bond of £200 to my overseer for the performance of my will as his mother should have done.

I make Edward my executor; if he fail or refuse I make William, and if he fail, Benjamin. I make my brother William Cock of Grays Inn my overseer, and for his pains 40s. To William my copyhold houses and lands in Burnham. To Benjamin my copyhold houses and lands called Edriches, Wisbiches and Pipers Hatche in the manor of Brightlingsea.

Witnesses: William Negus, William Smithe.

Proved 6 May 1599.

EVAN PRICE of Tendring gentleman, 18 May 1576.   [19/22]

To my very friend John Hastinges esquire my roan gelding and the grey colt of 4 years. To Mr Edmund Anderson of the Inner Temple, London, esquire, 40s. to bestow in a ring for a token of remembrance, and Thomas Lewes his servant 30s. likewise. To Joan Hedge a young heifer of 3 years. To my host Richard Seale of St Clement Danes (Middx.) 20s. over and besides all his charges. To every one of my servants a livery coat. The residue to my wife for life and my farm of Tendring and Brettes Hall [in Tendring] for life; if she marry only Brettes Hall. After her death my brother Davye Price shall have them to the use of his children, putting in sufficient sureties to bestow part in bringing them up in learning and in the meantime to put the rest forth for their most advantage, whereby they may have portion and portion like at their full age or at marriage. If he refuse, the goods to the use of Robert, son of my cousin Edward Lloyd of Hartesseth (Flints.) gentleman; if he refuse, to John Hastinges, whom I ordain my sole executor. I make Matthews Ewens of the Middle Temple gentleman my overseer. Witnesses: Matthew Ewens, John Overed.

Proved 3 August 1576.

JOHN PYNCHON of Writtle gentleman, 10 November 1573.   [16/38]

To be buried in Writtle church. To the reparations of the church 20s.

To Jane my wife my lands in Writtle and Bradwell-near-the-Sea for life; on condition that she bring up my children to full age or marriage, and that she pay yearly to William my eldest son at age so much of annuity with the revenue of my copyholds in Bradwell as amount to the yearly value of £20, to John Pinchon my second son and to Edward my third son at age each an annuity of £10, and to Elizabeth my daughter at marriage 500 marks, so that she make a sufficient release to my wife of her title to Cookes land in Roxwell and the profits due to her since my father's death and release to John Newton such right as she might have by any legacy of my late father of certain tenements by me to John Newton sold. To John Pinchon my lands called Whelers in Wike Street in the tenures of Robert Tunbridge and John Thornton and a field called Lowsford (containing 20 acres) in that of John Aware gentleman, after the decease of my wife; and or default of issue to Edward. To Edward my lands called Skigges and Turnors in the tenure of John Dockley, the great barn and the meads belonging in that of Thomas Reede's widow, and Clovilhill Croft and Challfe Hoopes in that of Hopkin, after the decease of my wife; and for default of issue to John. If my three sons die without issue, all my lands to Elizabeth.

Forasmuch as I am sundry ways indebted and leave the debts to be paid by my wife, I bequeath to her my lands called Fetches in Roxwell which I purchased of John Hawkin in the tenure of Stane and my lands in Bradwell purchased of Henry Drurie and his wife. To George Mannffeld and Denis his wife, my sister, my lands in Shenfield which I bought of old Symonde deceased. To my wife my farms [i.e. leases]

239

of the parsonages of Writtle and Roxwell and of the manor of East Hall and Shell Marsh and Garlmondes Marsh and the profits and the stock for life, paying the yearly rents and leaving the stock sufficient; after her death the residue of the term to William with the stock of cattle on the manor or farm of East Hall, i.e. 50 milch kine, 400 ewes and 20 rams, which cattle my wife have also for life.

To my singular good master Dr White, Warden of the New College of Winchester in Oxford, my best gelding, to make his choice, or else £10, most humbly beseeching him that, as he hath always been special friend and great good master to me and mine in my life, so he will continue to my wife and my poor children. To my loving friend Mr Bedell for a remembrance a ring of gold of the weight of 40s. For like remembrance to my loving friend Mr Tatem, vicar of Writtle, my best gown. The residue of my goods to my wife, whom I make my sole executrix, and my special good brother-in-law Mr Peter Osborne my supervisor, to whom I give for a remembrance a ring of gold of the weight of £3 6s. 8d.

Witnesses : Christopher Tatem, vicar, and Thomas Latley.

Memorandum. The will is written with my own hand in five pagines of paper and every pagine subscribed with my own hand—per me John Pinchon.

Proved 11 December 1573.

JOHN RAMPSTONE of Chingford gentleman, 15 February 1584.
[28/31]

To my daughter Mary 200 marks at marriage, a silver pot gilt, 3 kine and my grey nag. To Elizabeth and Ellen my daughters each £120 at marriage. To my son Rowland £30 at 22. To my beloved wife [not named] for life my freehold lands, except the house and the freehold at the Nether Street which I bequeath to Rowland; and after decease to Rowland, and for default of heirs to my three daughters. To Rowland the leases of marsh grounds in East Ham that I bought of my father-in-law, Mr William Gowge of [Stratford-le-] Bow [Middx.], and of Sir John Hungerford knight, and if my son be willing to sell the leases at any time my brother-in-law Mr Brockett shall have them before any other, giving £10 less than any other will give. To Thomas Stocke my servant marsh ground called Five Acres for 4 years, paying no more rent than I pay, on condition that he serve my wife for 2 years after his covenant year. To Elizabeth and Ellen each 6 silver spoons. To goodman Johnson 10s. and his wife 5s. To John Frissell my servant a cow and each of my other household servants 6s. 8d. To my brother Anthony £3. To my wife £300 to discharge my obligation to her friends to leave her worth so much when I die, and £50 for a more advancement of her living. To the poor of Chingford 13s. 4d. and of East Ham 13s. 4d. at the discretion of my friends goodman Muffett and Richard Reynoldes of East Ham. The residue of my goods to my wife. I ordain her, my loving brother Robert Rampstone, and my loving brother-in-law Mr William Brockett executors, and for their pains £5 each. I make my loving brother Thomas Rampstone my overseer, and for his pains my gold ring having hand in hand and heart in the middle. Witnesses : **Robert Heyward of East Ham**, Thomas Fulham of Chingford, Richard Pery the writer hereof.

Proved 15 October 1584.

ROBERT RAMPSTON of Chingford gentleman, 1 August 1585.

[29/40]

To be buried decently in Chingford church near the place where the bread is given. There be made a good and godly sermon by some learned and godly preacher at my burial, to whom shall be given 10s. To the poor people at the church at my burial £10. To my sister Elizabeth Capon yearly for life for her better maintenance £3. To Thomas Smith, son of my son-in-law Robert Smith, £5 to buy him books. To Matthew Lawsell, late one of the yeomen of the Queen's Majesty's Chamber, yearly for life 40s., of which the 20s. Robert Tyrrell gentleman requested me to give him shall be part. To my household servants men and women 10s. apiece. To 10 poor householders in Chingford whom my executrix shall think most meet 5s. apiece. The residue of my goods for life to Margaret my beloved wife, so as she do not marry again, whom I make sole executrix, provided that if she marry she shall take no benefit of any legacy and the portion that should have come to her shall remain to my next of kin. To John Abraham the younger of Sewardstone [in Waltham Holy Cross] husbandman 20s. I ordain my loving friends Thomas Wayte of London barber surgeon, Richard Goslinge of London draper, and William Benedick of London scrivener my supervisors, and 20s. apiece for a token of remembrance. Witnesses : Robert Smith gentleman, Nicholas Blencoe, William Benedick scrivener, Robert Rawdrey, Thomas Hickes, John Annesley.

Codicil, 2 August 1585. Whereas I have purposed for a yearly contribution to be made for ever to certain places in the counties of Essex and Middlesex and the city of London for the relief of the poor of Chingford £3, Waltham Holy Cross 40s., Loughton 20s., Chigwell 40s., Woodford 20s., Walthamstow 40s., West Ham 40s., East Ham 20s., Wanstead 20s., Leyton 20s., Enfield 40s., the poor of the prisons of Newgate 20s., the two Counters of Wood Street and the Poultry 20s., the Marshalsea in Southwark 20s., and the King's Bench in Southwark 20s., I have conveyed the reversion of my freehold lands to certain persons, my wife shall pay the £22. Witnesses : John Kytchyn, Richard Goslinge, William Benedick.

2 August 1585. I grant the same reversion to Thomas Gooche of Stratford-atte-Bow gentleman on condition that he pay the £22 to the wardens of the parishes and keepers of the prisons; and I devise the same lands to Nicholas Brooke of Waltham Holy Cross gentleman conditionally that he pay yearly the £22. Witnesses : William Shawe clerk, parson of Chingford, Matthew Lawsell gentleman, Ralph Tunstoll, William Benedick, John Kytchyn, Richard Goslinge.

Proved 10 August 1585.

241

MARGARET RAMPSTON of Chingford widow, 25 October 1590.

[34/66]

To be buried in Chingford church as nigh the place where my last husband Robert was buried as may be. I desire that Dr [Roger] Andrewes [vicar of Chigwell, 1605-06?] may be entreated to make my funeral and month's sermon and I give him 40s. for his pains. To the poor at the church the day of my burial £10, and a dinner to be made that day for such of my friends and neighbours as shall accompany me to the church. All the poor of Chingford shall have frize gowns or coats, i.e. gowns for the poor women and coats for the poor men. To the poor of Sowerby (Cumberland) where I was born 40s.

Whereas Robert Smyth, who married my daughter Frances against my will and without my knowledge, hath since the marriage been very many ways greatly by me advanced and yet not so contented hath most unjustly sued me in the Chancery upon supposed promises and troubled me divers ways, I take God to witness that he to my knowledge hath no cause so to do; yet I freely forgive him and his wife, and I pray God to forgive them and give them grace to repent, for all the matters which I have set down in my answer upon my oath in the Chancery are true. I have no meaning hereby to take occasion wholly to abridge my goodwill towards his children, but I pray God that he of his mercy do not punish the children for their parents' faults. And for their preferment I give £200 to be equally divided among their four children, Robert the eldest £50, Thomas my godson £50, Henry £50, and Blanche £50, each at 21; on condition that, if Robert Smyth or Frances or any of their children do at any time hereafter trouble, sue or hinder my son [in-law] Nicholas Blencowe concerning any lands or goods he shall have by my will or as executor to me, the gift of £200 shall be absolutely void. Whereas Robert Smyth did borrow £50 of Robert Rampston and £100 of me since and divers other sums by several obligations; whereas on his or her earnest entreaty and that of Nicholas Blencowe and James Spight, I took order with one Edmund Browne of Enfield [Middx.] for £240, which Smythe was indebted to Browne and for which he had become bound to Browne by 12 obligations, all which were assigned to me by Browne with Smythe's assent; and whereas I have lent money to Smythe and his wife for which I took no bond or bill; I will that, on a deed of release by Smythe to Blencowe, the bonds shall be delivered up to Smythe and be discharged of the debts. If he refuse to make such a release to Blencowe or if he sue or trouble him, my executor shall to the uttermost extremity, and that with as much speed as he can, put in suit all bonds and sue for such debts.

To Barnard Sympson my nephew and my household servant £50. To Dorothy Tolson my niece and servant 20 marks. To Mary Colyer my niece, now wife of Anthony Colyer, £10. To Jane dwelling on the Bankside, my sister's daughter's daughter, 40s. To Cecily Bawne sometime my servant 20s. To Mary, if I happen to die in this sickness, for her pains taken with me 40s. To my servants 10s. apiece, and to Anne Ruskins 20s. and one of my russet gowns. I give 20s. a year for 4 years to be bestowed on the mending of the highways in Chingford in such places as my executor shall think most needful. To two poor scholars in the Queen's College in Oxford 5 marks. To Mr William Shawe, parson of Chingford, 40s. To James Spight 5 marks and I release him a bill of 40s. which he oweth. To William Atkinson of the Temple £20 and £10 more to be by him given to Richard his brother at his discretion. To Richard Hutton of Gray's Inn £20.

I make Nicholas Blencowe my son and heir my sole executor, to whom I bequeath my goods and household stuff. I make William Atkinson, Richard Hutton, Thomas Wayte and William Benedict my supervisors, whom I desire to assist my son with their counsel, and for their pains £4 apiece and a mourning gown to Mr Atkinson's wife and to Waite and Benedict 40s. apiece and a mourning gown or cloak at their elections.

To Robert Jacson and John Barwys each 40s. to buy him a ring. To Robert Jacson my godson, son of Robert, 20s. to buy him books. To Mr William Woodall and his two sons, my good neighbours, 20s. apiece. To Agnes Blencow, my daughter and my son's wife, a nest of silver and gilt bowls and a nest of double gilt pots. To Frances Smythe my daughter £20 and my best gown, best kirtle and best petticoat on condition that if her husband do not perform the conditions in my will this legacy to be void. To Mistress Hutton, late wife of Anthony Hutton of Peareth (Cumberland), my elder gown of black cloth guarded with one guard of velvet lined with cotton and faced with velvet. I give 5 marks to be bestowed by my supervisors in books at the School of Peareth for the use of the scholars. To Richard Blencowe my nephew 40s. To Richard Hutton to give to such woman as he shall marry my chain of gold. Henry Blencowe shall pay his £20 which he oweth but not the interest and forbearance which is 40s. a year for 4 years. I will that Robert Smythe shall have a mourning cloak and his wife a mourning gown, Robert and Thomas Smyth, my grandchildren, a cloak, Henry Smyth a coat, and Blanche Smyth a gown, and every one of Nicholas Blencowe's children a mourning gown, cloak or coat. To Robert eldest son of Nicholas 40s., Nicholas his son £50 at 21, and Frances and Margaret his daughters £30 apiece at marriage. To Agnes Blencowe, my son's wife, a black mourning gown, my chamlet gown, a kirtle and a petticoat. To John Phillipps feltmaker 20 nobles. To the poor of St Olave in Southwark [Surrey] £3.

Codicil, 25 October 1590. Whereas by this will I had conditionally given certain legacies to Frances Smythe, wife of my son-in-law, and to him and their children, and yet he since continueth his wicked practices and misinformed my Lord Chancellor and others of me and my doings and procureth his Lordship to write hardly to me, I therefore and for other causes revoke such legacies to Frances, Robert and their children. To my nephew George Blencow, servant to her Majesty, 20 marks, my nephew Rowland Sympson a ring of 40s., and Henry Brewer 40s. and a colt.

Witnesses : William Atkinson, Richard Hutton, Dorothy Vernon, Alice Barwys, Nicholas Blencowe, Dorothy Tolson, Richard Blencowe, Barnard Sympson, Robert Ingham, Richard Hutton.

Proved 30 October 1590. Sentence, 19 February 1591, confirming Will in case between Nicholas Blencowe executor and Frances Smith *alias* Bateman.

THOMAS REDINGE of West Thurrock gentleman, 9 November 1592.

[37/21]

To be buried in the chancel of West Thurrock church near the place where Katherine my good wife lieth buried, and my executor to cause my grave to be covered with a stone. To the poor of West Thurrock £10 where most need shall be, every Christmas and Easter 20s. until the sum be paid. To the poor people of Pinner [Middx.] where I was born £4 according to the discretion of my executor and my loving sister Joan Edlyn. To Dorothy Rise my nurse 20s. To Agnes Pylgrome 5s. and Mary her daughter 6s. 8d. To Ralph Turner of Pinner £5. I forgive my brother Henry the £100 he oweth me, on condition that he make to my brother George the like assurance as he hath already made to me concerning the lease of Hedgestone Farm as also that other lease of Cockhills Field, to the intent that my good father's will may be performed. To George my son two tenements in Pinner Street and another in West End. To Richard my brother £10 to be paid when the legacy which my mother late deceased gave him doth end in manner as it was bequeathed to him. To Thomas his son £10. To Joan Edlyn my goddaughter £5 to be bestowed in plate; if she die before, to Audrey Edlin. To the daughters of my sister Girmill late deceased 40s. apiece (Joan Girmill excepted) and to Joan £10 at marriage. To Audrey Page, Margaret Legate, Rose Pinchon and Joan Edlin, my sisters, two angels apiece in remembrance of me to buy them rings. To Thomas Redinge my cousin and Master of Arts 20s. To Elizabeth Driwood, Audrey Page my goddaughter, and Audrey Edlin my sister's daughter 20s. apiece to buy them rings. To George my brother my tenement which I bought of my brother-in-law Thomas Haies in the tenure of William Hines, with the buildings, marshes and upland grounds; my parsonage, rectory or prebend of West Thurrock, with the buildings, barns and stables, tithes due to the parsonage, also the gift and presentation of the vicarage. To Frances my well-beloved wife £600, besides the thirds of my lands; her wearing apparel, linen and woollen, the silver bowl which her brother John Drywood gave her at her marriage, my silver salt, and the grey mare which I bought of her father-in-law with the side saddle, pillion and bridle. To Mr John Legatt my brother-in-law my lease of Buttes Farm in Hornchurch parish which descended to me by the death of Robert Redinge my brother. To Thomas Redinge my cousin, M.A., £80 in recompense of reckonings between us. The residue of my goods to George my brother, whom I make my sole executor, and I appoint Mr William Leveson my landlord and Mr John Legate overseers, and 20s. apiece for their pains. To every of my servants 6s. 8d. apiece and to young Humfrey Beckington my godson, 40s. Witnesses: Henry Pechye, Robert Weekes.

Proved 21 March 1593.

244

JOHN ROGERS of Walden gentleman, 27 November 1591.   [36/13]

To Anthony Calton of Butlers in Walden gentleman my sword and dagger of damask work. To Jane Bower servant to Anabel Goodwyn my hostess 20s. I forgive Richard Ogden and Richard Turner of Walden such money as they are indebted to me. To Thomas Edwardes and William Edwardes of Helston (Cornwall) and John Stevens, my sister's sons, each £5, so that they demand their legacies at the house of Anabel Goodwyn in Walden. To the poor folks of Walden £5. The residue of my goods to Anabel, whom I make my sole executrix. Witnesses : William Harrydaunce, James Croft notary public, Anthony Goodwyn.
Proved 4 February 1592.

HENRY ROLF of Kelvedon [Hatch] gentleman, 8 May 1602.   [47/12]

To Mary my daughter £500; the leases of my dwelling house in St Lawrence Lane in the city of London and from William Howe, my brother-in-law, of lands in Mucking, Horndon-on-the-Hill and Corringham called Cow Leaze, Chelley and Ringway Marsh, she paying yearly to the churchwardens and overseers of Mucking 40s. to be distributed among the poor; £500 to be paid as the same may conveniently be raised out of my estate; and my lands in Mucking holden of the manor of Mucking; and to her heirs, with successive remainders to my daughters Elizabeth and Anne, and to Henry, son of my brother Edmund Rolf, and his heirs. To my daughter Anne wife of John Crowch my freehold lands in Shenfield which I bought of John Woode esquire and his wife, and her heirs, with remainder to Elizabeth and my daughter Mary and their heirs and further remainder as aforesaid; my lease of houses new built by me in Grub Street in the city of London or suburbs, she paying or taking order for paying weekly a dozen of penny loaves being 13 to the dozen, in St Giles-without-Cripplegate church, during the continuation of the lease, among the poor inhabitants after morning prayer and other divine service every sabbath, and she and her husband making to Thomas Kelley citizen and embroiderer of London a lease for 21 years, as by several drafts thereof already drawn in my custody; the £200 remaining yet unpaid of my promised portion of £500 given in marriage with her to John Crowch; such portion of money as remaineth on account betwixt me and my cousin Edward Barkham and debt late of one Blieth deceased; also £200; all which legacies on condition that John Crowch, father to my son-in-law, shall according to his promise convey to his son and Anne lands of the yearly value of £80, whereof £50 a year to be for their present maintenance and £30 a year to come to them and their heirs after the decease of John the father. To William Pettus and Elizabeth his wife, my daughter, and their heirs, remainders to Anne and Mary and their heirs, then aforesaid, my messuage called Brizes, with the lands belonging in Kelvedon, Navestock and Doddinghurst; my lease of the farm called Jennynges, which one Fox now holdeth; and £500.

Whereas my brother Edmund oweth me and there will grow due to me at Michaelmas 1603 for money lent and for the arrerages of an annuity of £100 to me granted by Richard Beckham gentleman £300, and another £100 likewise to me due at Michaelmas 1604, I bequeath that £200, parcel of the £400, be paid by my brother to my executor to be bestowed, i.e. to keep in his own hands to the use of Susan Rolf and John Pettus, son and daughter of Elizabeth my daughter, to whom I bequeath the same, i.e. £50 each, £150, and other £50 residue of the £200, to be delivered to my son-in-law to the use of Henry son of John Crowch and Anne my daughter, to which Henry I give the said £50, and the other £200 residue of the £400 shall remain in the hands of Edmund to the use of Henry his eldest son, to whom I give £50, and the residue thereof, i.e. £150, to the use of Edmund's other children, to whom I give the same, to be distributed among them at 21 or marriage. Whereas my brother-in-law Thomas Lane oweth me £300, that he only pay to my executor towards the performance of my will £100, together with such [interest] thereof as shall be due at the time of my decease, and the residue of the £300 I bequeath among the children of Thomas and Mary his wife, my sister. Whereas my brother-in-law Thomas Atwood oweth me £206 on the mortgage of the lease of the house he dwelleth in and other debts, I give £50 thereof to Martha his wife, my sister, and if he pay my executor the residue of his debt within 4 years after my decease then the lease so mortgaged shall be delivered to him or otherwise reconveyed.

To my cousin Robert Rolf, now in house with me, £50, and Katherine his daughter £20 at marriage or 21; and such apparel of my own or my wife's as my executor shall think meet to him and Anne his wife. To William his son £5. To Robert son of William Mason £5. To Thomas son of Bridget Heath, my sister, and Margaret his sister, wife of William Lawes, and Anne wife of Christopher Story, each £5, and every other of my sister Heath's children 40s. To my brother Edmund and my sister Mary Lane each 50s. to buy a gold ring and to Edmund's wife 40s. for the like. To my brother-in-law Thomas Lane my best livery gown. To my cousin Edward Barckham £3 and Jane his wife 40s. to buy each a gold ring. To my godson Henry Harris, my goddaughter [blank] Warde, one of the daughters of [blank] Warde tailor, Elizabeth Codlinge my maid servant, Nicholas my manservant, each 20s., and Joan Staine my maidservant and Jerwood Eastrowe, Matthew Baker my servants 10s. apiece. To the poor inhabitants of Sperle (Norfolk) where I was born £5. To my cousins Joan wife of William Hammonde 40s., Margaret wife of Richard Wiberd 40s., and Mr John Pettus 50s. and his wife 40s., and to Mr Richard Luther and Mistress Martha and Mary wives of Richard and Anthony Luther, each 50s. to buy rings of gold. To the poor inhabitants of Kelvedon where I dwell 40s., Stondon 20s., Chipping Ongar 15s., High Ongar 15s., Navestock 20s., Doddinghurst 20s., South Weald 20s., and Blackmore 20s. To nurse Hilles wife of John Hilles 20s. and to my daughter [Anne] Crowche's nurse 10s. A bullock of the price of £3 shall be bought and distributed by the discretion of my executor, with 10 bushels of wheat and 6 barrels of beer, among the poor of the same parishes, or £8 at their discretion, provided that such persons as shall be at my funerals and be troublesome shall have no part. To my cousin Weld wife of Thomas Weld £5. To Susan one of the daughters of Henry Ducy £5 at 21 or marriage or otherwise towards her placing in service.

Whereas the lease of the manor of Mucking and lands in Mucking, Corringham and Horndon-on-the-Hill remaineth in me, I bequeath it to my very loving friends John Pettus esquire, Richard and Anthony Luther gentlemen, William Pettus merchant, and Adrian Moore citizen and haberdasher of London on trust notwithstanding that, whereas my brother-in-law William Howe by former agreements betwixt us was to pay me yearly for 12 years 100 marks for one year's payment only there is assigned to me the debt of £70 owing by one Thomas Staunton of Norwich beerbrewer and others, of which I have received £20, and of the residue of the 100 marks for 11 years, I will that, if Howe shall pay for 6 years the yearly payment of 100 marks and also £50 to my executor, then Pettus and the others shall dispose of the residue and the lease according to their best discretions as well for the payment of the rent on the lease as for the benefit of Howe and his children and their maintenance.

To my daughter Mary a double gilt bowl of silver which I bought of Richard Wythens, 12 beasts and 1 bull, 20 ewes, and 1 mare and her foal at Great Warley, with 1 grey nag at Bryses, my bedsteads and household goods in my house at Mucking or my house in St Lawrence Lane, with 2 featherbeds on the trundle bed in my hall chamber and my own bedchamber. To my daughter Anne Crowch 20 ewes at Great Warley, with 6 beasts at Shenfield, and a standing bedstead in my hall chamber at Bryses. My plate (except that before devised), jewels, gold and linen in my plate chest standing at my trundle bed's feet in my own bedchamber and the key thereof shall be delivered to my assured loving friend Mr Anthony Luther, to be kept by him until he and Richard Luther and their wives shall make an equal division of the same as also of my linen at Brizes into three parts; after which three lots or scrolls in parchment or paper shall be made to contain the part which every of my three daughters shall have, and be put into a hat, bonnet or other thing, where they shall not see what is contained therein but by chance take out such of the lots or scrolls as shall happen to them. The residue of my goods to Elizabeth my daughter and her husband William Pettus, whom I constitute my sole executor, and my well-beloved friend Anthony Luther and Mr Adrian Moore the overseers, and to Anthony for his pains £10.

Witnesses: John Pettus, [blank] Luther, Edward Josselyne, Richard Atwoode, John Partridge.

Proved 22 February 1603.

NICHOLAS ROOKES of Newport gentleman, 8 August 1578. [22/22]

To be buried in Newport churchyard by Joan my wife late deceased. To the poor men's box in Newport church 3s. 4d. To Henry my youngest son my houses and lands both free and copy in Newport. To William Burdall of Wiston [Suffolk] draper £40. To his children £10 to be divided among them at marriage. To Margaret Nayler my daughter £10. The residue of my goods to be divided among my sons Nicholas and Henry, whom I make executors. But I will that Henry shall not marry with Edy Whight, my kinswoman and late servant, which if he do he shall have no part of my lands or goods but all shall remain to Nicholas, as well as the executorship. To Richard Comfrett of Newport 10s., whom I make supervisor. Witnesses: Thomas Martine the elder, William Swynowe clerk [vicar of Newport?, rector of Virley, 1599-1633], George Yngisbie, Richard Yngisbie.

Proved by Henry, 30 May 1579.

JAMES ROWBOTHUM of Upminster gentleman, 1 February 1586. [30/51]

To my son William my manor of Little Bromefords with the appurtenances in Nevendon, Wickford, Ramsden Bellhouse and Ramsden Crays which I purchased of Henry Amcotes, my messuage late called Huntes and now the farmhouse, and the lands and messuages in Essex I purchased of George Heard; and in default of issue to Richard his eldest son on condition that he pay John, William and James Rowbothum, Elizabeth Dod, Agnes Hewes and Dorothy Rowbothum, Richard's brothers and sisters, £10 yearly for their lives in the porch of Upminster church; with successive remainders after Richard's death to his brothers and sisters on like condition; and after Dorothy's death, to William my brother, her father, on like condition to six of such as follow in remainder, viz. Richard son of William Wassher of Upminster, Thomas Wassher his brother, George son of Richard Carmarden of London, and Nathaniel, William and Anne Carmarden, his brothers and sister. I make my only executor my well-beloved son William, and I constitute for overseers Richard Carmarden and Thomas Sallter. Witnesses: Tristram Waters, John Waters, Thomas Sallter.

Proved 21 October 1586.

RICHARD SANDWITH of Orsett gentleman, 28 March 1576. [19/13]

To be buried in Orsett church. To Margaret my wife my household stuff in Orsett and Dagenham, my little nag, and 40s.; she pay John son of John Marshall, late of Dagenham, £10 which I owe him, which she shall have in her hands until he come of age. To the poor people of Orsett 10s. and Dagenham 10s. To my brother Robert Sandwith a ring of gold in value 30s. To John son of John Wicklief of St Martin-le-Grand, London, 40s. To my good lord and master, my Lord of Canterbury's grace, a ring of gold in value 40s., and I will that my wife pay him more £10 which I owe him, except he will be so gracious to her to remit it, which I hope he will. To my said cousin John Wicklife the elder a saddle having a seat of fustian anapes which I left at the sign of the Bell within Aldersgate. To Christopher Marshall my black gaskins and William Marshall my cut canvas doublet. To Buntinge a frize jerkin and to Oliver Eden another. To Mr Buskell for a funeral sermon 6s. 8d., and to James Gower, curate of Orsett, for writing my will 6s. 8d. The residue of my goods to my wife, whom I make sole executrix and Christopher Chiborne and Giles Buskell my overseers. Witnesses: James Gower writer hereof, Edmund Hurte.

Proved 1 June 1576.

GEORGE SAYER of St Peter, Colchester, the elder, gentleman, 22 January 1574. [For George Sayer esquire, see p. 125.] [20/25]

To be buried in St Peter's church by my first wife. Towards the repairing of the church 13s. 4d. To Richard Sayer my nephew £20 whereof he owed me £9; Agnes Sayer my niece £5; Henry Smythe my daughter's son £4 to make him a ring; and John Pye my son-in-law 40s. to buy him a ring of gold.

To poor maidens' marriages £5, i.e. 6s. 8d. to every one at the discretion of my executors within three years after my decease. To the poor of the same parish £5, i.e. every Friday 2d. apiece to such 12 poor people coming to the church to pray and hear divine service. To the poor prisoners in the Castle of Colchester 40s. to be paid every quarter 3s. 4d., and in the Moot Hall in Colchester 6s. 8d. to be paid quarterly 6d. There shall be given the five years after my decease 3,000 billets yearly to the poor people of Colchester.

To Elizabeth Johnson 20s. To every of my poor godchildren 12d. To Thomas Gibson my late servant 10s.; the rest of my servants 6s. 8d. apiece. To Mary Allen 10s. and a petticoat cloth; to Stace Peerson 13s. 4d. To the mending of the highway from Buttoll Hill to Myle Ende Went £3. To father Pyckas 20s.; to father Lewes 10s. and one of my old coats.

To Frances Sayer and Mary Sayer, my son's daughters, 200 marks each at 22 or marriage, on condition that they shall not be married without their father's consent before 22; and if either die unmarried before 22 their portions to be equally divided amongst my son's children. To Frances a gilt pot at marriage. To George son of George Sayer my son 100 marks at marriage; if he die leaving no issue, the legacies to his children be equally divided between Henry Smythe and my brother Robert Sayer's children. To Agnes Spisall 20s. To Thomas Sayer my son's child £200 at 22 or marriage; and my tenement wherein John Pye doth dwell and my tenement at North Gate where Greenewoodd late dwelt. After the death of George my son and Rose his wife my tenement wherein I dwell and my island adjoining to Shepen Grounde shall remain to Thomas. To Thomas an annuity of £20 out of my manor of Bowsers Hall in Aldham alias Little Fordham. To John Paynter the elder 10s. and a black coat cloth; to Anne Griffyne 10s. The residue of my lands and goods to George, whom I make my sole executor.

Witnesses: William Barkley, Richard Sawer, William Greene, John Fludde.

Proved 15 June 1577.

249

JANE SCOTT gentlewoman, 31 July 1595. [40/11]

Concerning all goods, money, jewels, etc., the most part whereof doth rest in the hands of Mr Thomas Josselyn of Willingale [Doe] esquire amounting to £200, I bequeath them to my well-beloved sister Abdias Scott, whom I make sole executrix. Witnesses : Francis Josselyn, William Fall, Maurice Hackett scrivener.

Proved 11 February 1596.

WILLIAM SCOTT of Chigwell gentleman, 20 November 1597. [For George Scott, see p. 126.] [42/40]

To be buried in Chigwell church near my late wife. To the poor of Chigwell 40s. My executor to pay all legacies as yet unpaid by the will of my late father George Scott. To my son George and his heirs my freehold lands in Chigwell and Lambourne. My son to make a lease to his brother Thomas of a field called Straddes lying among copyhold lands belonging to Billingbornes [in Chigwell] after my decease for the unexpired term in the lease of the manor of Woolhampton Hall [in Chigwell], paying 40s. a year, provided that if he grant it without George's consent the lease be void. To Thomas a bedstead that was my wife's father's in the gallery chamber, half a garnish of pewter, 3 gilt spoons, a brass pot, a spit, the lesser dripping pan, a small posnet, the long table in the parlour with the frame, 6 joined stools of the worser sort, the press in the old parlour, and such bedsteads and other implements and trash as is remaining at Bellingbornes, to be delivered to him at marriage if he marry with the good liking of my executor and overseers. To my son William such bedding and other furniture as he hath at Cambridge, 2 gilt spoons, a white silver spoon, my wearing apparel, a little gold ring on my little finger, and half a garnish of pewter, at 21; and my lease at Abridge which I bought of William Wilkins. To my son John at 21 such bedding and implements of house as are given him by his grandmother, and 2 gilt spoons, at 21; the other 6 gilt spoons unbequeathed to be equally divided between Edmund, Hugh and Harry my sons at 21. To my daughter Elizabeth wife of William Browne, above the £20 given by her grandmother, £100. To my two younger daughters Mary and Frances £100 each at 21 or marriage, and my executor to see them decently brought up, finding all things necessary until their legacies be due. My executor shall enter into a recognizance enrolled in Chancery to my overseers in £400 for the bringing up of Mary and Frances and payment of the £200, and shall pay a 40s. annuity to [blank] widow of Peter Greene. To my brother Robert and my sisters Crafford, Wentworth and Stone an angel of gold to make them each a ring. To every of my menservants 6s. 8d. and maidservants 3s. 4d. apiece. The residue of my goods to George, whom I make executor, and I appoint my loving brother-in-law Arthur Crafford and my cousin Hugh Base overseers, and to each 2 angels. Witnesses : William Scott, Robert Scott, Arthur Crafford, Hugh Base, George Bristo, Alexander Stowell.

Proved 30 May 1598.

THOMAS SEXTON of Great Maplestead gentleman, 6 October 1577.

[20/39]

To Jane my wife, late Jane Myller my servant, my manor or capital messuage called Byham Hall and the lands belonging in Great Maplestead, Little Maplestead and Gestingthorpe; and my lands called Goderich land and Pavyners in Little Maplestead; for life, with remainder to Mary and Susan our daughters. To my wife my goods, corn and cattle towards payment of my debts and bringing up our children. I make my wife executrix. Witnesses: William Vigorus, Peter Grene, Nicholas Martin, Geoffrey Griffin, John Wodborne.

Proved 19 October 1577.

JOHN SHIPMAN of West Ham gentleman, 8 January 1584.   [27/20]

To be buried in West Ham church. To Lucy my wife, besides the lands made over to her, my two houses called Copted Hall by Plaistow Cross in the occupation of James Best and Henry Best and 2 acres of upland called Purcelles Hill, for life, and after her decease to my cousin William White of Stratford Bow [Middx.]. To Miles Leedes my kinsman after my decease and my wife's 2 acres of upland at Hooke End. To William White my mansion house with the orchard and garden in Plaistow, 4 acres of upland called Bacon in East Ham, and 9 acres of marsh at Laymouth, after my decease and my wife's, provided that he pay £6 yearly for the relief of the poor inhabitants of West Ham to be distributed by the churchwardens and vestry. To my cousin John Pragle the younger dwelling by the butts in Plaistow my black house in Plaistow near Hooke Cross, 1 acre belonging near Hooke Field, and 2 acres of marsh called Capons adjoining to Many Gates. To Bess daughter of Edward Kimpton £5 and Lucy daughter of Robert Kimpton £5. To Thomas Banckes of West Ham gentleman £10. To my sons [in-law] George Kimpton and Edward Kimpton 40s. apiece to buy them a ring. To Knockar my servant 20s. and the rest of my servants within my house 6s. 8d. apiece. To Robert Wrighte 6s. 8d. and his son Robert 10s. To my goddaughter Jane daughter of George Kimpton 10s. and my other godchildren 2s. apiece. Witnesses: Thomas Banckes, Richard Shawe, John Doylwyn, Richard Moyle.

Memorandum, 9 January 1584. To John Dallinge 20s., Richard Knockar 20s., Robert Wright 30s. Witnesses: Thomas Banckes, John Pragle, William White, William Meriton. 9 January at 11 o'clock at night Mr Shipman gave to Miles Leedes his ring off his forefinger with a red stone. To Sir Thomas Lodge knight £3 to make a ring. To Thomas Smithe alias Tailor for his pains 6s. 8d. To James Best 5s. and his son Henry 6s. 8d. To his two maids Alice and Joan whatsoever he gave them in his will shall be made up to 20s. apiece and his servant Richard Shepperd shall have his gift made up to 6s. 8d. more than he first gave. He hath given Agnes wife of Miles Leedes 2 angels of gold to make a ring. Given in the presence of William White, John Doylwyn and Thomas Smithe.

Administration granted, 11 January 1584, to Lucy.

JOHN SMITHE of Tilbury [juxta-Clare] gentleman, 23 January 1591.
[35/23]

To be buried in Tilbury church. To my brother Robert Smithe my messuage called Gunnelles with the land belonging (containing 40 acres) in Stowmarket (Suffolk). To my brother Henry Smithe an annuity of £10 which I have during the life of Thomas Corbett. To my sister Martha Smith my lease for 3 years to come of Capons Fields, Christmas Crofts and Whesethedge, parcel of the manor of Vaws in Otten Belchamp, paying £3 6s. 8d. to me and Richard Warde. To my brother Henry Smithe my lease of certain land in Clare [Suffolk] on condition that he pay yearly during the life of my sister Katherine wife of Robert Elsinge 40s. and to my sister Anne wife of Robert Alington gentleman £10. To Anne a white garled cow. To my sisters Elizabeth wife of Robert Springe, Emme wife of Robert Simpson, and Mary wife of Richard Hardie, £5 each. To my kinsman William Russell, son of my sister Lora wife of one Morris, £6 13s. 4d. To my mother Katherine Smithe widow £10. The residue of my goods to my executors for the performing of my will. I ordain my executors my brothers Henry and Robert. Witnesses : Peter Poole, Henry Teboulde.
Proved 22 March 1591.

JOHN SMYTHE of Epping gentleman, 16 April 1570. [13/25]

To be buried in Epping church. To the poor men's box of Epping 6s. 8d. To Audrey my wife for life all the lands I have in Essex, and after her decease to Nicholas my son and his heirs; and for default of such issue the successive remainders of my manor of Haylees and Turkelees with Pritwell lands in Epping to Nicholas Saunderson and Elizabeth his wife, my daughter, and her heirs, and to Susan my daughter. To Nicholas my son my messuage called Weldbridge alias Gymbelles in North Weald Bassett, Bobbingworth, High Laver and Chipping Ongar; and for default of issue to Susan. To Nicholas my two messuages in Watling Street in the city of London in the tenures of Robert Nicoll and John his son; and for default of issue to Susan. To her 100 marks to be paid by Nicholas Saunderson at marriage. The residue of my goods to my wife and my son, whom I ordain my executors, and my nephew Wistan Browne supervisor. My son shall pay within 3 years after his mother's decease to Susan his sister £20. Witnesses : John Serle, James Barker, George Farnham, Silvester Asshby the writer.
Proved 21 August 1570.

THOMAS SMITH of Cressing Temple gentleman, 10 May 1563.
[7/11]

To [Mary] my well-beloved wife my whole term of years of the lease of the lands in Yorkshire which I have of the demise and grant of Sir Thomas Nevell knight, her father; and my goods, on condition that she shall bring up and find her children and mine in learning and virtue until 21, except my son Clement, for whom no part of the goods shall be employed; and as each of my children is 21 she shall pay of my goods £200 equally among them, except my daughter Clare Smith, who shall have no part of the £200; and the residue of my goods to my wife's own use. To her for life my parsonage of White Notley and the advowson, glebe and tithes, on condition that she yearly pay my servants John Dawson 40s. and Richard Culpeper 26s. 8d. for 12 years. In case my wife die before 12 years, Henry my son to have the parsonage, etc., until Clement is 21; if Clement die before 21 Thomas my son to have it until Henry is 21; and if Henry die before 21 William my son to have it until Thomas is 21; and if Thomas die before 21 Clare to have it until William is 21; with like condition to pay the two annuities. I bequeath my manor of Langford with the appurtenances and my messuages in Langford, Ulting, Wickham [Bishops], [Great?] Totham, Maldon, and Woodham Mortimer, so that my executrix shall take the revenues for 12 years to pay £200 to Clare at 21 or marriage; if she die before, Clement or my heir to have £100 at 21 and the other £100 to my sons equally; after the 12 years I give out of the manor annuities of £10 to Henry and £7 each to Thomas and William. I make my wife sole executrix and Mr [Richard] Weston, one of the justices of the Common Pleas, and Mr James Lorde of Danbury supervisors, and towards Mr Weston's pains £5 and my best gelding, desiring him most humbly to accept it in good part and as a poor remembrance of his very friend, and to Mr Lorde for his pains taken in my business before this time and now £10; if my wife refuse, my supervisors to be my executors and she to have half my goods. To Mary Filles, my wife's goddaughter, £10 if she shall be ordered by my wife when she marry.

Memorandum. The testator as well since the making of his testament as afore divers times and specially about the Feast of the Nativity of St John Baptist last, viz. 1563, and in the Feast of the Birth of Christ 1562, having conference with Mary his wife touching Clare and other his children, as well in his parlour as in his bed chamber at Cressing Temple, declared that, if Clare would not be obediently ruled as well in her bringing up as in her marriage by the said Mary her mother, she would have no part of his goods.

Witnesses: the said Mary Smithe, William Thomas, John Dawson, Thomas Pynkarde, Elizabeth Care, Alice Bailie, Mary Felis, Alice Saunders, with others.

Proved 8 April 1564 by Mary Smithe.

THOMAS SOMERVILDE of Stanford-le-Hope gentleman, 22 December 1589.   [35/13]

To a preacher for making a sermon at my burial 6s. 8d. To the necessity of the poor of Stanford 6s. 8d. and of Naunton (Glos.) where I was born 10s. To every of my godchildren 3s. 4d. I forgive Richard Thruxton such debts as he oweth to me. To Eugbuy Gatton esquire in consideration that he be overseer as my special trust is in him 20s. To my two loving brothers William and Giles Somervilde all my wearing

apparel, saddles, bridles, boots and spurs, 2 geldings, and £6, equally
to be divided. The residue to my loving and natural son Percival
Somervilde at 21; if he die before to my executor, paying Giles £7 and
to have the use of Percival's portion, bringing him up well and virtuously in good learning whereby he may be able to get his living with
honesty and to furnish him well during his nonage with victuals, apparel
and other necessaries, freely without any allowance therefor. I ordain
my sole executor William, and I desire Ewgbuy Gatton my overseer.
Witnesses: Richard Penn, Richard Wright, John Hunte notary, Daniel
Buck servant of John Hunt.

Codicil. To John Hunt of London notary public 3s. 4d.
 Proved 11 February 1591.

MATTHEW STEPHENS of Colchester gentleman, 2 March 1598.
[43/41]

To the parish of All Saints, wherein I dwell, £10, to be disposed by
my wife, my heirs, or the owners of my capital messuage wherein I dwell,
and the churchwardens yearly for the benefit of the poor of the parish
for ever.

To Priscilla my wife my houses and lands, free and copy, for life if
unmarried, the remainder to my heirs male; and for default of such
issue, the house I dwell in and the Walnut Tree House wherein Jacob
the carpenter dwelleth, with the copyhold called Huntes in Greenstead
to Priscilla my daughter for life, and after to William Stephens my
brother. If my wife die or marry and I have no issue male, the lands
called St Anne's and my house and lands at Wivenhoe (the enclosed
woods excepted) and my lands called Stephens in Ardleigh and Langham
to Elizabeth my daughter; my lands in Great Horkesley and my tenement
and lands in Lexden to Martha my daughter; my lands called Hunters
in Great Wigborough to Mary my daughter, she paying Anne for life
£4 a year; my lands called Abbotes Twenty Acres in Great Wigborough
and Peldon and my copyhold lands in Great Holland to Anne; and
after my daughters' decease all to William. To Martha for life a yearly
rentcharge of 40s. out of the lands given to Elizabeth. To my very good
uncle John Stephens of Ardleigh my tenement and lands in Ardleigh
called Coles in consideration that he bestow on Elizabeth what it pleaseth
him. If I die without issue male, I will to William my enclosed woods
in Wivenhoe which I purchased of Mr Barker, after my wife's decease.
To Robert Stevens my uncle 40s. To every one of my said daughters
£100 at 21 or marriage. To my wife for life the use of my plate and
household stuff so long as she is unmarried, and after her decease or
marriage to my five daughters to be divided part and part alike. I ordain
my wife sole executrix, and if she marry or die I ordain William and
my daughters my executors.

Whereas I, being one of the executors of Thomas Lawrence, lately
alderman of Colchester, with Martin Bessell alderman and William
Lawrence, by reason whereof certain money by agreement between our-
selves is remaining in my hands concerning which I am bound to them

254

in two obligations of £1,000 apiece, and they are bound to me in like manner, I appoint the right worshipful my very good friend Sir Thomas Lucas knight that my executors deliver to him all such money and the obligations, and I make him my executor for those matters only, with my brother [in-law] Robert Myddleton gentleman as an indifferent person. To Sir Thomas Lucas and my Lady Lucas each 40s. to make them a ring with the death's head. To my very good friends Mr Graie and his wife 20s. apiece. To my brother Bessell and his wife and my brother Myddleton 40s. apiece. To my loving brother John Stephens, my loving friends and kinsfolks Mr Thomas Reynoldes, my father-in-law Mr Myddleton, Mr Northey, Mr Lobell, and my uncles John and Nicholas Stephens, 10s. apiece to make them rings with this posy *Sis memor amici.* To Priscilla Davye 40s. and to Susan my maid 10s.

Witnesses: Thomas Reynolde, Robert Middleton, Ralph Northey, Henry Herringe, Henry Slinger.

Proved 13 May 1599. Note of further probate granted, 13 December 1626, to Elizabeth Gilberd *alias* Stephens, daughter of the testator.

WILLIAM STRACHIE of Walden gentleman, 8 November 1598.
[43/9]

To Elizabeth my wife 40 acres of customary lands, meadow and pasture at her choice where she will in Walden and Wimbish or either, to sell and surrender towards payment of my debts amounting to £240 and of such fines as shall be due to the lords of the manors; to her for life the residue of my customary lands, and after her decease to William my son. To her my messuage called Pellhams in Walden which I bought of Henry Leigh, and to pay in consideration thereof to Frances Strachie my daughter £20. To my wife for life my messuage and brewhouse in Kings Street in Westminster over against the Close in Middlesex, with the copper, brewing vessel, mill, washing tun, gyle tun, coolback and other utensils, and in consideration thereof to pay Frances, Elizabeth Strachie, Anna Strachie, Margaret Strachie, Abigail Strachie and Martha Strachie, my daughters, 200 marks each, viz. 25 marks every quarter during the twelve years after my wife's decease; if William decease without issue male, the remainder to John my son and his heirs male, paying likewise to my daughters. To Frances a bedstead over the great parlour, with certain pewter at my wife's appointment. To John a bedstead over the shop. To Thomas my son a bedstead over the buttery. To Alice Robinson my maidservant, in consideration of her long service, £10 and a bedstead over the buttery wherein Elizabeth Stocker use to lie or else some other at my wife's discretion, i.e. £3 6s. 8d. within 8 months after my decease, £3 6s. 8d. 6 months after, and £3 6s. 8d. at marriage if she marry with my wife's consent. The residue of my goods, household stuff, leases, jewels, linen, plate, brass, money, corn sown and growing, horses and other cattle, to my wife, whom I make sole executrix. Witnesses: Richard Frenche, Nicholas Clerke, and James Crofte notary public.

Proved 13 February 1599.

ALEXANDER SULIARDE of Stanford-le-Hope gentleman, 8 March 1572. [15/8]

To my well-beloved mother Joan Suliarde in sign of my dutiful good-will for a token 40 marks. To my brother Anthony Suliarde 20 marks. To my sisters Isabel Cheke and Martha Woodwarde 20 marks each. To my sister Jane Sulyarde who is yet unmarried 100 marks. The residue to my brother John Suliarde, whom I make my sole executor. Witnesses: John Pokyns clerk, William Woodwarde, Jane Suliarde, and Martha Woodwarde.

Proved 21 March 1572.

RICHARD THURSTON of Colchester gentleman, 17 February 1602.
[For Richard Thurston alderman, see p. 312.] [47/53]

To my loving friend Ralph Persyvall £10. The residue to my loving friend Thomas Clarcke citizen and haberdasher of London, whom I nominate my sole executor. Witnesses: Michael Pynder, John Smithe, Richard Chaundler and Thomas Tasker, servants of Robert Bankeworthe, scrivener.

Proved 23 July 1603.

RICHARD TURNOR of [Little] Parndon gentleman, 1 May 1597.
[41/77]

Whereas at this present I am towards the service of her Majesty and my country in Ireland, so as I cannot disjoin my body to any certain place of burial as those who have a more certain abiding as into the hands of God; therefore I mean frankly to offer it in this service for my country so to be buried wheresoever it pleaseth God to take me.

I appoint my dear and well-beloved wife Elizabeth my executrix and Edward Turnor, my eldest brother of Parndon, and my beloved brother-in-law Thomas Waterhows the younger of Whitchurch (Bucks.), gentle-man, my executors. To my wife £500, viz. £100 that William Sonner of Harlow Bury and his son owe me by their bond in the custody of my eldest brother, £100 that Search of Epping oweth me by like bond, £100 more owing me by a gentleman to whom my brother lent it whose name I have forgotten but appeareth by a bond also in his custody, £50 that my cousin John Wilkinson oweth me whereof my brother hath a bond, £50 that at my coming from London was in the hands of Mr John Morrie, and £100 owing me by the right honourable the Lady Bourgh the younger. If any of these debts, except the last because my wife knoweth best of the lending thereof and hath had many honourable promises for repayment, be such as my wife mislike, she shall make choice of any other money or debts owing me to the like value, and these specially named which she refusing shall be con-verted to such other uses as hereafter I appoint.

To my sister Elizabeth Turnor in consideration that she hath attended my wife £40 at marriage, provided that she match herself according to her mother's and my eldest brother's liking. To my eldest brother Edward my arras or tapestry hangings, in all five pieces of the story of Deborah and Barak, containing of Dutch ells, for by that measure I bought them, 135, which is of English yards about 101; and a basin and ewer of silver (the weight I certainly remember not), a deep round basin and ewer near the value of £20, 2 spout pots of silver, a bigger and a lesser, with serpents' heads, near to the value of £14, 2 big silver bowls which I bought at Brell [Brielle, Holland], near the value of £5, a bed of tawny silk, the tester of damask and the curtains of red taffeta, the bedstead, and an Irish rug of the same colour belonging to it; and lastly, for household stuff to the end I would furnish him one chamber, a pair of high copper andirons which usually stood in my great chamber. To my wife the rest of my plate and household stuff. Further she shall have the use of the plate, hangings and household stuff as well that otherwise bequeathed as to herself for life, if she remain a widow, but if she shall happen to marry, as I verily think she will not, I do out of the opinion that I have of her wisdom and care believe that she will make such a choice of these things which I have especially bequeathed to my brother as she will stand in no need; therefore I will that, on such marriage, this plate, hangings and household stuff be delivered to my brother according as I have bequeathed to him, but if she marry not she will so keep them as afterwards they may be likewise had for him, to whom by this it may appear I mean good. The rest of my plate and household stuff, according as before in like few words, to my wife. To her also her wearing jewels, as chains, borders, bracelets and rings.

Whereas I have more money that here yet I have bequeathed to the sum of £200 or £300, I will that as it is now in divers men's hands at use, some named in this, there be continued for 3 years after my decease £700 at like use, which is according to her Majesty's laws and not against God's as I am fully persuaded, for her maintenance, and after the 3 years to betake her to such £500 only as I have bequeathed to her.

To Thomas Waterhowse, my other executor, £10 as a token of my thankfulness to him for his travail therein. The residue to my eldest brother, to be well understood that his children should be the better for it, and I assure myself that they shall be so if he live, but if it please God to call him my desire is that he will take like order for them that I do for him to the end these things may come among them as a remembrance of us both, and so much the rather for the especial love I bear to one of his sons whom I christened, namely Arthur, for whom I have made in this no provision but leave it wholly to the disposition of his father. The peace of God be among us in this world to keep us from all contentions and in our souls to keep us by the precious merits of Jesus Christ, Amen.

[No witnesses.]

Proved 5 August 1597.

JOHN UPCHER gentleman, captain of 200 soldiers in the Low Countries, 26 March 1599. (Nuncupative.) [43/67]

He being in England and ready to go over into the Low Countries and after that in service in the Low Countries did before credible witnesses acknowledge that he was assured in marriage and contracted to Elizabeth daughter of William Lynne gentleman of Little Horkesley, and declaring how deeply he loved her and that he intended very shortly to marry her, and calling to mind the hazards and dangers which he was to undergo in the wars wherein he served, did by word of mouth declare that she should have all his goods.

Administration granted, 29 August 1599, to Elizabeth Lynne, spouse of the said John Upcher.

JOHN VENSTREE of Wivenhoe gentleman, 28 May 1591. [35/90]

Touching the disposition of my lease which I bought of Mr Richard Boillard of a house and lands in Hornsey (Middx.) belonging to the prebend of Brownswood which belongs to the cathedral church of St Paul which I hold for 52 years yet to come, for which I pay Mr Harrington esquire who hath the reversion of the same the yearly rent of £10, which lease I bequeath to my well-beloved wife Sarah. To her and my well-beloved friend Henry Best of London scrivener the messuage and lands belonging in Minster in the Isle of Sheppey (Kent) in the tenure of Thomas Benslyn, to the use of Sarah and Henry and their heirs. I constitute my wife and Henry Best to sell the house and orchard lately erected by me with the lands belonging in the tenure of John Deacon butcher. To my mother-in-law Alice Brewster in remembrance of my goodwill £5. To Richard Brewster gentleman, her husband, £5. To my very good friend Mr John Brewster £5. To my sister-in-law Ellen Bainham £3 6s. 8d. To Miles, Jane and Richard Exilby, children of Alice Brewster, each 10s. To Mr Thomas Harris tailor 40s. To my well-beloved sister dwelling at Rayleigh yearly 50s. for life. To Elizabeth Benslyn, widow of my cousin Thomas Benslyn of Sheppey, £10. To my well-beloved friend George Totty gentleman £10 to be abated and allowed to him in the last payments of £40 which he oweth me. To John Ayscough esquire £20. To the poor of Minster £10, St Dunstan-in-the-West in Fleet Street, London, £5, and Wivenhoe £5. To my wife the lease of the farm or tenement wherein I dwell called Rogers in Wivenhoe, with the goods, household stuff, plate, rings, jewels, corn and grain at Wivenhoe. The residue to my wife and Henry Best, whom I make executors, and overseer I make my very good friend William Crouch of St Dunstan, and for his pains £3 6s. 8d.

Witnesses: William Peckston scrivener, Robert Stephen, Thomas Mathewe, servant to Henry Best.

Proved 22 December 1591.

PHILIP WATKINS of Grays Thurrock gentleman. [No date.] (Nuncupative.)   [44/51]

To be buried in Grays Thurrock church. To Elizabeth my wife, Philip my youngest son, and Mary my daughter, each £33 6s. 8d. To my wife and her two children, Philip and Mary, each a cow, and 10 of my best hogs to be equally divided among them. To my wife the best and the worst featherbeds, 1 brass pot, 1 kettle, 2 chargers, 2 platters, 2 fruit dishes, 3 candlesticks, 1 salt, ½ dozen pewter spoons, 1 dozen trenchers, 2 tablecloths, ½ dozen napkins, ½ dozen hens and a cock.

Witnesses : John Beda, Richard Howmer. (He named William Watkins his son as executor.)

Administration granted, 17 June 1600, to Thomas Newman of St Catherine Creechurch near Aldgate, London, writer of the court letter, and Henry Barbor, clerk, vicar of Grays Thurrock, because William Watkins Vaughan [sic], son and executor during the minority of Thomas Watkins Vaughan and Alice Watkins Vaughan, children of the deceased, refused to act. Administration granted, 5 February 1602, to Elizabeth Watkins alias Heath, widow of the deceased.

JOHN WATSON of Rivenhall gentleman, 29 December 1584.   [29/3]

To the poor people of Rivenhall 40s. and Cressing 40s. To Catherine my wife £300, one-half of my plate and jewels (my chain only excepted) and one-half of my household stuff, and £50 a year for life, to be paid out of my eldest son's land. To William, my eldest son, my manor of Lanhams, Norfolkes and Mynges [in Peldon], both freehold and copyhold, the copies according to the customs of the manor, my farm in Peldon called Harveys and Billetes, £50, and my chain of gold (weighing 20 oz.), at 21. To John, Norton, Richard and Thomas Watson, the residue of my lands and chattels, the lease of the manor of Stoxes [in ?] only excepted, which I bequeath to my daughter Jane Watson, and £100, at 18; if she decease before, her portion to be equally divided among my four sons. To them all my money, jewels, plate and household stuff. I ordain William my sole executor and John Norton gentleman, John Duffelde and Robert Brudenell overseers, and for their pains each 5 marks, and they shall take the rents of my lands during William's minority and that of my other sons, and the use of the money, jewels, plate, and household stuff to their bringing up and benefit. Witnesses : Thomas Wilson, Samuel Cordall, Roger Debnam.

Administration granted, 27 January 1585, to the overseers, and 9 November 1597, to William.

THOMAS WHITNEY of Brook Walden in Walden gentleman, 24 January 1601.   [46/29]

To be buried in the south chapel in Walden church by my mother's grave, with some stone on my grave, the charge not exceeding £10. To Elizabeth my wife for life my lands in Walden free and copy, and my messuage and lands as well free as customary in Wimbish in recompense for her dower. My executors shall have all other my lands as well in London as elsewhere and the rents and profits until my son Thomas is 24 towards the payment of my legacies, to hold to Thomas and his heirs; and for default of such issue the remainders successively to Nicholas and to George, my sons, and their heirs. To my wife £6 a year for life. After my decease my executors shall divide into three parts my household stuff and my bedstead, tester, valances and curtains in the new chamber, my plate only excepted, and my wife shall have one part at her choice. To my daughter Anne Whitney £500 at 18 or marriage. To Thomas £500 and the said bedstead at 21. To my daughter Elizabeth £300 at 18 or marriage and the gilt bowl which Mistress Sutton her godmother gave her. To Nicholas £300 at 21. To George £300, also £20 in recompense of £20 which my brother George gave him by his will, and for this payment and satisfaction of which £20 I had consideration of my Lord and Mr [blank] to be paid to George at 21. To my brother Stutvile and my sister, his wife, Mr Hollande in Norfolk and Martin Stutvile a ring of gold of 40s. apiece. The consideration of my servants I refer to my executors. The residue shall be divided among George, Anne and Elizabeth, part and part like. My executors shall bring up all my children, and if my wife be desirous to have their keeping and bringing up then my executors shall pay her so much money as she and they shall agree upon. I make my brother Thomas and my wife's brother, Mr Richard Deane of London, James Crofte and Thomas Hedge my executors, to whom I give £10 apiece, and my supervisor, if it please him, my Lord and master [Lord Thomas Howard], to whom I give a piece of plate of £20. Witnesses: William Turnor and William Sothey.

Proved 7 May 1602.

JOHN WILFORDE of Barking gentleman, 22 September 1590. (Nuncupative.) [34/59]

Being weak and wounded in body, he said that his goods should be divided equally among his brethren and sisters, and that a scrivener should be sent for to set down in writing his will. Witnesses: Thomas Rudd of London salter, John Welles, John Colcloughe.

Administration granted, 28 September 1590, to William Wilford, son of the deceased.

THOMAS WILLIAMSON of Wimbish gentleman, 4 January 1562.
[5/31]

To Katherine my wife for life, in consideration that she keep herself unmarried and keep and bring up my children and hers honestly and virtuously until they be able to go to some science and godly mistery whereby they may the better live, my lands as well free as copy in Walden, Wimbish and Thunderley; and after her decease Anthony my son shall have my lands in Wimbish and Thunderley and my land in Walden called Prentis Mead. To Thomas my son my tenement in Castle

Street in Walden in the tenure of [blank] Wilson, 3½ acres of land at Mores Harp, 1½ acres of land in Bucknoll Lane in that of Margaret Brockley, and 3 acres of pasture in the Slade towards Little Walden in that of Thomas Colte. To George my son my tenement wherein Royse dwelleth lying without the bars towards the windmill in Walden, my tenement and orchard called Wren Park with 2 acres of pasture adjoining, 1 acre of land lying towards Duck Street in the tenure of Royse, 1½ acres lying under the windmill to Cambridge ward, 1 acre lying in length by Cambridge highway, 3 roods of pasture at Westley Wood corner in that of Thomas Cowete, and the tenement that Newborne dwelleth in, with the dovehouse, orchard and garden that William Gorsely hath. To Susan my daughter my bed in my great parlour and to Anthony my other bed in my other parlour, at their marriages. My wood and timber lying about Langfield (containing 5 acres) and Bowney (7½ acres) to be sold by my executrix and the money divided among my six daughters Mary, Judith, Susan, Annabel, Audrey and Katherine, except my best gown and best cloak which I will the one to my son Cotton and the other to Anthony, and Cotton to take his choice. To Gaselen my gown furred with fitches and to Francklyn my bible. If my wife be with child, it be partaker with my daughters part and part like. To Margaret Hanchet my servant at marriage 40s. If my wife marry, all lands, tenements and goods to her given to remain to my children before her marriage at the discretion of my supervisor. I ordain my wife my executrix and I desire my cousin Edward Thorowgood to be my supervisor, giving him 40s. Witnesses: Thomas Addam and Thomas Longe.

Proved 1 December 1562.

THOMAS WILLSONNE of Bocking gentleman, 24 February 1588.

[35/23]

To the poor of Bocking £5 and Stisted £5. Whereas Thomas Willsonne my father of Bethnal Green [Middx.] deceased did make me his sole executor and did bequeath divers legacies to his children which are not as yet by me paid; and whereas two leases yet enduring did accrue to me as executor, one of Bishops Hall and other lands in Stepney and the other of certain houses in St Martin-in-the-Fields by Charing Cross [Middx.]; out of the profits of which leases my will is that the said legacies and certain legacies by my will to my own children be paid; my executrix shall of the profits that first arise pay my father's legacies as yet unpaid amounting to £600, also pay after such legacies by me bequeathed to my daughter first to Susan at marriage or 21 £300, and to Elizabeth, Jane, Anne, Mary, Winifred, Frances and Dorothy each £200. To every of my servants dwelling with me 4 nobles. To my brother John Willsone a ring of gold with a death's head, and my sister, his wife, 4 angels to make a ring. To my sisters Bradburrie and Pigott each 4 nobles to make a ring, Barbara Lucas a ring of gold called a turquoise, Anne Haines a ring of gold with a child's face on it, Joan 3 angels to make a ring, and Elizabeth 3 gimmals of gold hanging together. To Dr Creake 4 angels for a remembrance to make a ring to seal with. To Thomas my eldest son a horn bordered about with silver parcel gilt. To Philip my son 4 angels to make a ring. To John Robinson my children's schoolmaster and Roger Debnam my tenant, each 4 angels, and my uncle Jeffery Brooke's wife 3 angels, each to make a ring. To my mother Simons a ring of gold with a death's head. To Henry Barr 40s. to make a ring. To goodwife Debnam my child's nurse 20s. To William Ungell 20s.

To my wife the issues of my lands so long as she remain unmarried; and after my son Thomas be 21 she shall pay him yearly 100 marks towards his maintenance. To her my goods to pay my debts and legacies and to see my children well and carefully brought up, and I make her my sole executrix. I appoint my well-beloved friends Mr Edward Thursbie and my uncle Mr Jeffery Broke my overseers, and for their pains 5 marks apiece.

Witnesses: Launcelot Browne doctor of physic, Jeffery Brooke, Humfrey Clarke, Thomas Juckes [Inckes?] grocer, Lewis Atmere, William Barnes.

Proved 31 March 1591 by Susan his widow.

ROBERT WINCHE of Woodford gentleman, 13 August 1590. [34/67]

To my well-beloved son Edmund my messuages in Waltham Holy Cross letten by lease for divers years to come to John Foxe of Enfield; my copyhold land in Edmonsea (being 4 acres) and a close of land abutting on Threstlinge Lane (1 acre) in Waltham letten also to John Foxe by licence of the lord of the manor of Waltham; my messuage called Frendes and 40 acres of land, meadow and pasture and a third part of a yard of land (4 acres) late parcel of a tenement called Hedgmans, and 3 parcels of meadow (1¾ acres), whereof one in Rowe Mead and the other two in Grobe Mead in the tenure of Christopher Peacocke in Waltham; my messuage called Huddes with 20 acres of land in the manor of Waltham late in that of Thomas Blenerhassett gentleman but now of William Symondes; all which I have surrendered to the lord of the manor by John Grene and Edward Grene, customary tenants, to the use of my will. To Edmund my messuage called Collins now divided into two houses, with 46 acres of land, meadow, pasture and wood in the tenure of myself and John Maltes; my messuage called Frythmans and 10 acres letten by lease, by licence of the lord of the manor of Woodford, to William Stakford, in the tenure of Thomas Covell; and my messuage called Sandishall alias Verlandes in that of widow Barthellnew; all in the manor of Woodford, which I have likewise surrendered by William Dimsdall and Robert Quickeko, customary tenants, on condition that he pay my wife an annuity of £6 13s. 4d. To Edmund also £100. To Daniel my son my lease of my house called the Three Crowns in Westcheap in London in the tenure of Basil Dighton. To my daughters Rebecca Bourey and Elizabeth Maultes each £50. To Anne Spaight my other daughter £50 on condition that Thomas her husband make her a sufficient assurance of such copyhold lands as standeth seised in his own right for her life, the remainder thereof to their heirs. To my three godchildren, Robert Maltes, William Edwardes and Elizabeth Bourey, each £3 6s. 8d. To the children of my sister Anne Barber £5 to be equally divided.

To the poor's box of Woodford [amount omitted]. There shall be bestowed in black cloth, funeral dinner and other charges touching my funerals £50, whereof those I will have to wear black, viz. my two executors, Magdalene my wife, Rebecca, Elizabeth and Anne and their husbands, Anne Barbor and her husband, my cousin Thomas Winch, Mr [Robert] Wright parson, Jane Peacocke and Ellen Edwardes, and such others as my executors shall think meet.

My plate, bedding, pewter, apparel, napery, linen and household stuff (the wainscot, hangings and glass in my mansion house only excepted) shall be equally and indifferently divided into three parts to Edmund, Daniel and my wife. She shall have her free habitation for life within these rooms of my messuage called Collyns, i.e. the kitchen chamber wherein she now lieth, the middle chamber next thereto, the reasonable use of the hall and kitchen for her business, and the liberty of the orchard and garden for her solace and recreation. The residue of my goods, money and marchands to Daniel. I make Edmund and Daniel my executors. To Mr Robert Wright parson, 6s. 8d. for a funeral sermon at my burial.

Witnesses : Edmund Greene, William Dymsdale, Robert Quicke.
Proved 19 October 1590.

MAGDALENE WINCHE of Woodford widow, 28 October 1592.
[36/81]

To be buried in Woodford chancel near my husband. To my son Edmund 2 bedsteads with the trundle beds in the kitchen chamber and the middle chamber in his house, 2 wainscot presses in the same chambers and 8 curtains in the chamber windows, the brushing board with the trestles, and court cupboard, with the hangings and painted cloth in the chambers, a great plated cupboard, a table, and 2 stone mortars in the kitchen. To my daughter Elizabeth Maltis my best featherbed. To her and my daughter Anne Spighte a pair of needlework valances with a pair of blue and yellow say curtains for a bed and my fair arras coverlet, for their lives, to use in childbirth, and to the survivor for ever. My gowns and wearing apparel with my linen be equally divided between my three daughters, viz. Rebecca Borie, Elizabeth and Anne. To Anne Borie my goddaughter £5 of that £10 her father John oweth me. To my daughter Borie's other five children 20s. apiece, viz. John, Thomas, Elizabeth, Ellen and Katherine, which is the remaining £5. To John Maltis my godson £5. To Sarah and Robert Maltis, children of my daughter Elizabeth, 20s. apiece. To Anne Spighte my goddaughter £5. To Ellen Edwarded my kinswoman 20s. To Margaret Barie my maid 10s. To the poor of Woodford £3. The residue to my son Daniel, whom I ordain my sole executor. Witnesses : Robert Wrighte and others.
Proved 5 November 1592.

EDWARD WINCHE of Woodford gentleman, 5 March 1603. [48/43]

To the poor people of Woodford where I now dwell, to such only as ordinarily receive the common alms there bestowed, £5. To Magdalene my wife an annuity of £40, on condition that she shall not claim any other portion of my lands in the manors of Woodford or Waltham Holy Cross nor sue my son Edmund for any dower. To him my lands freehold and copyhold. To my other two sons Thomas and Robert each £100 at 21 and to my three daughters Elizabeth, Magdalene and Mary each £100 at 21 or marriage; the use and profit of the £500 for 2 years after my decease shall be employed towards the payment of such fines as shall be imposed on Edmund for his copyholds, and afterwards to my wife for the bringing up and education of my children until 21 or marriage, my wife being bound with two other sureties in £800 to my executors for the payment of the legacies. To Edmund my books as well printed as written, and evidences and conveyances, desiring my executors to buy a strong and large chest with 3 locks and to place it in some convenient room in my dwelling house, my executors and my wife each to keep one key. To my loving friends and kinsmen Thomas Barbor citizen and salter of London and my brother Daniel Winche citizen and grocer of London each 6 of my best silver spoons for their pains, and I make them my executors. The residue (the glass, wainscot, presses, standing bedsteads, tables with frames, stools and forms of wainscot, chairs and court cupboards of wainscot in my dwelling house at Woodford excepted, which shall remain for Edmund's use when he is 21) to my wife. Witnesses : John Ryder notary public, and John Symons, Michael Havard and John Wandley, servants of the notary.

Proved 28 April 1604.

ROBERT WINCKFEILDE of Brentwood gentleman, 12 February 1600.
[44/17]

To the poor people of Great Warley 20s. and Brentwood 10s. The residue to Elizabeth my wife, whom I ordain my sole executrix. I make Jane Twine my daughter supervisor, and for her pains 20s. Witnesses : Nicholas Shereman, Robert Debney, Bridget Baily.

Proved 12 March 1600.

THOMAS WISEMAN of North End in Great Waltham gentleman, 20 November 1580. [For John and Anne Wiseman, see pp. 145-147.] [23/47]

To be buried in Great Waltham church next the north side in the upper alley.

To my daughters Elizabeth and Dorothy Wiseman 500 marks apiece at 21 or marriage. To Joan daughter of my son William deceased £40 at 20 or marriage. To Dorothy my wife for life, over and besides such lands as I have otherwise conveyed to her, my lands in Great Waltham, Great Dunmow, High Easter and Barnston, as well freehold as copyhold (a parcel of land in Great Waltham [common] field only excepted); with remainder to Thomas.

To Thomas my son my manor or messuage with appurtenances in Lambeth (Surrey) called Hether Rowe in the tenure of [blank] Bowyer esquire; two parcels of copyhold and pasture called Mexsawes and 1 acre of land in Fynes in Springfield; my lands in Great Baddow and Sandon as well free as copy called Grapnelles in that of Alexander Paschall; and my island called Ewsey [Osea in Great Totham] which I purchased of my Lord of Essex [Walter Devereux, 1st Earl of Essex]. To Thomas my stock and store of cattle, i.e. 20 milch kine and 100 ewes, which I have letten with my island to one Richarde; the crofts in Great Baddow called Apton Fields (containing 8 acres), a hope called Welles Hope (1 acre), and a parcel of mead adjoining Baddow Mead ($\frac{1}{2}$ acre) in the occupation of [blank] Read, on condition that he pay out of the same to the churchwardens of Great Waltham 40s. yearly at my mansion house in North End, viz. 20s. yearly in the necessary repairing of Waltham church and 20s. in deeds of charity within the circuit of North End by the discretion of 6 of the chiefest inhabitants of the same end; and the parcel of land in Chelmsford called Burgess Well in the occupation of [blank] Hubberd, so as my son pay an annuity which I have already granted out of the same.

To William son of William my son deceased a tenement and ferry in Rainham with two marshes adjoining in the tenure of [blank] Whodd, to hold after my wife's decease. To him my manor with appurtenances of Mucking Hall and a parcel of land adjoining called Taylors in Barling and Shopland, after the expiration of the lease which Henry Butler hath for 30 years for the yearly rent of £40, also yielding therefor yearly in the town of Chelmsford to me and my heirs 6 bushels of oysters, i.e. weekly during Lent a bushel; and the said fermor [lessee] shall repair the buildings and keep the dam at the fleet head as need shall require and have yearly upon the premises 10 loads of firewood to be spent there and sufficient timber for reparations, hedgebote, ploughbote, cartbote, gatebote and stakebote. To Thomas son of William my son my tenement in West Tilbury, East Tilbury and Mucking with the lands and marshes belonging in the tenure of John Prentis, after my wife's decease; and my manor, messuage or farm in Hatfield Peverel and Witham called Smalland Hall alias Marshes for 30 years after the lease which John Rowe hath, yielding therefor to me and my heirs £20 and 2 leads of cheese. I bequeath the manor and my manor or farm called Nabattes in Springfield in the tenure of John Bower to my wife for life, so as she keep herself unmarried, and after her decease or marriage the manor of Nabattes shall remain to Thomas for ever, and the manor of Smalland Hall to Thomas and his heirs male, and for default of such issue to William his son.

Touching my manors of Stisted and Milles in Stisted and my meadow called Hopkin Mead in Bockingham [in Copford], and my lands in Halstead which I purchased of Sir William Walgrave knight, which do amount to the third part of my lands in Essex, they shall descend to my heir by common law.

Whereas my son-in-law Thomas Gouge doth owe me by his bill £40, it shall be equally divided among his children by my daughter Clemence

265

deceased, his daughter Clemence Douge [*sic*] only excepted, for that I have otherwise considered her by my gift in my lifetime. To every of my household servants 10s. To my kinsmen Ralph and William Wiseman, my brother's sons, to my cousin Richard Everard of Walthambury, and to my sister Legat, a ring of gold worth 40s. apiece for a remembrance with a death's head therein and some writing as shall be thought good by my executor.

The residue to my wife and Thomas, whom I ordain executors, and my kinsmen John Glascockes of Roxwell gentleman, my son-in-law Thomas Gouge, and my kinsman Joseph Man of Braintree supervisors, and to each for their pains £10. To John Glascockes the [right of the] marriage of [my ward] John Wiseman son of William deceased, the marriage of which I have of the grant of the Queen's Majesty. If my goods and money shall not be sufficient to pay my debts and legacies, my plate and household stuff excepted, my executors shall receive the profits of my manor of Mucking Hall for 4 years after my decease. To John Welbecke and Joan Curtis my servants 40s. apiece.

Witnesses: Thomas Childe, William Cowlande, John Ellis, Thomas Lytle, Joseph Man writer hereof.

Proved 5 December 1580. Administration granted, 20 November 1598, to Ralph Wiseman, nephew of the deceased, Dorothy and Thomas now dead not having administered.

EDWARD WOULDE of Waltham Holy Cross gentleman, — December 1598. [43/32]

To be buried in Waltham church. To the poor people of Waltham £10. Towards the repairing of the church 40s. To the preacher at my burial 10s. To every of my servants 10s.

To Margaret my wife the following which are owed to me, viz. by Roger Bower of Waltham £150, Edward Stacie by bonds £130, my brother [in-law] Richard Meade £200, Mr Robert Hall £40, Reynold Etheredge £9, John Adames of Harlow 40s., James Crew 40s., Thomas Crew 18s., one Cracknell £4, William Campper of Hockley 180 quarters of wootes [oats], Mr Thomas Perrin of North Shoebury £16 10s., Mr Howe of Rayleigh £8, my fellow falconer £3, and Martin Maye of Waltham 40s.; also to her £133 6s. 8d. which Mr Drake is to pay by bond to be sealed by him for his last payment. To her my lease which I bought of Richard Walterer and my cattle except my grey gelding; my plate, jewels and other goods in my house; and my debentures in my hands. She shall pay all those debts which I have written in a schedule and annexed it to my will [not annexed to the registered copy].

To Francis Goodinge my kinsman £100, to be paid out of the bond that Mr Drake is to seal of £366 13s. 4d. To Anne Goodinge sister of Francis £20, to be paid out of the bond that Mr Drake is to pay for the first payment. To Katherine Almery £20 likewise. To Dorothy and Ellen Would my sisters £50 each likewise. To my cousin Peckeringe of London and his wife a ring of gold worth 10s. apiece. To Robert Finch my servant my russet cloak laid about with lace, my fustian doublets,

2 pair of breeches, and all my stockings except my silk stockings. The residue to my brother John Woulde, whom I make my sole executor.

Witnesses: Richard Meade, Roger Bowyer, Thomas Sutton.

Memorandum. My wife shall pay her children's portions which is £300 and the £10 which I have given to the poor, which is not expressed in the schedule. Witnesses: Roger Cooke, Roger Bowyer.

Proved 2 May 1599.

JOHN WRIGHT of Littlebury gentleman, 8 October 1590.   [36/27]

Touching such debts due to me by my attorney's book, I bequeath them to George Kirke my servant, he paying out of the same to his sister Beatrix Kirke my servant £5. To my servants John Kynnaston 40s., Thomas Michell 20s., and Nicholas Brande 20s. To the poor people of Littlebury 20s. and to the poor child Ruth Hurste 20s. To Margaret Hantler my goddaughter, 6s. 8d. The residue to Elizabeth my wife, whom I make my sole executrix. Witnesses: John Helie, Thomas Woodly, Denis Pallmer, Thomas Plummer.

Proved 13 April 1592.

EDWARD WYOTT of Tillingham gentleman, 25 July 1584. [For Edward Wyott esquire, see p. 147.]   [28/23]

At my burial there be made a sermon by some godly preacher, to whom 10s. To the poor people of Tillingham 40s. To Jane my wife for life my manor, farm or grange called Legates [in Tillingham] with the lands appertaining which I purchased of my father-in-law Walter Myldmay esquire, and after her decease to the child that she is now pregnant with, if any such child be, at 21, and my wife be dead before; and if she be not pregnant, to her. To her for life my lease of the manor of Tillingham and the parsonage, and after her decease likewise; the £500 that Walter Myldmaye oweth me, to be paid on 14 October next; and my reversion of the lease of the manor of Bradwell Hall during such time as I should have had it if I had lived after the decease of my mother. To my cousins Isaac, William and Edward Wyott, sons of my uncle deceased, £200 which I am to receive of my father-in-law on 14 October next, to be equally divided, and after my wife's decease out of my manor of Tillingham Hall and parsonage an annuity of £20 during the lease. To John Baker my man an annuity of £5 out of my manor or farm of Legates. To Richard Wheeler my servant £5 a year during his lease, to be deducted out of his rent. To every other of my men-servants 40s. and my maidservants 10s. To my brother [Sir William] Waldgrave and my wife's sister, his wife, 20s. apiece to make rings. To my very good friend Mr Bartholomew Averell my bay trotting gelding and 20s. to make a ring. To my cousins Arthur Capell 20s., Edward, John, Gamaliel, Robert, Francis, Anne and Mary Capell, each 10s. to make a ring as tokens of goodwill and friendship. To Robert Haines, my cousin Hains, and Thomas Harris each 10s. likewise. The residue to my wife, whom I make sole executrix. I name my very good uncles Henry Capell and Arthur Harrys esquires overseers, and for their pains 20s. apiece to make rings. Witnesses : Arthur Capell, Gamaliel Capell, Richard Wheeler, Thomas Barrett, Edmund Kinge, John Baker. Proved 21 August 1584.

WILLIAM YOUNGE of Thaxted gentleman, 1 November 1588.

[33/24]

To be buried in the chancel of Thaxted church. To the poor people of Thaxted 40s. on the day of my burial. To Joan Younge my daughter £100 out of the rents and profits of my messuages and lands in High Easter which I purchased of Edmund Weste esquire and Joan or Jane his wife and out of my stock of corn and cattle on the same; and a joined bedstead and a featherbed. To William my son presently after the decease of Elizabeth my wife my messuages and lands in High Easter free and copy called Bushes and Shortes, according to the custom of the manor of High Easter Bury; and for default of issue, according to the custom, to John and Christopher my sons equally to be divided. To William the said messuages and lands purchased during my wife's life, and after to John and Christopher to be equally divided; and for default of issue to remain to Robert my son. Thomas Reinouldes, my son-in-law, shall receive the rents and profits of the lands purchased of West to the use of William, until he is of lawful age, to bear the charges of keeping him at school, and the overplus shall remain in Robert's hands meanwhile to pay the same to William when he is of age. To Robert after my wife's decease my messuage called the Chequer in Thaxted; and for default of issue to remain to John and Christopher to be equally divided. To John and Christopher my lease of my farm in Navestock which I bought of John Grene, my father-in-law, and of Thomas Grene, my brother-in-law; if either die before its expiration, to remain to the survivor, to Robert and to Elizabeth my daughter to be equally divided. To Robert and Elizabeth each £100 out of the lease of the manor of Priors Hall alias the Parsonage of Thaxted which I bought of Robert Peter esquire at 18. To my wife the lease of the same manor. To her my household stuff, except such as is before bequeathed to Joan, on condition that she deliver to John, Robert, Christopher and Elizabeth at 18 so much as shall be worth £10 apiece or pay them each £10. To my brother Nicholas Younge my best doublet, my best cloak, and my gold ring or signet.

Touching such money as I am to pay to Thomas Pery, my wife's son, I leave so much money owing to me by sundry men as appeareth by sundry obligations and bills; and if this will not be sufficient, so much as shall be wanting shall be made up of my crop of corn and my barns, stocks and cattle in Thaxted; and the residue of my crop and cattle and of my plate and linen in Thaxted to my wife. I ordain Thomas Patteshall gentleman and Thomas Reynoldes my son-in-law as my executors, and for their pains each 40s.

Witnesses : Thomas Dockley, William Smithe, Edward Armiger.

Proved 10 February 1589.

5

MERCHANTS

FRANCIS ARCHER of Bocking clothier, 25 November 1578. [22/41]

To the poor people of Bocking £3 on the day of my burial at the discretion of my supervisors. To the reparation of Bocking church 10s. To the poor weavers and fullers of Bocking £3 10s. by the advice and appointment of the churchwardens and the collectors of the poor, i.e. yearly for seven years 10s.

To Amy my wife for life, in recompense for her dowry or third part of my lands and messuages, my messuage wherein I dwell, my two messuages in the occupation of John Fuller, my six messuages which I lately bought of Thomas Brokeman gentleman in that of Daniel Dobson, John Andrewe, Charles Hunt, Harry Coper, John Buntinge and Thomas Hardinge, and my two messuages in that of George Clarke, my son-in-law, and of Agnes Wickham widow, all in Bocking, my wife maintaining them in good reparations and suffering sufficient rooms for John Goodwin and Jacob Huet to occupy. To my wife for life my two tenements in Bocking in that of Thomas Miller and Edy Goodwin widow. After her decease I will that all be demised by George Clarke for 11 years, at such rents as they can be gotten and the rents to be paid the 1st year to Frances Archer, my son Robert's daughter, the 2nd, 3rd, 4th, 5th, 6th and 7th years [respectively] to Robert, Thomas, Joan, Margaret, Richard and Mary Archer, brothers and sisters of Frances, the 8th year to Edmund son of George Clarke and Priscilla my daughter, and the 9th, 10th and 11th years to Amy, Francis and Mary, sisters and brothers of Edmund; provided that, if any die before they have received their part, it shall be equally divided among the survivors, and that each repair the buildings in that year. To George and Priscilla Clarke my said messuages in the occupations of himself and Agnes Wickham after the end of 11 years, for ever. The reversion of the residue of the messuages to Robert. To him my messuage called the Greyhound which I bought of one John Pamer in Bocking. To Timothy my son my tenements, woods, meadows and pastures called Hawses in Halstead, 5 of my horses, 6 milch kine and 1 bullock, my grass there, my carts, ploughs, harrows, cart harness and plough harness, and the household stuff. To my wife my household stuff in my messuage, my bay gelding, and the residue of my milch kine and bullocks.

To John Goodwin and Jacob Hart, my two faithful servants, sufficient house rooms within my dwelling only to use the art of clothmaking for 14 years after my decease, also £20 each to remain in their hands for 12 years on condition that they stand bound to my executors in £40 for repayment at the end of 12 years. To every of my manservants 6s. 8d. and maidservants 10s. To the children of John Cawston of Lomysse [*sic*] beside Maldon £3 to be equally divided. The residue of my goods, wool, yarn, cloth, plate and money to George Clearcke, on condition that he pay my debts and legacies, excepting only my board and timber which shall be bestowed at the discretion of my executors. I ordain my wife and George my executors, and Edward Goldinge and Roger Debnam overseers and to each for their pains 10s.

Witnesses: Thomas Gilbert, Thomas Bacon, Edward Chissell, John Fuller, John Sparhawke, and other Edward [*sic*].

Proved 24 October 1579.

ANTHONY BARBER of Halstead clothier, 9 October 1568.   [11/22]

To Alice my wife my house which I purchased of John Browne of Chelmsford for her life, except the parlour, which Anthony my son shall have whensoever he shall think good for him or his wife to come into the country; and he or his wife shall have their easement on the backside, so they should live quietly together and one to be a comfort to another, and in their absence my wife shall have the parlour. To her £116, viz. £50 within half a year after my decease, she not to claim her dower or third, but if she doth claim it then she shall not have the £16 but £100 only and so to go her way. To her the best cow I have, she to take her choice; my implements of household stuff, except that in the hall, i.e. the table, cupboard, form, benchboard, stained cloths, a fire fork, and a pair of tongs, which shall remain in the hall to the use of him or her that shall next enjoy the same, except also my best bed in the parlour, which shall remain in the same; the great chest in the parlour; and 1 seam or quarter of wheat and as much malt and 10 load of wood in the yard, if there be so much at the time of my departing.

To Thomas son of John Bentall my son-in-law my house which I purchased of Nicholas Doorant of Stoke-by-Nayland (Suffolk) and a little backhouse with an oven adjoining; a house at the end of the yard, which I purchased of Richard Lynd late of Halstead which hath been sometime occupied for a weaving shop, also the garden place by the shop; to have the house immediately after the decease of Agnes Bentall his mother, who shall have it for life; and they shall have a sufficient watercourse for ever out of the yard through the garden and so by the lower end of the shop. To Thomas £5; to Magdalen daughter of John Bentall £20, and 6s. 8d. to be paid to her at 24; John to have the occupying of the £20, putting in reasonable security to my executors. If Agnes Bentall my daughter have any child more within a year after my decease, I give it £10. To John my second gown next my best; to Thomas Bentall my son-in-law my best gown; to Sybil my daughter, his wife, a cow, and if she have a child £10 to the same; to Anthony son of Thomas my house which I purchased of Thomas Sadlington of Castle Hedingham and £5 at 24. To the other five children of Thomas, i.e. Joan, Agnes, Ellen, Robert and William, £20 apiece at 24; and to Robert a cow. My wife shall have the said grounds freely a year after my decease on condition that John have a cow pastured on the ground and the milk one day and Thomas the other day; and Thomas and John shall have sufficient hedgebote on Pilgrims Farm during the said years for maintenance and fencing the ground. To four children which my kinsman Edward Hull of Stoke hath, £5 apiece at 24, and he shall have £10 in occupying the £20 until they come of age. To my god-children 3s. 4d. apiece.

To every servant that hath been with me a whole year 6s. 8d. (John Haberlee excepted) and 6s. 8d. to all who have been with me 7 years and have truly done their service and performed such covenants as they did make. To Mr Cliburye, vicar of Halstead, for a sermon at my burial, 5s. To 5 poor marriages which shall marry next in Halstead after my decease, 5s. apiece. My executor shall bestow at my burial in deeds of charity £10, whereunto two frize gowns be given to two poor men of which John Sawmon to be one if he be alive at that day, to help to bear me to the church, and to the other two that bear me 6s. 8d. apiece. To the poor people of Halstead £5, whereof 20s. to 20 aged and impotent persons by the discretion of my executor and the churchwardens and 20s yearly to 20 suchlike persons until the £5 be contented. To 10 of the poorest people of Little Maplestead, Earls Colne, Stisted, Castle Hedingham and Bocking 10s. each parish, to be paid at the discretion of my executor and two honest men of each parish. To John Badcock, my wife's brother, 20s. and to every of his children 12d.

Whereas John Haberlee oweth me 40s., I forgive it; and whereas Thomas Clarke of Witham clothier oweth me £240, if he pay £100 to my executor in such sort as it shall be due to my wife under my will, £40 more within 1½ years after my departure, and the other £100 within 4 years, my executor shall be content or else to receive it at such time as it be due. The rest of my goods to my son Anthony, whom I make my sole executor; I appoint John Atkyn my neighbour super-visor, and for his pains 13s. 4d.

Witnesses: John Baker tanner, Abraham Metcalf, Henry Johnson, William Clibury vicar, John Baker.

Proved 1 November 1568.

THOMAS BARKER of Colchester clothier, 27 February 1585. [29/19]

To Anne my wife my lands in Nayland and Stoke-by-Nayland (Suffolk) for life, my copyhold lands [no details] until my son John is 21. To my wife my lease of the lands and tenements of the manor of Shawes [in St Botolph, Colchester] which I bought of John Spencer until my son Richard is 21. To Thomas my son £20. To my sons John 100 marks and Richard 100 marks each at 21. If all my children die without issue, to my brother Richard's children [not named]. To Robert Cocke my servant 5 marks. To Elizabeth Coppin my kinswoman 40s., my sister Elizabeth Preston 40s. and not to her husband, George Preston my kinsman 40s. to his putting to some master, Richard Coppinge dwelling with Hawkins 20s. at 21, Thomas Coppinge my cousin 10s., John Spencer 40s., widow Briant 40s., my cousin Dorothy Preston 10s., Dorothy Knapp my maid 10s., Mary Goybie my maidservant 10s., John Moore my boy 5s., and Liberte Cranvyn 6s. To the poor of Colchester £3 6s. 8d.; to mother Lantherne 10s.

Provided that, if my wife be put out of my house within a year after my decease by Thomas, I revoke the legacy of £20 to him and give it to my wife. The residue to my wife for her better maintenance and to bring up my children honestly and in good education. I appoint my wife sole executrix and my supervisors my loving friends Mr John Pye and Richard Symnell, and to each £5 for their pains; Mr Pye to be guardian and to have the custody of the lands of my son Thomas to 14. Witnesses : John Fokes the elder, William Strickson, Elias Pilgrome.

Proved 5 May 1585.

THOMAS BARLOWE of St Nicholas, Colchester, alderman and grocer, 17 June 1591.   [37/29]

To be buried in St Nicholas' church. Such debts as I shall owe at the time of my death of right or in conscience or by my book of accounts under my own handwriting shall be paid by my executors. To the poor of every parish in the liberties of Colchester 5s., and the poor prisoners in the Castle of Colchester 6s. 8d., and the Moot Hall 3s. 4d., on the day of my funeral.

My goods, chattels, wares, implements, leases, plate, ready money and debts shall be divided into three equal parts according to the laudable custom of the City of London. One part I give to Joyce my well-beloved wife and her wearing apparel, both linen and woollen, with her rings and jewels; one third to Thomas, Robert, Agnes Burges, Elizabeth Weste, Frances Savage, Margery Barlowe, Mary Barlowe, John, Joyce Barlowe, Ester Barlowe, Eleanor Barlowe, Jane Barlowe and Avice Barlowe, my children, to be equally divided among them at their ages of 21 or marriage; the other third I reserve to myself to perform the legacies to my well-beloved brother William Barlowe £10, to my cousin John Whitehand 20s., and to my apprentices other than John Tillett 20s. apiece when their indentures shall expire. I most earnestly require my executor to do his best endeavour to pay to the executors of Acerbo Velutelli, merchant stranger deceased, £19 14s. 11d., and to the executors of Edmund Needham, grocer of London also deceased, £12 8s. 2d. If my said 13 children all depart out of this mortal life before their portions be due, the money shall be divided among my children's children then living. I make my well-beloved son-in-law William Savage sole executor and my well-beloved brother William Barlowe and my son-in-law Jeremy Burgis supervisors.

Witnesses : Thomas Catcher draper, Francis Kyd scrivener, William Lynes, Jeremy Burgis [vicar of Walton-le-Soken].

272

Codicil, 25 January 1593. Having before this time devised my will and now being sick but in very good remembrance (thanked be God) and calling to my mind sundry things which at the time was not in my remembrance; and whereas Thomas my son oweth me £300 and William my executor standeth bound with Mr Thomas Ketcher of London citizen for the payment to my executors, my intent is that before my will be proved he shall enter into a bond to my supervisors in £600 for payment of £300 to the use of my wife and children, also into another bond of £600 to my supervisors for the true execution of my will. Whereas Jeremy Burges clerk standeth bound in £[blank], which bond is in William Savadge's hands, he shall deliver it to my supervisors to the use of my children, provided that, if he refuse to enter into such bonds or to deliver the last bond to my supervisors, he shall not be my executor but I nominate Jeremy Burges with Robert my son, who shall enter into bonds of £1,000 to William Barlowe my brother, whom I nominate my supervisor.

Witnesses: William Banbridge clerk [rector of Greenstead-juxta-Colchester] and Thomas Fyrfan.

Proved the will and the codicil, 7 April 1593, by William Savadge.

JOHN BEASTE of Colchester merchant and alderman, 14 October 1573.
[17/2]

My executrix shall pay to the common preacher appointed in the town £20, i.e. 40s. yearly to be paid quarterly, and for want of such a preacher the £20 or so much as shall remain 40s. to be bestowed yearly on four sermons in Colchester, whereof two each in St Peter's and St James' churches. To the poor in the town and suburbs £200 for the succouring and relieving of the sick, diseased, impotent, aged and most needy persons in the town and suburbs, in wood, clothing or otherwise by the good discretion of my executrix, i.e. £20 yearly. If the hospital which the bailiffs and commonalty of the town have gone about to establish shall be erected within a year after my decease, she shall pay to the masters or governors of the hospital for the relief of such diseased, impotent and needy persons as shall be kept there £200, i.e. £20 yearly; and if the hospital be not erected within a year the £200 shall be paid by her towards the succouring of the said sick, diseased, impotent, aged and most needy persons in the town and suburbs.

To my cousin Benjamin Cleere alderman, son of John Cleere late alderman deceased, £5, and every of his children 40s.; my cousin Nicholas Cleere alderman, his brother, £5, and every of his children 40s.; my cousin Nicholas Cleere late alderman, £10; Thomas his son towards his exhibition at Cambridge £10; every of the other children of Nicholas 40s.; every of the children of my late cousin George Christmas esquire deceased 40s.; my cousin Robert Christmas £5; my cousin John Christmas, his brother, £5, and his daughter 40s.; my cousin Albane Clerke £5; my cousin Elizabeth Symcott £5, and every of her children 40s.; and every of the brothers and sisters of Albane and Elizabeth 40s. To Thomas Allfylde, son of Helen Allfylde, and to his sisters, the wives of Benjamin Thorpe, William Hills and Benjamin Fayrested, each £5. To widow Allfeld, late wife of John Allfylde of St James, £10 towards bringing up his children. To Thomas Nevard of Stratford [Suffolk] £5, and his sister now wife of Pounde £5. I forgive John Mircock of Fordham £10 which he doth owe me and which I lent him divers years past, and to every of his children 40s. To every of the children of William Christmas of Inworth 40s. at marriage or 18, and I forgive his debt of £28. To Thomas Roper of Alderkirk (Lincs.) £3 6s. 8d., and Anne Lambart his sister £3 6s. 8d. To my son-in-law John Birde £20, and Susan Cleere, Mary Birde and Mercy Birde, his sisters, £20 each, to be paid to such as are married or at marriage. To Robert Birde £10, William Mowlde £6 13s. 4d., and Anne Brande 40s., and I forgive her husband his debt of £13.

To John Decro my servant £5, Martin Besill my late servant 40s., Samuel Johnson, Robert Browne, Margaret Fyner and Alice Dynes, my servants, 40s. each, Adam Dynes sometime my servant 40s., and George Durburre my late servant £5.

Whereas my cousin John Christmas of Colchester gentleman by his indenture enrolled, dated 28 May last, sold to me the reversion of the manor of Barnhams with the appurtenances in Beaumont, Weeley and Thorpe, a mansion house, Plomers Grove, a marsh adjoining in the Old Hythe in St Giles, and divers other lands in Colchester, Lexden, Mile End, Boxted and Great Horkesley, after the decease of Bridget wife of George Dorrell esquire on a certain condition, I give the reversion to Joan my wife towards the performing of my will, and all other my houses and lands for ever. To the said William Christmas £5.

Provided that all the said legacies to those under 18 be paid either at 18 or marriage and not before. The residue of my goods and money to my wife, whom I name my sole executrix, and I name my trusty and loving friends George Sayer junior of Colchester gentleman and John Pye, one of the bailiffs of the town, supervisors, and for their pains £5 each.

Witnesses: Benjamin Clerk [*sic*], Richard Cooke, William Haull, William Mowlde, John Fludd.

Proved 22 January 1574.

JOHN BERIF of Colchester clothier, 13 March 1566.   [9/17]

To be buried in St James' church in Colchester. To Mr William Cole the preacher 6s. 8d., to make a sermon and to preach the glad tidings of the Gospel to the people at my burial. To the poor people in Colchester £10 to be distributed among them by my executors' discretion on the day of my burial.

To William my son and his heirs my messuage in which I now dwell in St James, with the four rentaries adjoining and with the cisterns, woad vats, leads and copper to the same belonging; and for want of issue successively to Augustine, Benjamin and Arthur my sons, and Anne Beriff my daughter, and their heirs. To Dorothy my wife for life my tenement and lands with a grove of wood in Elmstead which I purchased of my brother William Beriff; and for want of issue to the heir of myself and my wife and successively to Augustine and William and their heirs; also my lands, meadows and pastures called Meddowes in Elmstead which I purchased of William Huberd of East Bergholt [Suffolk] clothier; and for want of issue successively to William and Augustine. To Augustine my tenement in St James in which Thomas Ward weaver dwelleth; and for want of issue successively to William, Benjamin, Arthur and Anne. To my wife £40 which George Christmas esquire deceased did owe me, my best bedsteadle and a transom with curtains of blue and yellow, a great coffer, a silver bottle, and a spoon of silver all gilt. To William 300 marks, a silver salt gilt, a goblet of silver, 12 silver spoons, a standing cup of silver gilt, and 12 silver spoons with maidenheads, at 21; if he die before, to be divided equally among my children at 21; if all die, between the children of my brother Thomas. To Augustine 200 marks, 2 silver goblets, a silver salt gilt, and 2 silver pots at 21; if he die, between my children; if all die, between the children of my brother Augustine. To Arthur 200 marks, a silver salt parcel gilt, and 2 stone pots tipped and covered with silver all gilt at 21; if he die, between my children; if all die, between the children of Marian Lawrence my sister. To Benjamin 200 marks, 2 standing pieces of silver, a pot of silver and 2 spoons of silver with the apostles' heads at 21; if he die, between my children; if all die, between the children of Margaret Harrison, my late sister. To Anne 100 marks at 18 or marriage; if she die, between my children; if all die, between the children of my brother William. To William my household stuff, brass, pewter, linen, napery and bedding in my house, with my scales, beams and weights, all which shall be safely kept to his use and delivered by my executors at 21; if he die before, then successively to Augustine, Benjamin and Arthur at 21 and Anne at 18 being unmarried; if she die, to my wife; if she die they are to be appraised and sold by my executors and distributed among the poor people of Colchester. To William my lease of Poplar Meadow on the backside of my house; and my apparel except 3 of my best gowns and my best cloak. I forgive my brother Thomas the money he doth owe me. To Augustine my brother one of my best gowns as is faced with foins. To Thomas Hopton gentleman my best gown guarded with velvet and faced with budge. To Thomas Lawrence, my brother-in-law, my gown faced with gatten [goaten?]. To Benjamin Clere alderman my best cloak. To mother Lauton 40s.

Provided always that, if Arthur, Benjamin or Anne at 21 refuse to release to William my brother their right or interest in his capital messuage in the parishes of Trinity and St Giles, all the money, plate and other moveables bequeathed to them shall wholly remain to my executors towards the performance of my will. I charge my executors that they honestly and virtuously keep and bring up William, Augustine, Arthur, Benjamin and Anne in good education, learning and nurture until 21. The residue of my goods to my executors towards the performance of my will. I appoint my well-beloved friends Thomas Hopton and Thomas Lawrence my executors and Benjamin Clere my supervisor.

Witnesses : Robert Northen alderman, Nicholas Maynarde, John Lucas tanner, John Lloyde.

I further bequeath to my wife a trundle bed. To Augustine a posted bedsteadle to be delivered to such as shall have the bringing up of him; and to Arthur and Benjamin a featherbed. To my wife 4 wrought cushions. Witnesses : Nicholas Maynarde, John Lokis, Rowland [*sic*] Northen, John Fludd [for Lloyd?]

Proved 28 June 1566.

WILLIAM BERIFF of Brightlingsea merchant, 6 December 1577.

[21/22]

To be buried in the north chapel of Brightlingsea church. To Mr [Thomas] Simpson the vicar 6s. 8d. To 8 poor men to carry me to church 8s. To the poor inhabitants of this parish 20s. To the maintenance of the liberties and freedom of this parish 20s. To the poor people of St Nicholas, Colchester, 10s., and Elmstead 5s. To Anne my wife my free lands in Peldon, West Mersea, Langenhoe, Great Bromley and Great Bentley for life in recompense of her dower of such lands as I am seized of, and after her death John my son shall have these free lands called Quintines, Silvestres, Rowses, Heathehowse, Hearnes land, and Obangers. To my wife my copy lands in Peldon and West Mersea called Herblins, sometime one Merchantes, for life, and after her decease Herblins to William my son. To William my houses and lands free and copy in Brightlingsea. To John my tenements, lands, meadows, pastures and woods in Elmstead called Fennes, Wysemans, Adames, Pycardes and Frances, saving that my wife shall have for her own fire, upon the woods called Wysemans Heaths, 12 loads of wood every year for life and free egress and regress to fell them. To Bridget my daughter at 18 £60; if she die before, John and William to have the £60. To John a silver pot parcel gilt, a silver salt double gilt, a silver bowl parcel gilt, 6 silver spoons, a ring of gold with 3 stones, my wearing apparel, my 2 dags and target, and a bedstead. To William a silver pot parcel gilt, a silver salt double gilt, a silver bowl parcel gilt, 6 silver spoons, a ring of gold with my mark on it, and a bedstead. To Bridget a pot covered and footed with silver, 6 silver spoons, a ring of gold with a death's head on it, and a little silver salt parcel gilt. To Joyce Lambarde, my wife's daughter, after her decease, my garden in St Nicholas' parish, which I bought of George Harman, adjoining the woodyard belonging to the house sometime of Ralph Elkin her father. To William Wrenolde, my wife's son, a ring of gold with a white stone. The residue to my wife, whom I make my sole executrix. Witnesses : John Ayer, Richard Browne, Richard Carter, Robert Nicolson.

Proved 30 May 1578.

RICHARD BREWER of Halstead fishmonger, 11 March 1584. [29/39]

To be buried in Halstead church or churchyard. To Jane my well-beloved wife the house which I now dwell in and another free house called Hubberdes which I bought of one Mr Parker in Halstead, provided that she give to Joan Brewer my sister 40s. yearly for life, according to a deed dated 10 March 1584, and find her with meat, drink, lodging, apparel and houseroom. To Richard Turner my servant my horses and mares with their packsaddles for carrying fish, my apparel, and 20s. To Alice Crabe my servant 5s. To Joan Fenne my kinswoman 6s. 8d. To William Vygerouse junior 20s. The residue of my goods to Dame Frances Lady Poulet of Borley widow, whom I make my sole executrix. Witnesses: Robert Smithe senior, Thomas Mullynes, William Vigorous senior, Edmund Smythe.

Proved 24 August 1585.

JOHN BROOKE of Walden mercer, 16 October 1593.   [37/86]

To Cecily my wife my messuage wherein I dwell in Walden with the edifices, yards and gardens, and my lands in Walden called Gonters Croft, for life; and after her decease to Nicholas Brooke my brother; and he to pay my brethren and sisters living £5 apiece, provided that, if he decease without issue, the messuage be sold by Thomas Swallowe, Ralph Harison and James Crofte of Walden and the money be equally divided among them. To Richard, William, Fardinando and Nicholas my brothers each £10, and Anne wife of Thomas Pressland, Priscilla wife of John Badcocke, and Martha Brooke, my sisters, each £10. To the two children of Alice my sister, late wife of Robert Bates, each £3 16s. 8d. at 16. To Edward son of Richard my brother, £5. To Elizabeth Chamberlayne, my wife's kinswoman, £5. I freely forgive my brothers and Thomas Pressland what they owe me. To Richard Bushe of Walden 40s. and Gabriel his son £3. To Thomas Swanne my servant 40s. The residue of my goods, cloth ware, ready money, corn, and plate to my wife, whom I ordain sole executrix. Witnesses: James Crofte notary public, Joan Swallowe, Henry Leader, Roger Sergeant alias Sadler.

Proved 10 December 1593.

WILLIAM BUTTOR of Dedham clothier, 13 May 1593.   [38/80]

To my wife for life my house I dwell in with the land belonging, 3 acres of meadow in Hall Field, and the land in Ardleigh on the backside of Shellies house called Honts [Houts?], with remainder to my son Pearce. To him my West Field (containing 17 acres), provided that if it be tilth or in corn at my departure it shall be sown at my charge and when the time of harvest come to go to the performance of my will, and if it be with corn the corn to be sold; and he to give therefor to his brother Richard £10 and to [my daughter] Alice Morefewe £10. More to Pearce Semans Wood (18 acres) at Langham, with this condition that, in consideration of a reckoning between us that he do owe me, he pay my daughter Frances £30.

To my son Richard my house that Bates is in now in Ardleigh called

Honts, with the land belonging (6 acres) on the same side that the house stands on the highway; and in default of issue, with successive remainders to my daughter Morfewe, to William, and to my son Thomas Buttor's son. To Richard and Morfewe Hontes Wood in Ardleigh (12 acres) and to the longer liver and after to Richard's heir, with remainder to William, my son Thomas Buttor's son. To my daughter Morfewe Hontes Field in Ardleigh with a cottage thereon (about 5 acres), for life, with remainder to her eldest son then living, also my lease of one pykin [pightle] ground in Ardleigh on the one side of the same field (1 acre) called Long Scrope. To Pearce my lease of my farm called Porters in Ardleigh. Whereas my son Thomas doth owe me 100 marks by his bond, I give the 100 marks to Richard and Morfewe to be equally divided.

To my wife £100, and for her expenses for a year 5 seam of rye, my bay mare or whatever horse she will, my swine, 2 pots covered with silver, and the plate that she brought me; and Pearce shall deliver to her, in the wood that I have given him, every year for 6 years after my departure 8 loads of wood if she marry not again and dwell still where she now doth; also my household stuff that she brought me.

To Thomas a stone pot lipped with silver that was my father's and my silver salt. To Alice my daughter my silver goblet notwithstanding that my wife shall have the use of both while she liveth, if she marry not. To Thomas 5 silver spoons with lions at the end. To my daughter Alice Morfewe and to Richard 6 silver spoons each. To Thomas a cistern of lead to lay in oil, and my armoury that I am appointed to find. To John Morfewe my shearman's stuff that Stanton now hath and 2 pair of shears that Webbe hath. To Richard a featherbed, the best that was mine before marriage, a great long chest in the low parlour, and the bedstead in Thomas Annys' chamber. To my daughter Morfewe my next best featherbed and a cover of darnack work. To Richard another coverlet of darnack lined with canvas. My brass and pewter that was mine before marriage shall be equally divided between Richard and Morfewe. To Pearce my chest bound with iron and my book of Job. To Richard my bible. To Thomas Buttor my other great book of Erasmus of the Exposition of the Gospels and another small book of the Exposition of the Galations by Luther. To Richard my weights and beams.

To Dr [Edmund] Chapman [lecturer] of Dedham for a remembrance 20s. To Mr [Henry] Wilcocke [vicar] 20s. Pearce shall pay to my sister Myhills out of the profit of my farm every year while she live 20s., and 20s. now. To my poor neighbours in Dedham £6 13s. 4d. My executors shall take view of the poorest to go into their houses to see what lodging they have, and [?an, i.e. if] you shall find it too bare for any Christian you shall where you see most need is and the most honestest men provided for their lodging what you shall see they have most need of and provide for them, as far as your money will go, as to have a bed to lie in and a blanket and a coverlet of shreds or what you think good.

Provided that, if my wife shall go about any ways to take the benefit of a bond wherein I stand bound to leave certain lands, to be void of all my gifts and the land to Pearce presently and the rest to be divided between Alice and Richard. All these implements hereunder written shall remain in my house still, if my wife be therewith content, and she to have the use of them for the time she continue and dwell there, which I think will be so long as she doth live, and after her decease the house shall be still furnished with them still to him that it shall please God doth live to enjoy the house. Both tables in the hall with the forms and chairs, the press, and in the great parlour both the tables, the cupboards and the stained cloths; in the street parlour both the tables and the bedstead; in the buttery the cupboard; in the kitchen the table and frame, the dresser, the stained cloth, the salting trough, the querns, the lead and the pan. More to my wife, my napery as sheets and other linen, the rest of my bedding not before given, the hutches saving a danske chest I give to Alice, the rest of my household stuff, and my butter and cheese. To Romboull my man 10s., nurse Kinge 5s., widow Makin 5s., nurse Darby 5s., and Hassett 5s. The rest of my goods, as corn of my sollers, in the barn and on the ground, cattle, carts, tumbrils, and trace ploughs, to Richard and Alice equally to be divided. I make Pearce my sole executor, of whom I am in no doubt. [A few minor additional legacies to the same relations.]

Surrender, 16 October 1593, into the hands of John Whitlocke, John Neverd and John Boredge, tenants both of [the manors of] Dedham and Langham to the use of my will.

Witnesses: John Whitlocke, John Neverd, John Burredge.

Proved 19 November 1594.

PEARCE BUTTER of Colchester clothier, [blank] August 1599.
[44/68]

To my son William the houses and lands which my father gave me by will as also the field I purchased of Barker in Dedham (except the lease of the farm called Porters which I reserve to my son Peirce), and £160, at 21; also £40 on condition that he taketh to his wife my wife's daughter Anne Tomson, which is my desire, but if he refuse the £40 to her at marriage. To William my double gilt bowl, 3 silver spoons, my bell salt, and the rest of my household stuff at Brook House unbequeathed, a chest bound with iron at his grandfather's house, and my wood at Langham called Seamans Grove. To Peirce my lease of the farm at Ardleigh called Porters at 22, my tenement in Dedham wherein Cooke now dwelleth, and £150, at 22; and in default of issue to be divided equally among the rest of my children. To my son Daniel my lease which I purchased of Mr Thomas Godman called Brook House in the occupation of Anthony Whitinge who is to have the use of it in the meantime, paying such consideration for it as his father-in-law my cousin Henry Sherman shall think good; and in default of issue to James my son. To Daniel £60 at 22, also the £20 which his master Anthony Whitinge hath with him, at 22. My executors shall take out of the land £3 a year to buy wood for my mother-in-law for life. To John my son my houses and lands in Thorrington, free and copy, in the occupations of John Hubbert at 21, on condition that my executors shall pay yearly out of the rent to Dr [Edmund] Chapman, preacher of Dedham, £5 for 6 years; and in default of issue to William and on condition that he pay £100 to be equally divided among the rest of my children; also to John £60 at 22. To James my houses and lands in Great Oakley which I purchased of John Martyn, and the freehold land I purchased of Gilbert Rolf of Ramsey in the occupation of one Packman; also to James £100 at 22. The 40s. a year given to my brother Richard shall be taken out of the land at Oakley which I have given to James. To my daughter Anne Butter a branched damask board cloth with 12 napkins and a towel, her mother's child linen, the salt which was her mother's, 3 silver spoons, 1 of my silver tuns, the posted bed in the parlour at Brook House, the cupboard in the parlour, the table and stools, the settle to the bedstead, my tapestry carpet, 6 needlework cushions, and my pewter, with the chest it is in at Brook House. To my daughter Mary £200 at 20 or marriage but not before 18, and I commit the use of £100 to my executors for bringing her up and they shall allow her for the other £100 £8 a year during her minority; but if she die before 20, £150 to be equally divided among the rest of my children, £40 among my brother Thomas's children and my sister's children equally, £10 to William my brother Thomas's son, and £10 to the poor of Dedham towards the augmentation of the town stock.

Touching the household stuff which was my last wife's. To Anne Tompson 6 silver spoons, 1 silver tun, her mother's best carpet, 2 other best featherbeds, her mother's child linen, the table and the cupboard in the hall, 6 pair of the best sheets, the 2 chests and the livery table in the parlour, 6 of the best needlework cushions, and 1 flockbed. To John Tompson the household stuff in the wainscot parlour and 2 featherbeds, 1 flockbed, 6 thrum cushions, the table and the stools in the parlour, the long green carpet, the livery table in the hall, 4 silver spoons, 1 silver bowl, and 4 pair of sheets. To my sister Sarah Northie widow 40s. To William Tompson 4 silver spoons, his mother's best coverlet save two, the posted bedstead in goodman Clay's chamber, and the table upon the lodging chamber. To my daughter Mary Butter the field bedstead in the parlour, the long joined chest in the lodging chamber, 1 silver tun, 1 silver salt, 2 silver gilt bowls, and the rest of her mother's plate unbequeathed. To Anne Tompson, John Tompson, Sarah Tompson and Mary Butter her pewter and brass to be equally divided. The rest of her household stuff to be divided equally between Sarah, William and Elizabeth Tompson. My last wife's children's portions be paid them as in their father's will that they may be put out to the increasing of the stocks after they be bound apprentices and their masters to have the boys with their portions to yield them profit. Provided that, if my debts come short to discharge my will, the increase of the stock of Pierce, John and Mary Butter £100 shall go to making up the same, and if that be not sufficient to be indifferently defalked out of the portions of the rest of my children except William Butter, to whom I also give the £40 which I gave to Anne Tompson if she die before marriage. To my good friend Dr Chapman £13 6s. 8d. To Richard Butter my brother 40s. a year for life. To Samuel Butter my brother, Thomas Butter's son, £4 towards binding him apprentice. To my sister Morphewe 40s.

I appoint as my executors my loving friend Henry Sherman the elder and William Butter my son, and to Henry for his pains £6 13s. 4d., and as my supervisors my loving friends Dr Chapman and my cousin Haselwood, and to my cousin 40s. for his pains. To the poor of St James, Colchester, 40s., and of Dedham £3. The residue to be equally divided among the rest of my children.

Witnesses : John Stockes, John Bracewell and William Ball.

Proved 5 December 1600 by William Butter.

NICHOLAS CLERE of St James, Colchester, clothier and alderman, 24 February 1579. [22/25]

I require my cousin Mr [Nicholas] Challener [town preacher] to preach in St James' church four sermons for me, one at my burial and the others at such time as he shall think it most meet, and for his pains 40s. To the poor of the town £5 at or before my burial.

To my well-beloved wife Anne my head tenement in St James wherein I dwell and a rentary adjoining and now taken into the tenement on the west part, for life, and after her decease to my son Nicholas. Whereas I am possessed of a lease, for 30 years yet to come, of land called Mary Land (containing 4 acres) on the backside of my head tenement, made by the late Abbot of St John's, Colchester, and confirmed by the Queen's predecessors, I give it to my wife for life, with remainder to Nicholas. To her my tenement in St James which I purchased of Adam Dynes shearman until my son Thomas is 21, and if he die before 21 to my son William. To her my tenement, sometime three tenements, in Ballingdon near Sudbury for life, she also finishing at her costs a malting house adjoining; with successive remainders to William and to Thomas. My wife to have the profit and rents of my lands called Ponffild Lands, Cuttells Lands, my lands in Abberton, my groves in Greenstead and Wivenhoe, and the four rentaries adjoining my head tenement east and west until Nicholas is 21 and towards the education and bringing up of my children. To my wife for life my tenement in St James which I bought of my brother Benjamin Clere, wherein one Joice a stranger inhabiteth; with remainder to Nicholas. To him £40, my best silver salt, a goblet of silver, and 12 silver spoons marked in the tops with NC; to William £40; and to Thomas £40; all at 21. If my three sons die before 21, their portions to my three daughters, Mary, Anne and Jane, part and part like, and to each £40 at 21 or marriage. To my son-in-law Thomas Hasilwood my best gelding. To my daughters-in-law Anne Read, Margaret Hasilwood and Elizabeth Hasilwood each a bullock of 2 years. To my cousins John Clere my silk grograine jacket and Benjamin Clere an angel. To my maidservant Edith 5s. The residue of my goods to my wife, whom I make my sole executrix, and I appoint my well-beloved brother Benjamin Clere the elder my supervisor, and for his pains 40s.

Witnesses : Nicholas Challoner, Thomas Crosse, Percival Wylle.

Proved 19 June 1579.

GEORGE CROSSE the elder of Dedham clothier, 28 April 1602.
[46/48]

To Margaret my wife for life my tenement wherein John Bossett
dwelleth and my tenement on Peinsall Green wherein widow Webbe
dwelleth; also my corn, cattle and household stuff. To Margaret, Anna
and Sarah Crosse, my daughters, £10 each at 21 or marriage. To Edward
and William, my sons, £30 to be equally divided betwixt them at 21.
To John and Thomas, my sons, £40 to be divided, John within 3 months
after my decease, Thomas at 21. After my wife's decease the two tenements shall be sold and equally divided among my children. To George
my eldest son £30. To my wife £20. The residue of my goods to my
wife and George, whom I make my executors. Witnesses: Thomas
Clercke, John Pye.

Proved 4 June 1602.

THOMAS EASTEFEILDE *alias* LUCAS of Walthamstow moneyer, 9
July 1590. [34/53]

To be buried in Walthamstow church or churchyard. To the poor of
Walthamstow 20s. a year for 10 years to be distributed in bread at the
discretion of the vicar and churchwardens. To the reparations of the
church £3 6s. 8d. To the Company of Moneyers £3 6s. 8d. to make
merry withal or otherwise to be used at their discretion. To Alice my
well-beloved wife for life my dwelling-house, with so much land in
Walthamstow as shall be thought worth, at the discretion of my well-
beloved friends Richard Garnet, John Perine, John Reignoldes and
Thomas Catcher, £20 a year; but if she refuse the house and land £20
a year for life. To her 6 beasts, the third part of my moveables, and a
gelding or 4 marks to buy one at her own choice. To Alice, Anne and
Elizabeth, daughters of Thomas Catcher and Sabian his wife, £10 apiece
at 21, and Thomas and Sabian £10. To Thomas son of Robert Eastefeilde
£30 at 21; if he die before, to his father; my executor shall bring up
the child in learning and place him in some good occupation so near as
he can. To Agnes wife of Richard Merite of Stepney [Middx.] 40s. for
life, and after her decease to her sister Margaret for life. To my godchildren 12d. apiece. To my maidservants 5s. apiece. To Jane Aulsoppe
my wife's daughter 25s. a year for 4 years. To Agnes Woodcocke 10s. My
executor shall enter into bond of £200 to my overseers to perform
my will. To my son Francis Eastefeilde, whom I make my sole executor,
my freehold lands in Walthamstow and Limehouse in Stepney, and I
make John Reynoldes vicar of Walthamstow, Richard Garnett, John
Perrin and Thomas Catcher my overseers. Witnesses: Richard
Greenacres, William Johnson, Richard Coller.

Proved 22 July 1590. Sentence, 23 November 1590, confirming Will
in case between Francis Eastfield *alias* Lucas executor and Alice Eastfield
alias Lucas widow and Thomas Eastfield *alias* Lucas.

WILLIAM EATON of St Peter, Colchester, clothier, 31 October 1596.
[41/7]

To Margaret my well-beloved wife for life my tenement and tenteryard in my occupation, she to keep it tenant-like, provided that she enter
into an obligation of £100 to my supervisors not to take away the
wainscot but leave it with the glass and glass windows about the house,
with the brewing brass standing in the kitchen, to the use of my son
William; and after her decease to him and his heirs male; and for want
of issue successively to Alexander, John and Richard my sons and their
heirs male; if all die without heirs male, to be equally divided between
my daughters. If Margaret my daughter then living happen to have
children, she and her children also to have as good part of the rent
as the rest of the daughters of my sons; and my tenement and tenteryard
never to be sold but remain to the use of my will for ever; but if all
my children die without any children, one half of the rent to my supervisors part and part like, and after their decease to my cousin John
Eaton and his heirs, and the other half to the poor people of St Peter.

My household stuff shall be divided into two equal parts by my supervisors, whereof one to my wife and the other to William, and she to have
his during her life; and the half part of William shall be appraised by
three honest indifferent men, and she shall answer the goods or such
money as they be praised at. To William, Alexander, Margaret my
daughter, John and Richard £60 each, which my wife shall have the
use of until they are 15 towards their bringing up, she putting in sufficient
bond to my supervisors for their stocks, which shall be put out to the
best advantage, my sons to be apprenticed and their portions with the
use shall be paid at their age of 24, except for my daughter at 21. My
half part of the good ship Parnell shall be sold to the best advantage
towards the payment of my debts. To Peter Syman 5s. To the poor of
the parish 10s. To my cousins John Eaton 40s. and Richard, William,
Frances, Elizabeth and Mary Grene 10s. apiece. To Thomas Allen my
servant 40s. and Mary my maidservant 10s. The residue of my goods
to my wife, whom I appoint my sole executrix. I ordain my faithful and
well-beloved friends and cousins Mr Martin Bassell, alderman of Colchester, and Robert Searles, minister of the Word of God, supervisors,
and for a remembrance 40s. apiece to make a ring.

Witnesses: Richard Ewringe, Thomas Rigbe.

Proved 9 February 1597.

ROBERT ELDER of Boreham moneyer, 18 June 1571.   [14/48]

To be buried in the church of St Leonard in Shoreditch (Middx.). To
my well-beloved wife Sibyl my house named Porters and ground belonging (except a piece of pasture called God's Croft containing 4 acres) until
Edmund my eldest son and heir is 24; and in default of issue with successive remainders to John my second son, to Robert my son, and to the
rest of my sons and my daughters. To Thomas God's Croft. To John
and Robert two groves of wood called Phillis (8 acres) and Turtells (12

acres), with the felling of the wood for 6 years by even portions; and Richard Awsten, moneyer, my especial friend, shall fell the groves for their use; if they die before 6 years, to Cecily Elder and Emme Elder my daughters. To Cecily and Emme each 2 milch kine and £20 in the hands of my brother [in-law] William Perseley the younger. I ordain my wife my sole executrix. The residue of my goods to my wife. I make Richard Awsten of Hoxton [Middx.] moneyer and John Tenderinge of Boreham my overseers, and for their pains 20s. apiece. Witnesses : John Bockett, curate of Shoreditch, Thomas Haddon, William Roulff, George Symson, Thomas Ramsey, Hugh Williamson.

Proved 14 December 1571.

STEPHEN ELLINOT of Dedham clothier, 26 August 1591.   [35/83]

To Stephen my son my house I dwell in with my [out-]houses and lands after my wife's decease; and for lack of issue successively to Sarah my daughter and my wife and their heirs. To Stephen £20 at 21; and the use of the same towards his bringing up in my executor's hands from 16 to 21, to increase the £20. To Sarah £30 at 18. To my sister Elizabeth wife of Hugh May of this town £5. To Dr [Edmund] Chapman preacher of Dedham 20s. To Henry Wilcock minister and preacher of God's Word in Dedham 20s. To my brother Edward Ellinot 40s. and my sister Joan Wiles 20s. To the poor people in Dedham 40s. to be paid to the collectors of the poor in the minister's presence. Provided that the gift to my wife after my two children's decease without issue is on condition that she maintain my house in good reparations and that the party that shall marry her shall be bound with sufficient sureties to Charles Cardinall of Bromley gentleman, Christopher Burrowe of [East] Bergholt (Suffolk) yeoman, and Hugh May of Dedham clothier on the same condition. The rest of my goods to my wife, whom I make sole executrix, and the [above three] as supervisors. Witnesses : Henry Wilcok clerk, John Morffold, John Upcher, John Creake.

Proved 11 November 1591.

GRIFFEN ERNESBIE of Colchester clothier, 12 February 1591.

[35/29]

If Thomasine my wife be with child, to the child male or female £250 at 21 or marriage; if not with child, to my wife on condition she yearly for life give to the poor of the town 30s. If she happen to marry within 3 years after my decease, to Thomasine Thompson her daughter £20 at marriage or 21; if she do not marry within 3 years, Thomasine shall have but £10. Whereas the reversion of the messuage in the tenure of William Griffen stranger and the rentary in that of Peter Cowper weaver in St James after the decease of Agnes Earnesbie my mother do belong to me, if my wife be with child I demise them after my mother's decease to the child at 21; if not with child or the child depart before 21, my wife shall have the two houses after my mother's decease. Whereas William Thompson, my wife's son, hath by his grandfather's will, a

284

house given to him at 24 wherein goodman Cable dwelleth, he shall give his title to the house to Anne Thompson my wife's daughter, or my gift to him I disannul and give it to John Tompson my wife's son and his heirs, provided that John pay my wife during her life £5 yearly, also £10 to Elizabeth Thompson my wife's daughter, but if William sell it within 15 years my wife shall have it. To my brother-in-law Mr North £5. To the poor of Colchester £8 to be delivered to Mr Buckstone and Nicholas Clere. Whereas I have at Lambeth (Surrey) a lease of a house and certain seacoals and wood, I give them to my wife; and if my brother-in-law Mr Guie help my wife to sell them to the best advantage I give him £4. To my cousin Joan Buyson 20s. To my sister Guy and her children my term of years in the lease and houses which my father had of the Chamber of London on Lambeth Hill in London. Whereas I am to pay certain legacies given by my father's will, my wife shall discharge them as they grow due and for payment I give her the lease of the house at Halstead which my father had of Mr John Gooddaie. To my wife for life the tenement wherein Peter Cowper dwelleth, and after her decease, if William Thompson live to enjoy the house wherein William Griffen dwelleth, the house wherein Cowper dwelleth to Sarah Thompson and her heirs; if she decease before my wife, to Anne Thompson my wife's daughter and her heirs. The rest of my goods, money, plate, jewels and household stuff to my wife, whom I make my sole executrix; and I make my loving brother-in-law Mr North and my loving friend Mr Buckstone my supervisors to help her, and for their pains 40s. each. Witnesses: Thomas Hasilwood, Nicholas Clere.

Proved 14 April 1591.

CLEMENT FENNE of Pentlow clothier, 21 April 1563.   [6/29]

To be buried in the church or churchyard of Pentlow.

To Margery my wife my house called Bretts with the lands in the occupation of Thomas Dereman, also my house that John Hawkesawle occupieth, both for life; and after her death the former to remain to Thomas my son and his heirs and the latter to Clement my son and his heirs. To George my son my land in Nether Church Field which I purchased of Mr George Felton, a piece of marsh called the Further Marsh next Hills Meadow, and a piece of pasture called the Shrubbes, on condition that he discharge his mother during her life of 26s. 8d. a year for the rent due to Mr Felton. To my wife for life 3 acres of copy land in Mill Field in Foxearth; and after her death to Simon my son and his heirs. My household stuff to be equally divided between my wife and George my son. To him £20, a silver salt, 2 silver spoons and 3 beasts. To Thomas £10, 2 silver spoons and 2 beasts, at 21 or marriage. To Joan my daughter £10, my best silver goblet parcel gilt, 2 silver spoons, and 2 beasts to Simon and to Rose Fenne my daughter each 2 silver spoons and 2 beasts; all at 21 or marriage. To the repairing of Pentlow church 10s.; to the parson of Pentlow, Nicholas Bussh clerk, 3s. 4d.; to the poor of Pentlow 2 beasts, whereof 3s. 4d. yearly to the poor for ever. The rest of my goods to my wife, whom I make my sole executrix; and she shall have the profits of Pentlow Mill during the lease. I make John Wenden and Robert Brasington, John Fenne my brother [in-law] and William Raystone my brother-in-law my supervisors, and to the first two 6s. 8d. for their pains. Witnesses: Robert Brasington, John Fenne, William Raystone, Walter Bantofte and Nicholas Bushe.

Proved 12 August 1563.

GEORGE GEDGE of Boxted clothier, 11 May 1592.   [36/42]

To my cousin Thurston Ashley of Ipswich (Suffolk) my customary tenement called Porrettes with the lands, meadows and pastures in the occupation of Richard Barkar and John Ranck of Boxted holden of the manor of Boxted Hall, conditionally that he pay Agnes my wife for life 45s. quarterly To Anne Beaucham daughter of Prudence Beaucham £20. To George Brundishe the elder of Boxted, my sister's son, £20. To George Brewester my godson £20 at 21; if he die before, to be equally divided between his brothers and sisters at 21. To the children of my cousin Gilbert Spicer of London perfumer £20 to be equally divided. To the two sons of my niece Margaret Ward widow £20. To Judy Reade £5 and the £20 I owe her for the legacy of her father Jeffrey Reade at 21. To Elizabeth Brundishe £5 and her sister Anne Brundishe £5. To Thurston eldest son of my cousin Thurston and his heirs my house in Colchester in consideration of such travail and money as my cousin hath taken and disbursed about my affairs. To Katharine Meatam my niece a cow. My executrix shall save harmless Stephen Cole senior and William Bradley my neighbours for a bond wherein they stand bound to Mr Awdley of Berechurch for me. To my wife, whom I appoint my sole executrix, the lease of my house wherein I dwell, with my goods, cattle and corn, bestowing some part among such of my kindred that shall behave themselves towards her. She shall give to the repairing of the town house and enlargement of the same 20s. at such time as the parish begin to repair it. I appoint my loving neighbours and friends Stephen Cole senior and Samuel Warner of Boxted supervisors and to take bond of my cousin Thurston for payment of £135 to perform my legacies, and for their pains 10s. each. Witnesses: Philip Gilgate minister [Silgate in Newcourt's *Repertorium,* vicar of Boxted], John Humferey clothier, William Bradley, Benjamin Clere.

Proved 26 May 1592.

THOMAS GLOVER of Dedham clothier, 17 November 1596. [40/89]

To the poor of Dedham £10 to be put to the poor's stock and employed to the use of the poor with the rest of the stock now in their hands at the discretion of the governors of the same, always reserving the principal.

To Margaret my wife the occupation of my capital messuage, wherein I dwell, with the messuage adjoining in that of Richard Morse, the meadows and lands enclosed as lie together in the Hall Field and the common meadows of Dedham; the occupation of the outmeadows on the right hand of the lane and footpath leading from my house to the gate and lane next the gravel pits; and the use of my plate, jewels, painted cloths, ceilings, glass, benches, settles, trammels, bars of iron, oil, cistern, leads, coppers, implements and household stuff, beds and bedding in or to the mansion house fixed or belonging; all for life. Provided that if she marry she shall quietly depart and yield up the house, lands and the household stuff to my executors, and I give her £40 yearly. To her my cattle, corn growing and in the sollers, hay, ploughs, carts, harrows and other implements of husbandry, and my best bed. After her death or marriage my plate, my household stuff both woollen and linen, brass and pewter, beds and bedding not fixed to the house and before in use bequeathed to her, shall be equally divided among my children.

To William my son after her decease the capital messuage, with the barns and stables and gardens, a pightle called Tainter Field with the tainter, four meadows called Five Acre Meadow, Havels Meadow alias New Meadow, one on the north side of Tainter Field, and Watering Meadow, and the rest of the next meadow and hopyard southward to the path from the new footbridge to the river as is appointed to be divided hereafter in my son Edward's gift, and the said outmeadows. To William £200 at 21, and the occupation of my houses and lands in Dedham and Lawford not before bequeathed. To Thomas my son, after her decease, the house and lands and 1 acre in Broad Meadow in Dedham in the occupation of John Elmes, two fields by Hay Lane (containing 7 acres), 14 acres of land in Lawford in several parcels, all which I purchased of Robert Kettle and of Clement Wood; 4 acres of meadow called gores in Broad Meadow in Dedham and 3 roods of meadow adjoining called Crabtrees lying next the field sometime Richard Roome's and now Henry Coleman's; and a pightle on the east side of the said Coleman's field which I purchased of William Judye; also £200 at 21, and my tenement wherein John Pierson dwelleth in Dedham. To Edward my son after her decease the messuage wherein Richard Morse dwelleth in Dedham, with so much of the meadow on its west side as lieth from the new footbridge to the river to the meadow of Robert Sherman on the west; a pightle called Barley Field in Dedham and the two next meadows, Fen Meadow, and 10 acres of land in the Little Half Field called Gores; also £200 at 21. To John my son after her decease my tenement in Dedham Church Street which I purchased of Thomas Browne, 12 acres of land called Levettes Lenton in Dedham Hall Field, 3 acres of meadow called Gores Marsh with 2 pightles of meadow adjoining in the occupation of William Pettfeilde, a meadow called Stubbing in that of Simon Dawson, 3 roods of meadow called Stony Hill, and 3 acres in Broad Meadow; also £200 at 21. To my daughters Margaret Niccolson £40, and to Anne and Susan each £200 at 20.

To Dr Chapman £10, in consideration of my stipend yearly to be paid to him, after the rate of 50s. a year to be quarterly if he shall so long continue preacher of God's Word in Dedham. To Margery Darby my sister £10. To my brother Robert's seven children [not named] each

£3 at 21. To John Elmes my workman 40s., Richard Morse my weaver 20s., William Warner my weaver 10s., and Elizabeth Collen my servant 10s. To John Elminge my servant 20s. To my brother Robert my wearing apparel except my gowns. The residue of my goods to my said children equally to be divided. My well-beloved friend Edmund Sherman shall have the bringing up of my son Thomas and have him bound to him as an apprentice till 23, and to have the use and profit of his stock of money towards his good education and bringing up till 21, putting in sufficient sureties; and William Niccolson my son-in-law shall have my daughter Susan with her portion and bring her up till 20 or marriage, putting in bond.

I ordain my well-beloved brother William Glover of London executor, and for his pains my white nag, and he shall see my children brought up in the fear of God with the profits of their stocks which shall remain in his hands during their minorities. I appoint my well-beloved friends, Edmund Sherman and Henry Sherman of Dedham clothiers, supervisors, and for their pains 10s. each to their wives to be bestowed on rings of remembrance to wear for my sake.

Witnesses: John Effette, Richard Morse, John Elmyn, James Strachye.

Proved 11 December 1596.

THOMAS GRAYE the elder of Coggeshall clothier, 10 January 1602. [46/20]

To the poorest people of Great Coggeshall £3. To Thomas the youngest child of Thomas Gray my son my two tenements in Church Street. To John my son my lands free and copyhold. To Thomas my son my great chest or hutch in my chamber over the hall. My executor shall pay to the first child of my daughter Anne, if it shall please God to send her any, £20 at 21. To Thomas Gyon son of my daughter Margery deceased £20 at 21. To Anne Gyon his sister £10 at 21. To every one of my servants 3s. 4d. The residue of my goods to John, whom I ordain sole executor. I request my brother John Gray and my good friend Walter Owsolde to be overseers. Witnesses: Robert Anes, John Gray, Walter Owsolde.

Proved 11 February 1602.

JOHN GRIGGES of Manningtree, 2 November 1589. [34/33]

To be buried in the chancel of Mistley. Towards the reparations of Mistley church 40s. To Mr George Drywood, bachelor of divinity [rector of Mistley-with-Manningtree], my gold ring with the stone in it. To the poor of Salcott 40s. To Simon Dawson 20s. to be bestowed by him towards the maintenance of the town armour of Manningtree and 20s. towards the reparation of the almshouses of Manningtree.

To William Shortinge, Robert Shortinge, Agnes Shortinge and Mary Shortinge, the brothers and sisters of my cousin Stephen Shortinge, each

£3. To Alice, Stephen, Amy and Anne, Stephen's children, each 40s. To my cousin John Wynter 40s. to make him a ring. To Alice my wife if she overlive me, £5 to be delivered to Mr George Drywood, Simon Dawson, John Fenne, George Dowett and James Lyes to be put out for a stock for the relief of the poor of Manningtree for ever. I forgive John Carre the debts he oweth me, except 4 milch kine which he hath of mine which my wife shall have, if she shall dwell at Mistley or else not. To her if she overlive me my row of houses in the street in the market-stead of Manningtree for life, and after her decease to Barbara Carre my kinswoman, John's wife, except the lower open room now used for the Corn Cross or Corn Room, being under the west end of the two, and except free ingate, upgate and downgate to and from the place where the clock now standeth for the setting and mending of the same clock; and I give the said lower room to the use of the inhabitants for ever for the enlarging of the market place, they paying 1d. yearly rent for the same for ever. To Barbara £20. To Stephen Shorting my sealing ring of gold. The residue of my goods as well on the water as on the land to my wife. If I overlive my wife, to Mr George Drywood [and the four others] the row of houses to the use of the poor people of Manning-tree for ever, the revenues to their maintenance and relief; to Barbara my house in which widow Little dwelleth in Manningtree; and to Stephen Shorting my house wherein I dwell and the yard called the Quay Yard belonging, my house called the Brick House and the yard in Manningtree. To Thomas Goodfellow my servant 40s. To Mary Mytche £10. To Robert Bayfeild my wife's kinsman of Wendling (Norfolk) £10. To Mary Allen my wife's kinswoman the silver cup that was her father's. To Elizabeth wife of James Lyes 6 silver spoons. To the widow Little 20s. If I overlive my wife, the residue of my goods to Stephen Shortinge. I make my wife and him my executors and James Lyes my supervisor, to whom I give for his pains £10.

Witnesses: Robert Glaskock gentleman, John Holmes, Thomas Luffkin, James Lyes.

Proved 25 May 1590.

ROBERT JEGON of Coggeshall clothier, 8 November 1583.　[27/23]

To my son John my freehold tenement called Widdowsons in Stocke Street in Coggeshall. To my son Thomas my copyhold tenement called Tredgols held of the manor of Feering; my two tenements in the market-stead of Coggeshall wherein John Lee dwelleth, which I hold by convent seal of the manor of Much Coggeshall for the years yet to come and also other years I have in the same by a Duchy [of Lancaster] lease which is 31 years to come after my convent seal; also two tenements in Church Street being freehold, in one whereof Robert Smythe dwell-eth and widow Neale, in the other John Beacham; reserving to Joan my wife for life the profit of the last with the shop on the backside. To my son Ambrose my house wherein I dwell which I hold by convent seal of the manor of Much Coggeshall and my croft called Buttfield likewise held for the term of years in both to come; reserving to my wife her dwelling or otherwise the profits of both for life, she keeping them in sufficient reparations. To him my freehold tenement wherein my brother Roger dwelleth in Church Street called Swaines House, and the shop on the backside held by lease of the same manor; reserving the occupying of the weighing place there with a way to my wife or any other dwelling there during the years to come; and Roger shall have them until Ambrose is 21, paying him 20s. yearly; also to Ambrose my lease of my bailiwick of Feering, Portwicke and Kelvedon. To my daughter Elizabeth Adlyn 40s. to make her a ring. To my daughter Anne Noies £10. To Roger £4, my best coat, a pair of hose, a doublet and a shirt. To John my brother's son 13s. 4d. To the poor of Coggeshall 20s. To the poor scholars of the Queens' College in Cambridge 20s. To every of my servants in my house 12d. To my daughter Bridget £40. From the profit of the tenement in which John Beachem dwelleth my wife to pay Thomas at his commencing Master of Art £6 towards the charge of his commencement, but not if he never commence. To my wife 3 of my best kine or milch beasts, half of my household [stuff] and bedding, and £50. All which things and profits I give conditionally that she relinquish her dower. The other half to my sons equally to be divided, they giving Agnes and Bridget my daughters some part at their discretion. The stained cloths shall remain with the house, also the 3 bedsteads in the parlour, the chamber over the parlour and the chamber over the buttery. John shall have the custody and government of Thomas and to receive his rent, to see him brought up as my trust is in him and the government of Ambrose, to see him bound apprentice with some honest man, and to receive his stock with the profits of all other things given him. To John Beachem the elder some apparel or 10s. in money. I desire Thomas Hopper, Robert Litherlande and Thomas Gray to be my supervisors, and for their pains 3s. 4d. The residue of my goods to Ambrose and I appoint him my sole executor. Witnesses : Thomas Graye, John Gray.

Proved 31 January 1584.

RAYMOND KINGE of Harwich merchant, 7 October 1600.   [45/2]

To 20 poor folks in Harwich such as my executors shall think meet, by 20s. a year, and to the poor people of Dovercourt 20s. and Ramsey 20s.

To Helen wife of John Shrive and daughter of James Barker, my son-in-law, my house with the yard and garden which I purchased of Helen Morris in Harwich in the occupation of Charles Spincke. To Susan, daughter of James, my little house in Harwich which I had of Mr John Brocke and £10 at 22 or marriage. To Grace, Christian and Joan daughters and Anne youngest daughter of James, each £20 at 22 or marriage; to James his son at 23 and William his youngest son, each £20 at 21. To John son of John Scratton deceased and of Grace his late wife, my daughter, £20 at 22; to Raymond Scratton his brother £20 at 21. To Robert Goodwyn, son of my daughter Grace, £20 at 20. To Anne Scratton my house in Harwich which I bought of John Mylles with the backhouse and garden at 21 or marriage, and my executors to let it and have the rent till then. To Josan Kinge daughter of my son John £20 and a bedstead at 22 or marriage. To Anne Kinge daughter of John my house nigh Rookes Lane in Harwich with the outhouses and garden and two pightles that I bought of William Russell, Mr Markante of Colchester and John Jennynges of Harwich at 23 or marriage, and my executors to let it and have the rent. To John my son and Anne his wife the house wherein he dwelleth, for their lives, and after to Thomas their son and his heirs, and for default of such issue to Josan and Anne his sisters equally. To Thomas my copyhold lands in the manor of Dovercourt at 22, and my executors to hold them until then. To the three children of my kinsman Christopher Kinge 20s. apiece for their need, and no part to be delivered to their mother. To my cousin William Kinge, son of my brother Arthur, £5; my cousin William son of my sister Mary Kinge £5; and Raymond son of my cousin William £5 at 23. To father Grove 10s. To my neighbours mother Stevens and mother Cocke 10s. apiece. To Mr Hugh Branham [rector of Little Oakley] 10s. yearly for 6 years over and besides his wages. To John Forber £5. To widow Cowper 20s.

To my son John my storehouse called commonly a salthouse which I bought of Thomas Richmond adjoining the salthouse of Thomas Twytt in Castle [*sic*] parish in Harwich. To John one quarter and one half-quarter of my part of the hoy called the Anne of Harwich and of the tackle belonging; three quarters of my small ship or bark called the Phoenix of Harwich; and my small lighter with 2 small anchors and her mast, which lieth in Robert Goodwyn's yard, and as much old sail as will make her 2 sails. To John my greatest silver goblet, 6 silver spoons, a white silver cup, my small silver pot and my gilt cup; my best table standing in the parlour next the garden with 6 of my best joined stools, the bedsteadle in the westernmost chamber next the street, and my pair of blue silk curtains with the valance, my best kettle and great trivet, my shortest green carpet, my great green chest barred about with iron, and the square table in my great chamber over the hall with a green carpet belonging; and my apparel.

To Anne my wife one quarter and one half-quarter of the said hoy; and over and besides her apparel, jewels and plate which she brought with her, my best salt cellar of silver gilt, a cup of silver gilt, a white cup of silver, my great silver pot, and a little trencher salt cellar of silver, the bedstead in the chamber commonly called the King's Chamber, the new danske chest therein, and the pair of green silk curtains with the valance; and £100. If God shall send my ship called the Anne Frances of Harwich to return home in safety on the present voyage, another £100 to her to be paid by £10 a year. Which legacies of £200 I give on condition that she shall give good bond to my executors within 24 hours after my funeral not to have any of my tenements (except my mansion house for her dwelling for two years after my decease).

The residue of my household stuff (rye and other merchandises excepted) to be equally and indifferently divided into four parts, one each to my wife, John, Christian and Grace Goodwyn, provided that

Christian and Grace shall have to be equally parted between them my other two silver cups gilt and a white silver cup and that Raymond son of John shall have my six gold buttons. My wife and John shall pay him or her which shall have charge of Raymond at school and learning, keeping and government on every voyage which the hoy shall make to Newcastle out of the profits of every voyage 10s. apiece so long as he be kept at school. To my wife one quarter of the Phoenix in consideration that she bring up Raymond until he be put forth to some trade by my executors. To him my lands in Ramsey, and they shall have the rents till he is 24 and to account to him then. My wife shall have for her dwelling my mansion house wherein I dwell and the storehouse and other housing with the yard, garden and quay for two years after my decease, then to John for life, and after to Raymond, paying yearly to Thomas an annuity of £5. The legacies to John shall remain with my executor, James Barker, till Thomas Twytt his father-in-law enter into bond to my executors of so much money as yet remaineth unpaid of the portion that Thomas Twytt promised to pay to John in marriage with Anne his daughter. My ship called the Anne Frances and my merchandises shall be sold for the payment of my debts, funerals and legacies.

I ordain James Barker and John my executors.

Witnesses: Hugh Branham clerk, Michael Twytt, George Eastrike, John Forber.

Codicil, 7 January 1601. If in consideration of £5 due to me for money I have laid out for the affairs of the town of Harwich, the townsmen will not bestow on my kinsman William Kinge the pasturing of a cow in the marsh adjoining the town, then my executors shall give him £5. To Raymond brother of William £5. Whereas I was minded to give to Robert Goodwyn, my son-in-law, one third part of the Anne Frances, in consideration thereof I give him £40, if my executors sell the ship he shall have a third part, paying so much money above £40 as the third part shall come to after the rate that the ship shall be sold. Witness: John Forber, scrivener of the court letter of London.

Memorandum, manor of Dovercourt, of the surrender, 30 October 1600, by Raymond Kinge by the hands of John Forber of his lands to the use of his will.

Proved 23 January 1601.

ROBERT LAMBERT the elder of Colchester merchant, 14 September 1590. [36/69]

To the poor people within the liberties of the town of Colchester £5. To my loving friends, the preachers of God's Word, viz. Mr [George] Northey [town preacher of Colchester] 40s., Mr [Robert] Lewes [vicar of St Peter] 20s., Mr [Robert] Moncke [rector of Wakes Colne] 20s., Mr [Thomas] Upcher [rector of St Leonard] 20s. and Mr [John] Wilton [rector of Aldham] 10s.

To Anne my loving wife for life my capital messuage wherein I dwell and the barn piece of ground called the Purchase Orchard and meadow, which I bought of Edward Burton gentleman, and the use of the glass windows, ceilings, wainscots, locks, keys, bars and bolts of iron, ironworks, leads, cisterns, and hangings and other implements fixed or hung, also the use of the press in the chamber next the street and that beam with the pair of scales and those 500 lb. in weights of lead which I commonly weigh by; and after her decease to Thomas my son, and for default of issue successively to my sons Nathaniel and Robert. To her for life my freehold lands in Wivenhoe, with like remainders. To her for ever my capital messuage in the New Hythe of Colchester which I purchased of Edward Burton and Joan his wife; my two tenements in St Leonard in the New Hythe, whereof one was late in the tenure of William Rickes and the other in that of Lawrence Beane, and my lands which I purchased of Robert Bird, and after her decease to Nathaniel, and for default of issue successively to Robert and Thomas; my tenement in St Peter in North Street, late in that of John Norman, and my tenement in St Leonard which I purchased of Richard Langly, and after her decease to my daughter Elizabeth Bradshawe; and my lands which I purchased of John Clerke gentleman and Mary his wife in Peldon and Wigborough, and after her decease to Robert, and for want of issue successively to Nathaniel and Thomas. To Robert my messuage, lands, springhead, brewing-house, and a little parcel of meadow where the ballast quay doth stand I purchased of Robert Steven in St Leonard, and the vats, brewing vessels, coppers, cisterns, leads, pipes of lead, horsemill and millstones, and for default of issue to Nathaniel and Thomas; provided that my wife shall have the messuage and other premises until Robert is 24. To Robert £60 at 24, Thomas £50 at 24, and Bridget my daughter, wife of George Gowge, £50 at 24. To John my best silver piece which was his mother's.

Whereas my son-in-law Benjamin Clere is indebted to me in £52, also £50 more on his bond, if he pay the £50 to my executrix I give the £52 to Mary Clere my daughter. Whereas Richard Buckford my son-in-law doth owe me £23, on payment thereof I give it to Thomasine his wife, my daughter; if he deliver to my wife and Nathaniel, Robert and Thomas a general acquittance, my executrix shall pay him £40. To my godchildren 20s. apiece at 24 or marriage. To my grandchild Anna Buckford, daughter of my son-in-law Richard, £5 at 24 or marriage. To my brother John Lambert's children, James, John and Robert, £5 apiece, and to Margery £10, at 24 or marriage.

My wife shall have her legacies in satisfaction of dower. She bring up Thomas at her charge at the Inns of Court at his study for 4 years at the least after my decease. I charge my children to live lovingly together in the fear of God, be obedient to their mother, deal honestly and uprightly with all men, and be ordered quietly by good instruction of my wife, the which I desire the omnipotent God of his goodness and mercy to grant and to bless them all with his spiritual and heavenly blessing. The residue to my wife, whom I ordain my sole executrix. I heartily require my loving friend Mr Robert Mott, one of the bailiffs of Colchester, to be a friendly overseer, helper and counsellor to my executrix, and for his pains 40s.

Witnesses : Richard Symnell, William Turnor, John Richardes, Robert Elys.

Proved 7 September 1592.

CHRISTOPHER LANGLEY of Colchester merchant, 10 September 1601. [46/15]

To be buried in St Leonard's church.

To Margaret my loving wife my messuages and lands, customary and free, for life, a moiety of my ship called the Margaret and John of Colchester, a moiety of my ship called the Mary Anne of Colchester, three quarters of my ship called the Christopher and John of Colchester, a moiety of the ship called the Primrose of Colchester, two third parts of the ship called the Grace of God of Colchester, three quarters and one half-quarter of the ship called the Mary Rose of Colchester, and one quarter of my new ship now in building at Ipswich (Suffolk) by Robert Cole shipwright; and the rateable and like parts of the masts, sails, sailyards, anchors, cables, boats, furniture, munition and apparel to the ships belonging.

To John my son after my wife's decease the messuage wherein I dwell in Colchester Hythe with the orchard and two gardens; the messuage adjoining where in John inhabiteth and the yard or backside and garden; my lands and tenements called Marshalls in the parish and fields of Wivenhoe; and my customary messuages and lands in the parish and fields of Wivenhoe. To Anne [Cutter] my eldest daughter after my wife's decease three messuages in Colchester Hythe which I purchased of the widow Holte, and the residue of Nathaniel Lambert. To Margaret my second daughter, after my wife's decease, the messuage with the orchard and garden in Colchester Hythe which I purchased of [Thomas] Knevet, minister [rector] of Mile End in Colchester. To Rose my third daughter, after my wife's decease, five messuages together on Love Hill in St Leonard, two of which I purchased of Thomas Pisall of Brightlingsea, two of Philip Garret of Wivenhoe, and the other of Guntin of Lexden. To Mary my youngest daughter after my wife's decease my fair messuage and the orchard and garden in St Botolph which I purchased of John Barret weaver. If my son or any of my daughters be minded to sell or to make proffer of such sale of any of the same messuages or lands, on due proof made by two honest witnesses of good report and credit I give the same to my loving brother Jeffrey Langley of Colchester. To John the moiety or other part of the Margaret and Joan; to Anne one eighth part of the Primrose and the new ship, and the quarter of the same shall be employed for the better education of Christopher Cutter, her son and my godchild; to Margaret one half of one third part of the Grace of God; to Rose so much of the Mary Anne as with the half-third part which Henry Cleyborne now hath shall be one quarter.

If my wife shall hereafter marry, she shall only receive one third part of my messuages and lands for life for her dower and also one third part of my goods and shipping, and she shall surrender to my children the residue of their parts of the messuages, lands, goods and shipping. If she die intestate, whereby the shipping which I have bequeathed to her come to John, he shall in lieu thereof pay every of my daughters £150 apiece. To Margaret £10, Rose £20 and Mary £10 at marriage; to Rose a silver bowl and 5 silver spoons. If my wife continue in her widowhood until her death, such part of my household goods, plate and jewels as at her decease remain shall be by four honest men in Colchester, indifferently elected by my children, appraised and delivered to them an equal part. To Joan Langley my sister dwelling in Swadell [Swaledale?] (Yorks.) £10; my cousin Robert Langley of Hartlepool (Yorks.) £5; John, Margaret, Jeffrey and Christopher Langley, the four children of my brother Jeffrey, £40 apiece at marriage or 21. To my very friend Elizabeth wife of Henry Cooper citizen and grocer of London £5. To John Wallington, citizen and ironmonger of London, 20s. To my friend John Milly of London gentleman 10s.

To St Leonard's church in Colchester £5 to be bestowed on the church or steeple. To the poor, old, lame and impotent persons of the same parish £5. To Anne Holgrave, my wife's kinswoman, 40s.

I ordain my wife sole executrix, and I make my well-beloved friend the said Henry Cooper and my well-beloved brother Jeffrey overseers, whom I desire to be aiding my executrix, and for their pains £20 apiece. I desire John to be careful and diligent to my wife in effecting her business in marine causes to his uttermost ability as he tendered my blessing and will answer at the Day of Judgement. To Thomas Lowe minister [rector] of St Leonard 40s. To Bernard Hide citizen and salter of London £5. To Ralph Hide citizen and grocer of London 20s. to buy him a ring.

Witnesses : John Baker scr[ibe], William Wright, John Cooper, Henry Cooper, William Williamson, Barnard Hide, Ralph Hide, Elizabeth Cooper.

Proved 6 February 1602.

WILLIAM MARKES of St Mary, Maldon, clothier, 9 October 1582.
[25/45]

To Margaret my wife my goods, household stuff, stover and fuel in Maldon (my wool, yarn, horse and kine only excepted); £150 to be levied by my executors out of my other goods bequeathed to my three sons; also my ewes, rams, lambs and wethers and my hogs. My executor shall pay my wife £80 to the use of her four sons, Thomas, Abel, John and Nicholas, in payment of their legacies by the will of Thomas Hawkes their father. To my youngest daughter Agnes Markes £30 at 24. My wife shall have (if she will) such wool and yarn as is in my house at such prices as I paid for it, also my bay gelding with a white face, paying £4 to my executor. The residue of my goods to my three sons, viz. George my eldest, whom I nominate sole executor, and William and Edmund my second and youngest, equally to be divided between them; William shall have £9 in part payment of his portion which I delivered to Thomas Neverd his master, to be repaid when his apprenticeship be ended, the residue within a year, and Edmund to be paid within 15 months. I ordain Robert Heard and John Nashe to be overseers, and for their pains 20s. each. Witnesses: Robert Humfry, William Paine. Proved 22 November 1582.

WILLIAM MARTIN of Halstead clothier, 26 May 1573.   [17/29]

To be buried in Halstead church.

To William Cocksall gentleman, Henry Thomson, Lawrence Pilgrim, William Sadlington, Edward Turner, John Hunwick, William Sweting senior, John Barnarde, Thomas Digbye and John Vigorus, and their heirs, my tenements and lands which I purchased of Thomas Cooe called Cooes in Halstead in the tenure of Henry Greene, also my parcel of fen and pasture called Shellardes Fen in the occupation of Thomas Harvy which I bought of Sir Thomas Golding, upon special trust that they, their heirs and assigns shall employ the yearly profits towards the erecting and maintenance of a common Grammar School in the town of Halstead and a sufficient, meet and able schoolmaster for the bringing up and instructing of the children and young infants of such persons in the town and parish that will desire or require to be brought up in learning, if the inhabitants do at any time hereafter give for ever as much lands or rents as be of the yearly value of £3 6s. 8d. to make up the premises before bequeathed, now being of the yearly value of £6 13s. 4d., to the yearly value of £10, for the maintenance and stipend of the said schoolmaster. In the meantime I charge [the feoffees named] to employ the yearly profits amongst the poor people of Halstead until such further annual sum of £3 6s. 8d. be given, and not to let the premises for more than three years. The vicar and churchwardens and four of the chief inhabitants shall once every two years at the least in God's name require two or three of the nearest justices of peace to join with them to visit the school after its erection, and I give each churchwarden yearly for their diligence 20d.

To Agnes my wife my capital messuage wherein I dwell, two crofts of land belonging called Walshes and Chapel Croft and two crofts called Sparkes Croft and Giles Croft which I bought of Roger Martin esquire and other my lands in the occupation of Thomas Binde, my meadow near Towneforde Mill in that of John Atkin and Tanners Croft adjoining in that of William Rande, and two tenements which I bought of Thomas Clarke in that of George Barber and Anthony Blande, all in Halstead; for her life, in full recompense of her dower; with remainder to Anne widow of Thomas Clarke of Maldon deceased for life; and after her decease to remain to the said feoffees to employ the profits to the use of the school and stipend and to the poor of Halstead. Provided that, if there should not be given £3 6s. 8d. yearly to make up the yearly stipend of £10 for the schoolmaster before my capital messuage and lands should come into the feoffees' hands, £3 6s. 8d. of the profits shall be employed towards the erecting of the school and to make up the £10 and the overplus to be employed to the use of the poor. To John Archer, Robert Skath, John Salperwyck alias Gillam, John Bentall, Robert Smyth the younger, Thomas Norman, Thomas Kepe, John

296

Hobson, William Sewall and Thomas Lambert, and their heirs, my tenement and lands at Castle Hedingham which I bought of William Cooe in the occupation of Humphrey Lane, that they, their heirs and assigns shall employ two parts of the profits amongst the poor people of Bocking and the third part among the poor people of Castle Hedingham.

To William Sweeting my godson, son of William Sweeting, my messuage and lands in Halstead called Pichardes and Heithorne with a meadow now set with osiers at the end which I bought of Sir Thomas Golding in the occupations of William Sweting's father, Thomas Hunwick, Robert Osburne and John Tinges and myself. To Roger Martin my cousin my tenement and garden which I bought of Roger Martin esquire in Halstead in that of Edward Feling, on condition that he shall not practise any disturbance against my executors. My executors shall pay John Fortescue esquire £100 for redeeming certain lands in Great Thurlow (Suffolk) which I had of Thomas Potter. To the said William Sweeting the elder and John Burges my servant my lease of lands called Upper Priors, Nether Priours and Box Mill Meadow in Halstead equally between them, reserving one cow pasturing in the same lands for my wife and one cow pasturing for Henry Johnson.

To my wife my implements of household (except my plate) and 3 kine; and to Agnes Spurgeon her daughter 3 kine now with Richard Chote. To Roger Martyn my cousin £20 on condition as aforesaid and to his two daughters £10 each at marriage or 21. To William Martyn my cousin £20 and to his son £20 at 20. To William Buerell alias Borowgh my cousin £20.

To Richard Baker my servant £6 13s. 4d. and the said John Burges £10. To Mark Sadlington £20. To John Salperwyck alias Gillam £20. To William Vigorus £6 13s. 4d. To Avice Hall and Judith Abraham my maidservants £3 6s. 8d. each. To every one of my godchildren 12d. To the amending of the slough at the corner of Mr Jackman's wood towards Bocking 40s. To Robert Osborne £10 which William Sadlington doth owe me. To William Martyn my cousin £4 which Thomas Sampson of Colne oweth me. To Richard Sparrow my godson £3 6s. 8d. in satisfaction of such debts as his late father did claim of me. To Robert Smyth fuller, George Woodye, William Smyth weaver, Thomas Tokeley, Richard Sampson, John Ridenhall, William Ridenhall, John Harvy, John Abraham, Robert Enew and Richard Darmer, who have been my workmen, each 20s., also to John Baker the smith 20s. To my late servants Richard Merell 10s. and Henry Scotte, Henry Stedeman and William Stedeman each 13s. 4d. To Henry Scotte the elder £3 6s. 8d. To Edward Hawkin bailiff of the hundred [of Hinckford] 20s. To Ralph Huntman my godson 20s. To my wife so much wood as I have already bought. To John Stevens 20s. The rest of my goods to my executors, whom I name Francis Salperwyck alias Gillam, Thomas Sadlington and William Vigorus. I ordain John Atkin of Halstead supervisor, and for his pains 20s.

Witnesses : William Martyn, John Cogsh[i]ll, Robert Smyth, Edward Turner, John Archer, William Sadlington, Robert Snath, Henry Pole, John Shuntman, Thomas Rand, Thomas Foster.

Proved 2 July 1574. Sentence confirming Will in case between all three executors and Roger Martin.

JOHN MAYNARDE of St James, Colchester, alderman, 1 November 1565.   [12/15]

Alice my wife shall occupy my lands and mills free and copy for life, keeping them in sufficient reparations and maintain my woad house. To Joan Maynarde my daughter, after my wife's decease, my two mills called Stockes Mill and East Mill with the floodgate meadows in Colchester (containing 9 acres). To Elizabeth Maynarde my daughter my copyhold tenements and lands in West Mersea called Waldegraves, Bettes and Cokes; my mansion house which I dwell in with the ground belonging (6 acres) and my woad house called Cardes Hall with the leads and cisterns and the lands which I purchased with the woad house; my free tenement called Pylayes in Ardleigh and 20 acres of land and two grovets called Pylaies Groves (2½ acres); my three tenements in St Botolph which I purchased of Lawrence Coxsonne; my three tenements in Magdalen Street in Colchester; my free lands in Ardleigh by Crockleford Brook in the tenure of Henry Evered smith; my three parcels of copyhold ground (8 acres) at Dawndes Hill in Greenstead; and my tenement and garden in Hackney Lane in Colchester which I bought of Ardley. To Joan my tenement which I bought of Thomas Alfilde in St Botolph, sometime Mr Smalepeice's and after Alfylde's in the occupation of Vincent; after the decease of my wife. If both daughters die before her, all to remain to Julian wife of John Gerye of London, daughter of my brother Richard Maynarde deceased; and for default of issue to remain successively to Thomas, Henry, Nicholas, George and William, eldest, 2nd, 3rd, 4th and 5th sons of my brother Nicholas Maynarde. To Joan 300 marks, my best salt of silver, a standing cup of silver and gilt, 2 silver pieces, and 6 silver spoons at marriage. To Elizabeth 300 marks, a salt of silver, a nest of silver goblets gilt with a cover, and 6 silver spoons at marriage. To the children of my brothers Robert and Nicholas 40s. apiece. To the poor people in Colchester £6 13s. 4d. To the common preacher of Colchester 10s. To Julian wife of John Gerye of London pewterer £6 13s. 4d. To every of my covenant servants 5s. The residue to my wife, whom I make my sole executrix. I name my trusty and well-beloved friends in Christ John Beast and Robert Middleton of Colchester aldermen, overseers, and to each for their pains £5. Witnesses : Robert Northen, John Lucas, William Ram.
Proved 22 June 1569.

ALICE MAYNERD of St James, Colchester, widow, 5 May 1584.
                                                                         [28/18]

I have to the preferment of my two daughters in marriage before this time given the greatest part of my lands and goods, whom with their husbands and children I pray the Almighty God to bless, and for the small portion which remaineth in my possession I give the copyhold land which I hold of Sir Thomas Lucas, lord of the manor of Greenstead, containing 7 acres at Dawne Hill, to my executor to be sold for payment of such legacy as I shall give to the poor of this town and discharging of 20d. a week which I have given to my poor sister Elizabeth for life as also for the discharge of other legacies. To the poor people of the town of Colchester and liberties £13 6s. 8d. to be distributed in every parish, some at my burial. To my cousins Edward Maynerd, Robert Maynerd and Margery Briant, the children of Robert my late husband's brother, each £5. To Gillian Gerye, daughter of Richard Maynerd, and to William son of Nicholas Maynerd, both deceased, each £5. To the general preacher of the town of Colchester 40s. [George Northey]. To Thomas Fremlyn and Richard Symnell gentlemen, each £5. To Samuel Goodyer, scholar in Cambridge, 40s. My executor shall appoint some godly or learned preacher to preach four sermons in some country towns where the Gospel is not usually preached, and for each sermon 6s. 8d. To Edward Newman and Moses Gates my servants each 40s. so as they abide out their service with my executor, if he will keep them their times but if not then at their departure. To my grandchild John Nortoun £40 at 21. Although I have not herein set down any legacy to my daughter Joan's children, yet I have not forgotten them, for I have lately delivered into their father's hands £400 to be paid to them by him part and part like at their full ages. The residue to my son-in-law John Norton gentleman and Elizabeth my daughter his wife, which John I make my sole executor, and I appoint my son-in-law William Cardinall gentleman and my loving friend Mr John Pye my supervisors, and to each for their pains £5. Witnesses : William Tomson, Richard Symnell, William Hewer, Thomas Brabye.

Proved 11 July 1584.

NATHANIEL MORSE of Dedham clothier, 18 December 1590. [35/1]

After the payment of my debts, the rest of my goods shall be equally divided betwixt Joan my wife and my four children, Nathaniel, Michael, John and Susan Morse; and if my wife be now with child it shall have the like portion. I make executors my brother John Jeffrye and my good and loving wife. Witnesses : Roger Vaughan, Robert Barwicke, Thomas Upcher.

Proved 21 January 1591.

WILLIAM NEVERD of Dedham clothier, 18 September 1595. (Nuncupative.) [39/64]

To Mary, Anne and Susan Neverd his daughters each £20 at marriage or 21. To the poor people of Dedham 26s. 8d. at his burial. The rest of his goods to Anne his wife, whom he did make his sole executrix. Witnesses : Edward Clarke, John Lufkyn, with others.

Proved 25 October 1595. Administration granted, 3 May 1622, to William Bentley, husband of Mary Nevard alias Bentley.

THOMAS PEAYCOKE of Coggeshall clothmaker, 20 December 1580.
[23/50]

To be buried in St Katherine's aisle in Coggeshall church. My executors to buy the like stone that doth lie on my father's grave or my uncle Thomas Peaycoke by it and so to see it laid on my grave within thirteen months after my decease, and my grave to be made near to one of my uncles' graves but not to meddle with any of their graves. To Mr [Lawrence] Newman, vicar of Coggeshall, £5 to make a sermon at my burial and four more at his pleasure afterwards. To Mr Wilton 40s. to make two sermons in Coggeshall church at his pleasure. To Mr Henry Crane parson of Rivenhall 40s. to make a sermon there. To Mr [Robert] Lewis parson of Markshall 40s. to make two sermons there. There shall be given at my burial or within 6 days after to the poor people of Coggeshall £6 13s. 4d. at the discretion of my executors. They shall within two years after my decease purchase so much free lands as with £200 they may, the profit thereof to be bestowed among the poor people of Great and Little Coggeshall and so to continue unto the end of this uncertain world, and shall deliver a sure estate, feoffment and conveyance thereof to ten of the headboroughs of Coggeshall to the intent that the yearly rents and profits be bestowed among the poor people for ever as the same shall best be devised by learned counsel, within two years after my decease; and that the distribution be given by the consents of the collectors for the poor and the churchwardens viz. with one half of the rents and profits there shall be bought as much wood as it shall amount to betwixt Easter and the farthest day of August and with the other half a month before Lent as much white herring and red as it shall amount to. To the poor people of Clare (Suffolk) 20s., Feering 15s., Great Tey 10s., Markshall 3s. 4d., Earls Colne 10s., Halstead 10s., Pattiswick 5s., Stisted 6s., Bradwell 5s., Cressing 6s., Rivenhall 6s., Kelvedon 10s., Inworth 2s. and Messing 6s., to be delivered to the minister and 3 or 4 honest men of every parish to see the money given where most need shall be. To the prisoners of the Gaol of Colchester 20s. in bread, meat and drink, 6s. 8d. each week for 3 weeks.

To Joan my wife £100 on condition that she shall not claim her dower in any lands which I have heretofore sold to any person or which I am possessed of. She shall have for life her dwelling and the use of my tenement called Cobbes in West Street in Coggeshall which I bought of Thomas Coleman.

To Thomas Till and Joan his wife my messuage wherein he dwelleth and the tenement adjoining in Coggeshall for their lives and the longer liver, and after their decease to remain to Ambrose Tyll their son, and for lack of issue to Thomas his brother. The said Thomas, my son-in-law, and Joan shall hold a meadow called Poopes Leas (containing 5 acres) and Reyne Croft (32 acres) in Coggeshall which I hold by lease for 20 years after my decease; also £100. To Thomas Till son of Thomas and Joan and their heirs male my mansion house wherein I dwell situate at the Gravel in Coggeshall called Belles and Bevers [Beners?], with the buildings, yards and gardens belonging; and my two tenements adjoining which I purchased of Reynold Ferror and William Dell; and for lack of issue successively to Ambrose and to Richard Bynnyon and Anne his wife, my daughter, and the heirs male of each; also to Thomas son of Thomas and Joan the grounds and pastures on the backside of my mansion called Cowles alias Horse Leas (7½ acres) which I hold in fee farm, with like remainders; my customary meadow called Osiers and my customary lands called Mattresses and Lady Wood with an orchard in the same newly planted in Coggeshall which I hold by copy of court roll; the parcel of ground called Fynsons in Coggeshall which I hold by lease; my lands and pastures which I bought of William Fabyan gentleman called Buxgrove Lands in Coggeshall lying together by the highway from Earls Colne to Coggeshall to the Dovehouse Cross, with the houses, barns and stables thereon; and my meadow lying within Grigges in Coggeshall; all until Thomas is 26, so that Thomas the father or Joan shall not fell any wood or timber. To Ambrose £50 at 24 and Judith and Joan daughters of Thomas and Joan each £40 at marriage or 22; if any die before, to the rest of the children of Thomas and Joan by equal parts. To Thomas the son the lands called Croppes in Coggeshall, and a parcel of land called Sorrells (2 acres) in West Street which I hold in fee farm; with like remainders as my mansion house. To Richard Bynnyon and Anne my free lands and pastures called Brightes Fen and Newalles in Feering which I purchased of Mr Southwell; my lands, meadows and pastures called Samuelles and Jaglettes in Feering holden by copy of court roll of the manor of Feering Bury; my lease of the Dairy House with the lands belonging; my lease of the corn milne with the meadow belonging; and my lease of the house called Mr Harleston's house with 18 acres of ground belonging in Great and Little Coggeshall.

To Elizabeth, Tabitha and Anne daughters of Richard and Anne each £40 at 21 or marriage; if any die before, to the rest of the children of Richard and Anne by equal parts. To Judith Constantyne daughter of late Judith my daughter deceased £40 at 20; if she die before, to Richard Constantyne her father. To my cousin Robert Mott of Colchester 40s. and to his children 20s. apiece at 18. To Mary his sister 40s. To Robert Lytherland my lease of a croft, parcel of Over Church Field in Coggeshall lying by Church Lane near to Robert Jegons' house, and £5, and to his children 20s. apiece at 18. I give and freely forgive to John Lytherland £4 which he doth owe me, and to his children 10s. apiece at 18. To Elizabeth widow of [blank] Hulman 20s. and her children, except Thomas her son, 10s. at 18. To Susan and Judith sisters of Robert Letherland 30s. apiece. To the two daughters of William Osmonde, Anne and [blank], 30s. apiece. To John, Thomas and Elizabeth Hawkes 20s. apiece. To John Ocle 20s. yearly for life. To my cousin Martin of Clare [Suffolk] and his wife each 20s. and their children 10s. apiece.

To William Guyon my weaver 20s., William Lawraunce my tenant 20s., John Pyckett, Jonas Grene, John Burro, Anthony Osmunde, John Joyner, William Cavell, Thomas Cavell, and John Miles of Bradwell, each 10s., Thomas Clover 5s., John Gardiner my tailor, Thomas Richolde, Thomas Felsted, Richard Enowes of Colne, Reynold Ferror, Richard Todd the bailiff, George Lawrence and Thomas Burnet, each 10s., also to John Carter 40s. which he doth owe me. To Robert Colman

40s. and Thomas 20s. Also to William Fynche wheelwright, John Heywarde my tenant, John Fabyan my beerbrewer, and John Mott my tenant, each £5, William Haywarde my tenant 20s., John Colman my tenant £5, Anthony Litilbury 20s., and Thomas Aylewarde 20s.

To my brother Edmund Clarke and his wife each 40s. To William Tusser £5. To Andrew Trollope gentleman 40s. To William Gooday the elder 10s. To Thomas Hulman my servant £3 at 21, and if he die before, then to his brethren and sistern by equal parts. To John Walker my servant £3. I give £7 10s. to and among 30 of the poorest journeymen of the fuller's occupation in Coggeshall, i.e. to each 5s. To Thomas Browne £5.

To all these gentlemen and gentlewomen and other my friends, each a ring of gold with a death's head on it to the value as is appointed, i.e. my cousin John Peaycock and his wife 30s. apiece, Mr Humfrey Smythe and my cousin his wife 40s. apiece, Mr Matthew Smythe and his wife 30s. apiece. Mr Thursbie and his wife 30s. apiece, Mr Thomas Geynes and his wife 30s. apiece, Mr Deraughe 30s., Mr Byngham 30s., Mr Holmestede and his wife 30s. apiece, Mr Sparke of London 40s., Mr Davenaunte of London and his wife 40s. apiece, Richard Woodwarde and his wife 30s. apiece, and William Vigorus of Halstead and his wife 30s. apiece.

To the right worshipful Mr Justice Southcote and Sir William Cordell, Master of the Rolls, each £20, most humbly desiring their worships to take the pains to be overseers of my will; and if there shall arise any trouble between my executors or between any persons and them touching my will, Mr Justice Southcote and the Master of the Rolls shall have the hearing and determining of any such matter, without any suit of law.

The rest of my goods, debts, plate, household stuff and my ready money to Richard Bynyon and Thomas Till son of Thomas and Joan equally between them to be divided, which said Richard and Thomas the son I ordain my executors; provided that, as Thomas is under age, William Vigorus of Halstead shall as well receive to the use of Thomas the rents and profits of such lands, houses, lease lands, and other goods bequeathed to him as also shall join with my other executor in the execution of my will during such time as he shall come to 24, and then he shall make a true account to him; and further such money that shall be received by William Vigorus shall be laid in a chest with three locks and three keys standing in my mansion house, whereof he to have one key, Richard Bynnyon another, and Thomas Till the father another; and to William Vigorus for his painstaking 20 marks.

Witnesses : William Vigorus the writer, John Lee, John Browson, Stephen Pakmer, John Spencer, Robert Laston, Thomas Felsted, John Gardiner.

Proved 30 December 1580.

ROBERT PLATT of Chelmsford vintner, 27 January 1592.   [36/43]

To be buried in the chancel of Chelmsford church against the seat where Richard Nicoles now doth sit. To the poor inhabitants of Chelmsford and Moulsham 40s. and of Dullingham (Cambs.) 20s. To Richard Bateson of Moulsham one silver bowl called the white horse bowl. To Mary wife of John Nox a like bowl. To my cousin George Martendall 20s. To Thomas White my servant 40s. To Agnes Batcheler my cousin 20s. To John Ryson of Chelmsford my best gown. To my mother a piece of gold of 10s. To Mary wife of Christopher Taten £5. To my daughter Anne wife of Humphrey Weale £30 a year for 18 years, to be paid out of the lease of the parsonage of Dullingham, also my bed. To Joan my wife, whom I make my executrix, my lease of Dullingham. The residue of my goods to my wife. [No witnesses.]

Proved 10 May 1592. Administration granted, 12 July 1595, to Anne Weale alias Platt, daughter of the deceased.

ROBERT POYNTHAM of St Peter, Colchester, pewterer, 15 December 1596. [41/12]

To Joan my well-beloved wife my capital tenement in the parish of St Mary-at-the-Wall, Colchester, in the occupation of Arthur Jacksone my son-in-law, for her life, and to keep it in needful reparations; and after her decease successively to Rebecca my daughter for life and to Jacob Jacksone her son and his heirs. To my wife my tenement wherein Geese Wetton, stranger, chairmaker, dwelleth in St Peter, for her life; and after her decease successively to Elizabeth my daughter and her heirs and to Robert Jacksone, another of Rebecca's sons, and his heirs, To Rebecca £10. To Jacob, Robert and Elizabeth Jacksone, Rebecca's children, £10 apiece at 21 or marriage. To Elizabeth my daughter £30. To Rebecca half a dozen of my silver spoons and one of my stone pots tipped with silver. To Elizabeth my daughter my gilt salt and a stone pot lipped and tipped at the foot with silver. All which parcels my wife shall have for life. After her decease, to Jacob my bowl of silver and parcel gilt, she to have the use thereof. To my daughter Alice Hodsone £5. My ware both fine and base, new and old, brass kettles and tools whatsoever shall be sold by my executrix and supervisor towards my debts and legacies. My household stuff to my wife. I nominate her my sole executrix. I appoint my well-beloved friend Simon Goodwin of Ipswich my supervisor, and for his pains 20s. Witnesses: Thomas Melsam and Thomas Rigbe.

Proved 1 February 1597.

ROBERT RANDE of Manningtree merchant, 22 December 1572. [16/5]

To be buried in Mistley church, to the reparations whereof 40d. [sic]. To Henry Johnson, parson of Mistley, for a sermon at my burial 6s. 8d. To the poor people of Manningtree and Mistley 40s. to be distributed at the church at my burial. I will that there be 3 half barrels of beer provided, drawn and given out to the poor at the stalls in the street of Manningtree at the day of my burial. To 5 poor men of Manningtree to carry me to church 5s. among them. To my sister Margaret [Scott] towards the relief of her and her poor children £5. To my cousin

William Scott, my sister's eldest son, £10, my best cloak, coat and doublet. To my sister Agnes Morse widow £5. To my brother Thomas's wife for life for the relief of her three children £3. To my sister Margaret, my wife's sister, and my sister Agnes 20s. apiece. To Joan Cole my servant £5 at marriage, and if she die before, to Katherine Large my servant at marriage. To my godchildren 2s. 6d. apiece. To my cousin William Casye my best furred gown. To John Lucas gentleman 3½ yards of holland of 2s. the yard. To Margaret my wife my house wherein I dwell in Manningtree. Provided that, whereas Richard Pettit stands bound to me for a house and garden which he purchased, for the non payment of £5 a year until £30 be full paid, if he do not pay or make default in any payment my wife shall re-enter and take the house to her. The residue of my goods to my wife, whom I make my sole executrix. For overseer I appoint my beloved friend John Grigges, and for his own pains a hat price 5s. and my Chronicle book. Witnesses : John Lucas, John Grigges, William Sparkes.

Proved 7 February 1573.

WILLIAM RAVENS of Dedham clothier, 18 July 1580.   [23/51]

To my son Richard my occupation with all things belonging, to be sold by my executrix and whatsoever it misseth of £20 to be made up [to] £20 and paid to him £4 a year; and the tenement that Trafforde dwelleth in after his mother's decease. The rest of my goods whether corn, cattle, cloth or money to my wife. To my daughter Grace and her daughter Grace each a silver spoon, also to her daughter Grace a weanel to be let out by her parents to the best advantage to her use till she is 18. To my daughter Bridget and her daughter Elizabeth each a silver spoon, also to Bridget's two children a weanel likewise. To Richard 2 silver spoons. To my sister Baker 20s. To my son Carte my best cloak and to my son Page my best gown, desiring them to be supervisors. I make my wife my sole executrix. Witnesses : Ralph Starlinge, Gall Lewes, Richard Clarke, John Whitlock, Edmund Robinson.

Surrender, 19 July, into the hands of Ralph Starlinge and Robert Bytellburie and Habakkuk Page the bailiff [of the manor] to the use of the will. Witnesses : Habakkuk Page, Edward Cole.

Proved 29 December 1580 by [blank] widow and executrix.

JOHN RICHMOND of Walden mercer, 8 April 1597.   [41/24]

To be buried in Walden church. To Agnes my wife and her heirs my shops in the Market End in Walden which I bought of Joan Turner her mother. My messuage in Walden wherein I dwell shall be sold by my executrix for the performance of my will. To John and Thomas my sons each £40 at 21. The residue of my goods to my wife, whom I make my sole executrix, and supervisors I appoint my loving brothers Richard Richmond and George Adams and 5s. each for their pains. [No witnesses.]

Proved 30 April 1597.

To be buried in the chancel of Harwich church by Elizabeth my wife.

To John my eldest son my house which I dwell in, and if he die without heirs male to Robert my son, with remainder to be sold and the money to be divided among both my sons' children. To John my great bedstead in the parlour with the best covering of tapestry, a dumb bed with say curtains and the trundle bedstead under the great bed, with the long table and the frame, 6 stools, cobirons, court table and cupboard, my bare and empty joined chair, and the bare and empty chest, as they stand in the parlour. To Joan my wife my house that John now dwelleth in, for her life, with remainder to Robert my son and to John Garner my son-in-law part and part like. To my wife £50 to be paid in tallow as far as it will amount to at 27s. the hundred tried tallow and raw tallow at 20s. the hundred as I pay for it, and the best to be paid in money; my best posted bedstead in the parlour sollar with a trundle bedstead under it, a Spanish blanket of two coverings, one the second of tapestry, the other of wadmoll, at her choice; and the biggest copper kettle the which I try tallow in. The rest of my copper, brass, latten, pewter and iron shall be laid in three parts, my wife to have one third and her choice, the other two to John, Robert and Lucy Garner my children in equal parts. My linen shall be equally divided likewise. To my wife my silver and gilt tankard, 6 silver spoons next the best, and a pot footed, lipped and covered with silver and gilt that was Richard Smith's, my long table in the hall, with a long form and a joined chair, one danske chest, a great danske coffer, a karoby, and the great square table and frame in the parlour; with her apparel and jewels to her belonging. To Susan Cowper my daughter the house that Edward Keble dwelleth in; and after her decease to Daniel Verry, her eldest son, and £15, and my best silver goblet with 6 silver spoons, and the best pictured and gilt at the ends with the apostles. To Lucy Garner £15 and my silver and gilt bowl, a featherbed, and the great covering that lieth usually on the great bed in the parlour.

My barque called the Valentine, one half to John and a quarter to my wife freely paying nothing. Whereas John Alden my son-in-law bought half a quarter of Robert, he shall have the other half quarter, if it please God to deliver him home out of Spain; and if he be not delivered out of Spain out of captivity, as yet I hope in God by his providence he shall, the half quarter to remain to John Alden his eldest son, my godson, and he pay to his sister Josyan £6. To Robert one quarter of the Confidence, whereof he hath one quarter already, and the other quarter which is the half being mine to John Alden the younger, my daughter's son, paying to his brethren Peter, William and Thomas and Ellen his sister £3 apiece at 18. To Robert my lighter with her skiff freely, my best silver salt and my stone pot lidded, footed and lipped with silver, the billet that remains on his quay, saving 2,000 billet to my wife; the which he shall answer John Alden the elder for his half quarter of the Valentine and his quarter of the Confidence; such reckonings as is due to him as my books maketh mention of what his wife hath received and what remains, the coals being sold, he shall pay him in money. To Robert 2 sacks of alum lying at his house (containing in weight 400 lacking 5 lb.). Provided always that my wife shall not receive my legacy before she hath made a release of her dowry, the which release shall be required by my executors or their learned counsel. To my wife my little salt of silver and gilt and my bible. To Lancelot Russell my brother's son £5. To Simon Dawling that was my father's servant £5. To my servants George Persey, Richard Neve and Grace my maid 10s. apiece. To 20 poor householders 20s. To Mr Brandon [*sic*] 6s. 8d. for a funeral sermon, and 6s. 8d. for breaking of the ground in the chancel to the churchwardens. My wife shall have her dwelling in my house three months after my decease and the implements belonging to the candlehouse as knives, troughs, candle mould, candle spits and keelers for the tallow. I appoint sole executor Robert my son and supervisor John Gardener.

Witnesses: Hugh Branham clerk [vicar of Dovercourt-with-Harwich], Henry Gooding, Edmund Seman.

Proved 19 June 1587.

ROBERT SALMON [of Leigh], 3 September 1591.   [35/85]

To the poor of Leigh £6 13s. 4d. To Agnes my wife my house and land called Grymstons in Nevendon, for life, with remainder to my sons, two-thirds to Robert and one-third to Peter. To her my house that I dwell in called Jacke Andrewes with 2 acres called Normans Field on the east side of the church lane and a parcel of ground adjoining to my house on the north side called Sprange Field, and the dock to the house belonging, for life if she continue unmarried or if she marry then for so long as she dwell therein; but if she marry and do not dwell therein she shall have but one-third of it; with [successive] remainders (except Normans Field) to Robert, to Peter, to Thomas and to Nathaniel my sons. To her four tenements I have built upon my quay, then to Peter at 22. To her my house on my backside called the Repent, for life, with successive remainders to Thomas and to Nathaniel; my house called the Cappes by the Strand, for life, with like remainders, also Normans Field to Nathaniel and to Thomas; and one quarter of a new ship agreed to be builded at Ipswich between my son-in-law Lawrence Mower and me. To my wife and Robert my other ships and parts of ships that I have to be divided between them, conditionally to pay legacies to the rest of my children, i.e. Thomas and Nathaniel £60 apiece at 24, Mary Mower my daughter £60 2 years after my death, Martha Hall my daughter £100 [by detailed instalments] and Jacomyn Salmon my daughter £100 [likewise]. My wife shall allow yearly to Peter £100 for his maintenance at study in the university to the age of 22. To Edward Salmon my cousin 20s. and my sister Barrett £3. To Mr Wilkenson my ring and his wife 2 angels to make her a ring, my kinsman William Goodlad 2 angels, and my good friend Mr Rich 4 angels. To poor prisoners or any other whom my wife see to have most need £3, whom I ordain my sole executrix. I appoint supervisors William

Negus [rector of Leigh] and John Goodlad, and for their pains 40s. each.
Witnesses: Richard Goodlad, William Riddesdall.
Proved 25 November 1591.

AGNES SALMON of Leigh widow, 7 September 1596.　　[40/64]

To the poor of Leigh £5 to be distributed by Mr [William] Negus [rector] and goodman Peeke. To our pastor Mr Negus £3 and my table of death hanging by my bedside in the little parlour. To my old friend Mistress Wilkinson of London an angel and the ring of [off] my finger which I use to wear. To my good friend and neighbour Thomas Peeke of Leigh 20s. To my good friend Mr [Arthur] Dente, [rector] of South Shoebury, the wife of Thomas Dill, the wife of Henry Sayer, widow Dryver junior, widow Duffyll, the wife of Thomas Kensey, the wife of John Lowe, Agnes Hopwood my kinswoman, and my maidservant Margery, 10s. each. To my son Peter £60 to discharge my bond to his master, to my sons Robert, Thomas and Nathaniel £40 each, and to Jacomyne my Geneva bible. To my son Thomas a joined bedstead in the loft over the hall at 21. To Mary, Martha and Jacomyne 6 silver spoons each, and my yellow danske chest in the north loft with the linen equally to be divided. To Robert my silver salt and a silver cup. Out of my moveables, to Martha's two fatherless children, i.e. Samuel Hall at 21 and Martha Hall, at 18 or marriage, £10 each. The rest of my goods to be equally divided between my six children; if Robert, now being at sea, should die, his legacies to remain to his children Robert, Anne and Mary. To Margaret Barrett my sister-in-law 10s. I appoint as my executors my son Robert and Lawrence Mower and as my overseers my cousins John Goodlad and William Goodlad, and to each for their pains 20s. Witnesses: Richard Davysonne, Roger Jones.
Proved 23 September 1596.

EDMUND SHERMAN of Dedham clothier, 31 July 1599. [See next will.]　　[45/24]

To Anne my loving wife my house I dwell in with the meadow and lands, which I had by the surrender of Mr Humphrey Saxforde and Mr Robert Mawe gentlemen; my woodhouse and hopyard annexed which I bought of John Upchere; and my two fields next Ralph Cockes containing 6 acres, parcel of the land I bought of John Webbe; all for life. To her £100, my plate and household stuff excepting those particulars hereafter bequeathed, 6 of my best milch kine, my mare and my black gelding, 8 loads of hay, my rye in the barn, 3 seams of wheat, my wheat straw, my swine, my wood and broom in my yard, and my 2 weighing beams with my scales and my weights with my oil cistern of lead. To Edmund my son after my wife's decease the messuages and lands given her for life; my house and lands belonging (containing 7 acres) called Ryes wherein he dwelleth; and my shearman's occupation with the appurtenances. To Richard, Bezaliel, Samuel, John and

Benjamin each £50 at 24. To Anne Sherman my eldest daughter £50 at 21, my posted bedstead in my servants' chamber. To Sarah my daughter £50 at 21. To Hannah my daughter which I had by Anne my second wife £50 at 21. To Susan my daughter £50 at 21. To Mary my daughter £50 at 21. To my sister Judith Pettfield the tenement wherein Edmund Browne the tailor dwelleth, for life.

My house at the church gate wherein Mr Richard Ravens lately dwelt, 1½ acres of meadow in the Chilvall, my house that Robert Finch dwelleth in with the lands in his occupation, and my 7 acres of land called Thedomes Field adjoining, to be sold by my brother Henry Sherman and Simon Fenne my kinsman, clothier, of Dedham to the most advantage and delivered to my executrix for the performance of my will. My other lands, viz. the house that Greene the labourer dwelleth in and the field called Moncke adjoining, two fields parcel of the lands which I had of the surrender of John Webbe adjoining the house that Thomas Lucas dwelleth in, and 3 acres of land called the Grove adjoining the two fields to be let to the best advantage by my executrix and the money until my youngest daughter Mary is 20 to be likewise employed; and after she is 20 the house and land to John and the rest to Benjamin. To Samuel my two fields next to Ralph Cockes (containing 6 acres), after my wife's decease. To Bezaliel after her decease the tenement called Ryes on condition that he pay Richard £50. After my sister's decease the tenement given to her, to the Governors of the public Grammar School in Dedham and their successors for ever, to be employed for a dwelling house for a school master to teach children to read and write, who shall freely teach one poor child which shall be appointed from time to time by Edmund and his heirs for ever.

To my wife my malt. To Sarah, Hannah daughter of Anne my second wife, Susan, Samuel and John, 20s. apiece which was bestowed on them by their grandmother Cleere. To Elizabeth, Susan and Mary my maidservants 6s. 8d. apiece. To John Elmes my kinsman 10s. and Hazel Mores and Matthias Langley my menservants 10s. apiece.

All the rest of my goods shall be sold for the performance of my will. I constitute my wife my sole executrix. I ordain my loving friends Dr [Edmund] Chapman and Robert Lewys my brother-in-law supervisors, and to each for their pains 20s.

Witnesses : Robert Lewis, Henry Sherman, William Cole.

Codicil, 20 December 1600. To my three children, Anne Sherman, Bezaliel and Sarah, each 40s. which their grandfather Sherman gave them. To Dr Chapman £5 a year for 5 years if he continue so long in Dedham at 25s. a quarter. Witnesses : Henry Sherman, William Cole.
Proved 30 April 1601.

HENRY SHERMAN the elder of Colchester, 20 January 1590. [34/51]

To be buried in the parish church of Dedham. To Dr Chapman the preacher of Dedham £6. To Mr [Richard] Parker [vicar of Dedham] 40s. To the poor of Dedham £20 to be a continual stock for the poor to the world's end. It shall be ordered at the discretion of the Governors of the Free School of Dedham to take security for the principal.

To Henry my son my shearman's craft and the household [stuff] which he hath in his house already. To his children, Henry, Samuel, Daniel, John, Ezechiel, Phoebe, Nathaniel and Anne Shearman, each £5 at 22. To Edmund my son £10. To Edmund his son £13 13s. 4d. at 22. To Richard, Bezaliel, Anne and Sarah the children of my son Edmund each 40s. at 22. To Edmund my son my best cloak. To William Petfeilde my son-in-law £20, and his 3 children, Richard, Susan and Elizabeth, each £6 13s. 4d.

To Margery my wife £22; her household stuff which she brought me and that which we renewed and bought since we married; my broom, wood and logs; 20s. [*sic*]; and that £12 due to me from Tendring if my executors can recover it. She shall have her dwelling for 2 years in that part of the house wherein we dwell, viz. the lower parlour and the two chambers next Mr Ruddes and part of the backhouse if my son Robert do enjoy the house; but if it be redeemed he shall pay her £4 for 2 years. To her my tipped pot for her life and then to Judith my daughter.

To Robert £60 which I gave for the house wherein I dwell, lately Richard Kinge of Colchester beerbrewer; if the £60 be not paid according to bargain and sale at the time appointed I give the house to Robert. To him the copyhold called the Hebell (containing 15 acres) and 2 acres called Byrdes in William Petfeild's occupation; and £40. To Jane and to Anne Shearman, Robert's daughters, each £5 at 21. To Robert my household stuff which I had before I married, with the great cupboard in the parlour and the ceiling with the 3 tapestry cushions, my silver and gilt goblet, my best gown, and one sword and a bill. To Judith Petfeilde my daughter the chest and linen on the soller. To Henry my son 12 silver spoons. To my son-in-law Nicholas Fynce 40s. To the poor of All Hallows parish [in Colchester] 6s. 8d. To Robert the tipped pot which he hath. To Henry my armour, except that which I gave to Robert. If the £40 due to me by the executors of Richard Kinge be recovered, it be equally divided between Henry, Edmund, Robert and Judith. To Judith my sidesaddle and cloth to it. To Robert my saddle. To William Petfeilde my best gown save one. To Henry my best cassock hat and nightcap. To Christopher Stone a cloth doublet; to Caser an old pair of hosen; to Richard Fycher my old gown. To Edmund, Henry and Robert each 20s. in gold and to each of their wives the same. To Judith 20s. in gold. My goods to be equally divided betwixt Henry, Edmund and Robert. I ordain Henry and Edmund executors.

Witnesses: Richard Symnell, Oliver Pygge the elder, Nathaniel Bassack, Henry Osborne.

Codicil, 16 February. As to the £20 I gave to the poor, Henry shall have the occupying of it for term of his life, putting in surety to pay the principal and 40s. a year to their use to be bestowed in woollen and linen cloth. Witnesses: Oliver Pigge, Nathaniel Bassock.

Proved 25 July 1590.

HENRY STANDISHE of Waltham Holy Cross tanner 28 July 1589.
[34/12]

To my two daughters Agnes and Alice Standishe yet unmarried and unadvanced each £50 at 21 or marriage. To everyone to whom I have been chosen a witness at baptism 12d. apiece. To every manservant and womanservant each 3s. 4d. I give 20s. to be bestowed on the causeway in the highway between Smallinge Bridge and the Hermitage Bridge. The joined work, i.e. 3 bedsteads with a press in the chamber, a cupboard, a long table in the hall, the ceilings in the parlour and the stools there, the copper furnace in the kitchen, with powdering tubs, troughs and other implements in the buttery, kitchen and milkhouse, with the great iron racks in the kitchen, shall be distributed by my wife to my children, to all such of them as she by her motherly love and discretion shall think good. To Margaret my well-beloved wife £50. To John my son my tanhouse and the stock of leather tanned and untanned, vessels, barks, tools and implements belonging, also clapboard provided for the tanhouse, and my horses and geldings (except my team), to pay my debts and legacies. To my wife and John equally between them such crop of corn and hay growing at my decease and my team of oxen and horses. The rest of my goods to my wife, requiring her to be good to my children in their education and bringing up. To her in satisfaction of dower my house in which I dwell called Peacockes with the lands belonging, which I bought of John Hearde of London butcher, sometime John Brightes, and the lands I bought of Mr Welche (containing 30 acres) with the barn that I set up upon parcel of the said grounds called Kilcottes, for life; and after her decease, also with a close called Blackditch (6 acres) which I purchased of Wren's daughters and a close (3 acres) bought of John Alee, to Henry my son; and Kilcottes to Robert my son. The rest of my lands, also that called Wiggens bought of William Harison and Scotch Field (10 acres) and a close called Long Reach, to John. I make him my sole executor and supervisors I appoint my wife and Robert Leowin of Aemys Green carpenter, who married my wife's sister, and for his pains 10s. Witnesses : John Thompson writer of the court letter, William Kerwyn mason, Thomas Newman scrivener.
Proved 20 February 1590.

ROBERT STARLING of Dedham clothier, 27 November 1581.
[25/12]

To be buried in the church of that town where it shall please God to call me. To the poor people of Dedham £5 to be paid 20s. yearly. To Richard my son my lease of the mill, the meadows called the Raye, and both the woods called Burchettes which I hold of our sovereign the Queen, on condition that he quietly suffer Elizabeth his mother to enjoy such lands set down in indentures of covenant between me and Miles Dokare and others on the marriage of Mary, now Richard's wife. To him my lease of both the said woods which I hold of the Master of the Requests, on condition that he shall fell and deliver 10 loads of wood yearly to his mother. To him my lands in Ardleigh holden of the manor of Shawes [in Ardleigh]. To Elizabeth my daughter my tenement in Ardleigh with lands holden of the manor of Piggottes and my little tenement holden of the manor of Dedham; and the best bedstead in the parlour chember. To my wife my household stuff, except leads and coppers serving for brewing or dyeing and glass and ceiling appertaining to the house; and the use of my best bed for her life, and after it shall remain with the house to Richard. Of the two coppers at my house at Dodines Richard and Elizabeth my daughter shall have one each. To Joan late wife of my brother James Starlinge 20s. to be paid 4d. weekly. The rest of my goods to my wife, son and daughter to be equally divided. I make Richard my sole executor. Witnesses: Thomas Lufkyn, Miles Docker, Daniel Sheene.

Proved 31 March 1582.

WILLIAM STRACHIE of the New Hythe in Colchester merchant, 26 January 1569. [12/9]

To Joan my wife my mansion house with the barn and two tenements on the west side, my field called Purches, the orchard, and Labockes Meadow purchased of Nicholas Detchicke. The residue of my goods to my wife. I make my brother-in-law Thomas Williett of Sudbury [Suffolk], clothier, my executor. Witnesses: Benjamin Clere, Richard Symnell, Ralph Starlynge, Thomas Cletcher.

Administration granted, 7 April 1569, to Joan widow of the deceased.

THOMAS STRUTT of Pentlow clothier, 29 April 1585. [29/28]

To the poor of Pentlow 5s. To the hanging up of the bell in Pentlow 3s. 4d. To the poor of Poslingford [Suffolk] 10s. To Silvester Strutt my brother my houses and lands and £20. The residue to my executors, whom I make my two sisters Anne Strutt and Mary Strutt. I appoint my uncle Thomas Harvye my supervisor, and for his pains my bay gelding. Witnesses: John Crisall, Thomas Dereman, Thomas Harvye.

Proved 21 May 1585.

JOHN THOMSON of Colchester clothier, 27 February 1589. [33/50]

To Thomasine my wife my house wherein I dwell, for life, and after to John my son. To John and William my son each £100 at 24 or marriage. To my three daughters Thomasine, Anne and Sarah, £50 at 20 or marriage. To the child wherewith my wife now is at 24 or marriage. To the poor people of this town £5. To my brother William Thomson 40s. My wife shall the use of the money given to the children towards their bringing up, provided that she shall be bound with sufficient sureties in double the value to my other executor and my overseer for payment. The rest of my goods to her. I ordain her and my brother

311

William my executors and my brothers [in-law] Robert Bird and Richard Burgies my supervisors. Witnesses: Robert Byrde, George Northey, Richard Birgies.
Proved 23 May 1589.

WILLIAM THOMPSON of Colchester clothier, 21 September 1601.
[45/71]

To Anne my loving wife my houses and lands in Colchester for life. After her death, to William my son the house wherein I dwell and a little tenement adjoining in the occupation of one Fuller, except the folding shop with the chamber over it, parcel of my dwelling house; and 5 roods and a way to the ground from the gate there in Clay Lane extending to half the pond or watering there. To John my son my house in the occupation of John Laurence; two tenements of the same building in that of widows Madder and Wylie; and £50 at 24. To Thomas my son my house in that of William Sills and the above folding shop with chamber over it; and £50 at 24. To Robert my son my house in that of William Hall plumber; and £50 at 24. To Joseph my son my tenement in that of Robert Browne; and £50 at 24. Provided that, if any of my sons die without issue before 24, I give their house to my sons Nathaniel and Daniel equally; and to them £50 at 24. To my daughters Thomasine Thomsonne £50 at 20 or marriage. The rest of my goods to my wife, whom I make sole executrix, and overseer I make William. Witnesses: John Harris scr[ibe], Margery Haughton, Thomas Homes, Edward Neweman.
Proved 10 October 1601. Administration granted, 25 [blank] 1612, to William.

RICHARD THURSTON, alderman of Colchester, 22 June 1581. [For Richard Thurston gentleman, see p. 256.] [24/30]

To be buried in the churchyard of St Nicholas. To the poor of Colchester on the day of my burial 33s. 4d. To the Dutch congregation in Colchester £3 to the relief of their poor. To the impotent and poor of the town and liberties of Colchester £13 6s. 8d. to be bestowed in linen and woollen by the bailiffs.
To Catherine Mixa my servant 40s. at marriage. To Mary my daughter, wife of Elias Wortham, my best goblet. To William Wortham, my son [-in-law], the lease, which I bought of John Luson, of a warehouse at the New Hythe, at 21; if he die before, to be equally divided among my children, viz. Richard, Jeremy, John, Joan, Elizabeth, Priscilla and Susan.
All my wares whatsoever and a lease which I hold of John Wentworth esquire shall be valued and sold by such indifferent and honest persons as my friends William Sydaye gentleman and Thomas Raynoldes draper shall nominate, and the money as also my ready money and debts shall be equally divided between Elizabeth my wife and my children part

and part like, to my sons at 21 and my daughters at marriage; and all these portions shall remain in her custody until paid, on condition, that she shall enter into sufficient bond to my said trusty friends; and if she refuse to be bound then my supervisors shall have the custody, entering into bond with my very loving friends and neighbours Robert Mott alderman and Thomas Fyerfanne. To her towards the bringing up of my children my plate and household stuff. To her for life my lands in Nayland [Suff.], Wormingford, Great and Little Clacton and Colchester, and after her decease my 3 messuages and lands in Nayland and my messuage wherein I dwell in St Nicholas to William and his heirs; and for want of issue, the remainder to my other sons to be equally divided. To Richard after my wife's decease my house and lands in Wormingford which I bought of my brother Sidaye and my messuage in St Nicholas in the tenure of a Dutchman, with all implements in the house; with like remainder. After my wife's decease my house and lands in Great and Little Clacton shall remain to Jeremy; with like remainder. To Richard Wortham and Mary Wortham, Mary's children, each 40s. at marriage. To John after my wife's decease my 2 messuages in Weyre Street in Colchester and my 2 messuages in Mawdlyn Street in the suburbs; with like remainder. Provided that, if William shall at any time claim a messuage in St Botolph in the possession of William Welles glover and shall evict him, I revoke his legacies and give them to my wife. To Mr Northe, preacher of Colchester, 40s. as a token of my hearty goodwill to him. I ordain my wife sole executrix and William Sidaye and Thomas Raynoldes my supervisors, and to each for their pains 20s. To Thomas Tayler of Colchester gentleman 20s. for assisting my wife about the execution of my will; if she refuse to prove it, Sidaye and Raynoldes shall be executors.

Witnesses: Thomas Tailor, Robert Mott, Thomas Fyerfanne, Thomas Raynoldes. Proved 14 August 1581.

THOMAS TWYTT of Harwich the elder, merchant, 19 August 1599.
[46/4]

To the poor of Harwich £5, to be paid 20s. year. To Josian my wife, for life, my mansion house wherein I dwell, with the quay, and other edifices and after her decease to Michael my son; the messuage and ground, orchard and gardens that I purchased of William Cooper in West Street in Harwich, between the tenement late widow Beard's to the north and the Town Ground to the south, and after her decease to Michael; and the messuage called the Three Cups with the stable and a field called Stonewell Pightle with other edifices and gardens in the tenure of Anthony Syward, and after her decease to Thomas my son. To my wife one half of my household stuff, as bedding, plate and all other utensils; and £40. Provided that, if she decease before or within a year after my decease, the moiety of my plate be equally divided among my three daughters, Anne King, Sarah Jones and Bridget Haunkin and the residue of the moveables to Michael. To Thomas my messuage I bought of Richard Johnson alias Arnould with the brew

313

house, malting house, edifices, quays, and a pightle of ground lying without the South Gate of the town; the garden and the stable that I purchased of Peter Pettes, appendant sometimes of the capital messuage that I sold to Thomas Greene, in High Street; and a quarter of my ship called the Salomon with the tackling. I remit to Thomas £44 which he oweth me. To him my cask horses and carts and other utensils to my brew house and malting house appertaining, a green silk quilt, and a gold ring. To Michael my messuage, salt house, quay and appurtenances which I bought of John Gover of London; my messuage and salt house on the west side of the same, late John Jynnynges, in the tenure of widow Skynner; my salt house which I purchased of Thomas Riche-monde the younger; my two fields in Dovercourt which I purchased of Peter Pettes of Deptford (Kent) called Stonewell Fields in the occupation of George Castricke. To Anne King £87. To Sarah Jones one twelfth part of my hoy called the Apollo, and £20. To Bridget Haunkin the £20 which her father-in-law doth owe me, and £30 more. To Mr [Hugh] Branham [vicar of Dovercourt-with-Harwich] £4, whom I make super-visor. To Anne Branham £6. To widow Cooper 20s. and to my maid Susan 20s. The residue of my shipping, viz. three-quarters of the Salomon and the Apollo, to Michael. The residue of my goods, wares and fish to Michael, whom I constitute my sole executor. Witnesses: Raymond King, Hugh Branham clerk, John Forber writer of the court letter of London.

Proved 20 January 1602.

MICHAEL UPCHER of Dedham clothier, 10 June 1575.   [18/38]

To Mr [John] Worth [vicar of Dedham] for his pains in making an exhortation or sermon to the people assembled at my burial 20s. To the poor of Dedham and other towns adjoining by the discretion of my super-visors and other of my friends £10. To the dispersed strangers that are come into this realm for the profession of the Gospel £5.

To Joan my wife the house wherein I dwell and the land belonging that I bought of Richard Clerk the younger of Dedham, while she shall keep herself a widow and unmarried, and after marriage or decease to remain to Richard my son, on condition that he shall pay my debts and legacies. To my wife £100 on condition that she by her deed shall release her claim by her marriage to my lands in Stratford (Suffolk). To her and Richard my son my plate, bedding, brass, pewter, linen, napery, household stuff, and things belonging to husbandry, also my corn in my sollers and growing, cattle, hay, wood, broom and other fuel in my yards, all which shall be appraised by my friends hereafter named, to be equally divided betwixt my wife and Richard; provided that they shall not extend to any copper, pans, leads or cisterns hanging in my house or woodhouse or any glass, ceilings, settles or stainings which I bought with the house, but shall remain with it. If my wife shall couple herself in matrimony, her part shall be made up to £300 to be paid within a year after marriage, half part of goods bequeathed to be accompted in part of the £300.

To Richard a wood in Langham, and £100. To Michael my son the tenement and lands which I bought of William Darbie and £100 at 21. To Thomas my son my lands in Stratford which I purchased of Edward Furde gentleman, and to his heirs, and for want of such heirs to Michael. Nathaniel Morse, my son-in-law, shall have the custody and bringing up of Thomas to the age of 14 years and take the profits of the lands towards his virtuous education and godly bringing up and in setting him to school not only to write and read English but also to be further instructed in other good letters; if Nathaniel die before, I commit custody to Richard. To Thomas also £100 at 21. To every of my daughters, Sarah, Elizabeth, Susan and Judith, £100 at 21 or marriage, provided that, if my goods be insufficient, 100 marks. John Upcher, the younger, my brother, shall have the government and bringing up of Elizabeth and the occupying of her legacy during her nonage or marriage. In like manner I commit the bringing up and government of Judith and Susan with the occuping of their legacies to Stephen Upcher my brother and to my brother-in-law Warner the keeping of Susan. To Richard all things and instruments belonging to my occupation of shearman's science as shears, handles, shearboards, scraves, and cloth press.

To every servant abiding in my house 20s. I bequeath 4 broad cloths to apparel the poor householders and their children inhabiting in this town or elsewhere, to be cut out and given by the discretion of my executor and supervisors. To John Upcher the elder, my brother, £5. To John his son £5. To Anne Upcher his daughter 40s. at 21. To Gilbert Awcock my best gown. I bequeath a fine puke to be given amongst my friends. Shortly after my decease my goods shall be appraised by my trusty and loving friends, John Warner, Lewis Sparhauke, George Bigges, John Upcher, Stephen Upcher, Nathaniel Morse and William Warner the younger, and I earnestly request them to take pains to cast over my books of reckonings and bills of debts. The residue of my goods to Michael at 21. And that it may always appear what is the remnant and overplus of my goods not given, I desire them to make a true inventory quadripartite indented [the four parts to remain with groups of the friends and the executor]. I make Richard my sole executor, whom I straitly command to observe the advice of my supervisors, and if he wilfully and stubbornly refuse their counsel he shall lose all legacies. I make Lewis Sparhawke and George Bigges supervisors, and for their pains 40s.

Witnesses : William Ravens, Robert Hamme.

Proved 7 October 1575.

MICHAEL UPCHER of Dedham clothier, 25 January, 1585.   [29/12]

To my wife Frances my house and lands belonging in Dedham for 21 years (if she live so long) and if she be now with child, if male, to him and his heirs, and, if female, to my daughter Mary now born. To my wife 100 marks, all my household stuff, my mare and one cow. To Mary 100 marks at 20, but if my wife be with child with a daughter then she

315

should have the 100 marks and Mary to be void of it. To Dr [Edmund] Chapman, preacher of Dedham, £3. To Mr [Richard] Parker our pastor [vicar] 40s. To Mr Welch, preacher at Waldingfield [Suffolk], 20s. To Gilbert Alcock 30s. To the poor of Dedham to be paid 33s. 4d. a year till £5 be run up. To the maintenance of poor students at Cambridge that be well affected and sincerely seek God's glory 40s., to be distributed by the discretion of godly men, especially to those be gone out of this School of Dedham. To the children of my sister Sarah Wood wife of Clement Wood, to wit, Sarah, Elizabeth and Mary Wood, 20s. a apiece at 20. To my servant Agnes Clarke 10s. To Bridget Aylewerd, the girl is now with me, 10s. To goodman Anthony the tailor 10s. I ordain my sole executor my brother Richard Upcher and for his pains 40s. My uncles Stephen Upcher and John Upcher shall be my supervisors and each for their pains 10s. My wife shall not take away any of my glass windows nor the lead nor settle, but they shall abide with the house. Witnesses: Richard Parker, John Upcher, Nathaniel Morsse.

Codicil, written with the testator's own hand. My mother shall have my best cloak and my best hat. To George Bartle and Alice Bartle each 20s. at 22. If my wife be with child with a son, she shall have but £50 and my daughter other £50 and my son to have the rest which is £32 [sic] 13s. 4d.; but if she be with a son she shall have my house but 10 years and then the profit to the use of my son. My mother standing as witness, and Anthony [blank], Robert Fynce.

Proved 5 March 1585.

STEPHEN UPCHER of Dedham clothier, 20 September 1594. [38/67]

To the poor people of Dedham 3s. 4d. To Stephen my son my capital messuage wherein I dwell and the edifices, orchards and lands belonging called Brownes (containing 3 acres) in Dedham, on condition that he pay to my four daughters each £24, viz. to Anne within 1 year after my decease, Susan within 2 years, and to Alice and Lydia within 1½ years after marriage. Provided that, if Ralph Stereline my son-in-law shall within 2 years after my decease enfeoff Susan his wife with lands to the yearly value of £13, Stephen to pay and make up the £24 to £30 to Susan without fraud or coven. To Ellen my wife a featherbed and the bedstead whereon she lieth. To Stephen my lease of certain marsh grounds which I had of Sir Thomas Hennedge in Brightlingsea, provided that if Stephen shall refuse to execute my will I bequeath my houses, lands and marshes to my four daughters equally to be divided, paying to Stephen £100, and in this case the legacies to them to be void; and in case of his refusal I constitute my well-beloved friends Ralph King clerk [rector of Little Bromley] and Richard Upcher executors. I ordain Stephen executor, to whom I give the residue of my goods, and I ordain my said friends overseers and for their pains each 10s. Witnesses: John Upcher, Henry Sandford, Ralph Kinge.

Proved by Stephen Upcher the son, 15 October 1594.

316

EDWARD WATSON of Dedham clothier, 16 November 1600. [45/78]

To George Watson my brother my lands in Dedham and Langham, with the housen and appurtenances, paying £10 each to my sisters Mary and Elizabeth. To my uncle Bartholomew Watson £5 after the money be received of Mr Hear. To the poor of Dedham 20s. at my executors' discretion and 20s. to the poor of Ardleigh at my father's discretion. To my brother Mowse £10. To my mother a gown cloth and a petticoat cloth worth £3. To Mr Lufkyn £4, John Rande 30s., Joan Death 10s., goodman Ambler 20s., John Bundocke 20s. To my father 20s., my bed, a doublet cloth in my chest. To my sister Wight my chest and my brother Wight a jerkin and a pair of venetians. To Thomas Horsman 10s. The rest of my goods shall be to discharge my funeral. My executors, whom I name Mr Lufkyn and John Rande, both of Dedham, shall perform my will with the legacy coming to me from Mr Heare. Witnesses : John Whitlocke and John Garrington.

Proved 5 November 1601.

ROBERT WIELD of Langham clothier, 19 August 1600. [46/19]

To the reparations of Langham church about the new casting of the lead and covering of the aisle 20s. when done. To the overseers of the poor 60 lb. of coarse wool to be made into cloth for the clothing of such poor people this winter time as the overseers shall think have most need, and for the webbing and making it into cloth 20s.

To Margaret Bentley my daughter after my wife's decease my messuage in which I dwell with the lands belonging called Earles, with lands called Eastlands and a parcel of land called Five Acres in Langham, held of the manor by copy of court roll, for her life, the remainder to William her son. To Edward another of her sons my tenement and lands in Dedham which I purchased of Abraham Ham, held of the manor of Over Hall and Nether Hall in Dedham by copy, with 1 acre in North Mead in Langham called Coventryes Acre and 3 roods of meadow sometime belonging to a tenement called Jervayes; and his mother shall have the occupying thereof until he is 18, and then she shall pay him £6. To Bezaliel another of her sons my copyhold tenement, orchard and croft purchased of William Finkell in Dedham, with a parcel in North Mead called Bush Acre; and his mother shall take the profits until he is 18. To John another of her sons my tenement with the croft and orchard lately by me purchased of [blank] Page in Dedham, with a piece in North Meadow sometimes Litleburyes, and she shall take the profit until he is 18. To Margaret Bentley her daughter my tenement I purchased of Thomas Gull in Dedham at 18, and her mother to take the profits. To Elizabeth my well-beloved wife £86 13s. 4d., provided that, if she do not release her right of dower in lands in Hintlesham [Suffolk] by me lately sold, she shall lose my legacy. To Joan and Mary Smith my wife's daughters £6 13s. 4d. apiece at 18. To William £30 and Edward, Bezaliel, John and Margaret each £20 at 20. To my sister Hindes 40s.

To my sister London [Loudon?] 20s. and I forgive her husband such debts as he oweth me.

Presently after my death there shall be taken an inventory of my household stuff, bedding, linen and plate, one part to my wife and the other to be equally divided between the children of my daughter, to remain in her possession until they are 18. To William my broad looms in my occupation, on condition that he be bound an apprentice to the science of a weaver, and for default to Edward. My 6 milch kine, my nag, and such hay and stover at the time of my death in the barns of Earles, as be thought by indifferent men competent for the wintering of the cattle, shall remain there as a stock for my wife's use. She shall not lop or fell any of the oaks on the home grounds but shall preserve them for the increase of acorns. My desire is that, if any controversy shall arise between my wife and my daughter, they would be ordered by the advice of Robert Vigerous gentleman and Thomas Farrar clerk [rector of Langham]. To Richard Morse 20s. The residue of my goods to my daughter for performing my will and bringing my body decently to the earth, whom I make my sole executrix. I ordain Robert Vigerous and Thomas Farrer overseers, and 20s. apiece for their pains and to be helpers to my executrix.

Witnesses: Robert Vigerous, John Duke, Edmund Sebborne.
Proved 17 February 1602.

NICHOLAS WILBORE of Braintree draper, 27 November 1582.
[26/45]

To the poor people of Braintree 40s. To Anne my wife so long as she is a widow £20 yearly out of my tenement called the Chequer with that adjoining, my tenement in the Gawnte in which Joshua my son dwelleth with that adjoining [all in Braintree], my tenement called Wolves, and my lands I bought of Robert Polye called Copers Wood, Blumster Hamstall, the Slade, Crose Croft and a meadow called Whelers Fenn, all in Stisted; on condition that she shall bring up or see well placed Anne my daughter until 21 and to release her interest in the third part of the lands and tenements which I have now as well as those I have sold within 7 weeks after my departure. To my wife 8 loads of wood yearly to be felled at her own costs in Halls Grove; and her dwelling in the house I dwell in, with the commodities belonging, except the shop and two chambers over it, which Nicholas my son shall have. To him the bedstead and a table belonging to the chambers. To Thomas my son the house I dwell in after the said term; provided that, if he molest his brothers Joshua, William and Robert and not suffer them to to enjoy the copyhold lands I give them, it shall be lawful for them to enjoy the house. To Thomas my copyhold shop in the Market Place, my meadow called Skittes Hill, and my movable stall in the Market Place. To Joshua my house in the Gawnte in which he dwelleth, Halls Grove; and £60. To Nicholas my house called the Chequer with the tenement adjoining and the buildings, orchards and gardens belonging and for default of heirs to Robert. To Nicholas my field in Bocking End called Bartlettes

Croft, and for want of heirs to Thomas; and £100. To William my son one moiety of Wolves with the lands belonging in Stisted and Bocking, of my copyhold lands in Stisted, and of the lands I bought of Robert Polley; and for want of heirs to Robert. To him the other moiety; and for want of heirs to William. To him £100 at 22 and Robert £100 at 22. To Anne my daughter my house where Aylett dwelleth in Braintree; and £60 at 21; provided that, if she shall bestow herself in marriage to her utter undoing without her friends' consent, the £60 be bestowed on some piece of land, and she to have the rent thereof for life, and after her decease the land to remain to her children. To Joan my sister 40s. The rest of my goods, plate and jewels to my wife. I elect Nicholas to be my executor and my wife and Thomas to be my overseers. Witnesses : William Maynard, Elias Wortham, John Pondor, Richard Pattenson vicar.

Proved 16 September 15[8]3.

EDMUND WILLSONN of St. Leonard, Colchester, merchant, 2 January 1573. [16/2]

To our common preacher 10s. for a sermon at my burial. To the Hospital of Colchester £5. To the poor in the liberties of this town 20s. at my burial. I will that my household stuff which did not belong to my house at the time of my first purchasing nor do not belong to the house wherein I now inhabit, viz. all my plate, linen, bedding, brass, pewter, cupboards, tables, forms, presses, chairs and stools (excepting hereunder excepted), shall be equally parted into two indifferent parts, including my broken silver and plate; and Marian my wife shall have one part. To her £10, and my house at East Gate with the gardens and orchards, for life; on condition that she put in bond to my executors to keep the same well repaired and not to carry away any leads, doors, windows, glasses, wainscots, or anything belonging to the house; also £10 a year for her pension or dowry. She shall have 7 loads of wood yearly out of my wood at Ardleigh. To my brother George Allyn of London skinner my best puke gown, my ring with the death's head which I commonly wear, and 2 old angels. To his two daughters Elizabeth Chester and Allen Harteridge each 40s. To my apprentice Richard Nicoll £10 when his apprenticeship shall end, conditionally that he abide all the term. To Joan Nycoll his sister £10 at 21 or marriage. Out of the two parts of my household stuff be taken so much as be worth £4, which I will be bestowed between them. The poor widow Orris shall have my house wherein she dwelleth for life, so that she keep it in sufficient reparations; also 10s. To Thomas Whitman my sister's son £13 6s. 8d. The money which I have in my hands of Martha Robinson be made up £6 13s. 4d. and be delivered to my wife. To Simon my apprentice 20s. at the end of his years above the covenant. Out of the partition of my household goods there be reserved all things belonging to George Spisall of Brightlingsea. I will to remain to the house a posted bed standing in the guests' chamber with the hangings, wainscots, ceilings, glass windows, brewing vessel and tubs. The residue of my goods and lands to my son

Edmund, whom I ordain my only executor, and supervisor I appoint my loving brother [in-law] George Allyn of London. Witnesses: Donkyn Grynryg, Lewis Sparrowhawke, Michael Upchere.

Proved 14 January 1573.

JOHN WOOD of Dedham clothier, 8 March 1577. [20/12]

To Richard my eldest son my tenement called Stevens in Dedham and 20 acres of land called Dawes and Bromeleye in Lawford. My house, barns and lands in Kersey and Lindsey (Suffolk) to be sold by my executors, the money to be divided among my two sons Henry and George at 25. To Mary my wife my tenement called Pidgewells and 10 acres in Dedham, my lands called Foxes Pightles in Lawford, 1 acre of meadow in Stratford [Suffolk] holden of Sir John Syllyard with a free meadow there holden of the Earl of Oxford, 3 roods of meadow holden of Stratford Hall, and 1 acre of meadow holden of Sir John, for life; and after her decease to Robert and his heirs, with remainder [not successively] to Frances and Mary Wood my two daughters and their heirs. To John my farmhouse with the barns, stables, dovehouses and lands in Stortford (Herts.) and his heirs at 25, with successive remainders to Henry and to George. To my wife Crabtree Meadow in Stratford, for life, paying yearly to the churchwardens of Dedham 20s. for the poor people; and after her decease to the Governors of the Free Grammar School of Queen Elizabeth in Dedham for ever, paying yearly 20s. to the poor, reserving to me and my heirs free egress and regress through the meadow for carriage of my hay from my other grounds. To my wife my household stuff, plate, jewels, corn, cattle, hay, wood, ready money, and wool, yarn and cloth. I give £6 to be distributed among those honest poor men that are preachers of the Word of God as my executors shall think meet. To Mary my daughter my warehouse or salthouse in Harwich which I bought of one Peter Barnold at 21. To Frances £10 at 21. My executors to have the letting of my houses and lands during the minority of my children. To Thomas Wood my brother 10s. [sic]. I make my wife and my cousin Henry Sharman junior of Dedham clothier my executors, and for his pains £3. I make my well-beloved friend John Lucas of Manningtree my supervisor, and for his pains 20s. Witnesses: John Lucas, Henry Sherman senior, Thomas Alleyn, George Wood.

Proved 2 April 1577.

JOHN WOODHOWSE of Dedham clothier, 27 June 1570. [13/29]

To be buried in Dedham church. To the poor people of Dedham 20s. To Joan my wife my house that I dwell in, with my lands and meadows in Dedham, holden of the Queen as well those holden of [the manor of] Over Hall and Nether Hall, with the use of the hangings in the house, for life if she keep herself a widow; after her marriage or death to remain to Elizabeth my daughter and William Wrenche her husband,

320

for their lives; and after the decease of the longer liver to remain to John Wrenche their eldest son; provided that, if he die before his father or mother, to remain to Simon Wrenche his brother, and if Elizabeth die before John is 24, William shall give John, being not given to rioting, £20. To John Cooke son of Susanna my daughter £30 at 22; if he die before, to the youngest children of William and Elizabeth. To Simon and Elias Wrenche £5 each at 22, and to Phenenna, Anna and Elizabeth Wrenche £5 each at 18. To John Maskall 10s. at 22, Robert Maskall a coat cloth, Margaret Maskall a cassock cloth, Elizabeth Cukut 2 yards of broad cloth, Thomas Gladwyn 10s., and John Webbe the sexton a hose cloth. The residue of my goods to my wife on condition that she surrender at the next manor court of Over Hall and Nether Hall a piece of land that her father gave her, to the use of Elizabeth and William Wrenche, and after their death to John their son and his heirs. I ordain my wife and William Wrench my executors and give him 20s. I appoint my loving neighbour George Bigges supervisor and give him 10s. Witnesses: William Coole, Roger Vaughan and Robert Way junior.

Proved 6 October 1570.

Appendix A

Leases of Manor Farms to Yeomen

The following is a full record of the manors referred to in those P.C.C. Essex Wills, 1558-1603, which are not abstracted in this volume. In some cases the wills were made by non-resident lords owning several or many manors; but the testators (except for John Curtes) do not name the lessor and rarely give any details of the Hall and the demesne.

William Aylett of Rivenhall yeoman: manors of Rivenhall Hall and Kelvedon Hall (1581, proved 7 May 1538) [26/26].

Robert Badbye of South Ockendon: demesne of manor of Little Thurrock, held from the Queen, to repair farm and sea-walls (1582, pr. 1 Dec. 1584) [28/42].

Agnes Baker of Great Chesterford widow: demesne of manor of Walden (1569, pr. 9 March 1571) [14/11].

John Bentleye of Birdbrook: manor of Birdbrook and livestock (1567, pr. 2 Oct. 1567) [10/27].

Arthur Chapleyne of Finchingfield yeoman: Cornish Hall in Finchingfield (1590, pr. 11 Nov. 1599) [34/72].

John Clare of Thorrington: manor of Thorrington (1564, pr. 20 April 1574) [7/12].

William Creswell of Milton in Prittlewell yeoman: Milton Hall (1588, pr. 2 Feb. 1591) [35/12].

John Curtes of Bocking yeoman: manor of Cornish Hall in Finchingfield 'which I took this year from John Wentworth esquire and others' (1560, pr. 13 June 1560) [3/35].

Richard Cutt of Debden: Debden Hall and Abbess Hall (1592, pr. 6 Feb. 1593) [37/92].

Robert Fannyng of Barling yeoman: Mucking Hall [in Barling], Barrow Hall [in Great Wakering], and Resheley [Rushley Island] (1559, pr. 1 Mar. 1560) [3/19].

Henry Fuller of North Weald yeoman: manor of Paris in North Weald (1590, pr. 13 Nov. 1593) [37/76].

John Owghan sen. of Woodham Walter yeoman: manors of Burses in Thundersley and Bowers in Woodham Walter, 'which I have in reversion after the death of Thomas Hammond the elder' (1569, 22 Mar. 1569) [12/7].

John Peacock of Shopland yeoman: Shopland Hall (1589, pr. 24 Oct. 1589) [33/80].

Appendix B

Burials in Church

The following testators, in addition to those whose wills are abstracted in this volume, expressed the wish to be buried in their parish church; none, except William Newman, refers to monument or brass.

Elizabeth Awgar of West Ham widow, 'near Nicholas my husband' (1594, pr. 14 Jan. 1595) [39/6].

Agnes Baker of Great Chesterford widow (1569, pr. 9 Mar. 1571) [14/11].

John Bell of West Tilbury yeoman (1592, pr. 8 Dec. 1592) [36/90].

John Clare of Thorrington (1564, pr. 20 Apr. 1574) [7/12].

Grace Cocke, of St Leonard, Colchester, widow, 'near my husband' (1572, pr. 4 June 1572) [15/18].

Edward Cole of Braintree yeoman (1577, pr. 11 Oct. 1577) [20/38].

Thomas Dayniell of Barling fisherman, or in the churchyard (1597, pr. 19 Nov. 1600) [44/70].

Robert Fannynge of Barling yeoman, or in the churchyard (1559, pr. 1 Mar. 1560) [3/19].

Walter Harries of East Donyland mariner (1577, pr. 23 Jan. 1578) [21/2].

Christopher Johns of Harwich mariner, in Stepney (Middx.) church or churchyard (1578, pr. 3 Feb. 1579) [22/4].

William Newman, born in Harlow, in Harlow church (1602, pr. 2 Nov. 1602) [46/75].

John Owghan sen. of Woodham Walter yeoman (1569, pr. 22 Mar. 1569) [12/7].

Thomas Page of Brightlingsea mariner (1577, pr. 7 Feb. 1577) [20/5].

Robert Platt of Chelmsford vintner, 'in the chancel' (1592, pr. 10 May 1592) [36/43].

Agnes Rooke of Upton in West Ham widow, 'near where my late husband William Rooke lieth' (1572, pr. 26 Nov. 1573) [16/36].

Anne Sackvilde of Willingale Doe widow (1582, pr. 19 Apr. 1582) [25/13].

Robert Sadler of Kirby (1574, pr. 22 June 1574) [17/28].

Nicholas Sallowes of Brightlingsea mariner (1579, pr. 24 Jan. 1580) [23/1].

Appendix C

Ships and other maritime items

Every reference from the wills not abstracted above in this volume is given below. Nearly all the craft are very small. Many other Essex ships are mentioned in *Elizabethan Life: Home, Work and Land*, ch. 5 ('Shipping and Fisheries'), which has explanatory notes on the various terms, 'crayer', etc.

George Alchard of Harwich mariner: 'I authorize my father-in-law to demand my shares as master's mate in the *Salomon* on the voyage from Brazil' (1595, pr. 11 July 1595) [39/50].

John Benne of Leigh mariner: ¼ *Elizabeth* and part barque *Sayflower* (*sic*); part of *Dragon* (1575, pr. 27 Sept. 1575) [18/35].

Robert Birde of East Mersea ship master (no mention of ships) (1591, pr. 12 Mar. 1591) [35/19].

Henry Blacke of Brightlingsea mariner: crayer *Lion* (1565, pr. 20 May 1566) [9/13].

John Bonner sen. of Leigh mariner: ½ ship *Lyon* with ½ stock and profit of the voyage 'now in making'; crayer to be named *Susan* 'now in building' (1573, pr. 18 Feb. 1574) [17/9].

William Bonner of Leigh woollen-draper: ¼ ship *Dolphin* of Leigh (1591, pr. 15 Apr. 1591) [35/29].

Robert Bower of Leigh mariner: ½ ship *Seaflower*; ¼ ship *Marigold* (1590, pr. 2 Oct. 1591) [35/71].

Thomas Breadcake of Leigh mariner: ⅜ hoy *Elizabeth of Leigh* (1600 pr. 4 July 1600) [42/100].

John Butler of St Osyth yeoman: ware* *Peter* lying in Estnase in lordship of Great Clacton; ware *Wassell* in West nesse in same lordship; each 'with a boat belonging' (1582, pr. 16 Feb. 1583) [26/9].

Harry Churche of Southend in Prittlewell mariner: part crayer *Bridget*; part *Mary Gold*; part *Dreadnought* (1583, pr. 19 Nov. 1586) [30/63].

Richard Coulffe of Harwich mariner: ½ my venture in ship *Violet* 'to be sold after her return from Iceland'; ½ hoy *Philip and Jane* (1584, pr. 9 May 1584) [28/10].

---

* 'Ware', a fishing weir (cf. *Elizabethan Life: Home, Work and Land*, 72).

William Creswell of Milton [in Prittlewell] yeoman: $\frac{1}{8}$ ship *Pearl* (1588, pr. 2 Feb. 1591) [35/12].

Thomas Dayniell of Barking fisherman: trink† *Peter*; trink *Violet*; each 'with her trink right belonging' (1597, pr. 19 Nov. 1600) [44/70].

Thomas Debnam of Maldon mariner: 'intending a voyage to sea' (1600, pr. 3 Feb. 1601) [45/12].

William Fowle of Milton in Prittlewell yeoman: $\frac{1}{4}$ *Bersabey*; $\frac{1}{4}$ *Grace of God* (1569, pr. 10 Aug. 1569) [12/19].

Giles Freman of Leigh: $\frac{1}{2}$ barque *Freman*, 'to be sold when it shall please God to send her home' (1566, pr. 17 May 1566) [9/12].

Walter Harries of East Donyland mariner: cache [ketch] *John* 'and the profits coming out of the sea and all the North Sea fish in her, and a little boat' (1577, pr. 23 Jan. 1578) [21/2].

Christopher Johns of Harwich mariner: 'my house in the High Street next to the water, with the quay'; part ship *Mary Fortune* ‡ 'to my eldest son Christopher Jones' at 18; $\frac{1}{8}$ new ship *Centurion* (1578, pr. 3 Feb. 1579) [22/4].

Roger Jones [of Harwich]: 'if God send my ship well home'; 'to my brother [in-law] William Russell [see p. 305] my books and sea instruments except my astrolabe, which I give to my brother Christopher Jones' (1597, pr. 11 Apr. 1598) [42/30].

Humphrey Kytchen of Hadleigh miller: hoy *John* (1594, pr. 31 Oct. 1595) [39/64].

John Morse of Leigh mariner: $\frac{1}{4}$ ship *Speedwell*; $\frac{1}{3}$ ship *Phoenix*; $\frac{1}{3}$ 'ship now building at Maldon'; $\frac{1}{8}$ *Mary Fortune* 'with the stock at the coming home of the ship'; $\frac{1}{4}$ 'ship I have in building' (1575, pr. 3 May 1575) [18/22].

Thomas Morse of Leigh mariner: 'my ships' [no details] (1580, pr. 25 Feb. 1581) [24/8].

Joan Morsse of Leigh widow: part of *Anne Gallant*, 'so soon as the Lord shall bring her home'; part barque *Time* (1585, p. 16 June 1587) [31/38].

Lawrence Mower of Leigh: 'if it shall please God to send safely home such venture as I have in a good ship now abroad called the *Pleasure*' (1597, pr. 12 Jan. 1598) [42/6].

John Newporte of Harwich: part *Marigold*; part Anne *Frances*; part *Minion*, 'if she come home' (1570, pr. 23 Feb. 1572) [15/6].

Thomas Page of Brightlingsea mariner: crayer *Mary Grace*, 'with the stock and the profits of the voyage or voyages, of which I am in debt £20 for the setting forth of the *Mary Grace*'; boat *Ellen*, 'provided that it shall please Almighty God to send any misfortune to the ship that she should chance to be lost' (1577, pr. 7 Feb. 1577) [20/5].

Richard Pecocke of Shopland yeoman: $\frac{1}{4}$ monger *Nicholas*; ketch *Grace*; cock *Fetchfire*, 'with the dredges'; $\frac{1}{2}$ ketch *Mary Anne* (1579, pr. 13 Oct. 1579) [22/39].

John Peacock of Shopland yeoman: catch *Grace*, 'with the three cocks belonging' (1589, pr. 24 Oct. 1589) [33/80].

John Ropkin [of St Osyth] part barque *Thomas* (1576, pr. 22 May 1577) [20/18].

Robert Salmon [of Leigh]: 'my quay'; $\frac{1}{4}$ of a new ship to be builded at Ipswich; 'and all my other ships and parts of ships' (1591, pr. 25 Nov. 1591) [35/85].

William Shrive of Harwich mariner: $\frac{1}{4}$ hoy *Thomas of Harwich*; $\frac{1}{4}$ hoy *William of Harwich*; 'my small ferry boat' (1595, pr. 5 Dec. 1595) [39/76].

John Tyler of Leigh mariner: $\frac{1}{8}$ ship *Pearl*; $\frac{1}{3}$ ketch *Salamon* (1588, pr. 4 Jan. 1589) [33/17].

Richard Wade sen. of Brightlingsea mariner: $\frac{1}{4}$ crayer *Anne Gallant of Brightlingsea* (1575, pr. 15 March 1576) [19/4].

John Walker of Brightlingsea mariner: $\frac{1}{4}$ ship *Adoniah of London* [in] 'this voyage'; $\frac{1}{3}$ *George of Brightlingsea*. 'If the Almighty take me away with the ship and stock'. Dated 'aboard the good ship *Adoniah of London* in the river of Thames' (1589, pr. 6 Nov. 1589) [33/90].

Henry Wyatte of Salcott mariner: ship *John of Salcott* (1568, pr. 10 Apr. 1571) [14/18].

---

† 'Trink', a kind of fishing-net used in Thames (*O.E.D.*).
‡ For Jones, cf. *Eliz. Life: Home* (etc.), 62.

Index of Places

Parishes *not* in Essex are brought together under their own *counties*; all other parishes are in Essex. All references to manors and halls, churches (burials in and bequests to), advowsons, rectories, vicarages, rectors, vicars, curates, almshouses, mills, markets, parks, and schools are indexed under their parishes and also in the *Index of Subjects*. Testators' parishes are in **bold** figures.

Aldham, 133, 137, **234;** Bowsers Hall manor, 249; the Howe, 234
Althorne, 151-2; Herons a n d Countisbridge manor, 151-2
America, North, x
Ardleigh, 119, 201, **221-2**, 254, 277-9, 298, 319; vicar, 222; Moyes Hall manor, 119
Arkesden, 74, 106, 198
Ashdon, 137; A. manor, 3
Ashingdon, 182-3
Aveley, 101, 186, **226**

Baddow, Gt., 89(?), **90**, 91, 112, **117,** 140, 166; church, 117; Gt. B. manor, 117; B. Park, 117
Baddow, Lt., 123, **158**
Ballingdon, 281; B. Bridge, 205
Bardfield, Gt., 197, 220
Bardfield, Lt., 198, **220**
Barking, 54, 91, 130, **131,** 143, 260, 323; church, 131, 142; wards, 132; Eastbury Hall, 131
Barling, church, 323; Mucking Hall manor, 145, 265-6, 322
Barnston, 264
Bartlow, 137
Basildon, East Lee manor, 135
Beaumont, 274
Bedfordshire: Biggleswade, 9, 11; Eyeworth, 84; Luton, 98; Southill, 193
Belchamp, Otten, 45; Vaws manor, 253
Belchamp St Paul, **89**
Belchamp Walter, 45, 252
Benfleet, North, 191
Benfleet, South, 30, 173, 190-1
Bentley, Gt. and Lt., 169, 196, 276
Berden, 51
Berechurch, *see* Donyland
Bergholt, West, 50, 170; church, 50; W. B. manor, 3; Cookes *alias* Nether Hall manor, 50

Birch, Gt., 74, 87-8, 176; Gt. B. manor, 87; B. Hall with the Castle manor, 76; B. Heath, 76
Birch, Lt., **87**, 88; Lt. B. manor, 87-8; B. Hall, 88
Birchanger, 96, 98
Birdbrook, B. manor, 322
Blackmore, 137, **187**, 246
Bobbingworth, **160, 162**, 252; church, 161; rector, 161; B. Hall manor, 160; Blake and Upper Halls manor, 160-1
Bocking, 45, **133-4**, 179, 220, **261, 269,** 271, 319, 322; church, 133, 269; Dorewards Hall, Park, 134
Boreham, 2-4, 6, 67, 123, **139, 283-4;** church, vii; vicar, 140; B. Hall, 139; Culvers, 1; New Hall manor, 3, 6; Old Hall, 140; Wafer Hall, 3
Borley, 37, 39, **223;** church, rectory, 36-7
Boxted, **99, 168,** 274, **286;** church, 99; vicar, 286; R i v e r s Hall manor, 99, 222, **228**
Bradfield, 92, 102, 104, **202;** B. Hall manor, 46; B. Park, 46
Bradwell - juxta - Coggeshall, **87**, 103, **157**, 211, 300
Bradwell-juxta-Mare, 54, 219, 239; B. manor, 147-8, 267; East Hall manor, 240(?)
Braintree, 45, 133, 146, 178, 266, **318-9;** market, 318; B. manor, 10; Chequer, 318; church, 323
Braxted, Gt. and Lt., 81, 123, 207, 211, **230;** B. Lodge Park, 52
Brazil, 323
Brentwood, 15, 62, 100, 162, 190-1, **264;** fair, market, school, 15-16; White Hart, 190

Brightlingsea, **158, 276,** 294, 319, 324; church, 323
Bromley, Gt., 47, 276
Bromley, Lt., 188; rector, 316
Broomfield, 10, 11, 166; parsonage, 194; B. Hall manor, 10; Cross Keys, 166; Patching Hall manor, 11
Broxted, 73, 107; Chawreth manor, 57, 73, 107
Buckinghamshire: 178, 236; Ankerwicke, 40; Castle Thorpe, 172; Grove Place, 179; Whitchurch, 256; Wyrardisbury, 41
B u l m e r, 206, 223; Smeton Hall, 223
Bulphan, 191
Bumpstead, Steeple, 47, 57, **141-2,** 188; church, 141; rectory, 142
Bures, Mount, 137, 218
Burnham, 3, 10, 229; B. manor, 10; Mangapp manor, 3; Westwick H a l l and Estwick manor, 10
Burstead, Gt., 66, 181, 190, **195;** church, 195; B. G r a n g e, etc., manors, 13; **Blunts**walls manor, 30
Burstead, Lt., 32, 189-90
Buttsbury, 28, 32-4, 180, 195, **228;** rectory, 32; Imphy Hall, 30

Cambridgeshire: 8; Abington, 9; Bedwelhaye, 106, 108; C a m p s' Castle, 87(?); Croydon, 108(?); Dullingham, 303; Ely, bp. of, 30, 58; Ickleton, 106; Isleham, 11, 116; Kirtling, 11; Leverington, 57; Morden, Guilden, 105-6; Pampisford, 66; Sawston, 159; Shepreth, 35-6; Tydd, 57; W i s b e c h, 57, 141; Wratting, West, 197

330

Index of Persons

NOTE.—*Minor* variant spellings, e.g. Pakman (for Packman), Driwood (for Drywood) are neither noted nor cross-referenced. Clergy are distinguished. **Bold** figures denote testators.

333

Beard, Jn., 34; wid., 313
Beareman, see Beereman
Beast(e), Joan, 274; Jn., 22, **273**, 298; see also Best
Bea(u)cham, Anne, 286; Jn., 289-90; Prudence, 286
Becher, see Beecher
Beckham, Rich., 246
Beckington, Hum., 244
Beda, Jn., 259
Bed(d)ingefeild (Ben-), Mary, 102; Rob., 103; Tho., 79, 123; Wm., 101-2
Bedell (Beadell, Bedwell), Bridget, 65; Margery, 65; Mary, 65; Tho., 6, **56**, 129; Wm., 56-7; Mr., 240
Bedford, Earl of, see Russell
Be(e)che, Hen., 232; Tho. 232
Beecher, Hen., 16, 193
Beeke, Tho., 87
Beereman (Beare-), Rob., 87-9
Bell, Art., 219; Edw., 29, 31-2; Jn., 28-30, 32; Margery, 114; Wm., 28; —, 215-7
Benedict, Wm., 241, 243
Bendish, And., 57; Barbara, 57, 83; Eleanor, 57, 83-4, 195; Eliz., 57; Jn., 57, 73; Margery, 73; Margt., 57-8; Rich., 57-8; Rob., 57; Tho. 57, 58, 83-4, 195-6; Wm., 57-8; —, 57, 106
Bendlowes, Wm., 142
Beningfield, see Beddingefeield
Benne, Jn., 323
Bennett, Alice, 120; Jn., 76, 188; Rich., 231; mother, 97; —, 41, 150
Benslyn, Eliz., 258; Tho., 258
Bentall, Agnes, 270-1; Ant., 271; Ellen, 271; Joan, 271; Jn., 270, 296; Magdalen, 270; Rob., 271; Sybil, 270; Tho., 270; Wm., 271
Bentley, Bezaliel, 317; Edw., 317-8; Jn., 317, 322; Margt., 317; Mary 38, 299; Wm., 299, 317-8
Benyan, see Bynnyon
Berif(f), Anne, 274-6; Art., 274-6; Augustine, 274-6; Benj., 274-6

Bridget, 276; Dorothy, 274; Jn., **274**, 276; Wm., 22, 274-5, **276**
Berye, see Burie
Bessell (Besill, Bassell), Martin, 254, 274, 283; Mr. 255
Best(e) (Beest), Hen., 251, 258; Jas., 251; Jn., 157-8; see also Beaste
Bett, Hen., 232; Owen, 174
Bettenham, Dorothy, 48; Hester, 48; Jerome, 48; Judith, 47; Pet., 48; Sam., 48; Tho., 47
Bettes, Edw., 54; Tho., 130
Betune, Jn., 183
Bevis, Jn., 26
Bewell, Jn., 187
Bewleye, Tho., 182-3
Bewtie, Wm., 120
Bickerton, R., 192, Mary, 192
Bickner, Grace, 89; Jn., 147; Tho., 232
Biere (Bire, Byre), Hen., 212-3; Nich., 212-3
Bigges, Geo., 315, 321
Bilbroughe, Jn., 188
Billinge, Rich., 101
Billingsley, Hen., 81; alderman, 193
Binde, Tho., 296
Bird (Byrde), And., 171; Anne, 171; Beatrix, 171-2; Chris., 158, 171-2; Edw., 158; Eleanor, 158; Eliz., 171; Geo., 158, 171-2; Joan, 20; Jn., 171-2; 274; Jos., minister of Latton, 25; Mary, 171, 274; Mercy, 274; Phil., 171; Rich., 92, 138; Rob., 274, 293, 312, 323; Rose, 138; Sam., 171; Wm., 138, 158, 171
Bire, see Biere
Bishop, Ant., 7, 169; Mistress, 99
Blacke, Hen., 323
Blackmore, Jn., 59; Tho., 219
Blackston, Joan, 158; Jn., **158**
Bladwell, —, 191
Blake, Chris., 158; Giles, 158; Hum., 195; Rob., 195; Tho., **158**, 182-3
Bland(e), Ant., 296; Tho., vicar of Ramsey, 102; Tho., 25
Blanerhassett, see Blenerchasset
Blatche, Eliz., 236

Blenco(w)e, Agnes, 243; Frances, 243; Geo., 243; Hen., 243; Margt., 243; Nich., 241-4; Rich., 243; Rob., 243
Blener(c)hasset (Blan-), Eliz., 152-3; Rich, 152-3; Tho., 79, 122, 262; see Hassett
Blithe, Agnes, 48; —, 245
Bloyse, Phil., 138
Board (Bord), Phil., 45
Bo(a)the, Jn., 38; Margt., 38; —, 56
Bockett, Jn., curate of Shoreditch, 284
Bocking, Mr., 156
Bode, Edw., 226
Bog(g)as, Agnes, 177; Edw., 177; Rob., 178; 228
Boillard, Rich., 258
Bond, Ant., 188, Rob., 57
Boners, 'little' Nan, 21
Bonfield, Jn., 159; Wm., **159**
Bonham (Bonume), Jerome, 104; Rob., 156-7; Tho., 157; Wm., 157; Mistress, 155
Bonner, Jn., 226, 323; Wm., 323; —, 158
Boote, Geo., 146-7
Bord, see Board
Boredge (Burredge), Jn., 279
Boreman (Boor-), Nich., 214; Sir Wm., 85-6
Borie (Bourey), Anne, 263; Eliz., 263; Ellen, 263; Kath., 263; Jn., 263; Rebecca, 262-3; Tho., 263
Borne, see Bourne
Borowgh alias Buerrell, Wm., 297
Bossett, Jn., 282
Bostock, Anne, 147; Jn., 228
Boswell, Joan, 200; Jn., 12; Mr., 200
Boteler, see Butler
Bothe, see Boathe
Botley, Margt., 234
Boulton, Geo., 119
Bourdman, Tim., 183
Bourey, see Borie
Bourgh, Lady, 256
Bourne (Bo(w)rne), Eliz., 162; Jas., 160-2; Jn., 160-1; Margt., 160-1, **162**; Mary, 160, 162; Rich., 160, 162; Rob., 160-1; Wm., 10, 13, **160**, 161-2, 182; Mr., 86; see also Bawne
Bowde, Tho., 220

334

Bownest, Jn., 186
Bowswell, *see* Boswell
Bow(y)er, Edm., 77; Jane, 245; Jn., 265: Rob., 323; Rog., 266-7; —, 265
Bowzeye, Edw., 84
Boyton, Joan, 172; Jn., 172; Susan, 172
Brabye, Tho., 299
Bracewell, Jn., 281
Bradburie (-bery), Anne, 163; Barbara, 163, 214; Ellen, 163; Geo., 163; Hen., 58-9, 162, 163; Jane, 162: Margt., 58, 141; Marian, 162; Mary, 58; Math(y), 58, 73-4; Rob., 58, 141, 162-3; Susan, 58; Tho., 58; Wm., 58, 163-4; —, 261
Bradley, Wm., 286
Bradshawe, Brian, 99, Eliz., 293
Bradstreate, Tho., 99; Wm., 91
Bragg, Wm., 223-4; —, 217
Brampton, Mistress, 144
Bramston, Roger, 67; —, 67
Brande, Anne. 274; Jas., 92, Josias, 92; Nich., 267
Branham, Anne, 314; Hugh, rector of Lt. Oakley, vicar of Dovercourt, 291-2, 306, 314
Branton, Jn., 188
Brantwhat, Alex., 19
Brasie (Bracie, B r a c i), Audrey (Ethelreda), 131; Hamnet, 131
Brasier, Anth., rector of Ingatestone, 181, 236
Brasington, Rob., 286
Brathwaite, Jn., 195
Braybrooke, Jas., 35
Brea, Tho., 188
Breadcake, Tho., 323
Breadstreete, *see* Bradstreate
Bre(a)me, Art., 48-9, 132; Judith, 49; Rich., 155
Breder, Kath., 53
Brest, Barbara, 38
Bretland, Reg., 218
Brett, Anne, 25; wid., 71; —. 214
Bretton (Breattyn, Brytayne), Hen., 175; Wm., 190
Brewer (Bruer), And., 118; Hen., 243; Jane, 276; Joan, 277; Jn.,

195; Rich., 276; Rob., 147; Tho. 6
Brewster, Alice, 258; Anne, 235; Geo., 286; Jn., 235-6, 258; Rich., 258; Thomasine, 235-6
Briant (Bryan), Margery, 299; Rob., 49, 230; wid., 272
Bricke, —, 91
Brickit (Bryckett), Rob., 73-4
Bridge(s), Agnes, 167; Anne, 164-5; Ant., 164-5; Dorothy, 164; Edw., 164-5; Eliz., 164; Geo. 164-5; Hen., 194-5; Hum., 164-5; Joan, 15; Jn., 128, 164, **165**, 166-7, 234; Mary, 167; Mat., 166; Rich., 164-5; Sam., 164-5; Tho., 48, 67, 164-7; Wm., 166
Bridgman, And., 172; Eliz., 171-2; Rob., 176
Bright, Joan, 200; Jn., 200, 310; Mabel, 69; Ste., 70
Bringeborne, Rob., 116
Bristo, Geo., 250
Brith, —, 86
Broadwater, Nich., 165
Brocke (Broke), Eliz., 167-8; Jn., 8, **59**, 290; Mary, 59; Rich., **167**; Wm., 167, **168**; *see also* Broke
Brockett, Grace, 209; Wm., 240
Brockhurst, —, 86
Brockis, Jn., 86; Rob., 85
Brockley. Margt., 261
Brograve, Mr., 99
Broke, Hum., 81; Rob., 86; —, 140; *see also* Brock
Broke, *see* Brocke
Brokeman, Tho., 269
Brokes, Bart., 107
Broman, Jn., 15
Brooke(s), Cecily, 277; Edw., 277; Fardinando. 277; Jeff., 262; Jn., 84, 117, **277**; Martha, 277; Nich., 241, 277; Rich., 277; Sigismund, 72-3; Wm., 66, 277
Brookman, Anne, 198; Mary. 198
Broomley *alias* Lodge, Albon, 27
Broughton, And., 168; Audrey, 168; Chris., 168; Edm., **168**; Jn., 168; Wm., 168

Browffe, Wm., 84
Browne (Broun), Alice, 169; Anne, 59, 141, 169; Sir Ant., ix, 12, 14, 15-6, 60-4; Chas., 34, 36, 169; Connyngesby, 16; Edm., 50-1, 242, 308; Edw., 34, 59, 169; Dame Eliz., 17, 60-1; Eliz., 250; Ellen, 59; Frances, 170; Frs., 179, 237; Geo., 16, 60-1; 66, 178-9; Gertrude, 169; Hen., 16; Hum., 126, **169**; Jane, 17, 59, 61; Jerome, 86; Jn., 16-7, 59-63, 169, 270; Launcelot, 262; Kath., 61; Margt., 34, 169, 178-9; Mary, 60, 170, 179; Phil., 16, 141; Rich., 126, 139, 169-70, 183, 234, 276; Rob., 108, 139, 161, 169, **170**, 274, 312; Rog., 39; Rose, 126, 170; Susan, 169, 252; Tho., 45, 59, 70, 169-70, 191. 287, 302; Wm., 39, 59, 150, 169-70, 250; Sir Wistan (Weston), 14-7, **60**, 252; Mr., 250; —, 235
Brownsword, Hum., 149
Browson, Jn., 302
Brudenell, Rob., 259
Brugges, Prudence, 20; Wimond, 20
Brundishe, Anne, 286; Eliz., 286; Geo., 286
Brytayne, *see* Bretton
Buck, Dan., 254; Jn., 73
Buckford, Anna, 293; Rich., 293; Thomasine, 293
Buckingham, Mr., 168
Bucknam, —. 234
Buckstone, Mr., 285
Budgman, wid., 87
Buerell *alias* Borowgh, Wm., 297
Bugby, Jn., 167
Bugg(e)s, Edw., 85; Jn., 45
Bull, Ste., 27; Mr. 216
Bullington, Hen., 91
Bullman, Wm., 59
Bullocke, Edw., 179; Hugh, 144; —, 110, 143
Bundocke. Jn., 317; Rob., 52
Buntinge, Jn., 269; Tho., 165; —, 249
Burdall, Wm., 248
Burde, *see* Bird

335

338

Daye, Rich., 196; Wm., 186

Deacon, Jn., 258

Deane, Geo., 220

Death, Joan, 317

Debnam, Rich., 200; Rob., 264; Rog., 259, 270; Tho., 324; goodwife, 262

Debney, Rob., 264

Decesse, Tho., 53

Decro, Jn., 274

Dell, Wm., 300

Dellowe, Tho., 215

Denham, Jane, 75

Denne, Tho., vicar of Latton, 25-6

Dennis, Jn., 108; Mary, 187; Nich., 187; Tho., 100; Wm., 134, 187; —, 186

Dent, Art., rector of S. Shoebury, 307

Denny, Anne, 79; Dorothy, 79; Edm., 79; Edw., 79; Eliz., 79; Hen., 79, 184; Kath., 79

Dereham, Rob., 115

Der(e)(h)aughe, Edw., 79; Margt., 79; Mary, 24-5; Rob., 180; Wm., 24, 79; Mr., 302; —, 24

Dereman, Tho., 285, 311

Deresley *alias* Shaa, Mary, 128-9

Dericke, Mr., clerk, 110

Deryffall, Wm., 188

Detchicke, Nich., 311

Devell, Jn., 51

Devenishe, Harry, 194; Margt., 231

Devereux, Rob., Earl of Essex, 210; Walter, Earl, 265

Dickley, Anne, 188; Geo., 188; Jn., 188; Rob., 187, **188**

Dickon, Ralph., 69

Digbye, Tho., 296

Dighton, Basil, 219, 262; Jn., 41

Dill, Tho., 307

Dimsdall (Dym-), Tho., 45; Wm. 262-3

Dinglie, Anne, 122; —, 38

Dison, Joan, 189

Dixson (Dickson), Barbara, 110; Jn., 119

Dobson, Dan., 269; —, 39

Dobye, Agnes, 177; Jn., 177

Dobye *alias* Godfrey, Agnes, 177

Dockley, Jn., 239; Tho., 268

Dodd, Alice, 188; Eliz., 248; Geo., 188; Isabel, 188; Jn., **188**; Margt., 188

Dokare, Miles, 310-11

Domine, Mary, 159

Dondale, Hen., 25

Donne, Geo., 150; Sam., 58

Doorant, *see* Durrant

Dorrell, Bridget, 274; Geo., 274; *see also* Darrell

Dosset (Dow-), Agnes, 45; Amy, 45; Frs., 237

Dotterell, Tho., 183

Douse, Guy, 158

Dove, Tho., 150

Dow, Wm., 170

Dowett, Anne, 188; Geo., 188, 289

Downes, Anne, 208; Jn., 38

Downing, Edm., 107

Dowset, *see* Dosset

Doyl(i)e, Cope, 121; Edw., 144

Doylwyn (Dallinge), Jn., 251

Drake, Mr., 266

Drawater, Anne, 189; Ant., 189; Denis, 189; Joan, 189; Jn., **188**, 189, Jonas, 189; Oliver, 189; Seth., 189; Susan, 189

Drenter [Dreuter?], Jn., 45

Drury (Drewrie), Anne, 9; Audrey, 9, 11; Hen., 49, 239; Rob., 9, 11; Dr. Wm., 6, 9, 203; Mistress, 202-3

Dryver, wid., 307

Drywood, Eliz., 225, 244; Frances, 189-90; Geo., 190-1, 214, 288-9; Jn., 174, **189**, 190-1, 244; Nich., 190; Rob., 190-1; Tho., 190; Thomasine, 190; Wm., 190, 225

Duckett, Anne, 192; Ralph, **191**

Duckinton, Joyce, 68

Ducy, Hen., 247; Susan, 247

Dudley, Hen., Earl of Leicester, x, 3, 19

Duffelde (-fyll), Jn., 259; wid., 307

Duke, Jn., 318

Durburne, Geo., 274

Dun(e), Wm., 6, 177

Duninge, Jn., 174

Dunscombe, Chris., **192**; Grace, 192

Durbar, Geo., 158

Durden, Wm., 207

Durrant (Door-), Nich., 270; —, 212

Duttesbury, —, 159

Dyer, —, 184

Dyke, Tho., 71

Dymsdale, *see* Dimsdall

Dynes, Adam, 274, 281; Alice, 274

Dytchefielde, Edw., 166; Jn., 167; —, 167

Dyve, Douglas, 79

Eastefielde *alias* Lucas, Alice, 282; Frs., 282; Tho., **282**

Easton *alias* Carter, Amy, 135, 136; Dorothy, 135; Hester, 135

Eastrike, Geo., 292

Eastrowe, Jerwood, 246

Eaton (Eton), Alex., 283; Joan, 194; Jn., 283; Margt., 283; Rich., 283; Rob., 194; Tho., 194-5; Wm., **283**; —, 15

Ededropp, goodwife, 45

Eden, Oliver, 249

Edes, Jn., 34

Edgiot, Hen., 191; Jn., 189

Edlin, Audrey, 244; Joan, 244; Jn., 142; Tho., 244

Edmond(es) (Edmunds), Rob., 12; Tho., 173; —, 185

Edmondes *alias* Lawson, *see* Lawson

Edward VI, 10

Edward(es), Anne, 26; Ellen, 263; Rice, 234; Thos, 25, 245; Wm., 147, 263

Edwick, Tho., 220

Effette, Jn., 288

Egell, —, 201

Egerton, Sir Tho., 209

Eglesfylde, Margt., 173; Wm., 173

Ekin, Wm., 188

Elder, Cecily, 284; Edm., 283; Emme, 284; Jn., 283; Sibyl, 283; Rob., **283**

Elderton, Judith, 28

Elkin, Ralph, 276; Thomasine, 91

Ellinot, Edw., 284; Sarah, 284; Ste., **284**

Elliot, Clement, 132; Edw., 98, 154, 219; Jane, 98; Tho., 132-3; —, 97

Ellis (Elys), Edw., 12; Hen., 152; Jn., 59, 167, 266; Rob., 294; Wm., 161; —, 167

Elmes, Jn., 287-8

Elminge (Elmyn), Jn., 288

Elrington, Agnes, 192; Chris., 80-1; Dorothy, 80-1, Edw., 51, **80**, 81; Eliz., 193; Frs., 80-1; Jane, 80-1; Judith, 80; Law., 193; Rowland, 80-1, **192**; Tho., 80-1; Wm., 80-1, 193

Elsinge, Kath., 252; Rob., 252

Ely, bishop of, 58

Emery, Thomasine, 198; Tho., 198; Wm., 148

Enew, Rob., 297

Enowes, Rich., 301

Engledewe, see Ing-

Englishe, Jas., 66

Erington, Edw., 130

Ernesbie, Agnes, 284; Griffen, 284; Thomasine, 284

Ersewelle, Nich., 171-2

Essex, Earl of, see Devereux

Es(t)cott, Jn., 19, 70

Etheredge, Reynold, 266

Eton, see Eaton

Eustace, Hen., 79

Evans, Hen., 227; —, 69

Everard (-ed), Hen., 298; Rich., 266

Everton, Geo., 174-6

Eve(s), Reynold, 186; —, 206

Ewens, Mat., 239

Exilby, Jane, 258; Miles, 258; Rich., 258

Eyre (Ayer), E., 142; Jn., 276; —, 175

Eysam, Agnes, 187; Tho., 187

Fabyan, Jn., 302; Wm., 301

Fage, Edw., 236

Faierclyffe, Law., vicar of Haverhill, 57

Fale, Jn., vicar of Roydon, 192

Fall, Wm., 250

Fanne, Agnes, 162; Tho., 162

Fannyng, Rob., 322-3

Fanshawe, Hen., 144; Tho., 144; Mr., 143

Farmer, goodwife, 140

Farnham, Geo., 252

Farrar (Ferror), Reynold, 300-1; Tho., rector of Langham, 318

Farr(e), Benj., 195; Hen., 195; Rich., 195; Walter, **195**; Zacky, 117

Fawkes, Mat., 149

Fawvel, wid., 16

Fayrested, Benj., 274

Feling, Edw., 297

Felis, see Filles

Felste(e)d, Jn., 217; Tho., 301-2

Felton, Ant., 71; Geo., 285

Fenclyf, Wm., 185

Fenne, Clement, **285**; Geo., 285; Joan, 277, 285; Jn., 286, 289; Margery, 285; Rose, 285; Simon, 285, 308; Tho., 285

Fenner, Barnaby, 134

Fens(t)by(e), Wm., 184, 185

Fenton, Edw., 90, 91; Thomasine, 90

Fermery, Mr., 167

Ferne, —, 140

Ferris (Ferres), Dorothy, 222; Hen., 222; Mary, 222; Tho., 222

Ferror, see Farrar

Fewilliams, see Fitzwilliams

Fielde (Fylde), Jn., 78, 173

Filles (Felis), Mary, 253

Finche, Jn., 137; Rob., 266, 308; Wm., 302; Mistress, 61; —, 184; see Fynce

Finkell, Wm., 317

Fissher, Jn., 138; Rich., 125; Wm., 138; see Fycher

Fitche (Fytch), Anne, 82; Eliz., 81; Frs., 82-3; Margery, 147; Tho., 34, 36, 49, 82; Wm., 81, 82-3, 147; Mr, 56; Mistress, 38

Fitz - Williams (Few-), Philippa, 44; Sir Wm., 44, 109

Flammancke, Tho., 26

Fleminge, Anne, 90; Sir Frs., 211; Giles, 90-1; Mich., 132; —, 89

Flint, Rob., 21

Floode (Fludd), Jn., 22, 51, 84, 170, 249, 274, 276; —, 49

Folderinge, Jn., 117

Fo(l)kes, Jn., 272; Rob., 236; Tho., 236

Forber(e), Jn., 291-2, 314; Mr, 186

Ford (Foorde), Anne, 195; Audrey, 195; Eliz., 196; Jn., 83-4,

86, **195**; Kath., **83**; Margery, 83-4; Mary, 223; Mich., 223

Ford(h)am, Wm., 186, 209

Forster, Agnes, 54; Bridget, 53; Mich., 54; Tho., 69; Wm., 53

Fortescue (Fortyskue), Frs., 84; Geo., 84; Hen., 84; Isabel, 159; Jn., 159, 297; Kath., 159; Mary, 84; Mr, 159

Foster, Tho., 297

Fountaine, Wm., 230

Fowle, Wm., 324

Fowler, Jn., 15

Foxe, Jn., 262; Wm., 84

Frances, Mistress, 84

Francis, Edm., 230

Franck, Art., 85-6; Hen., 188; Jn., 128; Mary, 85; Rich., 85-6; Rob., 85-6, 128; Tho., **85-6**

Francklynge, Tho., 169

Freake, Edm., 96

Free, Anne, 172; Tho., 232

Freeman, Bart., 197; Cecily, 197; Eliz., 196-7; Gilb., 170; Giles, 324; Hen., **196**; Jn., 197; Margt., 197; Mary, 197; Ralph, 197; Tho., 196-7

Freeninges, Wm., 102

Frelove, Jn., 87

Fremlinge (-lyn), Eliz., 197; Joan, 197; Jn., 197; Rob., **197**; Tho., 197, 299

Frenche, Bridget, 198; Godfrey, 98; Jn., 110, 198; Rob., 188; Tho., **197**, 198

Frenchman, Jn., 65, 177

Freston, Rich., 71

Frissell, Jn., 240

Fromonte, Jn., 74; Tho., 74; Walter, 74

Fulham, Tho., 241

Fulkes, Rich., 119

Fuller, Hen., 322; Jn., 15, 21, 269-70; Tho., 197, 234; Wm., 173, 197, 212; —, 21, 130, 312

Fulnotby, Rob., 58, 164

Fulwood, Rob., 70

Furnes, Jn., 197; Tho., 197; Wm., 197

Furton, Clement, 76

Fycher, Rich., 309; see Fissher

Fy(er)fanne, Tho., 273, 313

Gough *alias* Gooche, Anne, 207
Gover, Jn., 314
Gower, Jas., curate of Orsett, 349; Rob., 28, 31-2
Gowge, Bridget, 293; Geo., 293; Wm., 240
Gouge, *see* Gooche
Gowlde, *see* Goolde
Goybie, Mary, 272
Graing, Jn., 91
Grave, Wm., 177
Gray, *see* Grey
Greaneleafe, —, 186
Gre(e)n(e), Anne, 207; Bryant, 207; Edm., 263; (Sir) Edw., 19, 262; Eleanor, 82; Eliz., 283; Frances, 283; Hen., 296; Jane, 207; Jerome, 207; Jn., 39, 80, 177, 262, 268; Jonas, 301; Margt., 207; Mary, 207, 283; Pet., 127, 250-1; Randall, 93; Rich., 207, 283; Rooke, 48-9, 82; Tho., 126, 268, 314; Wm., 125-6, 170, 224, 249, 283; wid., 250
Greenaces, Art., 208; Frances, 208; Rich., 208, 282
Greenacres *alias* Hammerton, Kath., 208
Gre(e)nley, Phil., 130, 144
Greenwood, Alice, 159; Jn., 150; Tho., 35-6
Gregose, Tho., 51
Gresham, Rich., 69; —, 168
Grevill, Anne, 30, 34; Chas., 34, 36; Edw., 30, 32; Griselda, 33; Jn., 30, 32, 34-5; Lod(o)wich, 29, 32-6; Margt., 30, 34; Pet., 34-5; Thomasine, 29-32, 36; Wm., 30
Grey (Gray), Alice, 208-9; And., 208-9; Anth., 208; Art., Lord of Wilton, 79; Edm., 208; Eliz., 209; Sir Hen., 103-4, 179; Jn., 48, 99, 288, 290; John Lord, 9; Jonathan, 209; Lady Mary, 9, 19; Mat., 209; Tho., 208, 209, 288, 290; Mr, 56, 255
Griffethe, Jn., 209; Mary, 209; Rich., 209; Rob., 119
Griffin, Anne, 249; Geoff., 251; Wm., 284-5

Grigges, Alice, 289; Jn., 288, 304
Grim(e)ston, Edw., 92, 102; Joan, 92
Grove, father, 291
Gryme, Nich., 84
Grynryg, Donkyn, 320
Gull, Tho., 317
Gullyver, H e n ., 25; Margt. 51
Gurney, Ant., 58
Guy (Guie), Jn., 229; Mr, 285
G(u)ynes (Gynnes), Eliz., 153; Hen., 152; Rob., 151-2, 157-8
G(u)yon, Anne, 288; Margery. 288; Tho., 288; Wm., 301
Gwye, Walter, 179
Gyfforde, *see* Gifforde
Gylbodye, Anne, 91
Gylman, —, 189

Haberlee, Jn., 271
Hacelinge, Parnel, 39
Hackett, Maurice, 250
Hackthrop, Rowland, 140
Haddon, Th., 284
Hadland (Hedland), Hen., 178; Rachel, 178
Hag(g)ar, Seth., 25, 51
Haies, *see* Hayes
Haines (Haynes, Heynes), Anne, 261; Rob., 267; Tho., 115, 183
Hale, Tho., 205; Wm., 201
Halesworthe, Agnes, 209
Hall (Haull), Anne, 34; Avice, 297; Eliz., 133; Godard, 91-2; Hen., 15, 17, 150; Jn., 169; Martha, 306-7; Pet., 157; Rich., 72, 86, 91; Rob., 75, 77, 79, 91, 92, 266; Sam., 307; Tho., 92; Wm., 91, 274, 312
Hall *alias* Price, Anne, 92
Hamden, Jn., 43
Hames, Jn., 49
Ham(me), Abraham, 317; Allen, 215-6; Rob., 315
Hammerton *alias* Greenacres, Kath., 208
Hammon(d), Dorothy, 227; Joan, 246; Jn., 216; Tho., 101, 322; Thomasine. 101; Wm., 246; —, 158
Hanchet, Margt., 261; Tho.. 117
Hancock, Davy, 214
Hanham, Gilb., vicar of Boreham, 140
Hantler, Marg., 267

Hanworth, Chris., 96
Harboroughe, Martha, Miles, 210; Rich, 210
Harbottell, Chris., 157; Joan, 92; Jn., 92; —, 156-7
Harde, Geo., 48-9
Hardie, Mary, 252; Rich., 252
Hardinge, Tho., 269; —, 217
Hare, Jn., 55-6; Rob., 38; Mistress, 55-6
Harker, Nich., 199
Harlakinden, Anne, 93; Eliz., 93; Geo., 93; Jn., 93; Rog. (or Rob.), 93; Rich., 93-4; Tho., 93-4; Wm., 93-4
Harleston(e), Anne, 122; Clement, 122; Jn., 94, 121-2; Mary, 94, 122; Tho., 94; Wm., 95; —, 301
Harman, Geo., 276; Mary, 132; Tho., 132
Harmer, Eliz., 110
Harper, Jn., 167; —, 7
Harrett, Rich., 208
Harrington (H e (a) r -), Anne, 96; Anth., 67; Hen., 223; Jn., 3-4, 51; Tho., 96; Wm., 188; Mr, 258
Harris (Harrys, Herrys), Alice, 197; Anne, 100; Art., 79, 95, 96, 100, 148, 151, 165, 208, 268; Edw., 95; Hen., 246; Isabel, 173; Jn., 312; Mary, 95, 100; Rob., 174; Rich., 115; Tho., 52, 68, 95, 197, 210, 258, 267; Vincent, x, 95, 151; Walter, 323-4; Wm., 95-6, 148, 204; —, 190, 202
Harrison, Alice, 229; Anne, 229; Eliz., 229, 238; Geo., 19; Jn., 182, 214, 229; Margt., 275; Mary, 229; Ralph, 277; Susan, 229; Tho., 237-8; Thomasine, 59; Wm., archdn. of Colchester, rector of Radwinter, 110
Harrydaunce, Wm., 245
Hart(e) (Huet), J a c o b, 269-70; Jn., 56, 232
Harteridge, Allen, 319
Hartley, Jn., 208
Harvey, Camilla, 211; Edw., 191; Eliz., 211; Frs., 8-9, 210; Jn., 211, 296-7, 311; Mary, 210; Tho., 205; Wm., 211; Sir Wm., 212

Harwood, Eliz., 233
Haselherst, Jn., 141
Haselwood, Eliz., 281;
  Jn., 17; Margt., 281;
  Tho., 191, 281, 285;
  —, 281
Hasset, Lady, 156; —,
  153, 279; see Biener-
  chasset
Hassoll, Jn., 154
Hast(e)ler, Rob., 196;
  Tho., 212
Hastings, Cath., wife of
  Earl of Huntingdon, 38
Hastinges, Jn., 239
Hatchman, —, 140
Hatleye, Jane, 232;
  Rich., 232
Haughton, Chris., 129;
  Geo., 129; Margery,
  312
Haunkin, Bridget, 313-4
Havard, Mich., 264
Hawden, Ralph, vicar of
  All Saints', Maldon,
  229
Hawes, Wm., 49, 146
Haveringe, Margt., 223
Hawkes, Eliz., 301; Jn.,
  301; Tho., 295, 301
Hawkesawle, Jn., 285
Hawkin(s), Edw., 297;
  Eliz., 147; Sir Jn., 91;
  Jn., 15, 239; wid., 81;
  —, 272
Hawtrie, Mary, 25
Hayes, Dorothy, 212;
  Edw., 212; Eliz., 212;
  Geo., 212-3; Hester,
  212; Jn., 212; Tho.,
  212, 244
Haymer, —, 110
Hayne, Morgan, 159
Haynes, see Haines
Hayword (wodd, Hey-
  ward), Anne, 34; Joan,
  200; Jn., 76, 117, 302;
  Rob., 241; Tho., 20;
  Wm., 44-5; 234; 302
Heard, see Herd
Hear(e), Mr, 317
Hearington, see Har-
Heath, Bridget, 246;
  Tho., 246
Hedge(s), Joan, 239;
  Margt., 222; Tho., 260
Heditche, Wm., 194
Hedland, see Hadland
Heidon, Sir Chris., 142
Heigham, see Higham
Helmey, Edm., 57
Hely, Jn., 267; Mr, 163
Henage (Hennedge), Sir
  Tho., 68, 316
Henry VIII, 10, 237
Henry, Geo., 188; Jane,
  21
Herbert, Wm., 17

Herd(e) (Heard), Geo.,
  101, 248; Jn., 103,
  215, 310; Rich., 248;
  Rob., 296; Wm., 101;
  Mr, 317; wid., 104
Herington, see Harington
Heritage, Hen., 6
Herne, Julian, 130
Herringe, Hen., 255
Herrys, see Harris
Hester, Joan, 236; Jn.,
  236; Tho., 236; Rich.,
  236; Wm., 236
Hewer, Wm., 299
Hewes, see Hughes
Hewet, Tho., 234; Wm.,
  86; wid., 86
Heynes, see Haines
Heyward, see Hay-
Hickes, Baptiste, 140;
  Mich., 140; Tho., 241
Hide, Ant., 134; Bernard,
  295; Ralph, 295
Hiegate, Dan., 77; Mary,
  76; Reynold, 75, 77
Higgons, Anth., 140
Higham (Hei-), Geo.,
  148; Jn., 95; Mary,
  184
Hildersham, Jn., 96
Hill(es), Chris., clerk, 48;
  Jn., 246; Nich., 9, 127;
  Thomasine, 223; Wm.,
  228, 274; nurse, 246
Hilsdon, Chris., 233-4
Hin(d)es, Wm., 244; —,
  317
Hithcok, Hen., 186
Hixson, goodwife, 140
Hoblethorne, Dame Eliz.,
  21
Hobson, Jn., 158, 297;
  Wm., 69
Hoby, Edw., 19, 69; Tho.
  Posthumus, 69
Hodge(s), Anne, 134;
  Jeremy, 134; Jn., 36;
  Naboth, 134; Philippa,
  134; Rowland, 179;
  Wm., 207
Hodgkine(s), Rob., clerk,
  95; Tho., 56
Hodilowe, Anne, 213;
  Barbara, 213; Edm.,
  213; Jn., 213; Kath.,
  213; Mary, 213; Tho.,
  213
Hodson (Hodge-), Alice,
  303; Dorothy, 25; Isa-
  bel, 65; Rob., 28, 65;
  Wm., 65, 226; nurse,
  65
Hogg, Pet., 91
Holden, Geo., 51; Jn.,
  51
Hole, Bedell, 154
Holgate, Rob., 58
Holgrave, Anne, 295

Holland, Jn., 221; Mr,
  260
Hollidaye, Wm., 218
Hollingsworth, Amy, 183;
  Law., 183
Holmes (Homes), Anne,
  176; Jn., 289; Tho.,
  312; Wm., 174; —,
  127
Holmsteede, Jn., 79; Mr,
  302
Holstock, Wm., 168
Holt, Wm., 105; wid.,
  294
Hones, Jn., 194
Hopkin(s), Jn., 68, 187;
  —, 239
Hopkinson, Edw., vicar of
  Nazeing, 237
Hopper, Rich., 210;
  Tho., 290
Hopton, Tho., 275
Hopwood, Agnes, 307
Horsman, Tho., 317
Horsnaile, —, 70
Horton, —, 212
Hovenden, Eliz., 213-4;
  Jane, 213-4; Mary,
  214; Rich., 213
Howard, Frances, 3, 28;
  Hen., 21; Lord Tho.,
  108-9, 150, 260; Lord
  Wm., 109
Howe, Anne, 104; Jn.,
  214; Martha, 214;
  Mary, 105, 214; Tho.,
  214; Wm., 104, 199,
  214, 245, 247; Mr,
  266; wid., 49
Howell, Rich., 19; Sam.,
  45
Howland, Jn., 83; Rob.,
  81; Mistress, 81
Howlett, Tho., parson of
  Chelmsford, 167
Howmer, Rich., 259
Hubbard (-ert), Edw., 96,
  98; Eleanor, 97; Eliz.,
  98; Frs., 98-9; Geo.,
  204; Jane, 96; Jn., 98,
  186, 279; Margt., 204;
  Miles, 99; Rich., 97-8;
  Thomasine, 98; Wm.,
  204, 275; —, 265
Hud(d)leston(e), Anne,
  88; Lady Dorothy, 15-
  7, 62, 64, 159; (Sir)
  Edm., 15-7, 62; Jn.,
  200
Huet, see Hewet, Hart
Huggens, Hum., 203
Hughes (Hewes, Huse),
  Agnes, 248; Jn., 231;
  Law., 90-1; Mary, 89
Hulke, —, 125
Hull, Edw., 271; Rich.,
  193; Wm., 134; —,
  236

344

346

347

348

Sallowes, Nich., 323
Sallter, Tho., 248
Salmon, Agnes, 306, **307;**
Anne, 307; Edw., 306;
Jacomyne, 306-7; Jn.,
194; Law., 194; Martha, 307; Mary, 307;
Nat., 306-7; Pet., 306-7; Rob., **306**, 307, 324;
Tho., 306-7; Mistress,
194; *see also* Sawmon
Salmon *alias* Smythe,
Law., 194
Salperwyck *alias* Gillam,
Frs., 297; Jn., 296-7
Saltonstall, Sir Rich., 121
Samforde, Tho., 233
Sammes, Jn., 95-6, 117,
151-2, 219, 228; Wm.,
235; —, 175
Sampson, Eliz., 122-3;
Frances, 122; Jn.,
121-3; Rich., 297;
Rob., **121**, Tho., 297
Samuell (-vell, -well), Geo.,
27; Mr, 126
Sandell, Edm., 124;
Eliz., 124; Leon., **123;**
Rob., 124
Sandes, Tho., 200
Sandford, Hen., 316;
Rob., 94
Sandwith, Margt., 248;
Rich., **248**; Rob., 248
Sansbury, Wm., 140
Sansom, Alice, 225; Joan,
225; Jn., 225; Margt.,
225; —, 217
Sare, Geo., 24; Rich., 24;
Tho., 24
Saunder(s), Alice, 253;
Anna, 234; Sir Edw.,
15; Elie, 230; Jn.,
234; Margt., 65; Wm.,
234
Saundershill, Edw., 28
Saunderson, Eliz., 252;
Nich., 252
Sava(d)ge, Edw., 70;
Frances, 272; Margery, 89; Repent, rector of Corringham,
236; Wm., 272-3
Saverie, Rich., 135
Savill, Hen., 210
Sawcer, Joan, 120
Sawmon, Jas., 225; Jn.,
271; *see also* Salmon
Saw(y)er, Rich., 170,
249
Saxforde, Hum., 307
Say(e), Rob., 118; —,
140
Sayer, Agnes, 249; Frances, 249; Geo., 125,
126,, 170, **249**; Hen.,
307; Mary, 249; Rich.,
126, 170, **249;** Hen.,

125, 249; Tho., 125-6,
196, 249
Scaroborough, Ste., 66
Scoller, Jn., 192
Scott (Skott), A b d i a s,
250; Chris., 221; Dorothy, 128; Edm., 127,
250; Eliz., 127-8;
Frances, 250; Geoff.,
140; Geo., **126, 128,**
250; Hen., 250, 297;
Hugh, 126-7, 250;
Jane, **250**; Joan, 127;
Jn., 16, 127-8, 250;
Margt., 303; Mary,
128, 250; Prudence,
127; Rich., 128; Rob.,
127, 150; Rog., 128;
Tho., 127, 150; Wm.,
126-8, **250**, 304; —,
6, 43, 147
Scratton, Anne, 290;
Grace, 290; Jn., 290;
Raymond, 290
Scrogges, Alex., 15
Scrogges *alias* Skeyef, *see*
Skeyef
Scudamore, Sir Jn.,
211-2
Seale, Rich., 239
Se(a)man, Edm., 306;
Hugh, 186
Seamer, Mary, 226
Se(a)rle, Grace, 215; Jn.,
74, 209, 252; Rob., 74;
Tho., 74
Searles, Rob., minister,
283
Sebborne, Edm., 318
Seborowe, Mabel, 183
Sedell, Rich., 6
Seintclere, Giles, 173
Segges, Margt., 204
Sell, Jn., 84
Selye, *see* Celye
Sergeant *alias* Sadler,
Rog., 277
Serle, *see* Searle
Settle, Jn., 178; Mat., 178
Sewall, Wm., 297
Sewster, Geoff., 74
Sex, Chris., 166
Sexton, Jane, 251; Mary,
251; Rich., 171; Susan, 251; Tho., **251**
Shaa, Anne, 10; Edm.,
128; Eleanor, 128;
Faith, 128; Judith,
128; Mary, 128; Philippa, 128-9; Rob., 128-9; Tho., 10, **128**, 129
Shaa *alias* Rochester,
Philippa, 128-9
Shaa *alias* Deresley,
Mary, 128-9
Sharman, *see* Sherman
Sharparow, Jas., 152
Sharpe, Jn., 45, 197

Shatswell, Wm., 231
Shawe, Rich., 6, 251;
Thurston, rector of
Theydon Mount, 42,
44; Wm., parson of
Chingford, 241, 243
Shaxforde, Tho., 233
She(a)ther, Edm., 194;
Wm., 101
Sheene, Dan., 311
Shelley, goodwife, 56
Shelton, Dan., 20, 77;
Grace, 20, 76
Sheppard (Sheap-), Jas.,
152; Jn., 48; Rich.,
251; Tho., 187; Wm.,
parson of Heydon, 73-4, 215
Sherman, Anne, 307-9;
Benj., 308-9; Bezaliel,
307-9; Dan., 309;
Edm., 288, **307**, 308-9;
Ezechiel, 309; Hannah,
308; Hen., 279, 281,
288, **308**, 309, 320;
Jn., 307-8; Judith, 309;
Margery, 309; **Mary,**
308; Nich., 264; Phoebe,
309; Rich., 307-8;
Rob., 309; Sam., 309;
Sarah, 309; Susan,
308; Genl. Wm., x
Shervile, Hen., 99
Shipman, Jn., **251**; Lucy,
251; Mr, 251
Shortinge, Agnes, 288;
Alice, 289; Amy, 289;
Anne, 289; Mary, 288;
Rob., 288; Ste., 288-9;
Wm., 288
Shrewsbury, **Earl of,** *see*
Talbot
Shrive, Helen, 290; Jn.,
290; Wm., 324
Shuntman, Jn., 297
Shyres, —, 208
Sibthorp, Anne, 129;
Chris., **129**; Elmer,
129; Jn., 129; Rob.,
129; Wm., 129
Sideye (Sydaye), Rich.,
126; Wm., 312-3
Silgate, *see* Gilgate
Siliard, *see* Suliarde
Sills, Wm., 312
Silvester, Sarah, 54
Simon(s) (Symon(s), Symonde), Bart., 96; Jn.,
264; Pet., 283; Rob.,
106; Wm., 262; —,
138, 147, 239, 262
Sim(p)son, Barnard, 242-3; David, 200; Emme,
252; Geo., 284; Joan,
130, 131, 236; Nich.,
130-1; Rich., **131;**
Rob., 131, 252; Rowland, 243; Susan, 131;

351

354.

355

Wiseman *alias* Strangman, Joan, 147
Withall, Mr, 58
Witham (Wittam), Hen., 118; Tho., 191; Wm., 118
Withie *alias* P o t t e r, Mary, 53
Wodborne, Jn., 251
Wode, Jn., 59
Wodham, Law., 214-5
Wolley, Emmanuel, 23, 26
Wolmer, Tho., 177
Wood (Whood), Agnes, 49; Clement, 287, 316; Eliz., 316; Frances, 320; Geo., 188, 320; Hen., 320; Jacob, 39; Joan, 54; Jn., 40-4, 68, 245, **320**; Margt., 44; Mary, 316, 320; Rich., 320; Sarah, 316; Tho., 48, 234, 320; —, 265
Woodall, Jas., 171; Rob., 243
Woodcocke, Agnes, 282
Woodford, Gamaliel, 26-7
Woodhowse, Joan, 320; Jn., **320**
Woodl(e)y, Tho., 164, 267; Mr, 162-3
Woodroff, Wm., 45
Woodward, Agnes, 187; Jn., rector of Ingatestone, 31-2; Martha, 256; Rich., 134, 302; Rob., 187; old, 159

Woodye, Geo., 297
Woolmer, Jn., 129
Woollwarde, Rich., 66
Wootton (Wotton), Dr. Nich., 107; Rich., 212; Tho., 108
Worcester, bishop of, 22
Worrlyche, Wm., 171
Worth, Jn., vicar of Dedham, 314
Wortham, Elias, 312, 319; Mary, 312-3; Rich., 313; Wm., 312-3
Worthlye, Joan, 167; Jn., 166
Woulde, Dorothy, 266; Edw., 266; Ellen, 266; Jn., 267; Margt., 266
Wratham, —, 159
Wratton, Jn., 236
Wraye, Sir Chris., 3-4, 6
Wregeswood, Tho., 101
Wren (Ren(n)e), W m., 92; —, 310
Wrenche, Anna, 321; Elias, 321; Eliz., 320-1; Phenenna, 321; Simon, 321; Wm., 320-1
Wrenolde, Wm., 276; *see also* Reynolde
Wright(e), Anne, 25; Eliz., 106, 267; Hum., 70; Jn., 15, 61-2, 106, 184, 218, **267**; Rich., 196, 254; Rob., 15. 251; Rob., parson of

Woodford, 263; Tho., 179; Wm., 134, 295; Mr, 13
Wrothe (Wrath), Dame Mary, 11; (Sir) Rich., 4, 6, 11, 154; Rob., 13, 129-30; Susan, 129-30; (Sir) Tho., 72, 130; Wm., 72-3; Mr, 144
Wybard, *see* Wiberde
Wykes, Hen., 157
Wylie, *see* Wilie
Wylle, Percival, 281
Wynge, Jn., 149
Wynter, Sir Edw., 24; Jn., 289; Wm., 24
Wyntroppe, Susan, 232
Wyott (Wyatte), Edw., 147, 148, **267**; Frs., 148; Hen., 324; Isaac, 148, 267; Jane, 267; Mary, 147-8; Wm., 148, 267
Wystock, Geo., 84
Wythens, Rich., 247
Wythers, Rich., 217

Yngisbie, Geo., 248; Rich., 248
York, dean of, 107
Yorke, Edm., 109; Rowland, 28
Younge, Chris., 268; Eliz., 268; Joan, 268; Jn., 168, 268; Nich., 268; Rob., 268; Tho., 227; Wm., 198; **268**

Index of Subjects

NOTES.—(1) *Occupations.*—All crafts, trades and occupations are brought together under 'trades and occupations'; cross-references are not made between subjects and occupations, e.g. mills and millers, schools and schoolmasters.

(2) *Unusual words* are indexed together under 'words, rare, archaic, or local'.

356

56, 59, 65, 67, 77, 89, 96, 100, 110, 112, 130, 136, 147
windows, *see* fixtures
wine, 193; pots, 7
woad-house, 156(?), 298; -vats, 274
wood, bequest of, *see* poor
woods, 5; (named), 12, 70, 76, 78, 95, 97, 135, 165, 278-9, 301; preservation of, 165, 225, 318; felling of, 64, 76, 105-6, 122-3, 132, 136, 174, 189-90, 202, 284, 301, 310; *see also* billet; clapboard
wool, 295
words, rare, archaic or local: balas, 1; budge, 275; bulchin, 160; capha, silk, 144; caul, 65; clapgate, 12; cloits,

149; coolback (brewing), 255; costed, 23-4; d o r v e d up, 64; dumb, 305; e d g e (hedge) of pearl, 7, 48;* foins, 275; fugar, satin, 23, 122; gatten (goaten?), 275; george, 2; gimmals, 261; ginnet spayed mare, 117; gorgonet, gold, 89; gyle tun, 255; hampstall, 118; hance, 84, 150; hardwick, 195; jaffen, 38; karoby, 305; knowe, 160; lanner, 50; marbet, 160; offcorn, 225; onycle, 58; peytrels, 49; porpentines, 4; prower, 180; pykin (pightle?), 278; quillets, 95; rode, 160; ronded/wort, 183; scraves (shearman's),

315; skene, 212; skillitory, 88; slips (spoons), 150; stainings, 314; steal, 84, 126; tonnel, 51; trink, 323; unthrift, ix, 164; wolverenes, 140, 162
writers of court letter of London, *see* trades (etc.)
writing, to learn, 315

Year Books, ix, 14
yeomen, x *et passim,* esp. 322

---

* 'edge, an edging or narrow border of goldsmithry for a head-dress, cap or bonnet' (from C. R. Beard's unpublished *Dictionary of Costume,* kindly supplied by V. & A. Museum).